Texts in Computer Science

Editors
David Gries
Fred B. Schneider

For other titles published in this series, go to
www.springer.com/series/3191

V.S. Alagar • K. Periyasamy

Specification of Software Systems

2nd edition

Prof. V.S. Alagar
Dept. Computer Science and Software Eng.
Concordia University
St. Catherine Street West 1515
H3G 1M8 Montreal, Québec
Canada
alagar@cs.concordia.ca

Prof. K. Periyasamy
Computer Science Department
University of Wisconsin-La Crosse
State Street 1725
54601 La Crosse, WI
USA
kasi@cs.uwlax.edu

Series Editors
David Gries
Department of Computer Science
Upson Hall
Cornell University
Ithaca, NY 14853-7501, USA

Fred B. Schneider
Department of Computer Science
Upson Hall
Cornell University
Ithaca, NY 14853-7501, USA

ISSN 1868-0941   e-ISSN 1868-095X
ISBN 978-1-4471-2644-7   ISBN 978-0-85729-277-3 (eBook)
DOI 10.1007/978-0-85729-277-3
Springer London Dordrecht Heidelberg New York

British Library Cataloguing in Publication Data
A catalogue record for this book is available from the British Library

Library of Congress Control Number: 2011922494

Cover design: deblik

Printed on acid-free paper

Springer is part of Springer Science+Business Media (www.springer.com)

Preface to the Second Edition

This is the second edition of the textbook in which most of the concepts introduced in the first edition are extended and updated, and a significant amount of new material has been added. While preserving the original intent of focusing on **software specification**, this edition emphasizes the practice of formal methods for **specification and verification activities** for different types of software systems and at different stages of developing the software systems. This expanded view is reinforced both in the organization of the book and in the presentation of its contents. The primary driving force for writing the second edition came from Springer-Verlag, London, who expressed a great desire and strong interest in catering to the growing needs of students and researchers in the area of Formal Software Engineering.

Background and Motivation

Although during the initial stages of formal methods research there was only a marginal use of formal methods in industry, new languages, techniques and tools developed during early 1990s have spurred great interest in adapting formal methods in industries. In fact, the 1990s witnessed an explosion of new developments in formal methods research. NASA Langley Research Center was the first hub of formal methods research and practice. The researchers at Langley focused on large scale commercial projects that are suitable for injecting formal methods. They felt that the industries were reluctant to use formal methods because of inadequate tools, inadequate background, and lack of adequate examples. However, this situation started changing gradually during 1995–2004 when new directions of research and development of tools in the three areas *Software Specification Methods*, *Model Checking*, and *Theorem Proving* provided a great spur for formal development activity in industries. Most notably, software engineers at nuclear power stations, aerospace and transportation industries used formal methods to formally specify and verify the properties of *safety critical* parts in systems. In 1998, the fully automatic driverless subway was launched in Paris Metro and, in 2006, the fully automatic driverless shuttle servicing the various terminals at Roissy Airport, Paris was launched. With success stories such as these arose a desire in academia and industries to learn formal methods more systematically. In order to choose a method that is appropriate for a specific application that demands concepts such as *causality*, *concurrency*, and *conflict avoidance* a certain level of expertise in formal methods education is necessary. Getting to know that it is possible to mix different abstractions from different languages to model heterogeneous systems is an asset for an efficient development process. Nowadays formal methods often are bundled up with tools, many available as open source software, to support architectural principles of generality and orthogonality. In view of these spectrum of changes and success stories, software engineers now have several case studies to learn from and choose languages and methods with a rich repertoire of appropriate concepts for their intended applications. In keeping up with this trend this second edition is offered. In writing this second edition, the expectation is that formal methods will be well integrated into the teaching of software engineering programs. In this hope, topics related to the integration of formal methods in software development process are discussed quite early in the text and are followed by presentations of abstraction principles, formalism definitions, notations of formalism, and a wide variety of fairly detailed specification examples.

What is New in the Second Edition?

Old material has been updated to improve both content and presentation. Some chapters in the first edition of the text have undergone extensive revisions. In some cases, an old chapter has been split into two or more chapters and in each of them extensive new material have been added. New chapters that discuss Object-Z, B-Method, and Calculus of Communicating Systems have been added. The entire book has been structured into six parts. The distinguishing features of this restructured and expanded second edition are as follows.

Part I The first part of the book introduces specification fundamentals. The material is presented in four chapters. An elaborate introduction to the role of specification is followed by discussions on specification activities and specification qualities. The first part concludes with a discussion on abstraction principles, illustrated with a domain abstraction example.

Part II The second part introduces the basics of formalism, automata notations used in formal languages, study extensions to the basic automata notation, and concludes with a discussion on the classification of formal specification techniques. This material is presented in four chapters. The chapters that discuss automata and extended state machine notations are almost self-contained. A variety of examples that arise in software construction are taken up for formal modeling using different variations of state machines. Top-down and bottom-up constructions of formal models, their sequential and parallel compositions are discussed and illustrated with examples.

Part III The third part of the book is entirely devoted to logic. Propositional logic, predicate logic, and temporal logic are treated in three separate chapters. The presentation focuses on introducing the logics as formal languages, and hence introduces their syntax, semantics, and reasoning methods in succession. The expressive power of predicate logic is illustrated for representing knowledge, policies, as well as serving as axiomatic system for program verification. For the latter purpose, Hoare axioms are presented and illustrated by verifying simple sequential programs. Temporal logic chapter gives a detailed discussion of the syntax, and semantics of linear temporal logic. Many examples from reactive systems and concurrent systems are chosen to emphasize the expressivity of the logic languages in specifying such systems and their properties. A discussion of axiomatic proof method and model checking are included.

Part IV Most of the model-based specification languages are based on set theory and first-order predicate logic. Therefore, it is essential to have a strong background in set theory and relations. This part of the book includes one chapter on set theory and relations. Most parts of this chapter are retained from the previous edition of the book.

Part V Three specification methods are discussed to illustrate the property-oriented approach to specifications. Two of the chapters, *Algebraic Specifications* and *Larch*, are left unchanged. The chapter *Calculus of Communicating Systems* is new and it discusses Milner's algebraic approach to specifying communication and concurrency. Some examples discussed in Temporal Logic chapter are drawn in here to strike a comparison between the two approaches. An effort has been made to make the discussion in this chapter simple, rigorous, and self-contained.

Part VI This part is devoted to model-based specification techniques. Four such techniques are described in detail. These are VDM-SL, Z, Object-Z and the B-Method. Material on VDM-SL and Z are retained from the previous edition of the book, while the bibliographic references have been updated. Two new chapters have been introduced, one for Object-Z and another for the B-Method. The material for new chapters are presented in the same style as in the old chapters. Also, the two new chapters include extensive examples and case studies, and provide a detailed tutorial of the techniques introduced in those chapters.

How to Use the Book

In the second edition of the book, we have added considerable new material and we have also restructured the chapters into various parts. Consequently, those who have used the first edition may see a different layout of the book. The book includes several different specification techniques grouped into various categories. In addition, it also includes chapters with necessary mathematical background for these techniques. Because of the diverse nature of these techniques, the book can be used by different groups of people for different purposes. Below we suggest a few streams of course offerings to fit different curriculum needs.

1. Chapters in Part I are required for further reading of the book.
2. Based on Part I, Part II, Chaps. 9, 10 of Part III, and Part IV a one-semester undergraduate course within a software engineering program can be given. This course is intended to be an Introduction to Formal Software Engineering Methods. The course can be extended into another semester by covering the material from one of the four specification languages discussed in Chaps. 16 through 19, and choosing a project in which the students would write a complete specification and analyze the specification. The examples and case studies given in these chapters would help the students to achieve this goal.
3. Chapters in Part II, Part III, and Chap. 15 from Part V can be offered as a one-semester course for senior undergraduate students or first year graduate students in computer science and computer engineering programs. This course is intended to be an Introduction to Formal Methods.
4. Parts V and VI are devoted to various formal specification techniques. Each chapter in these parts gives a thorough tutorial of one specification technique. Together with the mathematical fundamentals described in Part IV, each chapter in Parts V and VI can be individually used to teach a one-semester course on a particular specification technique. The course will introduce the formal method in some depth, choosing appropriate tools suggested in the bibliographic notes of these chapters. It is suitable to teach this course at senior undergraduate level or at the graduate level provided that the students are exposed to some of the mathematical fundamentals described in Parts I through IV before taking this course. Alternately, a quick overview of the fundamentals can be covered in few weeks and the rest of the semester can be spent on the syntax and semantics of the chosen specification technique.
5. An advanced graduate-level course can be taught using any one of the techniques discussed in Parts V and VI with emphasis on developing complete specification for a fairly large problem. This would involve refinement, proof obligation, and implementation.
6. Another option would be to teach an advanced graduate-level course that requires the students to critically compare the techniques in each group and write a report. For example, one course could be taught on model-based specification techniques, all chapters in Part VI. Students in this course will get an in-depth understanding of the techniques and also would be able to choose the appropriate technique for a given problem.
7. Practitioners of formal methods, especially those who use formal methods for industrial applications, can use this book as a reference. In particular, the chapters in Parts V and VI have been written in such a way that a practitioner who is familiar with one technique can quickly jump start with another technique with little time. The examples and case studies in each chapter in these two parts provide sufficient information for a practitioner to start writing the specification for a new application without much preparation time.

Intended Audience

This book is written to serve as a text book for students in Software Engineering, Computer Science, Computer Engineering and Information Systems Engineering. Software professionals who want to familiarize themselves with formal methods can use this book as a good reference. The wide coverage of various formal specification techniques and the tutorial nature of descriptions of each individual technique make the book as a good resource for formal methods, all in one place. The bibliographic notes given at the end of each chapter provokes the reader to expand their horizon beyond the materials discussed in that chapter along with information on tool support.

Acknowledgments

Our sincere thanks go to the editorial board of Springer-Verlag, London whose persistent persuasion gave us sufficient motivation to engage in this venture. Many people have assisted us in bringing out the second edition of this book. First of all, those who have helped us during the first edition deserve a second round of applause. During the extensive revisions and additions to the second edition we received great support from Lei Feng, Pankaj Goyal, Naseem Ibrahim, Diep Mai, Ka Lok Man, Mubarak Mohammad, Shiri Nematollaah, and Olga Ormandjieva. We express our sincere thanks for their dedication and timely support.

Preface

This is a textbook on **software specification** emphasizing formal methods that are relevant to requirements and design stages of software development. The aim of the book is to teach the fundamental principles of formal methods in the construction of modular and verifiable formal specifications. The book introduces several formal specification techniques and illustrates the expressive power of each technique with a number of examples.

General Characteristics

Traditional textbooks on software engineering discuss the difficulties and challenges that lie on the path from requirements analysis to implementation of a software product. Most of these books describe some techniques in detail and give hints on implementation of these techniques. Only a few among them deal with important software engineering principles and techniques, and discuss how a particular technique may be used to implement a given principle. There is very little exposure in these books to a rigorous approach to, or a systematic study of, the construction of verifiable software. Those who have acquired an understanding of the fundamental principles of software engineering from traditional textbooks will find the following characteristics of this book quite relevant to the practice of software engineering.

- *The book deals with specification.*
  The principal characteristic of this book is to discuss formalisms that provide a theoretical foundation for the principles of software engineering, and are appropriate to the requirements and design stages of software development. We discuss the concept of abstraction, the need for formalism in software development, the mathematical basis of formal methods, components of a formal system, specification languages, different levels of rigor in applying languages, and the need for tool support to use formal methods for different stages of software development. We discuss the relationship between specifications and implementations, as well as subjecting specifications to rigorous analyses and formal proofs.

- *The book emphasizes mathematical principles.*

  Formal approaches to software development can be understood and practiced by studying the mathematics they use. A primary objective of the book is to relate discrete mathematical structures to the study of abstract data types, and to bring students to the level
  of mathematical maturity where they can write and reason about small specifications.
  Once the students acquire the basic mathematical skills that a formalism is based on,
  mastery of formal specification languages, techniques for refinements, and proofs become easy to understand and apply. We believe that the use of tools and techniques
  become effective when their underlying principles are properly understood.

- *The book teaches formal specification languages.*

  Unlike many recent books that are devoted to one formal specification language, we
  discuss four specification languages to emphasize their design philosophies and their
  practical applicability. We also discuss formal specifications based on set theory and
  logic without regard to any specification language. The purpose here is to teach the
  reader that these mathematical abstractions form the formal basis of the four specification languages. The languages discussed in the book are OBJ3, VDM, Z, and Larch. We
  illustrate their expressive power for different classes of applications. We expect that our
  treatment of the subject will prepare the reader to learn more sophisticated languages and
  tools that may be developed in the future. It is our belief that mastery of these languages
  will allow the reader to choose the language that is suitable for a given application.

- *The book presents proofs.*

  Informal arguments conducted in conjunction with a formal specification often lead to
  a proof construction, which can be presented in a justifiable manner. Proofs ensure a
  measure of certainty on claims that can be made of specified system properties. We
  present proofs in rigorous as well as in formal styles. We avoid lengthy proofs, and put
  more emphasis on modeling, specification, and rigorous reasoning of the specifications.

- *The book presents engineering principles.*

  This book discusses the general principles for data refinement, operation refinement, and
  interface specification, and illustrates how these are constructed for particular specification languages. The presentation in the book aims to enable the reader to understand *why*
  a particular technique is important and *how* to apply the technique.

Audience

This book is designed to be used as a textbook by students of computer science, software
engineering, and information engineering. Software professionals who want to learn formal
specification languages and use formal methods in their work will find the material in
the book useful for serious self-study. The sections on bibliographic notes give a broad
account of work related to the topic discussed in each chapter; this should help software
professionals to identify industrial applications and learn from the experience reported on
the use of tools.

Background Knowledge

The book is designed for undergraduates, and beginning graduate-level students in computer science, computer engineering, software engineering, and information engineering. We assume that the reader has completed an undergraduate course in discrete mathematics. The reader must be fluent in programming and must have completed or must be doing a course in software engineering. An exposure to undergraduate-level theoretical computer science course, or attainment of a certain level of *mathematical maturity* which enables the reader to abstract, conceptualize, and analytically reason about abstracted concepts will be an asset.

Organization and Content

Several specification languages, formal methods, and tools based on them have been developed by different research groups. Some of these methods are practiced by industries and government organizations such as NASA. Books devoted to one particular specification language or method have been published recently. Organizing the essential material to explore four specification languages in one textbook poses a challenge. We have organized this textbook based on the view that a reader should learn the following:

- where and how to integrate formalism in the development process,
- a mathematical basis, and
- the formal specification methods.

These are organized as follows:

- The first three chapters debate the questions: Why do we study formal specification? How do we integrate formal methods in a development process? What are the attributes for a formal specification language?
- Chapters 4 and 5 introduce the concept of abstraction and formalism, and discuss extensions to BNF and finite state machines, the two formal notations that the reader might have used in earlier courses.
- Chapters 6 and 7 discuss specifications based on logic, set theory and relations, and include material on proofs. Although the examples subjected to proofs are small, the structure of formal proofs is brought out clearly. These two chapters must be read carefully by those readers who want to review their mathematical knowledge.
- Chapters 8–11 describe the specification languages OBJ3, VDM, Z and Larch. We discuss the algebraic-specification methodology in Chap. 8, and include a tutorial on OBJ3. In Chap. 9, we introduce VDM, a model-based specification language. Chapter 10 deals with Z, another leading model-based notation built around set theoretical foundation. In Chap. 11, we discuss Larch and Larch/C++ specification languages. Our goal is to treat specification languages from abstract to concrete levels. Whereas representational details are ignored in an algebraic-specification language, VDM and Z specification languages use abstract data types as models for representing information of software

systems. The Larch family of languages are geared toward interface specification, and clearly separate the shareable abstraction from the programming language details. In our opinion, these four languages are representatives of several specification languages used for specifying sequential systems, and their features can be utilized in different application areas.

While the material in the first seven chapters should withstand the passage of time, it is likely that some of the material in Chaps. 8–11 may become outdated because of changes to the specification languages. The language OBJ3 has been around for a number of years, and its design principles are sound. The reader is expected to learn these principles; the syntax of the language or how OBJ3 system interprets a specification are secondary. We have used the ISO standardized notation for VDM in this book. The Z notation is also being standardized by ISO; however, the standardization process is not yet complete. Therefore, we have adopted an earlier version of Z. The Larch Shared Language (LSL), in which abstractions are developed, resembles an algebraic-specification language. However, the semantics of LSL is based on first-order logic. Given the impressive LSL library constructed by Guttag and Horning, we do not expect the syntax and the semantics of traits in the library to change much. However, the Larch/C++ interface specification language may undergo changes. The reader is advised to refer to the web page for Larch/C++ maintained by Gary Leavens for any update on the language. Since interface specification must be related to programming, and C++ is widely used in industry, we hope that the choice of Larch/C++ bridges the gap between design and implementation issues to be resolved by software professionals.

Exercises

All chapters include a section on exercises. There are three types:

- Exercises based on the basic concepts and aimed at extending the basic knowledge; these exercises include specifications and simple proofs.
- Extensions to examples discussed in the chapter; these require integration of the material discussed in the chapter.
- Project-oriented exercises that require complete specifications and proofs.

Case Studies

Case studies are used in Chaps. 8–11 to illustrate the features of OBJ3, VDM, Z, and Larch specification approaches. Each case study is chosen to demonstrate the integration of different concepts and features from a particular specification language. For example, the *Window* specification discussed in Chap. 8 demonstrates the integrated use of modular development and parametric specification concepts in OBJ3. This specification can be incrementally extended with additional operations, views, and theories toward reusing it in the design of another window management system. The *Network* example given in Chap. 9 is a simple version of a communication network. We have given a rigorous proof that the specification supports safe communication of messages between any two nodes in the network. The *Automated billing system* example presented in Chap. 10 is an instance of a real-life commercial application, which can be extended to suit a more complex situation. The case study in Chap. 11 presents Larch/C++ interface specifications for the two Rogue Wave library classes RWZone, and RWFile. These two examples are chosen to illustrate the applicability of Larch/C++ specification language to software products in commercial class libraries. The case studies may be read at different times and may be adapted or reused for different purposes.

Lab Components

The material in Chaps. 8–11 may be taught with tool-supported laboratory projects. In order to ensure that the students use the tool effectively, the instructors must (1) provide a solid foundation on theoretical issues, and (2) give assignments on simple specifications which can be done by pencil and paper. This will give students sufficient familiarity with the subject matter before they start learning to use the tools. The differences in syntactic conventions, and even minor differences in semantics between the specification language and the language employed by the tool must be overcome by the student. This implies that laboratory projects may only be introduced closer to the end of teaching the language; only then can the students' knowledge be expected to grow.

How to Use the Book

This book has evolved from the lecture notes prepared by the first author eight years ago. The notes were revised every year both for content and style. From the experience gained by both of us from the same notes in teaching different courses at different universities, we made extensive revisions to the notes in the last two years. However, the overall structure of the notes has not changed. Since the structure has withstood changes to the specification language details, such as syntax, we are confident that the different sequences as suggested below would fit different curriculum needs:

1. Chapters 1 through 3 are required for further reading of the book.
2. Chapters 4 and 5 may be read partially as well as simultaneously.
3. Based on the first seven chapters, a one-semester (13–14 weeks) undergraduate course within a software engineering program or computer science program or computer engineering program can be given.
4. Depending on the mathematical background of students in an information engineering program, material from Chaps. 1 through 7 may be selected and supplemented with basic mathematics to offer a one-semester course.

5. A two-semester course for graduates or senior undergraduates in software engineering, computer engineering, computer science, and information engineering programs can be given as follows:
   (a) Chapters 1 through 7 may be covered in semester I. One of the following sequences for semester II may be followed:

   - Chapters 8, 9
   - Chapters 8, 10
   - Chapters 9, 11
   - Chapters 10, 11

6. An advanced graduate-level course can be given by choosing the material from Chaps. 8 through 11 and supplementing it with intensive laboratory sessions requiring the verified development of a large project. This type of course requires tool support; for example, LP can be used with Larch, a theorem prover such as EVES or PVS may be used with Z or VDM. The material in the book may be supplemented with published papers in the area.

Acknowledgements

Our sincere thanks go to the many students and people who have helped us to create this book. We are grateful to the students of COMP 648 Systems Requirements Specification at Concordia University, and 74.716 Formal Specifications and Design at the University of Manitoba, for pointing out many of the errors in previous versions of the lecture notes.

Our deepest sense of gratitude go to Darmalingum Muthaiyen, who critically read the entire book, and gave us valuable feedback and corrections. His thorough reading and suggestion for presentable style have contributed greatly to the current version of the book.

We sincerely express our thanks to Dennis Lovie, Jonathan Jacky, and Randolph Johnson for reading and providing critical reviews on the Z notation. In particular, we greatly appreciate Randolph Johnson's comments on the semantics of some of the notations which helped us improve the chapter to its current version. We followed up Dennis Lovie's suggestions on uniformity of names and descriptions in the examples, which enhanced the readability of the chapter.

Jimmy Cheng and David So helped us in typesetting the first version of lecture notes eight years ago. Many of the LATEX commands defined by them have been used in typesetting the current version of the book.

Finally, our thanks go toward everyone whose work has inspired us in writing this book.

Contents

Part I
Specification Fundamentals

Specification is an essential activity that encompasses the different stages of a software development process. The quality of a Software Requirements Document (SRD) is of utmost importance to bring in clarity and completeness to the development of the abstract model of a software product. The construction of software through the design and implementation stages also requires specification at a more detailed level. Learning to think with clarity and learning to abstract from natural language descriptions are hard; however, this is essential to break complexity barriers in the development of large software systems. In this part of the book the role of specification, specification activities, specification qualities, and abstractions for software construction are discussed. The learning outcomes from this module are the following:

- the nature and types of complexities in software construction
- the meaning of specification, why to specify, what to specify, and when to specify
- specification as a means of controlling the complexities
- inherent flaws in natural language specifications and how to avoid them
- what is a formal method, and how to choose one for integration in software development process
- support roles for administering formal methods in a project
- attributes of a formal specification language
- assessing the quality of a formal specification
- abstractions for software construction

Part 1
Specification Fundamentals

The Role of Specification

Software plays a prominent and critical role in large business applications, health care industry, technical endeavors in space missions, and control systems for airlines, railways and telecommunications. In turn, software affects every aspect of human endeavor including the control and delivery of most of the services that we depend on. The World Wide Web (WWW) has introduced new opportunities for business and social networking, while at the same time has raised concerns on security, privacy, and reliability of information content and its use. Software for managing these applications are complex to construct. The source of complexity of a software product lies in the identification of a set of adequate functional and non-functional requirements from domain analysis, specifying system integrity constraints, and gathering the vast amount of knowledge necessary to precisely describe the expected interaction of the software with its environment. When all requirements are not properly understood, recorded, and communicated within the development team, there is a gap between the documented requirements and the requirements actually needed for correct functioning of the system. The inability in mastering the complexity leads to this discrepancy, which is the root cause of software errors. Precise documentation of domain models and system requirements with sufficient detail to cover unexpected worst-case scenarios is a good defense against system errors. Formal methods can provide a foundation for describing complex systems, for reasoning about the behavior of software systems, and can be a complimentary approach to traditional software development methodologies.

More than three decades ago, Brooks [3] recognized the difficulties in developing large complex software and likened the development of large software system to a great beast thrashing in a tar pit. It was relatively easy to get hold of any particular component of the software, but pulling the whole out of the tar was nearly impossible. Ten years later, Brooks [4] wrote that not only has there been little change, but there is not even a "silver bullet" in sight: a method, a software tool, development in technology or management technique that would dramatically improve productivity. This situation was attributed to the *essential* difficulties that are inherent in the nature of software: *invisibility, complexity, conformity, changeability*. Since then the software industry has met many of these chal-

V.S. Alagar, K. Periyasamy, *Specification of Software Systems*,
Texts in Computer Science,
DOI 10.1007/978-0-85729-277-3_1, © Springer-Verlag London Limited 2011

lenges and made enormous progress in adapting to new techniques while on their way to successfully developing and deploying several large systems. While this was happening, the industry had to meet the demand for new software in complex application domains, such as nuclear and chemical process control, imaging and analysis, and pervasive computing. These applications demand *dependable* software, in the sense that the software be reliable, safe, and secure, in addition to being correct. The recent National Research Council report on "Software for Dependable Systems" [17] emphatically states that "*a system is dependable when it can be depended upon to produce the consequences for which it was designed, and no adverse effects, in its intended environment*". In social computing applications the effect of software is felt in the "*human, physical, and organizational environment in which it operates*". Consequently dependability should be understood in the broader context of environmental interactions, not just conformance to local system properties. The goal must be to define dependability criteria for a software at the outset and include that as a goal in the software development process activities. Accepting that there may be no "silver bullet" in this area, one of the promising approaches is to intensify the rigor with which requirements are gathered, analyzed, specified, and rigorous methods are integrated with the development life-cycle activities. Formal methods can play an effective role in not only tackling complexity but also help to achieve provably dependable systems.

Requirements engineering and domain analysis deal with gathering and analysis of requirements which eventually lead to a decision on "what to build". Each deserves serious study in its own right. We turn our attention to a study of specification as a means of dealing with the inherent difficulties stated above. After a discussion on software complexity, we explain the notion of specification and explain what aspects of software complexity can be controlled. The chapter concludes with a critique on natural language specification.

1.1
Software Complexity

Very large software systems contain several million lines of source code, and voluminous documentation. In the future, rarely will such systems be built from scratch. They will incorporate existing software components and will require numerous intermediate steps in putting them together. This process is reliable only when the behavior and interface of the integrated pieces are well understood. The details of such a large design do not and cannot be comprehended by one single person. Curtis et al. [11] define this scenario as psychological complexity. Basili [2] defines software complexity as "...*a measure of the resources expended by another system while interacting with a piece of software*". Both authors remarked then that the underuse of structured programming techniques seem to increase the difficulty of comprehension for a software engineer. Currently, automated tools that conform to standard coding practice and other techniques prevent use of non-structured programming. Also, most newer languages (relative to 1979/1980) would make it very hard to write non-structured code. Unfortunately neither structured programming nor recent programming practices would adequately address all the concerns related to complexity elimination. We discuss below factors that contribute to software complexity.

An understanding of the sources of complexity will help the software developer look for means of reducing the overall complexity and introduce simplicity in the construction of large software systems.

Structured programming techniques, which promoted the use of pre- and post-conditions, Hoare axioms, predicate transformers, and top-down design methodologies, provided some help to practitioners of those classical "formal" techniques. However, these techniques have not totally eliminated all the problems afflicting software development. The main reason is that these methods do not provide the structuring and encapsulation necessary to synthesize large-grain software components. Although new development methods are being practiced today, it still remains difficult to ensure the expected performance of a system in a context where the system will be used. This is attributed to the ever increasing complexity of developing software.

In order to be deemed useful, every software system should exhibit a certain behavior that is observable when the system is functioning in its environment. This observational behavior is the external projection of its internal effect. The correct behavior of the components and their interactions within the system structure cause the external acceptable interactions. When the components can be modeled in a simple way and the interactions are governed by well-defined deterministic rules, the overall behavior of the system becomes predictable to a high degree of accuracy. A system whose behavior is completely predictable from the properties of its individual parts is a *simple* system. Simplicity in this context does not rule out algorithmic complexity or software complexity as defined by Basili [2] and Curtis [11]; simple systems are characterized by total predictability and perhaps by short programs.

In contrast to simple systems, there are systems whose behaviors are not completely predictable. A system composed of many interconnected components may exhibit one or more properties which are not obvious from the properties of the individual components. This happens when either some of the components are difficult to model accurately or the interactions of components are governed by laws that are not well defined. As a result, the overall behavior of the system can only be predicted with some degree of uncertainty. Clearly, such systems are *complex* systems.

Different complex systems behave with varying degrees of complexity. For example, a weather forecasting system is complex due to the difficulty of formulating laws governing atmospheric storms; a software for monitoring and predicting the performance of stocks is complex due to the fact that there is no accurate model for economic trends. When such uncertainties are based on information-theoretic interpretation, the definition of complexity given by Parnas [27] matches the notion of (un)predictability applied to these systems.

Complex systems may be *open*, may *evolve*, may be *nested*, and may be *adaptive*. Examples of complex adaptive systems include nuclear process control and monitoring systems, financial systems, weather prediction systems, autonomic systems that self-monitor, self-protect, and self-repair, and human social networking systems. An important feature of complex system is *emergence*, the way complexity arises out of simple initial interactions. Congestion in Internet traffic is an emergent property. In the WWW almost any pair of pages may be indirectly connected through a diverse set of short direct links. This emergent property is a factor that rates the WWW as a complex system.

1.1.1
Size Complexity

Large software systems are built with a number of parts (modules). The size of such a system refers to the number of parts in the system, the number of requirements to describe each part, the number of interactions between parts, and the number of quality constraints on the collective behavior of the parts. According to Parnas [27], a system is complex if the shortest description of the system is long. Size is an important factor causing technical and psychological setbacks in the early stages of the software life cycle, and causing design and implementation errors at later stages of the software life cycle. The vast amount of information to be gathered and analyzed during the requirements specification stage can cause incorrect, and incomplete information to leak through the review process. According to Leveson [21], almost all accidents involving computerized process control systems are due to this kind of error caused by the size factor. In fact, understanding the dynamics and the conditions under which software systems grow is a major challenge for the information technology industry. The behavior of large sized systems is not only governed by the behavior of the individual parts but also by the collective interaction among the parts. The properties of these parts and the laws governing their interactions must be understood before linking other parts that interact with them. Removing conflicting properties and ensuring completeness of properties are hard to achieve in a large system. The classical "formal" techniques used for small programs do not scale up to suit these tasks in the production of large software systems.

1.1.2
Structural Complexity

There are two aspects to structural complexity: management and technical. Software process models suggest only the highest level system decomposition. Each phase in a life cycle is assigned a specific goal. People assigned to the different phases interact and oversee the production of products as dictated by the dependencies among the phases. Within each phase, the target product may be developed either in a top-down manner or by reusing and combining existing software. The breadth and depth of the hierarchy of the development team organizing and managing the development activities determine the structural complexity of managing the system. In addition, traditions and policies in a software development firm may regulate information flow between certain groups, thereby increasing the structural complexity.

The level of interaction, known as coupling, among the modules of a software system is another measure of its structural complexity. The number of levels in the hierarchy of coupling and the span of control reflect the amount of changes that may be required in dependent modules due to changing requirements. The way that modules are connected determine the structural complexity and it has a great impact on the usability, modifiability, and performance of the system.

1.1.3
Environmental Complexity

In computing, the term "environment" refers to the overall physical, systematic, or logical structure within which a computer or program can operate. Software environment is the term commonly used to refer to the particular combination of operating system, software tools, interface, database system, etc., through which a user operates or programs a system. Software environment is the sum total of requirements specification environment, design environment, implementation environment, testing and verification environment, and the deployment environment. In this discussion by "environmental complexity" we mean the complexity of the objects and their interactions in the deployment environment, the environment in which the software system is utilized. The complexity of this environmental aspect makes it hard to correctly determine the dependability attributes safety, security, and availability of the software. The complexity of other environments have an impact mainly on the functional correctness of the software, and this has been studied in some depth by computer science community. For dependable systems, such as reactive systems and safety-critical systems, functional correctness is only a part of the overall behavior. The fulfillment of the dependability contract between the system and its deployment environment squarely rests on how well the environment complexity is dealt with.

The client of a program is its environment, which can be either a user or another program. In the simplest situation the output from a program can be either a value to be consumed by the environment, or a state change in it. In either case the execution of a program affects the environment in which it is effective. A software's utilization in the environment that best fits its functional requirements may expose the weakness of the software, due to the non-fulfillment of the promised quality attributes. In order to earn the trust of the clients of the software, who are part of its environment, the attributes and constraints of the environment that regulate the acceptable software behavior in its environment must be included in the requirements and they must be rigorously analyzed during software development activities. Many software systems, such as the one described below, may affect our lives by causing injury if environmental constraints are not satisfied by system execution. Environmental analysis is absolutely essential for them, although the environmental constraints themselves may be complex to understand and specify. It is best to integrate the environment and system as one engineered artifact.

- *Reactive Systems*: A reactive system is different from traditional input–output systems. It may receive input at any time during its execution, provide outputs at different stages, and may be non-terminating. The two important properties of a reactive system are *stimulus synchronization* and *response synchronization*. Stimulus synchronization refers to the feature that the system accepts every stimulus (input) whenever it is received. Response synchronization refers to the ability of the system to respond to a stimulus in a timely fashion, in the sense that when the system response is received by the environment it is still in a position to use it. When the system responses are regulated by time constraints the system is called *real-time reactive* system. Violating time constraints may eventually lead to unsafe executions and deliver responses to the environment in

Table 1.1 Environment for safety-critical systems

Software System	System Objects	Environmental Objects	Nature of Complexity
Railway signaling system	Network of controllers	Trains, Gates, Actuators, Living Beings	Heterogeneous nature of objects, Time constrained and concurrent communication
Flight-guidance and Air-traffic control system	On-ground and on-board controllers, Navigation subsystem	Sensors for detecting atmospheric conditions, Unknown flying objects, Weather monitoring units, Humans	Asynchronous communication, Uncertainty in measurements, Unknown behavior of flying objects, failure prevention mechanisms
Nuclear power plants	Boiling water reactor controller, Waste and radiation manager, Corrosion detector and reducer	Humans, Places, Power Networks	Knowledge of and technology transfer from Nuclear Science and Nuclear Medicine, Automatic shutdown mechanism of power networks, and disaster control

untimely manner. Systems in which safe executions are paramount are called *safety-critical* systems. Examples of such systems include railway signaling systems, flight-guidance system and air-traffic control systems, and control systems for nuclear power plants. Table 1.1 describes three reactive systems that are safety-critical, the objects in each system, a set of environmental objects with which the system objects interact, and the nature of complexity for these systems.

In all examples cited in Table 1.1, environmental complexity, largeness, and inability to enforce timeliness in execution platforms add to the difficulty of constructing provably correct systems. Software systems that monitor atmospheric changes and predict the occurrences of floods, earthquakes, tornadoes, and hurricanes are *life-critical systems*. They communicate in real-time with systems that manage emergency relief operations. Thus, telephony and emergency health care are also associated with life-critical systems. A communication failure to connect a 911 call in an emergency may result in the loss of several lives.

- *Ubiquitous Computing Systems*: Ubiquitous computing refers to the invisible computation in the environment we are situated. Many devices in the environment surrounding the user compute results and convey responses by automatically tracking the activities of the user. The user by herself does not program, but may only hold a preprogrammed device to obtain the results of interest from the embedded computing and other devices. Most importantly the user may be unaware that she is being tracked in a computation scenario. The devices in the environment include sensors, controllers, and actuators. They are in general heterogeneous, with differing capabilities and complementary functionalities.

- *Context-aware Systems*: Context awareness is a term that originated with ubiquitous (also called pervasive) computing. Context-aware systems are not only pervasive but may have to deal with linking system changes with environmental changes subject to safety, security, privacy, and timeliness constraints. Understanding these constraints, formalizing them, and analyzing their impact on the software functionality must precede the development of software. Contexts that originate from the environment carry with them the knowledge about the environment. The abstraction of context, formal representation of it, and tracking context evolution are necessary for monitoring application behavior with respect to different contexts. Context, being related to human factors and environment, must be studied with great care for an application.

   In a formal approach to software development, it is necessary to

- formalize the environmental objects, their attributes and constraints and include them in the system specification,
- integrate the system and environmental model into one model in which each can observe the other and interact,
- verify that the system interaction with the environment does not violate the environmental constraints.

1.1.4
Application Domain Complexity

A *domain* refers to a particular field of *knowledge*. Banking, health care, transportation, communication and control, payroll, and E-commerce are some examples of domains.

   Domain complexity arises from the essential *intricacy of the knowledge* in that domain. In early 90's (and in times earlier than that) business software were using only common software solutions. Now, custom solutions are demanded. For example, E-commerce solutions must be customized. When business complexity grows, the custom software for a business application, which imbibes the complexity of the business domain, also increases. In many business applications, given the complexity of business model, "simple" software solutions will not adequately solve the problem. This means that a business software that provides a reasonably acceptable solution must necessarily be complicated. This complexity cannot be removed, but should be controlled. The software process model and the methods used in its different phases for constructing the business software brings in extraneous complexity through them. Incomplete models, inappropriate design, inefficient programming language, inaccurate programming, and incomplete validation are sources that bring in extraneous complexity. This second kind of complexity should be removed altogether. Formal domain modeling and domain analysis can help minimize this complexity. For example, in a software for business computing, business rules and business models can be formalized. This in turn will help to ensure the consistency of dynamically evolving business laws.

   Other sources that give rise to domain complexity are the following.

- *Interrelated domains*: Often software for application in one domain will require knowledge from other interrelated domains. For example, to *seek a medication* in the domain of on line health care system, a user interface domain is required, queries to database domain (patient database, medical database) are required, and a reference to on line health care policy domain is required. Thus, domain complexity is characterized by the number of interrelated domains, and the *depth* of the hierarchical relationship, involved in a software application in that domain.

- *Fuzzy boundary*: In many situations, an entity may belong to many domains. It is hard to delimit the operational ability for an entity and draw a strict boundary for an application in a domain.

- *Knowledge gathering and representation*: In general, it is impossible to know all objects in a domain, and all information about a known object. Thus knowledge acquisition for an application in a domain will necessarily be incomplete. In order to faithfully represent acquired knowledge, we need to invent a medium and it may be hard to invent such a medium. As an example, to automate a human enterprise, as is attempted in cognitive and behavioral sciences, the software cannot dodge this kind of complexity. The objects manipulated by the software are only models of the real objects belonging to the application domain. How to abstract those aspects of reality that should be part of the model on which the software construction can be based? For some application domains, the models can only be approximate. This may be due to an incomplete knowledge of the domain objects, or a severe limitation of the model, or a combination of both. Engineering applications use well-tested models that are supported by sound scientific theories. However, there is no cognitive model for a user; there is no exact model to represent the geometry, topology and properties of physical objects; there may not be an exact final model for weather as characterized by atmospheric ambiguities. In the absence of exact knowledge, it is very likely that many aspects of the domain may not be observable in the software; moreover, a number of observations projected by the software constructed from approximate models may not reflect reality.

1.1.5
Communication Complexity

The general communication problem involves knowledge (information) distributed among many *parties* (*people*, *processors*) and the need for the parties to communicate with each other in order to perform a task. The simplest version of communication problem is the two party scenario in which both know the task to perform, each party has a fixed amount of information I to share, and they communicate according to an agreed upon *protocol* P in attempting to perform the task. The communication in the protocol is a sequence of information exchanges, called a *run*. At each stage of the run, the protocol should determine whether the run terminates. If it terminates the protocol must specify the task accomplished. If the run does not terminate the protocol specifies which party should send information. The information sent at each stage will depend solely on the information exchanged by the parties until that stage. The communication complexity of this two party scenario for a given protocol P is the maximum *amount of communication* involved in the protocol P, the maximum is computed over all possible I. The communication cost of performing the task is the minimum cost of a protocol that performs the task, the minimum is computed over all possible protocols.

In a general software development factory, due to the size, the large number of internal structures and the heterogeneous nature of interrelated domains of the application domain, a group of people rather than just two persons will be assigned the task of developing a software system. Each person may play one or more roles in the activities associated with the development process. Describing, even informally, the protocol for information exchange in this scenario and specifying the amount of communication exchange in a run become hard. The complexity of protocols for cross-organizational development effort is much harder to assess.

The medium of communication can be one or more of verbal, graphical or textual. Sometimes, much of the information required during the early stages of software development is *tacit*. It is important that people involved in different phases communicate among themselves without *ambiguity*. When natural language is used for "written" technical reports, it is difficult to precisely state all the essential attributes of the product under development. When specification is expressed in a natural language and the design contains graphical constructs, it becomes difficult to relate descriptions in different media. When people use different notations within one phase, or different notations are used for different phases, due to semantic gaps agreements are hard to reach. Thus discovering a communication protocol and specifying it for guaranteed termination are hard tasks.

An immediate consequence of an imperfect protocol is that errors arise at early stages of the software life cycle. It is known that such errors are very likely to remain undetected until later stages and get amplified in the development process. Several empirical studies have confirmed that errors made in the requirements analysis phase are indeed significant. Moreover, design errors triggered by errors in the requirements analysis phase are more difficult to detect and correct; in fact, they cannot be fixed without first identifying their source in the requirements and then correcting the source.

1.2
Software Specification

Can software complexity be controlled by any systematic technique? We answer this question in two parts: (1) a proper specification can control and adequately contain certain types of complexity; (2) without specification software complexity is uncontrollable, especially for safety-critical systems. The second part of the answer is justified by the remarks of Brooks [4]. To justify the first part of the answer, we discuss below "what is a specification, why we need to specify, what to specify, and when to specify". The question "how to specify" is taken up in later chapters.

1.2.1
What is a Specification?

According to Chambers 20th century dictionary *specific* means *that pertaining to a particular species, specify* means *to be specific* and *specification* is the *act of specifying*. In Physical Sciences, terms such as *specific gravity, specific heat and specific inductive capacity* are defined to convey particular properties and characterize the behavior of physical substances in any context of their usage. In Engineering and in Architecture, the word specification refers to a statement of particulars describing the structural and behavioral details of the product to be developed. In the context of software development, all of the above meanings for specification can be carried over. In particular, software specification denotes a precise description of the system objects, a set of methods to manipulate them, and a statement on their collective behavior for the duration of their existence in the system to be developed.

1.2.2
Why Specify?

One of the main goals of software engineering is the production of software which successfully works in the environment where it is intended to be used. The development process of a large complex software system necessitates the gathering and the management of a vast amount of data on the application domain, processes, people and product descriptions. In order to cope with the numerous objects that arise and the enormous amount of information generated while managing them, *abstraction* and *decomposition* have been found to be useful tools. The principle of decomposition ensures that properties of the whole system follow from the properties of its parts. Abstraction principles, which are discussed in greater detail in Chap. 4, ensure that the specification has only key features, without a description on how they can be realized. For example, when several people work on a software project, decomposition and abstraction of tasks would bring forth precision and simplicity in expressing the interdependence and communication among objects. Therefore, you might choose to specify because you want a more precise statement or documentation of the requirements and system's interfaces, and would benefit members of software development groups by an abstract description of system design. That is, a specification provides a clear, concise medium of communication between designers, developers, and implementors. Tools can be applied to formal specifications to help find errors in the design and uncover boundary cases left unspecified. Other reasons would be

- *Completeness*: All situations, including exceptions and error handling, are to be specified for a communication protocol.
- *Controlling Complexity*: The system design is too large. It is necessary to decompose it, specify each part individually, and a method of putting them back together, known as *composition*, should be specified.
- *Contract Specification*: The user interface to a system (or program) is a contract and should be unambiguously specified.

- *Controlling Environment*: The system's obligation to its environment needs to be precisely stated in order that the client of the system can verify the satisfaction of this obligation after an interactive session terminates.

1.2.3
What to Specify?

Software life-cycle models decompose the entire development process into a series of phases and associate a specific task with each phase. Although the boundaries and the ordering of these phases differ in different models, the specification activity in each phase produces a more *precise definition* of system attributes. Hence, for each object its description, *properties*, and *operations* must be specified. For every pair of objects it is necessary to specify their interaction rules. Wing [34] stresses the distinction between *required*, and *permitted* behavior for system objects. Since a specification may allow different implementations, and the behaviors of implementations are not likely to be identical, it is safe to associate a specification with describing permitted behavior. Any one implementation may not capture all behaviors, but no implementation should be allowed to have a behavior outside the set of permitted behaviors. Wing [34] lists the following *what* list.

- *Properties of Objects*: An object in a specification is either *simple* or *structured*. Associate each object (entity) with a *type*. Investigate ordering, a simple form of relation, among objects. Associate abstract types with structured objects and thus define access methods. Specify the permitted sequence of access methods. State boundedness and invariant properties.
- *Correctness Condition*: A software system should maintain some global correctness condition. Examples include deadlock freedom and bounded growth of critical variables. Correctness condition should be verifiable at every stage of the development life cycle. If it cannot be verified at a certain stage, then one or more of the following situations have cropped up:

  1. The correctness condition is not expressed well in the specification notation. Change the notation or invent another syntax.
  2. The correctness condition is too strong. Back off and formulate a weaker condition with which the system development can progress.
  3. The stage that you are in the development process is not consistent with the previous stage in which the correctness condition was verified successfully.

- *Observable Behavior*: A system's interaction with its environment is observable. As an example, the error output from a C++ compiler makes an internal error, such as a register overflow, observable. A debugger may provide a deeper illumination of the observed behavior. Hence, what is observable is dependent upon the level of formalism that you use. A functional requirement may be specified by a set of functions. For each function the interface specifies "how to invoke the function" (*pre-condition*), and "what the output will be" (*post-condition*) when it is correctly invoked. State machines and defining state invariants on them are standard ways to specify the observable behavior of system entities and their interactions.

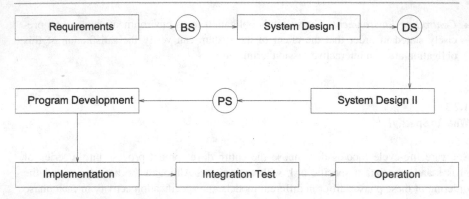

Fig. 1.1 A simple life-cycle model with specification phases

1.2.4
When to Specify?

From requirements to final implementation and delivery, system objects and their interactions are transformed from a high-level of abstraction successively through increasing
levels of concreteness to an executable program. Hence, we may regard specification as a
multi-stage activity rather than a one-time activity. We discuss here the specification activities with respect to a simplified life-cycle model shown in Fig. 1.1. In Chap. 2, we discuss
a life-cycle model in which formal methods is integrated in all phases of development
activity, from domain analysis to run-time environment.

In the simplified model, after the first phase of requirements gathering and analysis, a
software requirements document (SRD) is prepared. This serves as a *contract* between the
customer and the supplier. The first level software specification based on the objectives
stated in the SRD is a precise and unambiguous description of the *behavior* of the desired
system in terms of externally observable functional characteristics. Constraints of the system, if any, can also be specified as properties of the system. These remain *independent*
of any implementation or execution of the system. This first level specification is termed
behavioral specification, shown as BS in Fig. 1.1.

Following the behavioral specification, which describes WHAT is expected of the system, the next stage is to specify the *operational* characteristics and the *internal structure* of
the system. This specification level contains *more details* than the behavioral specification;
however, every care must be taken to ensure that external behavior as defined earlier is
preserved. This specification level, called *design specification* (DS), preserves the properties stated in the previous specification level, contains more details, probably motivated by
certain needs, and provides mechanisms needed to produce such a behavior. We may view
this specification as a more concrete description of the behavioral specification.

The first level design specification can be *refined* further by adding more and more details on data, action, control, and exception. Moreover, for each component in the design,
interaction between components and component interfaces can be specified in more detail
and further refined into a series of specifications. We consequently arrive at an interface

specification and a detailed design specification, which can be implemented as a program. The implementation language and the hardware configuration for its installation are chosen at the interface specification stage. Thus the specification exercise encompasses more than one phase of the software life cycle. We must keep in mind that modifying existing specifications and/or including new specifications may become necessary during any stage of system evolution. Specifications are subject to validation to ensure that they remain faithful to the intended need, as expressed in the requirements document and as required by the usage context.

The essential properties that characterize specifications created during the software development cycle are summarized as follows:

1. It must be possible to define the observable behavior.
2. The interface of a software component must be precise and simple.
3. The behavior of the whole must be expressible in terms of the behavior of the parts. Stated otherwise, it must be possible to compose specifications.
4. It must be possible to develop a program from the detailed design specification.
5. The design specification must contain a description of all behaviors expressed by the behavioral specification.
6. It must be possible to test for conformance—that a program satisfies its specification.
7. It must be possible to subject a specification to rigorous analysis; for example, given a specification and a property, it must be possible to determine whether or not the property is a consequence of the specification.

1.2.5
How to Control Complexity?

The most common and effective technique for dealing with complexity is *abstraction*. Different levels of abstractions will have to be employed to deal with system aspects (size, structure, operations), environment, domain, and communication. The software development team does not have much control over environment and application domain complexities. Application domain models, and knowledge-base support for environmental theories are necessary to help developers cope with these two complexities. The chosen abstraction should allow incremental absorption of requirements that emerge during the software development process or when the software is operational. Domain experts and environmental scientists should provide support for modeling interactions arising from evolving requirements.

Controlling Size Complexity

Software developers can deal with size through modular decomposition techniques which partition the world of objects into manageable collections. This allows the understanding of both the individual and the collective behavior of objects at a sufficiently high level of abstraction. Another approach is to use top-down functional decomposition with recursive definitions for abstracting the depth of a hierarchy in a structure chart. The depth of the hierarchy can be reduced by resorting to *incremental* abstraction. In this approach, the developer creates only the most critical details, and then expand them with additional details to promote user understanding and system needs. Another effective means to deal with size complexity is to *reuse* well-defined, well-understood, and well-tested software components. What is important here is the simplicity and correctness of interface specifications of reuse objects so that reusable components are best understood by understanding their interfaces, without having to know how they are implemented.

Controlling Structural Complexity

Structural complexity is best dealt with set theory, relations, and functions abstractions from Mathematics. Not only they provide an abstract *model* for structured objects, but also import with them the *theory* of sets, relations, and functions from Mathematics. For example, to describe a collection of similar, but distinct, objects having some common attributes, one can use the notion of *set*, without concern for the representation. If duplicates are allowed then *bag* (*multiset*) is an appropriate abstraction. If the objects are to be ordered, with respect to priority or partial ordering, then sequences or priority queues are appropriate abstractions. Dynamic properties of relational entities or any function or any structured entity can be abstracted using *algebras*. For example, the equation

$$insert(insert(s, e), e) = insert(s, e) \tag{1.1}$$

asserts that the property of a set that it has no duplicates is preserved by *insert* operation. To understand this equation, assume that s' denotes the set $insert(s, e)$. Now, substituting s' for $insert(s, e)$ in equation 1.1 will *rewrite* it as in 1.2.

$$inset(s', e) = s' \tag{1.2}$$

Hence, inserting e in set s' does not modify the set s'. Since this is true regardless of the element e and set s it follows that s' has no duplicates, hence a set. In specifying operations, it is best to use *declarative* rather than *operational* style. Algebras and Logics provide the notation with sufficient expressive power. Using quantified expressions, iterations over structures such as set members, can be specified. Describing specific search procedures can be postponed to the detailed design stage. Thus, the statement $\forall x \in X \bullet do f(x)$, describes function computations for each member of set X. The scope of quantification in quantified expressions must be understood. Both the expressions $\exists! x \in s \bullet P(x)$ and $\exists! x \bullet x \in s \wedge P(x)$ convey the meaning that there exists exactly one element of set s which satisfies the property P. It is best to keep function interfaces simple, by separating the normal behavior from error situations. That is, the total operational specification of a function is either its normal behavior specification or its error specification, but not both. Abstractly this is translated to (1.3).

$$TotalOp = NormalOp \vee ErrorOp \tag{1.3}$$

Controlling Environmental Complexity

The environment of a software system consists of entities that send stimuli to the system and receive responses from the system. The complexity of environmental entities and their interactions with system can be systemized through *contexts*. A context of the environment is a situation with a specific property that is true for that context. Discovering contextual information might help to eliminate a chunk of the environment as unnecessary for the specific application. In the design of GUIDE [8], an intelligent electronic tour guide, the environment of the software consists of the following objects:

- user, a visitor to explore a city
- information on the city, which includes places of interest, their locations, operational constraints, access constraints
- end system with which the user interacts to get environment information, and
- a wireless communication infrastructure.

Personal contexts for the user include her current location and her interests. Environmental contexts include local time of the day, and locations of city attractions. A property (constraint) of personal context may be "age of the person is at least 18 and interests are movies". A constraint of an environmental context may be "time of day is 17:30 and the nearest movie house is three blocks away and the movie starts at 18:00 hours".

Environmental analysis must be done to uncover environmental contexts and their constraints. Complexity may be reduced by using contexts as filters to extract system stimuli relevant to different contexts. The environmental objects may be partitioned such that objects in one partition have a common end system or require one common system response. Thus a separation of concerns is achieved for dealing with the size and structure complexity of the environment. The communication infrastructure for the end system must be chosen to serve efficiently in all contexts.

Controlling Domain Complexity

Domain engineering, which involves domain analysis and domain modeling leading to an organization of domain knowledge, is a necessary step to soft land domain complexity in software development process. Domain analysis involves identification and analysis of the applications, their detailed requirements, and the relations and data that exist in a specific domain [28]. The results of the domain analysis is a domain model which consists of knowledge about the domain and all its applications and its reusable components. For example, a car is an entity in the domain of automobile industry. A car contains many control systems such as *cruise control, anti-lock braking system, cooling and heating system*, and *security system*. A domain analysis for this domain should expose not only the functionalities and non-functional quality attributes of each individual system but also explore the role of smart sensors that may be shared by these systems. A common ontology language, called *ontology web language* (OWL) [30], can be used to formally represent the results of domain analysis. An ontology is a content theory about the sorts of concepts, their properties, constraints, and the relations between concepts that are possible in a specified domain of knowledge [9]. It provides terms for describing the knowledge about a domain capturing the intrinsic conceptual structure of the domain. The ontology thus represented can be carried down to design component-based systems.

Controlling Communication Complexity

Humans can follow organizational rules if they are clearly stated. However, rules for software development are subject to different interpretations. In order to ensure uniform interpretation of requirements, it is essential that the development team learns effective modes of communication which include precise notations, including formal notations, to communicate different views for the same entity. Ad-hoc notations, natural language intercepted with graphics, and/or pseudo code are not sufficient to discharge the demands placed on a design team. With natural languages and graphics, it is very easy to miss some situations, initial and boundary cases, and exceptions.

1.2.6
A Critique of Natural Language Specification

Specification must be documented using a representation technique that can unequivocally be understood and acted upon by all software engineers involved in the production of software. The discussion in Sect. 1.2.1 underlies that specification is not a one-time activity and clients of the specified product are different at different stages of the development cycle. There are several drawbacks to using an informal approach and a natural language description to specify software components intended for these clients. Natural languages are expressive but imprecise. It is possible to express any software property in a natural language, but the expression may be given different interpretations, or not understood at all. Natural language descriptions carry lot of noise, ambiguities, and contradictions, as pointed out by Meyer [22]. Noise refers to the usage of different words in a text to denote the same concept. For example, "nonempty sequence" of items is the same as "one or more" items. Although repetition is avoided in literary writing, in a technical document, observes Meyer, the same concept should be denoted by the same words, lest the reader be confused. Silence refers to undefined terms and undefined features of defined terms in a text. It is hard to analyze a natural language specification to detect this kind of error. Statements such as "event a happens after event b" is ambiguous, since the terms "happens" and "after" can be interpreted in more than one way. Another example is the usage of "up to" in the statement "an identifier can have up to eight characters". Informal descriptions, such as diagrams, have no inherent semantics unless accompanied by precise annotations. After illustrating these pitfalls of natural language descriptions through the text processing example first developed by Naur [24] and subsequently corrected by Goodenough and Gerhat [13], Meyer shows how the specification can significantly be improved through reasonable use of more formal specifications. We take up the study of formal specifications in later chapters.

1.3
Exercises

1. Give a natural language description of the features and functionalities of any two text editors you have used. How many deficiencies, as described in the text and in Meyer's paper [22], are found in your natural language specification?

2. Take a recipe description from a cook book. Determine the ambiguities, omissions, imprecision, and contradictions in it. How would you make it more precise? What environmental assumptions are necessary to implement the recipes ("bake the cookies", for example)?

3. What is the "domain" for an *Automated Teller Machine* (ATM)? Investigate the entities, their roles, properties, and interactions. Identify the different applications in that
   domain. Comment on the sufficiency of your domain analysis for these applications.
4. Study an *artificial pacemaker*, a medical device used to regulate heart beat. A first reference is http://en.wikipedia.org/wiki/Artificial_pacemaker. Investigate the "environment" in which it functions. Identify the contexts for its *safety*, *privacy*, and *reliability*.
5. Review a term project you have done and examine the stability of its design when a few
   of the requirements are changed. Are you able to do it from your design documentation
   and requirements specification? Explain the difficulties. Hint: You may wish to create a
   Traceability Matrix, which records and relates the objects from requirements and design
   in a meaningful way.

1.4
Bibliographic Notes

Complex physical systems exhibit emergent properties and a formal systematic study of
them have been undertaken by mathematicians and physicists [33]. Complex software systems, created by the combined efforts of many people, often lack a formal mathematical
model. Consequently, a thorough understanding of the interaction of the entire system is
hard to achieve. The seminal book by Brooks [3] and his observation [4] "one has to accept
that there is no silver bullet in this area" had a significant impact on software engineering
development practices. Beginning from the late 80's software developers embraced for
more systematic approaches founded on high-level programming paradigms, which are in
turn supported by mathematics, science and engineering. This is described in the report
[29] issued by the Computer Science and Technology Board, research done at SRI [10]
and at NASA [6]. In spite of systematic methods used in software development, modern
software with plug-in capabilities can be viewed as composite products, and hence they
carry the intrinsic product complexities [19] as well as emergent properties of the development environment. The challenge to providing a sufficient evidence of dependability
criteria and proving it in order to make claims on dependable software systems is discussed
in the report [17].

   With regards to the classification on the sources of software complexity we highlight
the three sources: environment, domain, and communication. The complexity they bring
into software development cannot be removed but should be tamed. In the Technical Opinion section of CACM [32], Wegner and Goldin have pointed out that artificial intelligence,
graphics, and the Internet could not be expressed by Turing machines, the basis of computation theory in Computer Science. The reasons are that in these areas of study interaction
between the program and the environment takes place during a computation, and are often
concurrent. As observed by Brooks [5], all intelligent systems must be situated in some
world (environment) and exhibit complex interactions if they have to produce any useful result. When such interactions cannot be adequately expressed within a computation
model then clearly a new conceptual framework is required. Milner [23] in his Turing
award lecture eloquently brings out the need for a new platform to express environmental

interactions. Consequently, we should agree that at the present level of knowledge environmental interactions cannot be modeled satisfactorily and computed correctly. That is the source of complexity and is hard to remove. Yet, as demonstrated by the successful development and deployment of the automatic train protection of Paris Metro [7], British Rail's signaling system [18] and the on-board avionics software for an Israel aircraft [14], a well-studied and regulated environment can be modeled and integrated faultlessly in software development.

As early as 1981, Neighbors [25] realized the necessity of modeling domain objects and analyzing their properties in developing reusable components for all systems in an application area. Domain-driven design [12] is a design paradigm for tackling the complexity trickling from domain into software development phases. To tackle domain complexity domain experts should be involved, not just at the beginning of domain modeling and requirements gathering, but throughout the development stages. Domain analysis must produce dependability criteria and certification standards for software in that domain.

Mobile computing, context awareness, and ubiquitous computing come together in many systems with which humans interact on a daily basis. Electronic Tour Guide (ETG) [8] is an example. This is a typical example in which domain complexity is compounded with the environmental complexity. Navigation using a map, retrieving context-dependent information, booking accommodation while on the go, and communicating with other visitors who have access to similar tour guides are some of the useful operations on a ETG. The main domain for ETG is *Tourism*. The interrelated domains are GUI (Graphical User Interface), wireless networking, sensor network, database, and navigation algorithms. As first remarked by Weiser [31], *"this is not GUI problem, ..., the problem is not one of interface, ..., this is not a multimedia problem, ... The challenge is to create a new kind of relationship of people to computers, one in which the computer would have to take the lead in becoming vastly better at getting out of the way so people could just go about their lives."* So, complexity of ubiquitous software, such as ETG, is quite high.

Communication complexity is now formally studied as part of Complexity Theory [20]. Taking lessons from the way the theorists formalize communication complexity, it is evident that even simple assumptions on the nature of communication and protocol lead to the conclusion that the complexity is quite steep and is hard to surmount in software development process.

With regards to the methods used in specifying software requirements, Alford [1] describes his Requirements Driven Development (RDD) method of system development based on a set of graphical and textual representations for capturing requirements and design. This method to systems engineering is supported by a set of tools for traceability analysis, to record design decisions, check consistency, and conduct reviews. It is believed that this method is widely practiced in industries. For complex systems, Henninger et al. [15, 16] provide useful checklists. These two papers describe the difficulties encountered in writing requirements specification for large and complex systems and discuss the specification techniques that are used for making requirements precise, unambiguous, consistent and complete. Parnas [26, 27] discusses complexity in the context of developing software for strategic applications and provides practical approaches to follow.

A good critique of natural language specification has been given by Meyer [22]. This article explains the "seven sins" of a specifier in using a natural language, reviews the types of errors uncovered in published papers [13, 24], and proposes a formal specification approach. The message of this paper is that a natural language specification, even when corrected and cleaned up by experts, will have flaws.

The article by Wing [34] must be read and re-read by all aspiring to become formal specification specialists. The merits, advantages, and limitations of most formal specification methods you will learn in later chapters of the book are brought out in this article.

References

1. Alford M (1985) SREM at the age of eight. IEEE Comput 18:4
2. Basili VR (1980) Quantitative software complexity models: a panel summary. In: Basili VR (ed) Tutorial on models and methods for software management and engineering. IEEE Computer Society Press, Los Alamitos
3. Brooks FP Jr (1975) The mythical man-month: essays on software engineering. Addison-Wesley, Reading
4. Brooks FP Jr (1987) No silver bullet: essence and accidents of software engineering. IEEE Comput 20(4):10–19
5. Brooks RA (1991) Intelligence without reason. MIT AI Lab Technical Report No 1293
6. Butler RW (1996) An introduction to requirements capture using PVS: specification of a simple autopilot. In: NASA technical memorandum 110255. Langley Research Center, Hampton
7. Carnot M, DaSilva C, Dehbonei B, Meija F (1992) Error-free software development for critical systems using the B-Methodology. In: Third international software symposium on software reliability engineering
8. Cheverst K, Davies N, Mitchell K, Friday A, Efstratiou C (2000) Developing a context-aware electronic tourist guide: some issues and experiences. CHI Lett 2(1):1–6
9. Chandrasekaran B, Josephson JR, Benjamins VR (1999) What are ontologies and why do we need them? IEEE Intell Syst 14(1):20–26
10. Crow J, De Vito BL (1996) Formalizing space shuttle software requirements. In: Proceedings of ACM SIGSOFT workshop on formal methods in software practice, San Diego, CA, January 1996
11. Curtis B, Sheppard SB, Milliman P, Borst MN, Love T (1979) Measuring the psychological complexity of software maintenance tasks with the Halstead and McCabe metrics. IEEE Trans Softw Eng SE-5(2):96–104
12. Evans E (2004) Domain-driven design: tackling complexity in the heart of software. Addison-Wesley, New York
13. Goodenough JB, Gerhart S (1977) Towards a theory of test data selection criteria. In: Yeh RT (ed) Current trends in programming methodology, vol 2. Prentice-Hall, Englewood Cliffs, pp 44–79
14. Harel D (1992) Biting the silver bullet: toward a brighter future for system development. IEEE Comput 25(1):8–20
15. Heninger KL (1989) Specifying software requirements for complex systems: new techniques and their application. IEEE Trans Softw Eng SE-6(1):2–12
16. Heninger KL, Kallander JW, Shore JE, Parnas DL (1980) Software requirements for the A-7E aircraft (second printing). NRL Memorandum Report No 3876, Naval Research Laboratories, Washington, DC
17. Jackson D, Thomas M, Millett LI (eds) Committee on Certifiably Dependable Software Systems, National Research Council, Software for dependable systems: sufficient evidence? http://www.nap.edu/catalog/11923.html
18. King T (1994) Formalizing British rail's signalling rules. In: FME'94: industrial benefit of formal methods. Lecture notes in computer science, vol 873. Springer, Berlin, pp 44–54

19. Kries B (2007) The future of product development. In: Proceedings of the 17th CIRP design conference. Springer, Berlin
20. Kushilevitz E, Nisan N (1996) Communication complexity. Cambridge University Press, Cambridge
21. Leveson NG (1991) Software safety in embedded computer systems. Commun ACM 34(2):35–46
22. Meyer B (1985) On formalism in specifications. IEEE Softw January:6–26
23. Milner R (1993) Elements of interaction. (Turing award lecture). Commun CACM 36(1):78–89
24. Naur P (1969) Programming in action clusters. BIT 9(3):250–258
25. Neighbors J (1981) Software construction using components. PhD thesis, Department of Computer and Information Science, University of California, Irvine
26. Parnas DL (1986) Can software for the strategic defense initiative ever be error-free? IEEE Comput 19:11
27. Parnas DL (1995) Fighting complexity. Invited talk. In: International conference on engineering complex computer systems, ICECCS'95, Fort Lauderdale, Florida, November 1995
28. Pressman R (2005) Software engineering: a practitioner's approach. McGraw-Hill, New York
29. Computer Science Technology Board (1990) Scaling up: a research agenda for software engineering. Commun ACM 33(3):281–293
30. Smith MK, Welty C, McGuinness DL (2004) Owl web ontology language guide. W3C recommendation, February 2004. http://www.w3.org/TR/2004/REC-owl-guide-20040210/
31. Weiser M (1993) Some computer science issues in ubiquitous computing. Commun CACM 36(7):74–84
32. Wegner P, Goldin D (2003) Computation beyond turing machine. Commun CACM 46(4):100–102
33. Complex System. http://en.wikipedia.org/wiki/Complex_system
34. Wing J (1995) Hints to specifiers. Manuscript CMU-Cs-95-118R

Specification Activities

2

The previous chapter provides a general discussion of the different stages of specification in the software development process. It was assumed that the discrete steps of the development process have been well-defined. That is, the activities, deliverables, reviews, and analysis procedures associated with each step have already been established. It was suggested that a specification of the products and processes can be added to each step of such a well-defined development process. This chapter addresses specific issues that should be considered, activities that should be initiated, and the roles that are to be assumed when specifications are *formal* due to the integration of *formal methods* into the existing software life-cycle process for a given project.

Formal methods refer to the use of rigorous techniques founded on mathematics, in particular on abstract algebra, discrete mathematics and logic, in the representation of information necessary for the construction of software systems. The word "formal" comes from "formal logic" in which reasoning is done by virtue of "structure" and independent of "content". The specifications in formal methods are "well-formed" statements in mathematics. Mathematical logic is used to specify a property that needs to be verified in the specified system. The property is true in the specified system if a set of inference rules in the logic can derive the property as a logical consequence. Each step of this deduction procedure follows from the preceding step when an inference rule is applied to it. Because content is not central to logical deduction, the inference procedure becomes a mechanical *calculation*. Thus, the verification process can be mechanized which in turn reduces reliance on human intuition. A formal method is to be preferred not just on its notations, but in its ability to adequately specify information and verify correctness of properties specified.

The word "method" comes from the context of engineering discipline and it denotes the *way in which a software process is to be conducted*. As stated in [20] in the context of system engineering, a method is defined to consist of an underlying *model* of development, *one or more languages, a defined set of ordered steps*, and *guidance* for applying these in a coherent manner. Model refers to the mathematical representation of the system. It is suggested by the chosen mathematical notation. For example, if set theory is chosen as the mathematical basis of formalism, then the expression $registered' = registered \cup \{Tom\}$ models the update operation when an item is added to a student file. By virtue of set the-

V.S. Alagar, K. Periyasamy, *Specification of Software Systems*,
Texts in Computer Science,
DOI 10.1007/978-0-85729-277-3_2, © Springer-Verlag London Limited 2011

ory semantics *registered'* = *registered* if *Tom* ∈ *registered*. Hence a formal specification language is a mathematically-based language, which has a well-defined syntax and semantics. The specification language must use the underlying mathematical objects as elements of the language and support formal verification. The expressive power of the language is brought out in the specification clarity, its support for removal of ambiguity and formal reasoning. These ultimately lead to an understanding of the system under development.

During the late 1980s and early 1990s, the initial stages of formal methods development, a *set of ordered steps* for system development was left undefined and no *guidance* (tool support) to practice safe specification was available. Since then formal methods have been maturing and several techniques and tools have been made available in public domain [29] to practice formal methods. They have been used successfully in engineering large complex systems [2, 3, 29].

2.1
Integrating Formal Methods into the Software Life-Cycle

Formal methods at different levels of formalization can be applied to any or all steps in the software development process. At some steps it may be sufficient to be rigorous, in the sense of being systematically precise without using the full power of mathematics and logic. As an example, in the late 1970s, Heninger and colleagues [14] at the Naval Research Laboratory introduced a tabular method to specify software system requirements. This method is rigorous, although not formal. In 1990, Van Schouwen [27] described a mathematical model and formalized the tabular methodology. Given the current maturity of formal [9, 29] methods, modern day software development practice can include formalization of behavioral specification, design specification, and program specification, and include a formal analysis of the system as well. Depending upon the type of project, it is necessary to decide the scope of formal methods to use and the level of formality desired at a particular phase in the development cycle. Based upon factors such as size of the project, application domain, scope of formal methods use, and level of formalism to be applied, it is necessary to determine the benefit-to-cost ratio of applying formal methods to the project prior to integrating formal methods in the development process.

Figure 2.1 is a process model in which formal method is integrated into all phases of life-cycle activities. This process model is to suggest the integration of formal methods in safety-critical systems development. It is assumed that domain experts construct a formal domain model which includes domain knowledge, concepts and ontologies, constraints among domain entities, and attributes of entities. A classification of different applications within the domain may also be included in the domain model. A set of requirements for a specific application is extracted from the domain model. The environment with which the system will interact is formalized and is combined with a formal specification of system requirements. The property to be formally verified in the system is formalized and is formally verified in the formalized system design. The verification is preceded by a formal

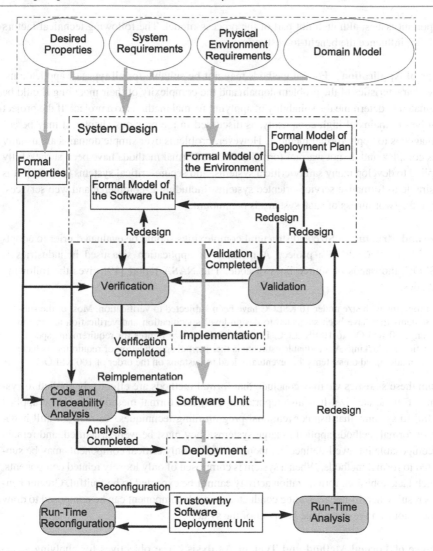

Fig. 2.1 Integrating formalism with process model

validation of system design to ensure that it has captured the stated requirements and environmental constraints. Such a validation may be an animation of the system being built. If validation fails the system design is to be redone. If verification fails the validation must be redone on the redesign. Only after verification is successfully completed the system implementation begins. Code analysis which includes tracing design units to implementation parts must be done before the system is deployed. Run-time configuration refers to the run-time system in the software deployment unit. If run-time analysis exposes errors a redesign of the system takes place. The level of formality and the choice of formalism are important issues, although not part of the process model. The following technical factors [19, 20] influence the benefit-to-cost ratio.

Type of Application   Formal methods may not be suitable for all types of applications. The characteristics of the problem domain and the complexity of their modeling should be evaluated to determine the suitability of applying formal methods to a project. If the project involves domains of high complexity, as discussed in the previous chapter, it may be advantageous to apply formal methods. However, problems over simple domains are usually less complex and do not warrant formal methods. Formal methods have been successfully applied to develop many safety-critical systems, and secure-critical systems [4, 8, 20]. It is desirable to formalize service-oriented systems, including E-commerce and web services, when trustworthiness of such systems is paramount.

Size and Structure   Size and structural complexities should be evaluated prior to adopting formal methods in a project. A measure of application size used in industries is KSLOC, thousands of source lines of code. The NASA report [19] gives the following statistics:

> Programs with size under 10 KSLOC have been subjected to verification. Most of the subsystems that have been subjected to design-level specification and verification are in the range 10 KSLOC to 100 KSLOC. However, precise size figures for requirements specification are lacking. A reasonable estimate is that formal specification of requirements have been attempted on systems that eventually lead to systems on the order of 100 KSLOC.

From these statistics we may conclude that formal methods are effectively applied to systems of moderate size. It is also reported in [19] that formal methods cannot be applied in full to systems that use conventional programming techniques. To reap the full benefits of formal methods applied to large systems, they must be well-structured, and remain decomposable into well-defined components so that only critical components may be subjected to formal methods. When a system is composed of only loosely related components, which lack cohesion, formalization activity cannot be expected to be fruitful. Greater benefits result when formal reasoning conducted on each component can be composed to draw conclusions on the composite behavior of the system.

Choice of Formal Method and Type of Analysis   The objectives for applying a formal method to a project must be clearly identified and documented. The development of safety-critical systems require the use of formal methods for specifying and analyzing critical components and their properties. An application which primarily uses the traditional structured development techniques may use formal methods only for the purpose of documenting data dictionaries. The objectives of these applications will have different impacts on the development process and consequently will influence different choices of formal methods.

Level of Formality   Methods such as manual inspection and walk-through conducted with the help of documents written in a natural language and supplemented by diagrams, equations, and pseudo code are not formal. Table-based specifications and diagrams used for object-oriented modeling [22] add more precision to natural language descriptions. These are only semi-formal notations. Specification languages such as Larch [11], VDM [17], and Z [24] have formal syntax and semantics, and also provide some mechanized support for syntax checking, semantic analysis and proofs. Methods such as B [1], PVS [21], and HOL [10] provide additional support for developing formal specifications, such as rigorous semantic analysis, refinement, and mechanized formal proof methods. Object-Z [23] and Alloy [16] integrate formal specification languages with graphical object modeling techniques. From the objectives of a given project, criticality of the application, project size, and available resources, the degree of formality suitable for the project must be determined and a choice be made from the above possibilities. The levels of formalization [20], in increasing levels of formality, are defined below.

1. A non-mathematical model of the system, such as data-flow diagrams, English text, and object diagrams, is translated to a mathematical description using notations from discrete mathematics and logic. An informal analysis of the specification may be done.
2. Formal specification languages with tools are used for syntactic analysis, pretty printing, and interpretation of the specification. Specification languages usually have built-in abstract data types that support specifying module interfaces, and object models.
3. Formal specification languages with formal semantics are used for specification. Tool support for analyzing specifications, say traceability analysis, and proof systems for mechanized verification are used.

Scope of Use   Formal methods can be used in one or more dimensions of the development process. The degree of formality may also be varied across the different dimensions.

1. *Selecting development stages:* Although formal methods can be applied to all stages of the development process, it is usual to apply it only selectively. Depending upon the level of verification rigor appropriate to a project, a subset of requirements and high-level design may be chosen to undergo the techniques of a formal method. Integrating formal methods during the requirements and design stages has the advantage of enhancing the quality of the software. This is because errors can be detected during the early stages of the development process, and the precision injected early on leads to formal verification and validation.
2. *Choice of components:* Higher levels of rigor may be called for to assess the quality of safety-critical components. To construct such components, formalism is not only necessary but a high degree of formality should be applied. Components that are not critical may be subjected to lower levels of rigor.
3. *System functionality:* A proof of correctness is required to establish that the system has the important properties required of it. Whenever the objectives of a project include such strict requirement, the functionalities of those components designed to meet such requirements should be formally verified.

Tool   It is not possible to apply formal methods with pencil and paper. To apply it with sufficient rigor, tool support is necessary. Since a tool may address one or more of the issues, developing a formal specification, syntax checking, semantic analysis, and theorem proving, the choice of tools for a project depends on all the factors discussed above. Tool support and good expertise are required to refine designs into programmable modules and conduct proofs on the correctness of refinements. Many tools are now available as open source software [9, 29] for practicing formal methods at almost all stages of the software development cycle.

2.2
Administrative and Technical Roles

Once a decision has been reached on adopting a formal method to a project, general guidelines be put in place to implement this decision before the project begins. The guidelines include mechanisms for documentation standards for improved communication, configuration management, and reuse of specifications. When the existing development process has well-defined steps, formal methods can be inserted at relevant steps in the entire process or it can be applied on a small scale to some of the steps. A pilot study may also be done to integrate formal methods to understand the steps where it is most effective, and train staff for these activities. Although the roles and sequence of activities of the staff depend on the specifics of the process model, a discussion of the roles based on a rough classification of roles is given below.

2.2.1
Specification Roles

System requirements, environmental objects and their constrained interactions, and the property to be verified in the software system are specified by those assuming specification roles. Naturally, these formal specifications are developed by groups of people who have a good understanding of the formal languages used for the specifications. A specifier may be the author as well as the analyzer for a specification unit. As an author, the specifier constructs the specification corresponding to a process or a product in a formal language. This activity involves a good understanding of language abstractions and the properties of the product or process. As analyzer, the specifier demonstrates the inherence of desired properties in the specification. In particular, the analyzer resolves inconsistencies and demonstrates the coherence of the specification. A specification may be refined to include more information. Whenever a specification is refined, it is required to establish the satisfaction of the refined specification to its source. This can be done by an informal analysis; however, within a strict formal framework, a proof is required.

In this role some staff are expected to field questions about tools, domain issues, and sufficiency of coverage, which arise during formalization and validation. They may assist users and other members of the development team in understanding the specification document. This may be done through natural language expositions and graphical illustrations to convey the meaning of formal constructs. In a typical walkthrough session, the specification staff shall demonstrate that there exist requirements in the SRD corresponding to every formal specification unit and vice versa. The goal of such sessions is to have demonstrated to the user that the formal specification document fully captures the requirements stated in SRD. The staff, in collaboration with other members of the team, may develop appropriate tools for traceability and reuse of specifications.

A formal specification, however, is not a panacea. Constructing a formal specification involves characterizing the intended correctness conditions. Missing on them, failing to state them correctly, and stating inappropriate conditions lead to surprising situations. Thus a specification will not, on its own, insure that no errors will be made, nor that the final product will be error-free. Since errors in a specification will have a detrimental effect on all future stages of software development, the specification must be analyzed to eliminate all errors. The kinds of errors to look for in walkthroughs and other forms of analysis include the following:

- missing, incorrect, redundant requirements,
- errors due to misuse of the specification language,
- logical errors in specifying correctness conditions,
- inappropriate inclusion of constraints in correctness conditions, and
- incorrect translation of requirements.

The role to be played here is to accumulate sufficient evidence to show that the formal specification is free of these types of errors. This role, commonly known as to *validate*, must be played with the collaboration of the end users. Ideally, the specification staff validate the specification by *executing* the specification in the presence of the customer.

Another important activity that the specification staff must undertake is to assist the test team understand and use the specification for designing functional tests for the software product. Since, after validation, the specification contains expected and correct functionalities of the product, the test team has the necessary information for testing the final product. The main advantage in playing out this activity is that the large amount of work involved during *a posteriori* error detection is replaced by a more scientific effort spent *a priori* during the construction of software.

2.2.2
Design Roles

An important role of a project staff is to be a design engineer. Design is concerned with constructing artifacts and assembling them together to produce the intended effect of a software product. Kapor [18] and Holloway [15] liken software designers to architects. The rationale is that architects have the overall responsibility for constructing buildings and engineers play a vital role in the process of construction. It is the architect who, upon receiving the requirements for constructing a house, produces a design which ultimately produces a "good" building that "pleases" the client. Engineers, taking directions from the architect, put things together by choosing components that are well tested. Similarly, in software systems, the designer is the architect who receives the validated requirements specification and produces a design to meet the overall needs of the user. In the house case, the components are the building materials, while in software development they are akin to the rooms and corridors of a house. The building materials of software development include previously built, tested and certified, programming languages, utilities, and middleware.

Although the design of the system begins with system requirements analysis, the design activity takes shape only after the components to be used in building the system are identified. The design activity proceeds according to project guidelines, and technical considerations planned for integrating formal methods in this stage. A formal design would involve several levels of *refinements*, starting from requirements specification. At each level, a refinement adds more details to the specification in the preceding level. The details may include data structuring details and/or algorithmic details. Part of refinement process is a proof that shows the behavioral satisfaction of the refinement to its predecessor. However, when the design is not fully formal the design team should ensure that critical components of the design are formalized. This is done by inventing state invariants, contracts on interface specifications, and other assertions on the design components, and expressing them in the same formalism used for requirement specification. This will enable a formal validation of the critical components in the design. However, if the chosen formalism cannot specify all aspects of the design, then different specification formalisms may have to be mixed. In [6], Object-Z and CSP are mixed to specify object-based system design. In [25], Z and timed CSP are combined to specify safety-critical systems. These two hybrid specification methods have successfully exploited the state machine semantic domains of Z and CSP. In situations when the underlying semantic domains are different the design team will face a difficult task in establishing semantic consistency and proving that design satisfies the requirements.

Regardless of whether a design is fully or only partially formal, a good design is one which can easily adapt to changes in the requirements and the environment. Toward achieving a good design, the design team should give strong considerations to the misgivings of domain specialists, even if they cannot substantiate these misgivings [15]. The design team should periodically meet with clients and specification staff to confirm changes in design caused by changes in specification. Thus, design staff play a pivotal role in software construction—they interact with clients, specification staff, and programming teams.

2.2.3
Implementation Roles

The term "implementation" is used in a broad sense to include code generation, code analysis, and deployment. A staff in implementation team is a programmer whose role will vary greatly depending upon the level of formality used and tool support. In case code generation is automated with the use of tools, as in B method, the programmer should undertake a traceability analysis to ensure that code covers the expected behaviors expressed in the design. Typically the generated code is written in some imperative language. For example, in B method the code is written using a B language sub-assembly, similar to an imperative programming language. In order to facilitate code generation on any target system, either the programmer has to translate installations or translation is done automatically to standard programming language. The programs obtained can then be compiled and assembled on the target machine to produce the executable software. In case the code generation is not automatic, the programmer's task is to take the designer's output and write programs consistent with the detailed design. It is the programmer's responsibility to ensure both correctness and efficiency in translating the design decisions into source code. However, it may happen that certain aspects of the design are difficult or impossible to implement. The programmer brings those design aspects which cannot be implemented to the attention of the design and specification staff. The rationale for unimplementable design aspects may be due to strong constraints and/or stringent requirements. They may traced back to the design and requirements, and rectified.

The programmer and the test engineer who developed specification-based testing collaborate in testing programs. The outcome of testing determines whether or not a program correctly interprets the requirements of the customer. In case of errors, the specification team is brought in for consultation. In particular, the programmer will make changes after the specification staff and the design team work out a new design. Model checking tools and test case generation tools are available [9] for this purpose. Traceability and run-time analysis are central to deployment of software. These activities exist even when formal method is not integrated with the development process.

2.3
Exercises

1. Enumerate the essential requirements of a communication channel between two processes. Identify safety and security properties.
2. Assume that software for Automated Teller Machine (ATM) is to be constructed following the process model in Fig. 2.1. Answer the following questions:

   • What is the domain of application? Enumerate a few domain entities, the attributes for each entity, and the relationship among the entities. What properties of entities govern security? Develop a property to be verified in the software implementing the ATM.
   • Describe the environment for ATM to function. What constraints are to be imposed by the software on the environment? What constraints the environment may impose on the software?
   • What software components should be formalized? For each formal unit state the property to be verified in it.

2.4
Bibliographic Notes

The factors to be considered for choosing specific tasks for formal methods application is discussed in the NASA reports [19, 20]. These reports outline the technical and administrative considerations that must be reviewed before integrating formal methods into a development process. It is stated in the report that for an effective application of formal methods to a project, the team responsible for applying formal methods must be trained in formal methods and tools. In a debate held at the Tri-Ada '94 [26], panel discussion the panelists argued that the expertise required to use formal methods can be gained through education and training courses spanning a few weeks. An understanding of the activities, skills and responsibilities associated with the roles involved in software development using formal methods is obtained from looking at the success stories [3] as well as learning from the failures [15].

Analysis and interpretation of formal specifications are enhanced with the help of tools. Several tools are available as open source software [29]. Tools specific to Z, Object-Z, VDM, and B method can be found in [9]. For Larch specifications, Guttag et al. [11] describes a syntax checker and a theorem prover. Larch Prover (LP) is a proof assistant incorporating several proof techniques for rewrite-rule theory. PVS [21] provides an integrated environment, formalism and methods supported by tools, for the analysis and development of formal specifications. Tool components include parser, type checker, browser, specification libraries, and integrated proof checker. The early work by Dick and Faivre [7] on black-box testing based on VDM specifications and Hierons [13] for generating test cases from Z specifications have led to study model-based testing methods. The report [12] compares many such tools from industry and academia.

Two excellent treatises on design are the book by Winograd [28], which is a collection of articles showing the diverse perspectives of software design, and the book by Dasgupta [5], which explores the logic and methodology of design from the computer science perspective. Holloway [15] draws lessons to software engineering from design failures in building physical structures, such as bridges and rockets. They are

- *Lesson 1*: *Relying heavily on theory, without adequate confirming data, is unwise.*
- *Lesson 2*: *Going well beyond existing experience is unwise.*
- *Lesson 3*: *In studying existing experience, more than just the recent past should be included.*
- *Lesson 4*: *When safety is concerned, misgivings on the part of competent engineers should be given strong consideration, even if the engineers cannot fully substantiate these misgivings.*
- *Lesson 5*: *Relying heavily on data, without an explanatory theory, is unwise.*

References

1. Abrial J-R (1996) The B-book: assigning programs to meanings. Cambridge University Press, Cambridge

2. Clarke EM, Wing J (1996) Formal methods: state of the art and future directions. ACM Comput Surv 28(4):626–643
3. Craigen D, Gerhart S, Ralston T (1995) Industrial applications of formal methods to model, design and analyze computer systems
4. Crow J, De Vitto BL (1996) Formalizing space shuttle software requirements. In: ACM SIGSOFT workshop on formal methods in software practice, San Diego, USA
5. Dasgupta S (1991) Design theory and computer science. Cambridge tracts in theoretical computer science. Cambridge University Press, Cambridge
6. Derrick J, Boiten E (2002) Combining component specifications in object-Z and CSP. Form Asp Comput, pp 111–127
7. Dick J, Faivre A (1993) Automating the generation and sequencing of test cases from model-based specifications. In: Woodcock JCP, Larsen PG (eds) FME93: industrial-strength formal methods, formal methods Europe. Lecture notes in computer science, vol 670. Springer, Berlin
8. De Vito BL, Roberts L (1996) Using formal methods to assist in the requirements analysis of the space shuttle GPS change request. NASA Report 4752, Prepared for Langley Research Center
9. Formal methods web page. http://formalmethods.wikia.com/wiki/Z_notation, May 2010
10. Gordon MJC, Melham TF (eds) (1993) Introduction to HOL. Cambridge University Press, Cambridge
11. Guttag JV, Horning JJ, Garland SJ, Jones KD, Modet A, Wing JM (1993) Larch: languages and tools for formal specifications. Springer, Berlin
12. Hartman A AGADIS: model-based generation tools. Technical report. http://www.agedis.de/documents/ModelBasedTestGenerationTools_cs.pdf
13. Hierons RM (1997) Testing from a Z specification. Softw Test Verif Reliab 7:19–33
14. Heninger KL et al. (1978) Software requirements for the A-7E aircraft. NRL Report 3876, Naval Research Laboratory
15. Holloway CM (1999) From bridges and rockets: lessons for software systems. In: 17th international system safety conference, Orlando, Florida, USA, pp 598–607
16. Alloy DJ (2002) A lightweight object modeling language. ACM Trans Softw Eng Methodol, 11(2):256–290
17. Jones CB (1990) Systematic software development using VDM, 2nd edn. Prentice-Hall International, Englewood Cliffs
18. Kapor M (1996) A software design manifesto. In: Winograd T (ed) Bringing design to software. ACM Press, New York, pp 1–9
19. Formal methods specification and verification guidebook for software and computer systems, vol I: Planning and technology insertion. NASA Report NASA-GB-002-95, Release 1.0, July 1995
20. Formal methods specification and analysis guidebook for the verification of software and computer systems, vol II: A practitioner's companion. NASA Report NASA-GB-001-97, Release 1.0, May 1997
21. Owre S, Rushby JM, Shankar N (1992) PVS: a prototype verification system. In: Kapur D (ed) Proceedings of the eleventh international conference on automated deduction (CADE), Saratoga, New York, June 1992. Lecture notes in artificial intelligence, vol 607. Springer, Berlin, pp 748–752
22. Rumbaugh J, Blaha M, Pramerlani W, Eddy F, Lorenson W (1991) Object-oriented modeling and design. Prentice-Hall, Englewood Cliffs
23. Smith G (2000) The object-Z specification language. Kluwer Academic, Norwell
24. Spivey JM (1988) Understanding Z, a specification language and its formal semantics. Cambridge University Press, Cambridge
25. Sühl C (2000) Applying RT-Z to develop safety-critical systems. Lecture notes in computer science, vol 1783. Springer, Berlin
26. TRI-Ada '94 formal methods panel summary. http://shemesh.larc.nasa.gov/fm/paper-tri-ada.html (04/16/2010)

27. van Schouwen AJ (1990) The A-7 requirements model: re-examination of real-time systems and an application to monitoring systems. Technical report 90-276, Department of Computing and Information Science, Queens University, Kingston, Canada
28. Winograd T (1996) Bringing design to software. Addison Wesley, New York
29. Wheeler DA (2010) High assurance (for security or safety) and Free-Libre/Open Source Software (FLOSS) ... with lots on formal methods/software verification. http://www.dwheeler.com/essays/high-assurance-floss.html (04/16/2010)

Specification Qualities 3

The process model introduced in Chap. 2 integrates the practice of formal method into all phases of life-cycle activities. Given the current maturity of formal methods, it is reasonable to assume that this process model is both practical and justified. Software development activity in this process model includes the formalization of software requirements specification, design specification, program specification, domain and environment specification, and analysis at different stages. The goal of this chapter is to explore the quality characteristics of these specifications that depend on the formal methods and the processes used in creating them.

The report IEEE 830 [9] recommends a standard practice for writing software requirements specification. It has enumerated many characteristics that taken together assess the quality of requirements specification. The report ISO/IEC 9126 [8], although intended as an OO design quality model, has influenced the development of general information quality benchmarks [10]. These information quality attributes seem to include the characteristics enumerated in IEEE830 [9]. In addition, the approach [10] can be adapted to assess the content of specification documents produced in the formalized life-cycle model and the quality of formalized content. This is the focus of discussion in this chapter.

Application of a formal method to software development activities results in a formal specification of those activities, and is used in subsequent stages of development. Thus, specifications arise from a need and are used to fulfill that need. Writing a formal specification for a given task requires a formal specification language in which the task is expressed. Thus the process involved in formalization is the choice of formal specification language and abstracting the given task in it. The product of this exercise is either a *model* or a *theory* of the task in the language. Thus, a quality seal on specification depends upon the *utility* factors of the specification document from the consumer perspective, *product* qualities of the model and theory expressed in the document from the system developer point of view, and *process* qualities of the language from specification developer point of view. In this three-way classification, we are assuming the *performance* quality to be part of *product* quality in virtue of the verifiable model created for it, and *manageability and operability* qualities to be absorbed by the *utility* factor. This chapter explores these three quality perspectives.

V.S. Alagar, K. Periyasamy, *Specification of Software Systems*,
Texts in Computer Science,
DOI 10.1007/978-0-85729-277-3_3, © Springer-Verlag London Limited 2011

3.1
Process Quality

In this section we first discuss the distinguishing characteristics of programming and specification languages and explore the attributes for a specification language, and then define a
process quality model. Most specification languages may include only a subset of these attributes. Consequently, when a formal method that has a limited repertoire of the attributes
is chosen by the specifier it may be impossible to express all the properties or behaviors of
the system in that specification language. The language may simply be too weak, or it may
not have the necessary constructs for specifying a particular feature of a particular system. It is therefore essential that the specifier diligently chooses an appropriate language to
specify the problem on hand. If the specifier is trained in using the formal language which
has sufficiently many attributes to meet the goals of formalization, then the quality of the
process can be expected to be high.

3.1.1
Why a Programming Language Cannot Serve as a Specification Language?

At requirements specification level, the specification expresses only *what* is to be done and
at later stages the specifications should address the issue *how* to do the tasks stated earlier.
It is clear from this distinction that a specification language should have declarative, rather
than control-centric expressive power. Both specifications and programs are formal objects.
A specification and the program that it specifies portray the behavior of some phenomena;
the only difference between the portrayals is in the level of detail. Whereas a specification
describes a property through a desired effect, a program conforming to this specification
achieves the desired effect thereby demonstrating the presence of the desired property in
the final product. This subtle relationship between a specification and a program satisfying
it should be maintained during all the stages of software development; otherwise many
decisions on data type structuring and control details may be taken too early and constrain
the development process. In terms of levels of abstraction, a program is a specification of
machine execution and a specification of the program is a statement on what that program
does without giving the details how it is accomplished.

  Imperative programming languages, such as C++, are control-centric; functional languages, such as LISP, are declarative, and in between lie *wide-spectrum* languages [3, 4].
A brief description of their level of formalism and a comparison of their roles in programming and specification are given below.

Imperative Programming Languages

  Imperative programming languages, such as C++, and Java, require algorithmic details,
execution sequence and data structure representations to be explicit in program descriptions. The program formally states a particular solution to the problem and may even state
the format in which the solution should be delivered to the user. We can consider a program as a model expressing the behavior of some entity—an algebraic formula, the square

root function, a banking system or an animation. Even at this level, the program may be regarded as a behavioral specification of its execution. So, programming languages are also specification languages at a certain level of abstraction. However, they cannot be used as specification languages throughout the software development process, for the following reasons:

1. Procedural programming languages do not separate functionality from implementation.
2. There is no referential transparency in imperative programming.
3. The data manipulated by a program must have a particular representation. If the representation is changed, a different program may be required. The representation of data has consequences for their access.
4. Both data and control spaces are deterministic. For example, the semantic interpretation of the abstract parse tree of a program can generate a behavior, and execution sequences, only if data and control information are complete. An analysis of the program with partial description is impossible.
5. Even if a program is modular and parameterized, strict type conformance may prevent the program from being extendible or reusable.
6. Over-specification is an aftermath in programming languages.

Declarative Programming Languages

A typical declarative language is LISP. LISP programs are declarative and consequently may be regarded as specifications. Such specifications, considered as *functional programs*, are executable. Historically, LISP has proved itself most useful in the task of creating working versions (prototypes) of complex systems. The language can be learnt easily and can be used effectively in describing complex problems and their solutions. Nondeterminism, selection and recursion are expressible in LISP. Moreover, LISP provides a small set of powerful constructs that can be combined to produce an abstract program. Such an abstract program is a high-level model with no consideration of control, sequencing or choice implied in an implementation. Functions written in this style have no side effects; that is, they correspond to the mathematical notion of a function—they produce the same value whenever invoked with the same arguments. A specification in pure LISP is easy to construct, understand and modify. It is easy to construct because of the small number of language constructs and rules. It is easy to understand because every use of a variable, within certain limits, yields the same value. This property, known as *referential transparency*, is a fundamental convention in the use of mathematical functions and expressions. Consequently, one does not require complex data flow analysis to determine what value a particular usage of that variable represents. This provides a conducive foundation for reasoning and verification. Another major advantage of pure LISP specification is its declarative nature—there is no over-specification. In particular, unnecessary sequentiality will not be expressed. This, combined with nondeterminism, facilitates the introduction of parallelism in lower-level programs. In spite of several attractive features, LISP cannot adequately serve as a language for specifying software systems. It lacks *encapsulation, modularity*, and *extensibility*, which are essential to contain design complexity.

Wide-Spectrum Languages

A specification can be executable, if suitable control abstractions are declaratively stated in the language. An executable specification is animated through this implementable feature. The concept of a wide-spectrum language was introduced by Bauer [3, 4] to serve this purpose. Declarative constructs in the language are used to write specifications and subsequent refinements toward concrete programs are obtained through binding and transformation. In essence, a wide-spectrum language consists of a base language plus syntactic extensions for various high-level constructs. The two-level framework is based on a formal semantics. It is machine-representable and interpretable. Programs in the verification system Eves [5] are specified, implemented, and proved using the wide-spectrum language Verdi, a variant of classical set-theory and an imperative programming language. One drawback of wide-spectrum languages is that they require many diverse language constructs to be defined within the same language consistently. A more severe drawback is that the language cannot forbid a specifier using control-centric features prematurely, thus over-constraining the specification.

3.1.2
Attributes of Formal Specification Languages

From the above discussion and the discussion in Chaps. 1 and 2 on the role of specification and specification activities, we conclude that a specification language embody the following characteristics:

Formalism   The semantic domain of the language is mathematics. Being a language for software development, it has a well-defined syntax for presenting the specification in a structured manner. The formal grammar of the language drives the well-defined syntactic units. A well-defined syntactic unit can be mapped to a semantic entity in the underlying mathematics. For example, the term $x \in S$ is a syntactic unit in Z language and its corresponding semantic entity is a value in $\{true, false\}$. The syntactic structures make the specification easy to read and comprehend, aid the specifier to state what needs to be stated within a structuring, and organize the specification into structured modular units.

Abstraction   The language has powerful primitives for defining and manipulating information and data at the logical level. Logical data definition should not imply any particular data representation. The language provides the definition of objects independent of the notions of "value" or "boundary". It should be possible to define an object by the set of associations through which it interacts with other objects. The language provides abstract operations that create, destroy, access and relate objects. For example, the predicate $s' = s \frown \langle x \rangle$ means that element x is added to the rear of a sequence. Thus, abstraction in the language promotes definitional (declarative) specification.

Abstraction can be applied incrementally to any desired level of detail. The language abstraction should allow the specification of normal behavior, error behavior, exceptions, and failures independent of each other, and provide constructs for composing these behaviors.

Using abstraction we can build models as well as theories, but that depends upon the specification language elements. A model is constructed by using mathematical structures, such as sets, relations, and sequences. By using a structure in a model, all mathematical operations of the structure become free for use, in the sense that the specifier does not have to define them. The language might use the same definitional symbols from mathematics. The advantage is that they are already defined and any one exposed to discrete mathematics can understand the specifications. The disadvantage is that the specifier may find some of the operations or properties as irrelevant for the application. An attempt by the user of the specification to introduce an irrelevant operation, although mathematically sound, may have unacceptable effect on the behavior specified.

As opposed to models, a theory builds only the properties that are expected in a system without borrowing heavily the structures from mathematics. For most of theory building, it is sufficient to borrow the fundamental theories, such as theory of natural numbers, the theory of reals, and the theory of ordering from mathematics. In theory building, a theory may be imported from a repository of theories, if there exists one. Importing theories may require discharging proofs in the theory being built.

A most celebrated example of theory for software engineers is a theory of stacks, captured by the two equations

$$pop(push(s, x)) = s, \qquad top(push(s, x)) = x \qquad (3.1)$$

The only subtlety here is that this is a theory of *infinite* (sized) stacks. For stacks of finite size, an elegant theory does not exist. In fact, theories are apt to describe infinite state systems. A finite state system can be described by a compact model.

Modularity   The language provides constructs for extending a specification through *enrichment* and *composition*. These features allow the construction of large and complex specifications by assembling smaller specifications; they also support modular design. Modularity combined with incremental specifications adds more expressive power to the language.

Nondeterminism   As part of its abstraction feature, the language may provide nondeterministic constructs for indirect data access and unrestricted choice from a specific list of actions. Descriptive reference for data is a nondeterministic construct in which the reference to an object is made through a list of attributes. So, nondeterminism gives more freedom at design level.

Inference Mechanism   The language allows inferring the behavior of objects in the model using system laws and defined actions. The inference mechanism "evaluates well-formed expressions" in the language and provides "meaning to the behavior displayed by the system".

Historical References   The language may provide facilities for time-dependent object interactions or action specification. This capability requires the ability to specify *time*, and associate time with object operations. By suitable extension, it may be possible to describe and analyze timed sequences of system states, and further reason about time-constrained

Table 3.1 Process quality specification categories

Level of Formality	Quality Vectors
1	$\{\langle 1, 1, k_{11}\rangle \mid 0 < k_{11} \leq 1\}$
	$\{\langle 2, 1, k_{21}\rangle \mid 0 < k_{21} \leq 1\}$
	$\{\langle 3, 1, k_{31}\rangle \mid 0 < k_{31} \leq 1\}$
2	$\{\langle 2, 2, k_{22}\rangle \mid 0 < k_{22} \leq 1\}$
	$\{\langle 3, 2, k_{32}\rangle \mid 0 < k_{32} \leq 1\}$
3	$\{\langle 3, 3, k_{33}\rangle \mid 0 < k_{33} \leq 1\}$

system properties at some or all future states. Without explicit mention of time temporal, operators may exist in the language to specify temporal properties of communicating objects.

3.1.3
A Model of Process Quality

The process quality is composed of the expertise of the specifier, the formal level chosen for the project, and the extent to which the specification tasks are completed. In Chap. 2, three levels of formal methods were defined. The level of formality chosen for the project is the level of the formal specification language. The attributes of the specification language are determined by the level of formality. The extent of coverage is the proportion of documents formally specified at any stage, and is a consequence of the set of attributes of the language and the expertise of the specifier. Thus, the process quality specification can be a vector $\langle i, j, k \rangle$, where i is the expertise level of the specifier, j is the level of formality, and k is the proportion of tasks formally specified. The expert level of the specifier can vary from 0 to 3. The first constraint on the vector $\langle i, j, k \rangle$ is $i \in \{0, 1, 2, 3\}$, $j \in \{1, 2, 3\}$, and $0 < k \leq 1$.

The constraint can be strengthened because the expertise level of the specifier should at least match or exceed the formality level of the project. That is, $i \geq j$ is an additional constraint on the process quality specifier. As the formality level increases, is it reasonable to expect the coverage level to increase? This need not be the case for all projects. That is why no constraint relating to the extent of coverage is imposed. Thus the process quality model has six categories of specification vectors. These are shown in Table 3.1.

3.2
Product Quality and Utility

The specification document is an outcome of the specification process. Its quality is to be assessed by investigating the extent to which the initial set of goals can be met. Assume that the following goals were set by the specifier:

- [G1] To succinctly state that a property holds.

- [G2] To precisely describe the interface of a component.
- [G3] To contain design complexity.
- [G4] To analyze hidden behaviors.
- [G5] To demonstrate that all required behaviors are inherent in the design.
- [G6] To localize the effects of change.
- [G7] To prove that a final product meets its requirements.

The assessment procedure is a validation, whether manual or using tools, to critically analyze the specification document and determine how much of the stated goals have been met and how well they have been met. The goal of validation process is to assess the quality of the specification document with respect to

- conformance of the specification document (model, theory) to stated goals, and
- its level of use and usability.

3.2.1
Conformance to Stated Goals

The following steps are essential for a fair assessment of specification document qualities.

Parsing   This form of analysis uncovers syntactic errors. At best it guarantees that a specification conforms to the syntactic rules of the formal specification language.

Type Correctness   Model-based specification languages and languages based on higher-order logic have strict typing conventions. Type checking uncovers semantic anomalies and inconsistencies. A consistent specification does not contain conflicting terms, conflicting attributes, and contradictory expressions. This form of analysis improves the quality of the specification document to the extent that every well-defined syntactic unit has a "value" in the semantic domain.

Once the specification document has successfully passed the above two steps, the rest of the analysis can focus on determining, either through inspection or using tools, the fulfillment of the stated goals.

Sufficient Completeness   Every requirement that needs to be described should have been expressed within the confines of the specification language. Implicit assumptions must be avoided; instead they must be stated explicitly either as axioms or constraints. The specifications should articulate through correctness conditions the environment or context in which input/output are to be given.

Precision   The specification must use appropriate language features to precisely and accurately portray the characteristics of the problem. Atomic operations, rather than complex operations, should be the norm in specifying system functionalities, because correctness conditions of atomic operations are simple to state and easy to verify. Composition rules provided by the language must have been used in specifying complex operations.

Structuring   Although there is no ordering in the specified units, it is better to organize the specifications into many hierarchical structures. A node in a hierarchy uses or requires the specifications of its children. This helps to eliminate undefined terms and concepts, and improves the accessibility of the specification document.

Operational Completeness   All possible behaviors, normal, errors and exceptions, must be part of an operational specification. Interface specifications become a contract between the user of a system and its implementer. The completeness property here is that the contract tells the user everything necessary to use the module and must tell the implementer everything necessary to implement it. A contract specification should be flexible so that at least one implementation becomes possible. It is better to use declarative style and introduce nondeterminism in specifying an operation. Every operation in the specification must eventually lead to an implementation.

Frame Problem   A specification language gives only the structuring needed to write down what the specifier wants. Often, in some specification languages what the specifier ignores or forgets to write has a *hidden* meaning. This implicit meaning has severe consequences on the local behavior of the specified unit where something was ignored, but on the behavior of the rest of the system. This is called *frame* problem, and must be thoroughly investigated in analyzing specifications. As an example, consider the precondition $x > 0 \wedge y > 0$ and the postcondition $x' < 10$ for a function specification. If the language semantics is "silent" on the scope of state variable y which is not present in the postcondition, then it is a frame problem. If the language semantics explicitly states that every state variable not part of a postcondition is not modified by the operation then there is no frame problem.

Animation   Simulation, animation, and direct execution offer the analyzer options to uncover errors, and execution-time inconsistencies. If the specification language is directly executable or can be interpreted faithfully then the set of executions should be examined for stated properties. This might lead to either strengthening or weakening or changing many specified constraints.

Logical Reasoning   It is possible to conduct logical calculations from the specification to ascertain whether certain properties are consequences of the requirements, and whether requirements have been interpreted correctly in the derivation of design and programs. Theorem proving, model checking, and proof checking are different forms of formal analysis to detect design faults, algorithmic errors, and internal inconsistencies.

Parsing and type checking are prerequisites to other analysis steps. Table 3.2 shows a correspondence between the stated goals and the assessment steps that achieve them.

Table 3.2 Analysis steps for stated goals

G1	G2	G3	G4	G5	G6	G7
Logical Reasoning (is it stated correctly?)	Operational Completeness	Structuring, Precision, Sufficient Completeness	Animation, Reasoning	Animation	Frame Problem Analysis	Sufficient Completeness, Logical Reasoning

Table 3.3 Product Quality Dimensions

Dimensions	Explanation
Accessibility	This refers to the extent to which information in the specification document is easily accessible or quickly retrievable for an application. As an example, given a stimulus (permitted by a requirement) it may be required to retrieve the specification for its response. (*Structuring*)
Adaptability	This refers to reuse of specification. Is it possible to apply the information content, either in parts or whole, to different tasks? Is it modifiable incrementally? (*Precision*)
Appropriate Coverage	The specification may say too little, that is, it is incomplete, or it can say too much, that is, it over-specifies (prescriptive rather than declarative), or it can be totally be irrelevant. (*Sufficient Completeness*)
Completeness	This refers to the extent to which the information in the specification document is not missing in the stated goals. (This includes both *sufficient completeness* and *operational completeness*.)
Concise Representation	The information is represented precisely and structured well. There is no redundancy and anomaly in the representation. (*Precision*)
Consistent Representation	There is no internal inconsistency, both in the language level and at the logical level. (*Logical Reasoning*)
Domain Conformance	The information in the document is credible and is fully supported by the domain knowledge.
Correctness	Is the information correct with respect to stated requirements? If the specification is executable, does it produce the intended behavior? (*Animation, Logical Reasoning*)
Interpretability	Is the specification language adequately expressive for the stated tasks? Is the information interpretable by a compiler and a program transformation tool? (*Parsing, Type Checking*)
Relevance	This refers to the applicability of the specification for design, or test case generation, and/or code generation activities?
Trust	Does the information include specification of non-functional requirements such as safety, security, privacy, and reliability criteria?
Timeliness	Is the information outdated or recent?
Understandability	How well the information in the document can be communicated to members of the development team?
Value	Will it eliminate further errors from creeping in? Will it decrease the cost of development?

3.2.2
Quality Dimensions and Quality Model

Specification document has two views: one as *information source* and another as a *service*. The information in the document, developed within the framework of a project, must be *useful* to subsequent stages of development in the same project. If possible it must also be

Table 3.4 Product quality perspective

Product-Service Quality	Conformance	Utility
Product Quality	*Soundness*	*Useful Information*
	• Completeness	• Appropriate Coverage
	• Concise Representation	• Relevance
	• Correctness	• Understandability
	• Consistent Representation	• Interpretability
Service Quality	*Dependable Information*	*Usable Information*
	• Trust	• Domain Conformance
	• Timeliness	• Accessibility
		• Adaptability
		• Value
		• Interpretability

usable (reuse) in other projects that share the same domain as the original project. Both use and usability are utility factors which are closely related to product quality. Since quality itself has been defined as fitness for use, or the extent to which the product serves the purposes of consumers (clients) it is appropriate to include use and usability factors along with the conformance attributes discussed earlier in defining product quality dimensions. Table 3.3 shows the dimensions for product quality model. The relationship between a dimension and the conformance attributes are explicitly shown in the table.

The choice of dimensions, as in Table 3.3, and the perspective of the product-utility quality factors shown Table 3.4 are suggested by the work of Khan et al. [10] on information quality model. The quality dimensions that are not directly related to conformance attributes have a relationship to service quality attributes. All factors that depend only upon the conformance attributes, otherwise are independent of how the information will be used, are divided into *soundness* and *dependability* quadrants. The soundness quadrant lists factors that assess the soundness of information in the specification product. The dependability quadrant is to assess the non-functional aspects associated with the information in the specification document. The factors that determine how the product will be used are split into *usefulness* and *usability* quadrants. Usability refers to the way the document may be used in general contexts, namely *reuse* of the product, whereas usefulness is restricted to the framework that mandated the specification task.

3.3
Exercises

1. Apply the attributes of a specification language to UML and document your experience.
2. Is UML a wide-spectrum language? Justify your answer.
3. Investigate the extent to which the analysis steps stated in Table 3.2 can be done for a UML specification that you have done.

4. Evaluate the quality of UML diagrams (use cases, class structure, statechart etc.) using the dimensions enumerated in Table 3.3.
5. Which subset of Java can be used as a specification language? Illustrate with examples.

3.4
Bibliographic Notes

There is not much work reported in assessing formal specification qualities. In [6], there is a brief discussion on the quality metrics to assess the formalization process undertaken for "requirements analysis of the space shuttle GPS change request". A change request (CR) will add new capabilities to the shuttle, based on Global Positioning System (GPS).

The classic work [2] on determining the goals of specification languages is the basis for the exposition of the attributes of specification languages in this chapter. The classification of process, product, utility qualities in the assessment of specification quality is largely suggested by the work of Khan et al. [10]. The book by Hauser [7] is quite helpful in formulating precisely the assessment factors of specifications. One of the earliest works on wide-spectrum languages for software development is that of Bauer [3, 4]. A similar work is the Program Development System (PDS) [11], based on EL1 (Extensible Language 1). The major difference between these works is their design principle—PDS provides an integrated prototyping environment, and Bauer's language leads to an implementation.

Several notions on (in)completeness in specifications are examined in [1]. This paper gives a classification of incompleteness based on the potential sources of errors in specifications. Wing [12] is a source of useful tips for the specifiers, analyzers, and teachers.

References

1. Alagar VS, Kourkopoulos D (1994) (In)completeness in specifications. Inf Softw Technol 36(6):331–342
2. Balzer R, Goldman N (1981) Principles of good software specification and their implications for specification languages. In: National computer conference, pp 393–400
3. Bauer FL (1976) Programming as an evolutionary process. In: Proceedings of the second international conference on software engineering, San Francisco, CA, pp 223–234
4. Bauer FL, Bauer M, Partsch P, Pepper P (1981) Report on a wide-spectrum language for program specification and development. Technical Report TUM-18104, Technical University, Munich, May 1981
5. Craigen D (1990) The Verdi reference manual. Technical Report TR-90-S429-09, Odyssey Research Associates, February 1990
6. De Vito BL, Roberts L (1996) Using formal methods to assist in the requirements analysis of the space shuttle GPS change request. NASA Report 4752, Prepared for Langley Research Center
7. Hausen HL (2007) Quality specification, testing and certification of bespoken, open source and commercial off-the-shelf systems. In: IFIP international federation for information processing. Springer, Boston

8. ISO (1991) ISO/IEC:9126 information technology-software product evaluation-quality characteristics and guidelines for their use. International Organization for Standardization (ISO)
9. IEEE (1998) IEEE recommended practice for software requirements specifications. IEEE Std 830-1998 (revision of IEEE Std 830-1993)
10. Kahn BK, Strong DM, Wang RY (2002) Information quality benchmarks: product and service performance. Commun ACM 45(4):184–192
11. Klausner A, Konchan TE (1980) Rapid prototyping and requirements specification using PDS. In: Gehani N, McGettrick AD (eds) Software specification techniques. Addison Wesley, Reading
12. Wing J (1995) Hints to specifiers. Manuscript CMU-Cs-95-118R

Abstraction

4

The concept of abstraction is imprecise. It cannot possibly be defined, but the notion of abstraction can be explained, illustrated, modeled, and understood. We begin this chapter by discussing different kinds of abstractions that have been proposed in mathematics and computer science. Next, we bring out the necessity of abstraction for software engineering and suggest different kinds of abstractions to learn for formalizing software development activities.

4.1
What Is Abstraction?

Some of the common forms for communicating our thoughts are speech, text and graphics. Of course there are other means of communications such as a sign language. Thoughts are *abstract* and exist in a subtle abstract medium. Spoken words, textual writings, and drawings are concrete expressions of thoughts. Abstraction is inherent to human nature, although bringing it to the right level of expression is hard. The issues involved in developing an abstraction can be summarized as follows. One thought can be described by different sets of words, and different textual writings denoting the same object may have originated from a single thought. In other words, abstraction is a *one-to-many* map. The medium in which an abstract object is specified has more constraints. For example, the syntax and semantics of the language used to describe the object impose certain constraints on the description. Consequently, representational *details are ignored* in abstractions. Finally, an abstraction cannot be fully understood by an observer unless the context in which the object originates is properly depicted. That is, abstraction implies *generality* and exists in an idealized mental state of the creator of the abstraction.

The need to create abstraction has existed for a long time. Abstraction has enabled artists, philosophers, mathematicians and scientists to capture essential features pervading several phenomena in abstract concepts. In modern times, engineers and business experts have realized that abstraction is a vital tool in coping with the design of large complex systems. The principal advantages of abstraction in software engineering are the attainment

V.S. Alagar, K. Periyasamy, *Specification of Software Systems*,
Texts in Computer Science,
DOI 10.1007/978-0-85729-277-3_4, © Springer-Verlag London Limited 2011

of *simplicity*, *generality*, and *precision* in the software development process and possibly *completeness* and *correctness* in the resulting product.

4.2
Abstractions in Mathematics

Abstractions by themselves have very little practical value until they are contextually related to real-world entities. In mathematics, abstract notations and concepts are invented to generalize and unify more concrete concepts. For example, in "abstract algebra" all the unifying properties of real numbers, complex numbers, and rational numbers are studied under the banner "fields"; the abstract generalization of algebraic properties of integers is studied under the title "rings". These are idealized abstractions. Real numbers correspond to mental idealizations of a mathematician; there is no tangible manifestation of a real number. The essential property of real numbers that "in between any two real numbers there is a real number" cannot realistically hold for angles, distances and time intervals that we measure in practice.

As opposed to idealized abstractions, there are mathematical abstractions that provide precision and expressivity to scientific and engineering descriptions. Concepts such as point, line and natural numbers are abstractions of the physical concepts "atom", "light rays" and "age". Vectors and tensors are abstractions used to deal with force and elasticity in engineering. These kinds of abstraction serve as *mathematical models* for certain aspects of real-world phenomena.

4.3
Fundamental Abstractions in Computing

The three most fundamental abstract concepts in computing are *algorithm*, *Turing machine* and *computability*. An algorithm is an idealization of a systematic mechanical process. The concept can be traced back to as far as the time of Euclid (300BC). It is remarkable that such a mechanical procedure has been conceptualized several centuries before computers were invented. In spite of its antiquity, the concept of algorithm came to be understood in a more universal fashion only after Alan Turing (1937) described this computational abstraction with the *Turing machine*.

A Turing machine is a piece of abstract mathematics and does not bear any resemblance to a physical machine. This *abstract machine* is obtained by ignoring all structural and physical properties of computing devices and focusing only on the common useful functionalities of these devices. Turing invented this abstraction to solve Hilbert's tenth problem characterized by the question "does there exist a general mechanical procedure which can solve any well-defined mathematical problem stated in a suitable format?". Turing gave a *specification* for stating the components of abstract machines and the rules governing the operations that can be performed on the machines corresponding to the stated problems.

Following the specification for any specific problem, the Turing machine for mechanically solving that problem can be realized. For example, Turing machines for performing arithmetic operations, symbolic comparisons, or any other complicated task can be constructed from a Turing specification, provided that these tasks can be described within the Turing abstraction framework. By composing such constructions, Turing specified a universal machine, which can simulate the behavior of any particular Turing machine. Finally, Turing showed that there is no mechanical procedure for deciding whether or not the universal Turing machine stops. The conclusion arrived at is that there can be no *one* algorithm applicable to *all* problems, nor for *all* Turing machines and for *all* their input. Thus, Turing concluded that Hilbert's tenth problem has no solution. This conclusion has a profound impact on related mathematical issues.

From Turing's abstraction principle, computer scientists and software engineers can learn the following essential benefits for software development.

1. Abstraction leads to an insight for a family of related problems and a class of algorithms;
2. abstraction is the basis for specification; and
3. simple solutions can be composed to obtain a result of far-reaching consequences.

The specification of a Turing machine uses terms such as "tape" and "internal states" that seem to correspond to the magnetic tape and the states of a real computer. This analogy helps us define a sequence of abstract machines $(m_0, m_1, \ldots, m_k)$. Each abstract machine consists, as in the case of Turing machines, of a set of states and transformations for effecting state changes. In a programming language, the state is the set of program variables and the transformations are the statements affecting the states. Thus, Turing machines are not only abstract machines but also serve as abstract models of programming languages and operational models of the algorithm concept.

The concepts abstract machine, abstract program, abstract programming language, specification and algorithm are all related to one another. Moreover, the concept of *computability* formulated by the logician Alonzo Church [1] is also related to the above concepts. The notion of "mechanical procedure" is fully abstracted in Church's thesis. The computability notion is a powerful functional and data abstraction achievable through "lambda calculus". Using this notion, abstract programs can be written as functions. The effect of these functions are derived from the rules of lambda calculus.

To capture computational behavior in a layer unconstrained by considerations of a machine architecture, Church considered a universe of objects called *functions* and provided a syntax for writing them. The arguments of functions are themselves functions. That is, functions and data are treated with no distinction. There exists a set of rewriting rules for manipulating function applications. Thus $f = gh$ implies that the result of the function g applied to the function h is another function f. This extends to self-application of a function. So, the lambda-calculus approach demonstrates the effect of recursion without explicitly writing recursive equations.

The Greek letter λ (lambda) is used to denote the abstraction of a function from the argument used to evaluate it. The letter x immediately following λ is a dummy variable in the expression $\lambda x \cdot f(x)$ and lambda binds this variable with its occurrences within its scope. That is, x is a place-holder into which any other entity (e.g. function) may be substituted.

Thus the notation $\lambda x \cdot f(x)$ abstracts the function f, which when acting on an argument a in the domain of f yields $f(a)$. That is,

$$(\lambda x \cdot f(x))(a) = f(a),$$

and consequently $\lambda x \cdot f(x) = f$. This captures the *function* for a range of values of the *datum* x; in Church's theory, the datum is viewed as a function. Similarly, $\lambda f \cdot f(x)$ abstracts the datum x and allows the set of functions to vary. Thus lambda expressions provide both function and data abstraction. For the expression $f(x)$, the lambda binding serves both syntactic and semantic roles. It states what is to remain *fixed* and what is allowed to vary. Because both syntax and semantics are succinctly conveyed, the lambda notation is formal and function application becomes a mechanical procedure.

The notation $\lambda x \cdot f(x)$ gives rise to abstraction by parameterization at the program level. For example, the expression $\lambda x \cdot (x^3)$ abstracts the "cubing" function for which there is no standard mathematical notation. However, if we set $C = \lambda x \cdot (x^3)$ then $C(a) = a^3, C(a+2) = (a+2)^3 = a^3 + 6a^2 + 12a + 8$. So we can interpret C to be the body of a *procedure* which evaluates the cube of its argument and x is its *formal parameter*. We can move toward more concrete notions by requiring the values of x to be integers and write the cubing function for integers by the lambda expression λx: integer $\cdot (x^3)$.

As remarked earlier, the power of lambda calculus lies in its ability to treat all objects as functions. A function can be composed with itself in a nested function. For example, the expression $\lambda f \cdot \lambda x \cdot f(f(x))$ abstracts x first and then abstracts f. As a consequence, it denotes a function which when applied to arguments g and a produces $g(g(a))$. Let us call this function TWO; that is,

$$\begin{aligned} \text{TWO} &= \lambda f \cdot \lambda x \cdot f(f(x)), \\ (\text{TWO}(g))(a) &= \lambda x \cdot g(g(x))(a) \\ &= g(g(a)). \end{aligned}$$

If $g = C$, then $(\text{TWO}(C))(a) = C(C(a)) = C(a^3) = (a^3)^3 = a^9$.

Using these abstractions, Church showed that every mechanical operation done in a Turing machine can also be done by using a suitable lambda expression. Hence Church's notion of computability, which is functional, is the same as that of Turing's mechanical operation, which is operational. This establishes a fundamental relationship between machines and functions.

4.4
Abstractions for Software Construction

The abstraction process contributes to almost all the activities of software life-cycle, as discussed in Chap. 2. Because of the heterogeneous nature of objects involved in software development process, no uniform method of abstraction can be practiced at all development stages. Jackson's remark [2] "*Abstractions are inverses of interpretations and provide a bridge between the informal domain and the abstract machine. The bridge must be carefully sited and chosen as narrow as possible.*" is central to the requirements generation stage from a domain model. In general, the kinds of abstractions we need for software development include *problem abstraction*, *domain abstraction*, *environmental abstraction*, *interaction abstraction*, *data abstraction*, *control abstraction*, *process abstraction*, *communication abstraction*, and *temporal abstraction*.

4.4.1
Problem Abstractions

Albert Einstein once said "If I had one hour to save the world I would spend the first 55 minutes in defining the problem." Problem definition should be precise, state the input, the constraints, and the output desired. Inventing models to represent real-world problems, and inventing efficient algorithms as part of models are key to problem abstraction. A model, usually a mathematical model, is a substitute for the real world. The model will have the "input information", and will have to be associated with "an information processor" to get "an output of expected results". As an example, graphs are appropriate models for problems in network, and communication domains. Input information and constraints in the problem will define the graph structure. Graph algorithms are processors and the result from the processor is the output to the problem. As an example of graph models consider "animals containment problem": the locations of n animals are given and it is required to construct a fence around these locations such that the cost of fencing is a minimum. The locations are input, and are abstracted as points in a plane. A fence is abstracted as a polygon in the plane. The constraint is that every point must be in the interior of the polygon, which translates to the requirement that the line segment joining any two points must be entirely within the polygonal boundary. The processor for finding the solution is an algorithm which constructs this polygon, called *convex hull*. It is necessary that the algorithm constructs a *minimum convex hull*, in which the perimeter of the polygon is the least possible. The output is the sequence of vertices of the polygon.

4.4.2
Domain Abstraction

Often a family of problems exist in a domain and a software solution for each one of them may be required. The problems in a domain are often related, sharing domain objects and their characteristics. Analyzing the domain, identifying its concepts, entities and their relationship, and understanding the critical properties of the domain are essential steps before extracting the requirements for a specific application in the domain.

Figure 4.1 shows the steps and artifacts in modeling a domain. The issues to be studied in domain analysis include:

- What entities and which properties of the entities are relevant for the specific application?
- How to abstract a chosen entity and its properties?
- What aspects cannot be abstracted and should be left to expert interpretation?

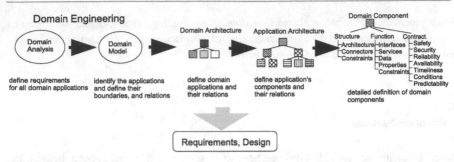

Fig. 4.1 Domain modeling

The result of domain analysis is a domain model, in which objects that may be shared by different applications within a domain are represented. The relationship of objects within each application, the boundaries between applications, and object semantics across boundaries are part of the domain model. From the domain model a domain architecture is developed. This is a high-level hierarchical description of different applications. One branch of this hierarchy is a specific application. Separating that branch and adding further details to it, one gets the application architecture, which in turn will lead to the concepts of *domain components*. Both functional and nonfunctional requirements gathered during domain analysis and classified in the application architecture are formally specified in domain components. Important types of nonfunctional requirements concern safety, security, timeliness, and reliability. Thus the domain model is the *knowledge* about the intended applications. We briefly explain these aspects through an example from Mohammad [3].

The example deals with the domain of automotive industry which will design, manufacture, and market motor vehicles. The domain model of the automotive industry will provide the domain description for design, manufacturing, and marketing. In the design of a car, many control systems such as *cruise control, stability control, anti-lock braking*, and *fingerprint-based security* may exist. As part of design description, the domain model will include descriptions for these control systems, the interaction (interference) among these systems, and nonfunctional (in particular criticality properties) aspects of the constituents of each system. In constructing software for one specific application, the domain model of that specific application becomes the feeder for requirements and design necessary for constructing that software. Such an application domain specific knowledge is abstracted through a *content theory*, known as *ontology*.

From the list of applications cited above for *car* domain, the ontology for *cruise control* application from Mohammad [4] is chosen for illustration in Fig. 4.2. The entity chosen for this example is the *controller*. The controller contains individual requirements instantiated from the functional and nonfunctional concepts. Relations between individuals are represented by properties. Two kinds of properties exist in the model: *has-property* and *request-property*. The controller has six functionalities: *enable, disable, resume, set speed, accelerate*, and *decelerate*. The quality attributes and constraints of these functionalities are given by a set of nonfunctional constraints. For example, there is a safety constraint that states "the cruise control is enabled only if the speed limit is between 30 mph and 90 mph". The request-property relation relates an individual of type *entity* to an individual

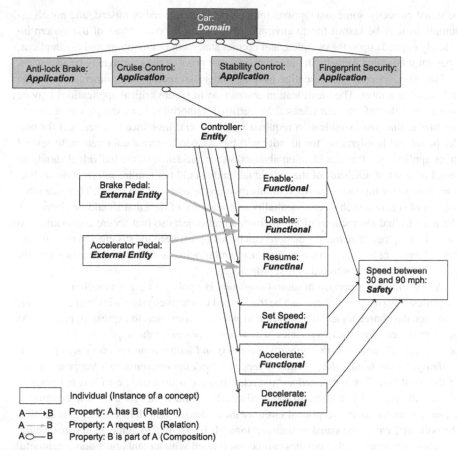

Individual (Instance of a concept)

A——→B   Property: A has B (Relation)
A - - →B   Property: A request B   (Relation)
A○— B   Property: B is part of A (Composition)

Fig. 4.2 Car ontology example focusing on the cruise control system

of type *functional* to indicate that the former is requesting the function provided by the latter.

The chosen abstraction of the domain results in one view of the domain, which will characterize the quality of software artifacts in subsequent stages of software construction. The view, as Jackson [2] calls it "chosen as narrow as possible", limits the information available in succeeding stages of the software development process. The critical consequence of this choice is a form of *incompleteness*—that is, the system would not be able to provide services on aspects that have not been included in this view.

4.4.3
Environmental Abstraction

Systems operate in some environment and in order to serve the clients in the environment systems must make assumptions about the environment. Often these assumptions may not be stated correctly, some assumptions might have been ignored or missed, and not all assumptions may be known for an environment. A proof of correctness of the system inevitably depends upon the complete and correct statement of environmental assumptions. They must be stated formally in order that a formal proof of the system may be attempted.

For many systems, such as online banking and social security, the authentication of an individual is a must. The identification abstraction in secure critical applications may be based upon the information released by certified authorities. For example, in accessing tax files online, the identification required will be social insurance number, and for border petrol and immigration, the identity will be passport and visa information. In several other applications, the identification abstraction for validation of the individual should be based on a set of attributes of the individual, and should not require information such as social insurance number or passport number which the user will not reveal. There are other aspects of security, such as confidentiality and integrity of data that should be abstracted. We need to find abstractions of the environmental objects so that secure communication based on cryptographic transformations can be set up between the system and the environment. Privacy of the client in the environment and timeliness of response demanded by the environment can be abstracted in first order logic.

An assumption, expressed in natural language, is a policy. Logic is a medium to formalize policies. Formalized policies can be transferred to become system's internal constraints. However, the chosen logical framework may not have constructs to express all policies. As an example, consider the two policies "P1: *a user may receive the response only if the user plays a role r*", and "P2: *the system should respond within a maximum delay of 5 units of time from the instant the stimulus is received from the environment*". Suppose the use of the word "may" is interpreted as "the relevant item is optional", then it is not possible to state the policy P1 in standard logic. Similarly, if the word "should" is interpreted to mean that under some exceptional circumstances the relevant item can be ignored, then the policy P2 cannot be stated in standard logic. It is essential to agree upon some natural language semantics so that policies can be interpreted without ambiguity and meaningful logical constraints can be written down.

Certain assumptions about the environment cannot be formalized. These include policies involving terms like *awareness*, *belief*, and *honest*. There is nothing gained by inventing predicates such $believes(honest(A), aware(B, valid(x)))$ to mean "A is honest, A believes that B is aware that x is valid". This kind of formalism does not read very different from the natural language and is hard to be transferred into constraints internal to the system.

4.4.4
System Abstractions

Abstraction at the requirements and design specification is suggested by the specification language of the chosen formal method. Data and function abstractions are ingrained in specification languages such as Z and VDM. These languages provide a means of abstracting observable state entities and specifying the operations to access or modify them.

Control abstraction necessary in these operations are abstracted through declarative constructs. Many specification languages provide notations to achieve operational completeness and enable incremental construction. The *schema calculus* feature in Z and Larch's *signal* clause can abstract exceptions and error situations. Refinement is a method to add more representational details to an abstraction. Schema refinements lead to parameterized procedures in implementation.

The state of the system is an abstract part of the observable behavior of the system. A state is transformed by the performance of an action. State transition rules are action abstractions. Each transition rule specifies the behavior of the system either with respect to an internal event or with respect to an environmental event. The overall behavior of the system is understood by following the sequence of transitions. Such a sequence is called a *thread of control*.

Process abstraction describes *what an abstract machine does* and not *how it works*. A process is an abstraction of a single thread of control. Specification languages such as Z, VDM, and B model *sequential computations*. That is, every computation is a single thread of control. Control abstractions must be included to explain the relevant flow of information. Control constructs can be abstracted in two ways:

1. The familiar programming language control constructs (such as *for* and *if then else*) are declaratively cast over arbitrary data types. For example, the construct "$\forall x \in S \land P(x)$ • *do A*" defines the action A for those elements in the set S satisfying a predicate P. The type and ordering are not of concern here.
2. New constructs can be introduced and their semantics defined using the specification language constructs; however, their implementation details are postponed to later stages.

The main difference between a process abstraction and a data abstraction is that the former is active whereas the latter is passive. All operations in a data abstraction can be passively accessed. However, process abstraction controls when or where an operation can be accessed. Both data and process abstractions require that access be made only through explicit interfaces. The interface specification of an abstraction describes the unchanging aspects of that abstraction.

Abstraction is also an invaluable tool for *program specification*, in which algorithmic and implementation-level data structures and controls need to be specified. A suitable choice of notation for algorithm specification is a combination of data abstraction, control abstraction, function abstraction and elements of logic. An implementation specification, often termed as pseudo code, can be written in an implementation language without strictly following the syntactic rules of the language. When the missing syntactic details and the input/output functions are inserted, the implementation specification becomes the source code in the chosen language.

4.5
Exercises

1. Give definitions using lambda abstraction for the following functions:

(a) one third of cubing;
(b) THREE, which takes a function f as an argument and produces a function which applies three times to itself;
(c) addition, multiplication, and raising to power n;
(d) composition of functions;
(e) the characteristic function Ψ, which associates for every subset A of X the predicate whose value is true over A and false otherwise.

2. Provide control abstraction for iterators of a binary tree.
3. Give ontologies, as in Fig. 4.2, for a *cooling-heating system* and an *anti-lock braking system* in the car domain. State the criticality properties of these two systems.

4.6
Bibliographic Notes

Abstraction for different stages of software development activity is discussed by Zimmer [10]. An account of abstraction process for software engineers in setting up the relationship among specification, application, and program is given by Turski and Maibaum [9]. Abstraction is described by Jackson [2] as a link between a description and the phenomena it describes. It should help the developer to look inward at the descriptions from the application domains and justify that the descriptions are faithful.

Domain analysis and modeling requires inventing abstractions that are appropriate for the domain of interest. Mohammad [3, 4] has given a rigorous approach to domain modeling. The approach constructs an ontology template, and uses it to formally derive components. The *Protege tool* [7] can be used to automate the process of generating OWL language [5] specification for the ontology. Since the ontology includes criticality properties of the domain of application, the components derived from the ontology inherit those domain-specific nonfunctional properties. That is, the "link", as described by Jackson [2], is strongly founded in the formal methodology of Mohammad [3, 4].

An excellent account of Turing machine and Church's lambda-calculus abstractions can be found in Penrose [6]. For an understanding of the seminal works of Turing [8], and Church [1], the reader can refer to any text book on Theory of Computation or Formal Languages.

References

1. Church A (1941) The calculi of lambda-conversion. In: Annals of mathematical studies, Cambridge, Mass
2. M. Jackson, Description is our business. Invited talk. In: VDM '91 Formal Software Development Methods; published as Prehn S, Toetenel WJ (eds) (1991) In: Lecture notes in computer science, vol 551, Springer, Noordwijkerhout
3. Mohammad M (2009) A formal component-based software engineering approach for developing trustworthy systems. PhD thesis, Department of Computer Science and Software Engineering, Concordia University, Montreal, Canada

4. Mohaamad M, Alagar V (2010) A component-based development process for trustworthy systems. J Softw Maint Evol, Res Pract, 1–20
5. Web ontology language. http://www.w3.org/2004/OWL/
6. Penrose R (1989) The emperor's new mind. Oxford University Press, London
7. Stanford University (2009) Protege. Stanford University/University of Manchester, Stanford/Manchester. Available at: http://protege.stanford.edu
8. Turing A (1937) On computable numbers with an application to Entscheidungsproblem. Proc Lond Math Soc (ser 2), 42:230–265
9. Turski WM, Maibaum T (1987) The specification of computer programs. Addison-Wesley, Reading
10. Zimmer JA (1985) Abstraction for programmers. McGraw-Hill, New York

Part II
Formalism Fundamentals

The term "formal method" refers to a package of a formal language, a formal development method, and tools to practice the formalism enshrined in the language and the method. In this part of the book a brief exposition to formalism is given, and it is followed by a discussion of the formal notation *automata* and its extensions. A broad classification of formal methods with a summary of tools available to practice them are included. The learning outcomes from this module are the following:

- formal systems, definition and examples
- automata, fundamental abstract machines
- extensions to automata
- examples of software models
- property-oriented vs. model-based specification languages

Formal Systems 5

Scientific experiments are of two kinds: (i) processes undertaken to discover things not yet known, (E1); and, (ii) processes undertaken to demonstrate things that are known, (E2). Scientific properties that have been observed will hold whenever the experiments are repeated with the same specifications, and under the same conditions. The results are independent of the scale on which the experiments are performed. Demonstrating the properties of a software system is analogous to conducting experiments of type E2. This can be done on a small scale, while establishing the properties of the software system through experiments on a reduced model of the system. However, the software development process is analogous to conducting experiments of type E1. This cannot be done on a small scale, or by employing a reduced model of the system. It is almost impossible to establish all the properties of a software system through the reduced model. It is therefore essential that software engineers get a direct exposure of the full-scale development process. On the other hand, a direct exposure of the full-scale development process may not be sufficient to reveal hidden properties of the system. A mid-way alternative is to adopt a certain degree of formality in software development. The motivation to espouse formal systems is driven by the quest for a foundation that is theoretically sound. A framework grounded on this foundation would contain the size and structural complexity of the system, provide a precise and unequivocal notation for specifying software components, and support a rigorous analysis of the relevant system properties. These observations are confirmed by the successful integration of formal methods in the development of large complex systems [3, 12].

A formal system consists of a *formal language* and a *deductive system*. The language may be introduced either informally or using a *metalanguage*. The metalanguage defines grammatical rules for formulating syntactically legal terms out of the symbols introduced in the formal language. The semantics of the language maps each syntactically legal term to a value in the chosen semantic domain. The language includes an "assertion part", usually some form of predicate logic. Assertions are used to write down precisely the behavior of the system under specification. Both syntax and semantics play a crucial role in the interpretation of assertions. A deductive system is part of the formalism. It is a machinery for conducting inferences in the construction of proofs from logical assertions. A sound deductive approach must include only correct representations, and correct mathematical reason-

V.S. Alagar, K. Periyasamy, *Specification of Software Systems*,
Texts in Computer Science,
DOI 10.1007/978-0-85729-277-3_5, © Springer-Verlag London Limited 2011

ing. Any slight deviation from the syntax and semantics may lead to paradoxical assertions. This must be avoided in the formal system; otherwise it will lead to self-contradictory conclusions in the deductive process. The challenge is to build formal systems in which syntax, semantics, and deductive mechanism do not allow contradictions to arise.

This chapter outlines the essential characteristics of a formal system. After a brief review of some of the formal systems studied in mathematics, science, and engineering, we discuss the components and properties of formal systems.

5.1
Peano's Axiomatization of Naturals—Formalization in Mathematics

Recall that abstraction "ignores details" and "generalizes" the domain being studied. With generalization, abstraction eliminates representational details; for example, Peano's axioms generalize natural numbers. The formal system of Peano [9], as stated below, uses set theory as the formal language, and logical axioms as the basis of inference.

Example 1 From the general point of view, natural numbers are the counting numbers. Our experience tells us that the set of natural numbers is infinite, and that for every natural number there is a unique next element. These observations are generalized by Peano's axioms which postulate the existence of a set P together with the map $succ : P \to P$ satisfying the following axioms:

A1 (axiom of infinity)   The map $succ$ is injective but not surjective. There is a bijection between P and P', where $P' = \{y|y = succ(x), x \in P\}$.
A2 (axiom of induction)   If $S \subseteq P, S \not\subseteq P'$ and $S' \subset S$, then $S = P$, where $S' = \{y|y = succ(x), x \in S\}$.

To understand the meaning of these axioms, one needs to invoke the semantics of terms such as injective, surjective and subset from the language of set theory and derive conclusions. There are four characteristics revealed in axiom A1:

1. P cannot be the empty set, because the empty set has no proper subsets.
2. An injective map from a finite set X to itself is also surjective. So, P cannot be finite.
3. Each element $x \in P$ is uniquely determined by the image $succ(x)$, since $succ$ is injective.
4. $P - P'$ is nonempty, for the map $succ$ is not surjective.

The following facts can be derived from axiom A2:

1. Since $S' \subset S$, S cannot be finite.
2. Since $S \not\subseteq P'$, S contains an initial segment of P.
3. S has a least element.
4. If $x \in S$, the integer $succ(x)$ also lies in S. The conclusion is that S must be all of P.
□

Mathematical formalisms can be imported into a formal method. The consequence is that the axioms of the mathematical formalism will constrain the specifications.

5.2
Model and Theory

One of the roles of abstraction, as discussed in Chap. 4, is to produce mathematical models and theories of the objects of concern. The strength of models and theories depend on the language used to build them. In this section, we compare the models and theories studied in Science, and Engineering. In Natural Science, Physical Science, Engineering, and Social Sciences, formal models are built by ignoring irrelevant details.

5.2.1
Formalization in Engineering

The foundation for building theories in Engineering is Applied Mathematics. For example, a mechanical engineer studies fluid dynamics using Navier–Stokes equation relating the velocity, density, pressure and the viscosity of a fluid. The formal representation of their relation is a partial differential equation and is the model of the fluid flow. This model is sufficient to understand the properties of fluid flow. However, the differential equation being non-linear is difficult to solve even with the use of powerful computers. Super-computers are being used as dedicated processors to analyze, understand and predict the behavior of fluid motion modeled by this equation. This is an example where the validation of a sound model may be extremely difficult. The predictive power of the model is constrained by an incomplete knowledge of the parameters of fluid flow and the limited computing power.

5.2.2
Formalization in Science

Scientists start their experiments by creating a formal representation of the domain. The representation includes a description of the domain objects and a rule-based discussion of the observed properties and behavior of domain objects. The descriptive part is the *model* of the domain and the rule-based discussion part represents the *theory* for the domain model. Informally, the theory of a model is a set of statements that can be made about the modeled domain. In practice, the set of all facts may be too large to enumerate. Consequently, only a subset of the facts is explicitly stated in the theory; the rest can be derived by exercising the rules underlying the model. Confidence in the model grows as theory predictions coincide with observed facts. Whenever a new observation contradicts the theory, both the theory and the model need to be modified or abandoned in favor of new ones.

An ancient model of the universe due to Ptolemy considered the Earth as stationary with the Sun, the Moon, the planets and the stars moving in circular orbits around the Earth. The theory of this model did not match the observed positions of the planets. The

Ptolemic model was then replaced by the Copernicus model in which the Sun was considered stationary, and the Earth and the planets moved around the Sun in circular orbits. Subsequently, Kepler modified the theory of Copernicus by postulating that the Earth and the planets moved in elliptic orbits around the Sun. The theoretical predictions of this revised model closely matched the celestial observations. Newton's laws of motion and theory of gravity generalized the previous predictive schemes. The axioms of Newton's theory of gravity were verified through experiments on the dynamics of terrestrial bodies, as well as through the observed outcomes in celestial mechanics. Other theories, such as Einstein's theory of relativity, accurately predicted the outcome of experiments well before the experiments became feasible. This evolutionary formalization process shows that scientific theories are acceptable only if they are found to be sound and free of contradictions.

Models in Social Sciences and Economics may also be formal, although they may lack accurate predictive power because of approximate modeling and incomplete knowledge. A naive solution is to exhaustively capture all the features of the modeled objects. Such a model goes against the principles of abstraction and defeats the purpose of theory building; the theory may even include contradictions. Hence, one has to compromise between the simplicity of the model on one hand, wherein only essential objects are modeled and essential axioms are stated, and the robustness of the model on the other hand, wherein the detailed features of the conceptual domain are captured.

5.2.3
Formalization Process in Software Engineering

The problem description, the specification of domain objects and their interdependence, and the program satisfying the specification represent models at different levels of abstraction. There is an underlying relationship among the models: A program characterizes how a solution to the given problem is arrived at. The specification is a higher level representation of the program it specifies. Representational and control details included in the program are not described by the specification. The description of a problem is part of the model describing the solution, it is integrated in the specification layer; that is, the specification layer describes both the model and the theory underlying the problem and its solution.

The specification thus serves the same purpose as a physicist's or an engineer's model. Therefore, a framework for building models and theories for software systems must be formal. The adequacy of the constructed model and theory must be established by showing that every intended behavior implied in the requirements is captured by the theory. Hence, in software engineering, formalization is a multi-step and repetitive activity:

1. Choose a formal framework within which specifications are to be built.
2. Construct a specification within the constraints of the syntax and semantics of the specification language.
3. Validate the specification against the requirements it is supposed to capture. If the intended properties are not consequent from the theory, the specification is modified, and the validation process is repeated until all the properties can be inferred from the specification. If a property cannot be deduced from the specification, step 2 is repeated.

If a requirement or property cannot be captured by the model, then the formalism is inadequate. In such a case, we go back to step 1 to choose another formalism.

5.3
Components of a Formal System

In this section the components of a formal system are explained with examples. The discussion is not specific to any formal language; rather it is to motivate the purpose behind the components.

5.3.1
Syntax

The syntax of a formal language is defined by a set of rules in a syntactic metalanguage. The set of rules, called *grammar*, depicts how basic objects, called *alphabet*, and constructs of the language, called *sentences*, are resolved and how more complex expressions, called *well-formed formulas*, may be constructed.

We use the standardized BNF [1, 8] convention for metalanguage notation. An alphabet is specified by writing the symbols within curly brackets {...}, separated by commas. A symbol can be a character, or glyph, or mark. A symbol is *uninterpreted*, in that it has no meaning in itself. Letters from various alphabets, digits, and special characters are often used as symbols. If an alphabet is clear from the context, we omit it in the description; otherwise we explicitly write it. As an example, $X = \{a, b, c\}$ is an alphabet with three symbols, a, b and c.

The grammar for a language is described by a number of rules. A rule names parts of the language, called non-terminal symbol of the language, and then defines it in terms of other non-terminal symbols and the symbols in the alphabet. The symbols of the alphabet are called terminals. They are atomic and cannot be refined by any definition.

Each non-terminal is introduced with a unique name, solely for the purpose of referring to it in other rules; the names are *not* part of the formal language. A non-terminal entity is followed by the symbol '=', the definition for the entity, and a semi-colon. A definition may consist of a sequence of items, where each item is either an alphabet or a non-terminal, and the items are separated by commas. A symbol from the alphabet is written within double quotes. When a non-terminal can be defined in more than one way, the different possibilities are listed and are separated by the symbol '|'. Examples 2, 3, and 4 introduce different elements, called *strings*, of a formal language.

Example 2 The entities *digit*, and *digits* describe strings with one or more digits.

> $digit$ = "0"|"1"|"2"|...|"9"|;
> $digits$ = $digit$ | $digit$,$digits$; $\qquad\qquad\qquad\qquad\qquad$ □

Example 3 The entities *twodigits*, and *threedigits* describe strings of a specific length.

> *digit*   = "0"|"1"|"2"| ... |"9"|;
> *twodigits*   = *digit,digit*;
> *threedigits* = *digit,twodigits*;

□

We need $n + 1$ rules to generate strings of length $n > 1$. However, we use a concise notation to denote strings of a specific length; for example, *digits(10)* denotes strings of exactly 10 digits.

We use meaningful identifiers to denote certain entities in the examples to follow. They are constructed according to the formal definition given in Example 4.

Example 4 We define two entities, *letter* and *digit*, and use them to create the entity *identifier*.

> *letter*   = "a"|"b"|"c"| ... |"z"|;
> *digit*   = "0"|"1"|"2"| ... |"9"|;
> *identifier* = *letter* | *identifier,digit* | *identifier,identifier*;

□

The examples illustrate the following features of the syntax definition method.

1. A formal syntax definition has three distinct uses:

   - it names the syntactic units through non-terminal symbols;
   - it defines the valid sentences of the formal language;
   - it shows the syntactic structure of any sentence in the language.

2. A grammar defines only one language.
3. The language being defined is *linear*. For example, a language to describe a knitting pattern cannot be defined under the metalanguage conventions described above.

5.3.2
Semantics

The sentences in the language defined by a grammar need to be attributed some meaning, if they are to be of any use. A formal system is useful only if each symbol and construct of its language component are meaningful. The *semantics* of a language determines how well-formed formulas can characterize certain properties by distinguishing those statements that are true of the conceptual domain. The definition of semantics boils down to a relationship between sentences and expressions specified in such a way that their truth values can be systematically extended to any statement in the language. In the context of a programming language, the structure of a program is determined by the syntax, and the nature of the computations is determined by the semantics of the language. However, the semantics of the language component of a formal system has more implication than programming language semantics. An important issue in the use of formal systems is *pragmatics*, which refers to the way in which the formal system is used. It is concerned with the different interpretations that can be given to associations between entities in the abstract model within the formal system and real-world objects. An interpretation of the formalization can be deemed faithful to its corresponding real entity, only if each property of that entity has been assigned a truth value by the semantics. In essence, the semantics of a language L is given by a structure (U, I), where U is a value domain (e.g., integers, real numbers, boolean) and the interpretation I is a mapping $I : L \to U$.

In Example 2, we can interpret each digit to correspond to the natural number it represents, and interpret a digit next to another as the usual decimal system. Under this interpretation, the well-formed formulas become the set of all natural numbers. However, other interpretations can be given to this language. Consider the case where we interpret each digit as a character, and the adjacent symbols as a concatenation of characters. This interpretation assigns a value from the domain of sequences to each well-formed formula of the language. However, every interpretation must remain consistent with the way the objects are manipulated according to the semantics of the language.

5.3.3
Inference Mechanism

The syntactic manipulation of well-formed formulas with little concern for their meaning is achieved by adding a deductive mechanism to the formal language. This deductive capability allows the derivation of new well-formed formulas from those that are present in the language. Deductive systems of interest for validation of system specifications are called *axiom systems*. The two components of an axiom system are the *axioms* and *the inference rules*. An axiom is a well-formed formula that is inherently valid within the formal system; it can be specified without reference to any other well-formed formula. The set of axioms forms a *basis* of the formal system allowing any other valid formula to be generated from the set by a systematic mechanical application of inference rules. An inference rule permits the generation of well-formed formulas as a consequence of other well-formed formulas.

Let L denote a formal language, and $x \in L$ be an axiom or any other well-formed formula. When applied to x, the inference rules produce zero or more well-formed formulas in L. We choose an arbitrary string x from the resulting language L, and repeat the process of applying inference rules. This will result in either an infinite number of new well-formed formulas being added to L, or the process to terminate after a finite number of iterations. We are interested only in those formal systems for which the language L is closed under this process. In this case, the resulting set L is called the *consequence closure* of the formal system.

Let σ denote the consequence closure operator, such that $\forall x \in L$, $\sigma(x)$ denotes the set of all well-formed formulas which can be derived from x through successive applications of the inference rules. Clearly σ maps sets of well-formed formulas in L into sets of well-formed formulas in the consequence closure of L. The following properties hold on σ:

Containment $\forall A \subset L, A \subseteq \sigma(A)$
Monotonicity $\forall A, B \subset L$, if $A \subseteq B$ then $\sigma(A) \subseteq \sigma(B)$
Closure $\forall A \subset L, \sigma(A) = \sigma(\sigma(A))$

A *theory* in a formal system is a set of statements A, $A \subseteq L$, such that $\sigma(A) = A$.

Example 5 We define a formal system to describe the *unary* representation for integers and addition and multiplication laws. The alphabet consists of the symbols $1, e, +$ and $\circ$. The well-formed formulas are defined by the following grammar:

nat	$= e \mid string\ of\ ones$;
string of ones	$= suc(e) \mid suc(string\ of\ ones)$;
suc(e)	$= 1$;
suc(string of ones)	$= string\ of\ ones, 1$;
sentence	$= (nat = nat + nat;) \mid (nat = nat \circ nat); \mid (sentence)$;

Axioms

1. $a = e + a$
2. $e = e \circ a$
3. $(x\ 1) \circ a = x \circ a + a$
4. $(x\ 1) + a = (x + a\ 1)$

Inference Rules

1. If $a + b = c$ is a well-formed formula, then (i) $suc(a) + b = suc(c)$, and (ii) $a + suc(b) = suc(c)$ are also well-formed formulas.
2. If $a \circ b = c$ is a well-formed formula, then (i) $a \circ suc(b) = c + a$ and (ii) $suc(a) \circ b = c + b$ are also well-formed formulas.

The sentence $111 = 11 + 1$ is a well-formed formula in the language. By the first inference rule, we have $suc(11) + 1 = suc(111)$. An application of the grammar rule gives the well-formed formula $111 + 1 = 1111$. This is, therefore, an immediate consequence of the assumption that $111 = 11 + 1$ is a well-formed formula. From the second part of the first inference rule, another immediate consequence is that $1111 = 11 + 11$ is also a well-formed formula. Assuming that $11 \circ 111 = 111111$ is a well-formed formula, an application of the second rule gives $11 \circ suc(111) = 111111 + 11$. By expanding $suc(111)$ and using Axiom 4 twice, we get $11 \circ 1111 = 11111111$ as another well-formed formula in the language. If we interpret e to be the digit *zero*, '1' to be the digit 1, a sequence of n 1's to be the natural number n, then it is straightforward to verify that $+$ and $\circ$ as defined here correspond to the addition and multiplication operations over natural numbers.   □

   As remarked earlier, the consequence closure of a formal system is the union of a set of axioms and a set of derivations of every subset for well-formed formulas using inference rules. The subset of well-formed formulas that we start with is called *premises* or *hypothesis*, and the well-formed formulas obtained by direct consequence of applying inference rules are called *derivations*. A statement is *provable* in a formal system if it has a proof constructed from the axioms using the inference rules. Within a formal system, the text of a formal *proof* consists of the hypothesis and the derivations, with logical steps, representing the application of inference rules, in between. Each logical step is an axiom or an immediate consequence of a previous step as determined by an inference rule. The conclusion represented by the last step of the proof is called a *theorem*. All axioms are true statements within the formal system. Every theorem other than an axiom requires a formal proof.

Example 6 Prove the theorem

$$111 \circ 111 = 111111111$$

within the formal system of Example 5. □

Proof

Step 1	$(x\ 1) \circ a = x \circ a + a$	Axiom 3
Step 2	$(e\ 1) \circ 111 = e \circ 111 + 111$	Substitution for $x(= e)$ and $a(= 111)$
Step 3	$(e\ 1) \circ 111 = e + 111$	Axiom 2
Step 4	$(e\ 1) \circ 111 = 111$	Axiom 1
Step 5	$1 \circ 111 = 111$	Definition of e
Step 6	$suc(1) \circ 111 = 111 + 111$	Inference Rule 2 applied to Step 5
Step 7	$(11) \circ 111 = 111 + 111$	Definition of suc
Step 8	$(11) \circ 111 = 11 + 1111$	Axiom 4
Step 9	$(11) \circ 111 = 1 + 11111$	Axiom 4
Step 10	$(11) \circ 111 = e\ 1 + 11111$	Definition of e
Step 11	$(11) \circ 111 = e + 111111$	Axiom 4
Step 12	$(11) \circ 111 = 111111$	Axiom 1
Step 13	$suc(11) \circ 111 = 111111 + 111$	Inference Rule 2 applied to Step 12
Step 14	$111 \circ 111 = 111111 + 111$	Definition of suc

Now apply Axiom 4 repeatedly to Step 14 and finally use definition of e followed by Axiom 1 to get the final result. □

It is clear from this example that the well-formed formulas are manipulated strictly according to the grammar rules, axioms and inference rules. That is, there is no interpretation assigned to the structures or their derivations. When the meaning for a string of n 1's is provided as the natural number n and e denotes 0, the formal operations provide the usual laws of addition and multiplication on natural numbers.

5.4
Properties of Formal Systems

A formal system is often constructed to fulfill a *need* and consequently the specifications within the system are subjective. The usefulness and validity of a formal system depend on the circumstances that called for the system. As opposed to mathematical models that may not exist in reality, entities within a formal system model real-world objects. In software engineering context, properties of a formal system such as consistency, completeness, and decidability, determine the expressiveness of abstractions, as well as the ability to infer properties of conceptual domain objects from the deductive mechanism of the formal system.

An essential feature of a formal system, as discussed earlier, is its use in deriving a formal proof for certain assertions that can be made within the system. The primary advantage of a formal proof is that each step in the proof is a derivation of one of the available well-formed formulas and consequently the proof process can be automated. In other words, checking the validity of a proof is a computable process. It can be done algorithmically and no evidence external to the formalized notions should be considered in deriving a proof. The consequence closure contains all the truth statements relevant to the formal system. However, it may not be complete in the sense that what is known to be true may not be provable within the formal system. Two factors contribute to this characteristic of incompleteness. The first comes from an incomplete formalization of knowledge about the application domain. The second is a form of incompleteness that is inherent in every formal system. These notions give rise to three important concepts: *consistency*, *completeness*, and *decidability*.

5.4.1
Consistency

The inference mechanism associated with a formal system enables us to determine whether or not a sentence x is derivable as a consequence of well-formed formulas in the formal system. Consider a formal system $F = (L, \sigma)$ where L is the formal language and σ is the consequence closure operator. If $x \in \sigma(L)$ we write $F \vdash x$. The symbol $\vdash$ is called the *syntactic turnstile*. A formal system is said to be *syntactically consistent* if for any given sentence x, $F \vdash x$ and $F \vdash \sim x$ cannot occur simultaneously. In other words, *at most* one of the sentences x or $\sim x$ can be deduced in F. In general, syntactic consistency is hard to establish. A formal system is *semantically consistent* if for each interpretation of a sentence there exists no mapping whose result produces both *true* and *false*. Semantic consistency is in general impossible to establish. Consequently, from a practical point of view, tool support is essential to examine inconsistency.

5.4.2
Completeness

It may happen that neither x nor $\sim x$ belongs to $\sigma(L)$. This occurs when x is a property not captured within the formal system. In such cases, we say x is *independent* of F. Whenever an essential property x is independent of F, x can be included in the formal system F, as an axiom, without violating the consistency of F. Thus, F can be extended by including sentences that are independent of F. Because axioms in F form a basis for F, a state is ultimately reached where the addition of one more axiom will violate the syntactic consistency of F. Every sentence in F is either derivable or refutable. This leads to the concept of *syntactic completeness*. That is, F is syntactically complete if for any given sentence x, either $F \vdash x$ or $F \vdash \sim x$. A formal system is *semantically complete* if for each interpretation of a sentence, every mapping of the sentence is either *true* or *false*. Completeness relates to the extensibility of a formal system, and consequently, its ability to capture more meaningful entities from its conceptual domain. Evaluating the completeness of a formal system is indeed a daunting task.

5.4.3
Decidability

In 1931, Gödel showed that any reasonable formal theory contains sentences that cannot be proved or disproved. This implies that it is impossible to certify that a formal system does not contain statements that are neither provable nor disprovable through its inference mechanism. There is no decision procedure to provide proofs for all true statements in a formal system, and some true statements do not have a proof within the system. Thus, the truth values of such sentences are *undecidable*. This result sets limits on deductive reasoning capabilities as applied to formal specifications. At the same time, the undecidability result guides the software engineer in specification building and reasoning. The software engineer cannot reject anything that is not deducible from axioms. On the contrary, a useful property that is not a consequence of the axioms should be added to the system specification and checked for consistency. If the added information is never used in subsequent design stages of the formal system, then it can be removed. Since the formal system must necessarily be broad, and hence is bound to be incomplete in Gödel's terms, the goal in designing a formal system focuses on consistency rather than on completeness. The construction of a formal system starts with a small and consistent set of axioms. The process progresses by discovering unspecified facts through formal deduction, gathering more knowledge on the domain, determining the independence of new facts, and augmenting the system with new facts.

5.5
Extended Syntactic Metalanguage

For many applications, such as specifying file formats, and document and protocol structures, the full power of a formal method is not necessary. A formal definition of syntax is sufficient. However, the syntax introduced in Sect. 5.3.1 is too simple to handle the complexities in document structures. In this section, an extended syntactic metalanguage is discussed for such purposes. We illustrate the metalanguage constructs for formally defining the syntax of complex documents.

The extensions to the syntactic metalanguage consist of adding one or more of the following items with each grammar rule: (1) an action; (2) a predicate; (3) metasymbols. We use upper-case letters for the metasymbol; for example, DIGITS(6), CHAR(10), and CIRCLE. These denote pre-defined object types. We assume that the grammar generating these entities have been defined already and are available for use in creating other entities. Another abbreviation used is $\{\ \}^n$, which denotes $n \geq 1$ repetitions of the symbol within curly parentheses. Thus, $\{WORDS\}^n$ denotes an entity representing a sequence of n *WORDS*.

Recently, a software in Visual Prolog has been developed by Axon [2] to provide an environment for *Idea Processor* (IP). In 1985, Hershey [6] introduced the commercial product *Idea Processor* to collect notes in the form of chunks of text, and rearrange them in groups to form an outline for an eventual expansion into a report. In 1986 Henderson [5] simplified many aspects of IP and gave a prototype in a functional programming language. We build on Henderson's simple concept that IP is defined as a collection of related ideas under a single title and introduce in Example 7 an extended metalanguage notation for formalizing the notion of ideas, and valid documents that can be processed by an Idea Processor.

Example 7 An idea within a document is a header and its associated text. The header is composed of an identifier and a name. The text associated with an idea consists of sub-ideas, and one or more paragraphs with text and diagrams. Each diagram has an identifier and a caption. An idea may have zero or more sub-ideas where each sub-idea has the same structure as that of an idea. A set of keywords is associated with an idea. For example, the following notes might be present in an idea processor document:

1. "specification in a natural language"
2. "ambiguities in natural language specifications"
3. "algebraic specification method"

   - "syntax and semantics of an algebraic specification language"
   - "an example"
   - "executing algebraic specifications"

The notes may include diagrams for illustration. The following interpretation is assumed for the upper-case symbols used in the formalism: NL denotes a new line; T denotes a tab (indentation). These actions are not explicitly described in the grammar. All other upper-case symbols are meaningful identifiers for pre-defined entities; for example, DIAG_ID means diagram identifier.   □

The formal definition of document given in Example 7 can be used to enforce the construction of structurally correct idea processor documents. However, the ideas expressed within a section should undergo a separate semantic validation.

The next example introduces a formal language for specifying *electronic forms*. In this example, an electronic form is a visual interface entity used for recording laboratory test results for the patients of a hospital.

Example 8 An electronic form, called *test_request_form*, records information on medical tests conducted on patients at different labs in a hospital. Although the details regarding the visual display of these forms may vary, their essential format can be abstracted sufficiently well to provide a screen specification for an electronic form. A typical *test_request_form* used in hospitals will have three sections: *test_information*, *patient_information* and *lab_information*. Within each section the data are grouped in a certain format. Figure 5.1 shows a typical form used in hospitals; Table 5.2 gives the grammar

Table 5.1 Grammar for Idea Processor documents

document	= NL, *DOC_TITLE*, NL, {*idea*}^{n};
idea	= *header*, NL, *text*, NL, *keyword*;
header	= *HEADER_NUMBER, HEADER_NAME*;
text	= {*sub − idea\paragraph,diagram\diagram,paragraph*}^{n};
sub-idea	= T, *idea*;
keyword	= {*WORDS*}^{n};
paragraph	= *line* | *line*, NL, *paragraph*;
line	= *WORDS* | *WORDS, line*;
diagram	= *drawing*, NL, *DIAG_ID, diag_cap*;
drawing	= *CIRCLE | RECTANGLE | DFD | FLOWCHART*;
diag_cap	= {*WORDS*}^{4};

Fig. 5.1 Test_Request_Form as seen on the screen

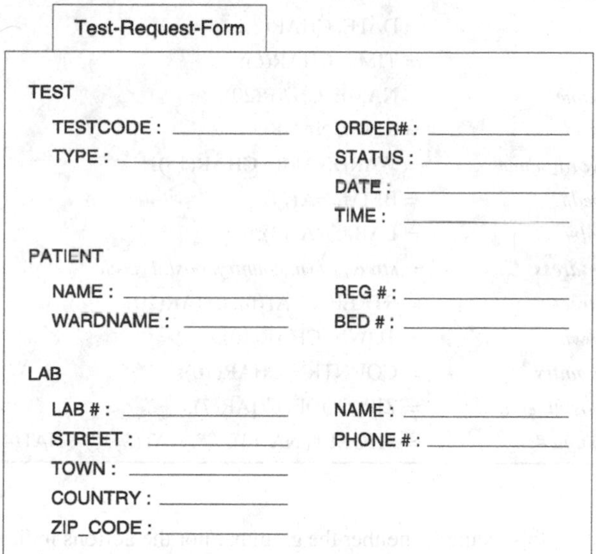

for the form. The grammar uses symbols from an alphabet, and pre-defined entities whose interpretations are as follows: the symbols ⟨L⟩, ⟨R⟩ force the visual display of the entities to which they are bound to occur, respectively, left-justified or right-justified on the screen. The visual display of the entity *test_request_form* is characterized by a well-formed formula from this grammar. Some grammar rules involve the specification of actions. These correspond to the semantic interpretations for the rules. For instance, the semantic interpretation for *test_request_form* at the completion of expanding the rule for *lab* corresponds to the action *CREATE_LABLAYOUT* associated with *lab*. This action activates the procedures for displaying on the screen the part of the form corresponding to the layout for the lab information.

Table 5.2 Grammar for Test_Request_Form

test_request_form	= test, NL, patient, NL, lab;
	{action: CREATE_WINDOW}
test	= TEST, NL, test_code: ⟨L⟩, order#: ⟨R⟩, NL, type: ⟨L⟩,
	status: ⟨R⟩, NL, date: ⟨R⟩, NL, time_ordered: ⟨R⟩, NL;
	{action: CREATE_TESTLAYOUT}
patient	= PATIENT, NL, name: ⟨L⟩, reg#: ⟨R⟩, NL, ward_name: ⟨L⟩, bed#:⟨ R ⟩, NL;
	{action: CREATE_PATIENTLAYOUT}
lab	= LAB, NL, lab#: ⟨L⟩, name: ⟨R⟩, NL, address: ⟨L⟩, NL, phone#: ⟨L⟩, NL;
	{action: CREATE_LABLAYOUT}
test_code	= TESTCODE, NAT(6);
order#	= ORDER#, NAT(20);
type	= TYPE, CHAR(15);
status	= STATUS, BITS;
date	= DATE, CHAR(8);
time	= TIME, CHAR(6);
name	= NAME, CHAR(20);
reg#	= REG#, NAT(8);
ward_name	= WARDNAME, CHAR(15);
bed#	= BED#, NAT(4);
lab#	= LAB#, NAT(3);
address	= *street, town, country, postal_code*;
street	= STREET, NAT(6), CHAR(20);
town	= TOWN, CHAR(10);
country	= COUNTRY, CHAR(10);
postal_code	= ZIP_CODE, CHAR(7);
phone#	= PHONE#, NAT(3), " ", NAT(3), " ", NAT(4);

In this example, neither the grammar nor the actions indicate *how* the electronic form is to be used; it only defines the structure of the form. The formal model can be "executed" to mimic the ways in which the form can be used in real-life situations. In Chap. 7, we construct a behavior model to demonstrate the correct user interactions and the corresponding responsiveness of the *test_request_form* software. □

5.6
Exercises

1. Let $A = \{a, b\}$ be the alphabet. Define a grammar over the alphabet A for which the language includes the strings ab, bba, and all strings that have ab and bba as substrings.

2. Let $A = \{0, 1\}$ be the alphabet. Define a grammar over the alphabet A for which the language includes only strings of even length.

3. Let $A = \{$ "0", "1", "2", "3", "4", "5", "6", "7", "8", "9", " $-$ ", "." $\}$ be the alphabet. The grammar is defined as follows:

```
F  = '-' FN | FN
FN = N | N '.' N
N  = D | D, N
D  = ''0'' | ''1'' | ''2'' | ''3'' | ''4'' | ''5'' | ''6'' | ''7'' |
     ''8'' | ''9''
```

The different symbols here are all abbreviations: F is the entity to be defined, FN is a fractional number, N is a sequence of digits, and D is a digit. Which of the following strings are produced by the grammar?

1. 5.26
2. -7.77
3. 3.-14
4. 4-5.16

4. There are two commands, **send**, and **reply**, for a simple electronic mailing system. Assuming that each message has a unique name, give specifications in extended BNF for these commands. The requirements are:

- A message can be sent by a user to one or more users in the system.
- A user can reply to only one mail at a time. The effect of reply is to compose a message, assign a unique name, assign a time-stamp, and send the message to the user from whom the original message was received.

5. Specify the structure of a **service contract**, as defined below, using extended BNF notation. A service contract has three sections. In the first section, a maximum of three services are listed. Each service has a **name**, a **parameter list**, **date** when the service is to be provided, and its **cost**. In the second section, one legal constraint pertaining to each of the services is stated. A constraint names a service and assigns a legal code (maximum four digits) to it. The third section lists the location (address) where each service included in the contract is to be provided.

6. Give an extended BNF for generating an electronic form for an Automobile Registration System, similar to the electronic form discussed in Example 8. The requirements are as follows:

- The form should have three sections: **Vehicle, Owner, Administration**.
- The information in the **Vehicle** section should include the make, model, year, serial number, engine capacity, factory price, and color.
- The **Owner** information should include the name, address, and phone numbers of the principal owner of the vehicle. It should also include the date of purchase and the purchase price of the vehicle.
- The **Administration** section should include the status of the vehicle (pleasure or business), date and place of current registration, registration number of the vehicle, registration fee, and expiry date of registration.

5.7
Bibliographic Notes

The metalanguage notation used in the text is derived from BNF (Backus Naur Form), a notation invented by Backus [1] and Naur [8], to define the syntax of Fortran and Algol 60 programming languages. The extended BNF, known as EBNF, is due to Wirth [11] and has been standardized by Scowen [11]. The YACC parser generator [4] produces translators for programming languages based on BNF descriptions. An interesting use of formal grammars for prototyping was suggested by Reisner [10] who used certain properties of the BNF notation to predict the complexity of a user interface. Many textbooks that treat comprehensively formal language theory use some variant of BNF, for example see [7]. The standardized EBNF manual provides a means to extend the standard EBNF, a useful feature to introduce new constructs in the syntactic metalanguage for formalizing complex structures.

Bringing in mathematical formalism into software development practices requires that true statements about the domain for which the software is developed must become axioms in the formal system. That is, the strings in the formal language are to be interpreted in such a way that if they become true in the domain then we have to accept that as theorems. The interpretation of every theorem must be a true statement. Choosing the right formalism is often problematic, because the axiom systems to be studied are suggested by the demands of the particular application domain.

References

1. Backus JW (1957) The FORTRAN automatic coding system. In: Proceedings of the AFIPS Western joint computer conference, pp 188–198
2. Bok C (2006) Developing an idea processor in prolog. Presented at the VIP-ALC Conference. http://web.singnet.com.sg/~axon2000
3. Formal Methods Web page, http://formalmethods.wikia.com/wiki/Z_notation, May 2010
4. Johnson SC (1975) Yacc: yet another compiler. Computer science technical report No 32, Bell Labs, Murray Hill, NJ
5. Henderson P (1986) Functional programming, formal specification, and rapid prototyping. IEEE Trans Softw Eng SE-12(2):241–250
6. Hershey W (1985) Idea processors. Byte 10(4)
7. Martin J (2003) Introduction to languages and the theory of computation, 3rd edn. McGraw-Hill, New York
8. Naur P (ed) (1963) Revised report on the algorithmic language Algol 60. Commun ACM 6(1):1–17
9. Peano G (1967) The principles of arithmetic, presented by a new method. In: van Heijenoort J (ed) From Frege to Gödel: a sourcebook of mathematical logic. Harvard University Press, Cambridge
10. Reisner P (1981) Formal grammar and human factors design of an interactive graphics system. IEEE Trans Softw Eng SE-7(2):229–240
11. Scowen RS (1998) Extended BNF—a generic base standard. Draft paper. http://www.cl.cam. ac.uk/~mgk25/iso-14977-paper.pdf (May 2010)
12. Wheeler DA (2006) High assurance (for security or safety) and Free-Libre/Open Source Software (FLOSS) ... with lots on formal methods/software verification. http://www.dwheeler. com/essays/high-assurance-floss.html (04/16/2010)

Automata

An automaton is an abstract machine that performs a task according to a specified set of instructions. It captures the behavior of a computer through its ability to read input, perform a sequence of step-by-step operations, and produce an output. Each step in a computation sequence is called a *state*. Given an input string, the machine reads the first (leftmost) symbol in its *initial* state and the state of the machine changes. The machine reads the next symbol at the new state and changes its state again. This process continues until the last symbol of the string has been read. The final state is the state reached by the machine after reading the last symbol from the input string. The last state characterizes the input string with respect to the machine. In general, an automaton, by virtue of states, is a useful abstraction for characterizing the behavior of a broad class of software and hardware systems. An automaton itself can be classified based on different perspectives:

- *finite* or *infinite*,
- *deterministic* or *nondeterministic*,
- *accepter* or *transducer*.

Finite automata are machines that have zero or a finite amount of memory, independent of input size. Since the number of states is finite and only a finite amount of information can be retained in each state, finite automaton cannot deal with situations in which information required is unbounded.

A *deterministic* automaton is one in which a state change leads to a unique next state. In a *nondeterministic* automaton, a state change leads to a state within a set of possible next states. It is known [7] that both deterministic and nondeterministic automata have the same computational power. Nondeterminism is a powerful tool in formal modeling and usually leads to a higher level of abstraction than deterministic models. In general, nondeterminism provides design freedom whereas deterministic model may constrain the design too early in the development process. Another merit of nondeterminism is that an implementation may be done in a concurrent or parallel computing environment. Formal methods for concurrent systems have constructs to specify nondeterminism. We will study one such formal method in Chap. 15.

An automaton whose output is either "yes" or "no" is called an *accepter*. For an input string, if the automaton outputs "yes", it means that the string is accepted (recognized)

V.S. Alagar, K. Periyasamy, *Specification of Software Systems*,
Texts in Computer Science,
DOI 10.1007/978-0-85729-277-3_6, © Springer-Verlag London Limited 2011

by the automaton; if it outputs "no", it means that the string is rejected by the automaton. This capability is sufficient for reasoning because, in formal reasoning, we are interested in knowing whether or not a property is true of the modeled system. An automaton which is capable of outputting a string of symbols, in response to an input string of symbols, is called *transducer*. In modeling the interaction of the environment with the system our interest will be to know the nature of system responses to environmental stimuli. We need a transducer to model such *observable* behavior. A finite automaton, whether it is an accepter or transducer, is called a *finite state machine*.

In this chapter we discuss the basic concepts of finite automata, and different notations used in modeling systems with finite state machines.

6.1
Deterministic Finite Accepters

The basic concepts of deterministic finite accepters are discussed in this section. The two important factors that characterize them are the lack of memory (or fixed memory independent of input size) and the predictable behavior at each state.

Definition 1 A *deterministic finite accepter* or *dfa* is defined by the tuple

$$M = (Q, \Sigma, q_0, F, \delta),$$

where

$Q(\neq \emptyset)$ is a finite set of states,
Σ is a finite set of input alphabet,
$q_0 \in Q$ is the initial state,
$F \subseteq Q$ is the set of accepting states,
$\delta : Q \times \Sigma \rightarrow Q$ is the transition function, where for every state $q \in Q$ and for every symbol $x \in \Sigma, q' = \delta(q, x) \in Q$.

An automaton can be represented either by a graph or by a table, which help follow the transitions. The graphical representation in Fig. 6.1 for the automaton in Example 1 is called the *state diagram*. In a state diagram, states are represented by rectangles, and directed arcs are used to represent transitions. The initial state is depicted with an incoming unlabeled arrow. A rectangle with two bounded lines is used to denote an accept state. For $q_i, q_j \in Q$, if $\delta(q_i, x) = q_j$ is the transition definition for state q_i, then in the graph the edge from state q_i to state q_j is labeled x. A dfa operates by starting from its initial state, recognizes the next input symbol, and makes a transition to the next state as defined by δ function. When all the symbols in the input string have been processed, the string is accepted if the machine is in one of its accept states; otherwise it is rejected.

Example 1 Consider the dfa

$$M = (\{A, B, C, D\}, \{0, 1\}, A, \{A, B, C\}, \delta),$$

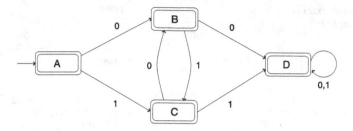

Fig. 6.1   State diagram of Example 1

where δ is given by

$$\begin{aligned}
\delta(A,0) &= B & \delta(A,1) &= C \\
\delta(B,0) &= D & \delta(B,1) &= C \\
\delta(C,0) &= B & \delta(C,1) &= D \\
\delta(D,0) &= D & \delta(D,1) &= D
\end{aligned}$$

This dfa accepts every binary string which does not have two consecutive 0's or two consecutive 1's. From the initial state A, the machine either transits to state B or state C depending upon the input being 0 or 1. If, in state C, the input symbol is 0, the machine has encountered two consecutive 0's, which must be rejected. This is why the transition at state B for input symbol 0 takes the machine to state D which has no outgoing edge. The state D is called a *trap* state, or an *empty* state denoted $\emptyset$. The transition from state C to state D is a mirror image of the transition from state B to state D. The transitions between states B and C are symmetric, allowing alternating 0's and 1's to be accepted.   □

The set of strings formed over the alphabet Σ is denoted Σ^*. From Example 1, it is clear that a dfa M defines a set of strings $L(M) \subset \Sigma^*$ accepted by it. The set $L(M)$ of accepted strings is the language associated with the accepter M. It is also clear that the string acceptance process is "algorithmic", and hence can be programmed. The interesting issue in formal methods is the dual of recognition, namely constructing a dfa model to solve a problem.

6.1.1
State Machine Modeling

A finite state machine (FSM) is formal and control-driven. With a formal state machine model, whether it is for a hardware or software module, it is possible to formally analyze it for the acceptance or rejection of a specified property. The only prerequisites are that the property to be verified is represented as a string of symbols, and the states with state transitions are precisely stated. In modeling systems, the notations and conventions of Definition 1 may not be followed strictly, as illustrated with the examples below.

Fig. 6.2 State diagram of
switch: Example 2

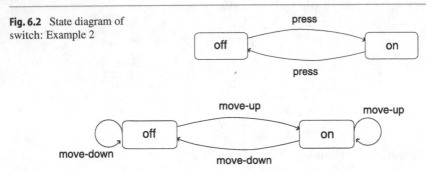

Fig. 6.3 State diagram of light switch: Example 2

6.1.1.1
Simple Switches

Switches are designed in many ways. In Example 2, we model two kinds of switches. In both models, the transition symbols are *actions* (stimuli from the environment). In this example, there is someone who "presses" the switch.

Example 2 The simplest switch we can think of is a "toggle switch", the one on a computer or its monitor. The device is either "off" or "on". When the switch is "on" and is pressed, it becomes "off", and the inverse operation is valid too. This behavior is shown in Fig. 6.2. For this example, the states are *off* and *on*, the alphabet has only one symbol, and the symbol is the "action" *press*. So, the first notational deviation is that transition symbols may be *actions* or *events* which may come from the environment.

For a light switch that is still designed in the old fashioned way, the switch can be "moved up" to switch on the light, and the switch is "moved down" to switch off the light. If the switch is moved up, any attempt to move it up should not cause any change in the state of the light. The behavior of this kind of light switch is shown in Fig. 6.3. The transition labels are the actions *move-up*, and *move-down*.   □

6.1.1.2
Language Recognizer

In constructing an automaton for recognizing a language, we use some form of reasoning similar to programming in a high-level language. Example 3 illustrates the logic for constructing the automaton in Fig. 6.4 for a language that includes all strings in alphabetical order over the alphabet $\{a, b, c\}$. Here the pattern is expressed by the property "alphabetic order". In constructing the dfa, notice that transitions are only *partial* in each state, which deviates from the definition of δ in Definition 1.

Example 3 Let $\Sigma = \{a, b, c\}$. A string $\sigma \in \Sigma^*$ is monotonic non-decreasing (monotonic, for short) if the characters in σ are in alphabetical order. Examples of monotonic strings in

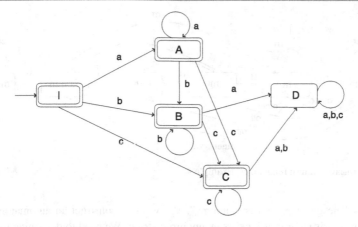

Fig. 6.4 Alphabetic pattern recognizer: Example 3

Σ^* are *aaa*, *abb*, *abcc*, *bbc*, *ccc*, whereas strings *abba*, and *ccb* are not monotonic. The problem is to construct a dfa over Σ which recognizes monotonic strings in Σ^*. An empty string is monotonic. Thus the initial state in the dfa is an accept state. All strings with only one character are monotonic. The first character of a monotonic string of length > 1 can be any one of *a*, *b*, *c*. Hence, from the initial state I, the automaton goes to state A, if the input symbol is *a*, goes to state B if the input symbol is *b* and goes to state C if the input symbol is *c*. The states A, B, and C are accept states. In state A, if the input symbol is *a* the transition should be from A to itself; if the input symbol is *b* the transition should be from A to B, and if the input symbol is *c* the transition should be from A to C. In state B, if the input symbol is *a* then it should be rejected. So we create a trap state D and define the transition from B to it for input *a*. In state B, either input *b* or *c* should lead, respectively, to accept states B and C. In state C, only input symbol *c* should lead to accept state C, and for other input symbols the transition should lead to state D. In state D, every input symbol should lead to D itself. The full dfa is shown in Fig. 6.4.   □

6.1.1.3
Pattern Matching

State machine is the natural formalism for constructing language parsers and text editing software. In text editing, pattern matching is a basic activity. A pattern is a fixed string of finite length. Pattern matching problem is "given a pattern p and a string s, find all substrings of s that match p". The two well-known solutions are Boyer–Moore [2] and Knuth–Morris–Pratt [6] (KMP) algorithms. The KMP algorithm constructs a finite state machine for the pattern p and then runs the string s on it to extract the matches. Example 4 explains a simple version of the method for the specific pattern "mummy". Definition 1 is adapted in many ways in this example: each state acts like a "memory bank", transitions in each state are only partial, and the label "other" denotes a set of symbols, and is used in the model to minimize the number of transitions in a state.

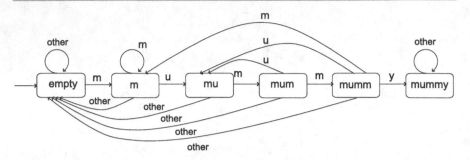

Fig. 6.5 "mummy" pattern recognizer: Example 4

Example 4 The given pattern is "mummy". We want to construct an automaton which will recognize this pattern, if it exists in any input string. We need to determine the states first. The information in a state should determine the substring recognized so far in the automaton. If we matched a part of the string so far that information is relevant for the state. Initially no string is recognized. Hence the initial state information is "empty string". Let us call the initial state *empty*. The automaton should stay in the initial state until it receives the input "m". When it receives "m" in state *empty*, it recognizes the substring "m" and hence makes a transition to the next state, say *m*. That is, at state *m*, it has recognized the prefix of length 1 of the pattern "mummy". Arguing like this, it is reasonable to conclude that we want the states to be *partial matches* to the pattern. The possible partial matches are "empty string", "m", "mu", "mum", "mumm", and "mummy". These are the *prefixes* of the string "mummy". So, the states are *empty, m, mu, mum, mumm, mummy*. Next, we must determine the input symbols and transitions. The three symbols in the pattern "mummy" are "m", "u", and "y". The input string may contain symbols other than the symbols in the pattern, and let us collectively call them *other*. For the sake of simplicity, we combine all transitions labeled by symbols from the set *other* into one single transition labeled by *other*. So, essentially there are a maximum of four possible transitions in a state, one for each pattern symbol and *other*. The transitions for the four cases in state *mumm* are discussed below:

1. If the symbol "y" is input in state *mumm*, we have a complete match, and so the automaton transits to state *mummy* and stays there. That is, a match is found in the input string and the rest of the input string is ignored.
2. If the symbol is "u" then the longest prefix of pattern that matches the suffix of the string "mum<u>mu</u>" is "mu". Hence the automaton should transit to the state *mu*.
3. If the symbol is "m" then the longest prefix of pattern that matches the suffix of the string "mum<u>m</u>" is "m". Hence the automaton should transit to the state *m*.
4. If the symbol is from the set *other* then the longest prefix of pattern that matches the suffix of the string "mumm<u>x</u>", where $x \in other$ is "empty". Hence the automaton should transit to the state *empty*.

Arguing similarly for each state, we determine the transitions of the automaton. The automaton constructed for matching the pattern "mummy" in any string over the alphabet $\{a, b, \ldots, z\}$ is shown in Fig. 6.5.   □

Fig. 6.6 Traffic-light model: Example 5

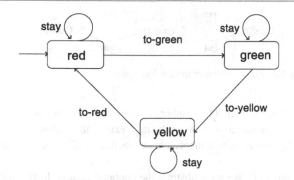

6.1.1.4
Traffic Light

A traffic light can be in one of the states {*red, green, yellow*} at any instant. Initially the traffic light may be in state *red* or in state *green* or in state *yellow*. Let us make an arbitrary choice and make *red* the initial state. After *some time*, it changes to *green*. It stays *green* for a while before changing to *yellow*. After staying *yellow* for a while, it changes to *red* again. This behavior is repeated *forever*. That is, initial state of the automaton is chosen arbitrarily from the set of states of the traffic light and the automaton has no final (accept) state. This is an important change that we have made now in dfa definition. Some external agent, called *controller* is necessary to control the duration of its stay in each state and finally to *stop* it from functioning. Here is an example where the entities *controller* and *light* have to communicate with each other. We will discuss this model of communication in Sect. 6.2.1. For the present, we model only the *forever* behavior of the light.

Example 5 The state names and transition labels are chosen to reflect meaningful terms in the application domain. The automaton has states $Q = \{red, green, yellow\}$, and its initial state is $q_0 = red$. The alphabet is the set events received by the traffic light from the controller. $\Sigma = \{stay, to\text{-}green, to\text{-}yellow, to\text{-}red\}$. At each state either the automaton "waits" in that state or transits to the next state. The language recognized by this automaton is σ^*, where σ is the sequence ⟨ stay, to-green, stay, to-yellow, stay, to-red ⟩ and $\star$ denotes 0 or more repetitions. If we replace the transition labels by the state names we get the sequence τ^*, where $\tau = \langle red, green, yellow \rangle$. We call σ^* the *trace* and τ^* "the *execution sequence*" of the automaton shown in Fig. 6.6. ☐

6.1.1.5
Finite Container

A container is an abstract data type for a collection of items. In many applications actual container size is not known in advance, yet a dynamic storage allocation algorithm allocates a fixed amount of container size. We can model such a bounded container by a state

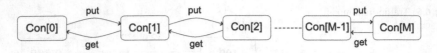

Fig. 6.7 Finite container model: Example 6

machine model. The number of states in the model is determined by the maximum allocated container size. At each state, except the initial state and final state, transitions are total. The transition labels are actions that modify the container state.

Example 6 We must abstract the container states. In the abstraction, the actual elements in the container are not of concern. Dynamically an item (request or data) is added to the container or removed from the container. Hence a state of the container is *container-size*. Initially, container is empty. If M is the maximum size of the container there is a state for size M (full container). Consequently, there are $M + 1$ states. Let us denote these states by $Con[0], Con[1], \ldots, Con[M]$. By putting one element in the container state $Con[k]$, $0 \le k < M$, the size of the container increases by one, which is the next state $Con[k + 1]$ of the container. No element can be put when the container state is $Con[M]$. An item can be removed only when the container is not empty. There is no accept state. Figure 6.7 shows the container dfa, and its formal definition is given below.

$$Container = (Q, \Sigma, q_0, \delta),$$

where

$Q = \{Con[0], Con[1], \ldots, Con[M]\}$
$\Sigma = \{put, get\}$
$q_0 = Con[0]$ is the initial state,
$\delta : Q \times \Sigma \to Q$ is the transition function defined as
$\delta(Con[k], put) = Con[k + 1], 0 \le k < M,$
$\delta(Con[k], get) = Con[k - 1], 0 < k \le M$

$\square$

6.1.1.6
Window Manager

A minimal set of operations for a window manager should be the creation of a new window, minimizing the window, maximizing the window, restoring the window, and closing the window. These are the *requirements* to be modeled. So, all the labels to the automaton are external *actions* that fulfill these requirements. Transitions in each state are only partial. The model is shown in Fig. 6.8.

Example 7 The states are suggested by the set of requirements. We need a state to abstract "new (standard size) window", a state to abstract "maximized window", we need two states to "hide" the new and maximized window, and one state to abstract "the

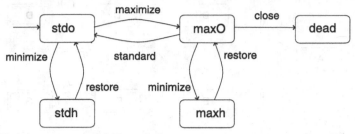

Fig. 6.8 Window-manager model: Example 7

end of window session". Hence the state machine consists of the set of states $Q = \{stdo, stdh, maxo, maxh, dead\}$ to, respectively, abstract the above situations. The initial state is $q_0 = stdo$. The set of actions is $\Sigma = \{maximize, minimize, restore, hide, close\}$. There is no accept state, and *dead* is a trap state. The state transitions are defined as follows:

$$\delta(stdo, maximize) = maxo \qquad \delta(std, minimize) = stdh$$
$$\delta(maxo, standard) = stdo \qquad \delta(maxo, minimize) = maxh$$
$$\delta(stdh, restore) = stdo \qquad \delta(maxh, restore) = maxo$$
$$\delta(maxo, close) = dead$$

The action *close* may also be defined in state *stdo*. The model may be extended with more states and transitions. For example, if "resizing" is required then a set of resize options must be specified. Corresponding to each resize option a new state is to be introduced. Transitions to new states can be defined as appropriate. Notice that in this high-level model the state variables which undergo change are hidden. It is possible to make them explicit and derive a new model, from which an implementation is possible. □

6.2
Nondeterministic Finite Accepters

A dfa is generalized in two ways:

- A string may label a transition.
- The transition function is generalized to a relation.

The second kind of generalization introduces *nondeterminism*, a powerful concept that often reduces the complexity in modeling and analysis. The generality of a nondeterministic finite acceptor (nfa) is brought out in the following ways:

- More than one transition in a state may have the same label. That is, transition δ in a state q for an input symbol x produces a subset of states $\delta(q, x) \subset Q$.
- A transition may be labeled by an *empty* string ϵ. Such a transition is a *silent* transition.
- A state $\emptyset$ is introduced for transition completeness.

Figure 6.9 shows a nfa with two accept states. Nondeterminism forces a choice for transitions at state A and at state F. The string 011 and 010 are both accepted at state D. The

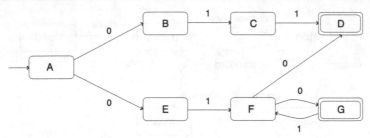

Fig. 6.9 Nondeterministic finite state automaton

Fig. 6.10 String acceptance in nondeterministic finite state automaton

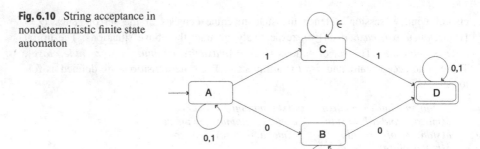

strings of type 010, 01010, 0101010, ... are accepted at state E. So the nfa accepts the set of strings $\{(01)^n 0 \mid n \geq 1\} \cup \{011\}$.

To determine whether a nfa would accept a given string, we start at the initial state and construct all the states the nfa could be in for successive symbols in the input string. Upon reaching the end of the string if the accept state is a member of the final set constructed then the string is accepted. For the nfa in Fig. 6.10, the strings ϵ, 0, and 1 are not accepted. Strings 00 and 11 are accepted. For the string 101101, the history of the set of states a is $\{A\}, \{A, C\}, \{A, B\}, \{A, C\}, \{A, C, D\}, \{A, B, D\}$, and $\{A, C, D\}$. The accept state D is in the final set of history, and hence the string 101101 is accepted by the nfa.

Apart from the nondeterminism introduced by the δ definition, there is another kind of nondeterminism in nfas. This is due to the ϵ transition in a state q. The semantics is that whenever state q is reached by some partial execution, the nfa makes another transition without reading any input symbol. It is always possible to eliminate ϵ-transitions while transforming a nfa to an equivalent dfa. The resulting dfa is in general more complex to comprehend. Example 8 explains this transformation process for the nfa in Fig. 6.11.

Example 8 We construct the dfa in Fig. 6.12 that is equivalent to the nfa in Fig. 6.11. In this construction, a state at which a progression for a symbol cannot be made is retained, while the state at which a progression is made will be replaced. That is, if $X = \{s_1, s_2\}$ is a state and $\delta(s_1, a) = \{s_3, s_4\}$ and $\delta(s_2, a)$ is not defined then $\delta(X, a) = \{s_3, s_4, s_2\}$. This convention is somewhat similar to the "product automata" transition definition. Alternately, we could have defined $\delta(X, a) = \{s_3, s_4\}$. This approach is somewhat similar to the convention of "synchronous product automata" construction. We discuss product automata

Fig. 6.11 Nondeterministic
finite state automaton with ϵ
transitions: Example 8

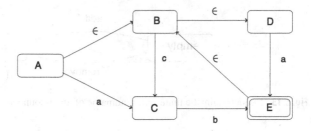

Fig. 6.12 Deterministic finite
state automaton equivalent to
Fig. 6.11 without ϵ

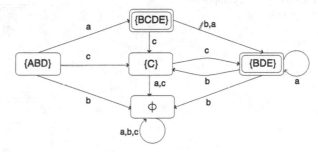

construction later on in the section as well as in later chapters. Either way we will end up
with an automata with no ϵ transitions.

- *Construct Initial State:* The initial state for the dfa is labeled with the *set of all states
  reachable* by reading only ϵ input in the initial state of the nfa. The states A, B, and D
  are reachable from the initial state A of the nfa through only ϵ transitions. Therefore,
  the initial state of the dfa in Fig. 6.12 is labeled $\{ABD\}$.
- *Recursively Construct other States* For each state in the dfa and for input symbol in the
  alphabet, construct next states. The rule is to consider all states reachable through direct
  transitions as well as after any number of ϵ-transitions. Hence, at the initial state symbol
  $\{ABD\}$ of the dfa
  - if the input symbol is a the next state is the set $\{BCDE\}$,
  - if the input symbol is b the next state $\emptyset$, the trap state, and
  - if the input symbol is c the next state is $\{C\}$.
  Repeating this step for each new state created in the dfa we get the dfa in Fig. 6.12. In
  the result there is no ϵ-transition. □

From software modeling perspective, nondeterminism is a powerful concept. Both $\emptyset$
states and ϵ-transitions may be suppressed, because transitions reflect only acceptable behavior. In Fig. 6.13, the behavior of an unbounded stack is modeled by a nondeterministic
automata. A stack is either empty or nonempty. These two situations are abstracted as the
states of the automaton. Removing an item from a nonempty stack may result either in an
empty stack or a nonempty stack. The action *remove* in state *nonempty* is nondeterministic.

Composing nfas In software modeling "divide and conquer" is a good solution approach
to follow. The problem to be modeled is divided into many sub-problems and a state machine model for each sub-problem is developed. The state machine model of the problem

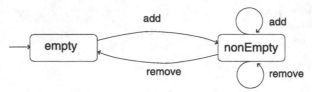

Fig. 6.13 Nondeterministic finite state automaton of an unbounded stack

Fig. 6.14 Choice composition
for automata

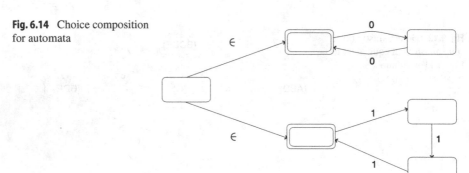

is obtained by putting together the state machine models of the sub-problems. The way in
which they are put together defines the "composition" rule and it is directed by the initial partitioning of the problem and the desired interaction between the sub-problems. In
a composition, ϵ-transitions play an important role. In Fig. 6.14, two dfas with different
behaviors are combined into a nfa with two ϵ-transitions. This is an example of "choice"
composition, the resulting nfa has either the behavior of one or the other. Choice composition is one of many different compositions, as discussed below.

When a nfa has multiple accept states, it can be converted to one with a single accept
state. This is achieved by relabeling all accept states as normal states and connecting them
to a new accept state using ϵ-transitions. So we may assume that the nfas we consider have
just one accept state.

Sequence   We want to construct the nfa M that performs the computation of nfa M_1
followed by the computation of the nfa M_2. The construction is done as follows:

- Define a new start state q_0 and a new accept state q_f.
- Add an ϵ-transition from q_0 to the start state of M_1.
- Add an ϵ-transition from the accept state of M_1 to the start state of M_2.
- Add an ϵ-transition from the accept state of M_2 to q_f.
- Change the original accept states of M_1 and M_2 to normal states.

Choice   We want to construct the nfa M that performs either the computation of nfa M_1
or the computation of the nfa M_2, but not both. The construction is done as follows:

- Define a new start state q_0 and a new accept state q_f.
- Add an ϵ-transition from q_0 to the start state of M_1 and to the start state of M_2.

- Add an ϵ-transition from the accept state of M_1 to q_f.
- Add an ϵ-transition from the accept state of M_2 to q_f.
- Change the original accept states of M_1 and M_2 to normal states.

Repetition We want to construct the nfa M^* that repeatedly performs the computation of nfa M. The construction is done as follows:

- Define a new start state q_0 and a new accept state q_f for M^*.
- Add an ϵ-transition from q_0 to the start state of M.
- Add an ϵ-transition from the accept state of M to q_f.
- Add an ϵ-transition from q_0 to q_f.
- Add an ϵ-transition from the accept state of M to the start state of M.
- Change the original start and accept states of M to normal states.

Example 9 A state machine model of a vending machine which dispenses *chips, chocolates*, and *drinks* is constructed by composing three simple machines *chips machine* (CS), *chocolate machine* (CE), and *drinks machine* (DS). In the composition, both choice and repetition constructions are used. The CS machine dispenses three kinds of chips, each costing 75 cents. Its behavior is modeled as a nfa, shown in Fig. 6.15(a). The labels "75c" and "press" are user actions and refer, respectively, to the user "inserting 75 cents" in the machine slot and "pressing a button" to get the chosen chips. The ϵ-transitions from state *chips-ready* to states *corn*, *potato*, and *banana* are simultaneously taken. The ϵ-transition from state *chips-basket* to *chips* is an internal transition. The transition labeled "other" is taken in the start state if 75 cents is not deposited in the machine slot. Although the state *chips-basket* is the accept state, the CS machine's behavior is indefinitely repetitive. The behavior of CE and DS machines, shown, respectively, in Fig. 6.15(b) and Fig. 6.15(c), can be understood in a similar manner. They repeatedly perform the actions of receiving exact change and the stimulus "press", and deliver the chosen product. Figure 6.15(d) uses the choice construction to compose the machines CS, CE, and DS into a nfa that models a general vending machine that repeatedly dispenses one of chips, chocolates, and drinks in each cycle of its operation. □

Intersection We consider two machines $M_1 = (Q_1, \Sigma_1, q_{10}, q_{1f}, \delta_1)$, and $M_2 = (Q_2, \Sigma_2, q_{20}, q_{2f}, \delta_2)$, without ϵ-transitions and define $M = M_1 \cap M_2$, which accepts a string x only if x is accepted by both M_1 and M_2. That is, the machine M *simulates* both M_1 and M_2. The construction of $M = (Q, \Sigma, q_0, F, \delta)$ is done as follows.

- Set of states: $Q = \{(p, r) \mid p \in Q_1, r \in Q_2\}$, all pairs of states, one from Q_1 and one from Q_2
- Alphabet: $\Sigma = \Sigma_1 \cap \Sigma_2$, symbols common to Σ_1 and Σ_2
- Initial state: (q_{10}, q_{20}), the pair of the start states of M_1 and M_2
- Accept state: (q_{1f}, q_{2f}), the pair of the accept states of M_1 and M_2
- Transitions: $\delta((p, r), x) = (\delta_1(p, x), \delta_2(q, x))$, defined only for symbol x that labels a transition at state p of M_1 and a transition at state r of M_2.

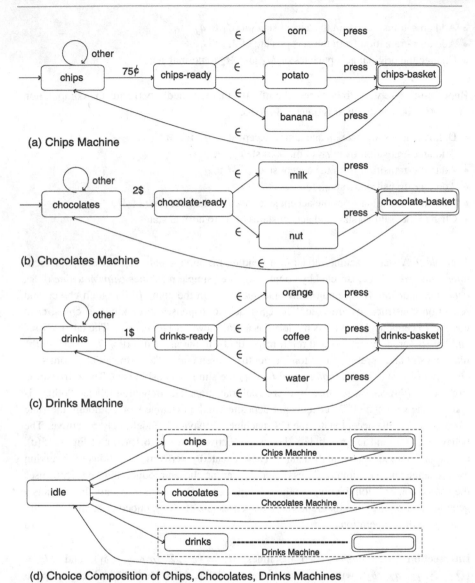

(a) Chips Machine

(b) Chocolates Machine

(c) Drinks Machine

(d) Choice Composition of Chips, Chocolates, Drinks Machines

Fig. 6.15 Nondeterministic composition of vending machines: Example 9

Figure 6.16(c) shows the intersection of the dfa in Fig. 6.16(a) and the nfa in Fig. 6.16(b). This example illustrates the principle that if one of the automaton in the intersection is a nfa then the resulting machine is necessarily a nfa. Definition of intersection may be relaxed by letting $\Sigma_1 \neq \Sigma_2$, and $\Sigma_1 \cap \Sigma_2 \neq \emptyset$. The only change in the previous definition of intersection is in the definition of transitions.

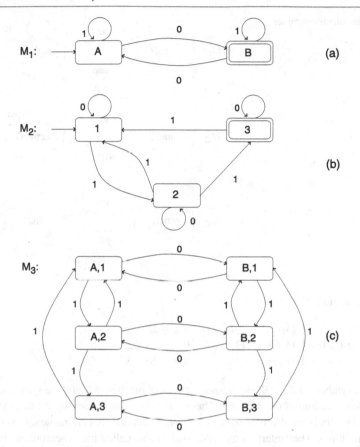

Fig. 6.16 Intersection—synchronous product

Generalized Intersection We consider two machines $M_1 = (Q_1, \Sigma_1, q_{10}, q_{1f}, \delta_1)$, and $M_2 = (Q_2, \Sigma_2, q_{20}, q_{2f}, \delta_2)$, without ϵ-transitions and define $M = M_1 \cap M_2$, which accepts (1) strings accepted by both M_1 and M_2, (2) strings accepted by M_1, but not accepted by M_2, and (3) strings accepted by M_2, but not accepted by M_1. That is, the machine M still *simulates* both M_1 and M_2. The construction of $M = (Q, \Sigma, q_0, F, \delta)$ is done as follows.

- Set of states: $Q = \{(p, r) \mid p \in Q_1, r \in Q_2\}$, all pairs of states, one from Q_1 and one from Q_2
- Alphabet: $\Sigma = \Sigma_1 \cup \Sigma_2$, symbols from both alphabets Σ_1 and Σ_2
- Initial state: (q_{10}, q_{20}), the pair of the start states of M_1 and M_2
- Accept state: $F = \{(q_{1f}, \star_2)\} \cup \{\star_1, q_{2f}\}$, where $\star_1$ can be some arbitrary state of M_1 and $\star_2$ can be some arbitrary state of M_2

Fig. 6.17 Producer–consumer model

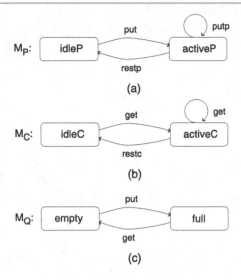

(a)

(b)

(c)

- Transitions: Let $\Sigma' = \Sigma_1 \cap \Sigma_2$.

$$\delta((p, r), x) = \begin{cases} (\delta_1(p, x), \delta_2(r, x)) & \text{if } x \in \Sigma' \\ (\delta_1(p, x), r) & \text{if } x \in \Sigma_1 \setminus \Sigma' \\ (p, \delta_2(r, x)) & \text{if } x \in \Sigma_2 \setminus \Sigma' \end{cases}$$

The action symbols in $\Sigma_1 \setminus \Sigma'$ are *internal* actions of machine M_1 and the symbols in $\Sigma_2 \setminus \Sigma'$ are internal actions of machine M_2. The symbols in Σ' are *shared* by the two machines. The shared symbols are abstractions for *synchronous* actions (or communications) between the two machines. The "intersection" operation is also called the synchronous "product" operation.

The intersection operation is symmetric. That is, $M_1 \cap M_2 = M_2 \cap M_1$. For any three machines M_1, M_2, and M_3 the transitive property $(M_1 \cap M_2) \cap M_3 = M_1 \cap (M_2 \cap M_3)$ holds only when the alphabets of the machines are identical, that is, if $\Sigma_1 = \Sigma_2 = \Sigma_3$. The transitive property does not hold for the generalized intersection operation. This is illustrated in Example 10.

Example 10 A producer process P generates data, and as it generates a datum it puts it in a buffer Q. A consumer process C removes one datum at a time from the buffer Q for its consumption. The synchronization here must ensure that process C does not consume more items than have been produced. Producer P should not add data into the buffer if it is full and that consumer C will not try to remove data from an empty buffer. The state machines M_P, M_Q, and M_C in Fig. 6.17, respectively, model the behavior of the three processes P, Q and C. The state machine model M_Q abstracts a buffer of size 1. The action *put* is shared between the models M_P and M_Q, and the action *get* is shared between the models M_C and M_Q. When process P produces an item, it attempts to "put" it into the buffer and it succeeds only when the buffer is empty. When process C attempts to "get" an item from the buffer, it succeeds only when the buffer is not empty. Consequently, in

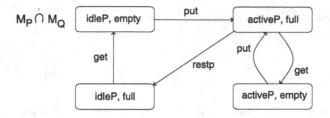

Fig. 6.18   Producer-buffer product: see Fig. 6.17

the product of the three machines M_P, M_Q, and M_C, there cannot be a transition labeled "put" in a state where "full" is part of state definition, and there cannot be a transition labeled "get" in a state where "empty" is part of state definition. Since process P starts the production before it can be consumed by process C, the synchronous product is defined by $(M_P \cap M_Q) \cap M_C$. Figure 6.18 shows the intersection $(M_P \cap M_Q)$. In constructing this machine, the action *restp* is internal to machine M_P, and actions *get* and *restc* are internal to machine M_Q. Figure 6.19 shows the intersection $(M_P \cap M_Q) \cap M_C$. In constructing this machine, the action *restc* is internal to machine M_C, and actions *put* and *restp* are internal to machine $M_P \cap M_Q$. Notice that in the product machine $(M_P \cap M_Q) \cap M_C$ action "put" never happens in states $(-, full, -)$, and action "get" never happens in states $(-, empty, -)$, where the symbol '$-$' stands for arbitrary states of M_P and M_C.   □

6.2.1
Finite State Transducers

An automaton that generates output symbols is called a transducer. Transducers in which output symbols are associated with transitions are known as Mealy machines [8]. Alternately, if the states in a transducer are associated with output symbols, the machine is known as a Moore machine [9]. We will continue to use the term finite state machines for transducers as well. From the state machine model, it is easy to recognize the type of machine that we use in the model.

Definition 2 A *finite state transducer* is a FSM

$$M = (Q, \Sigma_1, \Sigma_2, q_0, \delta),$$

where

$Q (\neq \emptyset)$ is a finite set of states,
Σ_1 is the input alphabet,
Σ_2 is the output alphabet,
$q_0 \in Q$ is the initial state,

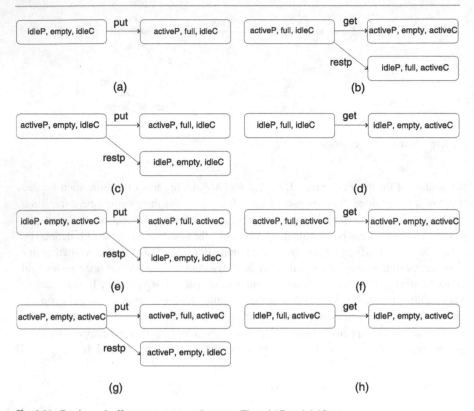

Fig. 6.19 Producer-buffer-consumer product: see Figs. 6.17 and 6.18

$\delta : Q \times \Sigma_1 \to \mathbb{P}(Q \times \Sigma_2)$, where for every state $q \in Q$ and for every symbol $x \in \Sigma$, $\delta(q, x)$ defines a set of pairs $\{(q', y)\}$. That is, the transition from state q to state q' produces the output y. This is also denoted by $q \xrightarrow{x/y} q'$.

In Fig. 6.20(a), the next state is uniquely defined for a given state, input, and output. Such a machine is called *pseudo nondeterministic* FSM. The nondeterministic FSM in Fig. 6.20(b) is equivalent to the deterministic FSM Fig. 6.20(c).

Modeling Controllers with Discrete and Continuous Behaviors   Finite state machine models are often used to model the behavior of controllers. A controller may interact with several objects in its environment. So, controller models must be constructed in order that its interaction models can be understood by manual inspection as well as reasoned about by mechanical means. Transducer models are helpful for user interactions. The interactions between a controller and its environmental objects may be either *discrete* or *continuous*. Two examples are discussed below to illustrate the features of typical controllers.

Fig. 6.20 Finite state
transducers

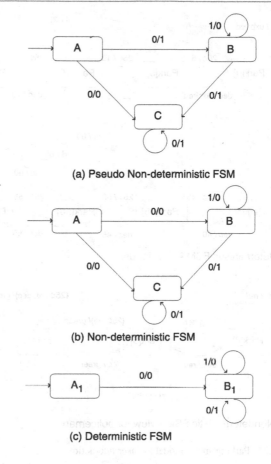

(a) Pseudo Non-deterministic FSM

(b) Non-deterministic FSM

(c) Deterministic FSM

Example 11 We consider a 60-minute parking-meter example and give a model of interaction between the parking meter and a user, and a different model of interaction between
the parking meter and a police officer.

A parking meter accepts 25 cents and one dollar coins. Feeding the machine with coins
of these types are denoted by the actions "25c" and "1d". The parking meter rejects all other
coin types. For 25 cents the parking time is 5 minutes and for 1 dollar the parking time is
20 minutes. The maximum parking time that can be bought at one instant cannot exceed
60 minutes. Each time the user feeds a coin into the parking meter, the user must be able
to observe the pre- and post-states of the parking meter. The parking meter should also
display at any instant the amount of parking time remaining. For the sake of simplicity,
we assume that the dial of the parking meter displays time in units of 5 minutes. This
assumption is justified because the minimum duration of parking time that can be rented
by the user is 5 minutes. The display handle's movement is atomic, happening once every
5 minutes. With these assumptions let us consider the set of states, input alphabet, output
alphabet, and transitions.

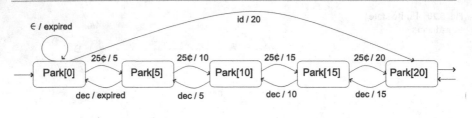

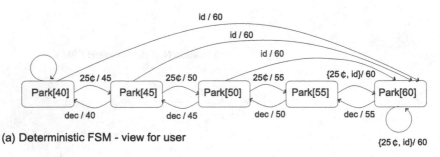

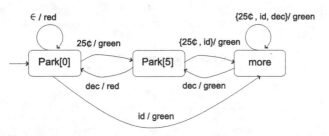

(a) Deterministic FSM - view for user

(b) Nondeterministic FSM - view for policeman

Fig. 6.21 Parking-meter model for user interaction

States: At any instant, the machine should display i, $i \in \{0, 5, 10, \ldots, 60\}$, where i is the time remaining for legal parking. So, the set of states is $Q = \{Park[0], Park[5], \ldots, Park[60]\}$

Initial State: $Park[0]$

Input: The user actions are feeding coins, denoted by $25c$ and $1d$. In the absence of a user interaction, the machine stays in its initial state by repeatedly triggering the ϵ-transition. The other parking-meter action is to decrement time (internally), denoted by dec. Although the time is continuously changing, due to the atomicity assumption, its internal action dec is made visible only at every 5 minutes. Hence $\Sigma_1 = \{25c, 1d, dec, \epsilon\}$, where $25c$ and $1d$ are user actions in feeding the parking meter, and dec is the action of the parking meter.

Output: The output generated by the parking meter in every state is the amount of time left for parking. The signal "expired" indicates that no more parking time is left. Thus, $\Sigma_2 = \{expired, 5, 10, \ldots, 60\}$.

Transitions: The parking-meter model is a deterministic finite state machine. In the description below, assume $i \in \{0, 5, 10, \ldots, 60\}$.

$$\delta(Park[i], x) = \begin{cases} (Park[0], \textit{expired}) & \text{if } x = \epsilon \wedge i = 0 \\ (Park[0], \textit{expired}) & \text{if } x = dec \wedge i = 5 \\ (Park[i - 5], i - 5)) & \text{if } x = dec \wedge i > 5 \\ (Park[i + 5], i + 5) & \text{if } x = 25c \wedge (0 \le i < 60) \\ (Park[60], 60) & \text{if } x = 25c \wedge i = 60 \\ (Park[i + 20], i + 20) & \text{if } x = 1d \wedge (0 \le i \le 40) \\ (Park[60], 60) & \text{if } x = 1d \wedge (45 \le i \le 60 \end{cases}$$

A police officer's view of the parking meter does not have to show all the states; instead it should project the view whether or not the parking time bought by a user has expired. It is sufficient to model the parking meter with three states $Park[0]$, $Park[5]$, and $Park[\infty]$, where $Park[0]$ is the initial state, $Park[5]$ is the state in which 5 minutes of parking remains, and $Park[\infty]$ is the state where more than 5 minutes of parking remains. The rationale for this choice of states is that a policeman should monitor the parking meter when the time remaining is not more than 5 minutes. The input alphabet is the same as in the previous model. The output alphabet Σ_2 is redefined as the set $\{red, green\}$ with two signals. The transitions are redefined as follows:

$$\delta(Park[i], x) = \begin{cases} (Park[0], red) & \text{if } x = \epsilon \wedge i = 0 \\ (Park[0], red) & \text{if } x = dec \wedge i = 5 \\ (Park[5], green) & \text{if } x = dec \wedge i = \infty \\ (Park[\infty], green) & \text{if } x = dec \wedge i = \infty \\ (Park[5], green) & \text{if } x = 25c \wedge (i = 0) \\ (Park[\infty], green) & \text{if } x = 1d \wedge i = 0 \\ (Park[\infty], green) & \text{if } (x = 25c \vee x = 1d) \wedge (i = 1 \vee i = \infty) \quad \square \end{cases}$$

Figure 6.21(a) shows part of the deterministic finite state machine model for user interaction (car driver parking a car), and Fig. 6.21(b) shows the nondeterministic finite state machine model for policeman's comprehension to perform his duty.

The parking-meter models have several incompleteness. They do not reveal how it will be used in ticketing a parking violation. In order to enforce ticketing for a parking violation, we need a model of policeman's monitoring the parking meter and require that only one car can be parked in the parking space associated with the parking meter. The policeman should issue the ticket only if the parking space is occupied when the parking meter displays "red". In order to enforce this property, we need to compose the three machines: (1) the state machine that models the policeman's view of the parking meter, (2) the state machine model of the policeman's duty, and (3) the state machine that models the policeman's view of the parking space. Below we sketch some of the details involved, leaving the rest for exercises.

Figure 6.22(a) shows a simple model of the policeman's monitoring behavior. It is a pseudo nondeterministic finite state machine with states $\{idle, active\}$. The initial state is

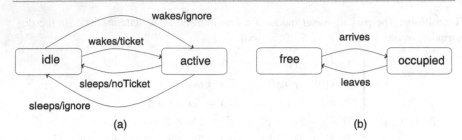

Fig. 6.22 Policeman's view of the parking space

idle. The transitions from state *idle* to state *active* are labeled by the action *wakes* with outputs *ticket* and *ignore*. The transitions from state *active* to state *idle* are labeled by the action *sleeps* with output symbols *noticket* and *ignore*.

A model of the policeman's view of the parking space is shown in Fig. 6.22(b). It is a finite state machine with two states {*free, occupied*}. The transition from state *free* to state *occupied* is labeled by the action *arrives*. The transition from state *occupied* to state *free* is labeled by the action *leaves*. Since the policeman should watch the parking machine and the parking space as a whole, the "police man machine" should be composed (in any order) with the nondeterministic "parking-meter machine" and the "parking space machine". The "intersection rule" for composition of state machines should be adapted to include the output of one machine with the other. We explain the procedure in Example 12. From the way composition is defined, it is understood that composition of state machines with outputs is not in general *commutative*. With the partial interaction scenario of the policeman monitoring the parking meter shown in Fig. 6.23, we should combine the arrival and departure of cars in the parking space in order to get the total interaction among the objects policeman, parking meter, and parking space.

Example 12 **States:**

$$Q = \{(idle, Park[0]), (idle, Park[5]), (idle, more), (active, Park[0]), (active, Park[5]),$$

$$(active, more)\}$$

Initial state: $(idle, Park[0])$

Input: Every input is a pair of labels, one that labels a transition of the "policeman machine" (PO) and the other that labels the "parking-meter machine" (PA).

Output: The output symbols are the output symbols of the "policeman machine", because the result of monitoring the parking meter is an action by the policeman. $\Sigma_2 = \{ticket, noticket, ignore\}$.

Transitions:

$$\delta(idle, Park[0]), (wakes, x) = \begin{cases} ((active, Park[0]), ticket) & \text{if } x = dec/red \\ ((active, Park[0]), ignore) & \text{if } x = \epsilon/red \\ ((active, Park[5]), ignore) & \text{if } x = \star/green \\ ((active, more), ignore) & \text{if } x = \star/green \end{cases}$$

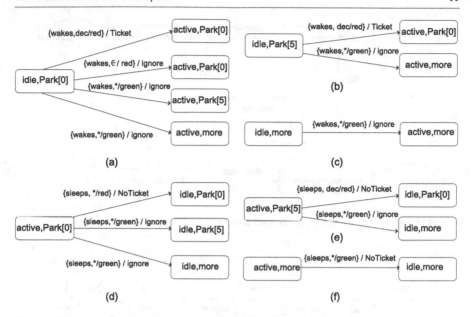

Fig. 6.23 Interaction between policeman and parking meter: Example 12

$$\delta(idle, Park[5]), (wakes, x) = \begin{cases} ((active, Park[5]), ticket) & \text{if } x = dec/red \\ ((active, more), ignore) & \text{if } x = \star/green \end{cases}$$

$$\delta(idle, more), (wakes, x) = \begin{cases} ((active, more), ignore) & \text{if } x = \star/green \end{cases}$$

$$\delta(active, Park[0]), (sleeps, x) = \begin{cases} ((idle, Park[0]), noticket) & \text{if } x = \star/red \\ ((idle, Park[5]), ignore) & \text{if } x = \star/green \\ ((idle, more), ignore) & \text{if } x = \star/green \end{cases}$$

$$\delta(active, Park[5]), (sleeps, x) = \begin{cases} ((idle, Park[0]), noticket) & \text{if } x = dec/red \\ ((idle, more), ignore) & \text{if } x = \star/green \end{cases}$$

$$\delta(active, more), (sleeps, x) = \begin{cases} ((idle, more), ignore) & \text{if } x = \star/green \end{cases} \qquad \square$$

An important feature to be observed of the parking-meter model is its discrete time behavior. Clock or timer is not explicitly modeled; instead we assumed that in each state there is a timer which runs for 5 minutes. When a state is entered through *dec* transition, the timer in that state starts decreasing, and when the state is entered through 25*c*, 1*d* transitions, the timer is initialized to 5 minutes.

In Example 13, we model the *hybrid* behavior of a controller that continually monitors the level of water in a tank and at discrete time instances commands the drain and water valves to open or close. The FSM model of the controller abstracts the continuous passage of time, not with timers, but with events. The nature of "water flow" is continuous. The flow of water into a tank is stopped or allowed through the actions of "opening" and "closing" of valves. These actions happen "instantaneously", and hence are "discrete time" events. Thus the FSM model in Example 13 captures the *hybrid* behavior of the water-level monitor.

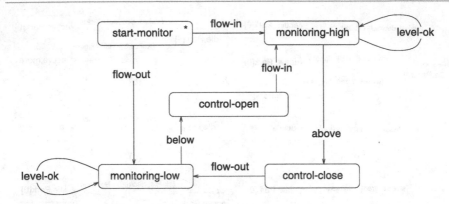

Fig. 6.24 Finite state machine for a water-level controller

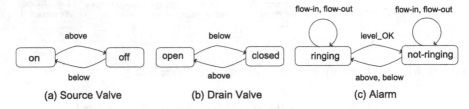

Fig. 6.25 Finite state machines for source valve, drain valve, and alarm

Example 13 The controller that monitors water level in a tank must ensure at all times that the water level is maintained between specified limits [*low*, *high*] in a tank. Whenever the level of water is at its maximum (denoted "high"), the controller should command the valve to open in order to drain the water. Whenever the level of water is at its minimum (denoted "low"), the controller should command the valve to close in order to allow the water to flow into the tank. Since water flow is a continuous phenomena, the monitoring act is a continuous action. Based on these requirements, the states and transitions are chosen for the FSM model in Fig. 6.24.

In its initial state, it may detect water flowing into the tank or flowing out of the tank. In the former case, it changes its state to *monitoring-high*, and in the latter case, it changes its state to *monitoring-low*. It stays in the *monitoring-high* state as long as the level of water is in the range [*low, high*]. If the water level exceeds *high*, it changes its state to *control-close*, wherein it will close the valve of the water pipe and open the valve of the drain pipe. This triggers the event *flow-out*, which takes the controller to the state *monitoring-low*. The controller stays in this state as long as the water level is above *low*. When the water level goes below *low*, it transits to the state *control-open*, where it will ensure that the valve for drain pipe is closed and the valve for water pipe is open. This triggers the event *flow-in* and the controller transits to the state of monitoring the water level at *monitoring-high*. Hence, the controller cycles through the activities of monitoring water levels, and controlling the valves of the source and the drain.   □

The FSM model in Fig. 6.24 includes assumptions about the behavior of the source valve and the drain valve. We specify their behaviors independently in Fig. 6.25. We add an alarm subsystem in the water-level control system to enrich the model and compose these models with the controller machine shown in Fig. 6.24. The semantics of composition clarifies the behavior of the composite machine whose components are the *controller, source-valve, drain-valve,* and *alarm*. When the water level is detected to be above *high,* the event *above* causes simultaneous transitions in four machines as follows: the controller machine changes state from *monitoring-high* to *control-close*; the *source-valve* changes state from *on* to *off,* signifying the closing of the water pipe; the *drain-valve* changes state from *closed* to *open,* to let the water flow out of the tank; the *alarm* changes state from *stop-ringing* to *start-ringing.* The system monitors the water level and the alarm is off while the water is flowing out. When the water level is detected to be below *low,* the event *below* causes simultaneous transitions in the four machines, causing the alarm to sound, the drain valve to close, and the source valve to open. The system returns to the state of monitoring the water-level while the water flows in, and consequently, the alarm stops.

6.3
Exercises

1. Construct a nfa with a single final state that accepts the set of strings $\{x\} \cup \{y^n \mid n \geq 1\}$.
2. A safe has a combination lock that can be in one of four positions 1, 2, 3, and 4. The dial can be turned clockwise (C) or anticlockwise (A). Assume that the correct combination to the lock is the sequence $\langle 1C, 4A, 3C, 2A \rangle$ and that any other combination will trigger an alarm. Devise a finite state machine to specify the behavior of the lock.
3. Construct a finite state machine for recognizing the pattern "raininspain".
4. Convert the nfa defined below to an equivalent dfa.

   States: $Q = \{q_0, q_1, q_2\}$
   Initial State: q_0
   Accept State: q_2
   Transitions:

   $$\begin{array}{ll} \delta(q_0, a) = q_1 & \delta(q_0, \epsilon) = q_2 \\ \delta(q_1, a) = q_1 & \delta(q_1, a) = q_2 \\ \delta(q_1, b) = q_0 & \delta(q_2, a) = q_2 \\ \delta(q_2, b) = q_2 & \delta(q_2, \epsilon) = q_1 \end{array}$$

5. Define state variables `max`, `hide`, and `active` of type Boolean for the state machine model of the window manager in Example 7. For each state in Fig. 6.8, specify the values for the state variables.
6. Give a state machine model of ATM with the following functionalities:

   - it reads a bank card
   - if it is a valid card, it provides two options for the user: *deposit, withdrawal*
   - if the option *deposit* is chosen, the following sequence of actions are possible:

- the machine gives three options: $20, $50, $100, and the user is allowed to choose only one option
- if the user chooses $20 option then a $20 must be fed into the machine, if the user chooses $50 option then a $50 must be fed into the machine, if the user chooses $100 option then a $100 must be fed into the machine, and any other action is illegal which will terminate user session and the card is returned
- if the option is exercised correctly, the machine returns a receipt and the card
- if the option *withdrawal* is chosen, the following sequence of actions are possible:
  - the machine gives three options: $40, $100, $200, and the user is allowed to choose only one option
  - choosing any other action is illegal which will terminate user session and the card is returned
  - if the option is exercised correctly, the machine returns cash, a receipt and the card

7. Assume that a machine produces *chips* and stores it in a warehouse (buffer). Whenever the chips (vending) machine CS in Example 9 dispenses a chip, it automatically gets a replacement from the warehouse. Discuss the interaction behavior between chips producer, buffer, and CS machine. What assumptions are necessary to ensure that the CS vending machine will always get replacement chips?

8. Specify the behavior of a printer and its monitor which function synchronously: the printer is controlled by the monitor to print one job at a time; the printer prints the header of a file and then prints its contents; while the printer is printing, all requests are received by the monitor, which maintains a queue of jobs; the monitor removes the first job in the queue when the printer is ready for printing.

9. Construct the state machine that shows the interaction between the policeman-parking-meter machine (Fig. 6.23) and parking lot machine (Fig. 6.22). In the model verify informally that when the parking space is *occupied*, the parking meter shows *red*, the policeman gives a *ticket* to the parked vehicle.

6.4
Bibliographic Notes

Automata and the variants of finite state machines have been studied for a long time in language theory, and formal specifications. Automata theory, languages, and Turing machine, which is an automaton with a tape, have been discussed in many books, most notably in [5]. It is known that every nfa has an equivalent dfa [5], yet nondeterministic finite state machines have more clarity and expressive power than deterministic finite state machines to model software interactions with its environment. The sound theory behind finite state machines lends to reasoning about a variety of issues such as reachability, recognition, and regulated executions. Their graphical representations, often called state diagrams, appeal both to the theorists as well as to practitioners. The size complexity, often experienced in graphical representations can be overcome by resorting to the pure algebraic representations. Conversely, when state diagrams are necessary to elucidate a theoretical investigation the graphical representation becomes an aid for better comprehension and deeper insight. Since state diagrams are graphs, the full power of graph theory is available for a formal analysis of its properties.

Many extensions to basic automaton have been studied during the last 50 years. Some of these we studied in this chapter, and another extension called "extended finite state machines" will be studied in the next chapter. The other kinds of automata that have the expressive power to model complex systems are *probabilistic automata* (PA), Büchi automata (BA), and *timed automata* (TA), and *real-time automata* (RTA). The probabilistic automaton (PA) introduced by Rabin [10] is a generalization of the nondeterministic finite automaton. A transition includes the probability that it might happen. Thus the automata is turned into a transition matrix or stochastic matrix. A probabilistic automaton recognizes Markov chains. PAs are useful for modeling evolving systems for which exact predictive rules may not exist. In 1962 Büchi [3] introduced a new automaton which is an extension of a finite state automaton to infinite inputs. It accepts an infinite input sequence if and only if there exists a run of the automaton which visits at least one of the final states infinitely often. Recall that in case of a deterministic automaton, there is exactly one possible run to the final state. The theory of Büchi automata is the basic formalism for model checking, which we study in Chap. 15. Alur and Dill [1] introduced TA, a variant of dfa that includes the notion of time. In this model, each input symbol occurs at a certain time. A state transition depends both on the symbol and the time at which the symbol is input. Time values are modeled by natural numbers. A TA includes a finite number of synchronous clocks and a boolean constraint on the clock values for each transition. A real-time automaton [4] (RTA) is a TA with only one clock that represents the time delay between two consecutive events. A transition is constrained by a guard, an interval of time within which the transition must be fired.

References

1. Alur R, Dill D (1991) The theory of timed automata. In: de Bakker JW, Huizing C, de Roever WP, Rozenberg G (eds) Real-time: theory in practice. LNCS, vol 600, pp 74–106
2. Boyer RS, Moore JS (1977) A fast string searching algorithm. Commun ACM 20:762–772
3. Büchi JR (1989) Finite automata, their algebras and grammars: towards a theory of formal expressions. Springer, New York. Published posthumously
4. Dima C (2001) Real-time automata. J Autom Lang Comb 6(1):3–23
5. Hopcroft J, Ullman J (1979) Introduction to automata theory, languages, and computation. Addison Wesley, Reading
6. Knuth D, Morris JH Jr., Pratt V (1977) Fast pattern matching in strings. SIAM J Comput 6(2):323–350
7. Martin J (2003) Introduction to languages and the theory of computation, 3rd edn. McGraw-Hill, New York
8. Mealy GH (1955) A method to synthesizing sequential circuits. Bell Syst Tech J 1045–1079
9. Moore EF (1956) Gedanken-experiments on sequential machines. Automata studies. Ann Math Stud 34:129–153
10. Rabin MO (1963) Probabilistic automata. Inf Control 6:230–245

Extended Finite State Machine

The FSM models we have considered, in spite of many extensions to basic automaton, fall short in many aspects. They have to be extended further, as broadly outlined below, in order to model complex system behavior.

- *State space*: The previous models become difficult to comprehend when the number of states and transitions increase. We need a notation to contain the state space complexity and help us develop state diagrams in *modular* and *hierarchical* fashion. Modularity helps *encapsulation* and hierarchy introduces *refinement*.
- *State variables*: The previous models do not allow *variables* in the model. We need to be able to introduce state variables in FSM models, and manipulate them in different states according to the transition logic. Introducing a state variable in the container model discussed in Example 6, Chap. 6, will enable us to observe the container size as a computed value, rather than just guess it from the state name. The model extended with variables will allow us to define a range of arithmetic and logical operators to manipulate state variables and trigger transitions based on logical primitives. It should also be possible to transfer variable values from one model to another model. In a sequential composition, a value output by one machine can be consumed by the other machine in the composition.
- *Generality of transitions*: The previous models allow only symbols or actions (events) as transition labels. With this convention, we cannot model requirements that involve *conditions*. With the introduction of variables, conditions may be used to label transitions with or without transition labels. As an example, with the introduction of the *timer* variable in the parking-meter model discussed in Example 11, Chap. 6, we can assert that the transition *dec* should be enabled when $timer = 0$. We can replace the label *dec*, if necessary, with the condition $timer = 0$.
- *Introducing output actions*: In a state, the output should be allowed to be any *instruction* or *action* rather than just symbol. Output instructions are internal to the model and output actions may be shared with another FSM model. It is better to use declarative, rather than operational, style for specifying actions.

The prime virtue of the FSM approach is that it can be used to model several layers of abstractions. We want to emphasize this aspect further in this chapter by introducing "top-down" and "bottom-up" FSM development. In a top-down approach, a state may be

V.S. Alagar, K. Periyasamy, *Specification of Software Systems*,
Texts in Computer Science,
DOI 10.1007/978-0-85729-277-3_7, © Springer-Verlag London Limited 2011

replaced with a finite state machine. If we want to prune a state machine view, we can combine states into a super-state, combine transitions as a result of it, and provide access points (selectors) for navigating specific transitions in the pruned FSM. Such an approach is similar to the transformation of a nondeterministic FSM to a deterministic FSM. These extended notations when combined with the operators "choice", "repetition", and "intersection" provide us with a rich language for modeling complex systems in a bottom-up manner. A FSM extended as explained above will be called an *Extended Finite State Machine* and has the following definition.

Definition 1 An *Extended Finite State Machine* (EFSM) is defined by the tuple

$$M = (Q, \Sigma_1, \Sigma_2, I, V, \Lambda),$$

where

1. $Q(\neq \emptyset)$ is a finite set of states. A state may be *simple* (atomic) or *composite*.
2. Σ_1 is a finite set of events.
3. $I \subset Q$ is the set of initial states. Every composite state will have an initial state.
4. V is the set of state variables. Every variable $x \in V$ is a global variable and can be accessed at every state $q \in Q$.
5. Λ is a finite set of transitions. A transition $\lambda \in \Lambda$ is $q \xrightarrow{e[g]/a} q'$, where $e \in \Sigma_1$, g is a condition, called *guard*, and $a \in \Sigma_2$ is an action. An action is either internal to the machine or a shared action. An action may be specified declaratively, say as a predicate. More than one action may be specified as a conjunction of predicates or just listing them within parentheses {...}. The guard must involve only constants and variables defined in (pre-)state q. In (post-)state q' the action a, if specified as a condition, must hold. If a is specified as an action then in state q' the result of the action must satisfy the state variables. A variable x affected in the transition specification $q \xrightarrow{e[g]/a} q'$ will be denoted x' in state q'.

All parts of a transition label are optional. For example, (1) if the label of a transition is e/a then g is interpreted to be true, and the transition is enabled when e occurs; (2) if the label of a transition is $[g]/a$ then the transition may be labeled by ϵ and is enabled only if g is true in state q; and (3) if the label of transition is e then the transition is enabled when e occurs in state q and there is no change in the variables at state q.

In models where the actions are specified as assertions involving the state variables, we ignore Σ_2 in the specification. A bounded buffer model is discussed in Example 1. It illustrates many of the extended notations mentioned above.

Example 1 A buffer is a queue of items, in which insertions are done at the *rear* of the queue and deletions are done at the *front* of the queue. So, in modeling a finite buffer, we need to introduce two variables r (rear) and f (front) of type $\mathbb{N}_0$, the set of non-negative integers, and a positive integer constant M that denotes the maximum size allocated for the buffer. The only two observable states of interest in modeling a buffer are those that, respectively, correspond to empty buffer and nonempty buffer. The condition $r = 0 \wedge f = 0$

Fig. 7.1 State diagram of Example 1

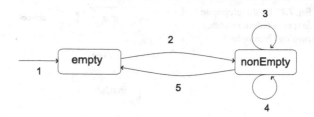

must be true in state *empty*. In state *nonEmpty*, the condition $0 < r \leq M$ is true. An item can be *put* in the buffer only if $0 \leq r < M$. Hence the *put* operation can be done in both states, the exception is when $r = M$, which happens in state *nonEmpty*. An item can be removed with *get* operation, if there is at least one item in the queue. That is, a *get* operation cannot be done in state *empty*. In state *nonEmpty*, a *get* operation will make the queue empty if the queue had only one item; otherwise the queue will be nonempty after *get* operation is done. After every *put* operation, the value of variable r is to be incremented by 1, and after every *get* operation, the value of variable f is incremented by 1. Hence the EFSM model shown in Fig. 7.1 is the tuple $B = (Q, \Sigma, q_0, V, \Lambda)$, where

$Q = \{empty, nonEmpty\}$
$\Sigma = \{put, get\}$
$q_0 : empty$
$V = \{size\}, size : \mathbb{N}_0$
$M \in \mathbb{N}$ is a constant.
$\Lambda :$ *Transition Specifications*
  1. $\xrightarrow{/\{f=0 \wedge r=0\}} empty$
  2. $empty \xrightarrow{put/r'=r+1} nonEmpty$
  3. $nonEmpty \xrightarrow{put[r<M]/r'=r+1} nonEmpty$
  4. $nonEmpty \xrightarrow{get[r \geq f+1 \wedge r<M]/f'=f+1} nonEmpty$
  5. $nonEmpty \xrightarrow{get[f+1=M]/\{r'=0 \wedge f'=0\}} empty$

$\square$

7.1
State Machine Hierarchy

A state machine M at one level of abstraction can be refined to another machine M' at a more concrete level by replacing a state q in M with a state machine q_M. Such a state where refinement takes place is called a *complex* state. A state that cannot be refined further is called a *simple* state. In a refinement of state q of machine M, all incoming transitions to state q can be dealt with in two ways: (1) they become transitions to the initial state (newly created) of the machine q_M, (2) they become direct transitions to sub-states of q. The outgoing transitions from q of machine M are replaced with new transitions, going out

Fig. 7.2 Basic telephone and first refinement of state *ringing*: Example 2

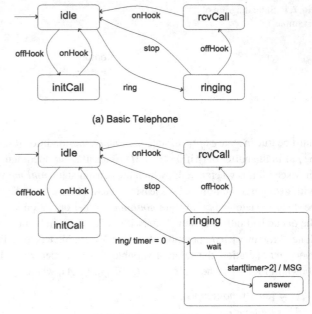

(a) Basic Telephone

(b) Refinement of state ringing

of the states of the machine q_M, to states in machine M. The resulting machine M' displays a more detailed behavior of the machine M. That is, state refinement leads from an abstract model to a concrete model and incrementally adds behavior. Example 2 discusses a simple abstract model of a telephone, and shows the refinements of two of its states.

Example 2 Figure 7.2(a) shows the EFSM of a basic telephone. The telephone is activated or deactivated by a user. In its initial state *idle*, if the telephone is activated by the event *offHook*, a call is initiated through an interaction with telephone exchange. The activity related to initiation of a call goes on in the state *initCall*. After a call is completed, the event *OnHook* returns the telephone from state *initCall* to *idle* state. During an incoming call, the telephone starts ringing at state *idle* and it may stop ringing after a while. The events *ring* and *stop* may happen alternately unless the telephone is picked up while it is ringing. The activity related to receiving a call goes on in the state *rcvCall* when the transition labeled *offHook* is enabled in state *ringing*. This basic behavior model is shown in Fig. 7.2(a). In this model, it is possible to refine all states. We discuss two successive refinements of state *ringing* and one refinement of state *idle*; rest are left for exercises.

First refinement of state *ringing*

State *ringing* can be refined by introducing an "answer" feature. That is, after a time delay an answering machine responds to the call with a message. The refined EFSM is shown in Fig. 7.2(b). The state *ringing* becomes a new EFSM with two states *wait* and *answer*. The state *wait* is its initial state, in which the machine waits for two units of time before the transition *start* takes it to state *answer*. In state *answer*, a message MSG is output. Therefore the basic telephone model is enriched as follows:

1. <u>Constant Introduction:</u> MSG: constant
2. <u>Variable Introduction:</u> $timer : \mathbb{N}$
3. <u>New Transition Specifications:</u>

$$idle \xrightarrow{\text{ring/timer=0}} wait$$

$$wait \xrightarrow{\text{start[timer>2]/MSG}} answer$$

With the semantics that the incoming transition to the complex state *ringing* becomes the incoming transition to the initial state *wait*, and an outgoing transition from state *ringing* will become an outgoing transition from every state in the refinement, only one of following behaviors is possible in the refined model.

- *message completed*: the answering machine outputs the message MSG and transition *stop* occurs to take the phone to the *idle* state, or
- *message interrupted*: while the message MSG is being output transition *offHook* occurs to begin the activity of receiving the call in state *revCall*, or
- *message not entered*: before transition *start* is enabled the transition *offHook* occurs that begins the activity of receiving the call in state *revCall*.

Refinement of state *idle* and second refinement of state *ringing*

The new state *answer* obtained in the first refinement of state *ringing* is refined to model both the announcement of the recorded message and the recording of the user message. The initial state in the refinement is *announce* and the other state is *record*. A new transition labeled by the event *toRecord* from state *announce* to state *record* is introduced. A variable *msgIn* of type Bool is introduced. The event *toRecord* should occur within one to five time units from the instant the announcement was started by *start* event. Its effect is to set the value of *msgIn* to true, signifying the presence of a recorded message. Hence, the refinement of state *answer* changes the transition specification

$$wait \xrightarrow{\text{start[timer>2]/MSG}} answer$$

to

$$wait \xrightarrow{\text{start[timer>2]/\{MSG,msgIn'=false\}}} answer$$

The new transition introduced by the refinement is

$$announce \xrightarrow{\text{toRec[timer<5]/msgIn'=true}} record$$

In order that a user can check for recorded messages in the *idle* state, we refine it to an EFSM with three states: *noMessg* (initial state), *Messg*, and *playing*. The status of the Boolean variable *msgIn* determines the state change at state *noMessg*. Figure 7.3 shows the refinements. $\square$

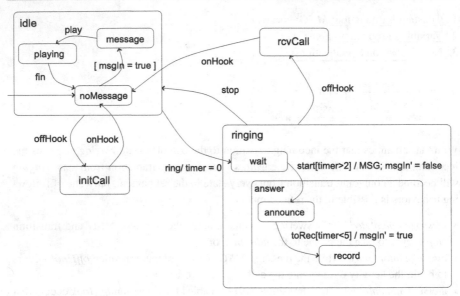

Fig. 7.3 Second refinement of state *ringing*: Example 2

7.1.1
Menu-Driven User Interface Model

EFSM is an appropriate formalism for modeling interactive systems. The grammar of electronic *test_request_form* in Table 5.2, Chap. 5 can be expanded in a top-down manner to
understand the user-interaction points in its structure. Although the form may be used in
different ways, an EFSM model can be given to constrain user-interaction behavior in
completing the electronic form in a manner that is consistent with the grammar. So, the
model that we construct includes states for user-interaction points, in addition to system
states induced by the grammar. The purpose of user-interaction points is to explicitly show
the stages of user interaction, a prime concept in user interface design. A user-interaction
point is an *environmental* state, and must be distinguished from an object state. In the
EFSM model, a circle is used to denote user-interaction points. A state representing a root
of a hierarchy of states is shown as a rectangle with two borders; all other states are shown
as simple rectangles. A rectangle containing an asterisk symbol denotes an initial state.

Initial Model
A *test_request_form* constructed according to the state transition diagram in Fig. 7.4 conforms to the rules of the grammar described in Table 5.2, Chap. 5. Corresponding to each
non-terminal of the grammar, there exists a transition leading to a state in the state transition diagram. For example, the transition *test* leading into *test-layout* corresponds to the
non-terminal *test*. Terminals are not included in the state transition diagram; they can be
mapped to concrete representations at the time of user interaction. Additional states, such
as *refresh and display*, and user-interaction points such as *choose* are included in the state
transition diagram to illustrate the steps in the design process.

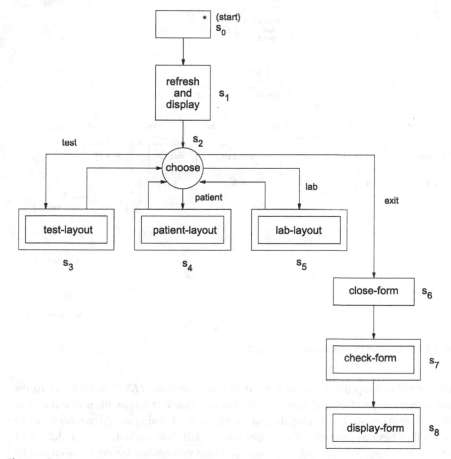

Fig. 7.4 State transition diagram for Test_Request_Form

When the event *enter_test_request_form* occurs in the initial state, the new state *refresh and display* is entered. The behavior in this state is the presentation of a refreshed window to the user. The transition from this state to the user-interaction point *choose* occurs automatically, where a user has a choice of creating one of the three layouts in *test_request_form*. The action *CREATE_TESTLAYOUT* is performed in state S_3: *test-layout*; the action *CREATE_PATIENTLAYOUT* is performed in state S_4: *patient_layout*; and the action *CREATE_LABLAYOUT* is performed in state S_5: *lab_layout*. These three states are super-states, and can be refined. The states S_6: *close_form*, S_7: *check_form*, and S_8: *display_form* do not correspond to grammar rules. These states correspond to the design steps describing the actions performed on the *test_request_form* after exiting from the process of completing the components of the *test_request_form*.

Refinement

Having developed a high-level model, the next step is to refine composite states. The refinement of the composite state S_3 is shown in Fig. 7.5. The terminal *TEST* in the grammar

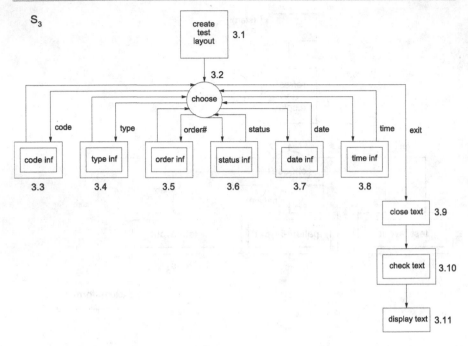

Fig. 7.5 Refinement of super-state S_3 in Fig. 7.4

rule for *test* is mapped to the concrete textual representation "*TEST*" in the form. At the user-interaction point entered from the initial state *create test-layout*, the user can choose one of several options for creating this part of the form. Choosing an option other than *exit* causes the object to enter one of the super-states—*3.3: code inf, 3.4: type inf, 3.5: order inf, 3.6: status inf, 3.7: date inf, 3.8: time inf*. These super-states are the states caused by transitions labeled by events corresponding to the non-terminals in the grammar rule for *test*. These super-states can be refined further using the grammar rules. The states *close text*, *check text*, and *display text* do not correspond to grammar rules; instead, they correspond to the design steps requiring further action on the completed form. Each super-state is further refined to a state transition diagram. This process continues until we arrive at state transition diagrams containing only simple states. See Fig. 7.6(b), which shows a refinement of the state *3.3: code info*.

Adding More Details

When semantically incorrect information or syntactically incorrect information is entered in the *test_request_form*, there needs to be a way of recovering from the error and continuing the activity from the latest valid state entered. This can be done by introducing a new state *abort*, and adding transitions from all other states to the *abort* state. Although the inclusion of this new state adds only little information to the model, the complexity of the model is significantly increased with the introduction of a large number of transitions. Once again, these can be resolved using hierarchical state structures as shown in Fig. 7.6(a). The highest level of the machine has two states, a simple state *abort*, and a super-state *normal*.

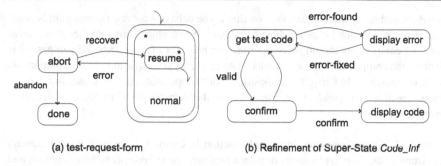

Fig. 7.6 Refining composite states

The super-state *normal* corresponds to the state machine shown in Fig. 7.4, and is further refined in Figs. 7.5 and 7.6(b). There are two initial transitions in Fig. 7.6(a) showing that *normal* is the initial state at the top level, and it also contains an initial state among its sub-states. At every level of refinement there is an initial state. The transition labeled *error* is from the super-state *normal*, and hence from all its sub-states, to the state *abort*. The transition labeled *recover* is from the state *abort* to the initial state of the state *normal*. The transition labeled *abandon* is from the state *abort* to the terminal state *done*.

7.2
Modularity and Bottom-up Construction

In many applications, there exists a *strong* interaction among domain objects, and the large number of domain objects and their features will make the interaction model quite complex. For example, in telephony if the handset of the telephone with a speaker phone attached to it is off the hook, both a busy dial tone and speaker noise are possible. In contrast, the interaction between the chips vending machine and the drinks vending machine modeled in Chap. 6 is *weak*, because if one of them is out of order it does not affect the outcome of the other machine. As in software design, modular modeling will help to reduce the complexity of modeling strong interactions. In case of weak interactions between objects, modular modeling is the natural choice. In general, modular modeling is the key for bottom-up construction of large models. Modularity reduces the complexity in modeling complex interactions and is likely to achieve completeness in the model. Example 3 illustrates this point.

A modular modeling starts at the domain level, where a model for each object is developed by exclusively focusing on its possible uses in the family of related applications in that domain. All objects that have potential interactions with a specific object are identified, and the nature of interactions are specified in the model. Each object may be encapsulated as a software *component*. A formal component definition, as given in [12, 13], will include the requirements specification and the desired properties of the object encapsulated in it. The component models of objects may be refined to bring out the detailed nature of interaction explicit in the models. These are achieved by introducing *shared events*, *shared variables,* and compatible *constraints* on them. The behavior for each component is specified using the extended state machine formalism. If two objects interact then their corresponding components should be composed. The behavior of the composed component is given by the composition of the extended state machines corresponding to the components in the composition. In Chap. 6, compositions for the operators *choice, sequential composition, repetition,* and *product* are given. We use the term "product" to denote generalized "intersection".

Example 3 While discussing domain abstraction in Chap. 4, a view of the car domain consisting of the four applications *anti-lock braking, cruise control, stability control,* and *fingerprint security* was introduced. The domain modeling phase for each application will produce a model for each entity of interest for that application and its relationship to different functional and nonfunctional requirements of that application. For each object in each application in the model, a component is designed. The behavior of each component is specified by an extended finite state machine. Below we illustrate these steps for the two applications *cruise control* and *anti-lock braking* systems, which have interacting events.

Cruise Control System (CCS)

The cruise control system (CCS) in a car is a multi-function computer system which automatically manages the speed of the car. It consists of four parts: *Accelerator pedal* (AP), *Brake pedal* (BP), *Dashboard* (DB), and *Controller* (CO). By stepping on to the AP the vehicle goes faster, and by releasing the pedal the vehicle slows down. So, AP has two states, which are named *idle* and *goFaster* as in Fig. 7.7(a). The transition specifications are

$$idle \xrightarrow{\text{accelerate}} goFaster$$

$$goFaster \xrightarrow{\text{accelerate}} goFaster$$

$$goFaster \xrightarrow{\text{releasePedal}} idle$$

BP has two states corresponding to 'brake is not applied' and 'brake is applied' as in Fig. 7.7(b). Its transition specifications are similar to that of AP.

DB is the interface to interact with CCS. It has four buttons with the following functionalities.

- *On* and *Off*: The *on* button gets the car ready to accept a cruising control command. The *off* button turns the cruise control off.
- *Set-Accel*: The Set-Accel has a dual function. If the car is at the enabling state, which means the *On* button has been pushed, then the cruising control will start and CCS will fix and maintain the speed that the car is currently driving. If the car is in cruise control state and the Set-Accel button is hit, then holding down the Set-Accel button will make the car accelerate faster.
- *Resume-Decel*: If the car driver hits the brake pedal while in cruising state, CCS will be at disable state. Hitting the Resume-Decel button at the disable state will command the car to accelerate back to the most recent speed setting. If the car is in cruise control state and the Resume-Decel button is hit, then holding down the Resume-Decel button will make the car decelerate.

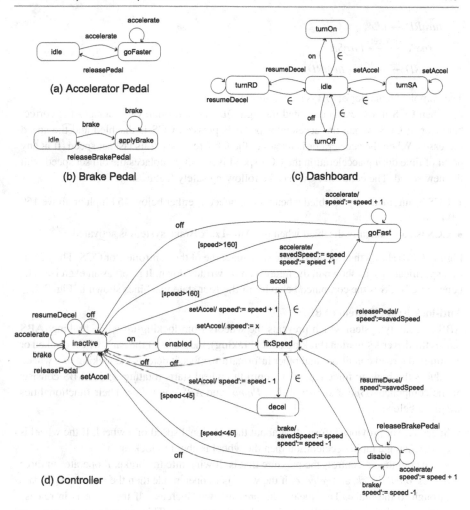

Fig. 7.7 Cruise control system

The transition specifications of DB are given below.

$$idle \xrightarrow{on} turnOn$$

$$idle \xrightarrow{off} turnOff$$

$$turnOn \xrightarrow{\epsilon} idle$$

$$turnOn \xrightarrow{\epsilon} idle$$

$$idle \xrightarrow{setAccel} turnSA$$

$$idle \xrightarrow{resumeDecel} turnRD$$

$$turnSA \xrightarrow{\epsilon} idle$$

$$turnRD \xrightarrow{\epsilon} idle$$

$$turnSA \xrightarrow{setAccel} turnSA$$

$$turnRD \xrightarrow{resumeDecel} turnRD$$

The complete behavior of DB is shown in Fig. 7.7(c).

When CCS in the car is activated through DB the controller, CO manages the correct behavior of CCS. When the accelerator pedal is pressed, CCS is disabled and the speed increases. When the accelerator is released, the CCS resumes at its last set speed. If at any point of time during acceleration the CCS speed is set, CCS replaces the old set speed with the new speed. The controller CO has the following safety features:

- CCS is automatically disabled when the car speed is either below 45 kmph or above 160 kmph.
- CCS is automatically disabled when the Anti-Lock Brake system is activated.

Figure 7.7(d) shows the extended finite state machine of the controller for CCS. The transition specifications, as shown in the figure, can be written down. It is left as an exercise. The behavior of CCS is the combined behavior of the four state machines shown in Fig. 7.7.

Anti-lock Brake System (ABS)

ABS is a safety system which prevents the wheels from locking up while braking. ABS senses the driver's situation (braking or not braking), the status of the car's wheel (locked or rotating), the road conditions and other information. Once it detects the locking of a wheel, it reduces the braking force repeatedly until the wheel starts rotating again. ABS consists of the components *Speed sensor*, *Valve*, *Pump*, and *ABS controller*. Their functionalities are given below:

- Speed sensor provides information about the rotational speed of a wheel. If the wheel is experiencing a rapid deceleration then the wheel is about to lock up.
- Valve component controls the pressure that is flowing into the brake. It operates in three modes, *open*, *block*, and *release*. If the valve is in open mode then the pressure will pass through to the brake. This means the pressure will increase. If the valve is in release mode then the pressure will be released from the brake. This means that the pressure will decrease. If the valve is in block mode then the pressure is prevented from raising further in case the driver pushes the brake pedal harder.
- Pump applies pressure.
- ABS controller component monitors the speed sensors and controls the system.

The ABS system works as follows. Every wheel has a rotational speed sensor which informs ABS when the wheel is locked due to heavy brake or sliding. ABS constantly monitors the speed sensors looking for decelerations in the wheels that are out of the ordinary. Just before a wheel locks up, it will experience a rapid deceleration. When ABS detects a wheel rotating significantly slower than the others, it actuates the valves to reduce hydraulic pressure to the brake at the affected wheel by switching to release mode. Thus it reduces the braking force on that wheel. The wheel then rotates faster. When the ABS detects that one wheel is turning significantly faster than the others, it instructs the pump to apply pressure and instructs the valve to switch to open mode. Therefore, the hydraulic pressure to

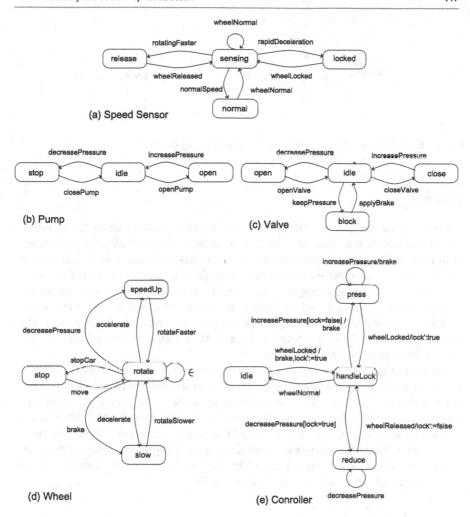

Fig. 7.8 Anti-lock brake system

the wheel is increased. Consequently, the braking force is reapplied and the wheel slows. This process is repeated continuously. This gives the system maximum braking power. The extended finite state machines for these component behaviors are shown in Fig. 7.8. Their transition specifications can be formally written down. See Exercise.

The event *brake* is common to both CCS and ABS models. When the event *brake* is triggered the ABS system will disable the cruise control. This happens when the ABS receives the event *wheelLocked*. The transition labeled by *wheelLocked* issues the event *brake* as an output response, which causes the cruise control to go to *disable* state. Therefore, if cruise control is active when the car is driven through an icy road and skidding happens then the ABS is automatically activated and it will apply the brake on the wheels, which eventually disables the cruise control. □

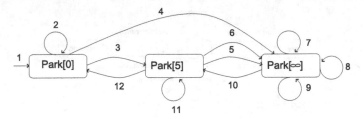

Fig. 7.9 Extended finite state machine model of timed parking meter

7.2.1
Simulation

A modular model is a *grey* box. Only those states, transitions, and variables that are necessary for an interaction are made observable. Rest of the details are hidden, usually in states or in internal transitions. Refinement of a modular model can add more details without affecting the interaction behavior. More details are added by the introduction of variables, new states while refining a complex state, and adding new transitions. So, a refinement *simulates* the behavior of the original model. In general, an EFSM M' simulates the behavior of an EFSM M, if M' can replace M in every environment of its interaction. The environment cannot distinguish between M' and M. We illustrate this principle for the Parking-Meter model in Fig. 6.21(b), Chap. 6.

We rename the state *more* by $Park[\infty]$. Informally, we want the new model of Parking Meter to allow any amount of parking time, provided coins are fed to satisfy parking requirement. The event *dec* is removed from the model; instead variable *feed* of type Boolean, and variables *timer* of type $\mathbb{N}$ are introduced in the refined model. The variable *feed* will be set to *true* whenever the Parking Meter is fed with a coin. The variable *timer* is assumed to mimic the behavior of a *real* timer, as in a stop watch. Once a time is set, the clock in the timer starts winding down. The specification of the refined model is given below. The timed parking-meter model is shown in Fig. 7.9.

$$PM = (Q, \Sigma_1, \Sigma_2, q_0, V, \Lambda),$$

where

$Q = \{Park[0], Park[5], Park[\infty]\}$
$\Sigma_1 = \{\epsilon, 25c, 1d\}$
$\Sigma_2 = \{green, read\}$
$q_0 : Park[0]$
$V = \{timer, feed\}, timer : \mathbb{N}, feed : Boolean$
$\Lambda : TransitionSpecifications$

1. $\xrightarrow{\text{[timer=0}\wedge\text{feed=false]/red}} Park[0]$

2. $Park[0] \xrightarrow{\epsilon\text{[feed=false]/red}} Park[0]$

3. $Park[0] \xrightarrow{25c\text{[feed=false]/\{(timer}'=\text{timer+5),(feed}'=\text{true),green\}}} Park[5]$

4. $Park[0] \xrightarrow{1d\text{[feed=false]/\{(timer}'=60),(feed}'=\text{true),green\}}} Park[\infty]$

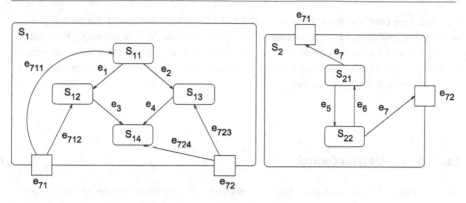

Fig. 7.10 Modeling message passing between finite state machines

5. $Park[5] \xrightarrow{25c[feed=true]/\{(timer'=timer+5),green\}} Park[\infty]$

6. $Park[5] \xrightarrow{1d[feed=true]/\{(timer'=60),green\}} Park[\infty]$

7. $Park[\infty] \xrightarrow{25c[feed=true]/\{(timer'=timer+5),green\}} Park[\infty]$

8. $Park[\infty] \xrightarrow{1d[feed=true]/\{(timer'=60),green\}} Park[\infty]$

9. $Park[\infty] \xrightarrow{[timer>5]/green} Park[\infty]$

10. $Park[\infty] \xrightarrow{[timer=5]/green} Park[5]$

11. $Park[5] \xrightarrow{[0<timer\leq5]/green} Park[5]$

12. $Park[5] \xrightarrow{[timer=0]/red} Park[0]$

Transition 11 is new in this model; it reflects the continuous passage of time. In the previous model, *dec* occurs only at intervals of 5 units of time. The states $Park[5]$ and $Park[\infty]$ are still abstract because the timer action is not explicit. Hence these two states are complex states and can be refined to explicitly model the timer behavior, as in a stop watch. See exercise.

7.3
Transition Points

In refining a state q of machine M, we allow all incoming transitions to state q become transitions to the initial state (newly created) of the machine q_M. An alternate approach is to allow direct transitions between a sub-state of one super-state and a sub-state of another super-state. The later semantics will require a transition to cross state boundaries and make the state diagram cluttered with transitions. To simplify the diagrammatic representation, *transition points* have been proposed by Selic, Gulleckson, and Ward [16]. This notation, illustrated in Fig. 7.10, supports the creation of transition points at the boundaries of super-states, and use of appropriate naming conventions for events flowing across these points. The transition e_7 from state S_{21} stops at the transition point e_{71} in S_2. The two transitions

e_{711} and e_{712} continue from the transition point e_{71} in S_1 to the states S_{11} and S_{12}. The semantics signifies that if the transition e_7 is triggered while S_2 is in state S_{21}, then either S_{11} or S_{12} will be the next state in the composed machine. The bonding between events e_7 and e_{711} (e_{712}) is established by the common transition point e_{71}. The semantics for transition e_7 at S_{22} is quite similar.

7.4
Case Study—Elevator Control

We construct a hierarchical state machine model for a simplified version of the elevator-control problem, attributed to Davis [2]. In arriving at a model, we will have illustrated all the modeling principles discussed in this chapter.

There are n elevators to service a building with m floors. The problem is to develop a formal specification describing the movement of elevators between floors while satisfying the following constraints.

1. Each elevator has a set of buttons, one for each floor. The one pressed lightens up, and causes the elevator to visit the corresponding floor. The illumination is switched off when the corresponding floor is reached by the elevator.
2. Each floor, except the ground floor and top floor, has two buttons, one to request for an elevator to go up, and one to request for an elevator to go down. These buttons illuminate when pressed. The illumination is switched off when an elevator, which can move in the desired direction, visits the floor.
3. When there are no requests to service, an elevator remains at the floor where it has been.

An important assumption is that the internal mechanism of the elevators guarantees that in-between two floors an elevator will keep moving without changing direction. There are three components to be modeled: elevator buttons, floor buttons, and elevator motion.

Elevator Buttons
The language for specifying the buttons, their states and transitions are defined below:

- $eb_{i,j}$: the button for jth floor in elevator i.
- $ebon_{i,j}$: the state in which $eb_{i,j}$ lightens up.
- $eboff_{i,j}$: the state in which $eb_{i,j}$ is not illuminated.
- $press\_eb_{i,j}$: the event-type that triggers the transition that occurs when $eb_{i,j}$ is pressed.
- $arrives\_at_{i,j}$: the event-type that triggers the transition that occurs when elevator i arrives at floor j.

The state transition diagram for elevator button $eb_{i,j}$ is shown in Fig. 7.11.

Floor Buttons
Each floor, except the ground floor and the top floor, has two buttons, one for calling an elevator to go up, and the other to call for an elevator to go down. The language elements required are:

- $fb_{b,j}$: the button at floor j for direction b.

Fig. 7.11 Finite state machine
for the jth floor button in
elevator i

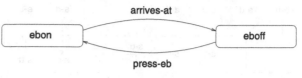

Fig. 7.12 Finite state machine
for the button at floor j for
direction b

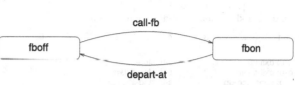

- $fbon_{b,j}$: the button $fb_{b,j}$ lightens up.
- $fboff_{b,j}$: the button $fb_{b,j}$ is not illuminated.
- $call\_fb_{b,j}$: the event-type that triggers the transition identifying that $fb_{b,j}$ is pressed.
- $depart\_at_{b,j}$: the event-type that triggers the transition that occurs when an elevator going in direction b leaves floor j.

The state transition diagram for floor button $fb_{b,j}$ is shown in Fig. 7.12. The state transitions for the buttons at the ground floor and at the top floor are similar to each other and can be derived from the diagram in Fig. 7.12.

Elevator Motion

The observable scenarios for an elevator, with respect to a floor i, are illustrated in Fig. 7.13, and enumerated here:

1. The elevator moves upwards without stopping.
2. The elevator moves downwards without stopping.
3. The elevator approaches from below, stops, and then continues upwards.
4. The elevator approaches from above, stops, and then continues downwards.
5. The elevator approaches from below, stops, and then continues downwards.
6. The elevator approaches from above, stops, and then continues upwards.
7. The elevator approaches from below, stops, and then waits in the idle state.
8. The elevator approaches from above, stops, and then waits in the idle state.
9. From the idle state, the elevator moves downwards.
10. From the idle state, the elevator moves upwards.

For an observer at a floor, an elevator can be in one of the following states:

1. *wait:* waits at that floor with its doors closed.
2. *stop-idle:* stops at that floor; this happens when there is no outstanding request to process.
3. *stop-up:* stops at the floor during its upward motion.
4. *stop-down:* stops at the floor during its downward motion.
5. *approach-up:* approaches the floor during its upward motion.
6. *approach-down:* approaches the floor during its downward motion.
7. *exit-up:* leaves the floor in its upward motion.
8. *exit-down:* leaves the floor in its downward motion.

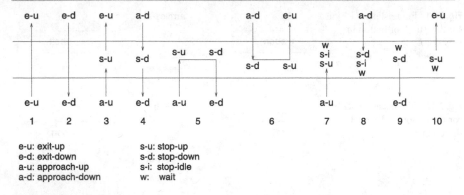

e-u: exit-up   s-u: stop-up
e-d: exit-down   s-d: stop-down
a-u: approach-up   s-i: stop-idle
a-d: approach-down   w: wait

Fig. 7.13 Scenarios for elevator motion observed at one floor

When an elevator stops at a floor, and there is no request to process, its doors remain open. The model assumes that the internal mechanism has a built-in sensor which slows (or accelerates) an elevator as required. In its upward motion, an elevator goes through the states *exit-up* and *approach-up* before entering one of the states *stop-up* or *stop-idle*. The transition labeled *reduce-speed* models this state change. The states *approach* and *exit* are observable when a button changes state.

The three states *stop-up, stop-down*, and *stop-idle* are combined to create the super-state *stop*; the two states *approach-up*, and *approach-down* are combined into the super-state *approach*; the two states *exit-up*, and *exit-down* are combined into the super-state *exit*. After stopping at a floor, an elevator leaves with its doors closed. The transition labeled *close-door* from the state *stop* to the state *exit* models this state change. Finally, when an elevator is called at a floor, and at that instant there is some elevator in the *wait* state, the elevator is made available. This is modeled by the transition labeled *call-fb(–,–)* from the state *wait* to the state *stop*. This generic model is shown in Fig. 7.14.

However, this model is inaccurate because of the fact that the semantics for a transition from a super-state S_1 to another super-state S_2 implies that the transition is from every sub-state of S_1 to every sub-state of S_2. This is remedied by showing the transitions relating all appropriate sub-states, as illustrated by Fig. 7.15. Whenever there is a call for an elevator, and there is an elevator in the state *stop-idle* at that instant, its state changes to either *stop-up* or *stop-down*; when there is no such request, it goes into the *wait* state. This situation is captured by the transitions labeled *called-from-up, called-from-down, change-direction*, and *no-request*. Figure 7.15 shows several additional transitions relating the sub-states of the state *wait* and the state *stop*. Note that the states *stop-up*, and *stop-down* can be modeled as complex states, and refined to capture the closing of the door of the elevator, as shown in Fig. 7.16.

Sequential Composition

The state transition diagrams for the elevator as observed at different floors can be composed cyclically (in the usual sequential composition the first and last machines are also composed) to obtain the state transition diagram for one elevator servicing a given number of floors. Let F_i denote the state machine for an elevator as observed at floor i. The

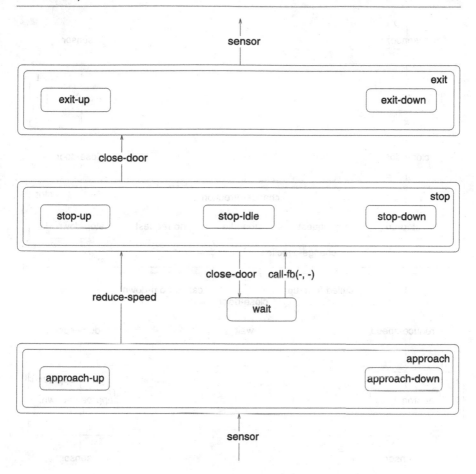

Fig. 7.14 Generic state machine model for elevator observed at one floor

transition from the state *exit-up* of F_i to the state *exit-up* of F_{i+1} corresponds to the case when the elevator is not stopping at the $(i + 1)$th floor in its upward motion. The transition from the state *exit-up* of F_i to the state *approach-up* of F_{i+1} corresponds to the case when the elevator is stopping at the $(i + 1)$th floor. Similar transitions exist between the state *exit-down* of F_i and the states *exit-down* and *approach-down* of F_{i-1}. The state machines corresponding to the ground and top floors are special cases; the states *exit-up* and *approach-down* do not exist in the machine corresponding to the top floor; the states *exit-down* and *approach-up* do not exist in the machine corresponding to the ground floor. Figure 7.17 shows the composed machine for an elevator servicing four floors. Only the states and transitions involved in the composition are shown.

For a building with several elevators with identical functionalities, the state machine specification for all the elevators is given by the product machine $E = E_1 \times E_2 \times \cdots \times E_k$, where E_i is the composed machine for elevator i, and $\times$ is the "generalized intersection" operation discussed in Chap. 6. The elevator system needs to be managed by a controller

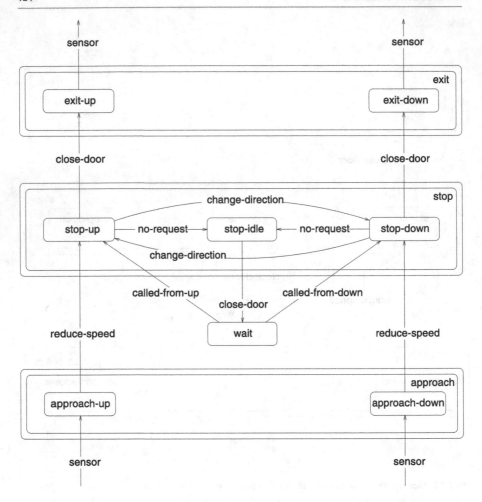

Fig. 7.15 Generic state machine model for elevator observed at one floor: refinement of Fig. 7.14

so that all requests are serviced in a fair way. This can be accomplished by the controller maintaining a queue of requests, so as to coordinate the movement of the elevators efficiently.

7.5
Exercises

1. Refine the state *rcvCall* in Fig. 7.2(a) to model the features (1) a received call may be put on hold for period x, $2 \le x \le 4$, and (2) a received call may be connected to a speaker.

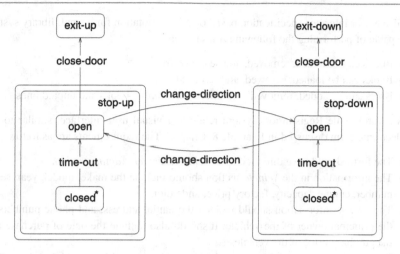

Fig. 7.16 Refinement of the states *stop-up* and *stop-down* in Fig. 7.15

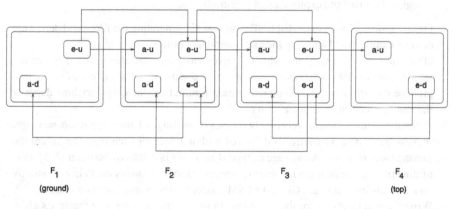

e-u: exit-up
e-d: exit-down
a-u: approach-up
a-d: approach-down

Fig. 7.17 State transition diagram for an elevator servicing four floors

2. Refine the states *Park*[5] and *Park*[∞] in Fig. 7.9 to explicitly model the *timer* behavior.

3. Modify the traffic light model in Fig. 6.6, Chap. 6 to satisfy the following constraints:

   - it stays in state *red* for three units of time,
   - it stays in state *green* for five units of time, and
   - it stays in state *yellow* for one unit of time.

4. Give an EFSM model for a bounded stack. Assume that the maximum size of the stack is $M > 0$.

5. Give a user interface specification based on EFSM notation for a small library system capable of performing the following transactions:

   - Books can be added, removed, and searched for.
   - Books can be loaned, renewed, and reserved.
   - Users can be added, removed, and traced for overdue books and unpaid fines.

6. An Automobile Registration System requires a visual user interface, similar to the electronic form discussed in Example 8, Chap. 5. The requirements are as follows:

   - The form should have three sections: *Vehicle, Owner, Administration.*
   - The information in the *Vehicle* section should include the make, model, year, serial number, engine capacity, factory price, and color.
   - The *Owner* information should include the name, address, and phone numbers of the principal owner of the vehicle. It should also include the date of purchase and the purchase price of the vehicle.
   - The *Administration* section should include the purpose of the vehicle (pleasure or business), date and place of current registration, registration number of the vehicle, registration fee, and expiry date of registration.

   Design a form, give an extended BNF grammar for generating the form, and derive the corresponding EFSM showing the user-interaction points.

7. Give a model of a *Cash Box* which receives cash, accumulates it and displays the total. Combine this model with *Chips Machine* discussed in Example 9 of Chap. 6 to produce the behavior "after completing each transaction, the chips machine deposits the money received by it in the cash box".

8. A communication channel receives two types of message, *A-message* and *B-message*. A message of type *A-message* is delivered within 3 units of time from the instant the message was received. A message of type *B-message* is delivered between [3, 5] units of time from the instant the message was received. All messages are delivered strictly on a first-in-first-out basis. Give an EFSM model for the communication channel.

9. Write the specifications for the transitions in the extended finite state machines given in Figs. 7.7(c), 7.7(d), and 7.8.

10. A home-heating system consists of a furnace, a thermostat, and a fan for blowing air. Temperature control is distributed, so that every room has a controller to maintain its temperature. When the temperature in a room goes below $t_r - 2$, where t_r is the desired room temperature, the furnace is turned on. When the temperature in the furnace reaches a certain limit T, the furnace is shut off and the fan starts blowing the hot air. The thermostat registers and monitors the room temperature. When the room temperature reaches $t_r + 2$, the furnace is shut off. The fan runs until the furnace temperature falls to $T - 5$. Assuming that $t_r + 2 \geq T$, give an EFSM specification for the system.

11. Arbiter is a mechanism for allocating resources efficiently in concurrent systems. The purpose of this exercise is to model an arbiter which allocates resources to two processes P and Q in such a way that every process eventually gets the requested resource. The following constraints apply for resource sharing between processes:

    - R is a finite set of resources

- for $r \in R$ there exists $t_r \in \mathbb{N}$, denoting the maximum utilization time
- a process can request the arbiter for any resource in R
- arbiter will accept all requests from P and Q
- every resource requested by a process should be allocated to it by the arbiter
- a process which received a resource r at time t must return it to the arbiter before time $t + t_r$.

7.6 Bibliographic Notes

Extended finite state machines have the expressive power to model complex system behavior. In order to use them well, their precise semantics must be understood. The Ptolemy approach [6] and Ptolemy II development framework [11] provide both semantics and tools for practical usage.

Statecharts [8] and Roomcharts [16] are the earliest two examples of visual formalisms for EFSM. Many different semantics [9] for Statechart formalism have been studied. An object-based variant of statechart, adapted and extended by the Unified Modeling Language [14], is now called UML statechart. Instead of using UML statechart facility, it is shown in [17] that a combination of using case diagrams and UML class diagrams can be converted to an extended finite state machine model. The resulting EFSM is used for generating test cases for black-box testing of the system implementing the model. The EFSM is further extended with a data flow modeling mechanism in [7] to the testing of interactive systems. The KIEL macro editor [15] (URL: http://rtsys.informatik.uni-kiel.de/~rt-kiel) is a latest graphical editor for the construction, modification, and revision management of statecharts.

The guards and variables in EFSM can include time variables that model discrete and continuous behavior of time. The semantics of real-time automata [4] and timed automata [1] have been tailored to study timed EFSMs. In [5], a variant of Roomchart has been used to model real-time behavior in UML.

The EFSM model is also used in behavioral specification of hardware models and in communication protocol specifications. In [10] communication protocols are modeled as hardware circuits using EFSMs with multi-way synchronization.

References

1. Alur R, Dill D (1991) The theory of timed automata. In: de Bakker JW, Huizing C, de Roever WP, Rozenberg G (eds) Real-time: theory in practice. LNCS, vol 600, pp 74–106
2. Davis N (1987) Problem # 4: LIFT. In: Fourth international workshop on software specification and design, IEEE Computer Soc, Los Alamitos
3. Denert E (1977) Specification and design of dialogue systems with state diagrams. In: Ribbons D (ed) International computing symposium. North-Holland, Amsterdam, pp 417–424
4. Dima C (2001) Real-time automata. J Autom Lang Comb 6(1):3–23

5. Douglass BP (1999) Doing hard time: developing real-time systems with UML, objects, frameworks, and patterns. Addison Wesley, Reading

6. Eker J, Janneck JW, Lee EA, Liu J, Ludvig J, Neundorffer S, Xiong Y (2003) Taming heterogeneity—the Ptolemy approach. Proc IEEE 9(12):127–144

7. Fantinato M, Jino M (2003) Applying extended finite state machines in software testing of interactive systems. In: DSV-IS 2003. LNCS, vol 2844, pp 34–45

8. Harel D (1987) Statecharts: a visual formalism for complex systems. Sci Comput Program 8:231–274

9. Harel D, Pnueli A, Schmidt JP, Sherman R (1987) On the formal semantics of statecharts. In: Proceedings of the second IEEE symposium on logic in computer science, pp 54–64

10. Katagiriy H, Yasumotoz K, Kitajimay A, Higashinoy T, Taniguchiy K (2000) Hardware, implementation of communication protocols modeled by concurrent EFSMs with multiway synchronization. In: Proceedings of the 37th conference on design automation (DAC'00), Los Angeles, USA

11. Lee EA (2009) Finite state machines and modal models in Ptolemy II. Technical report No UCB/EECS-2009-151, University of California at Berkeley, November 2009

12. Mohamad M, Alagar V (2010) A component-based development process for trustworthy systems. J Softw Maint Evol, Res Pract 1–20

13. Mohamad M, Alagar V (2010) A formal approach to for the specification and verification of trustworthy component-based systems. J Syst Softw

14. OMG Unified Modeling Language (OMG UML) (2009) Superstructure version 2.2

15. Prochnow S, von Hanxleden R (2007) Statechat development beyond WYSIWYG. In: International conference on model driven engineering languages and systems. ACM/IEEE, Nashville

16. Selic B, Gullekson G, Ward PT (1994) Real-time object-oriented modeling. Wiley, New York

17. Sinha A, Paradkar A, Williams C (2007) On generating EFSM models from use cases. In: Proceedings of sixth international workshop on scenarios and state machines (SCESM'07), pp 1–8

18. Zave P (1993) Feature interactions and formal specifications in telecommunications. IEEE Comput 20–30

Classification of Formal Specification Methods

8

Formal specification methods use languages with mathematically defined syntax and semantics, and offer methods to describe systems and their properties. The strength of a formal method rests on the level of formality and expressiveness afforded by its specification language, and availability of tools that support the method for developing the system in strict conformance to the system specification. So, a formal method may be placed in its category depending upon its strength and practical use, which in turn depend on the four pillars *mathematical basis*, *type of systems*, *level of formality*, and *tools support*.

8.1
The Four Pillars

The mathematical basis for a formal specification language is either one of the concepts *algebra*, *logic*, *set theory*, and *relations* or some combination of them. In order to reap the full benefits of a formal method, the specification language should provide formal extensional features to adequately address software engineering concerns and allow specifications to be composable from simple structured units, to be generic and parameterized, and to have well-described interfaces.

Systems can be broadly classified as *sequential*, *concurrent*, *distributed*, with or without *time* dimension. A specification language is often designed to best suit the need of a family of systems under one category in this broad classification. A reactive system may involve time constraints and exhibit concurrency. A transaction system, such as database systems and web-based service-oriented systems, is often distributed and involves timing constraints. Telephone switching systems, control systems, and transportation systems involve sequential as well as concurrent behavior and they may be governed by strict timing constraints. Such systems, because of their complex behavior, require languages that support constructs for specifying concurrent and time constrained interactions. It is not uncommon to combine one or more specification languages to specify such systems.

A mathematically based language is formal, yet it may or may not include a reasoning system for verifying system properties. To reason about system behavior, some form of logic is necessary. Two well-established approaches to verification are model checking and theorem proving. Model checking relies on building a finite model of the system and algorithmically checking that a desired property holds in the model. Theorem proving is an axiomatic technique in which the system is expressed as a set of axioms and a set of inference rules, and the desired property is expressed as a theorem to be proved. The proof appeals only to the axioms and the inference rules in developing a proof of the theorem. The verification method afforded by a specification language is closely tied to its mathematical basis. As an example, if the specification language is based on algebra then axiomatic verification, rather than model checking, is the choice of verification method.

Tools support is essential for integrating formal method with software development. The specification must be type checked, checked for syntactic correctness, and semantically analyzed. A specification that is syntactically and semantically error-free should be subjected to refinement and verification. The former requires both design-time and run-time tools. The latter will require either a model checker tool or theorem proving tool. Many specification languages aim for formal verification, and not for system development. There are many other specification languages which have development tools, but not verification tools. There are a few exceptions, such as PVS (Prototype Verification System) [24], which offer both development and verification support.

8.2
Classification

Based on the work of Wing [35], formal specification languages are broadly categorized as *property-oriented*, and *model-oriented*, which includes the *state-machine-oriented* case. A property-oriented approach builds a theory and it is essential to state everything that needs to be included in the theory. In a model-based approach, mathematical objects are used to build the model, and hence the properties of those objects can be freely used in the model.

8.2.1
Property-Oriented Specification Methods

Property-oriented category can be subdivided into two sub-groups, referred to as *axiomatic* and *algebraic*.

In an axiomatic approach, objects are built from types, and operations on types are given as assertions in first-order predicate logic. That is, axiomatic formal specification defines the semantics of functions of objects by a description of the relations between different objects and functions as axioms (predicate-logical formula). The language Anna [18] uses assertions to annotate Ada programs. These assertions serve to verify the correctness of Ada programs. TAM'97 (Trace Assertion Method) [17] is a formal method based on assertions for abstract specification of module interfaces. Axiomatic approaches naturally lend to verification based on theorem proving method. HOL (Higher-order Logic) [10] is a language that uses some kind of logical type theory in which system properties can be specified and verified. PVS language and tool [24] are based on classical typed higher-order logic. The Coq proof assistant [3] is widely used for checking assertions and for finding formal proofs from constructive proofs. Z specification language [31] may be viewed as a mixture of typed set theory and first-order logic, although Z is accepted as a model-based specification language.

As opposed to axiomatic approaches where logic enters to enrich an already rich mathematical basis, such as types, different kinds of logical specification languages exist. These are closer to logic than to systems they intend to specify. Examples of such languages include Temporal Logic [20] for reactive system specification, Interval Temporal Logic [23] for specifying concurrency, Durational Interval Logic [5] for specifying real-time behavior, and dL (differential dynamic logic) [25] for hybrid system verification. These languages extend the classical logic with new constructs, provide formal semantics, and give a set of axioms for verification. Tools for model checking temporal logic specifications include EMC [6], SMV (Symbolic Model Verifier) [21], and Spin [16].

In an algebraic approach, theory of objects and processes are defined as algebras. This method emphasizes the representation-free specification of objects and a declarative style of specifying their properties. An object is introduced as a set of definitions, and a set of *equations* defines the operations on the object. Terms in the language are terms in the underlying algebra and are uninterpreted. Equations are turned into *rewrite* rules for generating new terms in the specification. A property to be verified is to be stated as a term. If the stated property is a term in the algebra defined by the specification, the property holds for the specified system. That is, algebraic specification methods provide a language as well as a proof method. The best known algebraic specification language is OBJ3 [9]. The OBJ family of languages come with tool support for developing algebraic specifications and verifying stated properties. OBJ3 affords modularity, genericity through parameterization, and extendability through theory composition. Many other algebraic specification languages listed in [36], include ACSR (Algebra of Communicating Shared Resources) and ADL (Algebraic Design Language). The algebraic languages CCS [22] and μCRL [11] are widely used for specifying concurrent systems. A toolset for a process algebraic language is mCRL2 [2].

Larch [12] provides a two-tiered approach to specifying program interfaces. In one tier, mathematical abstractions introduce a first-order theory written in the conventional style of equational algebraic specifications. In the other tier, specifications are written in a predicative language using assertions on pre- and post-states of specified objects. Larch has a theorem prover, called LP.

8.2.2
Model-Based Specification Techniques

State machine models discussed in Chaps. 6 and 7 can be described as "model-based". Both Statecharts [13] and I/O Automata [19] support concurrency models. Statemate [14] is a tool for developing visual models and analyzing their properties. Statestep [4] is a finite state machine modeling tool which can be used with any state machine formalism. Disco [29] and Roomcharts [28] are based on statechart notation, and serve as specification and animation tools for modeling reactive systems.

Every formal specification language builds a "model" of the specified system. The significance of "model-based" languages is that the model of the system is built in terms of mathematical objects like sets, sequences, and relations. They provide an abstract description of the *state* of the system, together with a number of operations over that state. Mathematical objects, such as natural numbers, sets and relations are used to build a state model. An operation defined in a state is a function that modifies one or more state variables. Operation definitions use the underlying mathematical theory.

The most widely known model-oriented specification languages are Z [31], the B Method [1], and VDM [33]. Object-Z [30] is an extension of Z notation for modeling object-oriented system design. An extensive bibliography on Z and Object-Z are available in [36]. ProofPower [26] is a commercial tool that supports Z specification development and checks correctness properties in the specified system. The B method [1] is based on abstract machine formalism. The B-Toolkit comprises a suite of fully integrated software tools. They support formal development of software systems using the B Method. Rodin [27], an open source software, supports B specification, refinements, and proof. CSP (Communicating Sequential Processors) [15] is a state-based language for modeling concurrency. The tool Murphi [8] is both a description language and verifier for finite state concurrent systems.

8.3
Languages Chosen for Discussion

From the languages mentioned in Sect. 8.2, we have chosen a few to illustrate the full spectrum of specification languages. The list below includes indexes to the chapters where they are discussed.

1. *Mathematics for Software Construction* Chapter 12 demonstrate the usefulness of mathematical abstractions such as sets, relations, and sequences in software development. In particular, they lay the foundation for model-based specification methods.
2. *Property-oriented Languages and Methods* In Chaps. 9 and 10, we discuss propositional and predicate logics and illustrate specifications in assertional style. In Chap. 11, we discuss Temporal logic and use mainly linear temporal logic to specify concurrency and reactivity. We discuss model checking of temporal properties in state-based models. Algebraic specification method is introduced in Chap. 13 and OBJ3 specifications are developed. In Chap. 15, we discuss the elements of CCS, a process calculus for communicating systems. The two tiers of Larch and LP, Larch Prover, are taken up for discussion in Chap. 14.
3. *Model-based Languages and Methods* We have discussed state machine models in Chaps. 6 and 7. VDM specification language is discussed in Chap. 16, Z notation is discussed in Chap. 17, Object-Z language is introduced in Chap. 18, and the B Method is discussed in Chap. 19.

8.4
Bibliographic Notes

The property-oriented and model-based classification for specification languages is due to Wing [35]. The web page [36] is constantly updated and should be referred for formal methods practiced around the world. A set of tools for formal methods that have FLOSS (open source software) licenses are surveyed in [34].

References

1. Abrial JR (1996) The b-book—assigning programs to meanings. Cambridge University Press, Cambridge
2. Alexander M, Gardner W (eds) (2008) Process algebra for parallel and distributed processing. CRC Press, Boca Raton
3. Bertot Y, Castéran P (2004) Interactive theorem proving and program development. Coq'Art: the calculus of inductive constructions. Texts in theoretical computer science. An EATCS series, vol XXV. Springer, Berlin
4. Breen M (2005) Statestep specification technique: user guide, Version 2.0/2005-9-30, http://statestep.com
5. ChaoChen Z, Hoare T, Ravn AP (1991) A calculus of durations. Inf Process Lett 40(5):269–276
6. Clarke E, Emerson EA (1981) Synthesis of synchronization skeletons for branching time temporal logic. In: Logic of programs: workshop. LNCS, vol 131
7. Cooke J (1992) Formal methods—mathematics, theory, recipes or what? Comput J 35(5):419–423
8. Dill DL, Drexler AJ, Hu AJ, Yang CH (1992) Protocol verification as a hardware design aid. In: IEEE international conference on computer design: VLSI in computers and processors. IEEE Computer Society, Los Alamitos, pp 522–525
9. Goguen J, Einkler T (1988) Introduction to OBJ3. Technical report, SRI-CSL-88-9, SRI International, Meno Park, CA
10. Gordon MJC, Melham TF (1993) Introduction to HOL: a theorem proving environment for higher order logic. Cambridge University Press, Cambridge
11. Groote JF (1997) The syntax and semantics of timed CRL. Technical report SEN-R9709, CWI, Amsterdam
12. Guttag JV, Horning JJ, Garland SJ, Jones KD, Modet A, Wing J (1993) Larch: languages and tools for formal specification. Springer, New York
13. Harel D (1987) Statecharts: a visual formalism for complex systems. Sci Comput Program 8:231–274
14. Harel D, Lachover H, Naamad A, Pnueli A, Politi M, Sherman R, Shtull-Trauring R, Trakhtenbrot M (1990) Statemate: a working environment for the development of complex reactive systems. IEEE Trans Softw Eng 16(4):403–414
15. Hoare CAR (1985) Communicating sequential processes. Computer science. Prentice Hall, Englewood Cliffs
16. Holzmann G (1991) Design and validation of computer protocols. Prentice-Hall, Englewood Cliffs
17. Iglewski M, Kubica M, Madey J, Mincer-Daszkiewiczb J, Stencel K (2010) TAM'97: the trace assertion method of module interface specification (Reference manual). http://w3.uqo.ca/iglewski/public_html/TAM/SRC/tam-1.html (June 2010)
18. Luckham DC, von Henke FW, Krieg-Brückner B, Owe O (1987) ANNA: a language for annotating ada programs (reference manual). LNCS, vol 260

19. Lynch N, Tuttle M (1989) An introduction to input/output automata. CWI-Quart 2(3):219–246
20. Manna Z, Pnulei A (1992) The temporal logic of reactive and concurrent systems: specifications. Springer, New York
21. McMillan KL (1993) Symbolic model checking: an approach to state explosion problem. Kluwer Academic, Norwell
22. Milner R (1980) A calculus of communicating systems. LNCS, vol 92
23. Moszkowski B, Manna Z (1983) Reasoning in interval temporal logic. Technical report, Report No STAN-(2-83-969), Stanford University, CA
24. Owre S, Shankar N, Rushby JM, Stringer-Calvert DWJ (1999) PVS system guide, version 2.3. Technical report, Computer Science Laboratory, SRI International, Menlo Park, CA
25. Platzer A (2008) Differential dynamic logic for hybrid systems. J Autom Reason 41(2):143–189
26. ProofPower. http://www.lemma-one.com/ProofPower/index/index.html
27. RODIN project. http://www.bmethod.com/php/travaux-r&d-methode-b-projet-RODIN-en.php
28. Selic B, Gullekson G, Ward PT (1994) Real-time object-oriented modeling. Wiley, New York
29. Systä K (2010) DisCo: user manual (draft). http://disco.cs.tut.fi/animation/disco92/disco_tool_manual.fm.html (June 2010)
30. Smith G (2000) The object-Z specification language. Kluwer Academic, Norwell
31. Spivey JM (1992) The Z notation—a reference manual, 2nd edn. Prentice-Hall International, Englewood Cliffs
32. http://www.flowgate.net/?lang=en&seccion=herramientas
33. VDM portal. http://www.vdmportal.org/twiki/bin/view
34. Wheeler D (2010) High assurance (for security or safety) and free-libre/open source software (FLOSS). http://www.dwheeler.com/essays/high-assurance-floss.html (June 2010)
35. Wing JM (1990) A specifier's introduction to formal methods. IEEE Comput 23(9):8–24
36. Z notation. http://formalmethods.wikia.com/wiki/Z_notation

Part III
Logic

Logic is the basis for reasoning and inference. Logic is studied in its own right as part of many disciplines, including mathematics, philosophy, and computer science. In software engineering, logic is viewed as a formal language for modeling systems. Different kinds of logic are used for representing knowledge of the application domain, formalizing properties of the system under design, precisely formulating environmental constraints and its interaction with the system, and reasoning about critical properties in the system model. In this module, propositional logic, predicate logic, and linear temporal logic are discussed. The learning outcomes from this module are the following:

- logic as a formal specification language
- formal representation of knowledge and policies
- formal verification of sequential programs
- specifying reactive and concurrent systems
- model checking, a method for formally verifying a modeled system

Propositional Logic

9

Logic is a system for rational enquiry and is founded on axioms and inference rules for reasoning. Modern mathematical logic dates back to the works of Frege and Peano late in the 19th century. Examples of logic include classical *propositional logic, first-order logic, modal logics* and *temporal logics*. In this chapter, we investigate propositional logic. The focus is on how propositional logic can be used as a tool in the analysis and presentation of system requirements. This requires an investigation of how assertions are formulated and combined, whether assertions imply intended conclusions, and how to mechanically prove certain results from the stated axioms without assigning truth values to the formulas. We include in this chapter only brief and at times informal sketches of the language aspects of logic; however, we quote important results that are sufficient for the study of logic as a specification language.

9.1
Syntax and Semantics

A proposition is a statement which is either true or false, but not both. *Propositional logic*, the language of propositions, consists of well-formed formulas constructed from *atomic formulas* and the *logical connectives* $\wedge$ (*and*), $\vee$ (*or*), $\neg$ (*not*), $\Rightarrow$ (*if ... then*), $\Leftrightarrow$ (*if and only if*). The atomic formulas of propositional calculus are propositions such as "computer is intelligent", "program does not terminate' and "alarm rings forever". It is not the string of symbols in a proposition but the truth value of the assertion that gives meaning to the proposition. Thus, if P stands for "program does not terminate" and Q stands for "alarm rings forever", then $P \Rightarrow Q$ denotes the *compound* proposition "if program does not terminate then alarm rings forever", whose truth value is uniquely determined by the truth values of P and Q.

Table 9.1 gives the formal syntax of the language for propositional logic. The grammar does not show all possible names for propositions; for example, subscripted symbols and strings from the application domain are members of the set of terminals. There is an infinite collection of symbols that can be used to denote propositions, although only a finite subset

V.S. Alagar, K. Periyasamy, *Specification of Software Systems*,
Texts in Computer Science,
DOI 10.1007/978-0-85729-277-3_9, © Springer-Verlag London Limited 2011

Table 9.1 Formal language
for propositional logic

$terminals = \{P, Q, R, \ldots, \wedge, \vee, \neg, \Rightarrow, \Leftrightarrow, (,)\};$

$non\text{-}terminals = \{atomic\ formula, sentence\};$

$atomic\ formula = P|Q|R|\ldots;$

$sentence = atomic\ formula\ |$

$\qquad (, sentence,)\ |\ \neg, sentence|$

$\qquad sentence, \vee, sentence\ |$

$\qquad sentence, \wedge, sentence\ |$

$\qquad sentence, \Rightarrow, sentence|$

$\qquad sentence, \Leftrightarrow, sentence;$

Table 9.2 Truth table defining
semantics of propositional
logic

P	Q	$\neg P$	$P \vee Q$	$P \wedge Q$	$P \Rightarrow Q$	$P \Leftrightarrow Q$
T	T	F	T	T	T	T
T	F	F	T	F	F	F
F	T	T	T	F	T	F
F	F	T	F	F	T	T

is used at any instant. The logic operators observe precedence according to the following decreasing order: $\neg(highest), \{\wedge, \vee\}, \Rightarrow, \Leftrightarrow$. The expression $P \Rightarrow Q$ is sometimes written $Q \Leftarrow P$, and read "Q if P". The grammar together with the precedence rules describe what counts as *well-formed formulas*.

The semantics for propositional logic is obtained through a *model*, which assigns truth values, *true* (*T*) or *false* (*F*), to atomic propositions. The sentences in the language are evaluated in a model according to the interpretation shown in Table 9.2. A sentence is *true* in a model if the sentence under the truth assignment in the model evaluates to true. The interpretations in Table 9.2 hold even when P and Q are replaced by any formula in the language.

Two well-formed formulas P and Q are *equivalent*, written $P \equiv Q$, if and only if they have the same truth values under every interpretation. Notice that $\equiv$ is a metasymbol and is not part of the language. For example, $(P \Rightarrow Q) \equiv (\neg P \vee Q)$ can be verified using a truth table. There exist a number of equivalence rules that are useful in *simplifying* a well-formed formula. These include the distributive laws and DeMorgan's laws [1]. A sentence F is *satisfiable* if there is an assignment of truth values to the atomic propositions in F for which F is true. A sentence which is not *satisfiable* is *contradictory*. If, for a list of sentences L, every assignment that makes the sentences in L true also makes the sentence P true, we say P is a *semantic consequence* of L and write $L \models P$. The metasymbol $\models$ is termed *semantic turnstile*. If a sentence is true for every assignment F, it is termed a *tautology*, and we write $\models F$. For example, $P \vee false \Rightarrow P \wedge true$ is a tautology, and $P \vee true \Rightarrow P \wedge false$ is a contradiction. The statement $P \wedge true \Rightarrow P \wedge false$ is *contingent*; its truth value may be *true* or *false* depending on the truth values of its constituents.

9.2
Proof

A proof is a mechanism for showing that a given claim F is a logical conclusion of some set S of premises. In Chap. 5, we have introduced the notation $S \vdash F$ (F can be *derived* from S) to mean that there is a sequence of formulas $F_1, \dots, F_n$, with $F = F_n$, such that

- F_i is an axiom, or
- $F_i \in S$, or
- F_i is obtained from two previous F_js in the sequence $F_1, \dots, F_n$ by an application of modus ponens.

The sequence $F_1, \dots, F_n$ is called an S-derivation (or S-proof) of F. A $\emptyset$-derivation is simply a derivation. The axioms are tautologies. The proof system in propositional logic is *sound* in the sense

> if $\vdash F$ then F is a tautology,

and *complete* in the sense that

> if F is a tautology then $\vdash F$.

The purpose of a proof is to make explicit what is already implicitly present. A proof is presented in several steps, where each step logically follows from the preceding steps, and an axiom. The final step of the proof is the demonstration of the truth of the claim Q. A *formal* proof requires that all implicit assumptions are made explicit and the steps in the proof are shown with reference to the sources used in deriving each step.

There are two aspects in proving a result: proof construction, and proof presentation. The construction phase is often informal, and the presentation phase must be rigorous, if not fully formal. Although gaps may exist in a rigorous proof, they are usually easy to fill. Proof methods and their formal presentation in propositional logic framework are discussed below.

9.2.1
Reasoning Based on Adopting a Premise

Truth tables provide an exhaustive proof method for propositional logic. To prove a claim Q from the premises $P_1, P_2, \dots, P_k$, one constructs a truth table (all models) and verifies whether or not in every row of the truth table Q is true. That is, the relationship

$$P_1, P_2, \dots, P_k \models Q$$

must be verified in every model. Rewriting this statement as

$$P_1 \land P_2 \land \cdots \land P_k \Rightarrow Q$$
$$\equiv \neg(P_1 \land P_2 \land \cdots \land P_k) \lor Q$$

it is shown to be a tautology.

9.2.2
Inference Based on Natural Deduction

The natural deduction inference rules describe *valid* steps in a deduction process. A valid step is a pair (P, Q) of sentences such that Q logically follows from P. This is a purely syntactic method for deriving well-formed formulas from those that already exist. It is based on two sets of rules—one set introduces connectives and hence the rules are called *introduction rules*, and the other set eliminates connectives and hence the rules are called *elimination rules*.

Introduction Rules

∨-Introduction $\frac{\alpha}{\alpha \vee \beta}$ and $\frac{\beta}{\beta \vee \alpha}$

∧-Introduction $\frac{\alpha, \beta}{\alpha \wedge \beta}$ and $\frac{\alpha, \beta}{\beta \wedge \alpha}$

¬-Introduction $\frac{\alpha \vdash \text{false}}{\neg \alpha}$

⇒-Introduction $\frac{\alpha \vdash \beta}{\alpha \Rightarrow \beta}$

⇔-Introduction $\frac{\alpha \Rightarrow \beta, \beta \Rightarrow \alpha}{\alpha \Leftrightarrow \beta}$

Elimination Rules

∨-Elimination $\frac{\alpha \vee \beta, \alpha \vdash \gamma, \beta \vdash \gamma}{\gamma}$

∧-Elimination $\frac{\alpha \wedge \beta}{\alpha}$ and $\frac{\alpha \wedge \beta}{\beta}$

¬-Elimination $\frac{\neg \neg \alpha}{\alpha}$, $\frac{\alpha, \neg \alpha}{F}$

⇒-Elimination $\frac{\alpha, \alpha \Rightarrow \beta}{\beta}$

⇔-Elimination $\frac{\alpha \Leftrightarrow \beta}{\alpha \Rightarrow \beta}$ and $\frac{\alpha \Leftrightarrow \beta}{\beta \Rightarrow \alpha}$

Consider, for example, the first introduction rule for disjunction. This states that under the assumption that α has been proved, the disjunction of α with any other logical expression β is also proved. The validity of this inference rule comes from truth table interpretation: a disjunction is true in every interpretation where one of its disjuncts is true.

The introduction rules for conjunction and two-sided implication require individual proofs for their conjuncts. The conjunction elimination rules state that if $\alpha \wedge \beta$ has been proved, then both α and β are proved. Once again, the validity of this rule can be traced to truth table interpretation. To eliminate a disjunction, one has to have more information: the logical consequence of each disjunct. The implication elimination rule is also called the *law of excluded middle*.

Since these inference rules hold for arbitrary expressions α and β, whenever a proof step has expressions matching the pattern of the antecedent of a proof rule, that rule can be applied. For example, from $P \vee Q, \neg P$, and an application of conjunction introduction rule, infer $(P \vee Q) \wedge \neg P$. Apply the distribution law and simplify the consequence to $(P \wedge \neg P) \vee (\neg P \wedge Q)$. This expression reduces further to $\neg P \wedge Q$. An application of conjunction elimination rule proves $\neg P$ and Q. A more complex proof is shown in Example 1. Finding an appropriate proof strategy for proving results using these rules is not easy; it requires some expertise to choose the proper rule at each step.

Example 1 Show that

$$P \vee (Q \wedge R) \vdash (P \vee Q) \wedge (P \vee R)$$

Derivation steps:

1	P	premise
2	$P \vee Q$	$\vee$-Introduction
3	$P \vee R$	$\vee$-Introduction
4	$(P \vee Q) \wedge (P \vee R)$	$\wedge$-Introduction and from 2 and 3
5	$Q \wedge R$	premise
6	Q	$\wedge$-Elimination
7	$P \vee Q$	$\vee$-Introduction
8	R	$\wedge$-Elimination and 5
9	$P \vee R$	$\vee$-Introduction
10	$(P \vee Q) \wedge (P \vee R)$	$\wedge$-Introduction and from 7 and 9
11	$P \vdash (P \vee Q) \wedge (P \vee R)$	from 1 to 4
12	$Q \wedge R \vdash (P \vee Q) \wedge (P \vee R)$	from 5 to 10
13	$P \vee (Q \wedge R) \vdash (P \vee Q) \wedge (P \vee R)$	$\vee$-Elimination and from 11, 12

□

The strategy of natural deduction proofs is bottom-up. In Example 1, we first recognize that $\beta = (P \vee Q) \wedge (P \vee R)$ is to be derived from $\alpha = P \vee (Q \wedge R)$, and so we start with α. Noticing the structure of α, we attempt $\vee$-elimination rule and attempt the proofs for $P \vdash \beta$ and $Q \wedge R \vdash \beta$. We then attempt the two subproofs. The difficult part of the proof process is to find the most appropriate elimination or introduction rule for an application. That is, a program which attempts to prove a theorem may have to exhaustively search through the rules and apply all those whose patterns match. This strategy inevitably generates all the relevant theorems. In principle, there can be an infinite number of theorems and consequently bottom-up proofs cannot be efficiently automated.

9.2.3
Proof by Resolution

A *literal* is an atomic formula or the negation of an atomic formula. In the former case, the literal is *positive*, and in the latter case it is *negative*. If P_{ij}, for $i = 1, \ldots, n$; $j = 1, \ldots, m$, are literals, the disjunctions $C_i = P_{i1} \vee \cdots \vee P_{im}$, denoted by $\bigvee_{j=1}^{m} P_{ij}$, are clauses. The formula $F = C_1 \wedge \cdots \wedge C_n$, denoted by $\bigwedge_{i=1}^{n} C_i$, is in *conjunctive normal form* (CNF). For example, the sentence $(P \vee R) \wedge (Q \vee R) \wedge (P \vee S) \wedge (Q \vee S)$ is in CNF. For every formula F, there is an equivalent formula G which is in CNF.

Resolution is a simple syntactic transformation that can be applied to CNF formulas. For two clauses C_1 and C_2 of a formula F in CNF, the *resolvent* is defined as $R = (C_1 - \{L\}) \cup (C_2 - \{\bar{L}\})$, where

$$\bar{L} = \begin{cases} \neg P_i & \text{if } L = P_i \\ P_i, & \text{if } L = \neg P_i \end{cases}$$

The formulas F and $F \cup \{R\}$ are equivalent. The resolution inference rule consists of three parts:

resolution: $\quad \dfrac{\alpha \vee P, \beta \vee \neg P}{\alpha \vee \beta} \qquad$ (eliminate P),

chain rule: $\quad \dfrac{\neg \alpha \Rightarrow P, P \Rightarrow \beta}{\neg \alpha \Rightarrow \beta} \qquad$ (eliminate P),

modus ponens: $\quad \dfrac{P, P \Rightarrow \alpha}{\alpha} \qquad$ (eliminate P).

The rules eliminate an atom P from two formulas. These rules are suitable for constructing a *proof by contradiction*. To establish

$$P_1, P_2, \ldots, P_n \vdash Q$$

the proof proceeds by negating the conclusion Q (that is, by assuming that Q is false) and assigning the value *true* to each premise and showing a contradiction as a consequence of these assumptions. The contradiction establishes that $P_1, P_2, \ldots, P_n, Q$ cannot all be true simultaneously. The proof steps are:

1. Transform each premise and the negated conclusion (introduced as a new premise) into conjunctive normal form. Now each premise is a conjunction of one or more clauses and each clause is true.
2. Identify pairs of clauses which contain complementary literals; one contains an atom and the other contains its negation. Apply resolution to obtain the resolvent.
3. Apply repeatedly Step 2 until P and $\neg P$ are derived for some P, showing a contradiction. This completes the proof.

Example 2 Assuming that $P \Rightarrow Q$, and $R \vee P$ are axioms, show that $R \Rightarrow S \vdash S \vee Q$.

Proof

1. The premises are $P \Rightarrow Q, R \vee P, R \Rightarrow S$.
2. In conjunctive normal form the premises are $\neg P \vee Q, R \vee P, \neg R \vee S$.
3. The negation of the conclusion in conjunctive normal form is $\neg S, \neg Q$.

Clauses:

1.	$\neg P \vee Q$	premise
2.	$R \vee P$	premise
3.	$\neg R \vee S$	premise
4.	$\neg S \wedge \neg Q$	negation of conclusion
5.	$\neg S$	$\wedge$-elimination
6.	$\neg Q$	$\wedge$-elimination
7.	$R \vee Q$	(1), (2), resolution
8.	$\neg R$	(3), (5)
9.	Q	(7), (8)
10.	NIL	(6), (9)

Let us interpret the propositions in Example 2 as follows:

P: program does not terminate
Q: alarm rings forever
R: computer in not intelligent
S: computer runs forever

Now, the axioms are interpreted as follows:

1. If the program does not terminate, then the alarm rings forever.
2. Either the computer is not intelligent or the program does not terminate.

From this reasoning, we formulate a theorem: if "the computer runs forever" is implied by the fact that it is not intelligent, then either the computer runs forever, or the alarm rings forever. □

9.3
Consistency and Completeness

Propositional logic is both consistent and complete:

1. **Consistency or Soundness**—All provable statements are semantically true. That is, if a set of premises S syntactically entails a proposition P, then there is an interpretation in which P can be reasoned about from S. Formally, if $S \vdash P$, then $S \models P$. In particular, every theorem is a tautology.
2. **Completeness**—All semantically true statements are provable. That is, if a set of premises S semantically entails a proposition P, then P can be derived formally (syntactically) within the formalism. Formally, if $S \models P$, then $S \vdash P$.

There are two important consequences of completeness:

1. **Compactness**—If $S \models P$, then there is a finite subset S', $S' \subseteq S$ such that $S' \models P$.
2. **Decidability**—Given a finite set of propositions S and a proposition P, there is an algorithm which determines whether or not $S \models P$.

When a specification S is created within the propositional logic formalism, the decidability result confirms that S can be analyzed to demonstrate whether a property P holds in S or not. In Example 3, a set of requirements for checking out a book from a library is specified and analyzed for certain properties.

Example 3 The requirements for borrowing and returning a specific book from a school library are first stated informally and then formalized in propositional logic. The book can be in any one of the following four states: *on_stack*, *on_reserve*, *on_loan*, and *requested*. These are modeled by the propositions

- S—the book is on the stacks
- R—the book is on reserve
- L—the book is on loan
- Q—the book is returned

The constraints are

1. The book can be in only one of the three states S, R, L.
2. If the book is returned then it is on the stacks or on the reserve.

The propositional logic formulas for the constraints are:

1. $S \Rightarrow \neg(R \vee L)$
2. $R \Rightarrow \neg(S \vee L)$
3. $L \Rightarrow \neg(S \vee R)$
4. $Q \Rightarrow S \vee R$

Transforming the above formulas into CNF, we get the following four clauses:

1. $\neg S \vee \neg R$
2. $\neg S \vee \neg L$
3. $\neg R \vee \neg L$
4. $\neg Q \vee S \vee R$

We can derive the clauses shown in the table below.

(c1)	$\neg Q$	from (1) and (4)
(c2)	$\neg Q \vee \neg L \vee S$	from (2) and (4)
(c3)	$\neg Q \vee \neg R \vee S$	from (3) and (4)

No further clauses can be derived by resolution. Thus the empty clause cannot be derived and the set of formulas describing the requirements are satisfiable. Hence, the requirements are consistent.

Suppose we want to prove that the statement "if a book is on loan then it is not returned" is a consequence of the requirements. This is achieved by including the negation of the formula $L \Rightarrow \neg Q$ in the premises and applying the steps of the resolution principle to the clauses. Resolving $\neg(\neg L \vee \neg Q)$ with the premise we get the two additional clauses

(c4)	L
(c5)	Q

From (c1) and (c5) we derive the empty clause NIL. Hence the statement "if a book is on loan then it is not returned" is true in the model.   □

9.4
Exercises

1. Give a proof based on natural deduction for each of the following claims:
   (a) $(P \wedge Q) \wedge R \vdash P \wedge (Q \wedge R)$
   (b) $(P \vee Q) \wedge (P \vee R) \vdash P \vee (Q \vee R)$
   (c) $P \wedge (Q \Leftrightarrow R) \vdash (P \wedge Q) \Leftrightarrow (P \wedge R)$
   (d) $\vdash (P \Rightarrow (Q \Rightarrow R)) \Leftrightarrow ((P \wedge Q) \Rightarrow R)$
   (e) $(\neg P \Rightarrow Q) \wedge (R \Rightarrow (S \vee T) \wedge (R \Rightarrow \neg S) \wedge (P \Rightarrow \neg S) \vdash R \Rightarrow Q$

2. Use Proof by Resolution to prove

$$R \Rightarrow P \lor Q, \neg(R \land Q) \vdash R \Rightarrow P$$

3. In a departmental store, a cell phone is either in stock or out of stock. If it is in stock then either it can be put on display or it can be sold. A display model cannot be sold. A sold cell phone may be returned. A returned phone cannot be put on display, instead it is added to the stock. A cell phone can be in only one possible state at any instant. Give propositions for formalizing the constraints on cell phone and determine whether or not the stated requirements for selling a cell phone are consistent.

4. A formula ϕ is stronger than formula ψ if in every interpretation $\phi \Rightarrow \psi$ is true and $\psi \Rightarrow \phi$ is false. Which of the following statements are true?

   - $P \land Q \Rightarrow P$ is stronger than $P \lor Q$
   - $P \lor Q$ is stronger than $P \land Q$
   - $P \Rightarrow (Q \Rightarrow R)$ is stronger than $P \land Q \Rightarrow R$
   - $P \Rightarrow R$ is stronger than $(P \Rightarrow Q) \land (P \land Q \Rightarrow R)$

5. Given a propositional logic formula Ψ and an interpretation I that assigns a truth value for every proposition $P \in \Psi$. Write an abstract program that evaluates G under I.

9.5
Bibliographic Notes

Without logic it is hard to imagine the existence of computers and software systems. The impact of logic on programming and databases is discussed in [2], and different kinds of logics for modeling and reasoning in Artificial Intelligence is discussed in [3]. For a concise description of propositional logic, see the book by Priest [4].

Logic is at the core of rational thinking and human inference. Propositional logic is a simple vehicle to introduce basic properties of objects. A property, stated as an atomic statement, cannot be validated in the logic. Instead, propositional logic allows us to evaluate the validity of compound statements given the validity of its atomic components. Thus, a conclusion whose value is true may be drawn from an invalid statement or argument, and one whose value is false, from a valid sequence. Relational properties and properties of a collection of objects cannot be expressed in propositional logic.

References

1. Barwise J, Etchemendy J (1995) The language of first-order logic, 3rd edn. Center for the Study of Language and Information, Stanford
2. Grant J, Minker J (1992) The impact of logic programming and databases. Commun ACM 35(3):67–81
3. Hueth M (2004) Logic in computer science: modelling and reasoning about systems, 2nd edn. Cambridge University Press, Cambridge
4. Priest G (2000) LOGIC—a very short introduction. Oxford University Press, London

Predicate Logic

10

Although assertions can be combined in propositional logic, an intrinsic relationship to the primitive propositions cannot be stated. In this chapter, we introduce the first-order predicate logic with equality in which the intrinsic relationship of objects, and their attributes can be formalized. Formulas can be interpreted over structures rather than on simple values.

A predicate is a property or a relation that holds between individual objects within a specified world. Besides, operations are defined in predicate logic such that the result of an operation performed on one or more objects is an object in the same world. An example of operation on a set of individuals is "father-of". Because objects in the world can be individually or collectively accessed, we can make assertions about one or more objects in the world.

Predicate logic, like propositional logic, uses symbols to represent knowledge. These symbols represent *constants*, *predicates*, *variables*, and *functions*. A constant, such as *computer*, or *mary*, or *dense*, is intended to represent a specific object in the world or a specific property in the problem domain. A function symbol denotes an operation that may be performed on a (sequence of) individual objects to yield another object. A predicate symbol denotes a property or relation that holds for (a sequence of) individual objects. Every function and predicate symbol has an *arity*, indicating the number of arguments it requires. In addition, a symbol may be a variable intended to denote different individual objects.

Informally, the syntactic structure of a predicate is analogous to a parameterized procedure. It has a name and a set of arguments, which may be constants, variables, or functions. When the arguments are given values from certain domains, the predicate becomes a proposition which can be assigned true or false under a certain model. For example, $mammal(x)$ is a *unary* predicate. When the variable x is initialized to a *value* from the universe of mammals, the predicate $mammal(x)$ evaluates to true; for all other values of x, the predicate evaluates to false. Predicates having n-arguments express a certain relationship among the n objects modeled by the arguments. For example, $lessthan(a, b)$, $parent(x, y)$, $likes(a, b)$, and $ancestor(x, y)$ express binary relations; the predicate $quotient(a, b, c)$ defined by $c = a \ div \ b$ captures the ternary relation that c is the quotient when b divides a. The predicate $friends(father(x), mother(y))$ states that the father of x and the mother of y are friends. Here, *father* and *mother* are function symbols. All propositions are predicates.

V.S. Alagar, K. Periyasamy, *Specification of Software Systems*,
Texts in Computer Science,
DOI 10.1007/978-0-85729-277-3_10, © Springer-Verlag London Limited 2011

10.1
Syntax and Semantics

We assume the existence of predefined domains, *IDENTIFIER*, *VARNAME*, and *CONSTANT*. An uppercase letter $P \in IDENTIFIER$ denotes a predicate name, a lower case letter $f \in IDENTIFIER$ denotes a function name, and lower case letters $x \in VARNAME$ and $c \in CONSTANT$, respectively, denote a variable and a constant. Although some or all of the domains may be infinite, only a finite number of symbols from them will be used in constructing the predicate logic.

The formal language of predicate logic consists of *terms* and *well-formed formulas* (wff) or *well-formed expression*. The syntax of predicate logic defines terms and well-formed formulas. Terms are constants, variables, and functions $f(t_1, \ldots, t_k)$, where f is a function symbol, and t_is are terms. Formally, terms are recursively defined, as below.

$$t ::= x \mid c \mid f(t_1, t_2, \ldots, t_n)$$

An expression $P(t_1, \ldots, t_n)$ where P is a predicate symbol of arity n, and $t_1, \ldots, t_n$ are terms is a well-formed formula. In general, a well-formed formula ϕ is recursively defined as shown below.

$$\phi ::= P(t_1, \ldots, t_n) \mid (\neg \phi) \mid (\phi \wedge \phi) \mid (\phi \vee \phi) \mid (\phi \Rightarrow \phi) \mid (\forall x \phi) \mid (\exists x \phi)$$

The symbols $\forall$ (for all) and $\exists$ (exists) are quantifiers. Both quantifiers and negation ($\neg$) bind most tightly in the expressions. Some examples of well-formed formulas of predicate logic are

$\forall x \bullet \exists y \bullet (less(square(x), y))$,
$\forall x \bullet \forall y \bullet (likes(x, y) \Rightarrow marry(x, y))$,
$\exists x \bullet \exists y \bullet (airline(x) \wedge city(y) \wedge flies(x, y))$,
$\forall x \bullet \exists y, z \bullet (airline(x) \wedge city(y) \wedge city(z) \wedge flies(x, y) \wedge flies(x, z) \Rightarrow (y = z))$.

The last formula above asserts that every airline x flies to only one city. The meta symbol $\exists!$ may be used as a short hand to express uniqueness. That is, $\forall x \bullet \exists! y \bullet (airline(x) \wedge city(y) \wedge flies(x, y))$ expresses the same fact as the last formula above.

Constants, which are simple proposition symbols, and connectives are interpreted as in propositional logic. Each n-ary predicate is a boolean n-ary relation, with the name of the predicate usually designating a real-world object. Predicates are always used with the exact number of arguments. The existential ($\exists$) and universal ($\forall$) quantifiers are used for contextual binding. The domain of interest for which a variable is bound can be made explicit. The occurrences of x, y in the predicate $\forall x : jobs \bullet \exists y : queues \bullet (\neg executing(x) \Rightarrow has(y, x))$ are *bound*. In the formula $\exists y \bullet on(x, y)$, the variable y is bound but x is "free". Formulas in which every variable is bound are called *closed* formulas. Every closed formula can be interpreted as a proposition.

10.1.1
Semantics

The *meaning* to predicates and function symbols is assigned relative to a nonempty domain D. This domain is assumed to include all values that can be assigned to all variables in the language. The *interpretation* of an n-ary predicate p is a function that takes an assignment of values to the n arguments of p and returns *true* or *false*. An interpretation for a formula F assigns values to each free variable in F, and interprets each predicate in the formula as above. Thus, the meaning of a formula is an assignment of a truth value for each interpretation. The meaning of a formula is derived from the meanings of its subformulas:

1. If the formula is an atomic predicate $p(t_1, \ldots, t_n)$, the terms t_i are constants or free variables, the chosen interpretation assigns values to the variables, and then evaluates the predicate to *true* or *false*.
2. If the formula involves functions, these are evaluated to reduce the arguments of the predicates to constants before the predicate is evaluated.
3. An expression $E = E_1 \ op \ E_2$, where E_1 and E_2 are unquantified, is *inductively* evaluated — E_1 and E_2 are evaluated under the chosen interpretation and the semantics of op is applied to their truth values.
4. In an expression E of the form $\forall x \bullet E_1$, E_1 is evaluated and if the truth value remains the same for every value in the domain of interpretation, then E is *true*; otherwise E is *false*.
5. In an expression E of the form $\exists x \bullet E_1$, the domain of interpretation for E_1 is obtained by assigning a value from the domain of interpretation for E to x, and is used to evaluate E_1 inductively. If there exists at least value one value of x for which this process evaluates E_1 to true, the formula E also evaluates to *true*; otherwise, E evaluates to *false*.

Example 1 Consider the following predicate logic formula:

$$G(x, y) \Rightarrow \exists z \bullet (G(x, z) \wedge G(z, y))$$

We discuss four different interpretations for the predicate G.

Interpretation I_1

1. The domain D is the set of integers.
2. $G(r, s)$ is *true* if $r > s$.

The interpretation assigns to G the infinite collection of ordered pairs on integers (r, s), such that $r > s$.

  For this interpretation, the formula states that for any pair of integers x and y, if $x > y$, then there is some other integer z with the property $x > z$ and $z > y$. That is, z strictly lies between y and x. If $x = y$ or $y > x$, then $G(x, y)$ is *false*, and consequently, the formula is *true*. If $x = y + 1$, $G(x, y)$ is *true*; however, there is no integer z in between y and $x = y + 1$; hence, the formula has the value *false*. The formula is true for all interpretations, except when $x = y + 1$.

Interpretation I_2

1. The domain D is the set of positive integers.
2. The predicate $G(r, s)$ is true whenever r is a divisor of s.

For this interpretation, the formula states that for any pair of integers x and y, if x is a divisor of y, then there is some $z \in D$ with the property that x is a divisor of z, and z is a divisor of y. For $x > y$, the predicate $G(x, y)$ is *false*, and consequently, the formula is *true*. For some pair of positive integers x, y, $x \le y$, assume that $G(x, y)$ is *true*. The formula states that there is some positive integer z such that x divides z and z divides y. That is, z satisfies three properties:

- $x < z < y$;
- x divides z and y;
- z divides y.

If $x = 8$, $y = 24$, $G(x, y)$ is *true*, but there is no z satisfying the above three conditions. However, if $x = 4$, $y = 24$, $G(x, y)$ is *true*, and there exists $z = 8$ for which $G(x, z)$ and $G(z, y)$ are both *true*, and hence the formula is true. In general, the formula is false for some pairs (x, y), and is true for some other pairs (x, y). It is important to note that there are only a finite number of interpretations for the formula, because only finite number of values can be assumed by z in between x and y.

Interpretation I_3

1. The domain D is the set of real numbers.
2. $G(x, y)$ is true whenever $x \ge y$.

In between any two real numbers, there are infinitely many real numbers. Hence, the formula is true for all pairs x, y of real numbers. That is, there are infinitely many interpretations for the formula based on any pair of values assigned to the variables x, y of predicate G.

Interpretation I_4

This interpretation is based on natural numbers and their cartesian products.

1. $D = N \cup E$, where N is a subset of natural numbers, and $E = N \times N$.
2. The predicate $G(x, y)$ is *true*, if $x \le y \wedge (x, y) \in E$.

Under this interpretation, the formula states that if $(x, y) \in E$, then for some $z \in N$ the pairs (x, z), $x \le z$, and (z, y), $z \le y$ also belong to E. If we choose

$$N = \{1, 2, 3\}, \quad \text{and} \quad E = \{(1, 2), (1, 3), (2, 3)\}$$

then the formula is *true* for $x = 1$, $y = 3$, and $z = 2$. For several other assignments, such as $x = 2$, $y = 1$, and $z = 3$, the formula is *false*. In general, the formula is *true* if the free variables are assigned values from the domain $\{x, y : \mathbb{R} | x \le y\}$.   □

10.2
Validity, Equality, and Equivalence

An interpretation of a well-formed formula is called a *model* if the well-formed formula is true under that interpretation. A well-formed formula is *valid* if the formula is true under all interpretations. A formula is *invalid* if it is not valid. An example of a valid formula is $\exists y \bullet \forall x \bullet P(x, y) \Rightarrow \forall x \bullet \exists y \bullet P(x, y)$. An example of an invalid formula is $\exists x \bullet P(x) \Rightarrow \forall x \bullet P(x)$. To determine the validity of a first-order formula, normal forms are helpful. We discuss normal forms in Sects. 10.3 and 10.4.2.

A well-formed formula is *satisfiable* if there exists a model for it. All valid formulas are satisfiable, while some invalid formulas may be satisfiable. A well-formed formula is a *contradiction* or *unsatisfiable* if and only if it is false under all interpretations. In particular, a negation of a valid formula is unsatisfiable.

In software engineering, we use predicate logic formalism to formalize requirements, their properties, make assertions on state variables, and formally state invariant properties of the application domain. That is, in software engineering, a model is built "from outside the logic into the logic formalism", whereas in mathematical logic, a model is sought "from inside the logic to outside the logical realm". Keeping this distinction in mind, we affirm that formulas constructed by a software engineer are the software engineer's models of system requirements and the domain of interpretation of the logical formulas is the application domain in which the requirements arise. Thus for requirements specification using predicate logic, we may define the notions satisfiability and validity as follows:

- A formula in the specification is *satisfiable* if it can be interpreted to match a requirement in the requirements document.
- A formula in the specification is *valid* if it satisfies the stated properties in the application domain.
- A formula is *invalid* if it fails to satisfy the stated properties in the application domain.
- A formula is *contradictory* if its interpretation matches some requirements and fails to satisfy some others in the requirements document.

10.2.1
Equality and Equivalence

We introduce the binary infix predicate $=$ in the predicate logic. If s and t are terms, then $(s = t)$ is an atomic formula which may be true or false. This predicate satisfies the following equational axioms:

1. **Reflexivity** $\forall x \bullet x = x$;
2. **Commutativity** $\forall x, y \bullet (x = y) \Rightarrow (y = x)$;
3. **Transitivity** $\forall x, y, z \bullet ((x = y) \wedge (y = z)) \Rightarrow (x = z)$;

The operation of substituting one variable for another is a common practice in mathematics. In predicate logic, this must be done with some care. Formally, if S is a formula, t a term and x a variable, we define $S[t/x]$ (read "S with t for x") to be the formula obtained from S on replacing every free occurrence of x by t, provided no free variable of t is bound in S. If some free variable of t is bound in S, then each bound variable must be renamed so that it is not bound in S. When the substitution $[x/y]$ is applied to the formula $S : \forall x \bullet (x > 4) \wedge (y^2 = 4x) \Rightarrow (x > y)$, the bound variable x needs to be renamed, say to w, and then y is replaced by x in S. The expression $S[x/y]$ is $\forall w \bullet (w > 4) \wedge (x^2 = 4w) \Rightarrow (w > x)$.

Two formulas F and G are *equivalent*, written as $F \equiv G$, if they have the same truth value for all interpretations that are suitable for both F and G. If $F \equiv G$, and $x = y$, where x is a free variable in F and y is a free variable in G, then $F[t/x] \equiv G[t/y]$. That is, equivalent formulas remain equivalent when free terms in them that are equal are replaced by the same variable.

Example 2 We describe a predicate logic theory with equality for a projective plane in which lines and points satisfy the following properties: (1) two lines meet at a unique point, and (2) there is a unique line through any two points. A formula in extending this theory, in order to be valid, should not contradict any of the stated formulas.

The unary predicates *point*(x) (x is a point) and *line*(x) (x is a line) introduce points and lines. The binary predicate *lies_on*(x, y) relates the incidence property of point x to line y. The predicate logic formulas enforcing the properties are:

1. *domain distinction*
   (a) $\forall x \bullet (point(x) \vee line(x))$;
   (b) $\forall x \bullet (\neg(point(x) \wedge line(x)))$;
2. *incidence*
   $\forall x, y \bullet (lies\_on(x, y) \Rightarrow (point(x) \wedge line(y)))$;
3. *equality for lines*
   $\exists x_1, x_2 \bullet (\neg(x_1 = x_2) \wedge lies\_on(x_1, y_1) \wedge lies\_on(x_1, y_2) \wedge lies\_on(x_2, y_1) \wedge lies\_on(x_2, y_2)) \Rightarrow y_1 = y_2$;
4. *unique line*
   $\forall x, y \bullet ((point(x) \wedge point(y) \wedge \neg(x = y)) \Rightarrow \exists! z \bullet (lies\_on(x, z) \wedge lies\_on(y, z)))$;
5. *unique intersection*
   $\forall x, y \bullet ((line(x) \wedge line(y) \wedge \neg(x = y)) \Rightarrow \exists! z \bullet (lies\_on(z, x) \wedge lies\_on(z, y)))$.

$\square$

In Example 3, some truth-functional properties of a light switch are described in predicate logic. In doing it, the following points on translating natural language requirements are clarified.

- *temporal relations*: Words such as "sometimes", and "during" refer to the existence of some times at which a predicate is true of the objects of concern. Choose natural numbers for modeling discrete time and real numbers to model continuous time.
- *not both vs both not*: If we say that P and Q are "not both" true we need $P \wedge Q$ to be false. If we say that P and Q are "both not" true then both P and Q are false.
- *universe of discourse*: Quantifiers implicitly refer to objects in the universe of discourse defined for the model. In actual expressions, explicit reference to the universe of discourse may be absent.

- *quantification*: Universally quantified expressions typically involve conditionals. Existentially quantified *negated* conditionals are acceptable; however, existentially quantified conditionals should be avoided.
- *bound variables*: Bind all variables.

Example 3 This example specifies the sequence of discrete events affecting a light switch. A switch can be on or off at different times of a day. The status of the switch cannot be both on and off at the same time. Let $switch\_on(x)$ and $switch\_off(x)$ be predicates denoting that the status of the switch is on, and off, respectively, at time x. The universe of discourse is the same as domain of interpretation which is discrete time, assumed to be the set of natural numbers. Consequently, in any finite interval, there can be only a finite number of state changes for the switch. A translation of the requirements into predicate logic is given below:

1. The switch is in only one state at any time.
   (a) $\forall x \bullet (switch\_on(x) \lor switch\_off(x))$;
   (b) $\forall x \bullet \neg(switch\_on(x) \land switch\_off(x))$.
2. The predicate $on(x, y)$ denotes the property that the switch is on at the time points $x, x + 1, \ldots, y - 1$. The predicate $off(x, y)$ denotes the property that the switch is off at the time points $x, x + 1, \ldots, y - 1$.
   (a) $on(x, y) \equiv switch\_on(x) \land \neg\exists z \bullet (lessthan(x, z) \land lessthan(z, y) \land switch\_off(z))$;
   (a) $off(x, y) \equiv switch\_off(x) \land \neg\exists z \bullet (lessthan(x, z) \land lessthan(z, y) \land switch\_on(z))$.
3. If the state of the switch is on (off) at time y and the previous time it was in the same state was at time x, then the switch stays off (on) throughout the interval (x, y).
   a. $\forall x, y \bullet (switch\_on(x) \land switch\_on(y) \land lessthan(x, y)) \land \neg\exists z \bullet (switch\_on(z) \land lessthan(x, z) \land lessthan(z, y)) \Rightarrow off(x + 1, y)$;
   b. $\forall x, y \bullet (switch\_off(x) \land switch\_off(y) \land lessthan(x, y)) \land \neg\exists z \bullet (switch\_off(z) \land lessthan(x, z) \land lessthan(z, y)) \Rightarrow on(x + 1, y)$.
4. The predicate $from\_off\_to\_on(u_1, v_2)$ denotes the property that the switch is off at time u_1, and on at time v_2, where $u_1 < v_2$, and either (1) the switch remained off for the time points $u_1, u_1 + 1, \ldots, v_2 - 1$, or (2) every switch on is followed by a switch off in the interval (u_1, v_2). The predicate $from\_on\_to\_off(u_1, v_2)$ denotes the complementary property for the switch, when it is on at time u_1 and off at time v_2. We define the predicate $off\_on(u_1, v_2)$ to denote the property that every switch on is followed by a switch off, and the predicate $on\_off(u_1, v_2)$ to denote the property that every switch off is followed by a switch on and use them in defining the two predicates $from\_off\_to\_on$, and $from\_on\_to\_off$.
   (a) $off\_on(u_1, v_2) \equiv \exists v_1, u_2 \bullet (lessthan(u_1, v_1) \land lessthan(v_1, u_2) \land lessthan(u_2, v_2) \land off(u_1, v_1) \land off(u_2, v_2) \land on\_off(v_1, u_2))$;
   (b) $on\_off(v_1, u_3) \equiv \exists u_2, v_2 \bullet (lessthan(v_1, u_2) \land lessthan(u_2, v_2) \land lessthan(v_2, u_3) \land on(v_1, u_2) \land on(v_2, u_3) \land off\_on(u_2, v_2))$;
   (c) $from\_off\_to\_on(x, y) \equiv switch\_on(y) \land (off((x, y) \lor off\_on(x, y)))$;
   (d) $from\_on\_to\_off(x, y) \equiv switch\_off(y) \land (on(x, y) \lor on\_off(x, y))$.
5. If the state of the switch is on (off) at times x and y, $x \geq y$, then either it is on (off) throughout $[x, y]$ or every switch off (on) is followed by a switch on (off) in the interval $[x, y]$. The predicates $on\_on(x, y)$, and $off\_off(x, y)$ denote these properties.

(a) $on\_on(x, y) \equiv on(x, y) \vee \exists z \bullet (on\_off(x, z) \wedge off\_on(z, y))$;

(b) $off\_off(x, y) \equiv off(x, y) \vee \exists z \bullet (off\_on(x, z) \wedge on\_off(z, y))$.

□

10.3
More on Quantified Expressions

In writing predicate logic expressions for requirements, multiple quantifiers are often necessary. For example, the requirement "all printing jobs are assigned to one printer queue" can be translated to

$$\forall j : JOBS \bullet \exists p : PRINTERQUEUE \bullet assign(j, p)$$

To simplify the presentation of formulas, where the types of variables are obvious, the reference to types may be omitted. Thus,

$$\forall j \bullet \exists p \bullet assign(j, p)$$

is a shorthand for the formula above. Whenever all variables in a formula are universally quantified, the quantifiers may be dropped altogether from the presentation of the formula. For example, $\forall x, y \bullet P(x, y)$ is a closed formula, and can be written $P(x, y)$. Universal (existential) quantifier is a generalized conjunction (disjunction) operator. Consequently, negation can be moved in and out of quantified formulas by generalizing de Morgan's laws applicable to conjunction and disjunction. To enhance understandability, quantifiers can be interchanged or moved in front of a formula. Rules governing the movement of quantifiers are summarized below:

1. Moving negation out of quantifiers:
   (a) $\neg\forall x \bullet P(x) \equiv \exists x \bullet \neg P(x)$
   (b) $\neg\forall x \bullet \neg P(x) \equiv \exists x \bullet P(x)$
   (c) $\forall x \bullet \neg P(x) \equiv \neg\exists x \bullet P(x)$
   (d) $\forall x \bullet P(x) \equiv \neg\exists x \bullet \neg P(x)$
2. Driving quantifiers in front—If x does not occur free in Q then the following equivalences hold:
   (a) $\forall x \bullet P \wedge Q \equiv \forall x \bullet (P \wedge Q)$
   (b) $\forall x \bullet P \vee Q \equiv \forall x \bullet (P \vee Q)$
   (c) $\exists x \bullet P \wedge Q \equiv \exists x \bullet (P \wedge Q)$
   (d) $\exists x \bullet P \vee Q \equiv \exists x \bullet (P \vee Q)$
3. Moving quantifiers out—The following equivalences hold when x is bound in both P and Q:
   (a) $(\forall x \bullet P \wedge \forall x \bullet Q) \equiv \forall x \bullet (P \wedge Q)$
   (b) $(\exists x \bullet P \vee \exists x \bullet Q) \equiv \exists x \bullet (P \vee Q)$
4. Interchanging the order of quantification:
   (a) $(\forall x \bullet \forall y \bullet P) \equiv (\forall y \bullet \forall x \bullet P)$
   (b) $(\exists x \bullet \exists y \bullet P) \equiv (\exists y \bullet \exists x \bullet P)$

The quantifier rules can be used to put expressions with multiple quantifiers in *prenex* normal form, in which all quantifiers come first. As an example, the requirement "every procedure used by a program is stored in a reuse directory" has the predicate logic translation

$$\forall x \bullet ((procedure(x) \wedge \exists y \bullet (program(y) \wedge used\_by(x, y)))$$

$$\Rightarrow \exists y \bullet (reuse\_direc(y) \wedge stored\_in(x, y))).$$

When the quantifier rules are applied, the predicate logic expression is transformed to

$$\forall x \bullet \exists y \bullet \exists z \bullet ((procedure(x) \wedge program(y) \wedge used\_by(x, y))$$

$$\Rightarrow (reuse\_direc(z) \wedge stored\_in(x, z))).$$

10.3.1
Policy Language Specification

First-order predicate logic is the basis for Prolog [7] language, Datalog [6] programming for deductive database systems, and for several policy languages [1, 2, 4, 5]. We illustrate a few specification examples for role based access controls from Cassandra [1]. Access controls for heterogeneous distributed systems, such as electronic health records which are distributed large-scale databases, cannot be entirely based on the identification and authorization of individuals. This is because subjects may change their roles, may share files and resources and may wish to collaborate. Cassandra is a high-level policy language which is expressive, flexible and formal. Its semantics is based on Datalog, which is a subset of Prolog and both Datalog and Prolog are based on predicate logic.

A request to access a record or perform an action, or play a role must be authorized by the system. Based upon the submitted *credentials* and the policies, the system must deduce the request as a consequence in order to grant a request; otherwise the request is denied. This deduction process is driven by the inference engine in Datalog, which is somewhat similar to the proof by resolution discussed in Sect. 10.4.2. The basic operations are encoded as predicates and five of these special predicates are listed below. Any other operation or request in the system will be authorized only if it can be reduced to a subset of these special predicates which in turn should be resolved to be true. In the examples below both predicates and variables are shown in *italics* and constants are shown in typewriter font.

1. *permits(e,a)* indicates that the entity *e* is permitted to perform action *a*. If it is possible to infer

   permits(Alice, download(Clinical))

   from the policy base then the access control engine will grant Alice to perform the action of downloading the requested file.

2. *canActivate(e,r)* indicates that the entity *e* can activate role *r*. The property

   CanActivate(`Alice, Technician(pediatrics, Royal Victoria)`)

   must be inferred in the system in order to validate the role of `Alice` as a `technician` in `pediatrics` lab of `Royal Victoria` hospital.
3. *hasActivated(e,r)* indicates that the entity *e* has successfully activated role *r*. If the property

   CanActivate(`Alice, Technician(pediatrics, Royal Victoria)`)

   is inferred in the system then

   hasActivated(`Alice, Technician(pediatrics, Royal Victoria)`)

   is true in the system, and can be added temporarily to the policy base. This fact will be removed from the system when `Alice` terminates her interaction with the system.
4. *canDeactivate(e_1,e_2,r)* indicates that the entity e_1 can deactivate role *r* of entities e_2, if e_2 is currently active in role *r*. If

   hasActivated(`Alice, Technician(pediatrics, Royal Victoria)`)

   is true and a superior `Bob` of *Alice* has the right in the system to suspend the role of *Alice* then

   canDeActivate(`Bob, Alice, Technician(pediatrics, Royal Victoria)`)

   can be inferred in the system.
5. *isDeactivated(e,r)* indicates an automatic revocation of role *r*, if *e* had been active in role *r*. If

   hasActivated(`Alice, Technician(pediatrics, Royal Victoria)`)

   is true a system trigger might deactivate the role of *Alice*, thus making

   deActivated(`Alice, Technician(pediatrics, Royal Victoria)`)

   true in the system.

The basic syntax in Cassandra for defining a policy *H* is *H* ← *B* where *H* is a predicate and *B* is a conjunction of predicates. A policy definition is a rule that has the interpretation "apply policy *H* whenever *B* is true". Cassandra uses Datalogic syntax with constraints, involving a few extensions to predicate logic syntax. For example, the language uses the symbol "," instead of the "∧" symbol. The significance of Cassandra language is the provision of a set of basic *policy Idioms*, which are templates that occur repeatedly in specifying different policies. Below is an extract from [1].

Auxiliary roles: A logged-in user can read a file provided that the system can deduce she is the owner of that file. Ownership is here expressed with the auxiliary `Owner` role that need not be activated.

permits(x, `Read`(*file*)) ←

   hasActivated(x, `Login`()),

      canActivate(x, `Owner`(*file*))

Role validity period: A certified doctor, with certification issued at time t, can act in the role Doc() for a maximum period of one year.

$canActivate(x, \text{Doc}()) \leftarrow$

$\quad canActivate(x, \text{CertDoc}(t)),$

$\qquad \text{CurTime}() - \text{Years}(1) \leq t \leq \text{CurTime}()$

Separation of duties: A payment transaction requires two phases, initiation and authorization. Those phases have to be executed by two different people. The rule implementing the separation of duties states that an Authoriser of a payment must not have activated the Initiator role for the same payment. This restriction is implemented by the user-defined *countInitiators* predicate. Its definition is given by the second rule below. The *count(z)* function counts how many different values of z satisfy the body. Therefore, the parameter n is 0 only if x has not activated the Initiator role for the same payment.

$canActivate(x, \text{Authoriser}(\textit{payment})) \leftarrow$

$\quad countInitiators(n, x, payment), n = 0$

$countInitiators(count(z), x, payment) \leftarrow$

$\quad hasActivated(z, \text{Initiator}(\textit{payment})), z = x$

Role delegation: An administrator can delegate her role to somebody else by activating the *DelegateAdm* role for the delegatee. The delegatee can then subsequently activate the administrator role. The first parameter of the administrator role specifies who the delegator was. The second parameter n is an integer for restricting the length of the delegation chain: the delegatee can activate the administrator role only with a "rank" n' that is strictly less than the delegator's rank n but must be at least 0.

$canActivate(x, \text{DelegateAdm}(y, n)) \leftarrow$

$\quad hasActivated(x, \text{Adm}(z, n))$

$canActivate(y, \text{Adm}(x, n')) \leftarrow$

$\quad hasActivated(x, \text{DelegateAdm}(y, n)), 0 \leq n' < n$

With the following rule, the delegated role is automatically revoked if the delegation role of the delegator is deactivated.

$isDeactivated(y, \text{Adm}(x, n')) \leftarrow$

$\quad isDeactivated(x, \text{DelegateAdm}(y, n))$

We also need to specify who is allowed to deactivate a delegation role. In the first rule below, only the delegator herself has this power. In the second rule below, every administrator, with at least as high rank as the delegator, can deactivate the delegation.

$canDeactivate(x, z, \text{DelegateAdm}(y, n)) \leftarrow x = z$

$canDeactivate(x, z, \text{DelegateAdm}(y, n)) \leftarrow$

$\quad hasActivated(x, \text{Adm}(w, n')), n \leq n'$

Automatic trust negotiation and credential discovery: The following rule is part of the policy of a server holding the electronic health records (EHR) for some part of the UK's population. To activate the doctor role, x must be a certified doctor in some health organization org, and the organization must be certified.

$canActivate(x, \text{Doc}(org)) \leftarrow$

   $auth{:}canActivate(x, \text{CertDoc}(org)),$

      $org \diamond auth{:}canActivate(org, \text{CertHealthOrg}()),$

   $auth \in \text{RegAuthorities}()$

In the rule above, there is no location prefix in front of the first body predicate, so the doctor certification credential is required to already be in the local policy or have been submitted by x together with the role activation request. On the other hand, there is a location prefix $org\diamond$ in front of the second body predicate. The health organization credential is automatically requested from org. However, the health organization will allow this retrieval request only if its *canReqCred* policy allows it. With the following rule, the health organization specifies that it is willing to reveal its CertHealthOrg credential to certified EHR servers.

$canReqCred(x, y.canActivate(z, \text{CertHealthOrg}())) \leftarrow$

   $x \diamond auth{:}canActivate(x, \text{CertEHRServ}()),$

      $z = \text{Royal Victoria},$

      $auth \in \text{RegAuthorities}()$

10.3.2
Knowledge Representation

Structured system analysis, a graphical technique introduced in the 1970s by DeMarco [9], uses informal descriptions to explain graphical representations, and data dictionaries to explain the meaning and representation of data to be used in the software development process. Predicate logic formulas can be used to formalize data dictionary definitions and their integrity constraints. More generally, predicate logic formalism can be used to represent *knowledge* and reason about the represented knowledge. In Artificial Intelligence [8], knowledge structures are more complex and more expressive forms of logic are required for their representation and reasoning. We illustrate, in Example 4, the use of predicate logic to express the meaning of data, their constraints, and ability to query on the represented information in database studies.

Example 4 Let us consider a snapshot of World Cup 2010 database, which includes information on players, coaches, teams, games, and schedules. This database is quite large and certainly more advanced database tools than predicate logic tools are necessary to manage data and respond to queries. The list of teams is defined by a predicate *team*(x). By

Table 10.1 A partial schedule of matches

Team	Team	Date	Venue
USA	Slovakia	18 June	Johannesburg
Slovakia	Italy	24 June	Johannesburg
Portugal	North Korea	21 June	Cape Town
Germany	Serbia	18 June	Port Elizabeth

instantiating x over all participating countries, we get a collection of propositions, which are *facts* about participating teams. That represents *teams* database. As an example the set of propositions *team(USA)*, *team(Portugal)*, *team(Slovenia)*, *team(Slovakia)*, *team(Italy)*, *team(North Korea)*, *team(Germany)*, and *team(Serbia)* is a representation of "knowledge" on teams participating in 2010 World Cup. Similarly, unary predicates *city(x)*, *date(x)*, *player(x)*, and *coach(x)* should be introduced to model the knowledge on venues, dates, players, and coaches for games in World Cup 2010. Instantiating each predicate over respective domains would give sets of propositions that model knowledge on venues, dates, players, and coaches.

A game is played when there exist two teams who play on a day in a city. Knowledge on a game is captured by the predicate *game(x, y, z, w)*, where x, y are teams, z is a date and w is a city. Table 10.1 shows a partial list of games played. Similar n-ary predicates should be defined to capture other relationship that will exist in the database.

Representing knowledge using predicates

1. *memberof(x,y)* indicates that the player x is a member of the team y.
2. *coach(x,y)* indicates that the coach of the team y is x.
3. *game(x,y,z,w)* indicates that the teams x and y play on the date z at the city w.
4. *schedule(x,y,z)* indicates that the team x is scheduled to play on the date y at the venue z.
5. *plays(x,y)* indicates that the player x is to play on the date y.

Specification of the integrity constraints on data

1. A player is a member of only one team in the league.
   $memberof(x, y) \land memberof(x, y') \Rightarrow y' = y$.
2. A coach coaches only one team; a team has only one coach.
   $coach(x, y) \land coach(x, y') \Rightarrow y = y'$.
   $coach(x, y) \land coach(x', y) \Rightarrow x = x'$.
3. A team plays at most one game a day.
   $schedule(x, y, z) \land schedule(x, y, z') \Rightarrow (z = z')$.
4. No player of a team can be the coach of the team.
   $memberof(x, y) \land \neg coach(x, y)$.
5. Every game played by a team should appear in the schedule.
   $game(x, y, z, w) \Rightarrow scedule(x, z, w) \land schedule(y, z, w)$.
6. For every game, there are some players who do not play on the day of the game.
   $game(x, y, z, w) \Rightarrow \exists p, q \bullet (memberof(p, x) \land memberof(q, y) \land \neg plays(p, z) \land \neg plays(q, z))$.
7. There are players in every team who do not play consecutively scheduled games.

$(schedule(x, y_1, z_1) \land schedule(x, y_2, z_2) \land \forall y \bullet ((y_1 < y) \land (y < y_2) \land \neg \exists z \bullet schedule(x, y, z))) \Rightarrow \exists p \bullet (member(p, x) \land \neg(plays(p, y_1) \land plays(p, y_2)))$.

Querying the knowledge base

Database queries can be answered by using logic and set notation. As an example, the set $\{x \mid plays(x, 10\,April)\}$ gives the set of players who play on 10 April. To know which teams play on 10 April, we need to use the universal quantifier on venue to gather teams that play at different venues. This is best achieved using the "resolution" principle discussed in Sect. 10.4.2. An alternative approach is to use set theory notation and define the set $CITY = \{c \mid city(c)\}$, and use it in defining the set

$$\bigcup_{\forall c \in CITY} \{x \mid schedule(x, 10\,April, c)\} \qquad\qquad \square$$

10.4
Proofs

To illustrate the generalization of the axiomatic deduction system of propositional logic, let us revisit Example 2 and reason about the claims. Let a, b, c be three distinct points. That is, $point(a), point(b), point(c), \neg(a = b), \neg(a = c), \neg(b = c)$ are true. From the incidence assertion and the generalized inference rule "from p and $(p \Rightarrow q)$ infer q", we deduce that there exists unique lines z_1, z_2, z_3 such that the points a and b lie on z_1, the points a and c lie on z_2, and the points b and c lie on z_3. From the uniqueness property stated in the incidence assertion, $z_1 \neq z_2, z_1 \neq z_3, z_2 \neq z_3$. In addition to such proof rules of propositional logic, the predicate logic contains rules to deal with equality and quantifiers.

We now discuss two proof methods: natural deduction, and resolution. An essential step in a proof is syntactic substitution, which is described in Sect. 10.2.1 under the heading *Equality and Equivalence*.

10.4.1
Natural Deduction Process

Natural deduction involves four inference rules that correspond to the elimination and introduction of quantifiers.

Rules for universal quantification

1. *Universal Generalization*

$$(\forall\text{-}Introduction) \qquad \frac{c \in X \vdash P(c)}{\forall x \bullet P(x)} \qquad \text{where } c \text{ is arbitrary.}$$

If we choose an arbitrary element c of the domain X and prove $P(c)$ then we can infer $\forall x \bullet P(x)$. For example, if for an arbitrary student from the domain of students, it is proved that the student is registered in at least one course, then this property holds for every student in the domain.

2. *Universal Instantiation*

(∀-*Elimination*) $$\frac{\forall x \in X \bullet P(x), c \in X}{P(c)}$$ where c is arbitrary.

If P holds for all elements of the domain X, then it is true for any arbitrary element of the domain. The conclusion states that P can be treated as a proposition. For example, if X is the domain of prime numbers satisfying the property that every number from X can be written in the form $2^p - 1$, where p is a prime, then a prime number p can be found for any arbitrary element of X.

Example 5 Given the premises $P(a)$ and $\forall x \bullet (P(x) \Rightarrow \neg Q(x))$, prove $\neg Q(a)$. The steps are as follows:

1. $P(a)$ premise
2. $\forall x \bullet (P(x) \Rightarrow \neg Q(x))$ premise
3. $P(a) \Rightarrow \neg Q(a)$ ∀-*Elimination* in step 2
4. $\neg Q(a)$ modus ponens, steps 1, 3

□

Rules for existential quantification

1. *Existential Generalization*

(∃-*Introduction*) $$\frac{c \in X, P(c)}{\exists x \in X \bullet P(x)}$$ where c is arbitrary.

The rule establishes a disjunction over the elements of X, the domain of interest. The first hypothesis is that the set X is not empty, and the second hypothesis is that the property holds for some element of X. For example,

$pigeon \in \{dolphin, cat, pigeon\} \wedge bird(pigeon) \vdash \exists x$

$\in \{dolphin, cat, pigeon\} \bullet bird(x)$.

2. *Existential Instantiation*

(∃-*Elimination*) $$\frac{\exists x \in X \bullet P(x)}{P(c)}$$ for some c in the domain of interest.

In practice, it may be difficult to determine the particular value c from the domain for which $P(c)$ holds.

Example 6 Given the premises $\exists x \bullet P(x)$ and $\forall x \bullet (P(x) \Rightarrow Q(x))$, prove $\exists x \bullet Q(x)$. The steps are as follows:

1. $\exists x \bullet P(x)$ premise
2. $\forall x \bullet (P(x) \Rightarrow Q(x))$ premise
3. $a, P(a)$ ∃-elimination in step 1
4. $P(a) \Rightarrow Q(a)$ ∀-*Elimination* in step 2
5. $Q(a)$ modus ponens, step 3, step 4
6. $\exists x \bullet Q(x)$ ∃-introduction in step 5

□

Example 7 This example models the behavior of a queue which always contains at least one item, and which is never full. The proof steps using universal elimination and existential generalization are shown. We will show that $\exists x \bullet (queued(x) \wedge next\_to(x, c))$ follows from the following three premises:

1. $\forall x \bullet (received(x) \Rightarrow queued(x))$: every message received is put in a queue.
2. $\forall x \bullet (queued(x) \Rightarrow next\_to(x, c))$: the received message is next to message c in the queue.
3. $received(m)$: message m is received.

The proof steps are:

1. Using universal elimination from the first two premises, derive
   (a) $received(m) \Rightarrow queued(m) \dots$ premises (1) and (3).
   (b) $queued(m) \Rightarrow next\_to(m, c) \dots$ premises (2) and (3).
2. Apply *modus ponens* to premise(3) and formula 1(a) to derive $queued(m)$.
3. Apply *modus ponens* to premise (2) and formula 1(b) to derive $next\_to(m, c)$
4. Apply $\wedge$- introduction rule to the results of steps (2) and (3) to derive
   $queued(m) \wedge next\_to(m, c)$.
5. Apply $\exists$- introduction rule to derive the conclusion
   $\exists x \bullet (queued(x) \wedge next\_to(x, c))$. $\square$

In Example 7, we can weaken the third premise to $\exists x \bullet received(x)$ and keep the other two premises. Still, we can obtain the same conclusion. The proof requires $\exists$-elimination in the third premise, in order to follow the proof steps shown above. In applying existential quantification, a name that is not already in use should be substituted for the quantified variable. Otherwise, the proof may conclude with an irrelevant result.

10.4.2
Resolution

The resolution principle for propositional logic is extended to deal with predicate logic by considering quantified expressions in *clausal forms* and using *unification*, a substitution method for variables to obtain resolvent.

10.4.2.1
Clausal Forms

In order to apply resolution principle to first-order logic, the formulas must be in clausal form. A clause is a disjunction of literals with no literal appearing twice, and no existential quantifier and all universal quantifiers are at the left. We may omit universal quantifiers and bullets in writing clausal forms. An empty clause, denoted *Nil*, is unsatisfiable. A unit clause contains just one literal. An example of a clause is

$$\forall x \forall y \forall z (P(x, z) \vee \neg Q(z) \vee R(y, z))$$

Existential quantifiers in a formula are removed by a process known as *skolemization*, which preserves satisfiability, but not validity. A variable x quantified by $\exists x \bullet$ which is not itself within the scope of a universal quantifier, is replaced by a new constant (called a *Skolem* constant) in the domain of interest. However, if $\exists x \bullet$ is within the scope of universal quantifiers, say $\forall y \forall z \bullet$, then x is replaced by $f(y, z)$ where the Skolem function f represents the existence of a unique x for every pair of y and z. The following examples illustrate existential quantifier elimination by skolemization.

Example 8 In this example variable naming is done before skolemization.

$\forall x \exists y$	$hasmother(x, y) \wedge \exists x \forall y \neg mother(y, x)$	given formula
$\forall x \exists y$	$hasmother(x, y) \wedge \exists w \forall z \neg mother(z, w)$	renaming
$\forall x$	$hasmother(x, f(x)) \wedge \forall z \neg mother(z, c)$	skolemization

□

Example 9 In this example implication is eliminated before skolemization.

$\forall x \exists y$	$person(x) \Rightarrow hasmother(x, y)$	given formula
$\forall x \exists y$	$\neg person(x) \vee hasmother(x, y)$	implication elimination
$\forall x$	$\neg person(x) \vee hasmother(x, mom(x))$	skolemization

□

After skolemizing a formula, it is transformed to *prenex* normal form, in which the universal quantifiers are at the left. As an example, the prenex normal form of the formula

$$\forall x[P(x) \vee [\forall y[P(y) \vee P(f(x, y))] \wedge [Q(y, g(y)) \wedge \neg P(g(y))]]]$$

is

$$\forall x \forall y[P(x) \vee [[P(y) \vee P(f(x, y))] \wedge [Q(y, g(y)) \wedge \neg P(g(y))]]]$$

The expression obtained by removing all the universal quantifiers in a prenex normal is called the *matrix* of the given formula. This matrix is transformed into a conjunctive normal form by applying distributive laws. As an example, applying the distributive laws to the matrix in the above prenex normal form we get

$$\forall x \forall y[[P(x) \vee P(y) \vee P(f(x, y))] \wedge [P(x) \vee Q(y, g(y))] \wedge [P(x) \vee \neg P(g(y))]]]$$

The three clauses in this expression are

$$\{\{P(x), P(y), P(f(x, y))\}, \{P(x), Q(y, g(y))\}, \{P(x), \neg P(g(y))\}\}$$

Example 10 illustrates a resolution proof of validity.

Example 10 To prove the validity of a formula using resolution principle, the negation of the formula is converted to a CNF expression and then show that the clauses do not contradict. Consider the formula

$$\forall x[P(x, f(x)) \Rightarrow \exists y P(y, a)]$$

The negation of the above formula is

$$\exists x[P(x, f(x)) \wedge \forall y \neg P(y, a)]$$

Eliminating $\exists x$ will introduce a skolem constant c in the prenex form:

$$\forall y[P(c, f(c)) \wedge \neg P(y, a)]$$

The matrix in the normal norm has the following clauses:

$$\{\{P(b, f(b))\}, \{\neg P(y, a)\}\}$$

These two clauses do not contradict in any substitution for the variable y. That is, there is no contradiction. Therefore, we conclude that the formula

$$\forall x[P(x, f(x)) \Rightarrow \exists y P(y, a)]$$

is valid. $\square$

10.4.2.2
Unification

The resolution method requires that clauses be transformed so that two literals of opposite sign will have identical atoms. However, atoms may contain variable parameters. In this case, they can be made identical only when transformed by suitable substitutions. The process of finding a substitution and applying it to the clauses to be resolved so that the atoms in complementary literals are identical, is called *unification*.

Unification is applied to clausal forms. So, the set of expressions to which unification is applied consists only of atomic formulas or terms. It is known that for a given set of clausal forms, there exists a *unique* most general unifier (mgu). The algorithms that computes the mgu for a set of clauses iteratively builds up the mgu, by finding substitutions for one variable at a time. Unification is necessary for a general proof by resolution. For example, applying the substitution [f(t)/x] to the clauses $\{P(x), \neg Q(x, y)\}$ and $\{\neg P(f(t))\}$ allow us to resolve them to obtain the resolvent $\neg Q(f(t), y)$. Suppose we have the clause $L(x, y), P(y, z), R(z, w) \Rightarrow S(x, w)$, and three known assertions L(1,3),P(3,5), R(5,7), then the substitution [1/x, 3/y, 5/z] gives the new assertion S(1,7). The proof steps in Example 11 illustrate how the unifier is found for resolving clauses.

Example 11 The formula

$$C_1 \wedge C_2 \wedge C_3 \wedge C_4 \wedge C_5 \wedge C_6 \wedge C_7,$$

where

$$
\begin{aligned}
C_1 &= Q(w) \vee \neg T(a, w), \\
C_2 &= \neg Q(v) \vee \neg P(v), \\
C_3 &= \neg Q(u) \vee \neg S(u), \\
C_4 &= R(u) \vee S(u) \vee P(g(u)), \\
C_5 &= R(u) \vee S(u) \vee T(u, g(u)), \\
C_6 &= Q(a), \\
C_7 &= \neg R(a),
\end{aligned}
$$

is not satisfiable.

Proof:
Using resolution, the proof steps are:

1.	$Q(a)$	clause C_6.
2.	$\neg Q(u) \lor \neg S(u)$	clause C_3.
3.	$\neg S(a)$	substitution [a/u] and applying resolution to steps 1 and 2.
4.	$R(u) \lor S(u) \lor P(g(u))$	clause C_4.
5.	$R(a) \lor P(g(a))$	substitution [a/u] and applying resolution to steps 3 and 4.
6.	$\neg R(a)$	clause C_7.
7.	$P(g(a))$	applying resolution to steps 5 and 6.
8.	$R(u) \lor S(u) \lor T(u, g(u))$	clause C_5.
9.	$S(a) \lor T(a, g(a))$	substitution [a/u] and applying resolution to steps 6 and 8.
10.	$T(a, g(a))$	applying resolution to steps 3 and 9.
11.	$Q(w) \lor \neg T(a, w)$	clause C_1.
12.	$Q(g(a))$	substitution [g(a)/w] and applying resolution to steps 10 and 11.
13.	$\neg Q(v) \lor \neg P(v)$	clause C_2.
14.	$\neg P(g(a))$	substitution [g(a)/v] and applying resolution to steps 12 and 13.
15.	*NIL*	applying resolution to steps 7 and 14.

□

10.4.3
Decidability

As in propositional logic, there is a distinction between what is *true* and what is *provable*. A statement that is true under all interpretations may or may not be provable using a certain proof method. Provability depends on the proof method used, such as natural deduction or resolution. However, predicate logic is both sound and complete with respect to interpretations:

the Soundness Theorem If $S \vdash p$, then $S \models p$. That is, if p is provable from S, then it is a true statement.

the Completeness Theorem If $S \models p$, then $S \vdash p$. Every statement that is true in all models is also provable from the rules and axioms of the proof method.

Whereas propositional logic is decidable, predicate logic is algorithmically *undecidable*. That is, showing the validity of expressions and proving the satisfiability of an arbitrary predicate logic formula are much harder, because one has to consider all possible meanings to terms from the underlying structure, which may be infinite. There are predicate logic formulas that are satisfiable, but they do not have any model of finite size. This limits the extent to which proofs can be automated. In particular, mechanical theorem provers may not be able to derive proofs for certain complex programs. Strong heuristics to select proof strategies and methods to avoid complex predicate expressions that lead to undecidability are both essential in designing theorem provers.

10.5
Axiomatic Specification Examples

An axiomatic specification involves assertions based on variables of concern bound to the specified object. In Anna specification language, axioms are annotations to Ada statements. The annotated program in Example 12 is taken from [12]. In it, package `searching` introduces a type *intarray* and some operations on it. Each line of annotations in Anna uses the symbols "-", "|". The symbols =, <, <=, >= respectively denote the mathematical notations for "equality", "less than", "less than or equal to", and "greater than or equal to". These symbols are chosen to distinguish between Ada operators and Anna annotations. Annotations are formal statements relating the semantics of the program to first-order sentences, called *verification conditions*. Proving that the verification conditions are true is sufficient to prove the correctness of programs. The proofs in [12] are carried out using Hoare–Floyd [10, 14] logic, which we discuss in the next section. The IN clause expresses an entry condition; in this case the values in array a is sorted from m to n. The RETURN clause constrains the value returned by the function, including any side effects stated in RAISE clause. If there is no side effect, the exit clause OUT is used in Anna. In Example 12, the RAISE clause means that if the program terminates without meeting the condition in RETURN clause then the signal not_present is issued.

Example 12 PACKAGE Searching

```
TYPE intarray IS ARRAY(integer) OF integer;
FUNCTION bin_search(a:intarray; m,n,x:integer;
   RETURN integer;
--|WHERE
--|    IN sorted(a,m,n);
--|    RETURN k such that
--|        k >= m and k <= n and a[k] = x;
--|    RAISE not_present <=> IN not present(x,a,m,n);
--|END WHERE
--|  ...


END searching;
```

□

10.5.1
Hoare's Notation

In the seminal paper [14], Hoare introduced an axiomatic method for computer programming. In this section, we briefly survey this notation for specifying some imperative programs. The notation of Hoare, as currently used, is $\{P\}S\{Q\}$ where

- S is a program from an imperative programming language, similar to the style of Pascal, and
- P and Q are conditions on the variables used in program S.

The expression $\{P\}S\{Q\}$ is a *specification* of program S. This specification is *correct*, equivalently the expression $\{P\}S\{Q\}$ is true, if an execution of S starting in a state satisfying the condition P terminates, and the state in which the program S terminates satisfies the condition Q. P is called the *precondition* and Q is called the *postcondition* of the expression $\{P\}S\{Q\}$. For $\{P\}S\{Q\}$ to be true, the termination of program S is not necessary. So specification $\{P\}S\{Q\}$ is called *partial*. By establishing partial correctness and termination of program S separately, one proves the *total* correctness of program S.

Specification $\{P\}S\{Q\}$ serves to construct formal proofs of partial correctness once we observe that $P \wedge S' \Rightarrow Q$, where S' is the logical version of S. The deductive system due to Hoare [14] achieves this by building up proofs for every programming construct and logically putting them together. The notation $\vdash S$ from logic is used to mean that program statement S has a proof. In general, a rule in Hoare logic is of the form

$$\frac{\vdash S_1, \ldots, \vdash S_n}{\vdash S}$$

where the hypotheses $S_1, \ldots, S_n$ may include some theorems from mathematics in addition to Hoare logic theorems.

The assignment axiom The assignment axiom asserts the correctness of the assignment statement $V := E$, where V is a program variable and E is a well-formed expression. It asserts the fact that the value of V in the state *after* executing the assignment statement equals the value of expression E in the state *before* executing it.

The assignment axiom
$\vdash \{P[E/V]\}V := E\{P\}$

In specification refinement, it is necessary to strengthen the precondition and weaken the postcondition. The rules for strengthening the precondition and weakening the postcondition in the specification axiom are

Precondition strengthening
$\dfrac{\vdash P \Rightarrow P', \vdash \{P'\}S\{Q\}}{\vdash \{P\}S\{Q\}}$
Postcondition weakening
$\dfrac{\vdash Q' \Rightarrow Q, \vdash \{P\}S\{Q'\}}{\vdash \{P\}S\{Q\}}$

Conjunction and disjunction of specifications Two specifications about the same program can be split or combined using the following rules.

Conjunction of specifications

$$\frac{\vdash \{P_1\}S\{Q_1\}, \vdash \{P_2\}S\{Q_2\}}{\vdash \{P_1 \wedge P_2\}S\{Q_1 \wedge Q_2\}}$$

Disjunction of specifications

$$\frac{\vdash \{P_1\}S\{Q_1\}, \vdash \{P_2\}S\{Q_2\}}{\vdash \{P_1 \vee P_2\}S\{Q_1 \vee Q_2\}}$$

In order to prove the claim $\vdash \{P_1 \vee P_2\}S\{Q\}$ using the disjunction rule, a proof for $\vdash \{P_1\}S\{Q\}$ may be attempted first, and if it fails then a proof for $\vdash \{P_2\}S\{Q\}$ must be carried out.

The sequencing axiom A sequential composition of two programs S_1 and S_2, denoted $S_1 \circ S_2$, is a program S which starts execution with S_1 and after its termination, continues execution of S_2. A partial specification for S is derived from specifications of S_1 and S_2.

Sequential composition of specifications

$$\frac{\vdash \{P\}S_1\{Q\}, \vdash \{Q\}S_2\{R\}}{\vdash \{P\}S_1 \circ S_2\{R\}}$$

The conditional axioms The specification of conditional programs are given below. Let U denote the statement *if C then S*, and V denote the statement *if C then S_1 else S_2*. Assume that $\{P\}S\{Q\}$ is a specification for program S.

Axiom for conditional specifications

$$\frac{\vdash \{P \wedge C\}S\{Q\}, \vdash \{P \wedge \neg C\} \Rightarrow Q}{\vdash \{P\}U\{Q\}}$$

$$\frac{\vdash \{P \wedge C\}S_1\{Q\}, \vdash \{P \wedge \neg C\}S_2\{Q\}}{\vdash \{P\}V\{Q\}}$$

The repetition axiom The *while* construct used to repeatedly execute a program uses a *loop invariant* for program termination. Let U denote the program *while C do S*, and $\{P\}$ be the invariant of S whenever C holds. If the condition P holds once the execution of S begins then it holds in every execution of S. This implies that P must hold for U to begin execution, $P \wedge C$ must hold to begin execution of S, P should hold during every execution including when program U stops execution, and $P \wedge \neg C$ must hold when program U terminates.

Axiom for while program

$$\frac{\vdash \{P \wedge C\}S\{P\}}{\vdash \{P\}U\{P \wedge \neg C\}}$$

We discuss two simple programs below illustrating partial correctness criteria.

Program Exchange Given $X = a \wedge Y = b$ in the initial state of the program *BEGIN Z :=* $X; X := Y; Y := Z$ *END*, we want to prove that after termination of the program the condition $X = b \wedge Y = a$ is true. Let $P : X = a \wedge Y = b$ and $Q : X = b \wedge Y = a$. Using the sequential composition rule, the result is established if we have proofs for $\vdash \{P\}S_1\{Q_1\}$, $\vdash \{Q_1\}S_2\{Q_2\}$, $\vdash \{Q_2\}S_3\{Q\}$ for suitable Q_1 and Q_2, where S_1, S_2 and S_3 are, respectively, the assignment statements $Z := X$, $X := Y$, and $Y := Z$. Applying the assignment axiom on the specification $\{Q_2\}S_3\{Q\}$, we derive $Q_2 : X = b \wedge Z = a$. Applying the assignment axiom on the specification $\{Q_1\}S_2\{Q_2\}$, we derive $Q_1 : Y = b \wedge Z = a$. Applying once again the assignment axiom on the specification $\{P\}S_1\{Q_1\}$, we derive $P : Y = b \wedge X = a$.

Program Division   Assume that $a \geq b$ and $b > 0$ are integers. The quotient q and remainder r when b divides a satisfies the equation $a = b \times q + r$, $0 \leq r < b$. A simple program that uses additions to achieve division is

```
BEGIN
r := a
q := 0
while b ≤ r
    BEGIN
        r := r − b; q := q + 1;
    END
END
```

The precondition for the program is $\{P' : a \geq b \wedge b > 0\}$. The postcondition to be verified is $Q : (a = b \times q + r) \wedge r < b$. The postcondition after executing the first two assignment statements is $r = a \wedge q = 0 \wedge a \geq b > 0$, which satisfies the condition $P : a = b \times q + r$, and the loop condition $C : b \leq r$. In order to prove $\{P \wedge C\}S\{P\}$, where S is the body of the loop, it is sufficient to prove that P is a loop invariant. It is necessary to distinguish between the values of the variables prior to and after an operation, and is done by suffixing the variables with a prime to denote their values in the state after the operation. The substitution rule supports the renaming of variables in assertions. Write P as $P(q, r)$ to explicitly show its variation with q and r. After one iteration of the loop $r' = r - b$ and $q' = q + 1$, where r', q' denote the post state variables of r, p. $P(q', r') : b \times q' + r' = b \times (q + 1) + (r - b) = b \times q + r = a$. This proves the claim that P is loop invariant. Applying the while axiom, we derive the postcondition $\{P \wedge \neg C\}$, which equals $a = b \times q + r$, $0 \leq r < b$.

The Hoare notation is widely used in specifying interface specifications [13], and in specifying acceptable behaviors of abstract datatype operations [15]. Example 13 uses this assertions style to formally describe the status of a sequential file system before and after execution of statements modifying its status.

Example 13 A *file* is assumed to be a linear sequence of *records*, where the notion of record is primitive. The records of the file are sequentially numbered from zero. Thus $file_0, file_1, \ldots, file_{k-1}$ are the k records of a file at any instance. If $k < 1$, the file is empty and $file_j, 0 \leq j \leq k - 1$, refers to the j-th record of the file. Let *position* denote the current position of a cursor which is considered to be between two adjacent records. There is a sequence of records, LP, to the left of *position*, and a sequence of records, RP, to the right of *position*. If *length* denotes the number of records in the file, the statement

$S(position) : 0 \leq position \leq length$

is an invariant assertion. That is, $S(position')$ is true after every operation affecting *position*.

EMPTY_FILE $position = 0 \wedge length = 0$

MOVE_LEFT The cursor is moved to the left end of the previous record; if the file is empty the operation has no effect.

> precondition : $position > 0$
> postcondition : $(position' = position - 1) \wedge$
> $(length' = length) \wedge (file' = file)$

MOVE_RIGHT The cursor is moved to the right end of the following record; if the cursor is already at the right end of the last record in the file, the operation has no effect.

> precondition : $position < length$
> postcondition : $(position' = position + 1) \wedge$
> $(length' = length) \wedge (file' = file)$

INSERT_RIGHT Insert a new record r in the file so that the sequence of records to the left of the new position is {LP} and the sequence of records to the right of the new position is $\{r, RP\}$.

> precondition : $position < length$
> postcondition : $(position' = position) \wedge (length' = length + 1) \wedge$
> $\forall p \bullet ((0 \leq p < position) \Rightarrow file'_p = file_p \wedge$
> $(p = position) \Rightarrow file'_p = r \wedge$
> $(position \leq p < length) \Rightarrow file'_{p+1} = file_p)$

INSERT_LEFT Insert a new record r in the file so that the sequence of records to the right of the new position is {RP} and the sequence of records to the left of the new position is {LP, r}. The postcondition is similar to the previous operation except that $position' = position + 1$. The precondition is $position \geq 0$.

DELETE_LEFT Delete the record r to the immediate left of the cursor. If the file is empty, or if the cursor is at the left end of the first record in the file, then the operation has no effect.

> precondition : $position \geq 1$
> postcondition : $(position' = position - 1) \wedge (length' = length - 1) \wedge$
> $\forall p \bullet ((0 \leq p < position') \Rightarrow file'_p = file_p \wedge$
> $(position' \leq p < length') \Rightarrow file'_p = file_{p+1})$

DELETE_RIGHT Delete the record r to the immediate right of the cursor. If the cursor is at the right end of the last record in the file, or if the file is empty, then the operation has no effect.

precondition : $0 \leq position < length$
postcondition : $(position' = position) \wedge (length' = length - 1) \wedge$
$$\forall p \bullet ((0 \leq p < position') \Rightarrow file'_p = file_p \wedge$$
$$(position' \leq p < length') \Rightarrow file'_p = file_{p+1})$$

□

10.6
Exercises

1. Consider the two formulas $\forall x \exists y P(x, y)$ and $\exists y \forall x P(x, y)$.

   - Give an interpretation for which both formulas are true.
   - Give an interpretation for which the first formula is true and the second formula is false.

2. For each formula below determine whether or not it is valid.
   (a) $\forall x P(x) \Rightarrow P(a)$.
   (b) $(\exists x P(x) \Rightarrow \forall x Q(x)) \Rightarrow \forall x (P(x) \Rightarrow Q(x))$.
   (c) $\forall x \exists y P(x, y) \Rightarrow \exists y \forall x P(x, y)$.
   (d) $\forall x (P(x) \vee Q(x)) \Rightarrow (\forall x P(x) \vee \forall x Q(x))$

3. Give rules in Cassandra style for the following actions:

   - Alice owns the file GRADES. She delegates the Read right to all those who rank higher than her in the system.
   - A person x delegates her role of Administrator() to y for a period of 30 days. During this period y can activate this role but cannot delegate that role to anybody else.
   - All students of Loyola University get 15% savings on books purchased in ABC Stores during the month of September. In order to benefit from this promotion, student credentials will be validated automatically by the system.
   - Allow the deactivation of Admin() role of a person if the person is playing that role currently and has activated any other role.

4. Prove or disprove the claims below, using (i) natural deduction, and (ii) proof by resolution.
   (a) The following premises are given:
      (i) $\forall x \bullet (student(x) \vee teacher(x))$
      (ii) $\forall x \bullet (student(x) \Rightarrow (tall(x) \wedge loves(c, x)))$
      (iii) $\forall x \bullet (\neg small(x) \Rightarrow teacher(x))$
      (iv) claim: $small(c)$
   (b) $\forall x \bullet P(x) \vdash \exists x \bullet \neg P(x)$
   (c) $\vdash \exists x \bullet (P(x) \Rightarrow \forall y \bullet P(y))$

    (d) $P(a, b) \wedge \forall x \bullet (\exists y \bullet P(y, x) \vee P(x, y) \Rightarrow P(x, x)) \vdash P(x, a)$

5. The statements given below relate to computer accounts for students. Translate each sentence into a predicate logic formula; then transform each formula into an equivalent prenex normal form; finally, give the equivalent CNF for each formula:

    (a) Every student has a unique user name and password.

    (b) Every student owns 200 MB of disk space.

    (c) No student can have two different disk spaces.

    (d) A student may erase the disk space he/she owns.

    (e) A student may give the disk space to some other student, but not to two students simultaneously.

    (f) A student who receives the disk space from another student cannot erase the contents of the disk space.

6. From the premises

    (a) $\forall x \bullet (P(x) \Rightarrow Q(x))$

    (b) $\forall x \bullet \neg Q(x)$

    prove that $\forall x \bullet \neg P(x)$.

7. A directed graph is a 3-tuple (V, E, I), where V is a finite set of vertices, E is a finite set of edges, and I is a set of assertions denoting the incidence relationships between vertices and edges. For every vertex $v \in V$, the predicate $vertex(v)$ is true, and for every edge $e \in E$, the predicate $edge(e)$ is true. The predicates $first(x, e)$ and $second(y, e)$ denote the properties that the edge e is directed from vertex x to vertex y. Give a set of axioms and/or rules to specify the following properties:

- There is a path from vertex x to vertex y.
- There is a path between every pair of vertices in the graph.
- There exists a path of length k from vertex x to vertex y.
- There exists a partition of V into V_1, V_2, and V_3 such that $V_1 \neq \emptyset$, $V_2 \neq \emptyset$, $V_3 = \{c\}$, $V_1 \cup V_2 \cup V_3 = V$, and every path between a member of V_1 and a member of V_2 passes through c.

8. Assume the relationship as stated in the Parent Database shown below.

Child	Parent
alice	bob
mary	bob
lisa	andrew
edward	smith
bob	charles
smith	philip
andrew	charles

    (a) Express the Parent Database knowledge as propositions.

    (b) Assuming the constraints

$$parent(x, y) \Rightarrow \neg parent(y, x)$$

$$parent(x, y) \wedge parent(y, z) \Rightarrow \neg grandparent(x, z)$$

    determine all grandparents in the database.

(c) Write rules in Cassandra style for enforcing the following policies:

- Every action permitted to be performed by a child can be performed by the parent, and not by the grandparent.
- Actions permitted to siblings of a parent must be different.
- A parent can delegate a role to only one of her children.

9. Write pre and postcondition for the following operations on the file modeled in Example 13:

(a) *EXCHANGE*—The operation has no effect if *position* is either before the first record or after the last record in the file; otherwise, the records on either side of *position* are swapped.

(b) *COPY_LEFT(k)*—The operation has no effect if *position* is before the first record or $k \leq 0$; otherwise, the first k records to the left of *position* are copied to the right of *position* in the same order.

(c) *COPY_RIGHT(k)*—The operation has no effect if *position* is after the last record in the file or $k \geq 0$; otherwise, the first k records to the right of *position* are copied to the left of *position* in the same order.

10. Formally apply Hoare axioms to each program specification below and determine its correctness.

(a)

$$\vdash \{X = a \wedge Y = b\} X := X - Y; Y := X + Y; X := Y - X;$$
$$\{Y = a \wedge X = b\}$$

(b) Assume that you are given the theorems:

$$\vdash X \geq Y \Rightarrow max(X, Y) = X, \quad \text{and}$$
$$\vdash Y \geq X \Rightarrow max(X, Y) = Y.$$

Derive a proof for the program specification

$$\vdash \{T\} If X \geq Y \ then \ MAX := X \ else \ MAX := Y$$
$$\{MAX = max(X, Y)\}$$

(c) The precondition for the following program is $X = a \wedge Y = b \wedge S = 0$, where a and b are non-negative integers. Assume that $even(X)$ is true if X is an even integer, and *div* is integer division operation. Prove that the program terminates and the postcondition is $S = a \times b$.

```
while X ≥ 0 do
    begin
        while even(X) do
            begin Y := 2 × Y; X := X div 2; end;
        S := S + Y;
        X := X - 1;
    end
```

10.7
Bibliographic Notes

First-order predicate logic is a subject of great importance for software development where its formal notation and deductive systems are used to axiomatically specify system properties. Many automated theorem provers are based on predicate logic. For instance in the proof assistant Coq [3], formal proofs for proposition and predicate logic can be developed. Programming language Prolog [7] is built on top of Horn clauses, which express a subset of predicate logic. Prolog execution engine is driven by the unification principle. Several policy languages that use predicate logic formalism are surveyed in [4]. Specifying policies for heterogeneous open distributed systems that offer services to a large section of society, and proving that policies are respected in every system transaction are formidable tasks. Cassandra [1] with its formal foundation provides the scope of formally proving such system properties.

No axiom system in first-order logic is strong enough to fully describe infinite structures such as the natural numbers or the real line. In first-order logic, quantified variables range over individual elements, whereas in second-order logic, these variables can range over predicates and sets of individuals. Higher-order logic is the basis for powerful theorem proving tools such as HOL [11] and Isabelle [16].

References

1. Becker MY (2005) Cassandra: flexible trust management and its application to electronic health records. Technical report, UCAM-CL-TR-648, University of Cambridge, United Kingdom
2. Becker MY, Sewell P (2004) Cassandra: distributed access control policies with tunable expressiveness. In: POLICY '04: proceedings of the fifth IEEE international workshop on policies for distributed systems and networks. IEEE Press, New York, pp 159–168
3. Bertot Y, Castéran P (2004) Interactive theorem proving and program development. Texts in theoretical computer science. Springer, Berlin
4. Bonatti PA, Shahmehri N, Duma C, Olmedilla D, Nejdl W, Baldoni M, Baroglio C, Martelli A, Coraggio P, Antoniou G, Peer J, Fuchs NE (2004) Rule-based policy specification: state of the art and future work. Technical report, Dipatimento di Scienze Fisiche, Universit a di Napoli, Complesso Universitario di Monte Sant Angelo
5. Chen F, Sandhu RS (1996) Constraints for role-based access control. In: RBAC '95: proceedings of the first ACM workshop on role-based access control. ACM, New York, pp 39–46
6. Ceri S, Gottlob G, Tanca L (1989) What you always wanted to know about Datalog (and never dared to ask). IEEE Trans Knowl Data Eng 1(1):146–166
7. Clocksin WF, Mellish CS (1984) Programming in prolog using the ISO standard. Springer, New York
8. Davis R, Shrobe H, Szolovits P (1993) What is a knowledge representation? AI Mag 14(1):17–33
9. DeMarco T (1978) Structured analysis and system specification. Yourdon Press, New York
10. Floyd R (1967) Assigning meaning to programs. In: Mathematical aspects of computer science, XIX. American Mathematical Society, Washington, pp 19–32
11. Gordon MJC, Melham TF (1993) Introduction to HOL: a theorem proving environment for higher order logic. Cambridge University Press, Cambridge

12. Guaspari FD, Marceau C, Polak W (1990) Formal verification of Ada programs. IEEE Trans Softw Eng 16(9):1044–1057
13. Garland SJ, Guttag JV, Horning JJ (1990) Debugging Larch shared language specifications. IEEE Trans Softw Eng 16(9):1058–1075
14. Hoare CAR (1969) An axiomatic basis for computer programming. Commun ACM 12(10):576–583
15. Hoare CAR (1972) Proof of correctness of data representations. Acta Inform 1(1):271–281
16. Nipkow T, Paulson LC, Wenzel M (2002) Isabelle/HOL: a proof assistant for higher order logic, LNCS, vol 2283. Springer, Berlin

Temporal Logic

11

In classical logic, the predicate P in "if $P \wedge (P \Rightarrow Q)$ then Q" retains its truth value even after Q has been derived. In other words, in classical logic the truth of a formula is *static*. However, real-life implications are *causal* and *temporal*. To handle these, it must be possible to specify that "an event happened when P was true, moments after that Q became true, and now "P is not true and Q is true". This may also be stated using "states". We associate predicates with states such that a predicate is true in some state S and false in some other states. For example, the statements

P	the train is approaching the gate,
$P \Rightarrow Q$	if the train approaches the gate, the gate is lowered,
Q	the gate is lowered before the train is in the gate, and
R	the gate remains closed until the train crosses the gate

describe changes to the states of a control system that continuously maintains an ongoing interaction with the environmental objects train and gate. The program controlling the train and the gate, according to the specification stated above, is a reactive program. Reactive system refers to the reactive program together with its environment. Such systems are typically non-terminating, read input and produce output on a continuous basis at different system states, interact with other systems and devices in its environment, exhibit concurrent behavior and may have to obey strict timing constraints. For example, the statements P and R denote continuous activities, the statement Q involves the temporal ordering of the actions "gate closing" and "train arriving at the crossing", and the statements P and Q imply concurrency. Such statements cannot be formalized in classical logic. In order to formalize these statements in logic, we need to introduce constructs such as *next*, *always*, *after*, *since*, and *until* and provide semantics to terms involving them. With proper semantics, these terms can express ordinal, temporal, and causal relationships on events and state transitions, without reference to the actual times at which they happen. Temporal logic was developed by Pnueli [22] to describe such orderings. Many kinds of temporal logics exist today, some in which one can add timing constraint like "the gate must be lowered within 3 seconds after receiving the message that the train is approaching". The temporal logics introduced in the following sections are simple extensions of propositional and first order logic and do not involve real-time measurements.

V.S. Alagar, K. Periyasamy, *Specification of Software Systems*,
Texts in Computer Science,
DOI 10.1007/978-0-85729-277-3_11, © Springer-Verlag London Limited 2011

11.1
Temporal Logic for Specification and Verification

Temporal logics can support specification and reasoning at different levels of abstractions. They provide unified logical systems in which behavior specification, design specification, and implementation level details can be expressed and related in an intuitive manner.

1. *Requirements Description:* At the requirements level, propositions and predicates are determined to model the problem requirements, and temporal formulas are constructed to formalize the temporal properties of the requirements. In particular, functionalities that must be present "always", or "at some future instance", or "always from some future instance" can be stated as temporal logic formulas [15].
2. *Design Level Specification:* At the design level, the behavior of an object can be characterized by a sequence of states, and the events triggering the successive state transitions. Temporal logic formulas are used to assert properties that hold over (1) all sequences of states, (2) some sequences of states, and (3) some future state in some sequence. Temporal logic can be used to interpret sequential and concurrent actions [16, 17, 22].
3. *Program Specification:* An interpretation of a program using temporal logic becomes a temporal specification of the program [19, 22, 24]. Verification of program properties can be done by stating each property as a temporal formula and then showing that the specification satisfies the formula.
4. *Formal Verification:* The rules of temporal logic proof calculus are applied to show the correctness of a temporal logic specification with respect to more abstract system specifications [5–7, 16]. Even when the design specifications use a different formal notation, temporal logic may be brought in at formal verification stages, as done in model checking.

Many types of concurrent and reactive systems can be modeled in temporal logic and the critical properties of the system can be formally verified in the model. In particular, in the specification of concurrent or reactive systems, three important behavioral properties, termed *safety*, *liveness*, and *fairness* by Owiciki and Lamport [20], can be formally expressed.

- *Safety:* Informally, a safety property implies that *something bad will not happen*. Typical examples are:

   1. *the gate will remain closed while a train is crossing the gate*
   2. *water level in the boiler should be at least 3 meters, and the reactor temperature must be less than 3000 degrees.*

   Other examples of safety properties include

   3. *partial correctness*—the program does not produce stack overflow
   4. *mutual exclusion*—two processes are not simultaneously in the critical section
   5. *deadlock-freedom*—the program does not reach the state of deadlock.

- *Liveness:* Liveness property implies that *something good will eventually happen*. Typical examples are:

1. *whenever the gate is directed to raise, it will eventually do so*
2. *program terminates eventually.*

- *Fairness:* Fairness property implies that whenever an attempt is made to perform an action or request a service, it will eventually succeed. Typical examples are:

1. *starvation-freedom*, where a process does not wait forever to be serviced
2. *progress*, where every message sent in a channel is eventually received.

11.2
Concept of World and Notion of Time

The term "world" means a *frame* or a *state* and is characterized by a set of dimensions such as time, space, audience, and events. Natural language expressions are interpreted in *intentional logic* [4] by evaluating the expression over different *modes* that are worlds. In Example 1, taken from Wan [30], a pair (*month, location*) determines a world, which is a unit of time/space.

Example 1 An evaluation of the expression

E': the average temperature this month here is greater than 0°C

can be obtained by interpreting it along the dimensions *month* and *location*. The table below gives only a partial evaluation because there exists many locations not included in the table.

	Jan	Feb	Mar	Apr	May	Jun	Jul	Aug	Sep	Oct	Nov	Dec
Montreal	F	F	F	F	T	T	T	T	T	F	F	F
Ottawa	F	F	F	T	T	T	T	T	T	F	F	F
Toronto	F	F	T	T	T	T	T	T	T	T	F	F
Vancouver	F	T	T	T	T	T	T	T	T	T	T	T

$\square$

In temporal logic, "world" refers only to time points. A world is like a model at a specific moment in time that assigns truth values to atomic propositions. To navigate between the different worlds, an *accessibility relation* needs to be defined. With this relation as we navigate through the worlds, we are moving *through time*. So, when we refer to "time" we are not referring to absolute time (or clock time) but we are emphasizing only the temporal relation defined by the accessibility relation.

11.2.1
Temporal Abstraction

The accessibility relation may be explained through temporal abstraction. We describe this notion following the discussion in [18]. As we move from requirements specification, which is abstract, to a design specification, which is concrete, more details are added. An abstract specification may specify a component behavior as a state machine, emphasizing only on the correct sequence of actions. The times at which these actions must occur might have been left out, and may be added during the design of the component. In some cases, time information might be stated at the abstract level only at some states which are considered *time-critical*. The details of time left unspecified at other intermediate states should not affect the overall behavior of the component, in particular during the design stage when more detailed time information may be added. Even at the design stage, the stated times may not be the *exact* time points, rather only the time points that are *relative* to the stages through which the timed behavior evolves. The abstract specification represents a *temporal abstraction* of the more detailed behavior given by the design. Continuing this discussion, it is understood that the design represents a temporal abstraction of the program. A correctness condition should establish a relationship between these different formal representations of time.

In many problems such as hardware specifications and reactive system specification, each unit of time in an abstract specification corresponds to an interval of time in its concrete counterpart. It may be that a particular moment at the abstract level corresponds to some moment within an interval or to a set of adjacent time moments in the concrete level. Consequently, a correctness condition formulated at the abstract level, which involves only "coarse-grained" time must be consistent with the "fine-grained" time scale in the concrete level. This correspondence between the time scales is described by a function f, that assigns for every t_a in the abstract level a time point $t_c = f(t_a)$ at the concrete level such that the order of time is preserved:

$$\vdash \forall t_a, t'_a.(t_a < t'_a) \Rightarrow (t_c < t'_c)$$

The properties of time that should hold in the design will determine the function f. The inverse of f need not be a function, because many possible designs exist for an abstract specification. If f denotes the mapping from the requirements to the design and g denotes the mapping from the design to the implementation then the function $f \circ g$ is the time map from the requirements to the implementation. The advantage of temporal abstractions include

- irrelevant details about intermediate states are suppressed in the abstract level, and
- time scale is not absolute, and consequently a specification can focus on relative time points without being specific about "which" time points are in fact of interest.

11.2.2
Discrete or Continuous

When certain computations or actions need to be described as continuously varying, a dense model of time is appropriate. In such a case, the topology of time is that of real numbers or a subset of real numbers. When a property is present over a sequence of intervals, and in each interval the property persists in every sub-interval, then an interval and continuous model of time are used. When dealing with properties that are present only at certain time instants, a discrete model of time is chosen. In this case, the model of time is isomorphic to a subset of natural numbers.

11.2.3
Linear and Branching Models of Time

One may want to postulate that for any state (moment in time) there is either exactly one next state or several possible next states. The former case is called the *linear model* of time, and the latter case is called the *branching model* of time. The branching model is useful to handle uncertainty, and hence possible alternative futures. Properties such as "*p* is true *throughout every* possible future", "*p* is true *at the next time in some possible* future", "*p* is true *eventually in every* possible future", and "*p* is true *eventually in some possible* future" can be stated and reasoned about in branching time temporal languages.

11.2.4
Further Specializations of Time

In distributed computing and communication over shared networks, there is a need to make a distinction between *global* and *local* times. The other possibilities include *bounded time* and *interval time*. A bounded time applies to dense (discrete) model when a finite subset of real numbers (natural numbers) is chosen to model time. An interval time model has a discrete time structure, so that the next and previous intervals can be referred to. Within each interval, a property may hold in every sub-interval or only at specific discrete points. In addition, time modeled as intervals may be bounded or unbounded. As a result of this classification, many different models of time can be realized. Some of these include "discrete linear global time", "discrete branching local time", and "continuous branching interval time".

11.3
Propositional Temporal Logic (PTL)

PTL is a *discrete linear-time* temporal logic introduced by Pnulei [22]. The primary features are that (1) time structure at the abstract level is the set of non-negative integers, (2) for every moment in time there is only one future moment in time, and (3) only propositions are allowed in formulas.

In PTL, the set of propositional logic operators is extended with the temporal operators $\Box$ (*always*), $\Diamond$ (*eventually*) and $\bigcirc$ (*next*). Intuitive meanings of temporal operators used in first order formulas φ and ψ are given in the table below.

Formula	Intuitive meaning
$\Box\varphi$	φ is true in *all* future moments
$\Diamond\varphi$	φ is true at *some* future moment in time
$\bigcirc\varphi$	φ is true in the *next* moment in time
$\varphi\,\mathcal{U}\,\psi$	φ is true up and until some future moment when ψ becomes true

With the above intuitive meanings, we can formalize a few requirements as in Example 2.

Example 2

- Always, if an email is sent through the network, then it will eventually be delivered.

  $\Box(send\_email \Rightarrow \Diamond delivered)$

- If a car is parked and the meter has expired, then at the next moment it will be ticketed.

  $(parked \wedge meter\_expired) \Rightarrow \bigcirc ticket\_for\_violation$

- The university library never closes.

  $\Box library\_open$

- Always, after the machine gets a coin and the user press a button, it gives coffee or tea.

  $\Box(coin \wedge \bigcirc press\_Button \Rightarrow \Diamond(serve\_Coffee \vee serve\_Tea))$

- Always, after pressing a button the machine will serve coffee and then tea immediately afterward.

  $\Box(press\_Button \Rightarrow (serve\_Coffee \wedge \bigcirc serve\_Tea))$

- The gate remains closed until the train leaves the crossing.

  $gate\_closed\,\mathcal{U}\,train\_exits$

  □

11.3.1
Syntax

The vocabulary of temporal logic consists of a finite set *PROP* of propositional symbols. The logical connectives *true*, *false*, $\vee$, $\wedge$, and $\Rightarrow$ together with the temporal connectives $\bigcirc$, $\Diamond$, $\Box$, and $\mathcal{U}$ are added to the vocabulary.

The unary operators bind *stronger* than binary ones. Operators $\neg$, $\bigcirc$, $\Box$, and $\Diamond$ bind equally strong. As an example, the formula $\neg P\mathcal{U}Q$ is interpreted as $(\neg P)\mathcal{U}Q$. Temporal binary operators have stronger precedence over $\wedge$, $\vee$, and $\Rightarrow$. The formula $P \vee Q\mathcal{U}R$ is parsed as $P \vee (Q\mathcal{U}R)$. Parentheses should be inserted to override precedence.

The set of well-formed formulas of PTL, denoted $\textit{wff}_T$, is inductively defined as the smallest set of formulas satisfying the following rules.

1. We add a special proposition symbol *start* which is true only at the *beginning of time*. It is not meaningful to use *start* at any other state.
2. Every proposition P in *PROP* is in $\textit{wff}_T$.
3. The constants *true*, *false*, and *start* are in $\textit{wff}_T$.
4. If φ is in $\textit{wff}_T$, then (φ) and $T(\varphi)$, where T is a temporal operator, are also in $\textit{wff}_T$. The formulas $\neg(\varphi), \Box(\varphi), \Diamond(\varphi)$ and $\bigcirc(\varphi)$ are well-formed.
5. If φ and ψ are in $\textit{wff}_T$, then so are $(\varphi \vee \psi), (\varphi \wedge \psi)$, and $(\varphi \Rightarrow \psi)$.

As an example, the formulas $\varphi \Rightarrow \Box\Diamond(\psi \vee \chi)$, and $\varphi \wedge \Diamond(\psi \Rightarrow \varphi)$ are well-formed, whereas the formulas $\psi\Diamond\varphi$, and $\varphi \wedge \Box\chi \bigcirc \psi$ are not well-formed. Stating well-formed formulas in natural language may be quite cumbersome. For example, stating the formula $\Box((\varphi \Rightarrow \bigcirc\psi)$ in natural language is not that difficult: it states that at every moment in time the property "if φ is true then at the next moment ψ is true" holds. However, stating the formula $\Box(\varphi \wedge \Diamond\psi) \Rightarrow \Box (\varphi \Rightarrow \bigcirc\chi)$ in natural language is more difficult. A semantic model helps us to precisely interpret formulas and understand their meanings.

11.3.2
Model and Semantics

The time structure for PTL is $\mathbb{N}_0$, the set of non-negative integers. Each state $i \in \mathbb{N}_0$ is associated with a set of propositions that are *true* in that state. That is, the formal basis of the semantic interpretation of PTL is a *sequence* of propositional models. Formally, the models of PTL is defined by

$$\mathcal{M} = \langle \mathbb{N}_0, \pi \rangle,$$

where π maps state $i \in \mathbb{N}_0$ to $\pi(i) = s_i \subset \textit{PROP}$. $\mathcal{M}$ is called model variety. An alternate representation of the model variety is

$$\mathcal{M} = \langle s_0, s_1, s_2, \ldots \rangle$$

A pictorial representation of $\mathcal{M}$ is given below.

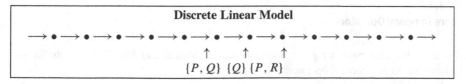

Discrete Linear Model

$\{P, Q\}$ $\{Q\}$ $\{P, R\}$

11.3.3
Formal Semantics

The semantics of PTL formulas for a model $\mathcal{M}$ is an interpretation relation

$$\models (\mathcal{M} \times \mathbb{N}_0) \mapsto \mathbb{B}$$

where $\mathbb{B} = \{true, false\}$. For a formula φ

$$\langle \mathcal{M}, i \rangle \models \varphi$$

is true if φ is satisfied at state s_i within the model $\mathcal{M}$. This satisfaction relation is built inductively, defined first for propositions, next for formulas involving classical logic connectives, and finally for general temporal formulas.

1. *Semantics of Propositions:* A proposition $P \in PROP$ satisfies $\langle \mathcal{M}, i \rangle$ iff $P \in s_i$. Formally,

   $$\langle \mathcal{M}, i \rangle \models P \text{ iff } P \in s_i$$

   The proposition *start* is true only at the beginning of time.

   $$\langle \mathcal{M}, i \rangle \models start \text{ iff } (i = 0)$$

2. *Semantics of Standard Logic Formulas:* We consider formulas involving $\{\neg, \wedge, \vee, \Rightarrow\}$.

   $\langle \mathcal{M}, i \rangle \models \neg\varphi$ *iff* $\langle \mathcal{M}, i \rangle \models \varphi$ *is not true.*

   $\langle \mathcal{M}, i \rangle \models \varphi \wedge \psi$ *iff both* $\langle \mathcal{M}, i \rangle \models \varphi$ *and* $\langle \mathcal{M}, i \rangle \models \psi$ *are true.*

   $\langle \mathcal{M}, i \rangle \models \varphi \vee \psi$ *iff either* $\langle \mathcal{M}, i \rangle \models \varphi$ *is true or* $\langle \mathcal{M}, i \rangle \models \psi$ *is true.*

   $\langle \mathcal{M}, i \rangle \models \varphi \Rightarrow \psi$ *iff if* $\langle \mathcal{M}, i \rangle \models \varphi$ *is true then* $\langle \mathcal{M}, i \rangle \models \psi$ *is true.*

3. Semantics of Temporal Logic Formulas: We consider formulas involving $\bigcirc, \square, \diamond, \mathcal{U}$.

   $\langle \mathcal{M}, i \rangle \models \bigcirc\varphi$ *iff* $\langle \mathcal{M}, i+1 \rangle \models \varphi$

   $\langle \mathcal{M}, i \rangle \models \square\varphi$ *iff* $\forall j (j \geq i) \langle \mathcal{M}, j \rangle \models \varphi$ *holds*

   $\langle \mathcal{M}, i \rangle \models \diamond\varphi$ *iff* $\exists j (j \geq i) \langle \mathcal{M}, j \rangle \models \varphi$ *holds*

   $\langle \mathcal{M}, i \rangle \models \varphi \mathcal{U} \psi$ *iff* $\exists j (j \geq i)$ *and* $\langle \mathcal{M}, j \rangle \models \psi$, *and*

   $\forall k (i \leq k < j) \langle \mathcal{M}, k \rangle \models \varphi$ *holds*

11.3.4
More Temporal Operators

We describe three more temporal operators below. Manna and Pnueli [17] includes an exhaustive list of temporal operators.

The *Unless* Operator $\mathcal{W}$

The formula $\varphi \, \mathcal{W} \, \psi$ (read φ unless ψ) states that φ is true unless ψ becomes true. The difference between *Until* and *Unless* operators is that in the former case ψ is *guaranteed* to be true at some future state, whereas in the latter case ψ may never become true. Consequently, $\varphi \, \mathcal{W} \, \psi$ specifies two scenarios: (1) ψ becomes true at some future state and the behavior is identical to the *until* operator, and (2) ψ never becomes true and consequently φ is true forever. Thus the formal semantics is

$$\langle \mathcal{M}, i \rangle \models \varphi \, \mathcal{W} \, \psi \text{ iff either } \langle \mathcal{M}, i \rangle \models \varphi \, \mathcal{U} \, \psi \text{ or } \langle \mathcal{M}, i \rangle \models \Box \varphi$$

The *Since* Operator $\mathcal{S}$

The formula $\varphi \, \mathcal{S} \, \psi$ (read φ since ψ) states that ψ has happened sometime in the past and φ has continuously held since then. Notice that in the model for PTL there is no moment in time that is less than 0. Thus the formal semantics is

$$\langle \mathcal{M}, i \rangle \models \varphi \, \mathcal{S} \, \psi \text{ iff } \exists j \, (0 \leq j < i) \langle \mathcal{M}, j \rangle \models \psi \text{ and}$$

$$\forall k \, (k \geq j) \langle \mathcal{M}, k \rangle \models \Box \varphi$$

The *Release* Operator $\mathcal{R}$

The formula $\varphi \, \mathcal{R} \, \psi$ (read φ release ψ) states that ψ has to be true at all states until and including the state at which φ first becomes true. If φ never becomes true then ψ must remain true forever. Notice that if φ becomes true at state s_i then ψ is not true from state s_{i+1} (unless something else happens), but we cannot assert anything about ψ after state s_i. Recognize that the *Release* operator is *the inverse* of the *Unless* operator.

Example 3 The formulas below are interpreted according to the above semantics.

1. *water_level_high* $\Rightarrow \bigcirc$*alarm_rings*: if the water level is high in state s_i, $i \geq 0$, then at state s_{i+1} alarm rings.
2. $\neg(\Box(get\_rank \wedge excel\_in\_sports))$: getting a rank in studies and excelling in sports is not always possible.
3. *system_down* $\Rightarrow \Diamond$*system_up*: if the system is down at state s_i then at some future state s_j, $j \geq i$ the system will be come back up.
4. *file_front* $\wedge$ *printer_on* $\Rightarrow (\Diamond start\_print \wedge printing \, \mathcal{U} \, file\_end)$: if the printer is on and the front of a file is received by it at state s_i then the printer will start printing the file at some future state s_j, $j \geq i$, and continue printing until the end of file is reached at some state k, $k > j$.
5. *execute_program* $\mathcal{W}$ *stackoverflow*: the program execution is continued unless there is stack overflow.
6. *cross_gate* $\mathcal{S}$ *gate_open*: the gate remains open since the train crossed the gate.
7. *arrived_at_terminal* $\mathcal{R}$ *driver_on_duty*: upon arrival of train at the terminal the driver on duty is released. $\qquad\qquad\Box$

11.3.5
Axioms

A sample set of axioms for PTL is given here. A set of axioms are grouped under a *law*. An axiom gives the equivalence between two PTL formulas. In general, many formulas equivalent to a given formula may exist. The axioms provide a basic set, using which the number of equivalent formulas may be reduced to those shown in the list below. For a complete list of axioms, principles of soundness, completeness, and axiomatization of systems consult [10, 17, 26, 29].

- *Absorption Axioms:* The absorption law removes operators whose effect are absorbed by other operators in a formula. If, always, it is true that φ is true infinitely often in a future time moment then it must be true at every future state starting at time 0. The converse is also true.

Absorption Law

$$\Diamond\Box\Diamond\varphi \equiv \Box\Diamond\varphi$$
$$\Box\Diamond\Box\varphi \equiv \Diamond\Box\varphi$$

- *Distributive Axioms:* The distributive law for $\Diamond$ distributes over *disjunction*, the distributive law for $\Box$ distributes over *conjunction*, and these laws are dual to each other. It should be noted that $\Diamond$ does not distributes over *conjunction*, and $\Box$ does not distribute over *disjunction*. Informally this can be reasoned about. For example, the formula $\Diamond\varphi \wedge \Diamond\psi$ asserts that eventually a state in which φ holds and a state in which ψ holds will be reached. But that does not mean that a state in which both φ and ψ are true will be reached. However, the operator $\bigcirc$ distributes over *conjunction* and $\mathcal{U}$ (until).

Distributive Law

$$\Diamond(\varphi \vee \psi) \equiv \Diamond\varphi \vee \Diamond\psi$$
$$\Box(\varphi \wedge \psi) \equiv \Box\varphi \wedge \Diamond\psi$$
$$\bigcirc(\varphi \wedge \psi) \equiv (\bigcirc\varphi) \wedge (\bigcirc\psi)$$
$$\bigcirc(\varphi\mathcal{U}\psi) \equiv (\bigcirc\varphi)\mathcal{U}(\bigcirc\psi)$$

- *Duality Axioms:* The duality rule for the next-step operator $\bigcirc$ says that it is dual to itself. Read it as "it is not the case that φ is true in the next step is equivalent to saying that it is the case that φ is not true in the next step". The duality rule for the future operator $\Diamond$ involves the always operator $\Box$, and conversely the duality rule for the always operator $\Box$ involves the future operator $\Diamond$. Read the duality rule for $\Box$ operator as "it is not the case that φ is always true is equivalent to saying that at some future time point φ is not true". Interchange the operators $\Box$ and $\Diamond$ in a rule to get (read) the other rule.

> **Duality Law**
>
> $$\neg \Box \varphi \equiv \Diamond \neg \varphi$$
> $$\neg \Diamond \varphi \equiv \Box \neg \varphi$$
> $$\neg \bigcirc \varphi \equiv \bigcirc \neg \varphi$$

- *Expansion Axioms:* Expansion axioms provide an *inductive* definition of temporal operators. As an example, if $\Diamond \varphi$ holds in the beginning, then either φ is true or $\bigcirc \Diamond \varphi$ is true in the beginning. In general, each law will assert the truth of a formula which does not involve a temporal operator in the current state, and it asserts the truth of the formula in the next state using the next state operator $\bigcirc$.

> **Expansion Law**
>
> $$\Box \varphi \equiv \varphi \wedge \bigcirc \Box \varphi$$
> $$\Diamond \varphi \equiv \varphi \vee \bigcirc \Diamond \varphi$$
> $$\varphi \, \mathcal{U} \, \psi \equiv \psi \vee (\varphi \wedge \bigcirc (\varphi \, \mathcal{U} \, \psi))$$

- *Idempotent Axioms:* The idempotent axioms eliminate the superfluous operator from a formula. For example, it is not necessary to say that "*always* a formula is always true".

> **Idempotent Law**
>
> $$\Box \Box \varphi \equiv \Box \varphi$$
> $$\Diamond \Diamond \varphi \equiv \Diamond \varphi$$
> $$\varphi \, \mathcal{U} \, (\varphi \, \mathcal{U} \, \psi) \equiv \varphi \, \mathcal{U} \, \psi$$
> $$(\varphi \, \mathcal{U} \, \psi) \, \mathcal{U} \, \psi \equiv \varphi \, \mathcal{U} \, \psi$$

- *Induction Axiom:* The axiom is similar to expansion law, applied to "implication". It asserts that temporal logic provides an inductive rule for proving assertions.

> **Induction Law**
>
> $$\vdash \Box (\varphi \Rightarrow \bigcirc \varphi) \Rightarrow (\varphi \Rightarrow \Box \varphi)$$

It is instructive to verify the equivalence of two formulas by proving that the semantic models of the formulas are identical. See exercises.

11.3.6
Formalizing Properties in PTL

We give examples showing propositional temporal logic characterizations for safety, liveness and fairness properties.

Example 4 Consider the *mutual exclusion problem* for two processes P_1 and P_2. A process has (1) a critical section, (2) a non-critical section, and (3) a section where it waits before entering the critical section. Let $wait_i$ denote that process P_i is in its waiting phase, and $criti_i$ denote that P_i is in its critical section. The *safety* property stating that P_1 and P_2 never simultaneously have access to their critical sections is expressed by the formula

$$\Box(\neg criti_1 \vee \neg criti_2)$$

The *liveness* property stating that each process P_i is infinitely often in its critical section is expressed by the formula

$$(\Box\Diamond criti_1) \wedge (\Box\Diamond criti_2)$$

A fairness property is that every waiting process will eventually enter its critical section. This property is also called *starvation freedom*. It can be expressed by the formula

$$(\Box\Diamond wait_1 \Rightarrow \Box\Diamond criti_1) \wedge (\Box\Diamond wait_2 \Rightarrow \Box\Diamond criti_2) \qquad\qquad \Box$$

Example 5 This example, called *Dining Philosophers*, is due to Dijkstra [8]. Five philosophers are sitting at a round table with a bowl of rice in the middle. The philosophers think, eat, and may have to wait before they eat. In between two neighboring philosophers there is only one chopstick. To take some rice out of the bowl and eat, a philosopher needs two chopsticks (eating by hand is forbidden!). So, a philosopher must take the chopsticks from the left and right side in order to eat. But if one philosopher keeps both chopsticks, the two neighbors will starve. The problem is to design a protocol for the dining so that the complete system is *deadlock-free*. That is, at least one philosopher can eat and think infinitely often. Additionally, some fairness is needed—every philosopher should be able to eat and think infinitely often. To specify deadlock-freedom, let us denote the philosophers by $0, 1, 2, 3, 4$. Let $wait_i$ be the proposition meaning that philosopher i is waiting. Let $occupied_i$ be the proposition that chopstick i is in use. The formula that expresses deadlock-freedom is

$$\Box\neg\left(\bigwedge_{0\leq i<5} wait_i \wedge \bigwedge_{0\leq i<5} occupied_i\right) \qquad\qquad \Box$$

Example 6 This example describes the temporal properties of a traffic light with phases R (red), G (green), and Y (yellow). We can consider the phases as "instances" (atomic). That is, a traffic light in phase R will go to the *next* phase G. That is, there is "nothing" in between R and G. We are not interested at "how long" the light will be red before turning yellow. With this assumption, the formula that expresses the "transition from *state* (phase) R to *state* (phase) G is

$$\Box(R \Rightarrow \bigcirc G)$$

However, if you want to consider *durations*, then "the traffic light remains red for sometime before turning green". Since we do not know for how long it will remain red, we can only state that eventually the light will become green.

$$\Box(R \Rightarrow \Diamond G)$$

If we want to be more descriptive of the behavior, we may say "once green, the light eventually becomes red after being yellow for sometime".

$$\Box(G \Rightarrow \bigcirc(G\mathcal{U}(Y \wedge \bigcirc(Y\mathcal{U}R))))$$

The traffic light is green infinitely often.

$$\Box \Diamond G$$

The traffic light is red only in a finite number of states.

$$\Diamond \Box \neg R \hspace{8cm} \Box$$

11.3.7
Specifications

In this section, we discuss methods for specifying communication and concurrency, and illustrate them in specifying reactive systems.

11.3.7.1
Communication and Concurrency

We consider a system involving several objects (components or agents) who may interact among themselves in order to achieve their goals. Essentially, each object is independent of the other, except when it needs a resource or information from another object in order to continue its activity. In a discrete time model, all components have a common global clock and have the same definition of next moment. In the discussion below, we let $Spec_A$ and $Spec_B$, respectively, denote the specifications of components A and B, $\langle \mathbb{N}_0, \pi_1 \rangle$ denote the model of $Spec_A$ and $\langle \mathbb{N}_0, \pi_2 \rangle$ denote the model of $Spec_B$.

True Concurrency The execution of components progress independently and simultaneously through the same sequence of states. This type of concurrency is called *synchronous*. There is no interaction between the propositions/formulas in $Spec_A$ and the propositions/formulas in $Spec_B$. The specification of the combined system that execute concurrently and synchronously is $Spec_A \wedge Spec_B$, whose model is $\langle \mathbb{N}_0, \pi \rangle$, where $\pi(i) = \pi_1(i) \wedge \pi_2(i)$, for $i \in \mathbb{N}_0$.

Example 7

$$Spec_A : \Box \begin{bmatrix} start \Rightarrow P \wedge \\ P \Rightarrow \bigcirc \bigcirc Q \wedge \\ Q \Rightarrow \bigcirc P \end{bmatrix}$$

$$Spec_B : \Box \begin{bmatrix} start \Rightarrow A \wedge \\ A \Rightarrow \bigcirc B \wedge \\ B \Rightarrow \bigcirc \bigcirc A \end{bmatrix}$$

The model for $Spec_A$ is $\langle \mathbb{N}_0, \pi_1 \rangle$, where

$$\pi_1(i) = \begin{cases} P & \text{if } i = 3k, k \geq 0 \\ Q & \text{if } i = 3k + 2, k \geq 0 \end{cases}$$

The model for $Spec_B$ is $\langle \mathbb{N}_0, \pi_2 \rangle$, where

$$\pi_2(i) = \begin{cases} A & \text{if } i = 3k, k \geq 0 \\ B & \text{if } i = 3k + 1, k \geq 0 \end{cases}$$

The model for $Spec_A \wedge Spec_B$ is $\langle \mathbb{N}_0, \pi \rangle$, where

$$\pi(i) = \begin{cases} A \wedge P & \text{if } i = 3k, k \geq 0 \\ B & \text{if } i = 3k + 1, k \geq 0 \\ Q & \text{if } i = 3k + 2, k \geq 0 \end{cases} \qquad \Box$$

Interleaving Executions   Two components execute independently; however, only one of the components can execute during a certain period of time. The model $\langle \mathbb{N}_0, \pi \rangle$ of this behavior is given by

$$\pi(i) = \begin{cases} \pi_1(i) & \text{if } A \text{ is executing} \\ \pi_2(i) & \text{if } B \text{ is executing} \end{cases}$$

Executions Triggered by Messages   Message passing can be specified in one of three possible ways.

- *Peer-to-peer communication:* An object A sends a message *directly* to another object B.
- *Broadcast Communication:* An object sends a message to several objects; however, it does not know the recipients of the message.
- *Multicast Communication:* This is a restricted form of broadcast, which specifies a constraint based on which the set of recipients are characterized. The sender does not know the actual recipients of the message.

Messages are sent through *channels*, which have the following characteristics:

- channel is *unidirectional*,
- channel does not lose messages, and
- messages are delivered in the order they are sent.

To specify interaction between components A and B through message passing, it is necessary to have two channels, one for component A to send messages to component B, and another for component A to receive messages from component B. We view the set of propositions in each specification to be partitioned into three sets *input*, *output*, and *internal*. A proposition $P \in output_A$ and a proposition $\bar{P} \in input_B$ are related by the connective $\Rightarrow$ to show the direction of flow of the message from component A to component B. Similarly, a proposition $Q \in output_B$ and a proposition $\bar{Q} \in input_A$ are related by the connective $\Rightarrow$ to show the direction of flow of the message from component B to component A. Depending upon the type of communication, quality of service criteria (QoS) and the medium of communication, the message is delivered in one of the following ways:

- the message is delivered *instantaneously*: $\Box[P \Rightarrow \bar{P}]$
- the message is delivered at the next moment: $\Box[P \Rightarrow \bigcirc \bar{P}]$
- the message is delivered at some future moment $\Box[P \Rightarrow \Diamond \bar{P}]$.

There exist other possibilities such as "the message is delivered at a *specific* time", or "the message is delivered within a certain interval of time" which we do not consider.

In Example 8, $send\_msg \in output_A$ and $rcv\_msg \in input_B$, and the communication specification states that message $send\_msg$ is sent by component A to component B. When it is received at the next moment in time, the proposition rcv_msg becomes true.

Example 8

$$Spec_A : \Box \begin{bmatrix} start \Rightarrow P \wedge \\ P \Rightarrow \bigcirc \bigcirc Q \wedge \\ Q \Rightarrow \bigcirc P \wedge \\ Q \Rightarrow send\_msg \end{bmatrix}$$

$$Spec_B : \Box \begin{bmatrix} rcv\_msg \Rightarrow A \wedge \\ A \Rightarrow \bigcirc B \wedge \\ B \Rightarrow \bigcirc \bigcirc A \end{bmatrix}$$

The communication specification is
$Spec_{AtoB}$:

$$\Box[send\_msg \Rightarrow \bigcirc rcv\_msg]$$

The specification of the message passing system is

$$Spec_A \wedge Spec_B \wedge Spec_{AtoB}$$

The behavior of the specification is best described by looking at its model. Component A is executed starting in its initial state. In the initial state P is true. The second line of $Spec_A$ ensures that Q becomes true at time point 2. The third and fourth lines of $Spec_A$ assert that the proposition $send\_msg$ is made true at time point 2, and P is made true at time point 3. From this moment on, P is true at time points $6, 9, \ldots,$ Q is true at time points $5, 8, \ldots,$ and $send\_msg$ is true whenever Q is true. The interaction specification *send_msg* $\Rightarrow \bigcirc rcv\_msg$ ensures that the proposition *rcv_msg* becomes true the moment after *send_ msg* is true. Since the proposition *send_msg* is true at time points $2, 5, \ldots$, the proposition *rcv_msg* becomes true at time points $3, 6, \ldots$. The first line of $Spec_B$ ensures that proposition A is true whenever proposition *rcv_msg* is true. The second line of $Spec_B$ affirms that proposition B is true the moment after proposition A is true. The last line of $Spec_B$ affirms that the behavior described thus far is repeated. Consequently, proposition A is true at time pints $3, 6, \ldots$, and proposition B is true at time points $4, 7, \ldots$. Notice that in the combined specification, the propositions *send_msg* and *rcv_msg* do not arise. That is, propositions in the sets $output_A$ and $input_B$ "cancel out", leaving the combined behavior to be described only by the propositions in $inner_A$ and $inner_B$. The models of specifications $Spec_A$, $Spec_B$, and $Spec_A \wedge Spec_B \wedge Spec_{AtoB}$ are given below.

Model of $Spec_A$

$$\pi_A(i) = \begin{cases} P & \text{if } i = 3k, k \geq 0 \\ Q & \text{if } i = 3k+2, k \geq 0 \\ send\_msg & \text{if } i = 3k+2, k \geq 0 \end{cases}$$

Model of $Spec_B$

$$\pi_B(i) = \begin{cases} A & \text{if } i = 3k, k \geq 1 \\ B & \text{if } i = 3k+1, k \geq 1 \\ rcv\_msg & \text{if } i = 3k+1, k \geq 1 \end{cases}$$

Model of $(Spec_A \wedge Spec_B \wedge Spec_{AtoB})$

$$\pi(i) = \begin{cases} P & \text{if } i = 0 \\ P \wedge A & \text{if } i = 3k, k \geq 1 \\ Q & \text{if } i = 3k-1, k \geq 1 \\ B & \text{if } i = 3k+1, k \geq 1 \end{cases} \qquad \square$$

11.3.7.2
Reactive System Specification: Rail Road Crossing Problem

We consider a *rail road crossing* instance of a reactive system in which event orderings are specified using temporal operators. In a general version of the problem, multiple trains are allowed to run in parallel while crossing gates and the communication between trains and controllers of the gates at the crossings have strict real-time constraints. But we consider a simple version in which time is abstracted by the "time moments (states)". Because in PTL only individual objects can be specified, we assume that there is one train which wishes to cross one gate which is monitored by one controller. When the train is approaching the gate, it informs the controller, which in turn instructs the gate at the crossing to close. The gate, upon receiving the instruction from the controller, closes before the train is in the crossing. When leaving the crossing, the train informs the controller, which instructs the gate to open. The gate, upon receiving the instruction from the controller, raises until it is fully open. The specification of this system should ensure the safety property "the gate remains closed while the train is in the crossing". The significant aspects of this problem are

- *reactivity*, whereby the controller interacts with the environmental objects train and controller,
- *concurrency*, whereby train actions and controller actions may overlap, and
- *asymmetry*, in the interaction pattern

Many specifications that satisfy the safety property can be given for this problem. Below one such specification is given, and an informal proof of the safety property is given. The events in the system are modeled as propositions, shown in the table below.

Train	Gate	Controller
tr_1: approaching	g_1: lowered	ct_1: receives "approaching" message from the train
tr_2: in the crossing	g_2: closed	ct_2: sends message "lower" to the gate
tr_3: is crossing	g_3: raised	ct_3: receives "exit" message from the train
tr_4: crossed the gate	g_4: open	ct_4: sends "raise" message to the gate

We need to specify the relationships among the events modeled as propositions. There exist many possible orderings of events which can characterize a safe system. Let us postulate the following behavior. We use the notation $\bigcirc^k$ to denote the kth next.

Behavior of Train

$$Spec_{train} : \Box \begin{bmatrix} tr_1 \Rightarrow \bigcirc^3 tr_2 \wedge \\ tr_2 \Rightarrow tr_3 \, \mathcal{U} \, tr_4 \wedge \\ tr_1 \Rightarrow \bigcirc^6 \Box \, tr_4 \end{bmatrix}$$

Behavior of Controller

$$Spec_{controller} : \Box \begin{bmatrix} ct_1 \Rightarrow \bigcirc ct_2 \wedge \\ ct_3 \Rightarrow \bigcirc ct_4 \end{bmatrix}$$

Behavior of Gate

$$Spec_{gate} : \Box \begin{bmatrix} g_1 \Rightarrow \bigcirc (g_2 \, \mathcal{U} \, g_3) \wedge \\ g_3 \Rightarrow \bigcirc g_4 \end{bmatrix}$$

Two types of interactions exist in the system: interaction between train and controller and interaction between controller and gate. We need to specify these interactions. The interaction specification $Spec_{train-controller}$ models the communication that takes "one unit of time", whereas the interaction specification $Spec_{controller-gate}$ models the communication that is "instantaneous". The rationale is that the gate object is "tightly coupled" to the controller and hence the message sent by the controller reaches the gate instantaneously, whereas the train object is quite independent from the controller object and hence the message sent by the train needs some time (>0) to reach the controller.

Behavior of Train–Controller Interaction The train informs the controller that it is approaching and this information is received at the "next moment" in time by the controller. The train also informs the controller that it has crossed the gate and this information is received at the "next moment" by the controller. This interaction specification is specified below.

$$Spec_{train\text{-}controller} : \square \begin{bmatrix} tr_1 \Rightarrow \bigcirc ct_1 \\ tr_4 \Rightarrow \bigcirc ct_3 \end{bmatrix}$$

Behavior of Controller–Gate Interaction The controller informs the gate to close and this information is received instantaneously by the gate. The controller informs the gate to raise and this information is also received instantaneously by the gate. This interaction specification is specified below.

$$Spec_{controller\text{-}gate} : \square \begin{bmatrix} ct_2 \Rightarrow g_1 \\ ct_4 \Rightarrow g_3 \end{bmatrix}$$

Initially *start* is true. At sometime in future the train is approaching. So the initial state specification is

$$Spec_{init} : start \Rightarrow \Diamond tr_1$$

Thus the full specification of the rail road crossing problem is obtained by "combining" the above specification units, which we write as

$$Spec_{railroad} \equiv Spec_{train} \wedge Spec_{controller} \wedge Spec_{gate} \wedge Spec_{train\text{-}controller} \wedge$$
$$Spec_{controller\text{-}gate} \wedge Spec_{init}$$

We need to verify in this specification the safety property "whenever the train is in the crossing the gate remains closed". From the semantics of $start \Diamond tr_1$, we infer that there exists $i \geq 0$ such that

$$\langle \mathcal{M}, i \rangle \models tr_1.$$

Applying the formal semantics to specifications, as shown in the box below, we get a formal semantic model of the railroad specification. In the box below we see that whenever tr_3 is true, g_2 is true. This proves the safety property for the given specification.

Model for rail road specification

$$\langle M, i \rangle \models tr_1$$
$$\langle M, i+1 \rangle \models cr_1$$
$$\langle M, i+2 \rangle \models ct_2 \wedge g_1$$
$$\langle M, i+3 \rangle \models tr_2 \wedge tr_3 \wedge g_2$$
$$\langle M, j \rangle \models tr_3 \wedge g_2, j = i+5, i+6, i+6, i+7$$
$$\langle M, i+8 \rangle \models tr_4 \wedge ct_3 \wedge g_2$$
$$\langle M, i+9 \rangle \models tr_4 \wedge ct_4 \wedge g_3$$
$$\langle M, k \rangle \models tr_4 \wedge g_4, k > i+10$$

11.3.7.3
Refinement

A specification $Spec'_A$ of component A is a *refinement* of $Spec_A$ of component A if every model of $Spec'_A$ is a *subset* of a model of $Spec_A$. Informally, a refinement reduces the number of possible models that satisfy a specification. Hence, successive refinements will lead to a fewer models and hence to a fewer implementations that are possible to verify. In PTL specification, any communication that involves $\diamond$ can be replaced by $\bigcirc$ operator to get a refinement. In particular, $Spec'_A : P \Rightarrow \bigcirc^4 Q$, $Spec''_A : P \Rightarrow \bigcirc^2 Q$, and $Spec'''_A : P \Rightarrow \bigcirc Q$ are some of the refinements of the specification $Spec_A : P \Rightarrow \diamond Q$. Depending upon the design goal, a suitable refinement must be chosen.

11.4
First Order Temporal Logic (FOTL)

The alphabet of PTL is extended to include a set of *predicate variables*, a set of function symbols, and a set of constants. In addition to the connectives in PTL, we add the universal quantifier $\forall$, and the existential quantifier $\exists$. We consider only a *partial* FOTL. A full account of FOTL can be found in [11, 17, 26].

The well-formed formulas in FOTL are defined as in Sect. 11.3.1, by letting predicates of arity ≥ 0 in wff_T and inductively defining the formulas in wff_T. Operator precedence remains the same as in PTL. Quantification over temporal formulas involves only one variable. As an example, we consider formulas such as $\forall x \bullet p(x) \Rightarrow \bigcirc q(x)$, and $\forall x \bullet (head(x) \geq 6) \wedge (tail(x) \neq null)$. Such formulas are called *monadic*. In full FOTL, a formula can have quantification over more than one variable, even allowing quantification over arbitrary structures such as sets and trees.

The semantics of FOTL formulas involve "interpretation" as in predicate logic and temporal semantics as in PTL. The time structure is still $\mathbb{N}_0$ and we consider only global time. Thus a model for FOTL formulas is

$$\langle \mathbb{N}_0, \pi, I \rangle$$

where I is an interpretation which assigns for every formula element a value in a certain domain. Thus, for each time moment $i \in \mathbb{N}_0$, $\pi(i) = s_i$ is the state in which the formulas are to be evaluated using the interpretation I. Denoting the value of a variable x (expression e, predicate p, formula f) in a state s by $s[x]$ ($s[e], s[p], s[f]$), the evaluation steps for formulas, not involving temporal operators, in an interpretation I are described below:

1. Step 1—Evaluating Expressions
   (a) An expression e is evaluated in a state s by assigning values to all free variables and associating meaning to basic constructs. The value of the expression $e = 2x - 3y$ in a state s is $s[e] = 2s[x] - 3s[y]$.
2. Step 2—Evaluating Predicates

(a) For the predicate $p(t_1, \ldots, t_n)$, where $t_1, \ldots, t_n$ are terms, define $s[p(t_1, \ldots, t_n)] = p(s[t_1], \ldots, s[t_n])$.

(b) Predicate formulas
- (i) $s[\neg p] = \neg s[p]$
- (ii) $s[p \vee q] = s[p] \vee s[q]$
- (iii) $s[p \wedge q] = s[p] \wedge s[q]$
- (iv) $s[p \Rightarrow q] = s[p] \Rightarrow s[q]$
- (v) $s[p \Leftrightarrow q] = s[p] \Leftrightarrow s[q]$

3. Step 3—Evaluating Quantified Formulas
    (a) $s[\forall x \bullet p] = \forall x \bullet s[p]$.
    (b) $s[\exists x \bullet p] = \exists x \bullet s[p]$.

For example, consider the interpretation $I : \langle x = -1, y = 3, z = 1 \rangle$ in state s for the formula $(x + y > z) \Rightarrow \bigcirc(y \leq 2 * z)$. Since $s[(x + y > z)]$ is true in state s, in the next state it is asserted that $(y \leq 2 * z)$ must become true. That is, in the next state there must exist an interpretation that makes the formula $(y \leq 2 * z)$ true.

11.4.1
Formalizing Properties in FOTL

In Sect. 11.3.6, we discussed formalization of safety, liveness, and fairness properties in PTL. In this section, we illustrate through examples formalization of some properties using quantified FOTL formulas. Example 9 formalizes some properties of a bi-directional communication channel. Example 10 is a formal specification of safety and liveness requirements of a queue module that may be shared between different processors.

Example 9 Consider the problem of sending and receiving messages over a communication channel. Let $\{a, b\}$ denote the set of end-points of a channel, and $e \in \{a, b\}$. Let

$$\bar{e} = \begin{cases} a & \text{if } e = b \\ b & \text{if } e = a \end{cases}$$

Let M denote the set of messages and $m \in M$ be any arbitrary message transmitted over the channel $\langle a, b \rangle$. The temporal logic formulas, given below, involve atomic formulas such as *accept*(m, e) and *deliver*(m, e) and temporal operators. They are quantified over the set of messages $M' = M \setminus \{\text{DISCONNECT}\}$, considered as a set of constants.

1. To state that a channel is operational at all time, it is sufficient to state that both end-points are accepting messages all the time.

    $\exists m, m' \bullet \Box \ (channel\_on(a, b) \Leftrightarrow accept(m, a) \wedge accept(m', b))$.

2. A channel cannot copy messages; if a message was delivered at some time, then it cannot be redelivered unless it was accepted again.

    $\forall m \bullet (deliver(m, \bar{e}) \Rightarrow \bigcirc\Box(\neg deliver(m, \bar{e}) \mathcal{W} accept(m, e)))$.

3. A channel cannot accept two different messages at the same end-point at the same time:

$$\forall m, m' \bullet \Box \ (accept(m, e) \wedge accept(m', e) \Rightarrow m = m')$$

4. A message accepted at e will be delivered at $\bar{e}$, unless $\bar{e}$ has accepted a disconnect message at a preceding time.

$$\forall m \bullet \Box \ (accept(m, e) \Rightarrow$$

$$\Diamond(\neg((\neg accept(\text{DISCONNECT}, \bar{e})\,\mathcal{U}\,(deliver(m, e))) \wedge$$

$$((\neg(deliver(m, \bar{e}))\,\mathcal{S}\,accept(\text{DISCONNECT}, \bar{e})))))$$

5. This axiom asserts the safety property that there can be no loss of messages in an active channel and that all messages accepted are eventually delivered. The messages are delivered at the end-point $\bar{e}$ in the same order in which they were accepted at the end-point e:

$$\forall m \bullet \Box \ (accept(m, e) \wedge \bigcirc\Diamond accept(m', e) \wedge$$

$$\neg(accept(\text{DISCONNECT}, \bar{e})\,\mathcal{U}\,deliver(m', \bar{e}))$$

$$\Rightarrow \Diamond((deliver(m, \bar{e}) \wedge \bigcirc\Diamond deliver(m', \bar{e})))$$

6. When a disconnect message is either accepted or delivered at one end, the channel stops functioning at that end.

$$((accept(\text{DISCONNECT}, e) \vee deliver(\text{DISCONNECT}, e)) \Rightarrow$$

$$\neg\exists m \bullet (\bigcirc\Box(\neg accept(m, e) \wedge \neg deliver(m, e)))) \qquad \Box$$

Example 10 is from Lamport [16]. It illustrates FOTL formalization of safety and liveness properties of a finite queue based on its states. The queue is a shared data type and hence PUT and GET operations may be initiated concurrently by more than one process. With the atomicity assumption and modeling concurrency as the interleaving of atomic operations, only one operation can occur on the queue at any specific time. That is, given the current contents of the queue, only one process can perform the PUT or GET operation on this state. A process uses GET to fetch a value at an instant; when the queue is empty, the process waits until another process puts a value in the queue.

Example 10 The capacity of the queue is max. The functions characterizing the queue states are defined below and the variables in the post-state are distinguished by suffixing them with a prime.

cur_queue:	the current state of the queue
putval:	argument to PUT. The precondition for PUT is *putval* $\neq$ nil and the post-condition is *putval'* = nil.
getval:	argument to GET. The precondition for GET is *getval* = nil and the post-condition is *getval'* $\neq$ nil.

enter(PUT), *enter*(GET), *exit*(GET) and *exit*(PUT) are boolean-valued functions signaling the initiation and termination of the operations.

Liveness Properties

1. The liveness property for the PUT operation is that it terminates. The element *putval* is inserted only if it does not cause an overflow; the symbol '*' denotes insertion at the rear.

   $enter$(PUT) $\land$ ($length(cur_queue) < $ max) $\Rightarrow$

   $\Diamond(exit$(PUT) $\land$ ($cur\_queue' = cur\_queue * putval$))

   $enter$(PUT) $\land$ ($length(cur_queue) = $ max) $\Rightarrow$

   $\Diamond(exit$(PUT) $\land$ ($cur\_queue' = cur\_queue$))

2. The liveness property for the GET operation is that it terminates only when a value is fetched from the queue. That is, if the queue is empty the operation waits until a value is put in the queue and then fetches the value.

   $enter$(GET) $\land \neg empty(cur\_queue) \Rightarrow$

   $\Diamond(exit$(GET) $\land$ ($getval * cur\_queue' = cur\_queue$))

   $enter$(GET) $\land empty(cur\_queue) \Rightarrow enter$(GET) $\mathcal{U}\ exit$(PUT)

3. When the queue is empty, some process will eventually put a value in the queue.

   $empty(cur\_queue) \Rightarrow \Diamond enter$(PUT)

Safety Properties

Safety properties assert what may or may not happen to the queue due to the actions PUT and GET. The state of the queue changes under the following situations:

1. *putval* $\neq$ *nil*, and PUT is invoked by some process on a queue that is not full;
2. GET is invoked by some process, and *cur_queue* is not empty.

Situation 1. Let ($enter$(PUT) $\land putval \neq$ nil) hold for *cur_queue*. The next state is *cur_queue'* which is the same as *cur_queue* when the queue is full or $cur\_queue' = cur\_queue * putval$. So, the temporal logic formula is

   $\Box((enter$(PUT) $\land putval \neq$ nil) $\Rightarrow$

   $((($length$(cur_queue) = $ max) $\land$ ($cur\_queue' = cur\_queue$))

   $\lor(($length$(cur_queue) < $ max) $\land$ ($cur\_queue' = cur\_queue * putval$))))$.

Situation 2. Let ($enter$(GET) $\land getval = $ nil) hold for *cur_queue*. The next state is *cur_queue'* which is the same as *cur_queue* when the queue is empty, or $cur\_queue = getval * cur\_queue'$. So, the temporal logic formula is

   $\Box(($enter$(GET) $\land getval = $ nil) $\Rightarrow$ (($empty(cur\_queue) \land empty(cur\_queue')$))

$$\lor (\lnot empty(cur\_queue) \land (cur\_queue = getval * cur\_queue')))).$$ $\qquad\square$

11.4.2
Temporal Logic Semantics of Sequential Programs

In this section, we consider the temporal logic semantics for simple sequential programs whose elements are the following:

- *Assignment Statement: $x := e$*
- *Composition of Statements: S_1; S_2*
- *Conditional Selection: if e then S_1 else S_2*
- *Repetition: while e do S*

Their formal meanings under Hoare logic have been discussed in Chap. 10. Below we give FOTL semantics to these constructs. The function $[[--]]$ assigns for each program element a well-formed formula in FOTL.

Semantics of Assignment Statement   Informally, this asserts that

- before the assignment is executed there exists some state s_i where an interpretation I_{s_i} exists,
- expression e is evaluated in the interpretation I_{s_i}, as $s_i[e]$ explained earlier, and
- the result of this evaluation is the result of interpretation $I_{s_{i+1}}$ applied to x, as $s_{i+1}[x]$ in state s_{i+1}.

The states s_i and s_{i+1} need not be shown explicitly; instead the $\bigcirc$ operator may be used.

Semantics—assignment statement

$$[[x := e]] = \exists I_{s_{i+1}} \bullet s_{i+1}[x] = s_i[e]$$

or

$$[[x := e]] = \bigcirc(x = e)$$

Semantics of Composition   Informally it asserts that at current moment the first statement is evaluated and the moment next to the termination of the first statement, the second statement is evaluated.

Semantics—sequential composition of statements

$$[[S_1; S_2]] = [[S_1]] \land \bigcirc[[S_2]]$$

Semantics of Conditional Statement   Let $I(e)$ denote the evaluation of test expression at state s_i, and assume that the evaluation does not take any time. If $I(s_i[e])$ is true then the expression $[[S_1; S_3]]$ is assigned a meaning in state s_i. If $I(s_i[e])$ is false then the expression $[[S_2; S_3]]$ is assigned a meaning in state s_i.

Semantics—conditional statement

$$[[(if\ e\ then\ S_1\ else\ S_2); S_3]] = (I(e) \Rightarrow [[S_1; S_3]]) \land (\lnot I(e) \Rightarrow [[S_2; S_3]])$$

Example 11 We derive a temporal formula for capturing the semantics of the following program:
```
begin
x:=2;
if (x>2) then x:=x-2 else x:=x+1;
y:=1/x;
end
```
Let *Prog* denote the program. Then

$$[[Prog]] = \bigcirc((x = 2) \land [[if \ldots]])$$

$$[[Prog]] = \bigcirc((x = 2) \land ((x > 2) \Rightarrow [[x := x - 2]]) \land ((x \le 2) \Rightarrow [[x := x + 1 \ldots]]))$$

$$[[Prog]] = \bigcirc((x = 2) \land [[(x := x + 1) \ldots]])$$

$$[[Prog]] = \bigcirc((x = 2) \land \bigcirc((x = 3) \land [[y := 1/x \ldots]]))$$

$$[[Prog]] = \bigcirc((x = 2) \land \bigcirc((x = 3) \land \bigcirc((y = 1/3) \land [[end]])))$$

$$[[Prog]] = \bigcirc((x = 2) \land \bigcirc((x = 3) \land \bigcirc((y = 1/3) \land true)))$$

$$[[Prog]] = \bigcirc((x = 2) \land \bigcirc((x = 3) \land \bigcirc((y = 1/3))))$$

$$[[Prog]] = \bigcirc(x = 2) \land \bigcirc \bigcirc (x = 3) \land \bigcirc \bigcirc \bigcirc (y = 1/3) \qquad \square$$

Semantics of Repetition Statement   The semantics is given by recursively using the conditional statement axiom.

Semantic—while statement

$$[[(while\ e\ do\ S_1); S]] = (I(e) \Rightarrow [[(S_1; (while\ e\ do\ S_1))]]) \land (\neg I(e) \Rightarrow [[S]])$$

Example 12 We derive a temporal formula that gives the semantics of

$$x := 1; \ while \ (x < 3) \ do \ x := x + 1; end$$

$$[[x := 1; \ while \ (x < 3) \ do \ x := x + 1; end]]$$

$$= \bigcirc((x = 1) \land [[while \ \ldots]])$$

$$= \bigcirc((x = 1) \land ((x < 3) \Rightarrow [[x := x + 1; \ while \ \ldots]]) \land ((x \ge 3) \to [[end]]))$$

$$= \bigcirc((x = 1) \land [[x := x + 1; while \ \ldots]])$$

$$= \bigcirc((x = 1) \land \bigcirc((x = 2) \land [[while \ \ldots]]))$$

$$= \bigcirc((x = 1) \land \bigcirc((x = 2) \land ((x < 3) \Rightarrow$$
$$[[x := x + 1; while \ \ldots]]) \land ((x \ge 3) \to [[end]])))$$

$$= \bigcirc((x = 1) \land \bigcirc((x = 2) \land \bigcirc((x = 3) \land (x \ge 3) \to [[end]])))$$

$$= \bigcirc((x = 1) \land \bigcirc((x = 2) \land \bigcirc((x = 3) \land [[end]])))$$

$$= \bigcirc((x = 1) \land \bigcirc((x = 2) \land \bigcirc((x = 3) \land true)))$$

$$= \bigcirc(x = 1) \land \bigcirc \bigcirc (x = 2) \land \bigcirc \bigcirc \bigcirc(x = 3) \qquad \square$$

11.4.3
Temporal Logic Semantics of Concurrent Systems with Shared Variables

We add to the communication primitives discussed in Sect. 11.4.2 a new one, called *communication through shared variables*. We are still restricting to global discrete linear time model. When two components A and B share some variables, we must specify how such variables are to be accessed and modified by each component. It is necessary that each component sees exactly the *same* values for the shared variables at every state; otherwise there will be anomalies in the computation. We should allow components to see modifications to the variables at any state, and read from and write to these variables, subject to the following restrictions:

1. Read and write operations are *atomic*, in the sense that these operations take unit amount of time and cannot be interrupted.
2. Only one component can write at any moment in time.
3. When a component is reading from a variable (writing on it) the other component cannot write on it (read from it).

11.4.3.1
Component Specification

We restrict to a single variable x shared between components A and B and use the notations x_A and x_B to denote the same variable x in respective components. With this convention, the communication specification for the shared variable x between components A and B will include $\Box(x_A \Leftrightarrow x_B)$. We specify restriction (3) as

$$\Box\neg(writing\_to(A, x_A) \wedge writing\_to(B, x_B))$$

and include it in the communication specification. The program region where the shared variable is accessed is the critical region of the program. Hence, restriction (3) is also equivalent to $\Box(\neg(criti_1 \wedge criti_2))$ (see Example 4). Thus, the communication specification for a single shared variable x is

$$\Box(x_A \Leftrightarrow x_B) \wedge \Box\neg(writing\_to(A, x_A) \wedge writing\_to(B, x_B))$$

The concurrent specification of components A and B interacting through a shared variable x, denoted $Spec_{A\|_x B}$, is

$$Spec_A \wedge Spec_B \wedge (\Box(y_A \Leftrightarrow y_B)$$
$$\wedge \Box\neg(writing\_to(A, y_A) \wedge writing\_to(B, y_B)))$$

We illustrate a mixture of communication mechanisms in the following two examples.

Example 13 Consider components A and B which share a variable y. Their specifications are given below:

$$Spec_A : \Box \begin{bmatrix} start \Rightarrow (x = 5 \wedge y_A = 14) \wedge \\ even(y_A) \Rightarrow \bigcirc(y_A = (y_A - x) \wedge \\ writing\_to(A, y_A)) \end{bmatrix}$$

$$Spec_B : \Box \begin{bmatrix} start \Rightarrow (w = 9) \wedge \\ odd(y_B) \Rightarrow \bigcirc(y_B = y_B + w) \wedge \\ writing\_to(B, y_B)) \end{bmatrix}$$

Let us denote the concurrent specification of components A and B as $Spec_{A\|_y B}$. To understand the behavior of $Spec_{A\|_y B}$ we need to calculate the predicates that are true at time points starting from 0. From the specifications $Spec_A$ and $Spec_B$ and the shared variable principle, the predicate $(x = 5) \wedge (y_A = 14) \wedge (y_B = 14) \wedge (w = 9)$ is true at time 0. Hence, the predicate $even(y_A)$ is true at time 0. Consequently, the second statement in $Spec_A$ is to be executed. This makes the predicate $(x = 5) \wedge (y_A = 9) \wedge (y_B = 9) \wedge (w = 9)$ true in state 1. Notice that the values of x and w remain unchanged, although this is not explicitly stated in the specification. In state 1, the predicate $odd(y_B)$ is true and consequently the second statement of specification $Spec_B$ is executed. This makes the predicate $(x = 5) \wedge (y_A = 18) \wedge (y_B = 18) \wedge (w = 9)$ true in state 2. Continuing the analysis for successive states, we notice that in even numbered states the predicate $even(y_A)$ is true, and the second statement of $Spec_A$ is executed. As a consequence, the value of y_A is decreased by 5, an odd amount, which makes y_A (and y_B) odd at the next state. In odd numbered states the predicate $odd(y_B)$ is true, and the second statement of $Spec_B$ is executed. As a consequence, the value of y_B is increased by 9, an odd amount, which makes y_B (and (y_A) even at the next state. Consequently the behavior of $Spec_{A\|_y B}$ is infinite, only one of the components is active at any one time, and the values of x and w do not change. After some calculations, the model $\langle \mathbb{N}_0, \pi \rangle$ of the concurrent specification $Spec_{A\|_y B}$ can be succinctly determined as shown below.

$$\pi(i) = \begin{cases} (x = 5) \wedge w = 9 \wedge y = 14 + 4k) & \text{if } i = 2k, k \geq 0 \\ (x = 5) \wedge w = 9 \wedge y = 5 + 4k) & \text{if } i = 2k - 1, k \geq 1 \end{cases} \qquad \Box$$

Example 14 In this example, we simulate the behavior of a game played by two persons *Alice* and *Bob* with a slot machine M. Both *Alice* and *Bob* interact with a slot machine M; however, they do not interact between themselves. The time points of their interactions overlap; however, the slot machine responds to them only after receiving input from both of them. The slot machine responds to both of them simultaneously, according to the following rules.

- The slot machine does not accept any amount less than $5.
- Both *Alice* and *Bob* specify amounts (> $5) they want to bet.
- *Alice* bets at every moment in time.
- *Bob* bets at the beginning and at every second moment in time.

- The slot machine M waits until both bets are received, and then does the following:

It determines the winner at the next moment (the moment after both bets are received), and sends an amount x subject to the constraint $(max - min \leq x \leq max)$, where max and min, respectively, denote the maximum and minimum of the two amounts bet by *Alice* and *Bob*.

11.4.3.2
Specifications

$$Spec_{Alice} : \Box \begin{bmatrix} start \Rightarrow req\_game(Alice, n) \wedge \\ req\_game(Alice, n) \Rightarrow \bigcirc req\_game(Alice, n) \wedge \\ \Diamond got\_result(Alice, n') \end{bmatrix}$$

$$Spec_{Bob} : \Box \begin{bmatrix} start \Rightarrow req\_game(Bob, m) \wedge \\ req\_game(Bob, m) \Rightarrow wait \wedge \\ wait \Rightarrow \bigcirc req\_game(Bob, m) \wedge \\ \Diamond got\_result(Bob, m') \end{bmatrix}$$

$$Spec_M : \Box \begin{bmatrix} [rcv\_bet(Alice, \bar{n}) \wedge rcv\_bet(Bob, \bar{m})] \Rightarrow \\ \bigcirc [choose(x \in \{max(\bar{n}, \bar{m}) - min(\bar{n}, \bar{m}), \ldots, max(\bar{n}, \bar{m})\}) \Rightarrow \\ \bigcirc((give\_result(Alice, x) \wedge give\_result(Bob, 0)) \vee \\ (give\_result(Bob, x) \wedge give\_result(Alice, 0)))] \end{bmatrix}$$

The predicate $choose(x \in S)$, where S is a set, asserts that a value x is chosen from the set, but does not specify exactly which element of the set is chosen and how it is chosen. Such a predicate introduces *nondeterminism* in the design. In $Spec_M$ the second line uses the predicate *choose* to specify that a value in the range $[max - min, max]$ is determined nondeterministically. The third line in $Spec_M$ states that once x is determined then in the next moment there is a *choice* of announcing the winner. The choice operator $\vee$ is introduced in the right hand side of $\Rightarrow$. The communication specifications are given below.

Communication Specifications

$Comms(Alice, M) : \Box(req\_game(Alice, n) \Rightarrow \Diamond rcv\_bet(Alice, \bar{n})) \wedge \Box(\bar{n} \Leftrightarrow n)$

$Comms(Bob, M) : \Box(req\_game(Bob, m) \Rightarrow \Diamond rcv\_bet(Bob, \bar{m})) \wedge \Box(\bar{m} \Leftrightarrow m)$

$Comms(M, Alice) : \Box(give\_result(Alice, \bar{m}) \Rightarrow \Diamond got\_result(Alice, n')) \wedge \Box(\bar{m} \Leftrightarrow n')$

$Comms(M, Bob) : \Box(give\_result(Bob, \bar{n}) \Rightarrow \Diamond got\_result(Bob, m')) \wedge \Box(\bar{n} \Leftrightarrow m')$

The full specification is

$Spec_{Alice} \wedge Spec_{Bob} \wedge Spec_M \wedge Comms(Alice, M) \wedge Comms(Bob, M) \wedge$

$Comms(M, Alice) \wedge Comms(M, Bob)$ □

In Examples 13 and 14, the communication specification fixes the interaction point of the components. The programs corresponding to such components, assuming that they start

at the same time and execute at the same speed, are expected to reach the specified interaction point at the same instant for "hand shaking". When programs that run at different
speeds share variables and the interaction specification states only mutual exclusion principle, a more thorough analysis of the shared variables becomes necessary. That is, different
interleaving executions must be analyzed. For a full account of the temporal semantics of
concurrent programs consult Pnueli [23].

Example 15 Programs $Prog_1$ and $Prog_3$ share the variable x, programs $Prog_2$ and $Prog_3$
share the variable y, and programs $Prog_1$ and $Prog_2$ have no shared variable. Assume that
the programs are started simultaneously at time 0. In these programs, the shared variables
are accessed only at the statements P_1, P_2, and P_3 as shown below.

$$Prog_1 : \begin{bmatrix} \vdots \\ P_1 :: x := x + 2; \\ \vdots \end{bmatrix}$$

$$Prog_2 : \begin{bmatrix} \vdots \\ P_2 :: y := y + 2; \\ \vdots \end{bmatrix}$$

$$Prog_3 : \begin{bmatrix} \vdots \\ P_3 :: \begin{cases} x := x - y + 1; \\ x := x + y + 1; \end{cases} \\ \vdots \end{bmatrix}$$

Using the temporal semantics (Sect. 11.4.2) for each program $Prog_i$, we create the temporal logic formulas $T(Prog_i)$. We may regard $T(Prog_i)$ as temporal specifications of the
component whose implementation is $Prog_i$. In such a specification, we can ignore variables
that are not accessed in the critical sections and identify $T(Prog_i)$ with $T(P_i)$. We can use
the semantics discussed above for the specifications $T(P_1)$, $T(P_2)$, and $T(P_3)$ to provide
a model of the concurrent execution of the program statements P_1, P_2, P_3. The program
$P_1 \parallel P_2$ exhibits pure concurrency, for they have no shared variables. Hence the model of
$P_1 \parallel P_2$ is the model of $T(P_1) \wedge T(P_2)$. The model for the concurrent program $P_1 \parallel_x P_3$
is calculated below from the model $T(P_1) \wedge T(P_3)$, subject to the interaction points. The
temporal specifications of P_1 and P_3 are

$$T(P_1) = \exists u \in Val_1(i). \bigcirc (x = u + 2)$$

$$T(P_3) = \exists a, b \in Val_3(j). \bigcirc ((x' = a - b + 1) \wedge \bigcirc (x'' = x' + b + 1)),$$

where $Val_1(i)$ and $Val_3(j)$, respectively, denote the set of values of state variables of program statements P_1 and P_3 at times i and j. We need to consider two situations: $i + 1 < j$,
which states that P_1 writes on variable x before P_3 commences execution, and $i > j + 1$,

which states that P_3 completes writing on variable x before P_1 starts execution. In the former case the behavior is

state $i + 1$ $(x = u + 2)$
state j $(x = u + 2)$
state $j + 1$ $(a = u + 2) \wedge (x = u - b + 3)$
state $j + 2$ $(a = u + 2) \wedge (x = u + 4)$

In the latter case the behavior is

state j $(x = a) \wedge (x' = a - b + 1)$
state $j + 1$ $(x' = a - b + 1) \wedge (x'' = a + 2)$
state $i - 1$ $(x = a + 2)$
state i $(x = a + 4)$ □

11.5
Formal Verification

Formal verification for temporal logic is of two kinds, known as *axiomatic* and *algorithmic*. In an axiomatic approach, a set of general axioms and a proof calculus [17] are formulated. They form the kernel to which more domain specific axioms and inference rules may be added. These axioms and inference rules are then applied to show the correctness of temporal logic specification with respect to more abstract system specification. In an algorithmic approach, a model of the system is constructed and an algorithm is developed to prove that the model satisfies the property, stated as a temporal logic formula. These two approaches are separate systems of studies in itself, which we pursue only in a small measure. The goal in this section is to outline the basic characteristics of these methods for FOTL and PTL and illustrate with simple examples.

In Sect. 11.5.1, we illustrate a version of axiomatic verification, that closely follows Hoare style axiomatization, applied to a simple planning system specified in FOTL. In Sect. 11.5.2, we introduce a model of the system specified by PTL formulas and give the algorithmic approach for verifying properties in the model.

11.5.1
Verification of Simple FOTL Specifications

We restrict to a simple subsystem of FOTL which consists of quantified temporal formulas that involve only the temporal operators $\square$, $\diamondsuit$, and $\bigcirc$. Since FOTL specifications are interpreted over linear states, in order to prove a property in the system it is sufficient to verify that the property holds at every system state. Let us write $\varphi(i)$ to mean that φ is true at the ith state of $\mathcal{M}$, the semantic model of the specification. If we can show

- $\varphi(0)$ is true, and

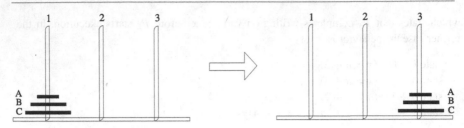

Fig. 11.1 Towers of Hanoi

- for any i establish $\varphi(i+1)$, knowing that $\varphi(i)$ is true,

then we know by induction Axiom (see Sect. 11.3.5) that $\varphi(i)$ is true for all $i \in \mathbb{N}_0$. It is this principle that we will use for formally verifying invariant properties, such as safety. We can recast the induction result using pre- and postconditions for actions at states. Let $a_1, a_2, \ldots$ be a sequence of actions performed at states $s_1, s_2, \ldots$. If P_i is a precondition and Q_i is the postcondition for action a_i at state s_i, and $\mathcal{T}(a_i)$ is the temporal logic specification of the system at state s_i, it is necessary to verify that $P_i \wedge \mathcal{T}(a_i) \Rightarrow Q_i$, and $Q_i \Rightarrow P_{i+1}$, where P_{i+1} is the precondition for action a_{i+1} at state s_{i+1}. This formulation is similar to the Hoare style axioms for verifying correctness of sequential programs discussed in Chap. 10.

Example 16 Planning problems require the construction of a series of actions such that the goal can be achieved by executing those actions in a certain order. Temporal logic can be used to specify actions and their ordering in planning problems. We consider the Tower of Hanoi problem to illustrate the methodology.

> Three pegs p_1, p_2, and p_3 and three disks A, B and C are available. Initially the three disks are stacked on peg p_1, with the smallest disk A on top and largest disk C at the bottom. It is required to plan a move of the disks from peg p_1 to peg p_3, using peg p_2 as a temporary storage area, such that after every single move, the disks are ordered with the largest one at the bottom.

A configuration refers to the collection of pegs and the ordering of disks on them. The initial and final configurations are shown in Fig. 11.1. We assume that each peg p has a "largest" disk D attached to its bottom. This disk cannot be moved. Denoting the size of a disk x by $size(x)$ we have the constraint

$$size(A) < size(B) < size(C) < size(D_p) = \infty$$

We abstract each peg with disks stacked in it in increasing order of size from its top to its bottom as a *stack* of linearly ordered items. All actions on a peg, according to the problem requirement, should satisfy this property. That is, "items from top to bottom in a stack are linearly ordered, in decreasing order" is an *invariant* property of the Hanoi system. Once this is recognized, we want to provide a temporal logic specification of a stack that satisfies this invariant property, and then use the stack operations to define the move actions for solving the Hanoi problem.

Stack Specification   Let $(\mathcal{D}, \prec)$ be a linearly ordered domain. That is, for any two values v_1, v_2 in $\mathcal{D}$, either $v_1 \prec v_2$ or $v_2 \prec v_1$ can hold. A stack contains elements from $(\mathcal{D}, \prec)$, subject to the invariant property stated above. Assume that $\mathcal{D}$ has an infimum $-\infty$, and a supremum ∞. That is, $\forall v, v \in \mathcal{D}$ the property $-\infty < v < \infty$ holds. Stack operations should satisfy the invariant property. In the stack specification shown below, *curr_stack* denotes the current stack configuration.

Operation	Specification
TOP	argument is *curr_stack*
	it returns a value $v \in \mathcal{D}$.
	precondition is *true*
	let φ denote the predicate
	$v = \infty$ if *curr_stact* is empty
	$v = TOP(curr\_stack)$ if *curr_stack* is not empty
	in the postcondition
	$\varphi \wedge (curr\_stack' = curr\_stack)$
ADD	adds an element to the current stack.
	arguments to ADD are *addval* $\in \mathcal{D}$, and *curr_stack*.
	precondition is $addval \prec TOP(curr\_stack)$
	postcondition is $TOP(curr\_stack') = addval \wedge$
	$(curr\_stack' = addval * curr\_stack)$
REMOVE	removes the element from top of the stack
	argument is *curr_stack*.
	precondition is *curr_stack* is not empty.
	postcondition is $(TOP(curr\_stack) * curr\_stack' = curr\_stack)$

Proving Invariant Property   Let $I(s)$ denote the invariant property of the stack: "items from top to bottom in a stack s are linearly ordered, in decreasing order". $I(empty)$ is trivially true. We need two basic axioms on ordered sequences to prove that stack operations preserve the invariant property $I(s)$. Let $\sigma = \langle v_1, v_2, \ldots, v_k \rangle$, $v_i \in \mathcal{D}$ be a strictly monotonic increasing sequence. That is

$$v_1 \prec v_2 \prec \cdots \prec v_{k-1} \prec v_k$$

If $v \prec v_1$ then the sequence $v * \sigma$, where $*$ denotes insertion at the front of the sequence, is also strictly monotonically increasing. This follows from the transitive property of $\prec$. If the element v_1 (in general, any v_i) is removed from the sequence, the rest of the sequence remains ordered. These properties are stated below for insertion and deletion of items in a stack of ordered items.

Ordered Stack—Insertion Axiom
$$\frac{I(s), x \prec TOP(s)}{I(x * s)}$$

Ordered Stack—Deletion Axiom

$$\frac{I(s), s = x * s'}{I(s')}$$

From the postcondition of *TOP* operation, infer $curr\_stack' = curr\_stack$. Hence, it follows that *TOP* operation preserves the invariant property:

$$I(curr\_stack') = I(curr\_stack)$$

When the precondition of the *ADD* operation

$$I(curr\_stack) \wedge (addval \prec TOP(curr\_stack))$$

is satisfied from the insertion axiom, it follows that $I(curr\_stack')$ holds after termination of *ADD* operation.

The precondition of *REMOVE* specification is $curr\_stack$ is not empty. So, we infer

$$curr\_stack = x * curr\_stack',$$

where $x = TOP(curr\_stack)$. Combining $I(curr\_stack)$ with this result, we derive

$$(curr\_stack = x * curr\_stack') \wedge I(curr\_stack),$$

and from the deletion axiom we derive $I(curr\_stack')$.

Hanoi Specification   We give a temporal specification of actions. The basic action is a move, which is described using stack operations. Each move is atomic, in the sense that its execution cannot be interrupted and it takes one unit of time to complete it. The move action has parameters x and y which represent, respectively, the configurations of the peg from which the top disk is moved and the configuration of the destination peg in which the disk is placed. It is advantageous to have the notation $x = TOP(x) * rest\_of(x)$ for a nonempty configuration. If the configuration x is empty then $x = TOP(x) = D_x$.

Move Action:: move(x,y)

$$\langle v = TOP(x); \quad ADD(v, y); \quad REMOVE(x) \rangle$$

Using the stack specification, the meaning of action $move(x, y)$ can be formally written as

$$move(x, y) \Rightarrow \bigcirc((TOP(y') = TOP(x)) \wedge (rest\_of(y') = y) \wedge (x' = rest\_of(x))),$$

where x' and y' denote the post states of peg configurations x and y. For the sake of simplicity, we use a "horizontal notation" to display the status of a (stack) peg x, as in $u * w * D_x$, for which $TOP(x) = u$ as and $rest\_of(x) = w * D_x$.

1. *Initial Configuration:*
   Initially, disks A, B and C are in peg p_1, with A at the top, on top of disk B, disk B on top of disk C which is on top of the bottom disk D_{p_1}. The pegs p_2 and p_3 are empty.

```
                    Initial Configuration
        p₁ : A * B * C * D_{p₁}
                                    I(p₁) ∧ I(p₂) ∧ I(p₃)
        p₂ : D_{p₂}    p₃ : D_{p₃}
```

$$p_1 : A * B * C * D_{p_1}$$
$$p_2 : D_{p_2} \quad p_3 : D_{p_3} \quad\quad I(p_1) \wedge I(p_2) \wedge I(p_3)$$

2. *Goal Specification:*
The goal is to have disks A, B and C stacked on peg p_3 in the same order as in the initial state. The goal configuration is specified as follows:

```
                    Goal Configuration
        p₁ : D_{p₁}    p₂ : D_{p₂}
                                    I(p₁) ∧ I(p₂) ∧ I(p₃)
        p₃ : A * B * C * D_{p₃}
```

$$p_1 : D_{p_1} \quad p_2 : D_{p_2}$$
$$p_3 : A * B * C * D_{p_3} \quad\quad I(p_1) \wedge I(p_2) \wedge I(p_3)$$

3. *Planning:*
Starting with the initial configuration, the goal configuration is achieved by a sequence of moves as specified below.

$$move(p_1, p_3) \wedge \bigcirc move(p_1, p_2) \wedge \bigcirc^2 move(p_3, p_2) \wedge$$
$$\bigcirc^3 move(p_1, p_3) \wedge \bigcirc^4 move(p_2, p_1) \wedge \bigcirc^5 move(p_2, p_3) \wedge$$
$$\bigcirc^6 move(p_1, p_3)$$

4. *Verification:*
For each move operation, we have to (1) verify that the precondition is true, (2) calculate the postcondition, and (3) prove that the invariant is preserved. We should also prove that when all the moves are completed, the goal configuration is reached.

Verification for the first move: $move(p_1, p_3)$.

We substitute $[p_1/x, p_3/y]$ in $move(x, y)$ definition.

```
            First Move Action:: move(p₁, p₃)
        ⟨v = TOP(p₁);   ADD(v, p₃);   REMOVE(p₁)⟩
```

Initially, p_1 is not empty. From the postcondition of TOP operation, infer $v = TOP(p_1) = A$. Since $TOP(p_3) = D_{p_3}$, and $size(A) < size(D_{p_3})$ is true, the precondition of the operation $ADD(v, p_3)$ is true. From the postcondition of $ADD(v, p_3)$ we infer $TOP(p_3') = v \wedge p_3' = v * p_3$. By atomicity assumption, we have the result

$$\bigcirc((TOP(p_3') = A) \wedge (rest\_of(p_3') = p_3) \wedge (p_1' = rest\_of(p_1)))$$

Notice that we could have obtained the above result directly from the temporal specification of $move(x, y)$. Applying deletion axiom for $REMOVE(p_1)$ we get $I(p_1')$, and

Table 11.1 Hanoi Configurations

Time	Action	Configuration	Time	Action	Configuration
0	$move(p_1, p_3)$	$p_1 : A * B * C * D_{p_1}$ $p_2 : D_{p_2}$ $p_3 : D_{p_3}$	4	$move(p_2, p_1)$	$p_1 : D_{p_1}$ $p_2 : A * B * D_{p_2}$ $p_3 : C * D_{p_3}$
1	$move(p_1, p_2)$	$p_1 : B * C * D_{p_1}$ $p_2 : D_{p_2}$ $p_3 : A * D_{p_3}$	5	$move(p_2, p_3)$	$p_1 : A * D_{p_1}$ $p_2 : B * D_{p_2}$ $p_3 : C * D_{p_3}$
2	$move(p_3, p_2)$	$p_1 : C * D_{p_1}$ $p_2 : B * D_{p_2}$ $p_3 : A * D_{p_3}$	6	$move(p_1, p_3)$	$p_1 : A * D_{p_1}$ $p_2 : D_{p_2}$ $p_3 : B * C * D_{p_3}$
3	$move(p_1, p_3)$	$p_1 : C * D_{p_1}$ $p_2 : A * B * D_{p_2}$ $p_3 : D_{p_3}$	7		$p_1 : D_{p_1}$ $p_2 : D_{p_2}$ $p_3 : A * B * C * D_{p_3}$

applying insertion axiom for $ADD(v, p_3)$ we get $I(p'_3)$. Since the move operation does not change the state of p_2, $I(p'_2) = I(p_2)$. Thus, we have calculated the configuration at time moment 1, and proved that the first move operation preserves the invariance property $I(p_1) \land I(p_2) \land I(p_3)$.

Starting at the configuration at time 1 and following the above steps for the operation $move(p_1, p_2)$, we will arrive at the second configuration and will prove the invariant property $I(p_1) \land I(p_2) \land I(p_3)$. Calculations at successive time points are shown in Table 11.1.   □

11.5.2
Model Checking

Model checking is an *algorithmic* technique for verifying finite state concurrent systems. Model checking method has successfully been applied to verify hardware designs, communication protocols, and reactive system properties. It is a rich field of study in which theory blends with practical techniques to verify safety and liveness properties of complex systems. Because model checking can be *automated*, it may be preferred to axiomatic verification method. However, model checking has some limitations as well. In this section, we discuss some basic principles of model checking with PTL and FOTL formulas.

The first step toward model checking is to create a formal model of the system and specify the property to be verified in the model. The formal model that is used for reactive systems is a state transition graph, called *Kripke structure* (KS). A KS resembles a state machine that we have seen in Chaps. 6 and 7, yet they are more general. Essentially, a KS has a set of states, a set of initial states, a set of transitions between states, and for each state a set of properties that are true in that state. Every state must have a transition. There is no accepting state. The language used to describe the properties in each state and label the transitions go toward defining the richness of the KS. In reactive and concurrent system models, input may be received at more than one state and the program need not terminate. This is why in KS there is no accepting state and more than one input state is allowed. In our study, we will restrict to PTL and simple FOTL formulas for stating the properties and labeling the transitions. Example 17 informally explains the construction of KS for a set of FOTL formulas. We use the notation x' to denote the variable x in a post state.

Example 17 We want to formally represent the computation of the program P

$$\langle x' = (x + y) \ mod \ 3; \ y' = (y + 1) \ mod \ 3\rangle$$

over the domain $V = \{0, 1, 2\}$ as a Kripke structure. The two program statements are to be executed as an atomic unit. A state represents "variable-value" pairs. That is, $\langle x = v_1, y = v_2\rangle$, where $v_1, v_2 \in V$ is a state, which is written (v_1, v_2). We associate the formula $x = v_1 \wedge y = v_2$ with the state (v_1, v_2). Thus the set of all states for the given variables over the domain V is

$$V \times V = \{(0, 0), (0, 1), (0, 2), (1, 0), (1, 1), (1, 2), (2, 0), (2, 1), (2, 2)\}.$$

Let $(x = 0 \wedge y = 2)$ be the initial state. Program P that defines the relationship between (x, y) and (x', y') is the *transition* relation for the KS. That is, executing the program at the initial state gives the next state $x' = 2 \wedge y' = 0$. So, in KS, there is a transition from state $(x = 0 \wedge y = 2)$ to $(x = 2 \wedge y = 0)$. The transition relation for the KS is the set of ordered pairs of vertices related by the execution of P. So, the KS that models the computation P is

- *set of states:* $S = V \times V$
- *set of initial states:* $S_0 = \{(0, 2)\}$
- *transition relation:*

$$R = \{((0, 2), (2, 0)), ((2, 0), (2, 1)), ((2, 1)(0, 2)), ((0, 0), (0, 1)), ((0, 1), (1, 2)),$$

$$((1, 2), (0, 0)), ((1, 1), (2, 2)), ((2, 2), (0, 0)), ((0, 0), (1, 1))\}$$

- *properties:*

$L((0, 0)) = \{x = 0 \wedge y = 0\}$	$L((0, 1)) = \{x = 0 \wedge y = 1\}$
$L((1, 0)) = \{x = 1 \wedge y = 0\}$	$L((1, 1)) = \{x = 1 \wedge y = 1\}$
$L((2, 0)) = \{x = 2 \wedge y = 0\}$	$L((2, 1)) = \{x = 2 \wedge y = 1\}$

$$L((0, 2)) = \{x = 0 \wedge y = 2\}$$
$$L((1, 2)) = \{x = 1 \wedge y = 2\}$$
$$L((2, 2)) = \{x = 2 \wedge y = 2\}$$ □

Formally a Kripke structure over a set of atomic propositions AP is a four tuple $KS = (S, S_0, R, L)$ where

1. S is a *finite* set of states.
2. $S_0 \subset S$ is the set of initial states.
3. R is a *total* transition relation on S, that is, for every $s \in S$ there is an s' such that $R(s, s')$.
4. L associates with each state s, a set $L(s) \subset AP$ of propositions that are true in that state.

A path in the structure KS from state s is an infinite sequence of states $\langle s_0, s_1, s_2, \ldots \rangle$, where $s = s_0$, and $R(s_i, s_{i+1})$ holds for all $i \geq 0$. Every state in KS is reachable from the initial state. In Example 17, the only path that starts in the initial state $(0, 2)$ is $(0, 2)(2, 0)(2, 1)$.

11.5.3
Program Graphs, Transition Systems, and Kripke Structures

In computing literature, especially in the field of formal modeling and verification, many different, but related, models are constructed. Program graph (PG) is a directed graph model constructed from a program description [1]. The vertices are program states, and a directed edge formalizes state change under a constraint. The semantics of state transitions is the "guard/action" paradigm that was introduced for EFSMs in Chap. 7. So, for all practical purposes, a PG is a EFSM in which typed variables appear as guards for transitions. In PG, the program statements are the interpretation functions which define evaluation of variables in a state. The semantics of the transition $s \xrightarrow{[g/\alpha]} s'$ is that a nondeterministic choice is made at state s to select a transition that satisfies g, the action α is executed according to the evaluation defined by I, and the transition results in state s'. Program graphs can be combined exactly the same way that EFSMs are combined, except that for concurrent programs the proper semantics of concurrency must be followed to combine their respective graphs. Program graphs of concurrent programs with shared variables must be combined using the *interleaving* semantics. That is,

$$\frac{s_1 \xrightarrow{[g/\alpha]} s_1'}{(s_1, s_2) \xrightarrow{[g/\alpha]} (s_1', s_2)}$$

$$\frac{s_2 \xrightarrow{[g/\alpha]} s_2'}{(s_1, s_2) \xrightarrow{[g/\alpha]} (s_1, s_2')}$$

and the interpretation combines the interpretations of the two programs. We denote the interleaving program graph of PG_1 and PG_2 by $PG_1|||PG_2$. Example 18 illustrates this principle.

Example 18 The program graphs PG_1 and PG_2 corresponding to the program statements $P_1 : x := x + 2$, and $P_2 : x := x * x$ are shown in Fig. 11.2. The programs P_1 and P_2 have the shared variable x. Interleaving semantics apply for shared variables. Applying the semantics for interleaving we get the graph $PG : PG_1|||PG_2$ shown in Fig. 11.2. $\square$

Fig. 11.2 Program graphs and their product: Example 18

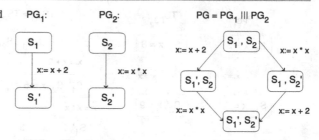

A transition system (TS) over a set of propositions AP is almost identical to the Kripke structure (KS) over AP, the only exception is that a TS may be *infinite*. The states of TS are called *locations*, and the state transitions are caused by atomic actions. In an infinite TS, the set of locations S, the set of propositions AP, and the set of actions are infinite. The semantics of a transition from location s to location s', written $s \xrightarrow{\alpha} s'$, is that a transition from state s is selected *nondeterministically*, the action α is performed, and the location s' is reached. The outcome of this selection process cannot be predicted a priori. Similarly, if the TS has more than one initial state, the start state is selected nondeterministically.

Because a finite TS is a KS, every location of TS is a tuple containing evaluations of variables. In general, a location of TS is of the form $\langle s, p_1, p_2, \ldots, p_k, \rangle$, where p_i are propositions (or simple predicates of the form $b = 1$) that are true in that location, and s is a local name for the location. Comparing the semantics of PG and TS, it is evident that the state transition semantics can be given to transitions in PG and get the transition system TS_{PG} of a program graph PG, as described below:

- For each location s of PG create the locations $\{\langle s, (v_i, a_i)\rangle \mid v_i \in V\}$ of TS_{PG}, where a_i is the evaluation of a variable v_i in location s.
- Corresponding to a transition $s \xrightarrow{[g/a]} s'$ in PG, g must satisfy the evaluation of variables at s and a must satisfy the evaluation of variables at s'. Let $p_1, p_2, \ldots, p_k$ denote the evaluations that satisfy g at s, and $q_1, q_2, \ldots, q_k$ denote the result of applying the action α on $p_1, p_2, \ldots, p_k$, the transition rule becomes

$$\frac{s \xrightarrow{[g/\alpha]} s'}{\langle s, p_1, p_2, \ldots, p_k\rangle \xrightarrow{\alpha} \langle s_1', q_1, q_2, \ldots, q_k\rangle}$$

The transition systems TS_{PG_1}, TS_{PG_2}, and $TS_{PG_1 \parallel PG_2}$ of the program graphs constructed in Example 18 are shown in Fig. 11.3.

Notice that

$$TS_{PG_1} \parallel TS_{PG_1} \neq TS_{PG_1 \parallel PG_2}$$

The reason is that the interleaving product of transition systems assume that the programs are truly concurrent, and share no variable. Therefore, in model checking systems with shared variables, we should compute the interleaving program graphs from the programs

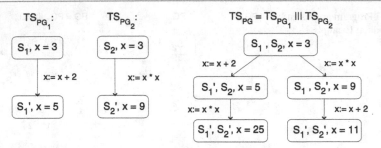

Fig. 11.3 Transition graphs corresponding to the program graphs in Fig. 11.2

Fig. 11.4 Program graphs for the mutual exclusion programs in Example 19

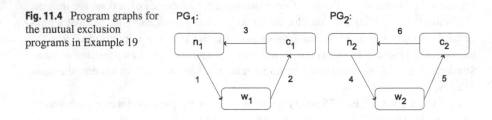

and then create its transition system. With this background we now look at the *mutual exclusion* algorithm of Peterson [21].

In Example 19, processes P_1 and P_2 share the three variables x of type $\{1, 2\}$, and b_1 and b_2 of type Boolean. In order to enter the critical section, a process waits, gets the token, enters the critical section and performs its action, releases the token and exits into noncritical section. The main interest is on the shared variables in order to prove the safety property, as stated in Example 4, Sect. 11.3.6. So we abstract away from the computations in noncritical sections and focus only on the conditions for performing the action in the critical section. The situations are abstractly denoted with states containing the propositions c_i, n_i, w_i, as explained below:

c_i : process P_i is in the critical section
n_i : process P_i is not in the critical section
w_i : process P_i is waiting to enter the critical section

Thus, for the program graph PG_i of process P_i, the locations are c_i, n_i, w_i, and the set of variables is $V_i = \{x, b_1, b_2\}$, $i = 1, 2$. The variables b_i indicate the current location of process P_i. That is, $b_i = w_i \vee c_i$, and is set when P_i wants to wait. Initially we assume $b_1 = b_2 = false$. If $x = i$ then process P_i may enter its critical section. The program-graphs generated from the program descriptions of P_1 and P_2 in Example 19 are shown in Fig. 11.4.

Example 19

P_1:	P_2:
loop forever	**loop forever**
(*noncritical actions*)	(*noncritical actions*)
⋮	⋮
(*request to enter critical section*)	(*request to enter critical section*)
$\langle b_1 := true; x := 2 \rangle$	$\langle b_2 := true; x := 1 \rangle$
(*waiting*)	(*waiting*)
wait until $(x = 1 \vee \neg b_2)$	**wait until** $(x = 2 \vee \neg b_1)$
(*(action in critical section*)	(*(action in critical section*)
do critical section od	do critical section od
(*release*)	(*release*)
$b_1 := false$;	$b_2 := false$;
(*noncritical section*)	(*noncritical section*)
⋮	⋮
end loop	**end loop**

The specification of the program graphs PG_1 and PG_2, in the notation of EFSM, are given below.

$$PG_i = \{Q_i, \Sigma_i, V_i, \Lambda_i\}, i = 1, 2$$

where

$Q_i = \{c_i, n_i, w_i\}$

$\Sigma_i = \{\}$

$V_i = \{x, b_1, b_2\}, x \in \{1, 2\}, b_1, b_2 \in \{true, false\}$

Λ_1 : *Transition Specifications for PG_1*

1. $n_1 \xrightarrow{[true/(b_1=true \wedge x=2)]} w_1$
2. $w_1 \xrightarrow{[(\neg b_2 \vee x=1)/...]} c_1$
3. $c_1 \xrightarrow{[true/(b_1=false)]} n_1$

Λ_2 : *Transition Specifications for PG_2*

4. $n_2 \xrightarrow{[true/(b_2=true \wedge x=1)]} w_2$
5. $w_2 \xrightarrow{[(\neg b_1 \vee x=2)/...]} c_2$
6. $c_2 \xrightarrow{[true/(b_2=false)]} n_2$

Figure 11.5 shows the program graph PG which is the product of the program graphs PG_1 and PG_2 given in Fig. 11.4. The graph PG is constructed using the interleaving semantics on PG_1 and PG_2. In this graph, we find that the only ways to reach the state $\langle c_1, c_2 \rangle$ are to try transitions from states $\langle w_1, c_2 \rangle$ and $\langle c_1, w_2 \rangle$. However, in state $\langle c_1, w_2 \rangle$, $x = 1 \wedge b_2 = true$ is true, whereas the guard condition for transition (labeled 5) at that state is $\neg b_1 \wedge x = 2$, which is false. Similarly, in state $\langle c_2, w_1 \rangle$, $x = 2 \wedge b_1 = true$ is true, whereas the guard condition for transition (labeled 2) at that state is $\neg b_2 \wedge x = 1$, which is false.

Fig. 11.5 Product of program graphs for the mutual exclusion programs in Example 19

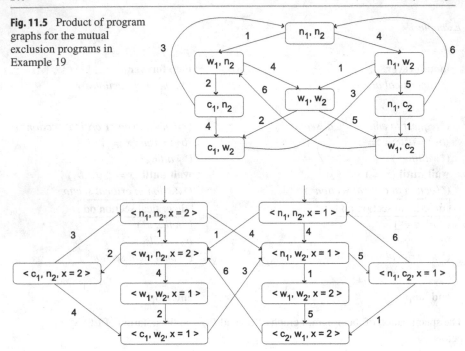

Fig. 11.6 Transition System for the mutual exclusion programs in Example 19

Consequently the state $\langle c_1, c_2 \rangle$ is not reachable. That is, in all states of the program graph *PG* the property $\neg(c_1 \wedge c_2)$ is true. This proves the safety property of Peterson's mutual exclusion algorithm.   □

The transition system for the program graph in Fig. 11.5 is shown in Fig. 11.6. Notice that the state (n_1, n_2) of the program graph corresponds to the two states $\langle n_1, n_2, x = 1 \rangle$ and $\langle n_1, n_2, x = 2 \rangle$ of the transition system. This is due to the reason that in the noncritical section n_1, the variable x is set to 2 and in the noncritical section n_2, the variable x is set to 1, and consequently in the combined state (n_1, n_2), the variable x can take either value. The transition specifications for both figures are identical.

In summary, a KS is a TS, a PG can be transformed to a TS, and a EFSM is a TS. That is, a TS, also called *labeled transition systems* (LTS), is the most general formal model for describing concurrent and reactive systems. When we start with a program, we construct its PG and then derive its TS. When we start with a model, say EFSM, then we may regard it as a PG and then derive the corresponding TS. Since we are dealing only with finite state concurrent and reactive systems, we will be dealing only with finite transition systems, which are Kripke structures.

A model checking algorithm is a *decision procedure*, which for a given model and a property should output "YES", if the model satisfies the property or output "NO" if the model fails to satisfy the property. When a Kripke structure is the formal model, we need to include "accept" states in it in order that the algorithm may recognize the acceptance

Fig. 11.7 Büchi automaton: Example 20

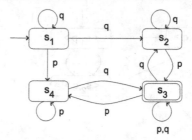

of the stated property. Moreover, the property itself may be stated as "something never happens", which requires a verification for infinite number of time points. The structure, known as Büchi Automaton (BA) [3], has the following attractive properties necessary for model checking.

- A Kripke structure can be transformed into a BA by simply making every state in KS an accepting state, and adding a new initial state.
- A BA is a finite state automaton extended to accept/reject infinite strings. Consequently, PTL formulas which are infinite strings can be recognized by a BA.
- PTL properties can be turned into Büchi automata.
- It is *easier* (linear time) to check if a BA accepts any string at all.
- It is known that Büchi automata are closed under union, intersection and complementation. This means that there exists an automaton that recognizes exactly the complement of a given language, and an automaton that recognizes the intersection of two automata. An equivalent statement is that the class of Büchi recognizable languages is closed under boolean operations.

11.5.4
Model Checking using Büchi Automata

A Büchi automaton is a finite state machine $\mathcal{A} = (Q, \Sigma, q_0, F, \delta)$ which accepts *infinite* strings. The notation $(ab)^{\omega}$ denotes the infinite repetition of the finite string ab, and the notation $(ab)^*$ denotes any arbitrary, but finite, repetitions of string ab. A *run* σ is an infinite sequence of states $s_0, s_1, \ldots, s_n, \ldots$, where s_0 is an initial state, and (s_i, s_{i+1}) is a transition in the BA. For a run σ, let $Inf(\sigma)$ denote the set of states that occur infinitely often in σ. The run σ is *accepted* by the BA if $Inf(\sigma) \cap F \neq \emptyset$, where F is the set of accept states of the BA. That is, some accept state must be *visited* infinitely often in the run σ.

Example 20 The automaton in Fig. 11.7 is a BA which has one accept state s_3. Example runs are s_1^{ω}, $s_1^* s_2 s_3^{\omega}$, and $s_1^* s_4^* s_3^{\omega}$. For the run $\sigma_1 = s_1^* s_2 s_3^{\omega}$, $Inf(\sigma_1) = \{s_3\}$ and hence the run σ_1 is an accepting run. For $\sigma_2 = s_1^* s_4^* s_3^* s_2^{\omega}$, $Inf(\sigma_2) = \{s_2\}$, and $Inf(\sigma_2) \cap \{s_3\} = \emptyset$. Hence the run σ_2 is not an accepting run. The string that corresponds to the accepting run $s_1^* s_2 s_3^{\omega}$ is $q^* q p^{\omega}$. It is easy to verify that the automaton accepts the strings in which both p and q appear infinitely often. □

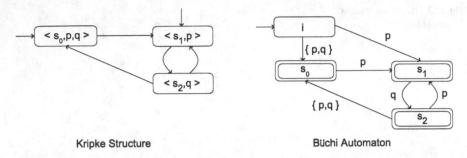

Kripke Structure   Büchi Automaton

Fig. 11.8 Büchi automaton corresponding to a Kripke structure

The language $\mathcal{L}(\mathcal{A})$ is the set of strings accepted by $\mathcal{A}$. Every PTL formula is accepted by a Büchi Automaton. Consequently, a PTL formula can be expressed as a Büchi automaton. However, the converse is not true, because Büchi automaton can capture properties not expressible by PTL.

A Kripke structure (S, R, S_0, L), where $L : S \rightarrow 2^{AP}$, can be transformed to a Büchi automaton $(Q, \Sigma, q_0, F, \delta)$ as follows:

states: $Q = S \cup \{i\}$, (all states of the Kripke structure plus one new state are the states of the automaton)

alphabet: $\Sigma = 2^{AP}$ (alphabet is the set of propositions used in the labelings of the transition system)

initial states: $q_0 = \{i\}$ (initial state is the new state created in Q)

accept states: $F = S$ (all states of the Kripke structure become final states of the automaton)

transitions: $\delta(s, \alpha) = s'$, $s, s' \in Q$ if and only if (s, s') is a transition in R and $L(s') = \alpha$

Figure 11.8 gives a Kripke structure and its corresponding Büchi automaton. The property to be verified can also be given as Büchi automata. Figure 11.9 shows the basic PTL formulas and their corresponding BAs. To reduce the number of transitions in a BA representation, we annotate the transitions as in Fig. 11.8. We can use boolean expressions, rather than a subset of propositions for annotation. Each transition annotated in this manner actually represents several transitions, where each transition corresponds to a truth assignment for AP that satisfies the boolean expression. As an example, when $AP = \{p, q, r\}$, a transition labeled $p \wedge \neg r$ matches labeled with $\{p, q\}$ and $\neg r$.

Model Checking Procedure   Model checking is an algorithmic way of determining whether or not a system satisfies a stated property. There are several model checking procedures [6]. One of them, called *automata theoretic method*, is based on the following observation. A system modeled as Büchi automata S satisfies the property specified as another Büchi automata $\mathcal{P}$ when

$$\mathcal{L}(S) \subset \mathcal{L}(\mathcal{P}) \tag{11.1}$$

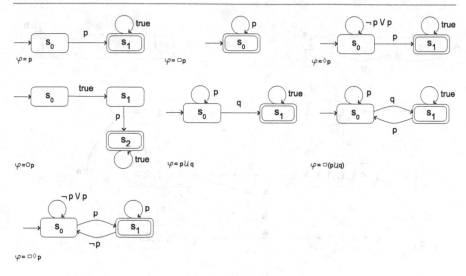

Fig. 11.9 Büchi automata corresponding to PTL formulas

That is, the behavior of the modeled system is contained within the behaviors allowed by the property. The relation (11.1) can be rewritten as

$$\mathcal{L}(\mathcal{S}) \cap \overline{\mathcal{L}(\mathcal{P})} = \emptyset \tag{11.2}$$

This means that any behavior disallowed by the property is not contained within the behaviors of the system. If the intersection in (11.2) is not empty, any behavior in it is a counterexample to the claim.

Computing Product of Büchi Automata   The method for computing the intersection of finite automata does not work for computing the product of Büchi automata. Finite automata accept only finite words, whereas Büchi automata accept infinite words. An infinite word that is accepted by the product of two Büchi automata should visit the accept states of each automaton infinitely often. It is therefore necessary to record in every state of the product machine a *tag* indicating whether the product automaton is checking for an accept state of the first automaton or the second automaton. The product automaton accepts the string only if it switches the focus (as indicated by the tags) from the second to the first (or equivalently, from the first to second) infinitely often. That is, the accept states of the product automaton are precisely those where "switching back and forth" happens. The formal construction is given below.

The product of two Büchi automata $\mathcal{A}_i = (Q_i, \Sigma, q_{0i}, F_i, \delta_i)$, $i = 1, 2$, is $\mathcal{A} = (Q, \Sigma, q_0, F, \delta)$, where

- *states:* $Q = Q_1 \times Q_2 \times \{1, 2\}$
- *initial states:* $q_0 = \{(s_1, s_2, 1) \mid s_1 \in q_{01}, s_2 \in q_{02}\}$

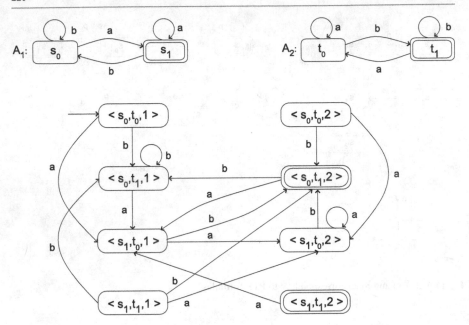

Fig. 11.10 Product of two Büchi automata

- *transitions:* For $a \in \Sigma$,

  $(s_1, s_2, 1) \xrightarrow{a} (s_1', s_2', 1)$ if $s_1 \xrightarrow{a} s_1', s_2 \xrightarrow{a} s_2'$, and $s_1 \notin F_1$.

  $(s_1, s_2, 1) \xrightarrow{a} (s_1', s_2', 2)$ if $s_1 \xrightarrow{a} s_1', s_2 \xrightarrow{a} s_2'$, and $s_1 \in F_1$.

  $(s_1, s_2, 2) \xrightarrow{a} (s_1', s_2', 2)$ if $s_1 \xrightarrow{a} s_1', s_2 \xrightarrow{a} s_2'$, and $s_2 \notin F_2$.

  $(s_1, s_2, 2) \xrightarrow{a} (s_1', s_2', 1)$ if $s_1 \xrightarrow{a} s_1', s_2 \xrightarrow{a} s_2'$, and $s_2 \in F_2$.

- *accept states:* $F = Q_1 \times F_2 \times \{2\}$ (or $F_1 \times Q_2 \times \{1\}$)

We write $A_1 \otimes A_2$ to denote the product automaton of the Büchi automata A_1 and A_2. Figure 11.10 shows two Büchi automata and their product.

When we transform a Kripke structure to a Büchi automaton, we make every state of the Büchi automaton an accepting state. Therefore, in this approach we ignore the tags. In general, tags are necessary for computing the product of any two Büchi automata. When we use boolean expressions to label the transitions of the automata, the transition relation is to be modified to reflect the equivalence of boolean expression for simultaneous transitions. That is, for the transitions $s_1 \xrightarrow{\alpha_1} s_1'$, and $s_2 \xrightarrow{\alpha_2} s_2'$, the simultaneous transition $(s_1, s_2) \xrightarrow{\alpha} (s_1', s_2')$ exists in the product automata if and only if $\alpha_1 \equiv \alpha_2 \equiv \alpha$.

Based on our discussion so far, the model checking procedure using Büchi automata is as follows:

1. Construct the Büchi automaton $\mathcal{A}_{sys}$ for the system.
2. Construct the Büchi automaton $\mathcal{A}_{\neg \varphi}$ for negation of the property φ to be verified.

Fig. 11.11 Büchi automata
corresponding to the formula
$\varphi = \Box(p \Rightarrow \bigcirc\Diamond q)$

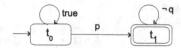

3. Compute the product $\mathcal{A}_{sys} \otimes \mathcal{A}_{\neg\varphi}$.
4. If there is no accepting run (a cycle through an accepting state) in the product automata, declare that the property φ is true in the system sys. This is justified by (11.2). Otherwise, the property φ is not true in the system sys, and every accepting run in the product automata is a counterexample to the claim.

Example 21 illustrates the model checking steps using the emptiness criteria in the product of two Büchi automata.

Example 21 We want to verify the property $\varphi = \Box(p \Rightarrow \bigcirc\Diamond q)$ in the Büchi automaton shown in Fig. 11.8. The steps are shown below:

1. Let B_{sys} be the Büchi automaton in Fig. 11.8.
2. We need to transform $\neg\varphi$ into a *normal form* in which all negations are pushed inside the temporal operators. We use the duality axioms (see Sect. 11.3.5) successively:

$$\begin{aligned}
\varphi &= \Box(p \Rightarrow \bigcirc\Diamond q) \\
\neg\varphi &= \neg\Box(p \Rightarrow \bigcirc\Diamond q) \\
&= \Diamond\neg(p \Rightarrow \bigcirc\Diamond q) \\
&= \Diamond(p \wedge \neg\bigcirc\Diamond q) \\
&= \Diamond(p \wedge \bigcirc\neg\Diamond q) \\
&= \Diamond(p \wedge \bigcirc\Box\neg q)
\end{aligned}$$

The Büchi automaton $B_{\Diamond(p \wedge \bigcirc\Box\neg q)}$ is shown in Fig. 11.11.
3. We construct the product automaton. In the state t_2 of the automaton $B_{\neg\varphi}$, the only transition is labeled by $\neg q$, which is not a label of any transition in the automaton B_{sys}. Hence, in the product automaton, there is no transition from any state $(*, t_1)$, where $*$ is a state of B_{sys}. The transition $t_0 \xrightarrow{true} t_0$ matches with any transition in B_{sys}, and the transition $t_0 \xrightarrow{p} t_1$ labeled p can be taken simultaneously with the transitions in B_{sys} that have label p. The product automata $B_{sys} \otimes B_{\neg\varphi}$, as shown in Fig. 11.12, can be constructed in this manner. Since there is no cycle through the accepting states in the product automaton, we conclude that the property φ is true in the Büchi automaton shown in Fig. 11.8. □

11.6
Exercises

1. Express $(\Diamond\varphi)$ using $\mathcal{U}$ operator. Express $\Box\varphi$ using $\Diamond$ operator.
2. Give natural language statements for the following formulas:

Fig. 11.12 Product of the Büchi automata in Figs. 11.8 and 11.11

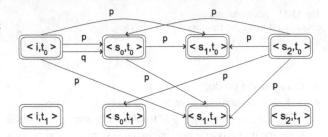

- $\Diamond(\varphi_1 \mathcal{U} \varphi_2)$
- $\Diamond\varphi_1 \mathcal{U} \varphi_2$
- $\Box\varphi \Rightarrow \Diamond\psi$
- $\neg\Box(x > 1)$
- $(\neg q\mathcal{U} p) \vee \Box p$
- $\Diamond(\varphi \wedge \bigcirc\neg\varphi)$

3. Give temporal logic formulas for the following statements:
   (a) It is always true that at some future moment only one of φ or ψ becomes true.
   (b) Initially $x > 0, y > 0$, at some future moment $x > y$ is true and it stays true unless y becomes negative.
   (c) A printer completes the printing of a file within a finite amount of time.
   (d) Only one user can use the printer at a time.
   (e) The gate eventually opens after the train exits from the crossing, provided the gate does not receive close message from the controller within 3 time units from the instant the train exits.
   (f) It is not the case that the channel delivers two identical messages in successive steps.
   (g) Whenever the input number is odd, the execution never terminates.
   (h) Whenever the parity bit is 1 in a register, the register contents do not change for the next two steps.
   (i) Events p and q alternate infinitely often.
   (j) Event p should eventually followed by event q or event r but not by both.
4. Write a fairness condition for Dining Philosopher's problem (Example 5) in PTL.
5. Prove or disprove the following equivalences:

   - $\Box\varphi \equiv \bigcirc(\Box\varphi)$
   - $\Diamond(\varphi \wedge \psi) \equiv \Diamond\varphi \wedge \Diamond\psi$
   - $\bigcirc\Diamond\varphi \equiv \Diamond\bigcirc\varphi$
   - $\Box(\varphi \Rightarrow \psi) \equiv (\Box\varphi \Rightarrow \Box\Diamond\psi)$
   - $(\bigcirc\varphi \Rightarrow \psi) \Rightarrow \bigcirc(\varphi \Rightarrow \psi)$

6. Prove the equivalences stated in Sect. 11.3.5.
7. Define the temporal operator $\mathcal{N}$ (**atnext** [14]), to be used as $\varphi\mathcal{N}\psi$, using the basic temporal operators. It has the meaning "φ holds at the nearest future time point where ψ holds". Either prove or give a counterexample for the following formulas:

   - $\Box\varphi \Rightarrow \varphi\mathcal{N}\psi$

- $\Box(\varphi \Rightarrow \varphi \mathcal{N} \psi)$
- $\Box(\varphi \mathcal{N} \psi) \Rightarrow \Box \Diamond \psi$

8. Below is a temporal specification for two components A and B that communicate through messages.

$$Spec_A : \Box \begin{bmatrix} start \Rightarrow \varphi \\ \wedge \varphi \Rightarrow \bigcirc \psi \\ \wedge \psi \Rightarrow \bigcirc \varphi \\ \wedge \psi \Rightarrow \bigcirc \bigcirc send\_msg \end{bmatrix}$$

$$Spec_B : \Box \begin{bmatrix} rcv\_msg \Rightarrow \bigcirc \vartheta \\ \wedge \vartheta \Rightarrow \bigcirc \eta \\ \wedge \eta \Rightarrow \bigcirc \vartheta \end{bmatrix}$$

Give a model of the following concurrent specifications:

(1) $Spec_1 :: Spec_A \wedge Spec_B \wedge \Box[send\_msg \Rightarrow \bigcirc rcv\_msg]$

(2) $Spec_2 :: Spec_A \wedge Spec_B \wedge \Box[send\_msg \Rightarrow \Diamond rcv\_msg]$

Prove that $Spec_1$ is a refinement of $Spec_2$.

9. In the previous question suppose $send\_msg$ is changed to $send\_msg(t)$, where t is a token and it is either 0 or 1. Component B should send an acknowledgement (a simple message with no parameter) to component A if the value of token is 1. With this change, rewrite the concurrent specifications in Exercise 8.

10. With respect to the rail road crossing specification in Sect. 11.3.7.2 do the following:

(a) Give formal semantics for the following formulas:
   (i) $g_4 \, \mathcal{W} \, tr_1$
   (ii) $g_4 \, \mathcal{S} \, tr_3$
   (iii) $tr_1 \, \mathcal{R} \, g_4$

(b) Modify the railroad problem requirements: The system allows two trains, one controller, and one gate. When one train is in the crossing or busy crossing the gate, and the controller receives "approaching" message from the other train the controller should instruct the gate closed until both trains exit the crossing. However, both trains should not share the crossing at any moment. Give a specification for this problem.

11. Specify a *signal* object with the behavior that in the initial state it is *red*. When it receives a message at some time it changes to *yellow* at the next instant. It stays yellow until it receives a message to turn *green*. It stays *green* unless it receives a message that will turn it *red*. This behavior is repeated infinitely often. Modify the requirements of the rail road crossing problem in Sect. 11.3.7.2 as follows:

(a) The controller informs the signal about the status of the gate through different messages.

(b) If the signal is *red* and it receives the message from the controller that "the gate is open", it continues to stay in that state. When it receives the message that the "gate is lowered", it turns *yellow* in the next time moment. When the signal is *yellow*, if it receives the message "gate is closed" from the controller, it turns *green* at the same time moment. When it receives the message "gate is raised" it changes to *yellow* at the next time moment. If it receives the message "gate is open" when it is *yellow*, it changes to *red* at the same moment.

(c) The train observes the signals and modifies its behavior. If it observes *red* signal it will *stop* before reaching the crossing. If it observes *yellow* it will *slow down* before reaching the gate. If it observes *green* it will either maintain its normal speed or *resume_normal* speed.

Give a formal specification for the reactive behavior of train, controller, signal, and gate components. Give a formal model of the system and informally infer from your model the satisfaction of the safety property.

12. This exercise is concerned with specifying a plain old telephone system: a system consisting of a finite number of telephones, where communication between two telephones is possible through a *channel*. All telephones are connected to one channel. Each telephone has a unique number. The state of a telephone is determined by the truth values of the following set of predicates: *on-hook(x)*, *off-hook(x)*, *dial-tone(x)*, *ringing(x)*, *busy-tone(x)*. A user can perform the following actions: *lift-handset(x)*, *replace-handset(x)*, *dial-number(x,y)*. When a number *y* is dialed in a telephone *x*, either there is a busy tone at the telephone *y*, or the telephone *y* rings. In the latter case, either the phone is eventually picked up or it is not picked up. If the telephone is picked up, the telephone is said to be connected, and if the telephone is not picked up there is no connection. In such an operation no other telephone is affected.

(a) Give temporal logic formulas for a set of constraints on the telephone system. Example constraints are "a telephone is either on-hook or off-hook, but not both", and "a phone cannot have a busy tone and not be connected to some number".

(b) Give a temporal logic specification for placing a call that results in a successful connection. Give a channel specification, as complete as possible, so that you can provide the full specification of processing a telephone call. Verify using the formal model of the system that every call made by a telephone is connected unless the telephone at the destination is busy.

13. Give temporal logic semantics for the program below:

```
begin
x:=0;
y:=3;
while (x <= y) do
{
  if even(x) then <y:=y+x; x;=x+1>
              else <y:=y-2;x:=y+x;>
}
end
```

14. Modify the requirements of Example 14 as follows: the slot machine sends a randomly chosen amount *x*, which is either (*max* − 2) or (*min* + 2), as long as the cash balance in the slot machine remains greater than (*max* + *min*) (of the previous round). Once the balance falls below this limit it continues to send an amount 0, until its balance is

once again at least $(max + min)$. This behavior is repeated forever. Give the complete specification of the slot machine interaction with its players.

15. *Craps* is a gambling game which eventually terminates. A player, say *Alice*, plays the game using a machine that generates *random numbers* to simulate the roll of a pair of dice. The rules of the game and declaring the result of the game rest with a referee (R), an automatic device, with whom *Alice* and her random number generating (RAG) device communicate. Each time *Alice* asks RAG for a number, RAG delivers the referee R an integer in the range $[1, 7]$ and the name *Alice*. To simulate a throw on a pair of dice, *Alice* will ask RAG at two successive moments. The device RAG takes one moment of time to generate the number and one moment of time to deliver it to R. Two moments after the judge receives the necessary information, it will announce the result to *Alice*, and *Alice* will receive the result the moment after it is sent by R. The referee has set down the following rules for playing the game.

- Let a and b denote the random numbers received after *Alice* requests for it.
- Let $s = a + b$
- If $s = 7$ or $s = 11$, R announces that *Alice* is the winner. The game is over.
- If $s = 2$ or $s = 3$ or $s = 12$, R announces that *Alice* is the loser. The game is over.
- In all other cases R requests *Alice* to play again.
- *Alice* should request RAG at two successive moments to get new numbers.
- Let a' and b' be the numbers received by R.
- Let $s' = a' + b'$.
- If $s' = 7$ the referee announces that *Alice* is the loser. The game is over.
- If $s' = s$ the referee announces that *Alice* is the winner. The game is over.
- The referee follows the rules from Step 5 until the game is decided.

Give a temporal logic specification for playing this game. HINT: Define the operator *while* :: $\varphi \, \mathcal{W} \, \psi$ meaning "φ holds at least as long as ψ holds", and use it to specify the loop.

16. In software design, the *publisher–subscriber* design pattern is often used. This problem is on modeling the behavior of *publisher–subscriber*. Component C_p is *publisher* of information, and components $C_{s_i}, i \geq 0$ are subscribers to information published by C_p. Give a model of the following behavior.

- *subscribe:* A component repeatedly sends message *enroll( )* to the publisher C_p until it receives an acknowledgment *enrolled(i)*. The publisher assigns the ID i to the component, and is named C_{s_i}.
- *publish:* The publisher C_p sends out (broadcasts) information ϑ at *odd* time moments $t \geq 3$, to all components who are enrolled at time $k, k < t$.
- *release:* A component C_{s_i} repeatedly sends message *release(i)* to the publisher C_p until it receives an acknowledgment *released(i)*. The publisher removes ID i.
- *membership:* A component that received an acknowledgment *enrolled(i)* is a subscribed member from the moment of enrollment to the moment of release.

Prove the following properties:

- *safety property:* Only subscribers should receive the information published by the publisher.

- *liveness property:* All subscribers receive the same information.

17. Construct the program graph and the transition system corresponding to the program

```
begin
while (x > 1)
if (x > y) then x:=x-y;
if (x <= y) then y:=y-x;
}
end
```

18. Consider the two actions

$$P_1 :: \langle y := y - x; x := x + 2 \rangle$$

$$P_2 :: \langle x := y + x; x := x - 2 \rangle$$

as programs that share the variables x and y. Construct

- the program graph PG_1 and PG_2 of the programs P_1 and P_2
- the program graph of $PG_1 |||PG_2$
- the transition systems TS_{PG_1}, TS_{PG_2} and $TS_{PG_1|||PG_2}$ corresponding to program graphs PG_1, PG_2, and $PG_1|||PG_2$

Is $TS_{PG_1} |||T S_{PG_2} = T S_{PG_1|||PG_2}$

19. Model check the formula $\Diamond(r \Rightarrow p \vee \neg q)$ on the Büchi automaton model shown below.

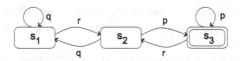

20. Transform the Kripke structure (S, R, S_0, L) defined below to a Büchi automaton and model check the formula $\Diamond(p \vee t)$ in it.

$S = \{s_0, s_1, s_2, s_3, s_4\}$,
$R: s_0 \xrightarrow{\alpha_1} s_1, s_2 \xrightarrow{\alpha_2} s_1, s_2 \xrightarrow{\alpha_3} s_4, s_3 \xrightarrow{\alpha_2} s_0, s_3 \xrightarrow{\alpha_1} s_2, s_4 \xrightarrow{\alpha_3} s_0$
$L: L(s_0) = \{p, s\}, L(s_1) = \{r, s\}, L(s_2) = \{q, r\}, L(s_3) = \{p, q\}$,
$L(s_4) = \{p, t\}$, where p, q, r, s, t are propositions.
$S_0 := \{s_0, s_4\}$

11.7
Bibliographic Notes

Modal logics [4, 13] and temporal modalities [25] are the foundations on which the temporal logics are based. Linear temporal logic was introduced by Pnueli [22]. Since then a variety of temporal logics have been studied, most notably CTL (Clock Temporal Logic) [2, 9], CTL*, and Lamport's Temporal Logic of Actions [16]. Both CTL and CTL* are branching time logics. CTL* subsumes both CTL and LTL. There are logics based on them for industrial usage. These include IBM Sugar based on CTL, Intel FORSpec based on LTL, PSL (IEEE-1850 standard) that incorporates features from CTL*, and the TLA+2 tools. In PSL, it is possible to write both property-oriented and model-based specifications.

Temporal logic is most suited for specifying the behavior of reactive and concurrent systems. The behavior of such systems, considered as traces, are collections of infinite words which constitute an ω-language over an alphabet. This connection between LTL formulas and ω-languages was first studied by Sistala et al. in [27]. This seminal work lead to model checking using Büchi automata which recognizes ω-languages.

The term model checking refers to a collection of methods for the automatic analysis of properties, such as safety, liveness, and fairness in reactive and concurrent systems. The input to model checkers are always *abstract models* of the system. A positive verdict from a model checker is of "limited value" because of possible (and potential) *incompleteness* in the model, approximations that might have lead to contain the complexity of the model, and limitations imposed by available resources. The positive aspect of getting a negative verdict is that the counter-examples produced by the model checker are invaluable in debugging complex systems. Testing community use model checkers just for this feature. On the whole, model checking has the following strengths:

1. It is a systematic approach and is an automatic verification procedure.
2. Many tools are available; for example SPIN system developed by Holzmann [12] received an award for its outstanding performance. Consequently, model checking has become portable and scalable to industrial applications, requiring only a moderate level of expertise in the formal notations used.
3. Many systems, some fairly large, have been model checked. It is now done *routinely* on a widespread basis for verifying properties of large systems composed of both hardware and software.
4. There is a wide networking community of users, researchers, and developers. They continue to produce new techniques and tools.

However, there are still a few problems with this approach.

1. It supports only *partial* verification. That is, only one property can be checked at any one time. In order to check fairness and safety, two independent invocations to a model checker is necessary.
2. Positive verdict of one property cannot guarantee that the system is free of other errors.
3. It is restricted to verifying stated properties in finite state models, and not on actual systems.
4. It is not suitable for infinite state systems. Many real world systems may not be finite state systems. Many techniques, such as *predicate abstraction*, *partial order reduction*, and *symbolic representations* are known [1, 6] to reduce infinite state systems to finite state systems. Not all these techniques are fully automated.
5. State explosion is a common problem. A reactive system may not terminate and a concurrent system may have many asynchronous processes. The formulas required to rep-

resent the state spaces of such systems are usually quite complex, making the state space hard to contain within manageable size.

The result of Sistala and Clarke [28] on the complexity of LTL model checking sets limits on what is practically feasible. Model checking is done *only* on an abstract model which cannot be built automatically. Because of the disadvantages listed above, standard validation procedures such as testing are necessary to ensure that the implementation adequately reflects the properties verified by a model checker as well as properties that are not model checked.

References

1. Baier C, Katoen JP (2007) Principles of model checking. MIT Press, Cambridge
2. Ben-Ari M, Pnueli A, Manna Z (1983) The temporal logic of branching time. Acta Inform 20:207–226
3. Büchi JR (1960) On a decision method in restricted second order arithmetic. Z Math Log Grundl Math 6:66–92
4. Carnap R (1947) Meaning and necessity. Chicago University Press, Chicago. Enlarged Edition 1956
5. Clarke EM, Emerson EA, Sistala AP (1986) Automatic verification of finite state concurrent systems using temporal logic specifications. ACM Trans Program Lang Syst 8(2):244–263
6. Clarke EM, Grumberg O, Peled DA (1999) Model checking. MIT Press, Cambridge
7. Courcoubetis C, Vardi M, Wolper P, Yannakakis M (1992) Memory efficient algorithms for the verification of temporal logic properties. Form Methods Syst Des 1:275–288
8. Dijkstra E (1965) Solutions of a problem in concurrent programming control. Commun ACM 8(9):569
9. Emerson EA, Clarke EM (1980) Characterizing correctness properties of parallel programs using fixpoints. In: Automata, languages, and programming. Lecture notes in computer science, vol 85, pp 169–181
10. Gabbay D, Pnueli A, Stavi J (1980) The temporal analysis of fairness. In: Proceedings of the seventh ACM symposium on principles of programming languages, January 1980, pp 163–173
11. Gabbay D, Hodkinson I, Reynolds M (1994) Temporal logic: mathematical foundations and computational aspects. Oxford logic guides, vol 1. Clarendon, Oxford
12. Holzmann G (2003) The SPIN model checker: primer and reference manual. Addison-Wesley, Reading
13. Kripke SA (1963) Semantic considerations on modal logic. Acta Philos Fenn 16:83–94
14. Gröger F (1986) Temporal logic of programs. EATCS monographs on theoretical computer science. Springer, Berlin
15. Lamport L (1983) What good is temporal logic. In: Proceedings of IFIP'83 congress, information processing. North-Holland, Amsterdam, pp 657–668
16. Lamport L (1994) The temporal logic of actions. ACM Trans Program Lang Syst 16(3):872–923
17. Manna Z, Pnueli A (1992) The temporal logic of reactive and concurrent systems—specifications. Springer, New York
18. Melham TF (1989) Formalizing abstraction mechanisms for hardware verification in higher order logic. PhD thesis, University of Cambridge, August 1989
19. Moszkowski B (1986) Executing temporal logic programs. Cambridge University Press, Cambridge

20. Owiciki S, Lamport L (1982) Proving liveness properties of concurrent programs. ACM Trans Program Lang Syst 4(3):455–495
21. Peterson GL (1981) Myths about the mutual exclusion problem. Inf Process Lett 12(3):115–116
22. Pnueli A (1977) The temporal logic of programs. In: Proceedings of the eighteenth symposium on the foundations of computer science, Providence, USA
23. Pnueli A (1981) The temporal semantics of concurrent programs. Theor Comput Sci 13:45–60
24. Pnueli A (1986) Applications of temporal logic to the specification and verification of reactive systems: a survey of current trends. Lecture notes in computer science, vol 224
25. Prior A (1957) Time and modality. Oxford University Press, London
26. Rescher N, Urquhart A (1971) Temporal logic. Springer, Berlin
27. Sistala AP, Vardi M, Wolper P (1983) Reasoning about infinite computation paths. In: Proceedings of the 24th IEEE FOCS, pp 185–194
28. Sistala AP, Clarke EM (1985) The complexity of linear propositional temporal logic. J ACM 32(3):733–749
29. Stirling C (1992) Modal and temporal logics. In: Handbook of logic in computer science. Oxford University Press, London
30. Wan K (2006) Lucx: Lucid Enriched with context. PhD thesis, Concordia University, Montreal, Canada

Part IV
Mathematical Abstractions
for Model-Based Specifications

Model-based specification techniques not only provide a mechanism to construct an abstract model of the application being specified but also give refinement techniques to derive design and implementation from the model. In order to construct such an abstract model, to reason about the model and to provide sufficient syntactic structures for refinement, most model-based specification techniques use set theory notation and first-order predicate logic. A chapter in Part III of the book covers predicate logic. Set theory and relations are discussed in detail in this part. The following are the learning outcomes from this part:

- notations for sets, relations and functions
- simple specifications using sets
- reasoning with sets
- various types of relations and functions
- examples of specifications using relations and functions
- sequences and their representations
- examples of specifications using sequences

Part IV
Mathematical Abstractions
for Model-Based Specifications

Set Theory and Relations

12

The main goal of this chapter is to demonstrate the usefulness of mathematical abstractions such as sets, relations, functions, and sequences in software development. In particular, the chapter lays the foundation for the specification languages presented in the next four chapters.

Software systems deal with real-world objects, their attributes, and their interactions. Collections of such objects are abstracted as *sets* or *sequences*, and the interactions between pairs of objects are abstracted as *relations* or *functions*. When such abstractions are not created and used in software development, the modeling of real-world objects may be influenced by implementation details.

Sets correspond to structures for providing truth values to propositions and predicates. Each n-ary predicate $P(x_1, x_2, \ldots, x_n)$ is interpreted over a structure $R \subseteq U^n$, where U is the universal set, such that the predicate is true for tuples in R. The domain R consists of all relations $r(x_1, x_2, \ldots, x_n)$ for which $P(x_1, x_2, \ldots, x_n)$ is true. For a unary predicate $p(x)$ the domain is the set of values of the argument x for which $p(x)$ is true. This view of sets of objects, and relations, implicitly defined by predicates over the objects, is useful in introducing the notion of *type* and defining *type invariants* in the specification of software systems.

12.1
Formal Specification Based on Set Theory

The vocabulary, the syntax, and the semantics of the formalism are borrowed from set theory. The syntax includes the notation for set presentation, set membership, and set extension. The semantics conduces to reasoning about specifications based on the notation.

V.S. Alagar, K. Periyasamy, *Specification of Software Systems*,
Texts in Computer Science,
DOI 10.1007/978-0-85729-277-3_12, © Springer-Verlag London Limited 2011

12.1.1
Set Notation

A set may be presented by enumerating its elements. Thus,

$status = \{idle, on, off\}$

introduces the set *status* whose elements describe the three possible states of a process. To introduce a set which cannot be enumerated but whose membership criterion can be asserted, we use the "let" construct. For instance, we describe sets using the following statements: "Let *Person* denote the set of all persons registered in an employment registration bureau" and " Let *P* denote the set of printers". Such definitions may be used in defining other sets. We also use standard mathematical notations such as $\mathbb{N}$ to denote the set of natural numbers.

The set comprehension notation is used to introduce sets obtained by specializing nonempty sets that have already been defined. For example, the set

$\{x : \mathbb{N} | 1 < x < 1000 \wedge prime(x)\}$

introduces the finite set of prime numbers in the range $1 \ldots 1000$. The set

$retired = \{e : \text{Person} | age(e) \geq 65\}$

refers to the set of persons who have reached the age of 65.

In this chapter, we adopt the notion that *types* are *maximal* set of values. In general, specification languages have built-in types; some provide facilities to construct complex types. An object is associated with a type, and an identifier is used to denote the object. When a type denotes a *maximal* set of values, an object can belong to only one type. Within this framework there is no notion of subtyping. The set constructors, $\cup$, $\cap$, $--$ are also used as type constructors. The expression $x : retired \cap male$ introduces a variable denoting a male retired person. The two expressions $x \in retired$, and $x : retired$ have the same meaning.

The *powerset* of a set S, denoted by $\mathbb{P}S$, represents the set of all subsets of S. It serves as the type for collections of objects. To formalize statements such as "let X and Y denote two sets of retired people", it is sufficient to write $X, Y : \mathbb{P}\ retired$. The set membership operation $\in$ may be used to determine subset relationships. For instance, $(\forall e : X \bullet e \in Y) \Rightarrow X \subset Y$. If T is a type and $S \subset T$, we assert that $P(x)$ is true for some $x \in S$, by writing

$\exists x : T \bullet x \in S \wedge P(x),$ or

$\exists x : S \bullet P(x)$

The declaration $e : X - Y$ introduces a variable of type $X - Y$, that is, a variable whose values belong to the set X, but not to the set Y.

A set cannot represent an ordered collection of objects. Information that require some ordering are represented using *n*-tuples. If x and y are elements of sets X and Y then the ordered pair (x, y) is an element of the *Cartesian Product type* $X \times Y$. The cartesian product notion can be generalized:

$$X_1 \times X_2 \times \cdots \times X_n$$

is the set of all n-tuples $\{x_1, x_2, \ldots, x_n\}$, where $x_i \in X_i$. Two n-tuples $\{x_1, x_2, \ldots, x_n\}$, and $\{y_1, y_2, \ldots, y_n,\}$ are *equal* if $(x_1 = y_1 \wedge x_2 = y_2 \wedge \cdots \wedge x_n = y_n)$. The ordering of components in a cartesian product is meaningful. The cartesian products $T \times T \times T$, $T \times (T \times T)$, $(T \times T) \times T$ correspond to different sets. Set equality is extended to cartesian products. Two tuples are equal if and only if their corresponding components are equal. If $S, T \subset X \times Y$, then $S = T$ if and only if they have the same tuples. The data type *date* can be modeled using cartesian product as follows:

date = Year $\times$ *Month* $\times$ *Days,*   where

Year $= \{x : \mathbb{N} \mid 2000 \leq x \leq 4000\}$,

Month $= \{Jan, Feb, Mar, Apr, May, Jun, Jul, Aug, Sep, Oct, Nov, Dec\}$,

Days $= \{x : \mathbb{N} \mid 1 \leq x \leq 31\}$.

This type includes some invalid tuples such as $(2000, Feb, 30)$. To exclude invalid values for a type, we need *type invariant*. These are described in detail in Chap. 16.

12.1.2
Reasoning with Sets

Proofs about sets are constructed from the semantics of set operators introduced in the previous section. Natural deduction is the frequently used proof technique. It uses the following axioms for set operations.

1. *empty set*
   A basic axiom of set theory is that the empty set, denoted as $\emptyset$, exists and has no elements:

$$\frac{\emptyset}{\forall x : S \bullet x \notin \emptyset}$$

   This axiom uses the set membership operator $\in$, which is axiomatized next.

2. *membership*

$$\frac{e \in S}{S \neq \emptyset}$$

$$\frac{e = x_1 \vee \cdots \vee e = x_k}{e \in \{x_1, \ldots, x_k\}}$$

$$\frac{\exists x : S \mid P(x) \bullet a[x] = e}{e \in \{x : S \mid P(x) \bullet a[x]\}}$$

The first axiom states that if there exists an element in a set, then the set is not empty. The second axiom is applicable for set enumeration. The third axiom applies for set comprehension.

3. *subset*

$$\overline{\emptyset \subseteq S}$$

$$\frac{\forall x : S \bullet x \in T}{S \subseteq T}$$

$$\frac{S \subseteq T \wedge T \subseteq U}{S \subseteq U}$$

4. *equality*

$$\frac{S \subseteq T \wedge T \subseteq S}{S = T}$$

5. *membership in powerset*

$$\frac{S = \emptyset}{\mathbb{P}S = \emptyset}$$

$$\frac{T \subseteq S}{T \in \mathbb{P}S}$$

6. *membership in cartesian product*

$$\frac{e_1 \in X_1 \wedge \cdots \wedge e_n \in X_n}{(e_1, \ldots, e_n) \in X_1 \times \cdots \times X_n}$$

7. *equality of tuples*

$$\frac{x_1 = y_1 \wedge \cdots \wedge x_n = y_n}{(x_1, \ldots, x_n) = (y_1, \ldots, y_n)}$$

8. *union, intersection, difference*

[*union*]
$$\frac{x \in (S \cup T)}{x \in S \vee x \in T}$$

[*distributed union*]
$$\frac{x \in \bigcup S}{\exists X : S \bullet x \in X}$$

[*intersection*]
$$\frac{x \in S \cap T}{x \in S \wedge x \in T}$$

[*distributed intersection*]
$$\frac{x \in \bigcap S}{\forall X : S \bullet x \in X}$$

[*difference*]
$$\frac{x \in S - T}{x \in S \wedge x \notin T}$$

Example 1 Prove (i) $S \subset S \cup \{e\}$, and (ii) if $e \in S$, $S = S \cup \{e\}$.
Proof of (i):

1. $S = \emptyset$. From the first axiom for empty set, infer $\emptyset \subset \emptyset \cup \{e\}$.
2. $S \neq \emptyset$.

   - From $x \in S$, infer $x \in S \vee x \in \{e\}$ ($\vee - introduction$)
   - From the union axiom and the previous step, infer $x \in S \cup \{e\}$

3. From 1 and 2, infer $S \subset S \cup \{e\}$.

Proof of (ii):

1. $S \subset S \cup \{e\} \ldots$ proved in (i).
2. From $x \in S \cup \{e\}$ and the union axiom, infer $x \in S \vee x \in \{e\}$.
3. If $x = e$ from the premises and from the second subset axiom, infer $S \cup \{e\} \subset S$.
4. If $x \neq e$ and $x \in S \cup \{e\}$, from the second axiom for set membership infer $S \cup \{e\} \subset S$.
5. From set equality axiom, and steps 3 and 4, infer $S = S \cup \{e\}$.   □

From Example 1, it follows that sets $X = \{3, 7, 3, 5, 8, 5\}$ and $Y = \{3, 5, 8, 7\}$ are equal. Reordering or introducing duplicate elements in a set will not create a different set.

12.1.3
A Specification Example

A Computer Assisted Education-Tool (CAET) is a multi-user environment for distance learning. A simplified version of CAET is specified in the following example. The focus is on abstracting application domain objects such as users, access rights, files, and user commands.

Example 2 Some of the requirements of CAET are stated informally and formalized using set notation.

1. *User Categories*—There are four classes of users: *author, teacher, student and administrator*. An author, who can be a teacher but not a student, prepares lessons. A teacher can be an author but not a student or an administrator. An administrator has special privileges for managing accounts of students registered for courses offered by CAET and hence cannot be an author, teacher, or student. The categories of users are modeled by sets.

   Let u denote the set of all user names, and *curusers* denote the set of all current users; *author, teacher, student and administrator* denote the sets of all authors, teachers, students and administrators in CAET.

   $(curusers \subseteq u) \wedge$

   $(curusers = author \cup teacher \cup student \cup administrator) \wedge$

   $(author \cap student = \emptyset) \wedge$

$(teacher \cap student = \emptyset) \wedge$

$(teacher \cap administrator = \emptyset) \wedge$

$(student \cap administrator = \emptyset) \wedge$

$(author \cap administrator = \emptyset)$

2. *File categories*—Three are three categories of system files: 1) lessons and quizzes; 2) class list and grade list for students; 3) author list and teacher list. Authors, teachers, and students can access files in the first category; teachers and administrators can access files in the second category, and only administrators can access files in the third category. The specification models the structure of the *file store*, and not the structure of the files in the file stores.

Let *file_store_a* denote the type of file store exclusively owned by administrators. All administrators have the same set of privileges for files in *file_store_a*. The store is a collection of ordered pairs:

$file\_store\_a = \mathbb{P}(administrator \times ad\_files),$

where *ad_files* is the type of file names owned by the administrators.

Let *file_store_b* denote the type of file store jointly owned by teachers and administrators, containing the set of class lists and grade lists. A class list is created by an administrator who authorizes the teacher of the section to read or copy the list. A teacher can access only the class list of his/her section, and cannot modify the list. The grade list for the class can be created and modified by the teacher of the section only; an administrator can only view the grades. File access privileges are asymmetrical with respect to the class of users. The type of *file_store_b* corresponds to the union type of two sets of ordered pairs:

$file\_store\_b = \mathbb{P}(administrator \times (teacher \times class\_files)) \cup$

$\mathbb{P}(teacher \times (administrator \times grade\_files))$

where *class_files* and *grade_files* are file names for class and grade lists, respectively.

Let *file_store_c* denote the type of file store that may be jointly accessed by administrators, teachers and students. The files in this store are exclusively created by authors, and hence may be modified only by the authors. Students and teachers can read the files or copy the files into another file store. The file store has the type

$file\_store\_c = \mathbb{P}(author \times course\_no \times lesson) \cup$

$\mathbb{P}(author \times course\_no \times quiz)$

where *course_no* is the type defining the set of courses, *lesson* and *quiz* denote types of file names containing lessons and quizzes. The implication of this model is that several lesson files and several quiz files may be created by several authors for one course. In addition, the authors may own other auxiliary files. The type of auxiliary files is modeled as collections of ordered pairs (*user*, *file*):

$aux\_file\_store = \mathbb{P}(curusers \times file\_names),$

where *file_names = quiz* ∪ *lesson* ∪ *class_files* ∪ *grade_files* ∪ *ad_files*.

3. *File store access rights*—Each file category can be accessed by a designated set of users. This requirement is described by the type

$$fsar = \mathbb{P}(file\_store \times \mathbb{P}(curusers)),$$

where

$$file\_store = file\_store\_a \cup file\_store\ b \cup file\_store\_c \cup aux\_file\_store$$

4. *Access rights*—The set

$$privileges = \{read, write, edit, copy, execute, nil\}$$

defines all possible access rights in the system. A user can have one or more of these rights for a file. Thus, access rights for files are described as a collection of triples (u, f, A), such that user u has the rights enumerated in set $A \subseteq privileges$ for the file with name f.

$$ufar = \mathbb{P}(curusers \times file\_names \times \mathbb{P}(privileges)).$$

5. *Access rights invariants*—
   (a) It is a requirement that the access rights granted to users for certain files remain compatible with the file store rights granted to user categories.

   $$\forall x : ufar \bullet ((u, f, A) \in x \Leftrightarrow$$
   $$((f \in file\_store\_a \wedge u \in administrator) \vee$$
   $$(f \in file\_store\_b \wedge (u \in administrator \vee u \in teacher)) \vee$$
   $$(f \in file\_store\_c \wedge u \in authors) \vee$$
   $$(f \in aux\_file\_store \wedge u \in curusers)))$$

   (b) Files containing lessons and quizzes must remain accessible to users of CAET. The author of a lesson or quiz must be able to read, write, edit, and copy the files containing the material.

   $$\forall x : file\_store\_c \bullet ((a, c, l) \in x \Rightarrow$$
   $$\exists y : ufar \bullet (a, l, A) \in y \wedge$$
   $$\forall z : curusers \exists w : ufar \bullet ((z, l, B) \in w \wedge B \subseteq \{read, copy\})))$$

   A similar assertion can be made for a quiz file in *file_store_c*.

6. *Transferring access rights*—For every file in *aux_file_store*, the owner of the file has all the privileges on the file. Any user who is not an owner of a file can have the same privileges if granted by the owner. A user u_1 can grant to another user u_2 certain privileges $B \subseteq privileges$ on a file f such that (u_1, f) exists in *aux_file_store*. To describe accesses granted by users, we introduce the type:

$$grant\_access = \mathbb{P}(curusers \times curusers \times file\_names \times \mathbb{P}(privileges))$$

such that

$$\forall g : granted\_access \bullet (g = (u_1, u_2, f, B) \Leftrightarrow$$
$$B \subseteq privileges \wedge \exists x : aux\_file\_store \bullet (u_1, f) \in x)$$

7. *State invariants*—The *state* of CAET at an instant is characterized by a set of users, a collection of files in the file stores and access rights of users on the files in the stores. Both *file_store_c* and *aux_file_store* may keep different versions of the same file. However, versioning of files in other file stores are permitted subject to certain constraints. For example, a lesson prepared by an author may be revised by another author. A revision is an ordered pair $((a, c, l), (a', c, l'))$. Versioning is described by the following types:

$$\mathbb{P}(L \times L), \quad L = \mathbb{P}(author \times course\_no \times lesson)$$
$$\mathbb{P}(Q \times Q), \quad Q = \mathbb{P}(author \times course\_no \times quiz)$$
$$\mathbb{P}(A \times A), \quad A = \mathbb{P}(curusers \times file\_names)$$

These types are constrained by the following invariants:

$$sucl : \mathbb{P}(L \times L); \; sucq : \mathbb{P}(Q \times Q); \; suca : \mathbb{P}(A \times A);$$
$$sucl \subseteq file\_store\_c \times file\_store\_c \wedge$$
$$sucq \subseteq file\_store\_c \times file\_store\_c \wedge$$
$$suca \subseteq aux\_file\_store \times aux\_file\_store$$

8. *Operations*—We specify only two operations, namely file creation, and file deletion. Other operations are included in the exercises at the end of the chapter. We use unprimed and primed variables to denote, respectively, the state before and after an operation.

   (a) *File creation*—Let

   $$storea : file\_store\_a,$$
   $$storeb : file\_store\_b,$$
   $$storec : file\_store\_c,$$
   $$auxstore : aux\_file\_store, \text{ and}$$
   $$ur : ufar$$

   denote the status of the stores. Files may be created by any user. For example, an administrator can create a new file in three different ways:

   (i) A file to be used exclusively by administrators is protected from all other user categories and is maintained in *storea*. The other file stores are unchanged. Assuming that the syntax of *create* command is *create userid, file, status*, it has the following effect:

   $$(command = create) \wedge (userid \in administrator) \wedge (status = ad\_protect)$$
   $$\Rightarrow (storea' = storea \cup \{(userid, file)\} \wedge (storeb' = storeb) \wedge$$

$$(storec' = storec) \wedge (auxstore' = auxstore) \wedge$$
$$(ur' = ur \cup \{(userid, file, privileges)\}).$$

(ii) An administrator may create a file to be shared with some teacher and hence the file is added to *storeb*. Assuming that the syntax of *create* command is

$$create\ userid_1, userid_2, file$$

its effect is specified as follows:

$$(command = create) \Rightarrow ((userid_1 \in administrator) \wedge$$
$$(userid_2 = teacher) \Rightarrow ((storea' = storea) \wedge$$
$$(storeb' = storeb \cup \{(userid_1, (userid_2, file))\}) \wedge$$
$$(storec' = storec) \wedge (auxstore' = auxstore) \wedge$$
$$(ur' = ur \cup \{(userid_1, file, \{read, copy\}),$$
$$(userid_2, file, \{read, copy\})\}))).$$

(iii) An administrator may create a file in *auxstore* for general usage. Assuming that the syntax of *create* command is

$$create\ userid, file$$

its effect is

$$(command = create) \Rightarrow$$
$$(auxstore' = auxstore \cup \{(userid, file)\}) \wedge$$
$$(storea' = storea) \wedge (storeb' = storeb)$$
$$\wedge (storec' = storec)$$

(b) The *delete* command is used to remove an existing file from a filestore. Deleting the file *filename* requires annulling access rights on the file for user *userid* and annulling the granted rights on the file. We use variables *storeu* and *storeg* in the following formulas, where

storeu: *ufar*

storeg: *granted_access*

Let *remove_privilege(userid, filename)* be the predicate

$$\exists B : \mathbb{P}\ privileges \bullet$$
$$\{userid, filename, B\} \in storeu \Rightarrow$$
$$(storeu' = storeu - \{(userid, filename, B)\}) \wedge$$
$$\exists u : curusers, \exists C : \mathbb{P}\ privileges \bullet$$
$$(\{userid, u, filename, C\} \in storeg \wedge C \subseteq B) \Rightarrow$$
$$(storeg' = storeg - \{(userid, u, filename, C)\})$$

(i) The effect of the *delete* command on student files is

$$(command = delete) \land (userid \in student) \Rightarrow$$
$$((auxstore' = auxstore - \{(userid, filename)\}) \land$$
$$(stored' = storea) \land (storeb' = storeb) \land$$
$$remove\_privilege(userid, filename)$$

(ii) An author may delete files from *storec* or from *auxstore*:

$$(command = delete) \land (userid \in author) \Rightarrow$$
$$((\exists c : course\_no \bullet (storec' = storec - \{(userid, c, filename)\}) \oplus$$
$$(auxstore' = auxstore - \{(userid, filename)\}) \land$$
$$(stored' = storea) \land (storeb' = storeb) \land$$
$$(storec' = storec)) \land remove\_privilege(userid, filename)$$

where the operator $\oplus$ denotes the exclusive-or operation, which enforces that only one of the two deletions occurs. The effect of the *delete* command for other categories of users and files can be described in a similar fashion.   □

12.2
Formal Specification Based on Relations and Functions

A direct way to express a relationship between two objects is to construct the ordered pair of the two objects. When the relationship is specialized, as in the case when only one object is related to another object, a function is more appropriate to express the relationship. Relationships among several objects can be expressed as ordered tuples. Symbol tables, dictionaries, and database information are all instances of relations.

12.2.1
Relations and Functions

Binary relations model objects that relate members of two sets. If X and Y are sets, then $X \leftrightarrow Y$ denotes the set of all relations from X to Y:

$$X \leftrightarrow Y = \mathbb{P}(X \times Y)$$

We use the notation $r : X \leftrightarrow Y$ to denote a relation r from X to Y. Binary relations can express one–one, one–many, and many–many dependencies between members of the two sets. For instance, "an account-holder holds only one current account" is a one–one relationship between *account_holders* and *current_ accounts*, "a student takes several courses" is a one–many relationship between *student* and *course*, and "patients are allocated to different labs for tests" is a many–many relationship between *patient* and *lab*.

All set operations, except union, can be meaningfully applied to the relations r, s : $(X \leftrightarrow Y)$. The two other operations are

1. *inverse*—The inverse relation $s = inverse(r)$, of relation r, can be computed by the rule

$$(x, y) \in r \Leftrightarrow (y, x) \in s$$

2. *composition*—The composition rule constructs a new relation from two given relations. The composite relation $w = r \circ u$ can be constructed by the rule

$$r : (X \leftrightarrow Y); u : (Y \leftrightarrow Z)$$
$$w : (X \leftrightarrow Z)$$
$$(x, z) \in w \leftrightarrow \exists y \in Y \bullet (x, y) \in r \wedge (y, z) \in u$$

The composition rule plays a significant role in specifications, especially when relations defined on a set are applied repeatedly to the set. Let r^n be defined as the composition of r^{n-1} with r, where r^0 is the *identity relation*. The relation $r^{re} = r \cup r^0$ is *reflexive*; the relation $r^{sy} = r \cup inverse(r)$ is *symmetric*; the relation $r^+ = \bigcup r^n$ is the *transitive closure* of r. In fact, r^+ is the smallest transitive relation containing r. For instance, if *flies* : $(city \times city)$ is a relation describing the property that $(x, y) \in flies$ if there is a direct flight from city x to city y, then the transitive closure relation *flies*$^+$ contains all ordered pairs such that there is a flight (direct or indirect) between each pair of cities. The relation *flies*^{sy} contains the tuples (x, y), such that a direct flight from x to y and from y to x exists.

A *total function* f from X to Y, written $f : X \rightarrow Y$, maps every element of X to exactly one element of Y. When f is defined on only a proper subset of X, f is called a *partial function*. The set of all total functions from X to Y is denoted by $X \rightarrow Y$ and the set of all partial functions from X to Y is denoted by $X \nrightarrow Y$. Functions can be defined recursively, and functions can take functions as arguments, and functions can return other functions.

A function specification may either be *implicit* or *direct*. An implicit specification defines *what* is to be computed, whereas a direct specification defines explicitly *how* the result may be computed. Implicit specifications are more abstract, and shorter in description than direct specifications. Another compelling argument for implicit specification is that the computational model and algorithms for arriving at the result can be postponed to later stages of the design process. Implicitly defined function must include preconditions and postconditions. When the function is applied to arguments satisfying the precondition, its results should satisfy the postcondition. The function cannot be applied to arguments not satisfying the precondition. We do not consider the consequences of partial functions for which certain terms in the precondition are undefined. The appropriate logic dealing with partial functions is discussed in Jones [2].

The syntax for implicit and direct function specifications vary from one specification language to another. However, the semantics confirms to the pattern described above. Example 3 illustrates the difference in the respective specification styles.

Example 3 The greatest common divisor (*gcd*) of two positive integers x, y is the largest integer among the common divisors of x and y. A formal specification for *gcd* is

$$gcd : \mathbb{N} \times \mathbb{N} \rightarrow \mathbb{N}$$

pre $x > 0 \land y \geq 0$

post $d > 0 \land ((d\ div\ x) \land (d\ div\ y) \land \neg \exists s \bullet ((s\ div\ x) \land (s\ div\ y) \land d < s))$

An implicit definition of the *gcd* function is constructed from three other function definitions. The predicate *divides*(x, y) is a truth-valued function, the function *common_divisors* maps a pair of nonnegative integers to the set of their common divisors, and *max* maps a set of positive integers to their maximum:

$divides : \mathbb{N} \times \mathbb{N} \rightarrow Bool$

$divides(x, y) == y\ mod\ x = 0$

$common\_divisors : \mathbb{N} \times \mathbb{N} \rightarrow \mathbb{P}\mathbb{N}$

$common\_divisor(x, y) == S$

post $\forall r \in S \bullet (divides(r, x) \land divides(r, y))$

$max : \mathbb{P}\mathbb{N} \rightarrow \mathbb{N}$

$max(S) == r$

post $r \in S \land \neg \exists y \bullet (y \in S \land r < y)$

$gcd : \mathbb{N} \times \mathbb{N} \rightarrow \mathbb{N}$

$gcd(x, y) == r$

pre $x > 0 \land y \geq 0$

post $r = max(common\_divisors(x, y))$

A direct function specification for *gcd* is given below. A proof that the function specification satisfies its requirements (definition) is given in Sect. 7.2.4.

$$gcd(x, y) = \begin{cases} x, & \text{if } y = 0, x > y \\ gcd(y, x\ mod\ y), & \text{if } x \geq y > 0 \\ gcd(y\ mod\ x, x), & \text{if } 0 \leq x < y \end{cases}$$ $\quad\square$

12.2.2
Functions on Relations

The *domain* of a relation $R : X \leftrightarrow Y$, written as *dom R*, is the subset $A \subseteq X$ defined by

$A = \{x : X \mid \exists y : Y \bullet (x, y) \in R\}$.

Hence, the domain of a relation can be defined as a function:

$dom : (X \leftrightarrow Y) \rightarrow \mathbb{P}X$.

In particular, when the relation R is a function, the argument of the function *dom* is R, a function, and the image of *dom* is a *set*. Functions such as *dom* that take functions as arguments are called *higher-order functions*.

The *range* of a relation $R : X \leftrightarrow Y$, written as *ran R*, is defined similarly as the subset $B \subseteq Y$,

$$B = \{y : Y \mid \exists x : X \bullet (x, y) \in R\}.$$

That is, $ran : (X \leftrightarrow Y) \to \mathbb{P}Y$ is also a higher-order function. Example 4 uses higher-order functions in specifying time-dependent events in a reactive system.

Example 4 Let E denote the set of all event *names* used in describing a computer system. An event $e \in E$ is said to *occur* if there is a time interval during which the effect of e is realized. Assigning values to variables, ringing a bell, and activating a print operation are examples of events.

1. *Event occurrence*—An event occurs continuously during an interval of time. Moreover, an event can occur several times during system execution. To model these requirements, we need a continuous model of time as discussed in Chap. 11. Let R denote the time domain. Since occurrence implies *discrete instances*, the kth occurrence of an event is associated with a beginning time and an ending time. We conceive the event occurrences as higher-order functions:

   $$\text{TIME}_1, \text{TIME}_2 : E \to (\mathbb{N} \to \mathbb{R})$$

   so that

   $$\forall e : E \bullet \text{TIME}_1(e), \text{TIME}_2(e) : \mathbb{N} \to \mathbb{R} \text{ and}$$

   $$\forall n : \mathbb{N} \bullet \text{TIME}_1(e)(n) = t_n, \text{TIME}_2(e)(n) = t'_n \text{ with } t'_n \geq t_n.$$

   The initiation time of the nth occurrence of event e is t_n and its completion time is t'_n. By including the constraint that $t'_n \geq t_n$ as part of the specification, we satisfy the safety requirement that terminations can be observed only for initiated events.

2. *History of variables*—Variables assume different values at different points in time. For each variable $v \in V$, the function *ASSIGN* produces the event $ASSIGN(v)$. The event $Assign(v)$ assigns a value from the domain *DOM* to the variable v. Since $ASSIGN(v)$ is an event, it may occur any number of times; for each occurrence, it takes a certain amount of time to complete assigning a value to v. $\text{TIME}_1(ASSIGN(v))(k)$ and $\text{TIME}_2(ASSIGN(v))(k)$ denote the start and completion times of the kth assignment to v.

   $$\text{ASSIGN} : V \to E,$$

   $$\text{VALUE} : V \to (\mathbb{N} \to DOM),$$

   $$\forall v : V \bullet (\text{VALUE}(v) : \mathbb{N} \to DOM),$$

   $$\forall v : V \bullet (\forall k : \mathbb{N} \bullet (\text{VALUE}(v)(k) \in DOM))$$

   The value $v_k \equiv \text{VALUE}(v)(k)$ is the value assigned to variable v during the interval

   $$[\text{TIME}_1(\text{ASSIGN})(k), \text{TIME}_2(\text{ASSIGN})(k)].$$

Fig. 12.1 Relationship among VALUE, ASSIGN and TIME functions

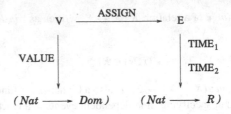

The value v_k remains unchanged in the interval

$$[\text{TIME}_2(\text{ASSIGN})(k), \text{TIME}_1(\text{ASSIGN})(k+1)].$$

The diagram in Fig. 12.1 shows the relationship among VALUE, ASSIGN, and TIME functions.

3. *Measure of events*—The functions $COUNT_1$, $COUNT_2$ are higher-order functions producing counting functions for each event $e \in E$. For $t : \mathbb{R}$, $COUNT_1(e)(t)$ is the number of initiations of e *strictly before* time t, and $COUNT_2(e)(t)$ is the number of observed completions of e *strictly before* time t.

$$\text{COUNT}_1, \text{COUNT}_2 : E \to (\mathbb{R} \to \mathbb{N})$$

$$\forall e : E \bullet (\text{COUNT}_1(e), \text{COUNT}_2(e) : \mathbb{R} \to \mathbb{N}) \Rightarrow$$

$$\forall e : E \bullet (\forall t : \mathbb{R} \bullet (\text{COUNT}_1(e)(t), \text{COUNT}_2(e)(t) \in \mathbb{N})),$$

where $COUNT_2(e)(t) \leq COUNT_1(e)(t)$.

The higher-order functions $LAST_1$, and $LAST_2$ are defined as follows:

$$LAST_1, LAST_2 : E \to (\mathbb{R} \to \mathbb{R}).$$

$$\forall e : E \bullet (\forall t : \mathbb{R} \bullet (LAST_1(e)(t), LAST_2(e)(t) \in \mathbb{R}))$$

$LAST_1(e)(t) = t_1$ if $t_1 < t$ and event e was last initiated at time t_1. Similarly, $LAST_2(e)(t) = t_2$ if $t_2 < t$ and event e was last completed at time t_2. An interesting relationship among these six functions is that

$$LAST_1(e) = TIME_1(e) \circ COUNT_1(e), \quad LAST_2(e) = TIME_2(e) \circ COUNT_2(e)$$

In database applications, it is sometimes required to construct sets of objects satisfying a given property, and to redefine attributes on subsets of objects. These operations may be specified using the restriction and overriding operators.

The operator $\lhd$ restricts the domain, and the operator $\rhd$ restricts the range of relations. The operators are defined as functions:

$$\lhd : \mathbb{P}X \times (X \leftrightarrow Y) \to (X \leftrightarrow Y)$$

$$\forall S : \mathbb{P}X, R : X \leftrightarrow Y \bullet$$

$$S \lhd R = \{(a, b) \mid a \in S \land (a, b) \in R\}$$

$\rhd : (X \leftrightarrow Y) \times \mathbb{P}Y \rightarrow (X \leftrightarrow Y)$

$\forall T : \mathbb{P}Y, R : X \leftrightarrow Y \bullet$

$R \rhd T = \{(a, b) \mid b \in T \wedge (a, b) \in R\}$

$S \lhd R$ filters tuples $(a, b) \in R$ for which $a \in S$ and produces the result relation. $R \rhd T$ filters $(c, d) \in R$ for which $d \in T$ and produces the result relation.

Given

$rel = \{(1, x_3), (4, x_2), (5, x_6), (7, x_6), (9, x_8)\}$

$S = \{4, 7, 9\}$

$T = \{x_3, x_6\}$

the expression $S \lhd rel$ corresponds to the relation

$\{(4, x_2), (7, x_6), (9, x_8)\},$

and the expression $rel \rhd T$ corresponds to the relation

$\{(1, x_3), (5, x_6)\}.$

Two other useful derived operators are $\lhd\!\!\!- $ and $-\!\!\!\rhd$, the subtraction operators for the domain and range of a relation, respectively. $S\lhd\!\!\!- R$ filters tuples (a, b) of R for which $a \notin S$. $R-\!\!\!\rhd T$ filters tuples (c, d) of R for which $d \notin T$. The following relationships are observed on the operators.

$S\lhd\!\!\!- R = (X - S) \lhd R$

$R-\!\!\!\rhd T = R \rhd (Y - T).$

It follows from these definitions that $S \lhd R$ and $S\lhd\!\!\!- R$ are complementary and partition the relation R. That is,

$R = (S \lhd R) \cup (S\lhd\!\!\!- R),$

$(S \lhd R) \cap (S\lhd\!\!\!- R) = \emptyset.$

Similarly,

$R = (R \rhd T) \cup (R-\!\!\!\rhd T),$

$(R \lhd T) \cap (R\lhd\!\!\!- T) = \emptyset.$

The *union* ($\cup$), *intersection* ($\cap$) and *difference* ($-$) operators are functions:

$\cup, \cap, - : \mathbb{P}(X) \times \mathbb{P}(X) \rightarrow \mathbb{P}(X)$

Union and intersection are *commutative* and *associative*; but difference is neither commutative nor associative. Commutativity and associativity allow any number of sets to be combined in any order; that is, both union and intersection can be applied to more than two sets. Although the meaning for intersection and difference applied to relations can be carried over from set theory, the meaning for union should be given in such a way that it will ensure that the result is a relation. When $dom\ f \cap dom\ g = \emptyset$, the union of the two relations $f, g : X \leftrightarrow Y$ is the set union $f \cup g$. In particular, if f and g are functions, then $h = f \cup g : X \rightarrow Y$ is also a function:

$$h(x) = \begin{cases} f(x), & x \in dom\ f, \\ g(x), & x \in dom\ g. \end{cases}$$

When $dom\ f \cap dom\ g \neq \emptyset$ and f and g yield different results for some values in their common domain, "f overrides g" or "g overrides f". The relational overriding $f \oplus g$ defines a relation which agrees with f outside the domain of g, and agrees with g in the domain of g. For functions f and g, the overriding of f with g is the function $h = f \oplus g$, such that

$$h(x) = \begin{cases} g(x), & x \in dom\ g \\ f(x), & x \in dom\ f - dom\ g. \end{cases}$$

$$\forall f, g : X \rightarrow Y \bullet (f \oplus g = (dom\ g \vartriangleleft f) \cup g). \qquad \square$$

12.2.3
Reasoning

Functions can be analyzed for various properties: total or partial, *injective, surjective*, or *bijective*, and more importantly for satisfaction of their specifications. In this section, we focus on the latter aspect, and discuss three methods for reasoning.

12.2.3.1
Proof by Cases

When conditional expressions are used in an explicit function definition, a case by case analysis is required. This proof technique is used when two functions have to be compared or composed over their common domain.

Example 5 Prove that neither $f(n) > g(n)$, nor $f(n) < g(n)$, holds for all values of $n \geq 0$, where $f, g : \mathbb{N} \rightarrow \mathbb{N}$,

$$f(n) = \begin{cases} n^2, & \text{if } 0 \leq n \leq 4, \\ n, & \text{if } n > 4 \end{cases}$$

and

$$g(n) = 2n + 3.$$

Proof: To compare the functions in their full domain, it is necessary to compare their definitions case by case:

Case 1: $0 \leq n \leq 4$.

$$f(n) - g(n) = n^2 - 2n - 3 = (n-3)(n+1).$$

Hence, for $n \geq 3$, $f(n) \geq g(n)$, and for $0 \leq n < 3$, $f(n) < g(n)$.

Case 2: $n > 4$.

$$f(n) - g(n) = -(n+3) < 0. \text{ So, } f(n) < g(n).$$

A case by case proof is useful in showing the satisfaction of a direct function definition to its specification. Example 6 shows one such proof. □

Example 6 Prove that the specification:

$abs : \mathbb{Z} \rightarrow \mathbb{N}$

$v = abs(m)$

post $v \geq 0 \wedge (v = m \vee v = -m)$

is satisfied by the direct function definition:

$abs(m) == if \ m < 0 \ then \ -m \ else \ m$

Proof:

1. $m \in \mathbb{Z}$.
2. $m < 0 \vee m \geq 0$.
3. from $m < 0$ and the function definition,
   (a) $abs(m) = -m$.
   (b) infer $m < 0 \wedge abs(m) = -m$.
   (c) from the postcondition of the *abs* function and the previous step infer $v = -m \wedge v \geq 0$.
4. from $m \geq 0$ and the function definition,
   (a) $abs(m) = m$
   (b) infer $m \geq 0 \wedge abs(m) = m$.
   (c) from the postcondition of the *abs* function and the previous step infer $v = m \wedge v \geq 0$.
5. $m \in \mathbb{Z} \Rightarrow (abs(m) \in \mathbb{N} \wedge ((abs(m) = -m \wedge m < 0) \vee (abs(m) = m \wedge m \geq 0))$ □

12.2.3.2
Proof by Induction

Mathematical induction is founded on *the well-ordering property*, which states that every nonempty set of nonnegative integers has a least element. Induction is applied to prove propositions of the form $\forall n \ P(n)$, where the universe of discourse is the set of nonnegative integers. We consider two versions of the induction principle below, and a third version in Sect. 7.3.3.

Induction—version I

An inductive hypothesis $P(n)$ expresses a property to be proved for every nonnegative integer. The basis step consists of proving $P(0)$, while the inductive step is to prove that $\forall n\, P(n) \Rightarrow P(n+1)$. From these two steps, we conclude that $P(n)$ is proved for all $n \geq 0$. We express the proof steps as an inference rule

$$P(0);$$

$$[\textit{first-ind}] \quad \frac{m \in \mathbb{N},\ P(m) \vdash P(m+1)}{\forall n : \mathbb{N} \bullet \vdash P(n)}$$

Example 7 Prove that the function $f(n) = n! - 2^n$ is positive for $n \geq 4$.
Proof:

1. $n \in \mathbb{N}$ and $P(n) : n! - 2^n > 0$.
2. $P(4) : 4! - 2^4 > 0$ is *true*.
3. $P(m)$ is *true*, $m \geq 4$.
4. $m! - 2^m > 0$, from step 3.
5. $(m+1)! - 2^{m+1} = (m+1).m! - 2.2^m$.
6. $m + 1 > 2$, from step 3.
7. $(m+1)(m! - 2^m) > m! - 2^m$, from steps 4 and 5.
8. $P(m+1)$ is *true*, from steps 4 and 6.
9. $P(m) \Rightarrow P(m+1)$.
10. From steps 2 and 9 infer $P(n)$ is *true*.

Induction—version II

This version of induction is more powerful than the first version. When it is required to prove $P(m)$, the inductive hypothesis $P(n)$ is permitted to hold for all predecessors of m. That is, the inductive proof requires the proof for $(P(1) \wedge \cdots \wedge P(m)) \Rightarrow P(m+1)$ for every positive integer m. The rule is

$$P(0);$$

$$[\textit{second-ind}] \quad \frac{m \in \mathbb{N},\ (\forall m, m < n \Rightarrow P(m) \vdash P(n))}{\forall n \in \mathbb{N} \vdash P(n)}$$

Although these two versions of induction are equivalent, the second one is more powerful and simpler to apply. Let us consider the specification for the greatest common divisor (gcd) function and its direct function definition given in Sect. 7.2.2. The postcondition in the specification can be rewritten as

$gcd(x, y) = d$
post $divides(d, x) \wedge divides(d, y) \wedge \neg \exists s \bullet ((divides(s, x) \wedge divides(s, y) \wedge d < s)$ $\square$

A proof that the direct definition for gcd satisfies its specification is shown in Example 8. This example also illustrates the use of induction for recursively defined functions.

Example 8 The two basic results that we use are

1. P1: Every non-zero integer is its own divisor and divides 0.
2. P2: For nonnegative integers a and b, where $b \leq a$, there are integers q and r such that $a = b.q + r, 0 \leq r < b$.

The proof uses these results, and the second version of induction, and proceeds by case analysis based on the constraints introduced in the function definition.

1. Let $P(m, n), m > n$ be the proposition that the direct function definition for gcd(m,n) satisfies the postcondition in the specification.
2. Basis: $P(m, 0), m \geq 1$
   (a) from the first case, $y = 0$ in the function definition, $gcd(m, 0) = m$.
   (b) To prove that m satisfies the postcondition:
       (i) $S = common\_divisor(m, 0) = \{m\} \cdots$ from P1.
       (ii) $\neg \exists s \bullet (s \in S \wedge m < s)$ is *true*.
       (iii) infer m satisfies the postcondition.
       $P(m, 0)$ is proved.
   (c) Inductive step: $P(m, n)$ is true. That is, the direct function definition for gcd(m,k) satisfies the postcondition of the specification for $0 \leq k \leq n < m$). We must prove $P(m, n + 1)$.
       (i) Rewriting the inductive step

       $$g = gcd(m, n) \wedge divides(g, m) \wedge divides(g, n) \wedge$$

       $$\neg \exists s \bullet (s \in S \wedge \wedge divides(s, m) \wedge divides(s, n) \wedge g < s).$$

       (ii) From the inductive hypothesis, infer $n + 1 \leq m$.
       (iii) From P2, if $m = (n + 1).q + r$, then $0 \leq r < n$.
       (iv) Infer from the previous step that if d divides m and $n + 1$, then d divides r. Hence, $gcd(m, n + 1) = gcd(n + 1, r), 0 \leq r < n + 1$.
       (v) By the inductive hypothesis, $P(n + 1, r)$ is true. That is, $gcd(n + 1, r)$ satisfies the postcondition of the specification.
       (vi) Infer that $gcd(m, n + 1)$ satisfies the specification. That is, $P(m, n + 1)$ is true.
       (vii) The inductive step is proved.
       (viii) Infer $P(m, n)$ for all $n, m > n$. □

12.2.4
A Specification Example

Functions are mathematical objects and consequently have the important property of substitutivity. After a function has been defined, it can be used in any context where it is appropriate. Function composition, overriding, and the possibility of defining functions with functions as arguments make the functional approach to specification both elegant and expressive. Example 9 is a simplified and adapted version of the security model discussed by

McLean [3]. The specification below formally explicates security by constructing formal models of objects and security policies using relations and functions.

Example 9 A computing environment consists of a set of *objects* O such as programs, files and system utilities, and a set of *subjects* S such as users and programs that access and manipulate the objects. Security involves the enforcement of rules governing the accessibility of objects by subjects. Subjects and objects are usually hierarchically classified and the security level is determined by the position of subject(object) in the hierarchy. Below, the model and security requirements are stated informally and then specified.

1. *Type*—A subject is assigned certain rights against an object in the system. So, there is a ternary relationship to be captured here: the tuple $(s, x, a), s \in S, x \in O, a \in A$ denotes that s has access a on object o. Hence, $M = \mathbb{P}(S \times O \times A)$ models all access right combinations.

2. *Security functions*—Every object has a unique *security level classification* and every subject has a unique *security level clearance*. These may be modeled by functions: there exist security level functions $f : S \to \mathbb{N}, g : O \to \mathbb{N}$, where $f(s)$ gives the *security level clearance* for the subject $s \in S$, and $g(o)$ gives the *security level classification* for the object $o \in O$.

3. *Information flow*—Information flows from *lower security levels* to *higher security levels*. If $f(s) > f(t)$, then the subject t can transfer its information knowledge, including its access rights, to the subject s.

4. *System state security*—The state of system M is minimally secure only if subjects that are allowed to access an object have a higher clearance level than the object. Formally, this security requirement translates to:

$$\forall m : M \bullet ((s, x, read) \in m) \Rightarrow f(s) > g(x).$$

A stronger security condition for state M is that every subject s having *read* access to an object x, and having *write* access to an object y, must satisfy the constraint $g(y) > g(x)$. That is, information can be passed from a lower level object x to a higher level object y. Formally,

$$\forall m, n : M \bullet ((s, x, read) \in m) \land ((s, y, write) \in n) \Rightarrow g(y) > g(x)$$

In particular, an object from a lower security level can be copied into an object from a higher security level by a subject who has *read* access to the former object. Formally,

$$\forall m : M \bullet ((s, x, read) \in m) \land \exists y : O \bullet ((g(y) > g(x)) \Rightarrow copy(s, x, y)$$

5. *Constraints on access rights*—We define the following higher-order function to specify constraints on access rights assigned to subjects.

$$F : S \to (O \to A)$$
$$\forall s \in S, F_s : O \to A$$

There is a function F_s for each subject $s \in S$, and $F_s(o)$ gives the access rights assigned to s for object o. The constraint that two subjects s_1 and s_2 have the same rights for an object o_1 is specified as

$$F_{s_1}(o_1) = F_{s_2}(o_1)$$

The set of objects for which a given subject s has only "write" access is given by

$$\{s : S, o : O | (F_s(o) = \{write\}) \bullet o\}$$

Specifying the operation of canceling all access rights assigned to a subject s on the objects in the set X, $X \subset O$, requires the overriding function. Define the function

$$G_s(o) = \begin{cases} \emptyset, & o \in X \\ F_s(o), & o \notin X \wedge o \in A \end{cases}$$

The function

$$H : S \rightarrow (O \rightarrow A), \text{ such that}$$
$$H_s = F_s \oplus G_s$$

defines the modified access rights.

6. *Secure flow of information*—Let $flows : S \leftrightarrow S$ be a relation on S with the interpretation that $(a, b) \in flows$ or $flows(a, b)$ if $f(a) < f(b)$. That is, information may flow from a subject of lower security clearance to a subject of higher security clearance. The relation is reflexive and transitive. The reflexive closure relation $flows^*$ contains all tuples (a, b) such that information flows from subject a to subject b either directly or through a sequence of subjects. The set $B = ran(A \lhd flows)$, such that $A \subset S$, gives the set of subjects whose information is reachable from members of A. Similarly, the set $C = dom(flows \rhd A)$ is the set of subjects from whom information can reach members of A. Information from members of A cannot reach the set of subjects $D = ran(A \ntriangleleft flows)$. The set $E = dom(flows \ntriangleright A)$ is the set of subjects whose information can flow to members of A. Two subjects s, t belong to the same security level if $(s, t) \in flows^*$ and $(t, s) \in flows^*$. It is easy to prove that

$$\forall A, A' : \mathbb{P}(S) \bullet (ran(A \lhd flows) \cap ran(A' \lhd flows) = \emptyset \leftrightarrow A \cap A' = \emptyset)$$

7. *Secure object transfer*—The content of information flow is an object (file or program) and it is characterized by a sequence of *read*, and *write*. If $(a, b) \in flows$ and subject a owns an object y, then the actual flow of y from a to b can be formalized as

$$\forall(a, b) : flows \bullet (\exists m, n : M \bullet (m = (a, y, write) \wedge$$
$$n = (b, z, read) \wedge g(z) > g(y)))$$

Since a owns y, $f(a) > g(y)$ and $n \in M$ implies $f(b) > g(z)$. Hence the constraint $g(z) > g(y)$, enables the copying of y into z without violating the security constraint $f(b) > f(a)$.   □

12.3
Formal Specification Based on Sequences

Sets, relations and functions do not imply any *ordering* on the objects modeled. Sequences are ordered collections of objects. A sequence is appropriate for modeling container entities, such as queues, for which the ordering of items is meaningful.

12.3.1
Notation

A sequence is characterized by a function $f : \mathbb{N} \to X$. The elements of the sequence can be enumerated as $f(1), f(2), \ldots, f(n)$; it is usual to write f_n for $f(n)$. The element f_n is the nth element of the sequence defined by f. Since the images $f(i)$ and $f(j)$ may be equal, a sequence may include the same element more than once. For instance, let $X = \{a, b\}$, and $f(i) = a$ if i is odd, and $f(i) = b$ if i is even. The infinite sequence is composed of alternate a's and b's.

The set of all functions of type $\mathbb{N}_1 \to X$ characterizes the set of all sequences over X:

$$seq[X] \stackrel{\triangle}{=} f : \mathbb{N}_1 \to X$$

A finite sequence is a function f whose domain is a finite initial segment of $\mathbb{N}_1$.

$$f : \{1, 2, \ldots, n\} \to X$$

The notation $seq[X]$ also denotes the type of sequences defined on a finite set X. When $X = \emptyset$, $seq[X]$ is the empty sequence. If $|X| = k(> 0)$ and the initial segment of $\mathbb{N}$ is $\{1, \ldots, n\}$, $seq[X]$ consists of all sequences of length n, where each sequence has elements from the k-element set X. There are k^n sequences in $seq[X]$.

One important consequence of the above definitions is that every element of a sequence $s : seq[X]$ is of type X. A finite sequence can be described by an orderly enumeration of the elements:

$$\langle s_1, s_2, \ldots, s_i \rangle, i \leq |X|$$

The number of elements in a finite sequence s is denoted by $\# s$. We also use the notation $s_i, 1 \leq i \leq \#s$ to denote the ith element of the sequence s.

12.3.2
Sequence Operators

Two sequences of the same element type can be composed to form a single sequence in such a way that the order of each sequence is maintained, and the elements of one sequence follow the elements of the other. The composition operator $\frown$, representing *concatenation*, is defined as

$$\frown: seq[X] \times seq[X] \to seq[X]$$
$$\forall s, t : seq[X]$$
$$\forall i : 1 \leq i \leq \#s \ (s \frown t)_i = s_i$$
$$\forall i : 1 \leq i \leq \#t \ (s \frown t)_{i+\#s} = t_i$$

The function # which assigns to each sequence its number of elements is *additive*; that is,

$$\#(s \frown t) = \#s + \#t$$

A *subsequence* of $f : \{1, 2, \ldots, n\} \to X$ is described by $f \circ r$, where $r : \{1, 2, \ldots, n\} \nrightarrow \{1, 2, \ldots, n\}$ is an increasing injective partial function. For example, $s_1 = \langle x_3, x_4, x_5, x_6 \rangle$, $s_2 = \langle x_2, x_5 \rangle$ and $s_3 = \langle x_1, x_6, x_8 \rangle$ are subsequences of $s = \langle x_1, x_2, x_3, x_4, x_5, x_6, x_7, x_8 \rangle$; however, $s_4 = \langle x_6, x_3, x_7 \rangle$ is not a subsequence of s. The sequence s_2 is obtained by composing the function $f(i) = x_i, 1 \leq i \leq 8$ with $r(1) = 2, r(2) = 5$. There is no function r which can be composed with f to obtain the sequence s_3. If $r_1, r_2, \ldots, r_k$ are subsequence functions with disjoint ranges then the subsequences $f \circ r_1, f \circ r_2, \ldots, f \circ r_k$ are disjoint. The ranges of the functions r_1 and r_2 defined by $r_1(1) = 2, r_1(2) = 5, r_2(1) = 1, r_2(2) = 6, r_2(3) = 8$ are disjoint. Notice that $s = f \circ r_1$, and $s' = f \circ r_2$ are disjoint sequences.

To compare sequences we must define an *order* on X and then extend this definition for sequences of any length. Let $(\leq, X)$ be a *totally* (*linearly*) ordered set. Using the symbol $\preceq$ to denote ordering on sequences, we define $\langle x_i \rangle \preceq \langle x_j \rangle$ if $x_i \leq x_j$ in X. Sequences having only one element are comparable and can be sequentially enumerated. For $s, t : seq[X]$, if $s = \langle x_1, x_2, \ldots, x_k \rangle$ and $t = \langle y_1, y_2, \ldots, y_k \rangle$ we define $s \preceq t$ if $x_1 \leq y_1$ and $\langle x_2, \ldots, x_k \rangle \preceq \langle y_2, \ldots, y_k \rangle$. A strict inequality can be defined:

$$s \prec t \stackrel{\triangle}{=} (\#s < \#t) \vee (\#s = \#t) \wedge (s \preceq t)$$

Thus, $\langle 1, 3, 5 \rangle \preceq \langle 1, 3, 7 \rangle \prec \langle 1, 3, 7, 9 \rangle$.

Another operation is to rearrange a sequence. If two sequences $s, t : seq[X]$ of length k have the same elements, there is a permutation $p : \{1, 2, \ldots, k\} \to \{1, 2, \ldots, k\}$ such that $s_i = t_{p(i)}, i \in \{1, 2, \ldots, \#s\}$. For example, for sequences $s = \langle 1, 3, 5, 3, 7 \rangle$ and $t = \langle 3, 5, 7, 3, 1 \rangle$, there are two permutations; one of them is defined by $p(1) = 5, p(2) = 4, p(3) = 3, p(4) = 1, p(5)3$. The problem of finding the permutation for a linear ordering on the elements of a sequence is analogous to sorting. We define below several functions on sequences. Other functions are defined in the exercises. We denote the nonempty sequence type by $seq_1[X]$.

1. The function *first* returns the first element of a nonempty sequence.

$$first : seq_1[X] \to X$$
$$first(s) \stackrel{\triangle}{=} s_1$$

2. The function *next* accepts a nonempty sequence and returns the sequence following its first element.

$$next : seq_1[X] \rightarrow seq[X]$$
$$(next(s))_i = s_{i+1}, 1 \le i \le \#s - 1$$

That is, *next(s)* is the sequence

$$\langle s_2, s_3, \ldots, s_k \rangle.$$

Notice that $next(s) = \langle\rangle$ if $\#s = 1$.

3. The function *locate* returns true if a given element is an element of the sequence; otherwise it returns false. Recursive definitions such as the one given below can be shown to define a unique function.

$$locate : seq_1[X] \times X \rightarrow \text{Boolean}$$
$$if \#(s) = 1 \text{ then } locate(s, a) \stackrel{\triangle}{=} s_1 = a$$
$$if \#(s) > 1 \text{ then } locate(s, a) \stackrel{\triangle}{=} (first(s) = a) \vee (locate(next(s), a))$$

4. The function *find* returns the smallest index at which a given object is located in the sequence; if the object is not found, the function returns 0.
   $find : seq_1[X] \times X \rightarrow \{0, 1, \ldots N\}$, where N denotes the length of the longest sequence in $seq_1[X]$.

$$find(s, a) \stackrel{\triangle}{=} \begin{cases} 0, & s_i \neq a, i \in 1, 2, \ldots, \#s \\ k, & s_i \neq a, i \in 1, 2, \ldots, k-1, s_k = a, k \le \#s \end{cases}$$

5. The function *find_all* returns a sequence of indices of a sequence at which locations the given argument is found.

$$find\_all : seq[X] \times X \rightarrow seq[\mathbb{N}_1]$$

where $\mathbb{N}_1 = dom(seq[X])$.

$$find\_all(s, a) \stackrel{\triangle}{=} \langle j_1, \ldots, j_k \rangle$$

which describes the sequence of locations in sequence s at which there is a match for a.

Example 10 shows that the function *find_all* can be recursively defined using the other functions defined above.

Example 10 The goal is to define $find\_all(s, a)$ using functions defined on sequences. Since an empty sequence contains no element, *find_all* returns an empty sequence if s is empty. When s is nonempty, either the given element a is not in s or it is found in one or more locations. In the former case, the result returned is an empty sequence. In the latter case, there is a first match at a location k, which is found by the function $find(s, a)$.

It is necessary to construct the result as a sequence. We construct an intermediate result sequence t in which k is inserted. The sequence s is now split at location k, the elements $s_1, \ldots, s_k$ are discarded, and the sequence $s^{(1)}$ is constructed with the remaining elements of s. The sequence obtained recursively from $find\_all(s^{(1)}, a)$, is concatenated to t. This is not the final answer; to understand why, we illustrate the steps of the function $find\_all$ with an example:

For $s = \langle 1, 3, 7, 1, 8, 11, 3, 4, 1, 15 \rangle$, and $a = 1$ $find\_all(s, a)$ should produce the sequence $r = \langle 1, 4, 9 \rangle$.

The steps for constructing r are

1. $locate(s, a) = true; find(s, a) = 1; split(s, find(s, a)) = s^{(1)} = \langle 3, 7, 1, 8, 11, 3, 4, 1, 15 \rangle$
2. $locate(s^{(1)}, a) = true; find(s^{(1)}, a) = 3; split(s^{(1)}, a) = s^{(2)} = \langle 8, 11, 3, 4, 1, 15 \rangle$
3. $locate(s^{(2)}, a) = true; find(s^{(2)}, a) = 5; split(s^{(2)}, a) = s^{(3)} = \langle 15 \rangle$
4. $locate(s^{(3)}, a) = false; \langle \rangle$ is returned
5. The temporary sequence t is $\langle 1, 3, 5 \rangle$
6. The sequence r is the sequence of partial sums of the sequence t.

A definition for sequence t is

$temp : seq[X] \times X \rightarrow seq[N_1]$
$temp(s, a) = t, \quad$ where
$t \overset{\Delta}{=} if\ locate(s, a)\ then$
$\langle find(s, a) \rangle \frown find\_all(split(s, find(s, a)), a)$
$else \langle \rangle$

The definition for $split$ is

$split : seq[X] \times \{1, \ldots, N\} \rightarrow seq[X]$
$split(s, k) = s^{(1)}, \quad$ where
$s_i^{(1)} = s_{i+k}, 1 \leq i \leq \#(s) - k$

The definition for the sequence of partial sums is

$part\_sum : seq[N_1] \rightarrow seq[N_1]$
$part\_sum(t) = if\ t = \langle \rangle then \langle \rangle else$
$if\ next(t) \neq \langle \rangle then \langle head(t) \rangle \frown part\_sum(\langle head(next(t)) + head(t) \rangle \frown$
$(next(t))) \ else \langle head(t) \rangle$

Finally, the function $find\_all(s, a)$ is defined as the composite function $part\_sum \circ temp$. $\square$

12.3.3
Proofs

The definition of sequences imposes an ordering on the elements of a sequence. We can thus refer to the first element of a sequence, and to the rest of the sequence. The first element of the rest of a sequence is the second element of the sequence. The successive elements of a sequence are indexed by terms of the form $succ^k(0)$. This suggests the applicability of induction to structures constructed using a finite number of generators.

The induction rules discussed in Sect. 7.2.3 are based on the generators *zero*, and *succ* for natural numbers. A finite sequence may be viewed as generated by $\langle\rangle$ and $\frown$. These two generators are sufficient for generating all finite sequences. For example, the sequence $\langle 1, 5, 3 \rangle$ may be generated by the successive concatenations:

$\langle\rangle$; $\langle 3 \rangle \frown \langle\rangle$; $\langle 5 \rangle \frown \langle 3 \rangle \langle\rangle$; $\langle 1 \rangle \frown \langle 5 \rangle \langle 3 \rangle \langle\rangle$

The empty sequence $\langle\rangle$ is analogous to *zero*, and the operator $\frown$ is analogous to *succ*. We consider *zero* as the index for an empty sequence, and for a sequence of *oldindex* elements, we consider $succ(oldindex)$ as the new index concatenated to the sequence. We reformulate the induction rule *first_ind* for sequences.

$$P(\langle\rangle);$$

$$[seq\_ind] \quad \frac{e \in X, s \in seq[X], P(s) \vdash P(\langle e \rangle \frown s)}{s \in seq[X] \vdash P(s)}$$

A sequence allows multiple occurrences of an element to be distinguished by their ordering. A set neither allows multiplicity nor imposes an ordering on its elements. A *bag* or a *multiset* allows multiplicity, but no ordering. When only multiplicities, but not ordering, are required to be recorded, the *bag* type should be chosen. In the following discussion, we develop a simple theory for bags and show its relationship to the theory of finite sets and sequences.

For a finite set X, the type $Bag[X]$ is the set of all bags defined on X. The definition $b : Bag[X]$ introduces a bag b, which records ordered pairs of elements from X and their occurrence counts.

$$b = \{(x_1, n_1), \dots, (x_k, n_k)\},$$

where $x_i \in X, n_i > 0$.

We use the set notation $\in$ for bag membership, and $\perp$ to denote an empty bag. The following functions are defined on bags:

1. *Add a member*—This function adds an entry (e, k) to a given bag. If a tuple of the kind (e, n) exists in the bag, the multiplicity of e is incremented by k; otherwise, the given pair is included in the bag.

   $add : Bag[X] \times (X \times \mathbb{N}) \to Bag[X]$
   $add(\perp, (e, k)) = \{(e, k)\}$
   $add(b, (e, k)) = b'$
   post$\neg(\exists(a, n) \in b \bullet a = e) \to b' = b \cup \{(e, k)\}$
   $\vee(\exists(a, n) \in b \bullet a = e) \to b' = b - \{(e, n)\} \cup \{(e, n + k)\}$

2. *Test for membership*—Given an element $e \in X$, this function returns true if an ordered pair for e is included in the given bag; otherwise, the function returns false.

   $locate : B[X] \times X \to \mathbb{B}$

Fig. 12.2 Setseqbag

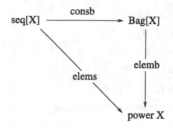

$$locate(b, e) = \exists(a, n) \in b \bullet e = a$$

3. *Extract elements from the base domain*—This function extracts the elements of the basic domain for a bag, constructing a set of the elements while ignoring their occurrence counts.

$$elemb : Bag[X] \to \mathbb{P}X$$
$$elemb(\bot) = \emptyset$$
$$elemb(add(b, (e, k))) = if\ locate(b, e)\ then\ elemb(b)$$
$$\quad else\ elemb(b) \cup \{e\}$$

4. *Multiplicity of a base element*—The multiplicity of a base element e in a bag b is 0 if e is not in $elemb(b)$; otherwise it is determined by a unique entry in b.

$$count : Bag[X] \times X \to \mathbb{N}$$
$$count(\bot) = 0$$
$$count(add(b, (e, k)), a) = (e \neq a \wedge count(b, a)) \vee (e = a \wedge (k + count(b, a))$$

5. *Bag construction from a sequence*—Given a sequence, this function records the elements and their occurrence counts as ordered pairs, ignoring the ordering on the elements of the sequence.

$$consb : seq[X] \to Bag[X]$$
$$consb(\langle\rangle) = \bot$$
$$consb(e \frown s) = add(consb(s), \langle e, 1 \rangle)$$

The *elems* function constructs a set containing all the elements of a sequence, ignoring the ordering on the elements and their occurrence counts.

$$elems : seq[X] \to \mathbb{P}X$$
post $Y \in \mathbb{P}X \wedge \forall i \bullet (1 \leq i \leq \#s \wedge s[i] \in Y)$

We claim that the three functions *elems, elemb, consb* are related by the commutative diagram shown in Fig. 12.2. We consider a simple example before giving a proof by induction for this claim.

$$X = \{a, b, c, d\}; s : seq[X]; t : Bag[X]$$

$$s = \langle b, c, b, a, b, a \rangle$$
$$t = \{ (a, 2), (b, 3), (c, 1) \}$$
$$elems(s) = \{a, b, c\} \subset X$$
$$consb(s) = t$$
$$elemb(b) = \{a, b, c\} \subset X$$
$$elems(s) = elemb(consb(s)) = (elemb \circ consb)(s)$$

Proof:

The proof is by the induction rule [*seq_ind*] stated previously in this section.

1. *Basis step.*

   $$elems(\langle \rangle) = \emptyset \dots \text{definition of elements}$$
   $$consb(\langle \rangle) = \perp \dots \text{definition of } consb$$
   $$elemb(\perp) = \emptyset \dots \text{definition of } elemb$$
   $$infer\ elems(\langle \rangle) = (elemb \circ consb)(\langle \rangle)$$

2. *Inductive step.*
   Assume that for $s : seq[X], s \neq \langle \rangle$

   $$elems(s) = (elemb \circ consb)(s)$$

   To complete the inductive step, it must be shown that

   $$\forall e \in X \bullet elems(e \frown s) = (elemb \circ consb)(e \frown s)$$

   There are two cases to consider: $e \notin consb(s)$ and $e \in consb(s)$.
3. *Case 1: $e \notin consb(s)$*
   The right-hand side in step 2 is rewritten using the definition for *consb*:

   $$elemb(consb(e \frown s)) = elemb(add(consb(s), \langle e, 1 \rangle))$$

   Using the definition of *elemb*, rewrite the right-hand side as

   $$elemb(consb(s)) \cup \{e\} = (elemb \circ consb)(s) \cup \{e\}.$$

   By inductive hypothesis, rewrite the right-hand side as

   $$elems(s) \cup \{e\} = elems(s) \cup elems(\{e\}) = elems(e \frown s).$$

4. Case 2: $e \in consb(s)$
   Since $locate(consb(s), e)$ is *true*, we rewrite the right-hand side in step 2 as $elemb(consb(s))$, using the definition of *elemb*. By the inductive hypothesis, we rewrite this as $(elemb \circ consb)(s) = elems(s)$. Using the equality property of sets, we infer that $elems(s) = elems(e \frown s)$.
5. The proof for the inductive step is now complete. By the [*seq_ind*] principle of induction, the proof of the claim follows.

12.3.4
A Specification Example

In Chap. 5, we introduced formal definitions for the data types involved in an *Idea Processor*. In this section, we define several functions on these data types.

Let *word* be a basic type denoting the set of all words to be included in a dictionary. A finite sequence of words is a basic unit of ideas, called *note*. The type of this basic unit is defined as *note = seq[word]*. We define the ordering on the words as in a dictionary such that two words $w_1, w_2 \in word$ can be compared: $w_1 < w_2$ if w_1 precedes w_2 in the dictionary. This represents a *total order* on *word*. The ordering can be extended to sequences of words, as explained in Sect. 7.3.1. The functions *first, next, locate, find* and *find_all* defined in Sect. 7.3.2 apply to this sequence. An *idea* is recorded as a set of notes; that is, *idea* : $\mathbb{P}X$, where $X = \{n : note \bullet n\}$ is a collection of *note*. Based on these data types, we define functions for manipulating ideas.

$$
\begin{aligned}
create \ &: \rightarrow idea \\
add \quad \ &: idea \times note \rightarrow idea \\
remove \ &: idea \times note \rightarrow idea
\end{aligned}
$$

create is a null-ary function producing an empty database of type *idea*. The other functions are

$$
add(t, n) \stackrel{\triangle}{=} t \cup \{n\}
$$
$$
remove(t, n) \stackrel{\triangle}{=} t - \{n\}
$$

Since t is a set type, adding a note which already exists in t, or removing a note which does not exist in t, produces acceptable behavior. Since the elements of t are of type sequence, explicit methods can be given for testing membership in t. We introduce these primitives, *empty* and *is_member*, to operate on ideas.

$$
\begin{aligned}
empty \quad \ &: idea \rightarrow \mathbb{B} \\
is\_member \ &: idea \times note \rightarrow \mathbb{B}
\end{aligned}
$$

Since *create* produces an empty set of ideas, *empty(create)* is *true*; however, *empty(add(t, n))* is *false*. Applying *is_member* on an empty set of notes has the following result:

$$
is\_member(create, n) = (n = \langle \rangle)
$$

Using these functions, the definitions of *remove* and *add* may be rewritten:

$$
remove(t, n) \stackrel{\triangle}{=} \text{if } is\_member(t, n) \text{ then } t - \{n\} \text{ else } t
$$
$$
add(t, n) \stackrel{\triangle}{=} \text{if } is\_member(t, n) \text{ then } t \text{ else } t \cup \{n\}
$$

To define *is_member(t, n)* for any nonempty set of notes, we need an equality relation for sequences. We can either use the ordering $\preceq$ defined on sequences or the function *find_all*.

In the latter case, the function $is\_member(t, n)$ can be specified as follows:

$$equal : note \times note \to \mathbb{B}$$

$$equal(m, n) \triangleq elems(m) = elems(n) \wedge$$

$$(\forall w : word \bullet find\_all(n, w) = find\_all(m, w))$$

$$is\_member(t, n) \triangleq \exists m : note \bullet (m \in t \wedge equal(m, n))$$

From the above functions, we can prove the following properties:

1. $add(remove(t, n), n) = t = remove(add(t, n), n)$
2. $add(add(t, n), n)) = t$
3. $add(add(t, n_1), n_2) = add(add(t, n_2), n_1)$

12.4
Exercises

1. Using the set axioms given in Sect. 7.1.2, give a formal proof for the following or disprove by giving a counterexample:

   (a) $\dfrac{A \times B = A \times C}{B = C}$

   (b) $\dfrac{\mathbb{P}X = \mathbb{P}Y}{X = Y}$

   (c) $(A - B) - C = (A - C) - (B - C)$

2. Let $S \in \mathbb{P}X$. Define the function:

   $$put : X \times S \to S$$

   $$put(e, s) = \{e\} \cup s$$

   Prove the following properties on the function put:

   (a) S is generated by $\emptyset$ and put.
   (b) $e_1 \in put(e, s) = (e_1 = e) \vee e_1 \in s$.
   (c) $put(e_1, put(e, s)) = put(e, put(e_1, s))$.

3. Specify the following constraints and operations for Example 2:

   (a) A student can own a maximum of 20 files. The author of a lesson can own a maximum of 50 files. An administrator can own a maximum of 100 files.
   (b) A student is able to read and copy a quiz file. The author of the quiz is able to read, write, edit, and copy the quiz file.
   (c) When the *view* command is invoked by a user, only the file store for which the user has access rights can be seen. Moreover, the status of the file store remains unchanged.
   (d) Specify the access rights invariant for quiz files in *file_store_c*.
   (e) Specify an operation to be invoked by a teacher that modifies the contents of a grade file.

(f) Specify an operation to be invoked by students to copy a lesson file into a student auxiliary file.

4. Let *courses* denote the set of courses offered in a department. Registering for a course may require prerequisite courses. Write a specification which produces *seq_courses*, a sequence of courses from the set *courses* satisfying the following properties: (1) every course in *courses* occurs in the sequence *seq_courses*; and (2) if $c_1 = seq\_courses[i]$, and $c_2 = seq\_courses[j]$, and $i < j$, then course c_1 is a prerequisite for course c_2.

5. Let S denote the set of students in a residential college. The college has k dormitories $d_1, \ldots, d_k$. Every student lives in some dormitory, and no student can live in more than one dormitory. A collection $P = \{S_1, \ldots, S_j\}$, where $j \le k$, $S_i \subset S$ is the set of students living in dormitory d_i, and $1 \le i \le j$, is an instance of a model for students and the dormitories where they live. Do the following:

    (a) Give the type definition for P.
    (b) State formally the following constraints: (1) every student lives in some dormitory; (2) no student lives in more than one dormitory.
    (c) Give the specification of a function to remove a student from the dormitory.
    (d) Given two students $a, b \in S$, determine the dormitories to which they belong. If they belong to two different dormitories, then merge the two dormitories into one dormitory.

6. Prove the following claim made in Example 9:

$$\forall A, A' : \mathbb{P}(S) \bullet (ran(A \lhd flows) \cap ran(A' \lhd flows) = \emptyset \leftrightarrow A \cap A' = \emptyset).$$

7. For any finite set X and for some $n > 0$, prove or disprove the claim that

$$\emptyset \cup X \cup X^2, \ldots, X^n$$

defines all sequences of length not exceeding n on X.

8. For a finite sequence type, define the following functions:

    (a) *min* that finds a minimum among the elements of the sequence.
    (b) *swap* that exchanges the elements in two given locations of the sequence.
    (c) *rotate* that cyclically shifts right the elements in the sequence.
    (d) *reverse* that uses *rotate* to reverse the ordering of elements in the sequence.
    (e) Prove $reverse(s_1 \frown s_2) = reverse(s_2) \frown reverse(s_1)$.

12.5
Bibliographic Notes

We included a preliminary mathematical review of sets and relations to clarify the specification notation. For a more detailed review of the fundamental concepts of discrete mathematics, the reader is referred to Alagar [1] and Rosen [4].

Specifications based on sets and relations are model-based, while implicit functional specifications are property-oriented. The Z notation [5] is based on set theory and the semantics for Z specifications are assigned from set operations. VDM specifications [2] can be written in a pure functional style, with or without sets and relations. These formal notations are discussed in Chaps. 16 and 17.

References

1. Alagar VS (1989) Fundamentals of computing—theory and practice. Prentice Hall, Englewood Cliffs
2. Jones CB (1990) Systematic software development using VDM, 2nd edn. Prentice hall international series in computer science
3. McLean J (1990) The specification and modeling of computer security. IEEE Comput 23(1):9–16
4. Rosen KH (1990) Discrete mathematics and its applications, 2nd edn. McGraw Hill, New York
5. Spivey JM (1988) Understanding Z: a specification language and its formal semantics. Cambridge University Press, Cambridge

Part V
Property-Oriented Specifications

Specifications based on logic and algebra are known as property-oriented specifications. In this module, algebraic specification methodology is discussed and illustrated with OBJ3 specification language. The other two specification languages discussed are Larch, a two-tier language useful for interface specifications, and CCS (Calculus of Communicating Systems) for specifying communication and concurrency. The learning outcomes from this module are the following:

- algebraic abstractions
- structuring algebraic specifications
- parameterized algebraic programming
- Larch Shared Language
- Larch Interface Language
- proofs in Larch
- CCS operators
- CCS language-syntax and semantics
- reasoning with equivalence and congruence relations

Algebraic Specification

13

Algebraic specification emerged in the 1970s as a formal specification technique for specifying data structures in an implementation-independent style. This approach has given rise
to several specification methods providing techniques for *data abstraction*, *theory formulation*, *analyzing specification properties*, *modular development*, and *hierarchical composition*. Algebraic specification is founded on equational logic, and the underlying semantics
is derived from algebra, where different mathematical structures such as groups, rings,
and fields are studied. In this chapter we look at how to construct algebras for specifying
various software artifacts.

13.1
Algebra and Specification

An *algebra* can be considered as a collection of sets, together with operations on the sets. If
we regard sorts (types) as sets, we get the equation *Algebra = Sorts(Types) + Operations*. If
we represent a system as a collection of sets and describe the functionality of the system by
equations on operations defined on the sets we obtain an algebra. The resulting algebra may
be viewed as an *algebraic specification* of the system. For instance, we may view a system
as a collection of objects $O_1, O_2, \ldots, O_n$, where each O_i is modeled as a set. We describe
the functionality of object O_j by a set f_j of functions. The algebraic specification of a
software system expresses the collective behavior of the objects through a set of equations
on the functions.

The justifications for viewing a system specification as an algebra include the following.

- An abstract axiomatic specification of a program is given by its algebra. To understand
  this paradigm, let us consider the conventional view of programs put forth by Wirth [13]:
  Algorithms + DataStructures = Programs. An abstraction of the program-level data
  structure is obtained by composing *sorts*, types based on set-theoretic constructs. The
  resulting abstractions are termed *Abstract Data Types (ADT)*. We abstract algorithmic
  details by disregarding *how* operations are performed, and emphasizing *what* they perform. This abstraction corresponds to the operations on sorts. We thus obtain the abstraction *Sorts + Operations* corresponding to *DataStructures + Algorithms*. Having defined

V.S. Alagar, K. Periyasamy, *Specification of Software Systems*,
Texts in Computer Science,
DOI 10.1007/978-0-85729-277-3_13, © Springer-Verlag London Limited 2011

Algebra as *Sorts + Operations*, it follows that *Algebra* is an abstraction of *Programs*. In other words, a program can be specified as an algebra.

- The terms of an algebra are free of representation constraints. The effect of operations on the terms of an algebra are expressed by axioms. Axiomatic definitions are more abstract than model-based definitions.
- Since an algebra is an abstract model of a program, we are able to describe programming tasks and reason about them, before deriving a concrete representation of the algebra, that is, another algebra or program.
- In general, we can derive several concrete representations for an algebra. Consequently, programs describing *dissimilar* objects and sharing a common *structure* correspond to an algebra.

Example 1 introduces a simple abstract algebra.

Example 1 Let S denote a set with four operations *right, left, below, above* defined on it. The axioms constraining these operations are

1. $left(right(x)) = x = right(left(x))$
2. $above(below(x)) = x = below(above(x))$
3. $right(above(x)) = above(right(x))$
4. $left(above(x)) = above(left(x))$
5. $right(below(x)) = below(right(x))$
6. $left(below(x)) = below(left(x))$

The set S together with the operations and the axioms, define an algebra $\mathcal{U}$. We describe three different concrete structures that are modeled by $\mathcal{U}$; i.e., $\mathcal{U}$ is a specification of the structures. □

Example 2 gives three algebras which are the concrete representations of algebra $\mathcal{U}$ defined in Example 1.

Example 2 1. Lattice points—Algebra $\mathcal{L}$
Let $L = \{x, y | x, y \in \mathbb{Z}\}$ with four operations *rightnext, leftnext, abovenext* and *belownext* defined on it:

$\forall p \in L$

$\quad rightnext(p) = (x + 1, y)$

$\quad leftnext(p) = (x - 1, y)$

$\quad abovenext(p) = (x, y + 1)$

$\quad belownext(p) = (x, y - 1)$

It is easy to verify that the axioms of algebra $\mathcal{U}$ are true for this interpretation. The elements of set L have a representation, and consequently the algebra $\mathcal{L}$ is more concrete than algebra $\mathcal{U}$.

2. Linear Transformations—Algebra $\mathcal{T}$

Let us consider the integer matrix A:

$$A = \begin{pmatrix} 1 & 2 & 4 \\ 3 & 5 & 7 \\ 6 & 8 & 9 \end{pmatrix}$$

Let CRS be the cyclical right-shift operation on columns (elements of column 1 are moved to column 2; elements of column 2 are moved to column 3; elements of column 3 are moved to column 1).

$$\text{CRS(A)} = \begin{pmatrix} 4 & 1 & 2 \\ 7 & 3 & 5 \\ 9 & 6 & 8 \end{pmatrix}$$

Let CBS be the cyclical counter-clockwise-shift operation on rows (elements of row 1 are moved to row 2 and so on). Let CLS denote the cyclical left-shift operation on columns, and CAS be the cyclical clockwise-shift operation on rows.

$$\text{CLS(A)} = \begin{pmatrix} 2 & 4 & 1 \\ 5 & 7 & 3 \\ 8 & 9 & 6 \end{pmatrix}$$

$$\text{CAS(A)} = \begin{pmatrix} 3 & 5 & 7 \\ 6 & 8 & 9 \\ 1 & 2 & 4 \end{pmatrix}$$

$$\text{CBS(A)} = \begin{pmatrix} 6 & 8 & 9 \\ 1 & 2 & 4 \\ 3 & 5 & 7 \end{pmatrix}$$

The axioms of the algebra $\mathcal{U}$ can be verified for these operations applied to matrix A. The axioms hold when these operations are applied to any $n \times n$ matrix. Algebra $\mathcal{T}$, for $n \times n$ matrices with these four operations, is a concrete model of algebra $\mathcal{U}$.

3. Strings—Algebra $\mathcal{S}$

Consider a set S of strings over an alphabet. Define CROT and CLOT to be the cyclical right shift and cyclical left shift of characters in a string. For instance, CROT($abac$) = ($caba$), and CLOT($abac$) = ($baca$). The two other operations on set S are identities LID, and RID. It is straightforward to verify the axioms of algebra $\mathcal{U}$ for algebra $\mathcal{S}$ under this interpretation. □

The mathematical machinery of algebras and the generality achievable in this framework allow algebraic specifications be written as mathematical objects in an accurate, unambiguous, and implementation-independent manner. The fundamental concepts of algebras are introduced in the next section through their mathematical foundations. We include an informal introduction to the concepts, avoiding mathematical details, and illustrate the concepts with several examples.

13.2
Algebras—A Brief Introduction

A *many-sorted algebra* is an abstract structure consisting of a family S of sets and a family $\Omega = \{\Omega_1, \Omega_2, \ldots, \Omega_k\}$, $\Omega_i \cap \Omega_j = \emptyset$, where Ω_i is a set of operations with arguments and results belonging to the sets in S. The sets in S correspond to sorts, and Ω corresponds to a family of operator names. The pair $\langle S, \Omega \rangle$ forms a *signature*. Each operation in Ω_i has the same type; this type represents the *scheme* of the operator.

Example 3 In Example 1, algebra $\mathcal{U}$ is 1-sorted or homogeneous. The signature of $\mathcal{U}$ is $\langle T, \Omega \rangle$, where

$T = \{S\}$

$\Omega = \{right, left, above, below\} : S \rightarrow S$

There is only one sort and one scheme.   □

In order to handle ADT's rigorously in software engineering contexts, we need to consider many-sorted or heterogeneous algebras. For example, the stack structure can be adequately described by considering the set of stacks, the set of element type it holds, for example integers or strings, and the set of booleans to describe equality relationship on items. Notice that algebra S in Example 1 is an inadequate description of strings because many useful operations on strings could not be described in that homogeneous algebra.

Example 4 In this example, we consider a file of records storing some database information. The three concepts to be abstracted are *file*, *record*, and *information*. We choose the three sorts *file*, *record*, and *infor*, each corresponding to one database concept. Some of the operations that we consider are

- *insert*: to add a record in a file,
- *delete*: to remove a record from a file,
- *trash*: to purge a file, and
- *update*: to revise information in a record.

A signature for the algebra of transactions is $\langle S, \Omega \rangle$, where

$S = \{file, record, infor\}$

$\Omega = \{\{insert, delete\} : file \times record \rightarrow file$

$\quad\quad \{update\} : file \times record \times infor \rightarrow file$

$\quad\quad \{trash\} : file \rightarrow file\}$

The four operators in this example are grouped into three schemes.   □

13.2.1
Homomorphisms

A *homomorphism* is a structure-preserving map between two algebras. We first deal with homomorphisms of homogeneous algebras and then introduce homomorphisms of heterogeneous algebras.

Homogeneous Algebras A *homomorphism* is a map between two algebras preserving various algebraic properties. For example, if an operation $*$ is defined on two sets X and Y, then the map $f : X \to Y$ is a homomorphism if, for all $x, y \in X$, $f(x * y) = f(x) * f(y)$. If X has an *identity* element e, satisfying the property $x * e = x$ for all $x \in X$, then $f(e)$ is an identity for Y. The proof follows from the definition of homomorphism. If X contains an identity element e, an element $x \in X$ may have an *inverse* $x^{-1} \in X$ satisfying the property $x * x^{-1} = e$. If e' is the identity in Y which is the image of e in X, then

$$e' = f(e) = f(x * x^{-1}) = f(x) * f(x^{-1}).$$

Hence, $f(x^{-1}) \in Y$ and is the inverse of $f(x) \in Y$. Moreover, if the operation $*$ is commutative (associative), then f preserves the commutative (associative) property in Y. The following theorem summarizes these results.

Theorem *If $f : \langle X, * \rangle \to \langle Y, * \rangle$ is a homomorphism and e is an identity for X, then $f(e)$ is an identity for Y. If for all $x \in X$ for which an inverse $x^{-1} \in X$ exists, $f(x^{-1}) \in Y$ is an inverse of $f(x) \in Y$. The map f preserves commutative and associative properties, if any.*

Example 5 Consider the set of two-dimensional vectors on real numbers $\mathbb{R}$, with the operation $+$ (vector addition) defined as

$$\langle x, y \rangle + \langle a, b \rangle = \langle x + a, y + b \rangle.$$

The operation $+$ is both commutative and associative. The vector $\langle 0, 0 \rangle$ is the identity element and $\langle -x, -y \rangle$ is the inverse of vector $\langle x, y \rangle$. Define $f : \mathbb{R} \to \mathbb{R}$ by

$$f(\langle x, y \rangle) = \langle Ax + By, Cx + Dy \rangle,$$

where A, B, C, D are constants. The map f is a homomorphism. To prove it, show that $f(\langle x, y \rangle + \langle x', y' \rangle) = f(\langle x, y \rangle) + f(\langle x', y' \rangle)$. Since $f(\langle 0, 0 \rangle) = \langle 0, 0 \rangle$, the identity is mapped onto itself. Since $f(\langle -x, -y \rangle) = \langle -Ax - By, -Cx - Dy \rangle = -(\langle Ax + By, Cx + Dy \rangle) = -f(\langle x, y \rangle)$, f maps the inverse of $\langle x, y \rangle$ to the inverse of $f(\langle x, y \rangle)$. The homomorphism preserves commutative and associative properties. Notice that f is a linear transformation defined on 2×2 matrices. $\square$

If a homomorphism $f : X \to Y$ is an onto mapping from X to Y, f is called an *epimorphism*. For example, consider $(\mathbb{N}, +)$, the algebra of integers under addition and $(\mathbb{N}_n, +)$, the algebra of integers under addition modulo n. Define the map $f : \mathbb{N} \to \mathbb{N}_n$, $f(a) = a \bmod n$. The map is onto; that is, for every $k \in \{0, 1, \ldots, n-1\}$, there is a $j \in \mathbb{N}$ such that $j \bmod n = k$. For $a, b \in \mathbb{N}$, since $(a + b) \bmod n = (a \bmod n) + (b \bmod n)$, the map f is a homomorphism. Hence f is an epimorphism.

If a homomorphism $f : X \rightarrow Y$ is one-to-one, it is called a *monomorphism*. A homomorphism which is both an epimorphism and a monomorphism is called an *isomorphism*. Isomorphic algebras have essentially the same structure - only their names are different.

Example 6 Consider the set $X = \{0, 1, \ldots, 2^k - 1\}$ with addition modulo 2^k and the set Y of k-bit binary digits with addition modulo 2. Define the map $f : Y \rightarrow X$, where f maps a binary digit to the natural number it represents. For two binary digits $b_1 \neq b_2$, $f(b_1) \neq f(b_2)$. For every number in X there exists only one binary digit. Hence f is an isomorphism.   □

Example 7 Consider algebra $\mathcal{U}$ with operators *right*, *left*, *above*, *below* and algebra $\mathcal{T}$ with operators CRS, CLS, CAS, CBS defined in Example 1. Define a homomorphism $f : \mathcal{U} \rightarrow \mathcal{T}$, which maps an element of algebra $\mathcal{U}$ to an $n \times n$ matrix of algebra $\mathcal{T}$, and maps operators as follows:

$f(right) = \mathsf{CRS};\ f(left) = \mathsf{CLS};$

$f(above) = \mathsf{CAS};\ f(below) = \mathsf{CBS}.$

A term of the form *above(x)* in $\mathcal{U}$ will be mapped by f to the term $f(above)(f(x)) = \mathsf{CAS}(m)$ in algebra $\mathcal{T}$. The axioms are mapped accordingly. For example, the axiom $above(below(x)) = x = below(above(x))$ will be mapped to $\mathsf{CAS}(\mathsf{CBS}(m)) = m = \mathsf{CBS}(\mathsf{CAS}(m))$. Similarly, we can define homomorphisms from $\mathcal{U}$ to $\mathcal{L}$ and from $\mathcal{U}$ to $\mathcal{T}$.   □

Heterogeneous Algebras   The software development process involves designing complex data types composed from basic data types such as integer, boolean, array, and record. For instance, a database file may be composed from set and record data types. In such a case, a file operation should preserve the operations on sets and records. This situation characterizes a heterogeneous homomorphism. Informally, a homomorphism F, from an algebra A with signature $\Sigma_A = \langle S_A, \Omega_A \rangle$ to an algebra B with signature $\Sigma_B = \langle S_B, \Omega_B \rangle$, maps each sort $s \in S_A$ to a sort $F(s) \in S_B$, and each operator $h \in \Omega_A$ to an operator $F(h) \in \Omega_B$, such that each scheme θ of Ω_A is mapped to a scheme $F(\theta)$ of Ω_B, in which the arity of scheme θ is preserved. For example, if the domain of scheme θ is

$S_1 \times S_2 \times \cdots \times S_k,$

then

$\forall x_1 \in S_1, x_2 \in S_2, \ldots, x_k \in S_k,$

$F(h(x_1, x_2, \ldots, x_k)) = F(h)(F(x_1), F(x_2), \ldots, F(x_k))$

F preserves the arity and the types of the operators.

Example 8 Consider algebra $\mathcal{S}$ with signature $\langle S_1, \Omega_1 \rangle$, and algebra $\mathcal{C}$ with signature $\langle S_2, \Omega_2 \rangle$, where

$S_1 = \{Stack, Elm\}$

$\Omega_1 = \{\{push\} : Stack \times Elm \rightarrow Stack$

$\{pop\} : Stack \rightarrow Stack$

$\{top\} : Stack \rightarrow Elm$

$\{newstack\} :\rightarrow Stack\}$

$S_2 = \{Container, Item\}$

$\Omega_2 = \{\{put\} : Container \times Item \rightarrow Container$

$\{get\} : Container \rightarrow Item$

$\{newc\} :\rightarrow Container\}$

Define a map $F : S_2 \rightarrow S_1$, such that $F(Container) = Stack$, $F(Item) = Elm$, $F(put) = push$, $F(newc) = newstack$, and $F(get) = top$. It is easy to verify that F is a homomorphism from C to S. For example, F maps the term $put(newc, i)$ to $push(newstack, e)$. $\square$

13.3
Abstract Data Types

Informally, an abstract data type D is a set S of data structures and a collection Ω of services provided by them. The abstract data type D is modeled by an algebra $\mathcal{A}$ over the signature$\langle S, \Omega \rangle$. The set S consists of the sorts needed to construct D. The operations in Ω correspond to abstract algorithmic procedures manipulating the modeled data.

The syntactic structure of data type D is determined by the signature of algebra $\mathcal{A}$, and the semantics is derived from the notion of *computation structure*. The computation structure is a many-sorted algebra in which all elements of set S can be denoted by *ground terms*. A term of a sort may refer to nullary functions, functions defined in the algebra, and free variables. Every such term must be reduced to a ground term. The conjoint interpretation of all the ground terms give the computation structure of the data type modeled by algebra $\mathcal{A}$.

Assuming that *Elm* corresponds to *Nat*, the sort of natural numbers, some of the ground terms of algebra S modeling a stack data type in Example 8 are

1. *newstack*—an empty stack.
2. $push(push(newstack, zero), succ(zero))$—a stack with two elements, $succ(zero)$ on top of *zero*.
3. $top(pop(push(push(newstack, zero), succ(succ(zero)))))$—the top element of a stack containing *zero*.

Fig. 13.1 The data type *Natural*

Spec: *Natural*;
Sorts: *Nat*;
Operations:
    zero :→ *Nat*;
    succ : *Nat* → *Nat*;
    add : *Nat* × *Nat* → *Nat*;
    mult : *Nat* × *Nat* → *Nat*;
Variables:
    a, *x* : *Nat*;
Axioms:
    $add(zero, a) = a$;
    $add(succ(x), a) = add(x, succ(a))$;
    $mult(zero, a) = zero$;
    $mult(succ(x), a) = add(mult(x, a), a)$;

Fig. 13.2 The data type *Stack*

Spec: *Stack*;
Sorts: *Stack*, *Nat*;
Operations:
    zero :→ *Nat*;
    succ : *Nat* → *Nat*;
    newstack :→ *Stack*;
    push : *Stack* × *Nat* → *Stack*;
    pop : *Stack* → *Stack*;
    top : *Stack* → *Nat*;
Variables:
    s : *Stack*, *n* : *Nat*;
Axioms:
    $pop(newstack) = newstack$;
    $top(newstack) = zero$;
    $pop(push(s, n)) = s$;
    $top(push(s, n)) = n$;

13.3.1
Presentation

A *presentation* of an abstract data type is a signature together with a set of *axioms*. The axioms characterize the properties of the data type within a many-sorted logical formalism. Usually, this formalism is restricted to a first-order logic with equality. Frequently, properties characterized by choices may be written as conditional equations using *if-then-else* expressions. The example in Fig. 13.1 is a presentation of the data type of natural numbers; it is a 1-sorted specification. A presentation for the stack algebra discussed in Example 8 is shown in Fig. 13.2. This presentation includes the sort *Nat*; it is a 2-sorted specification.

In a presentation, information is organized in the following sequence:

- The name of the presentation, which may include the name of a generic parameter of some sort, is given in **Spec** clause.
- The **extend by** clause is optional; it enumerates the names of presentations introducing sorts that are required in defining this presentation.
- The **Sorts** clause introduces the names of sorts defined in the presentation.
- The **Operations** clause introduces the operations on the sorts. The order of listing the operations is not important.
- The **Variables** clause introduces variables of sorts introduced earlier for writing axioms. The order of listing the variables is not important.
- The **Axioms** clause lists the axioms constraining the operations. The order of their listing is not important.

The name of the presentation must be unique. The sort names associated with formal parameters, if any, must be specified. The name space for sorts and presentations are not distinct; that is, a sort defined in a presentation may have the same name as the presentation. For instance, the name of the presentation in Fig. 13.2 is *Stack* which is also the name of a sort introduced in the presentation. It is more convenient to name the sort differently from the presentation defining it. The **extend by** clause is essentially the import list which includes all presentations of which reference is made in this presentation. The sorts and operators introduced in these included presentations can be used freely in defining new sorts. The operator names, introduced as functions, can only refer to the distinguished sorts defined in the presentation and those that have been introduced in the presentations mentioned in the **extend by** clause. The functions may be partial or total. The axioms define the operations in terms of their relationships and are universally quantified over the sorts introduced in the **variables** clause. An algebra denoted by a presentation *satisfies* the axioms in the presentation if for each axiom $t_1 = t_2$ the two terms t_1 and t_2 denote the same element of the algebra for each possible assignment of values to the variables in the terms. Hence, the two terms

$$push(newstack, succ(zero))$$

and

$$push(pop(push(newstack, zero)), succ(zero))$$

are equal. The equality symbol '=' is often *overloaded*; in the context of "*if a = b then x else y*", '=' is a relational operator. When a and b are terms of the same sort, the axiom $a = b$ means that a and b are *congruent* (*equivalent, have the same value*). A term a occurring in an expression e can be substituted by a term b to give an expression e' equivalent to e. This substitution rule allows *rewriting* of equations. The axiom $a = b$ may be viewed as the rewrite rule $a \Rightarrow b$ meaning that the right-hand side b is substituted wherever the left-hand side a occurs in expressions. Rewriting can be used to reduce equations to *ground terms*, that is, terms with no variables. An expression containing no variable can be evaluated to a term in the algebra; this term can be associated to a unique sort. In order to obtain expressions containing only ground terms that cannot be reduced any further, the specification should have *constructors*. We discuss such specifications in the next section.

Fig. 13.3 Specification for a
simple set

Spec: *Simpleset*;
extend Boolean **by**
Sorts: S;
Operations:
> $empty :\rightarrow S$;
> $insert : Nat \times S \rightarrow S$;
> $member : Nat \times S \rightarrow Bool$;

Variables:
> $s : S; n, m : Nat$;

Axioms:
> $member(n, empty) = false$;
> $member(n, insert(m, S)) = (m = n) \vee member(n, S)$;
> $insert(n, insert(m, S)) = insert(m, insert(n, S))$;

13.3.2
Semantics

For a given signature there exists a collection of algebras and several possible homomorphisms among them. An algebra $\mathcal{I}$ of this collection is an *initial* algebra if for every other algebra $\mathcal{A}$ in this collection there exists a unique homomorphism from $\mathcal{I}$ to $\mathcal{A}$. If an initial algebra exists in the collection, it is unique up to an isomorphism. That is, if there exists more than one initial algebra in the collection then there exists an isomorphism between each pair of initial algebras; see Goguen [6]. The initial algebra can also be understood through equality of terms in the algebra: in the semantics of the initial algebra two variable-free terms denote different objects unless it can be proved from the stated axioms that they denote the same object.

Another frequently used semantic model is the *final (terminal) algebra*. The final algebra is the term algebra satisfying the stated axioms of the presentation and having the smallest number of terms. There is a unique homomorphism from any other algebra satisfying the axioms to the final algebra. The final algebra can also be understood through the inequality of terms: in the semantics of the final algebra, two variable-free terms of the same sort denote the same object unless it can be proved from the stated axioms that they denote different objects. The difference between these two semantics is illustrated in Fig. 13.3, which extends the presentation Boolean in Sect. 13.4.

The initial initial algebra semantics for the presentation in Fig. 13.3 is the *bag* of natural numbers. The terms $insert(2, S)$ and $insert(2, insert(2, S))$ yield different values, and correspond to the semantics of initial algebra. The final algebra semantics for this presentation is the *set* of natural numbers. Two sets are different if the function *member* gives different results on the sets for at least one member. Since $member(2, insert(2, empty))$ and $member(2, insert(2, insert(2, empty)))$ are both true and $member(n, insert(2, empty))$ and $member(n, insert(2, insert(2, empty)))$ are both false for $n \neq 2$, the terms $insert(2, empty)$ and $insert(2, insert(2, empty))$ denote the same object, namely the set with only one member, the number 2.

In this book, the initial algebra semantics is considered in defining algebraic specifications.

13.4
Properties of Algebraic Specifications

In this section we study reasoning by term rewriting, extension of many-sorted specifications, classification of operations, and the adequacy of algebraic specifications.

13.4.1
Reasoning

Presentations can be analyzed to establish a property that holds for all objects of a sort defined in the presentation as well as to identify inconsistent requirements. *Equational reasoning* and *induction* are the techniques frequently used in such analysis. The first-order axioms serve the role of a verifier for the properties of the data type. The induction method is quite similar to the structural induction technique discussed in Chap. 12. We briefly outline equational reasoning based on term rewriting for the data types *Nat* and *Bool*. The presentation for *Bool* is shown in Fig. 13.4. The two constant functions *true* and *false* are the values of the sort *Bool*.

Example 9 illustrates the reduction of algebraic equations to some canonical form using axioms as rewrite rules.

Example 9 An expression with variables is reduced to a variable-free expression by using the axioms as rewrite rules. In rewriting an expression e, a subexpression f of e is matched against the left-hand side t_1 of an axiom $t_1 = t_2$, and if it matches, then f is replaced by the right-hand side t_2.

1. To simplify the expression

   $$add(succ(succ(zero)), succ(succ(a))),$$

   the following steps are done:
   (a) Identify the axiom in the presentation *Natural* that is appropriate for application. In this case, we choose the axiom $add(succ(u), v) = add(u, succ(v))$. The term $succ(zero)$ is matched with u, and the term $succ(succ(a))$ is matched with v in the left-hand side of this axiom. When substituted for u and v, the right-hand side of the axiom when substituted gives the rewritten expression:

   $$add(succ(succ(zero)), succ(succ(a))) \Rightarrow$$
   $$add(succ(zero), succ(succ(succ(a))))$$

Fig. 13.4 The data type *Bool*

Spec: *Boolean*;
Sorts: *Bool*;
Operations:
  true, *false* $:\rightarrow Bool$;
  not $: Bool \rightarrow Bool$;
  *_and_* $: Bool \times Bool \rightarrow Bool$;
  *_or_* $: Bool \times Bool \rightarrow Bool$;
  *_impl_* $: Bool \times Bool \rightarrow Bool$;
  _==_ $: Bool \times Bool \rightarrow Bool$;
Variables:
  $x, y : Bool$;
Axioms:
  false $= not(true)$;
  true $= not(false)$;
  false $= false$ *and* x;
  $x = true$ *and* x;
  true $= true$ *or* x;
  $x = false$ *or* x;
  x *or* $y = y$ *or* x;
  x *and* $y = not(not(x)$ *or* $not(y))$;
  x *impl* $y = (not\ x)$ *or* y;
  $x == y = (x$ *impl* $y)$ *and* $(y$ *impl* $x)$;

(b) One more application of the same axiom, with u matched to *zero*, and v matched to $succ(succ(succ(a)))$, rewrites the above expression to

  $add(zero, succ(succ(succ(succ(a)))))$

(c) We then use the first axiom $add(zero, a) = a$, to get the equivalent expression

  $succ(succ(succ(succ(a))))$

This expression is variable-free and cannot be reduced further.

2. It can be verified from the axioms in the presentation *Natural* that the expressions:

  $mult(succ(succ(0)), a)$ and

  $add(add(0, a), a)$

are equivalent.

3. From the first two axioms of the *Boolean* presentation given in Fig. 13.4, it can be proved that

  $x = not(not(x))$,

  $not(x$ *or* $y) = not(x)$ *and* $not(y)$.

The proof consists of two steps:

Fig. 13.5 Data type *Ternary* enriches *Natural*

> **Spec:** *Mod3_enrich_natural*;
> **extend** *Natural* **by**
> **Sorts:** *Ternary*;
> **Variables:**
> $x : Ternary$;
> **Axioms:**
> $succ(succ(succ(x))) = x$;

(a) Substitute *not(x)* for x, *not(y)* for y in the axiom *x and y = not(not(x) or not(y))*:

$$not(x) \ and \ not(y) = not(not(not(x)) \ or \ not(not(y)))$$

(b) The result $x = not(not(x))$ is used in the right-hand side:

$$not(x) \ and \ not(y) = not(x \ or \ y) \qquad\qquad\qquad \square$$

13.4.2
Extending Many-Sorted Specifications

It is sometimes convenient to reuse an existing specification by incrementally adding more functions and axioms. Larger presentations can be constructed by reusing already defined sorts. The **extend by** clause is used to construct a larger specification with or without the introduction of new sorts. The extended version inherits the sorts, operations and axioms defined in the original presentation. If $SP_1 = \langle \langle S_1, \Omega_1 \rangle, E_1 \rangle$, then the expression

Spec SP = extend SP_1 **by sorts S Operations** Ω **Axioms** E

denotes the specification $\langle \Sigma, E_1 \cup E \rangle$, where $\Sigma = \langle S_1 \cup S, \Omega_1 \cup \Omega \rangle$.

The specification given in Fig. 13.5 extends *Natural*, defined in Fig. 13.1. The new sort *Ternary* is a subsort of *Nat*. The operators *zero, succ, add and mult* are also defined for the new sort *ternary*. There is no new operator defined. The new axiom enforces that every multiple of 3 is reduced to *zero*. Instead of the axiom written in Fig. 13.5, we could have included any one of the following axioms:

$succ(succ(succ(zero))) = zero$

$add(x, add(succ(x), succ(succ(x)))) = zero$

An extension of the many-sorted specification *Stack* given in Fig. 13.2 is shown in Fig. 13.6. The specification extends the sort *Stack* with operations *size* and *push*1. For the objects of the sort *Bstack* all the operations of *Stack* are available. In the extended specification, a new element can be pushed onto the stack only if the number of elements on the stack does not exceed the maximum size M. It would be appropriate to hide the *push* operation from the users of the *Boundedstack* specification.

Spec: *Boundedstack*;
extend *Stack* **by**
Sort: *Bstack*;
Operations:
     $M :\to Nat$;
     $size : Bstack \to Nat$;
     $push1 : Bstack \times Nat \to Bstack$;
Variables
     $s : Bstack$; $n : Nat$;
Axioms:
     $size(newstack) = 0$;
     $push1(s, n) = if\ size(s) < M\ then\ push(s, n)\ else\ s$;
     $size(push1(s, n)) = if\ size(s) < M\ then\ 1 + size(s)\ else\ M$;

Fig. 13.6 Specification for a *bounded stack*

13.4.3
Classification of Operations

The operations for an abstract data type may be divided into *constructors* and *non-constructor operations*. Informally, constructors are operations that generate objects of the abstract data type, whereas non-constructor operations describe the functionality of the objects of the data type. Another way to view this is that constructors provide data abstraction, while non-constructors provide procedural abstraction. The operations may be classified as follows :

1. *Primitive constructors:* These operations take no input and create objects of their abstract date type. Examples are *zero* of *Natural*, *empty* of *Simpleset*, *true* and *false* of *Boolean*, and *newstack* of *Stack*.
2. *Constructors:* These operations take objects of their abstract date type as input and create other objects of their corresponding abstract data type. For example, *succ*, *add*, and *mult* are constructors for *Natural*, and *and or impl*, and $==$ are constructors for *Boolean*.
3. *Mutators:* These operations modify objects of their abstract data type. For example, *push*, and *pop* are mutators for *Stack*, and *insert* is a mutator for *Simpleset*.
4. *Observers:* These operations take objects of their abstract data type and zero or more objects of other abstract data types, and return results of other abstract data types. For example, *member* is an observer operation for the objects of the sort *Simpleset*, and *size* is an observer operation for the objects of the sort *Bstack*.

Primitive constructors create only objects of their type. For example, *empty* of *Simpleset* produces an empty bag. The other objects are produced by constructors and mutators. For instance, *insert* of *Simpleset* produces different objects of the sort *Simpleset* depending on the natural numbers inserted in the object. All constructors are assumed to be total functions.

13.4.4
Adequacy

Adequacy is a context-dependent notion. To satisfy the requirements imposed by a context of usage, sufficient set of operations for a data type should be provided. For example, we have not provided operations for comparing natural numbers in *Natural*. When we include these operations, sufficient axioms to characterize the properties of the additional operations should be included. From such an enriched specification it is possible to infer more information about natural numbers. Still, there are other operations such as integer division producing quotient and remainder that cannot be performed in this extended specification. In general, we decide whether a specification is adequate by identifying the operations that are mandated in the user requirements. We then provide

- a sufficient number of operations for describing the objects and their modifications in the context of their usage; and
- a sufficient number of axioms to capture the behavior of objects.

A rule to achieve a reasonable degree of adequacy, given by Liskov and Guttag [11], is to include operations from at least three of the four classes discussed in the preceding section. An abstract data type specification should include primitive constructors, observers, and either constructors or mutators. Notice that immutable types such as *Natural* have only constructors, whereas mutable types such as *Stack* have mutators. The axiom part should include axioms describing the effect of each observer operation over each constructor/mutator. We illustrate these concepts in the specification *Orderednatural* shown in Fig. 13.7 and in the specification *NatTree* shown in Fig. 13.8.

The data type *Orderednatural* extends *Natural* with three observer operations. The effect of an observer operation on constructor pairs is shown in Fig. 13.7. For the data type *NatTree* the primitive constructor is *empty*, *node* is a constructor, the operations *left*, *right* are mutators, and *content*, *isempty*, *isfound* are observers. The effect of the observer operations on the constructor is described in three axioms. We could include additional axioms such as $content(left(node(x, n, y))) = content(x)$, but such axioms are implied by the stated ones. Operations such as *content*, *left*, *right* are not meaningful for an empty binary tree. Hence, although terms of the form *content(empty)*, *content(left(empty))*, *content(right(empty))*, *content(left(right(empty)))* are in the initial algebra of *NatTree*, they do not correspond to any element in *Nat*. That is, this algebra does not represent the computation structure of naturals. Informally, terms of the form *content(empty)*, *left(empty)*, *content(right(empty))* denote incorrect function applications. This can be handled by adding one axiom for each kind of erroneous term. The set of axioms in Fig. 13.8 is therefore not adequate. An alternative way of remedying this inadequacy is to restrict the algebra to contain only terms that are determined by axioms to be valid. We look at this alternative in Sect. 13.6.

Fig. 13.7 Specification for *orderednatural*

Spec: *Orderednatural*;
extend *Natural* **by**
Operations:
  $eq : Nat \times Nat \to Bool$;
  $lt : Nat \times Nat \to Bool$;
  $le : Nat \times Nat \to Bool$;
Variables:
  $x, y, z : Nat$;
Axioms:
  $eq(zero, zero) = true$;
  $eq(zero, succ(x)) = false$;
  $eq(succ(x), zero) = false$;
  $eq(succ(x), succ(y)) = eq(x, y)$;
  $lt(zero, zero) = false$;
  $lt(zero, succ(x)) = true$;
  $lt(succ(x), succ(y)) = lt(x, y)$;
  $le(x, y) = eq(x, y) \vee lt(x, y)$;

Spec: *NatTree*;
extend *Orderednatural* **by**
Sorts: *Tree*;
Operations:
  $empty :\to Tree$;
  $node : Tree \times Nat \times Tree \to Tree$;
  $left, right : Tree \to Tree$;
  $content : Tree \to Nat$;
  $isempty : Tree \to Bool$;
  $isfound : Tree \times Nat \to Bool$;
Variables:
  $x, y : Tree$; $n, m : Nat$;
Axioms:
  $isempty(empty)$;
  $\neg isempty(node(x, n, y))$;
  $left(node(x, n, y)) = x$;
  $right(node(x, n, y)) = y$;
  $content(node(x, n, y)) = n$;
  $\neg isfound(empty, m)$;
  $isfound(node(x, n, y), m) = (m = n) \vee isfound(x, m) \vee isfound(y, m)$;

Fig. 13.8 Specification for a *binary tree*

13.5
Structured Specifications

It is convenient to design specifications in a structured fashion by refining and composing existing modules of specifications. The **extend by** clause may be used for the incremental

Fig. 13.9   The data type *Word*

Spec: *Primitivesort*;
extend Boolean **by**
Sorts: *Word*;
Operations:
$\_==\_$: *Word* × *Word* → *Bool*;
$\_\leq\_$: *Word* × *Word* → *Bool*;

development of complex specifications. We select a subset of requirements from the *Idea Processor* example discussed by Henderson [10] to illustrate the incremental specification process.

The primary purpose of an Idea Processing System (IPS) is to support users in organizing and sharing ideas on different subjects, providing facilities for editing and retrieving items of cognitive content. An IPS provides editing operations such as *add, modify, delete*, and *merge*, storage and retrieval operations, and a display operation for a selected group of ideas. Chapter 5 includes a formal grammar for defining the structure of objects in an IPS. In Chap. 12, we have given a functional specification for some of the operations in IPS. Neither of these formalisms specified all the data types in an IPS. In the following discussion, we specify all the abstract data types for an IPS; however, we include specifications for editing functions only.

Requirements and model: An IPS is a database of *ideas*, where each *idea* is associated with one topic of interest. An idea is a collection of major ideas pertaining to that topic, and each major idea is referred to as a *group*. We model an idea, which is a collection of groups as a *list*. A group may be composed of other major ideas. In order to distinguish between the major ideas within a group, each group is required to have a *heading*. The *body* of a group may include other major ideas and/or a *note*, a description of the major idea under the chosen heading. A note is a sub-idea modeled by a sequence of words. Sub-ideas are identified by unique *keywords*. Sub-ideas can be moved around within a group and one or more sub-ideas can be merged within a group. An IPS allows the creation and manipulation of ideas toward composing them into a major text.

Primitive sort: We need a primitive data type to capture the notion of words. Let *word* denote this sort, in which we define two observer operations "$==$" (equality) and "$\leq$" (less than or equal). We interpret $w_1 \leq w_2$ to mean that word w_1 precedes w_2 in alphabetical order.

Presentation of note: We define *note* as a sequence of words. We follow the abstraction from Chap. 12 for data type sequence. Figure 13.10 shows the specification of the sort *Note*. We have chosen the representation 0 for *zero*, 1 for *succ(zero)*, and + for *add* for the functions in sort *Nat*. The operations *length*, *eq*, and *head* are observer operations. The operations *addf*, *tail*, *cat* are mutators, and *empty* is the only constructor. Writing one axiom for each observer operation over each mutator and constructor, we obtain a collection of 12 axioms. Notice that the effect of the operation *tail* on an empty sequence is to produce an empty sequence, and the effect of the operation *head* on an empty sequence is undefined.

In Chap. 12, we defined the precedence relation for sequences, so as to establish a partial ordering on all sequences. The following signature and axioms may be added to the presentation in Fig. 13.10.

Spec: *Sequence*;
extend *Natural*, *Primitivesort* **by**
Sorts: *Note*;
Operations:

$empty :\rightarrow Note$;
$addf : Word \times Note \rightarrow Note$;
$tail : Note \rightarrow Note$;
$head : Note \rightarrow Word$;
$cat : Note \times Note \rightarrow Note$;
$length : Note \rightarrow Nat$;
$eq : Note \times Note \rightarrow Bool$;

Variables:

$u, v : Note$;
$x, y : Word$;

Axioms:

$length(empty) = 0$;
$length(addf(x, u)) = 1 + length(u)$;
$eq(empty, empty) = true$;
$eq(empty, addf(x, u)) = false$;
$eq(addf(x, u), empty) = false$;
$eq(u, v) = (head(u) == head(v))$ and $eq(tail(u), tail(v))$;
$head(addf(x, u)) = x$;
$tail(empty) = empty$;
$tail(addf(x, u)) = u$;
$cat(empty, u) = u$;
$cat(u, empty) = u$;
$cat(addf(x, u), v) = addf(x, cat(u, v))$;

Fig. 13.10 The data type *Note*

$pred : Note \times Note \rightarrow Bool$;

$pred(u, u) = false$;

$pred(empty, addf(x, u)) = true$;

$pred(addf(x, u), empty) = false$;

$pred(u, v) = (head(u) \leq head(v)) \vee$
$(((head(u) == head(v)) \wedge pred(tail(u), tail(v)))$;

Presentation of sub-ideas: (keyword, note): Each note is associated with a unique keyword of type *word*. We focus on specifying the sort (*keyword, note*) shown in Fig. 13.11. It has one constructor *pair*, and three observers *eqp*, *first*, and *second*. The function *first* extracts the keyword from a pair (*keyword, note*), and the function *second* extracts *note* from a pair (*keyword, note*). The equality operator *eqp* uses the equality operator "==" defined for the sort *word*, and the observer operator *eq* defined for the sort *note*.

Fig. 13.11 Specification of
Orderedpair (*word*, *note*)

Spec: *Orderedpair*;
extend Sequence **by**
Sorts: *Ordpair*;
Operations:
> *pair* : *Word* × *Note* → *Ordpair*;
> *first* : *Ordpair* → *Word*;
> *second* : *Ordpair* → *Note*;
> *eqp* : *Ordpair* × *Ordpair* → *Boolean*;

Variables:
> *s* : *Word*; *t* : *Note*; *p*, *q* : *Ordpair*;

Axioms:
> *first*(*pair*(*s*, *t*)) = *s*;
> *second*(*pair*(*s*, *t*)) = *t*;
> *eqp*(*p*, *q*) = (*first*(*p*) == *first*(*q*)) *and*
> *eq*(*second*(*p*), *second*(*q*));

Presentation of a set of (keyword, note): There are several design options for storing and manipulating elements of the sort *note*. One option is to form classes of elements of the sort *note*, so that elements in the same class are equivalent, in having the same keyword. Another alternative is to merge the elements of sort *note* having the same keywords into a single note. We follow this option and specify a set of sub-ideas as a set of ordered pairs (*word*, *note*). Figure 13.12 shows the presentation for such a set. The operations include

- the familiar set operations *insert*, *delete*, *membership*,
- an operation *match* to determine whether or not two sub-ideas have the same keyword, and
- an operation *merge* to put together by concatenation those sub-ideas that are related by a common keyword.

Notice the disadvantage of the merge operation (a mutator)—the two sub-ideas do not exist anymore as separate entities. To remedy this situation, one can create new sets using the *copy* constructor.

Presentation of a group: A *group* is an ordered pair (*note*, *item*), where an *item* is modeled as a discriminated union of *note* and *group*. The *Orderedpair* presentation in Fig. 13.11 needs to be modified for the new sorts that make up the *group*. The operations *headline* and *body* for a group in Fig. 13.13 are similar to the operations *first* and *second* defined for the sort *Orderedpair*. The two observer operations *is_note* and *is_group* distinguish between the different types of objects within a group.

Finally, the database of ideas is modeled as a list of groups in Fig. 13.14. Each element in the list is an idea, which can be accessed through the *head* operation. An idea can be inserted using the *insert* operation; an idea can be deleted using the *delete* operation.

Several other operations for an idea processor have been discussed by Henderson [10]; some of them are mentioned in the exercises.

Spec: *Setofpairs*;
extend *Ordpair* **by**
Sort: *Setp*;
Operations:

    emptyset :$\to$ *Setp*;
    insert : *Ordpair* $\times$ *Setp* $\to$ *Setp*;
    delete : *Ordpair* $\times$ *Setp* $\to$ *Setp*;
    member : *Ordpair* $\times$ *Setp* $\to$ *Bool*;
    size : *Setp* $\to$ *Nat*;
    merge : *Ordpair* $\times$ *Ordpair* $\times$ *Setp* $\to$ *Setp*;
    match : *Ordpair* $\times$ *Ordpair* $\to$ *Bool*;

Variables:

    s, *t* : *Setp*; *x*, *y* : *Ordpair*; *n* : *Nat*;

Axioms:

    member(*x*, *emptyset*) = *false*;
    member(*x*, *insert*(*y*, *s*)) = *eqp*(*x*, *y*) $\vee$ *member*(*x*, *s*);
    match(*x*, *y*) = (*first*(*x*) = *first*(*y*)) $\wedge$ (*second*(*x*) $\neq$ *second*(*y*));
    merge(*x*, *y*, *s*) = *if* *member*(*x*, *s*) $\wedge$ *member*(*y*, *s*)
                      $\wedge$ *match*(*x*, *y*) *then*
                        insert(*ordpair*(*first*(*x*), *cat*(*second*(*x*), *second*(*y*))),
                        delete(*y*, *delete*(*x*, *s*)));
    size(*empty*) = 0;
    size(*insert*(*x*, *s*)) = *if* *member*(*x*, *s*) *then*
                    size(*s*) *else* 1 + *size*(*s*);
    size(*delete*(*x*, *s*)) = *if* *memeber*(*x*, *s*) *then*
                    size(*s*) $-$ 1 *else* *size*(*s*);
    delete(*x*, *emptyset*) = *emptyset*;
    delete(*x*, *insert*(*y*, *s*)) = *if* (*x* == *y*) *then* *s*
                    else *insert*(*y*, *delete*(*x*, *s*));

Fig. 13.12 Specification of a set of sub-ideas

13.6
OBJ3—An Algebraic Specification Language

In the preceding section, we discussed algebraic specifications without restriction to any specification language. In this section we introduce OBJ3, an algebraic specification language described by Goguen and Winkler [7], and illustrate the features of the language with several examples.

OBJ3 is a wide spectrum functional programming language that is rigorously based upon order-sorted equational logic. OBJ3 system consists of the OBJ3 specification language, an interpreter and an environment for executing specifications. The philosophy underlying the design of OBJ3 is incremental and modular development of specifications that are executable, reusable, and composable. This goal is achieved by providing three kinds of en-

Fig. 13.13 The data type
Group

Spec: *Nordpair*;
extend: *Setofpairs* **by**
Sorts: *Group*;
Operations:
    headline : *Group* → *Note*;
    body : *Group* → *Item*;
    makeg : *Note* × *Item* → *Group*;
    is_note : *Item* → *Bool*;
    is_group : *Item* → *Bool*;
Variables:
    n : *Note*; *t* : *Item*; *p* : *Group*;
Axioms:
    headline(*makeg*(*n*, *t*)) = *n*;
    body(*makeg*(*n*, *t*)) = *t*;
    is_note(*headline*(*p*)) = *true*;
    is_group(*body*(*p*)) = ¬*is_note*(*body*(*p*));

Spec: *List*;
extend *Nordpair* **by**
Sorts: *Idealist*;
Operations:
    null :→ *Idealist*;
    insert : *Group* × *Idealist* → *idealist*;
    head : *Idealist* → *Group*;
    tail : *Idealist* → *Idealist*;
    delete : *Group* × *Idealist* → *Idealist*;
    isin : *Group* × *Idealist* → *Bool*;
Variables:
    f, *g*, *h* : *Idealist*; *a*, *b*, *c* : *Group*;
Axioms:
    head(*insert*(*a*, *null*)) = *a*;
    head(*insert*(*a*, *insert*(*b*, *null*))) = *head*(*insert*(*a*, *null*));
    tail(*insert*(*a*, *null*)) = *null*;
    tail(*insert*(*b*, *insert*(*a*, *null*))) = *insert*(*a*, *tail*(*insert*(*b*, *null*)));
    delete(*a*, *null*) = *null*;
    delete(*a*, *insert*(*b*, *f*)) = **if** *a* = *b* **then** *f* **else** *insert*(*b*, *delete*(*a*, *f*));
    isin(*a*, *null*) = *false*;
    isin(*a*, *insert*(*b*, *f*)) = **if** *a* = *b* **then** *true* **else** *isin*(*a*, *f*);

Fig. 13.14 Specification for a list of ideas

tities in the language: *object*, *theory*, and *view*. An object encapsulates executable code. A theory defines properties that may be satisfied by another theory or object. The *module*

```
obj FLAVORS is sort Flavor .
    op first : Flavor Flavor -> Flavor .
    op _second_ : Flavor Flavor -> Flavor .
    ops Chocolate Vanilla Strawberry : -> Flavor .
    vars X Y .: Flavor .
    eq first(X,Y) = X .
    eq X second Y = Y .
endo
```

Fig. 13.15 Definition of the Object FLAVORS

concept refers to an object or a theory. A view is a binding (mapping) between a theory and a module. For specification execution, OBJ3 system uses the *term rewriting*, a reduction process to evaluate expressions with respect to a defined object.

An OBJ3 specification is an *algebra* and functionalities of the system are algebraic expressions, such that every expression is valid in this algebra. OBJ3 follows the initial algebra semantics. To determine whether the system under development conforms to a certain behavior, we write an algebraic expression characterizing that behavior, and use the interpreter to check whether this expression is reducible to *true*. This procedure is performed in the OBJ system in two steps:

1. *Creation of rewrite rules or equations*
   An interpreter constructs the rewrite rules from the axioms and introduces them to the system database.
2. *Reduction*
   A program then extracts the rewrite rules from the database and applies them to the given expression.

The result of reducing an expression is either an atomic value (*true*, *false*, etc.) or a term which is irreducible in the algebra.

13.6.1
OBJ3 Basic Syntax

The fundamental unit of OBJ3 is the *object*, which encapsulates executable code. Syntactically, the definition of an object starts with the keyword obj, and ends with the keyword endo. The identifier of the object appears immediately after the keyword obj; the keyword is follows the name; thereafter appears the body of the object.

An example of an unparameterized *sort* is shown in Fig. 13.15. The specification of an object consists of the following five components:

1. *Defining sorts*
   The object (*module*) name FLAVORS, and the sort (type) name Flavor are introduced in the first line of Fig. 13.15. By convention, object names are written in upper-case

letters and sort names start with an upper-case letter. A sort in OBJ3 is similar to a type in Pascal or Ada. The object declaration

```
obj NUMBER is sorts Nat Rat .
```

introduces the object NUMBER and two sorts with sort names Nat and Rat. Blank spaces are a requisite.

2. *Defining operations*

Operations can be defined in three different styles:

- *functions* (standard form)

```
op first : Flavor Flavor -> Flavor .
```

- *mixfix operations*

This kind of definition uses place-holders, indicated by an "underscore" character, to indicate where arguments should appear. For example, the following is a mixfix definition.

```
op _second_ : Flavor Flavor -> Flavor .
```

The operation can be used in an expression like X second Y. As another example, the definition

```
op _ _ : Bit Bits -> Bits .
```

can be used to create a bit string. A typical expression using this syntax is 1 011 whose result is 1011.

- *constants*

A constant is an operation with arity 0. For example,

```
ops Chocolate Vanilla Strawberry : -> Flavor .
```

The keyword ops is used for introducing more than one operation. It is more convenient to use parentheses to separate operations in complex cases as in:

```
ops (_+_) (_-_) : IntExp IntExp -> IntExp .
```

3. *Declaring variables*

A variable is declared using the keyword var. More than one variable of the same sort can be introduced using the keyword vars as in:

```
vars X Y : Flavor .
```

By convention, variable names start with an upper-case letter.

4. *Defining axioms*

Axioms are referred to as *equations*; the following are examples of axioms.

```
eq first (X, Y) = X .
eq X second Y = Y .
```

5. *End of specification*

The keyword endo marks the end of the specifications for the object. There is NO period after endo!

The OBJ3 interpreter accepts the specification of the object FLAVORS line by line, parses it, creates the set of rewrite rules and introduces into the system database under the name FLAVORS. We have now defined a module FLAVORS. We may define other object modules with their own respective algebraic specifications. All objects are sequentially introduced into the OBJ3 database.

13.6.2
Built-In Sorts and Subsorts

OBJ3 is based on strong sorting-every symbol has a sort or can be associated to a sort. Sorts are introduced in OBJ3 with the syntax

    sorts ⟨*Sortids*⟩

as in

    sorts Nat Int .

13.6.2.1
Built-in Sorts

The OBJ3 system includes a library comprising of several built-in sorts. These represent frequently used abstract data types, and include the following pre-defined modules:

- TRUTH-VALUE provides the constant truth values true and false.
- TRUTH enriches TRUTH-VALUE with the operations ==, =/=, and if _ then _ else _ fi.
- BOOL provides the boolean logic operators and, or, xor, prefix not, and infix implies.
- IDENTICAL, which can be used instead of BOOL checks for literal identity of terms without evaluating them.
- NAT provides natural numbers.
- NZNAT provides non-zero naturals.
- INT provides integers.
- RAT provides rational numbers.
- FLOAT provides floating point numbers.
- ID provides identifiers; it includes lexicographic ordering, and all the operations available in BOOL.
- QID is similar to ID, except that the identifiers start with an apostrophe symbol; for example, 'a, 'b, '1300, and 'anyidentifier. It has no built-in operation.
- QIDL provides identifiers with apostrophes, and includes all the operations available in BOOL; in addition, it includes lexicographic ordering.

These pre-defined sorts may be imported in the specification of a user-defined module.

13.6.2.2
Order-Sorted Algebra

One of the main features of OBJ3 is the introduction of subsorts. This supports the treatment of partial operations, multiple inheritance and error handling. OBJ3 can be used to formally specify a hierarchy of object-oriented software components.

A sort s' is a subsort of the sort s, written s' < s, if the value of the domain s includes that of s', and the operations of s are available to s'. The basic syntax for a subsort declaration in OBJ3 is

```
subsort s' < s .
```

The subset partial ordering can be established among locally defined and imported sorts. For example,

```
subsort MyRat < MyInt < MyReal .
```

where MyInt is a subset of MyReal, and MyRat is a subset of MyInt. Thus, any operation defined for the sort MyReal is available to variables of the sorts Myint and MyRat. The following examples illustrate the subsort relation:

1. The sort Nznat defining positive integers is a subsort of the sort Nat defining natural numbers.

   ```
   subsort NzNat < Nat .
   ```

2. A nonempty list is a subsort of a list.

   ```
   subsort NeList < List .
   ```

3. A bounded stack is a subsort of a stack.

   ```
   subsort BStack < Stack .
   ```

4. A nonempty tree of naturals is a subsort of a tree of naturals.

   ```
   subsort NeNatTree < NatTree .
   ```

Subsorting ensures correct function application to variables of appropriate subsorts, and induces the reasoning process to handle exceptional situations properly:

- The division operator is defined only for NzNat; we thus avoid division by 0.
- The *head* operation defined for *Idealist* in Fig. 13.14 can be restricted to a nonempty list.
- The *size* operation is meaningful only for a bounded stack Bstack, a subsort of the Stack sort.
- The operations *left*, *right*, *content*, and *isfound* defined for the sort *NatTree* in Fig. 13.8 can be redefined to be restricted to *NeNatTree*, the sort characterizing nonempty trees of natural number.

The order-sorted algebra also supports multiple inheritance such that a subsort may have more than one distinct supersort.

13

13.6.2.3
Import Clause

An OBJ3 module can be divided into smaller units so that each unit can be understood, analyzed and reused independently. A hierarchical relationship is explicitly introduced to bring out the dependency of a module on other modules. Whenever module A has to use the sorts and operations declared in module B, module B must be explicitly imported in module A. Since a module can import several other modules, OBJ3 can be used to provide *multiple inheritance*, an important feature of object-oriented programming. Notice that in this hierarchy higher level modules *include* lower level modules.

OBJ3 incorporates four modes for importing modules, **protecting**, **extending**, **including** and **using**. The abbreviations **pr**, **ex**, **inc**, and **us** can be used to denote the corresponding modes of importation. By convention, if a module X imports a module Y that imports a module Z, then module Z is also imported into module X; that is, the *imports* relation is a transitive relation. The meaning of the import modes is related to the initial algebra semantics. The semantics for the four modes are as follows:

- `protecting` (no junk, no confusion)

```
obj X is
    protecting Y .
    . . .
endo
```

X imports Y, and Y is protected. No new data item of sorts from module Y can be defined in this module. The signature of module Y cannot be changed; that is, no new operation with sorts of module Y as domain can be introduced. Moreover, a function already defined in module Y cannot be redefined. However, the signature of module Y can be used in defining operations in X. That is, there is neither junk data nor confusion introduced in the imported clause. The module NATTREE in Fig. 13.16 protects the imported modules NAT and BOOL. The subsort relation asserts is that *Nat* (naturals) is a subsort of *Nebtree* (nonempty binary tree), which in turn is a subsort of *Btree* (binary tree).

- `extending` (no confusion)

```
obj X is
    extending Y .
    . . .
endo
```

If module X imports module Y, and module Y is extended, then new data items of sorts from Y may be defined in module X. However, the operations in module X do not redefine any function already defined in module Y. This implies that new operations can be added to extend the behavior of module Y in module X. This is illustrated in the module *ORDLIST*.

```
obj ORDLIST is sort List .
    extending LIST .
    op insert : List Nat -> List .
    vars I J : Nat .   var L : List .
```

```
      eq insert(null, I) = (I null) .
      cq insert(I L, J) = if I > J then (J I L)
                                    else (I insert(L, J)) .
   endo
```

- using

```
   obj X is
      using Y .

         . . .
   endo
```

If module X imports module Y in the using mode, then there is no guarantee in the sense that new data items of sorts from module Y may be created, as well as old data items of sorts from module Y may be redefined. This import mode is analogous to code reuse in object-oriented paradigm. OBJ3 implements using by copying the imported module's top-level structure, sharing all of the modules that it imports. Hence, the sorts defined within a given module are required to have distinct names, and all copied operations are required to be uniquely identified by their name and rank.

- including

```
   obj X is
      including Y .

         . . .
   endo
```

If module X includes module Y, then module Y is incorporated in module X without copying. This is the only difference between the using and including modes.

It is important to note that OBJ3 does not check whether the user's import declarations are correct. The consequences of an incorrect import declaration can be serious, leading to incomplete reductions in some cases, and insufficient reductions in others.

13.6.2.4
Declaration of Attributes

It is convenient to consider certain properties of an operation as attributes and declare them within the syntax of the operation. These properties include axioms like associativity, commutativity, and identity. Declaring the attributes of an operation influences the order of evaluation, and parsing.

Associativity and Commutativity   The following example illustrates the declaration of associative operations.

```
   op _or_ : Bool Bool -> Bool [assoc] .
   op __ : NeList List -> NeList [assoc] .
```

Expressions involving an associative operator do not require parentheses; for example, we can write

```
(x or y or z)
```

instead of

```
(x or (y or z))
```

Binary infix operations can be declared as *commutative* with the attribute comm, which is semantically a commutativity axiom, implemented by commutative rewriting. Axioms such as

```
eq x + y = y + x
```

lead to non-terminating rewrite rules. Care must be exerted to avoid such axioms, and include the commutativity property as an attribute for the operation eq. A binary operation can bear both commutative and associative attributes.

Identity   The identity attribute can be declared for a binary operation; for example, in

```
op _or_ : Bool Bool -> Bool [assoc id: false] .
```

the attribute

```
id: false
```

gives the effect of the identity equations

```
(B or false = B)
```

and

```
(false or B = B).
```

Identity attributes can be constants such as 0 for + and 1 for *, as well as ground terms such as *nil* for list addition, and *emptyset* for set union.

13.7
Signature and Equations

An OBJ3 module or theory is constructed following the syntactic conventions explained in the previous section. The signature includes the definition of subsorts, and the modes for imported modules. The syntax for expressions should be consistent with the signature of operations as defined in the module and in the imported modules.

```
obj NATTREE is sorts Nebtree Btree .
   protecting NAT .
   protecting BOOL .
   subsorts Nat < Nebtree < Btree .
   op empty : -> Btree .
   op node: Btree Nat Btree -> Nebtree .
   op left: Nebtree -> Btree .
   op right : Nebtree -> Btree .
   op content: Nebtree -> Nat .
   op isempty: Btree -> Bool .
   op isfound : Btree Nat -> Bool .
   vars X Y : Btree . vars N M : List .
   eq isempty(empty) = true .
   eq not isempty(node(X, N,Y) .
   eq left(node(X,N,Y)) = X.
   eq right(node(X,N,Y) = Y.
   eq content(node(X,N,Y) = N.
   eq not isfound(empty,N) .
   eq isfound(node(X,N,Y),M) = (M = N) or isfound(X,M)
                                       or isfound(Y,M) .
endo
```

Fig. 13.16 Definition of the binary tree object

13.7.1
Signature of a Module

The signature of an object consists of the sorts, the subsort relations (optional), the import list of modules (optional), and the operations available on the object. The signature of module NATTREE in Fig. 13.16 introduces two sorts Nebtree and Btree, representing a nonempty tree of natural numbers, and a tree of natural numbers. The module NATTREE imports the built-in modules NAT and BOOL. With the introduction of subsort Nebtree, the functions left, right, content, and isfound become total functions defined only for Nebtree. However, all the operations defined for Btree remain available for Nebtree as well. All the operations defined for Nebtree remain available for its subsort Nat; however, they are not meaningful for Nat.

Every term in the algebra generated by NATTREE is either a natural number, or a nonempty tree, or a tree. This ensures the closure property for the algebra. A comparison of this specification with the specification *NatTree* shown in Fig. 13.8 reveals that the terms content(empty), left(empty), right(empty) do not form part of this new algebra.

13.7.2
Equations

The ability to write equations (axioms) requires an understanding of the operators used. Similar to the classification of operations discussed in the Sect. 13.4.3, OBJ3 operations can also be broadly divided into two groups: **Constructors** and **Observers**. Notice that no axioms are defined for basic constructors. An observer cannot modify the values of an object. The operational semantics corresponds to *reduction* by term rewriting. The reduction of an expression is carried out by matching the expression or a sub-expression of the expression with the left-hand side of an equation, and then replacing the matched sub-expression with the corresponding right-hand side of the equation. An expression that already contains only basic constructors cannot be reduced any further. Any other expression can be reduced to an expression containing only the basic constructors. For example, the expression

> *content (left (node (node (empty, 1, empty), 3,*
>   *node (node (empty, 5, empty), 7, node (empty, 9, empty)))))*

is rewritten using the equation

```
eq left(node(X,N,Y)) = X .
```

to

> *content(node(empty,1,empty)) = 1*

and then further reduced to 1 by using the equation `content(node(X,N,Y)) = N .`

A conditional equation may be created using `cq` instead of `eq` when declaring the equation. For example,

```
cq min(X,Y) = X if X < Y else Y fi.
cq isTriangle(A,B,C) = true if A < B + C and
   B < A + C and C < A + B .
```

The operational semantics for rewriting conditional equations is as follows: first, a match for the left-hand side of the expression is found; next, the conditional equation is evaluated by substituting the bindings obtained from the match; if it evaluates to *true*, then the rewriting is done as described above for the right-hand side of equations. The evaluation strategy in the OBJ3 system is guided by the declaration of attributes, which in fact, can affect both efficiency and termination.

13.8
Parameterized Programming

In Sect. 13.5, we constructed a specification for an *Idea Processor* using data type specifications that are specific to the needs of that application. To maximize the potential for reuse, data type specifications must remain as self-contained and general as possible. In this section we discuss how OBJ3 specifications can be constructed to have such properties.

Abstract data types such as set and sequence arise as basic building blocks of more complex data types in various applications. Sets of integer, sets of real, and sets of sequences,

Fig. 13.17 A simple theory

```
th TRIV is
     sort Elt .
endth
```

```
th PREORDERED is
     sort Elt .
     op _<=_ : Elt Elt -> Bool .
     vars E1 E2 E3 : Elt .
     eq E1 <= E1 = true .
     cq E1 <= E3 = true if E1 <= E2 and E2 <= E3 .
endth
```

Fig. 13.18 The preordering theory

for instance, do not require separate specifications. The set operations can be abstracted independently of the element type. It would be convenient to be able to specify a set of elements of type E by using a parametrized specification module $SET[T]$ where T is a formal parameter which can be mapped to sort E. OBJ3 provides a parametric specification mechanism: types(sorts) are used to parameterize types (sorts), in a way analogous to the use of types to parameterize functions and procedures in programming languages. The intent of parameterized programming is to decompose the code into parameterized components. At the specification level, objects, theories, views and module expressions provide formal support for writing parametric specifications. A theory can be used to define the interface and properties of a parameterized module. A view expresses that a certain module satisfies a certain theory in a certain way by binding actual parameters of a module to a theory. Instantiating a parameterized module, using a particular view as an actual parameter, yields a new module. Module expressions involving interacting modules, can be formally evaluated with no side-effect.

13.8.1
Theories

Theories express the properties of a module or an object; they provide a means for describing entities that cannot be defined in terms of objects. OBJ3 theories have the same structure as objects; they describe sorts, operations, variables and equations. Theories can import other theories and objects, and can also be parameterized. The difference between objects and theories is that objects are executable, while theories only define properties. Figure 13.17 shows the simple theory TRIV, which is pre-defined in OBJ3; TRIV introduces the new sort Elt.

A theory of a pre-ordered set is shown in Fig. 13.18.

```
view TRIV-TO-FLAVORS from TRIV to FLAVORS is
    sort Elt to Flavor .
    op newop to first .
endv
```

Fig. 13.19 Mapping from theory TRIV to object FLAVORS

Fig. 13.20 Mapping from
theory PREORDERED to
NAT

```
view NATORD from PREORDERED to NAT is
    sort Elt to Nat .
    vars X Y : Elt .
    op X <= Y to X < Y or X == Y .
endv
```

13.8.2
Views

A *view* describes the association between a *theory* and an *object*, such that the sorts of the theory are mapped onto the sorts of the object, while preserving the subsort relation. The operations of the theory are mapped onto the operations of the object. A view is a homomorphism from the algebra described by the theory to the algebra described by the object. In Fig. 13.19, TRIV-TO-FLAVORS is the name of the mapping, TRIV is the theory and FLAVORS is the object. The view NATORD in Fig. 13.20 describes the *less-than or equal-to* ordering on *NAT*.

13.8.3
Parameterized Modules

The theories of parameterized modules must be defined earlier in the sequence modules that use those theories are presented to OBJ3 system. Parameterized modules are declared as follows:

```
obj NAME[X ::THEORY1]
```

or

```
th NAME[X ::THEORY1]
```

With such a declaration, the sorts, operations and equations of THEORY1 become visible to the module NAME. An example of a parameterized module defining a partial order is shown in Fig. 13.21. This module imports the object BOOL in protecting mode, and hence the sort Bool is visible within the module. The two operations introduced in the module define the partial order and the equality relation on sort Elt belonging to the theory TRIV. The specification in Fig. 13.14 can be adapted to a parameterized module LIST[X::TRIV].

Modules can have more than one parameter; a two-parameter module has the following signature:

```
obj POSET[X :: TRIV] is protecting BOOL .
  op _<=_ : Elt Elt -> Bool .
  op _=P=_ : Elt Elt -> Bool .
  vars X Y Z : Elt .
  eq X <= X = true .
  eq X =P= X = true .
  eq (X <= Y) and (Y <= X) = X =P= Y .
  eq (X <= Y) and (Y <= Z) = X <= Z .
  endo
```

Fig. 13.21 The partially ordered parametric object POSET

```
obj ORD-PAIR[S :: TRIV, T :: TRIV] is sort OrdPair .
  protecting POSET[S] .
  protecting POSET[T] .
  protecting BOOL .
  op pair : Elt.S Elt.T -> OrdPair .
  op first : OrdPair -> Elt.S .
  op second : OrdPair -> Elt.T .
  op eqp : OrdPair OrdPair -> Bool [comm ] .
  var Et : Elt.T . var Es : Elt.S . vars P Q : OrdPair .
  eq first(pair(Es, Et)) = Es .
  eq second(pair(Es, Et)) = Et .
  eq eqp(P, Q) = (first(P) =P= first(Q)) and
                (second(P) =P= second(Q)) .
  endo
```

Fig. 13.22 A parameterized module for *Orderedpair*

```
obj NAME[X :: THEORY1, Y :: THEORY2]
```

If the two theories are the same, we can write:

```
obj NAME[X Y :: THEORY1]
```

The parameterized module in Fig. 13.22 has two parameters S and T satisfying the theory TRIV. Notice that this module imports POSET[S], and POSET[T] in protecting mode. Hence all the properties of partial ordering are available without any change in the module ORD-PAIR. This module generalizes the *Orderedpair* specification shown in Fig. 13.11; it allows the components of the ordered pair to belong to two different sorts.

13.8.4
Instantiation

Instantiation of a parameterized module replaces its formal parameters by the actual parameters. Each theory is replaced by the corresponding actual module, using the views to bind the actual parameters to the formal parameters. Instantiation avoids multiple copies

of imported modules. Instantiating the module BAR, with the formal parameter X mapped
to the object FLAVORS, can be carried out using one of the following constructs:

```
obj BAR[X :: TRIV] is sort Flavor .
```

by the object FLAVORS, one of the forms given below can be used:

- The view is used as actual parameter:

```
BAR[TRIV-TO-FLAVORS ] .
```

- An unnamed view is used as actual parameter:

```
BAR[view from TRIV to FLAVORS is endv] .
```

- The default view from TRIV to FLAVORS is used as actual parameter:

```
BAR[FLAVORS] .
```

When an instantiated algebra is used in several contexts and in reduction, it is convenient
to name the algebra using the *make* command; for example,

```
make BAR-FLAVORS is BAR[TRIV-TO-FLAVORS] endm .
```

where BAR-FLAVORS is the name given to the instantiated object BAR[TRIV-TO-
FLAVORS]. The *make* command allows us to instantiate a module only once, and simplifies *module expressions*.

Using the default view from TRIV to NAT the parameterized module ORD-PAIR may
be instantiated with NAT as actual parameter to get a module expression for the object
POINT:

```
make POINT is ORD-PAIR[NAT,NAT] endm .
```

Using different default views, from TRIV to NAT, and from TRIV to BOOL, the parameterized module ORD-PAIR can be instantiated with the actual parameters NAT, and BOOL
to obtain the module expression:

```
make PAIR-NATBOOL is ORD-PAIR[NAT,BOOL] endm .
```

Using the default view from TRIV to POINT, we can obtain the module expression:

```
make LINE-SEGMENT is ORD-PAIR[POINT,POINT] endm .
```

In Fig. 13.23, we define the parametric module SEQUENCE, which can be instantiated
to obtain different sequences; for example,

- a sequence of natural numbers is defined by the module:

```
make SEQUENCE-OF-NAT is SEQUENCE[NAT] endm .
```

- The *word* entity in the *idea processor* example can be modeled using the built-in sort
QID for identifiers. We can then define the data type *note* as a sequence of words, with
the module:

```
make SEQUENCE-OF-WORDS is SEQUENCE[QID] endm .
```

```
obj SEQUENCE[X :: ELEMS] is sort Seq .
   protecting POSET[X] .
   protecting NAT .
   protecting BOOL .
   subsort Elems < Seq .
   op empty : -> Seq .
   op __ : Seq Seq -> Seq [assoc id: empty] .
   op tail : Seq -> Seq .
   op head : Seq -> Elems .
   op length : Seq -> Nat .
   op equ : Seq Seq -> Bool [comm] .
   vars U V : Seq . vars X Y : Elems .
   eq length(empty) = zero .
   eq length(X U) = succ(length(U)) .
   eq head(X U) = X .
   eq tail(empty) = empty .
   eq tail(X U) = U .
   eq equ(empty, empty) = true .
   cq equ(U, empty) = false if U =/= empty .
   cq equ(U, V) = equ(tail(U), tail(V))
      if U =/= empty and V =/= empty and head(U) == head(V) .
   cq equ(U, V) = false
      if U =/= empty and V =/= empty and head(U) =/= head(V) .
endo
```

Fig. 13.23 A parameterized module for sequence

- the ordered pairs (*key, note*) in the *IdeaProcessor* example can be characterized by the module:

```
make ORD-PAIR[QID, SEQUENCE[QID]] endm .
```

13.8.5
Module Expression

A *module expression* is an expression of an OBJ3 specification which may consist of a homogeneous or a heterogeneous algebra. Evaluating a module expression involves only functions applied to arguments; there is no variable, no assignment and no side-effect. Module expressions form a formal basis for software reuse. They allow the definition, construction, and instantiation of modules, as well as various forms of module modification. Thus, a given module can be reused in various contexts. The three major combination modes for modules are: *instantiation*, *renaming*, and *sum*.

- *Instantiation* is discussed in the previous section.
- *Renaming* is used to create a new module by renaming the sorts and operations of an existing one. In Fig. 13.24, the sort *Element* is renamed to Newelement. In Fig. 13.25, the sort Flavor is renamed to Vegetable, the operation first is renamed to newfirst and the operation second to newsecond. Renaming is applied to a module expression postfix after the symbol "*", creating a new module with the specifications of the preceding module.

```
th NEWELEMENT is
    using ELEMENT * (sort Element to Newelement) .
endth
```

Fig. 13.24 Renaming sorts

Fig. 13.25 Renaming sorts
and operations

```
FLAVORS * (sort Flavor to Vegetable .
    op first to newfirst .
    op _second_ to _newsecond_ .)
```

- *Sum* constructs a union of objects; it creates a new module by composing the specifications of all the components of the sum. The expression A + B creates a module which incorporates the union of axioms, variables, operations, and sorts of both modules A and B.

13.9
Case Study—A Multiple Window Environment

We develop an OBJ3 specification for managing a screen with multiple windows, where each window is associated with a set of geometrical shapes. For the sake of simplicity, the requirements are restricted to windows associated with squares.

13.9.1
Requirements

A screen is a rectangular area which contains a collection of windows. Each window in the screen is a rectangle with its sides parallel to the axes of the screen. A window is associated with the collection of square shapes drawn within it. When the window is moved to a different location within the screen, the square shapes associated with it are also moved without any change to their relative positions inside the window. One is required to provide the following functionalities for window objects and square shapes:

1. Create a window.
2. Determine whether the cursor is within a given window.
3. Select a window identified by the cursor.
4. Move a window to a specified location within the screen.
5. Determine whether two windows overlap.
6. Add a window to the collection of windows.
7. Associate a list of squares with a given window.
8. Add a square to the list of squares associated with a window.
9. Translate a square horizontally within a window.
10. Translate a square vertically within a window.

Fig. 13.26 Coordinate axes
for window environment

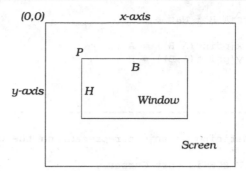

13.9.2
Modeling

We define the coordinates of a point in the screen as a pair of natural numbers. We model the cursor as a point. A rectangle is constructed from a point indicating its top-left corner, and two natural numbers denoting its breadth and height. We specialize the rectangle object by extending it with new operations and axioms to obtain a square object. Similarly, we specialize the rectangle object to model a window.

We define a parametric object which takes one parameter to model a list of elements of some sort. This object can be instantiated to obtain lists of squares, and lists of windows. We model a screen as a list of windows, where each window is associated with a list of squares.

The position of a point on the screen is given with respect to coordinate axes, where the origin is at the top-left corner of the screen, the x-axis as the horizontal axis and the y-axis as the vertical axis, as shown in Fig. 13.26.

13.9.3
Formal Specifications

```
***  **********************************************************
***                   SIMPLE   WINDOW   SYSTEM              ***
***                     OBJ SPECIFICATION                   ***
***  **********************************************************

*** an object representing the two coordinates of a point.

obj POINT is sort Point .
  protecting NAT .

  op point : Nat Nat -> Point .
  op x     : Point -> Nat .
  op y     : Point -> Nat .
```

```
  vars A B : Nat .

  eq x(point(A,B)) = A .
  eq y(point(A,B)) = B .

endo

*** ----------------------------------------------------------- ***

*** defining an object representing the click at a point.

obj CURSOR is sort Cursor .
  protecting NAT .
  protecting POINT .

  op cursor : Point -> Cursor .
  op move   : Cursor Nat Nat -> Cursor .
  op x      : Cursor -> Nat .
  op y      : Cursor -> Nat .

  vars X Y : Nat . var P : Point .

  eq x(cursor(P)) = x(P) .
  eq y(cursor(P)) = y(P) .
  eq move(cursor(P),X,Y) = cursor(point(X,Y)) .

endo

*** ----------------------------------------------------------- ***

*** defining an object representing a rectangle.

obj RECTANGLE is sort Rectangle .
  protecting NAT .
  protecting POINT .

  op rectangle : Point Nat Nat -> Rectangle .
  op locate    : Rectangle -> Point .
  op breadth   : Rectangle -> Nat .
  op height    : Rectangle -> Nat .

  op topleft   : Rectangle -> Point .
  op topright  : Rectangle -> Point .
  op downleft  : Rectangle -> Point .
  op downright : Rectangle -> Point .

  var P : Point . vars B H : Nat .

  eq locate(rectangle(P,B,H)) = P .
  eq breadth(rectangle(P,B,H)) = B .
  eq height(rectangle(P,B,H)) = H .

  eq topleft(rectangle(P,B,H))  = P .
  eq topright(rectangle(P,B,H)) = point(x(P) + B, y(P)) .
```

```
  eq downleft(rectangle(P,B,H)) = point(x(P), y(P) + H) .
  eq downright(rectangle(P,B,H))= point(x(P) + B, y(P) + H) .

endo
```

*** --- ***

*** defining an object representing a square.

```
obj SQUARE is
  extending RECTANGLE * ( sort Rectangle to Square ,
                          op rectangle to square ) .
  protecting NAT .
  protecting POINT .

  op square : Point Nat -> Square .
  op side   : Square -> Nat .

  var P : Point . vars B H S : Nat .

  cq locate(square(P,B,H)) = P if B == H .
  cq side(square(P,B,H))   = B if B == H .
  eq locate(square(P,S))   = P .
  eq side(square(P,S))     = S .
  cq square(P,B,H) = square(P,B) if B == H .

endo
```

*** --- ***

*** defining an object representing a window.

```
obj WINDOW is
  extending RECTANGLE * ( sort Rectangle to Window ,
                          op rectangle to window ) .
  protecting NAT .
  protecting BOOL .
  protecting POINT .
  protecting CURSOR .

  op move     : Window Point  -> Window .
  op contains : Window Cursor -> Bool .
  op cross    : Window Window -> Bool .

  vars B H : Nat . vars P : Point . var C : Cursor .
  vars W W1 W2 : Window .

  *** move window to a specified location.

  eq move(W,P) = window(P, breadth(W), height(W)) .

  *** true if the window contains the location of the cursor

  eq contains(window(P,B,H),C) = x(C) >= x(P) and
```

```
                                  x(C) <= (x(P) + B) and
                                  y(C) >= y(P) and
                                  y(C) <= (y(P) + H) .
```

    *** two windows cross each other if one of them has a
    *** corner which is contained in the other window.

```
    eq cross(W1,W2) = contains(W1,cursor(topleft(W2))) or
                      contains(W1,cursor(topright(W2))) or
                      contains(W1,cursor(downleft(W2))) or
                      contains(W1,cursor(downright(W2))) .
```

endo

*** --- ***

*** a parameterized object LIST which takes one parameter.

```
obj LIST[X :: TRIV] is sort NeList List .
  protecting NAT .
  protecting BOOL .
  subsorts Elt < NeList < List .

  op null      : -> List .
  op __        : List List -> List [assoc id: null] .
  op __        : NeList List -> NeList .
  op tail _    : List -> List .
  op head _    : NeList -> Elt .
  op empty? _  : List -> Bool .
  op length _  : List -> Nat .
  op copy      : List List -> List .

  var X : Elt . vars L L1 : List .

  eq empty? null = true .
  eq empty? L = L == null .
  eq length null = 0 .
  eq length(X L) = length(L) + 1 .
  eq head(X L) = X .
  eq tail(null) = null .
  eq tail(X L) = L .
  eq empty?(copy(null,L)) = true .
  eq tail(copy((X L),L1)) = L .
```

endo

*** --- ***

*** defining a view from the pre-defined theory TRIV
*** to the object WINDOW

```
view WIN from TRIV to WINDOW is
  sort Elt to Window .
endv
```

```
*** creating an object representing a list of windows.
*** instantiating the parameterised object LIST.

make WINLIST is
  LIST[WIN] * ( sort List to Winlist ) .
endm

*** -------------------------------------------------------- ***

*** defining an object representing a screen.

obj SCREEN is sort Screen .
  protecting BOOL .
  protecting CURSOR .
  protecting WINDOW .
  protecting WINLIST .

  op screen  : Winlist -> Screen .
  op winlist : Screen -> Winlist .
  op addwin  : Screen Window -> Screen .
  op overlap : Screen Window -> Bool .
  op select  : Screen Cursor -> Window .

  var B : Cursor . var W : Window .
  var WL : Winlist . var S : Screen .

  eq winlist(screen(WL))  = WL .
  eq winlist(addwin(S,W)) = W winlist(S) .

  eq overlap(screen(null),W) = false .
  eq overlap(S,W) = cross(head(winlist(S)),W) or
                    overlap(screen(tail(winlist(S))),W) .

  eq select(screen(WL),B) = if contains(head(WL),B)
                            then head(WL)
                            else (select(screen(tail(WL)),B))
                            fi .

endo

*** -------------------------------------------------------- ***

*** defining a view from the pre-defined theory TRIV
*** to the object SQUARE

view SQUAR from TRIV to SQUARE is
  sort Elt to Square .
endv

*** creating an object representing a list of squares.
*** instantiating the parameterized object LIST.

make SQUARELIST is
```

```
  LIST[SQUAR] * ( sort List to Squarelist ) .
endm

*** ------------------------------------------------- ***

*** defining an object representing the shapes in a window.
*** the object associates a window with a list of squares.

obj WINDOWSHAPES is sort Windowshapes
  protecting NAT .
  protecting BOOL .
  protecting POINT .
  protecting CURSOR .
  protecting WINDOW .
  protecting SQUARELIST .

  op windowshapes      : Window Squarelist -> Windowshapes .
  op win               : Windowshapes -> Window .
  op squarelist        : Windowshapes -> Squarelist .
  op squarewithin      : Square Window -> Bool .
  op addsquare         : Square Windowshapes -> Windowshapes .
  op htranslatesquare  : Square Window Nat -> Square .
  op vtranslatesquare  : Square Window Nat -> Square .

  var W : Window . var SL : Squarelist .
  var WS : Windowshapes . var S : Square .
  var P : Point . vars L X Y : Nat .

  eq win(windowshapes(W,SL)) = W .
  eq squarelist(windowshapes(W,SL)) = SL .

*** determine if a square fits within a window.

  eq squarewithin(square(P,L),W) =
       contains(W,cursor(topleft(square(P,L)))) and
       contains(W,cursor(topright(square(P,L)))) and
       contains(W,cursor(downleft(square(P,L)))) and
       contains(W,cursor(downright(square(P,L)))) .

*** add square to list of squares if within the window.

  eq addsquare(S,WS) =
       if squarewithin(S,win(WS))
       then windowshapes(win(WS), (S squarelist(WS)))
       else WS fi .

*** translate square horizontally if fits in window
*** at new location.

  eq htranslatesquare(square(P,L),W,X) =
       if squarewithin(square(point(x(P) + X, y(P)), L), W)
       then square(point(x(P) + X, y(P)), L)
       else square(P,L) fi .
```

```
*** translate square vertically if fits in window
*** at new location.

eq vtranslatesquare(square(P,L),W,Y) =
        if squarewithin(square(point(x(P), y(P) + Y), L), W)
        then square(point(x(P), y(P) + Y), L)
        else square(P,L) fi .

endo
```

*** -- ***

13.10
Exercises

1. Define a homomorphism on the set of n-dimensional vectors of real numbers. Hint: See Example 5.
2. Give an algebra for representing a queue of elements. Identify the different schemas needed. Hint: See Example 8.
3. Define a presentation for the algebra characterizing a queue, as requested in Exercise 2, including a set of axioms.
4. Define the operation *position* for the data type *note* shown in Fig. 13.10; the operation determines the position of a given word in a note. Use the already defined operations in your definition of *position*.
5. A collection of sub-ideas is specified as a set in Fig. 13.12. What property is violated if a *copy* function, which makes copies of sub-ideas, is introduced? What data type is appropriate if two sub-ideas having the same key are required and must be considered together to form a single sub-idea? Rewrite the complete specification for the collection of sub-ideas with the proposed changes.
6. Use the signature of the specification in Fig. 13.10 to write a function *mentionsall*, which takes two arguments n, n' of type *note* and returns a sequence composed of *words* occurring in note n as well as in note n'.
7. Use the signature of the specification in Fig. 13.10 to write a function *replaceall*, which takes three arguments w, w' of type *word*, and n of type *note*, and replaces all occurrences of the word w by the word w' in the note n.
8. Give a parametric specification for a binary tree. Define (1) a view for constructing a binary tree of natural numbers, and (2) a view for constructing a binary tree of identifiers. Give reductions for printing the contents of the tree in pre-order and post-order traversals.
9. Extend the specification discussed in the case study for a multiple window environment, as follows:
   (a) Give a specification for constructing ordered pairs of points. Include operations to determine whether or not the second component of the pair is (1) above, (2) below, (3) to the left, (4) to the right, (5) above and left, (6) above and right, (7) below and

right, and (8) below and left of the first component. Give sufficient equations for the axioms.

(b) Give specifications for a *line segment* object. A line segment is a straight line of finite length. Include operations for translating a line segment parallel to the coordinate axes.

(c) Use the `ORD-PAIR[S::TRIV, T::TRIV]` parametric specification given in the text to derive modules for constructing (1) points, and (2) line segments. Hint: Construct appropriate views, and use the renaming mechanism.

(d) Include the following operations for the `WINDOW` object: (1) *fulltop* to extend the height of the window upto the top of the screen, (2) *fullright* to extend the breadth of the window to the right upto the screen boundary, (3) *fulldown* to extend the height of the window up to the bottom of the screen, (4) *fullleft* to extend the breadth of the window to the left upto the screen boundary, (5) *fullscreen* to resize a window so as to fill the entire screen. Include sufficient axioms.

(e) The rectangles considered in the case study have their sides parallel to the coordinate axes. Consequently, the intersection of two rectangles forms a rectangle. The parameters P, B, H of the rectangle, formed by the intersection of any two rectangles $R = rectangle(P_1, B_1, H_1)$, and $R' = rectangle(P_2, B_2, H_2)$ is determined by the dimensions and the relative positions of rectangles R and R'. Introduce operations and axioms for determining the intersection of two rectangles.

(f) Introduce one more sort for the rectangle object to denote its color. Assume that a window may be white or blue. The color of a window W_1 is white when the window is created. It changes to blue when another window W_2 hides part of window W_1. Introduce the notion of hiding and write axioms that are to be satisfied by windows on a screen.

(g) Use the `OBJ3` interpreter to verify that the horizontal and vertical translation axioms in `WINDOSHAPES` are commutative and transitive. In addition, verify that vertical and horizontal translations commute.

(h) Introduce sorts for triangle and circle objects. Make a list of triangle objects, and a list of circle objects. Associate these lists with window objects.

13.11
Bibliographic Notes

Data abstraction was first discussed within the *class* concept of the SIMULA programming language [4]. The algebraic approach to specification of data types can be traced back to several papers published in mid 70's, including Goguen, Thatcher, Wagner, and Wright [6], and Guttag and Horning [9]. A formalization of abstract data types within a many-sorted algebra based on initial algebra semantics was done by the ADJ-group, and reported in Goguen, Thatcher, Wagner [5]. Since then, several algebraic specification languages have been designed, and several books and papers have been written on the theoretical as well as the practical aspects of algebraic methodology for software specification. Wirsing [12] gives a comprehensive survey of algebraic specification theory and methods.

The specification language CLEAR, developed by Burstall and Goguen [3] was the first language designed for constructing structured algebraic specifications. The seminal paper of Burstall and Goguen [2] on *"putting theories together"* has influenced the design of several other algebraic specification languages, in particular the OBJ family. The design of OBJ, initiated by Goguen, was carried through by several researchers [7]. The parameterization concept introduced in the design of OBJ3 was influenced by CLEAR.

References

1. Bergstra JA, Heering J, Klint P (1989) Algebraic specification. ACM, New York
2. Burstall R, Goguen J (1977) Putting theories to make specifications. In: Proceedings fifth international joint conference on artificial intelligence, pp 1045–1058
3. Burstall R, Goguen J (1981) An informal introduction to specifications using CLEAR. In: Boyer R, Moore J (eds) The correctness problem in computer science. Academic Press, San Diego, pp 185–213
4. Dhal OJ, Myhrhang B, Nygaard K (1970) Common base language. Norsk Reguesentral, Oslo
5. Goguen J, Thatcher J, Wagner E (1976) An initial algebra approach to the specification, correctness and implementation of abstract data types. In: Yeh R (ed) Current trends in programming methodology, vol IV. Prentice-Hall, New York, pp 80–149
6. Goguen JA, Thatcher JW, Wagner EG, Wright JB (1977) Initial algebra semantics and continuous algebras. J ACM 24:68–95
7. Goguen J, Winkler T (1988) Introducing OBJ3. Technical report SRI-CSL-88-9, SRI International, August 1988
8. Guttag J (1975) The specification and application to programming of abstract data types. PhD thesis, Department of Computer Science, University of Toronto, Ontario, Canada
9. Guttag JV, Horning JJ (1978) The algebraic specification of abstract data types. Acta Inform 10:27–52
10. Henderson P (1986) Functional programming, formal specification, and rapid prototyping. IEEE Trans Softw Eng SE-12(2):241–250
11. Liskov B, Guttag J (1989) Abstraction and specification in program development. MIT Press, Cambridge
12. Wirsing M (1990) Algebraic specification. In: van Leeuwen J (ed) Handbook of theoretical computer science. North-Holland, Amsterdam
13. Wirth N (1976) Algorithms + data structures = programs. Prentice-Hall, New York

Larch

14

A specification of the system under development must include a description of the boundary between the system and its environment. This boundary characterizes the *interface* of the system. The components in a system interact with each other through their interfaces. It is crucial that each interface specification describes precisely the forms of communication that are permitted at the interface, their causes and effects. Understanding the interface of a component should provide insight into the nature of the system being specified. This is particularly important for systems exhibiting similar behavior, with different interfaces.

Each interface language is designed to deal with information that can be observed by client programs written in a particular programming language. Formal specification languages studied in the previous three chapters are general-purpose languages; they are suitable for design specifications. The refinement techniques associated with model-oriented specification languages provide a methodology for deriving a detailed specification, close to the final implementation. However, to be able to use Z, or VDM-SL, as an interface language, an interface refinement relation is required to bridge the semantic gap between the specification language and the programming language to be used to implement the refined module. This refinement relation must express assertions about program states, and implementation specific notions such as exceptions. It is unlikely that all features of a programming language can be captured in such an interface refinement relation. To describe the behavioral characteristics of a software system, we need a language in which the interfaces of the system components and the externally observable behavior of each system component can be formally specified. The works of Wing [11, 12], and Guttag and Horning [6] on Larch specification languages are geared toward this goal.

14.1
The Two Tiers of Larch

Larch provides a two-tiered approach to specification of program interfaces:

- In the *interface tier*, a Larch Interface Language (LIL) is used to describe the behavior of a program module written in a specific programming language. LIL specifications

V.S. Alagar, K. Periyasamy, *Specification of Software Systems*,
Texts in Computer Science,
DOI 10.1007/978-0-85729-277-3_14, © Springer-Verlag London Limited 2011

provide the information needed to understand and use a module interface. LIL refers to a family of specification languages. Each specification language in the LIL family is designed for a specific programming language. Specifications are written in a predicative language using assertions on the pre- and post-states.

- In the *shared tier*, the Larch Shared Language (LSL) is used to specify state-independent, mathematical abstractions which can be referred to in the interface tier. These underlying abstractions are called *traits*; a trait defines a multi-sorted first-order theory, and is written in the conventional style of equational algebraic specification.

The philosophy behind this two-tiered approach is best summarized by Wing [12]:

> We believe that for specifications of program modules, the environment in which a module is embedded, and hence the nature of its observable behavior, is likely to depend in fundamental ways on the semantic primitives of the programming languages... Thus we intentionally make an interface language dependent on a target programming language, and keep the shared language independent of any programming language. To capitalize on our separation of a specification into two tiers, we isolated programming language dependent issues—such as side effects, error handling, and resource allocation—into the interface language component of a specification.

Larch's two-tiered approach makes it possible to express programming language dependent properties using syntax and semantics which corroborate with the underlying programming language. Constructs are provided for expressing programming language dependent properties such as parameter passing, side effects, exceptions, and concurrency using the syntax and semantics of the underlying programming language. Each LIL has a mechanism for referencing the formal parameters in the specification of an operation using the same syntax and semantics as in the underlying language. The semantics for the primitive terms used in the interface specification is provided by traits in the shared tier.

Larch's two-tiered approach has the advantage of providing separation of concerns between the two tiers. According to Guttag and Horning [6], the complex parts of the specification are to be kept in the shared tier, where mathematical abstractions necessary for the interface specifications are defined. Although some of these abstractions may be very specific to applications, a large number of them will exhibit general characteristics. Such abstractions may be reused in various applications. The semantics of LSL is simpler than most of the interface specification languages. Consequently, specifiers are less likely to make mistakes in LSL traits. The Larch Prover (LP) [6] can be used to verify the validity of claims about semantic properties of LSL traits. The interface tier may be specialized for use with a particular programming language. The concepts and constructs of the chosen programming language may be used to describe resources provided to the module, state changes, computed results, and exceptions. By understanding the interface specification and overlooking its implementation, a class can be reused in a black-box fashion. From the experience reported by Alagar [1] it seems that Larch has the potential for effectively immediately and unintrusively integrated into current industrial processes for effective reuse of commercial class libraries such as Rogue Wave [10].

Several specification languages for the interface tier have been proposed in recent literature. These include:

- LCL [6] tailored to the C language,

- LM3 [7] tailored to Modula-3,
- Larch/Smalltalk [5] for Smalltalk,
- Larch/Ada [3] for Ada, and
- Larch/C++ [8] for C++.

We present a brief tutorial on Larch shared language and discuss some of the salient features of Larch/C++ in this chapter. There are some pragmatic considerations in introducing Larch/C++. C++ provides support for data abstraction, encapsulation, polymorphism, and inheritance. The widespread use of C++ in industry warrants that any effort to unintrusively integrate formal methods in software development as well as reuse of specifications are most likely to succeed if targeted at C++.

14.2
LSL—Larch Shared Language

This section introduces LSL, Larch Shared Language. The founders of Larch, Guttag and Horning [6] give an excellent exposé of LSL; we conform to their style and liberally add several examples.

14.2.1
Equational Specification

The unit of encapsulation in LSL is a trait, which introduces some operators and specifies some of their properties. There are two kinds of symbols in such a description: *operators* and *sorts*. An operator is similar to the programming language concepts procedure, function, and method. A sort is analogous to the notion of type in programming languages. When we discuss a trait, the terms operators and sorts will be used; in the context of discussing programming language issues, we use the term type. Sorts are disjoint sets of values, and are used to denote the domain and range of operators. LSL operators are *total* functions.

Traits are constructed in a *monotonic* fashion: we first define basic traits, and then use them in constructing larger ones. A trait, once constructed, can be put in LSL library and reused in contexts where their properties are meaningful. The LSL handbook of Guttag and Horning [6] contains a collection of traits, many of which we reuse in our examples. Two basic traits that are often required are Boolean and Integer, which, respectively, define a theory for boolean values and a theory for integers. The logic operators *true*, *false*, ¬, ∨, ∧, ⇒, and ⇔, as well as some overloaded operators *if_then_else_*, = are pre-defined in the language; that is, the traits defining these operators are implicitly included in every trait. Figure 14.1 shows an LSL trait *SetTrait* specifying the properties of a set. The example is similar to a conventional algebraic specification as introduced in Chap. 13. The name of a trait is distinct from the names of all sort and operator identifiers defined in the trait, for example *Set*.

14

    SetTrait(Set, E): **trait**
       includes *Integer*
       introduces
          emptyset: $\rightarrow$ *Set*
          insert: E, Set $\rightarrow$ *Set*
          delete: E, Set $\rightarrow$ *Set*
          unionn: Set, Set $\rightarrow$ *Set*
          member: E, Set $\rightarrow$ *Bool*
          subset: Set, Set $\rightarrow$ *Bool*
          size: Set $\rightarrow$ *Int*
      asserts
       Set **generated by** *emptyset, insert*
       Set **partitioned by** *member*
       $\forall\, x,\, y : E,\, s,\, t : Set$
         $\neg(member(x,\ emptyset))$
         member(x, insert(y,s)) == $(x = y) \lor$ *member(x,s)*
         member(x, delete(y,s)) == $(x \neq y) \land$ *member(x,s)*
         member(x, unionn(s,t)) == *member(x,s)* $\lor$ *member(x,t)*
         subset(emptyset, s)
         subset(insert(x,s),t) == *member(x,t)* $\land$ *subset(s,t)*
         subset(delete(x,s),t) == *subset(s,t)*
         unionn(s, emptyset) == *s*
         unionn(s, insert(x,t)) == *insert(x, unionn(s,t))*
         size(emptyset) == *0*
         size(insert(x,s)) == *if member(x,s) then size(s) else 1+size(s)*
    implies
       S **partitioned by** *subset*
       $\forall\, x,y: E,\, s,t: S$
       insert(x, insert (x,s) == *insert(x,s)*
       insert(x, insert(y,s)) == *insert(y, insert(x,s))*
       subset(s,t) $\Rightarrow$ *(member(x,s)* $\Rightarrow$ *member(x,t))*
      converts *delete, unionn, member, subset*
       exempting $\forall\, i : E$
       delete(i, emptyset)

Fig. 14.1 An LSL trait for finite Sets

A trait contains a collection of operator declarations, or *signatures*, which follows the keyword **introduces,** and a collection of *equations*, which follows the keyword **asserts.** Each operator is a total function that maps a tuple of values from its domain sorts to a value from its range sort. Every operator used in a trait must have been declared. Signatures are used to type check the *terms* in a trait. Sorts are not explicitly declared; they are implicitly introduced through the signature of the trait.

The specification of *SetTrait* includes the trait *Integer* which is defined in the LSL handbook [6]. The included *Integer* trait gives information about the operators $+$, $-$, 0, and 1, which are used in the right-hand side of equations. The *body* of the specification is composed of the set of equations, the **implies**, **converts** and **exempting** clauses following the reserved word **asserts**.

An equation is of the form $x == y$, where x and y are terms of the same sort. An equation of the form $x == true$ can be abbreviated by simply writing x. The first equation in *SetTrait* is an abbreviation for $\neg(member(x,emptyset)) == true$. Similarly the fifth equation is an abbreviation for $subset(emptyset,s)==true$. Equations 10 and 11 affirm the essential property that a nonempty set can contain only distinct elements. Equations 2 to 9 define the mathematical properties of set membership for sets constructed using the basic constructor *insert*, and non-basic constructors *delete*, and *unionn* (set union).

The semantics of $=$ and $==$ are exactly the same; only their syntactic precedence differs to ensure that expressions are parsed in an expected manner without the use of parentheses. The operator $=$ binds more tightly than $==$.

All operators in *SetTrait* are in *prefix* notation, the familiar notation for function definition in mathematics. Operators can also be defined in *mixfix* notation. The symbols "__" in an operator definition indicates that the operator will be used in mixfix notation. For example, the operator *member* in *SetTrait* could also be defined using the binary infix operator $\in$. The signature for this infix operator is

$$\_ \in \_ : E, Set \rightarrow Bool$$

Using this signature the second equation can be rewritten as

$$x \in insert(y, s) == (x = y) \vee x \in s.$$

Mixfix operators can be used to enhance the readability of specifications; for example, it is preferable to use $\_+\_$ than to use *plus* as an operator. Precedence rules in Larch ensure that terms are parsed as expected. The precedence scheme for operators is given below; operators are listed such that the ones most tightly bound come first:

- postfix operators consisting of a period followed by an identifier, such as $\cdot$ *front*,
- all other user-defined operators and built-in boolean negation,
- the built-in equality operators, $=$ and $\neq$,
- the built-in propositional connectives, $\vee$, $\wedge$, $\Rightarrow$, and $\Leftrightarrow$,
- the built-in conditional connective $if \_ then \_ else\_$,
- the equation connective $==$.

Infix terms with multiple occurrences of an operator at the same level, and without parentheses, associate the operators from left to right. For example, the equation

$$x == y \cdot a \cdot b \cdot c + front(z) = u \wedge v$$

is equivalent to the term

$$x == (((((y \cdot a) \cdot b) \cdot c) + front(z)) = u) \wedge v.$$

A trait is *well-formed* if it is syntactically correct and the terms in the equations are legal and are successfully parsed. The semantics of Larch traits is based on multi-sorted first-order logic with equality, rather than on an initial, terminal or loose algebra semantics as

Fig. 14.2 Specification of
Abelian groups

$$\overline{Abegroup(+, -, T)\text{: \textbf{trait}}}$$
introduces
$$0 : \to T$$
$$\_ + \_ : T, T \to T$$
$$- \_ : T \to T$$
$$\_ - \_ : T, T \to T$$
asserts
$$\forall\, x, y, z : T$$
$$x + (-x) == 0$$
$$x - y == x + (-y)$$
$$x + 0 == x$$
$$x + y == y + x$$
$$x + (y + z) == (x + y) + z$$

used by algebraic specification languages. A *theory* is a set of logical formulas with no free variable. A well-formed trait denotes a theory in multi-sorted first-order logic with equality. The theory contains the equations of the trait, the conventional axioms of first-order logic with equality, and the logical consequences that follow from the axioms. Formulas in the theory follow only from the presence of assertions in the trait—never from their absence. The theory associated with a trait including other traits corresponds to the union of its theory and those of the included traits. For instance, the theory associated with *SetTrait* contains all consequences of the equations given in Fig. 14.1 and of the equations defined for *Integer* and the traits that implicitly define the logic operators.

SetTrait does not provide all information about sets:

1. It does not state how sets are to be represented.
2. Procedures to implement the operators are not stated.
3. It does not explicitly state all the mathematical properties of sets—some of them can be inferred from the equations and others cannot be inferred.

The first issue can be settled at the implementation stage. The second issue is taken up during the development of interface specifications. The claims made in an LSL specification can be checked; if they are proved to follow from the specification, then it brings out the extent of completeness intended by the specifier.

A trait definition need not correspond to the definition of an abstract data type definition since an LSL trait can define any arbitrary theory of multi-sorted first-order equational logic. For example, a trait can be used to define abstract states of an object, or a first-order theory of mathematical abstractions such as partial orders and equivalence relations. Figure 14.4 shows specifications for pre-ordered sets, partially ordered sets, and totally ordered sets. The mathematical concept of Abelian group, a set with a binary operation "+" and its inverse "−", having 0 as the identity element, is specified in Fig. 14.2. The algebraic structure of rings having a unit element 1 is specified in Fig. 14.3. This specification includes the trait characterizing the Abelian group and adds a binary operation "∗", which is transitive and distributive with respect to the binary operation "+". Notice that 0 is the identity element for the "+" operation, and 1 is the identity element for the "∗"

Fig. 14.3 Specification of rings

$$\begin{array}{l}
Ring(\ast, T)\text{: } \textbf{trait} \\
\quad \textbf{includes } Abegroup \\
\quad \textbf{introduces} \\
\qquad 1 : \rightarrow T \\
\qquad \_ \ast \_ : T, T \rightarrow T \\
\quad \textbf{asserts} \\
\qquad \forall\, x, y, z : T \\
\qquad\quad x \ast (y + z) == (x \ast y) + (x \ast z) \\
\qquad\quad x \ast 0 == 0 \\
\qquad\quad x \ast 1 == x \\
\qquad\quad x \ast (y \ast z) == (x \ast y) \ast z
\end{array}$$

operation. The operation "+" is commutative, while the operation "∗" is not defined to be commutative.

14.2.2
More Expressive Specifications and Stronger Theories

Equational theories are not adequate to specify abstract data types. A trait defining an abstract data type introduces a *distinguished sort*, also called the *principal sort* or *data sort*. In such traits, an explicit reference to the operator symbols that generate values of the data sort and a mechanism to recognize equivalent terms of the data sort can be provided. These are achieved in LSL by adding **generated by** and **partitioned by** clauses.

In *SetTrait* the **generated by** clause states that all values of the sort *Set* can be represented by terms composed solely of the two operator symbols *emptyset* and *insert*. Asserting that sort S is generated by a set of operators *Ops* means that each term of sort S is equal to a term whose outermost operator is in *Ops*. This corresponds to the "no junk" principle of the initial algebra semantics of algebraic specification languages. The operators in *Ops* are referred to as the *generators* of sort S. This clause justifies a *generator induction schema* for proving properties of the distinguished sort. In the case of natural numbers, *0* and *succ* are the generators. These generators combined with the total ordering property for natural numbers provide the induction scheme. Similarly, the **generated by** clause strengthens the theory of *SetTrait* by adding an inductive rule of inference which can be used to prove properties for all *Set* values.

The **generated by** clause of *SetTrait* asserts that any value of the sort *Set* can be constructed from the operator *emptyset* by a finite number of applications of the operator *insert*. We can thus use induction to prove the following property:

$$\forall s : Set, size(s) \geq 0$$

Basis of Induction:

$size(emptyset) = 0$ is true.

Induction step:

$$\forall s : Set, x : E \bullet size(s) \geq 0 \Rightarrow size(insert(x, s)) \geq 0$$

This claim is proved using the last equation from the theory of *SetTrait*.

The operators of an abstract data type in Larch can be categorized as *generators*, *extensions*, and *observers*. Generators produce all the values of the abstract data type. Extensions are the other operators whose range is the distinguished sort. Observers are those operators whose domain include the distinguished sort and whose range is some other sort. As remarked in Chap. 8, a good heuristic for writing axioms is to write one equation defining the result of applying each observer or extension to each generator. This provides a sufficient coverage of the abstract data types, as it assumes all possible values.

A **partitioned by** clause asserts that the operators listed in that clause form a complete set of observers for the trait. Intuitively, it states that two terms are equal if they cannot be distinguished by any of the observers. All equal terms form one equivalence class. Observers partition the set of all terms into equivalence classes so that for any two terms observers can determine whether or not they belong to the same equivalence class. For the *SetTrait* example, this property can be used to show that the order of insertion in the set is immaterial. The terms $insert(x, insert(y, s))$ and $insert(y, insert(x, s))$ are equal for all values $x, y : E, s : Set$. A **partitioned by** clause gives a new axiom justifying a deduction rule in proving properties about the trait. Hence, the **partitioned by** clause in *SetTrait* adds the deduction rule

$$\forall x : E \bullet (x \in s = x \in t) \Rightarrow s = t$$

This deduction rule can be used to prove the property

$$\forall x : E, s : Set \bullet insert(x, insert(x, s)) == insert(x, s)$$

To prove this property, we need to discharge the proof

$$\forall y : E \bullet member(y, insert(x, insert(x, s))) = member(y, insert(x, s))$$

The proof steps are:

1. From Equation (2) in *SetTrait*, infer

   $$member(y, insert(x, s)) == (x = y) \vee member(y, s)$$

2. From Equation (2) in *SetTrait*, infer

   $$member(y, insert(x, insert(x, s))) == (x = y) \vee member(y, insert(x, s))$$

3. Applying Equation (2) again to the right-hand side, we obtain

   $$member(y, insert(x, insert(x, s))) == (x = y) \vee ((x = y) \vee member(y, s))$$

4. The right-hand side of step 3 can be further reduced to

   $$(x = y) \vee member(y, s)$$

5. The result follows from step 4 and the right-hand side of step 1.

14.2.3
Composing Traits

LSL traits can be composed using the **includes** clause. A trait that includes another trait is textually expanded to contain all operator declarations, constrains clauses, **generated by** clauses, and axioms of the included trait. The meaning of operations and equations in the including trait are made clear by the meanings of operations and equations in the included traits. The constants 0, and 1, and the operations "+" in *SetTrait* are defined in the included trait *Integer*. The operator *size* cannot be defined without this inclusion.

Traits describing specific theories and defined separately can be reused within other traits where such theories are appropriate. For example, the trait *TotalOrder* becomes more structured by including the trait *Poset*. This is consistent with the mathematical property "if every pair of elements of a partially ordered set are comparable, then it is a totally ordered set". Thus when an ordering such as set inclusion is needed in a theory, the trait *Poset* can be included; whereas, when a total ordering theory is to be imposed on structures, the trait *TotalOrder* can be included. When both partial order and total order theories are required in another theory, both *Poset* and *TotalOrder* can be included. The LSL handbook available in Guttag and Horning [6] contains traits built by reusing simpler traits in a monotonic fashion.

14.2.4
Renaming

While reusing traits, sort names and operator names can be renamed as in parametric substitutions. The trait *Poset* shown in Fig. 14.4, is included in the trait *TotalOrder*. There is an implicit dependency on the operators $<$ and $\leq$. Since there are different partial orders for different sorts, we can rewrite the header of the *Poset* trait as

   Poset$(T, <, \leq)$: **trait**.

Now the reference

   includes *Poset*(*int* **for** T, $<$ **for** $<$, $\leq$ **for** $\leq$)

in the trait *TotalOrder* gives the theory of a total ordering on integers. Note that the operators $<$, and $\leq$ are overloaded—for any trait T, and for the trait *Integer*.

Using renaming, a set of integers can be obtained from the trait *SetTrait* shown in Fig. 14.1 as follows:

   includes *SetTrait*(S, *int* **for** E)

In addition, the operator *subset* can be replaced by the customary mathematical symbol $\subseteq$, using the following statement.

   includes *SetTrait*(S, *int* **for** E)($\subseteq$ **for** *subset*)

Fig. 14.4 Specifications for ordering relations

Preorder(◇, T): **trait**
  includes *Boolean*
  introduces
    $\_ \diamond \_ : T, T \rightarrow Bool$
  asserts
    $\forall x, y, z : T$
      $x \diamond x$
      $x \diamond y \wedge y \diamond z \Rightarrow x \diamond z$

Poset(T): **trait**
  includes *Boolean*
  introduces
    $\_ < \_ : T, T \rightarrow Bool$
    $\_ \leq \_ : T, T \rightarrow Bool$
  asserts
    $\forall x, y, z : T$
      $\neg (x < x)$
      $x \leq x$
      $x < y \wedge y \leq z \Rightarrow x < z$
      $x \leq y \wedge y < z \Rightarrow x < z$
      $x \leq y \wedge y \leq x == x = y$
      $x \leq z == x < z \vee x = z$
  implies
    $x \leq y \wedge y \leq z \Rightarrow x \leq z$
    Preorder(≤ **for** *◇)*

TotalOrder(T): **trait**
  includes *Poset*
  asserts
    $\forall x, y : T$
      $x < y \vee y \leq x$

In general, the syntax for renaming is *Tr(x* **for** *y)*, denoting the trait *Tr* in which every occurrence of *y* is replaced by *x*, where *y* is a sort or an operator. The renaming is propagated in the signature of *Tr* to the operators where *y* appears. The theory of a trait is not changed due to renaming, because the theory is a logical consequence of the assertions in the trait.

14.2.5
Stating Checkable Properties

An LSL trait is a precise formal description of a specifier's intended object, that is, an abstract structure or an abstract data type. When an object is not properly conceptualized, its specification may not faithfully reflect the intended behavior of the object. An LSL trait, which is syntactically correct, may have semantic errors. These errors cannot be detected in the way that programs are debugged, for LSL traits cannot be executed. Consequently, specifiers are provided with LP, the Larch Proof assistant, using which errors in LSL traits can be debugged. Nevertheless, there is no basis against which correctness of an LSL trait can be established.

To gain confidence in LSL traits, the trait should be checked for the satisfaction of intended properties. Three important properties that should be checked are *consistency*, *completeness*, and *theory containment*.

14.2.5.1
Consistency

An LSL trait is consistent if and only if its theory does not contain a *contradiction*; that is, the theory must not contain the equation *true* == *false*. In general, consistency is hard to prove and is undecidable. The inconsistency of a trait is often much easier to detect. When an inconsistency is detected the trait must be debugged for errors. However, when no inconsistency is detected, we cannot assume the specification to be consistent.

14.2.5.2
Theory Containment

If a property which is not explicitly stated as an equation can be shown to be a logical consequence of the equations, then that property is contained in the theory of the trait. LSL traits can be augmented with checkable claims in order to verify whether intended consequences actually follow from the axioms of a trait. These checkable claims are specified in the form of assertions which are included in the **implies** clause of the trait and which can be verified using LP. For example, the property

$$\forall s, t : S, x : E \bullet subset(s, t) \Rightarrow ((member(x, s) \Rightarrow member(x, t))$$

can be claimed for the trait *SetTrait* shown in Fig. 14.1. The assertion can be added to the trait in the **implies** clause. Proving this claim increases the confidence in the theory predictive capability of the trait, and helps to establish other properties in traits that include this trait. The **implies** clause can be used to specify a theory with equations, generator clauses, partitioning clauses, and references to other traits.

14.2.5.3
Completeness

A theory is complete if every sentence in the theory can be reduced to either *true* or *false*. LSL trait theories need not be complete—sometimes, some characteristics of certain operators may be deliberately omitted. Such intentional incompleteness may provide

Fig. 14.5 LSL trait for stack

StackTrait(E, Stack): **trait**
    introduces
       new: → *Stack*
       push: Stack, E → *Stack*
       top: Stack → *E*
       pop: Stack → *Stack*
       isEmpty: Stack → *Bool*
    asserts
       Stack **generated by** *new, push*
       Stack **partitioned by** *top, pop, isEmpty*
       ∀ *s: Stack, e: E*
         top(push(s,e)) == e
         pop(push(s,e)) == s
         isEmpty(new)
         ¬ *isEmpty(push(s,e))*
    implies
       converts *top, pop, isEmpty*
       exempting *top(new), pop(new)*

some flexibility in writing interface specifications. However, it is useful to state verifiable claims about completeness; this is done in the **converts** clause. The claim **converts** *top, pop, isEmpty* states that the equations in Fig. 14.5 fully define the operators *top, pop,* and *isEmpty* of *StackTrait.* However, the meaning of the terms *pop(new),* and *top(new)* are not defined. The **exempting** clause documents the absence of equations for these terms; that is, it lists the terms that are not claimed to be defined. The **converts** and **exempting** clauses together provide a means of stating that an LSL trait is *sufficiently* complete. For the *Set-Trait* example, intuitively, the **converts** and **exempting** clauses assert that the specification of each of the operators *delete, union, member,* and *subset* is complete in the sense that any term involving these operators can be reduced to a term not involving these operators. The only exception to this rule is the term *delete(x,emptyset).* For example, any term *t* whose outermost operator is *unionn* can be reduced to a term *s* involving only the operators *emptyset* and *insert,* provided that *t* has no subterms of the form *delete(x,emptyset).*

14.2.6
Stating Assumptions

Recall that in VDM every operation has pre- and postconditions. The satisfaction of the precondition is essential for invoking the operation. In Larch we document the precondition for proper usage of a trait with the **assumes** clause. Assumptions stated in **assumes** clause must be *discharged* by a formal proof.

The specification of a stack given in Fig. 14.5 is quite general. It can be specialized to specify an integer stack by renaming the sorts in its definition. For example, the specification

$RStackTrait(E, Stack):$ **trait**
    includes $StackTrait, Integer$
    introduces
        $count: E, Stack \rightarrow Int$
        $\_\leq\_: E, E \rightarrow Bool$
    asserts
        $\forall s: Stack, a,b: E$
            $count(a, new) == 0$
            $count (a, insert(b, s)) == count(s) + (if\ b \leq a\ then\ 1\ else\ 0)$

Fig. 14.6 A specialization of stack

$NStackTrait(E, Stack):$ **trait**
    assumes $Totalorder(E)$
    includes $StackTrait, Integer$
    introduces
        $count: E, Stack \rightarrow Int$
    asserts
        $\forall s: Stack, a,b: E$
            $count(a, new) == 0$
            $count (a, insert(b,s)) == count(s) + (if\ b \leq a\ then\ 1\ else\ 0)$
    Implies
        $\forall a,b:E, s:Stack$
            $a \leq b \Rightarrow count(a,s) \leq count(b,s)$

Fig. 14.7 A specialization of stack with assumption clause

$IntegerStack:$ **trait**

includes $Integer, StackTrait(Int, Stack)$

introduces a stack of integers. The operators defined in the *Integer* trait are quite distinct from the operators in *StackTrait*. Consequently, there is no inheritance of integer properties in *StackTrait*. Therefore, *StackTrait(Int, Stack)* needs no assumptions on integers.

Let us consider the specification of a stack of integers in which the elements who do not exceed the integer on top of the stack is of interest. This requires an extension to *StackTrait* dealing with integers and an operator for counting the number of elements in the stack having the stated property. Writing the specification as shown in Fig. 14.6, the operator $\leq$ is used in defining *count*; however, the properties of $\leq$ are not stated within the specification. We should not define $\leq$ within *RstackTrait*, because the properties would be required by the trait that includes *RstackTrait*. The properties of the operator $\leq$ are "assumed" in *Rstack-Trait*, with an explicit statement in the **assumes** clause. The specification in Fig. 14.7 states in the **assumes** clause that the theory of *TotalOrder(E)* is assumed. Since *TotalOrder(E)*, shown in Fig. 14.4, defines the properties of $\leq$ through its **includes** clause and its equation, we do not have to introduce the operator $\leq$ in *NstackTrait*. With the assumption that

E is totally ordered, one can state and prove properties for the operator *count*; for example, *count* is monotonic in its first argument. This is stated in the **implies** clause.

The theory of the trait *NStackTrait* is the same as if *Totalorder* was included in the trait. The only difference is that whenever *NStackTrait* is included or assumed in another trait, the assumption on *Totalorder* must be discharged with a proof. For example, consider defining another stack trait which includes *NStackTrait* and introduces the operator *height*, which counts the number of elements in the stack. Intuitively, it is clear that

$$\forall a : E, s : Stack, count(a, s) \le height(s)$$

is true. The proof of this claim requires discharging the proof obligation on the assumed total order property for integers. Proofs become simpler when included traits include assumed traits—that is, no separate proof is necessary. For example, using the trait *Totalorder* from Guttag and Horning [6], we notice that it is also used in the trait *Integer* which is included in *NStack(E,Stack)*, and can therefore discharge the proof syntactically. In other situations, LP can be used to discharge the proof.

14.2.7
Operator Overloading

In mathematics, operators such $=$, $\le$, and $+$ are often used to denote operations on different kinds of objects: for example, A + B, where A and B are integers, reals, rationals, or matrices. The operators have precise meanings in their contexts of usage. One of the advantages of operator overloading is to avoid excessive proliferation of operators, as this may limit the extent of understanding and clarity. LSL has several built-in overloaded operators and operators can also be overloaded by users.

The operators $=$, $\neq$, and *if__then__else* are built-in and overloaded; they have consistent meaning in all traits where they can be used. Users can introduce overloaded operators in the **introduces** clause and provide equations in the **asserts** clause to disambiguate their meaning. For example, consider the trait *Rational* shown in Fig. 14.8. The operator $\le$ is introduced in the **introduces** clause; it takes two rational numbers and returns *true* or *false*. Equation 3 in the **asserts** clause defines the ordering on rationals. The symbol $\le$ on the right-hand side of the equation relates integers. The context of usage unambiguously provides the meaning of $\le$. However, it is also possible to state the context in assertions: for example, equation 3 could be written as

$$(r \le s) : Rat == (deno(r) \neq 0) \wedge$$
$$(deno(s) \neq 0) \wedge$$
$$((nume(r) * deno(s)) : Int \le (nume(s) \wedge deno(r)) : Int$$

The operators $+$, $-$, and $*$ can be overloaded to define addition, subtraction, and multiplication, respectively, for rationals.

Fig. 14.8 LSL trait for
rational

Rational(Int,Int): **trait**
  includes *Integer, TotalOrder(Int)*
  introduces
    cons: Int, Int → Rat
    deno: Rat → Int
    nume: Rat → Int
    _≤_ : Rat, Rat → Bool
  asserts
    ∀ *x, y : Int, r, s : Rat*
      deno(cons(x,y)) == y
      nume(cons(x,y)) == x
      r ≤ s == (deno(r) ≠ 0) ∧ (deno(s) ≠ 0) ∧
        *(nume(r) * deno(s) ≤ nume(s) * deno(r))*
  implies
    TotalOrder(Rat)
    exempting ∀ *r : Rat*
    deno(r)=0

Fig. 14.9 An enumeration
trait

Flavor: **trait**
  introduces
    chocolate: → Flavor
    vanilla: → Flavor
    strawberry: → Flavor
  asserts
    chocolate ≠ vanilla
    chocolate ≠ strawberry
    vanilla ≠ strawberry
    chocolate ≤ vanilla ≤ strawberry

14.2.8
In-line Traits

LSL provides a shorthand for writing traits in-line. Three such examples are *enumerations*, *tuples*, and *union*. The trait *Flavor* shown in Fig. 14.9 defines three distinct constants, and an operator to enumerate them. This trait can be succinctly defined as

  Flavor **enumeration of** *chocolate, vanilla, strawberry*

The tuple notation is similar to the notation used for the fixed-size record type in Pascal. It introduces fixed-size tuples of a sort. The *Point* trait in Fig. 14.10 introduces a tuple with three fields. There are two operators associated with each field, one for extracting the field from the tuple, and another to change the value of the field. A shorthand definition for this trait is

  Point **tuple of** *xcoord, ycoord, zcoord*: *Int*

Fig. 14.10 A tuple trait

Point: **trait**
  introduces
    [_,_,_]: Int, Int, Int → Point
    xcoord: Point → Int
    ycoord: Point → Int
    zcoord: Point → Int
  asserts
    Point **generated by** *[_,_,_]*
    Point **partitioned by** *xcoord, ycoord, zcoord*
      ∀ *x,y,z: Int, p: Point*
      [x,y,z].xcoord == x
      [x,y,z].ycoord == y
      [x,y,z].zcoord == z

TransModes: **trait**
  includes
    Mode_tag **enumeration of** *atomic_trans, long_trans*
  introduces
    atomic_trans: A → TransModes
    long_trans: L → TransModes
    _.atomic_trans: TransModes → A
    _.long_trans: TransModes → L
    tag: Transmodes → Mode_tag
  asserts
    TransModes **generated by** *atomic_trans, long_trans*
    TransModes **partitioned by** *.atomic_trans, .long_trans*
      ∀ *t:A, T:L*
      atomic_trans(t).atomic_trans == t
      long_trans(T).long_trans == T
      tag(atomic_trans(t)) == atomic_trans
      tag(long_trans(T)) == long_trans

Fig. 14.11 A union trait

The union shorthand introduces a discriminated union of two sorts, as in the definition of union types in some programming languages. For a variable of union sort, we need a tag to identify its individual sort. Consequently, the union sort is finitely generated by the components of an enumerated sort. The sort *TransModes* in Fig. 14.11 is the union of two sorts *A* and *L*. The name *atomic_trans* of sort *A* and the name *long_trans* of sort *L* serve as the two field names for the sort *TransModes*. That is, a transaction type *TransModes* is either an atomic transaction or a long transaction. A shorthand definition for this trait is

  TransModes **union of** *atom_trans: A, long_trans: L*

$String(E, C)$: **trait**
  includes *List*
  introduces
    $\_\_ [\_\_] : C, Int \rightarrow E$
    prefix $: C, Int \rightarrow C$
    removePrefix $: C, Int \rightarrow C$
    substring $: C, Int, Int \rightarrow C$
  asserts
    $\forall\, e : E,\, s : C,\, i,\, n : Int$
      $\neg(member(e, emptyset))$
      $tail(empty) == empty$
      $init(empty) == empty$
      $s[0] == head(s)$
      $n \geq 0 \Rightarrow s[n + 1] = tail(s)[n]$
      $prefix(empty, n) == empty$
      $prefix(s, 0) == empty$
      $n \geq 0 \Rightarrow prefix(e \dashv s, n + 1) = e \dashv prefix(s, n)$
      $removePrefix(s, 0) == s$
      $n \geq 0 \Rightarrow removePrefix(s, n + 1) = removePrefix\,(tail(s), n)$
      $substring(s, 0, n) == prefix(s, n)$
      $i \geq 0 \Rightarrow substring(s, i + 1, n) = substring(tail(s), i, n)$
  implies
    $IndexOp(\dashv$ **for** *insert*$)$
    C **partitioned by** *len*, $\_\_ [\_\_]$
  converts *tail, init*

Fig. 14.12 LSL trait for string

14.3 More LSL Examples

We discuss four LSL trait examples to illustrate the features of Larch shared tier. The first example develops a theory of files; the second builds a theory of iterators which can be used in specifying different C++ collection classes; the last two examples are related to *internationalization* issues in software engineering, wherein accommodating different cultural conventions for representing and dealing with time and date are addressed.

These examples require the LSL library trait *String* given in Guttag and Horning [6]; for reference, it is reproduced in Fig. 14.12. The trait *String* models a string as a list of elements. The sort of string is C, and the sort for elements is E. The trait implicitly includes the properties of the sort *Int*, and includes the trait *List* shown in Fig. 14.14, in which the operators *empty, tail, init, head*, and $\dashv$ are defined. The operator $\dashv$ inserts an element to the front of a given list; the rest of the operators have meanings similar to the list operators defined in Chap. 5. The operator $\_\_ [\_\_]$ extracts the element from a given position of a string; the other operations have their intuitive meanings.

File: **trait**
> **includes** *String(Byte, Data)*
> *File* **tuple of** *name:Name, data:Data, mode:Mode*
> *Openfile* **tuple of** *file:File, data:Data, mode:Mode, fpointer:Int*
> *Mode* **enumeration of** *READ, WRITE, READ_WRITE*
> *readeffect* **tuple of** *ofile: OpenFile, reddata:Data*
> **introduces**
>> *create: Name, Mode → File*
>> *open: File, Mode → OpenFile*
>> *flush: OpenFile → OpenFile*
>> *error: OpenFile → Bool*
>> *read: OpenFile, Int, Int → readeffect*
>> *write: OpenFile, Data, Int → OpenFile*
>
> **asserts**
>> ∀ *f:File, opf:OpenFile, mode, m:Mode, nm:Name, i, p:Int, dat:Data*
>> *create(nm, m) == [nm, empty, m]*
>> *open(f, READ) == [f, f.data, READ, 1]*
>> *open(f, READ_WRITE) == [f, f.data, READ_WRITE, 1]*
>> *open(f, WRITE) == [f, f.data, WRITE, len(f.data)]*
>> ¬*(error(flush(opf)))* ⇒ *(opf.data = opf.file.data)*
>> *read(opf, i, p).reddata == prefix(removePrefix(opf.data, p), i)*
>> *read(opf, i, p).ofile == [opf.file, opf.data, opf.mode, p + i]*
>> *write(opf, dat, p) == [opf.file, prefix(opf.data, p) ‖ dat ‖*
>> *removePrefix(opf.data, p + len(dat)), opf.mode,*
>> *p + len(dat)), opf.mode, p+len(dat)]*
>
> **implies**
>> ∀ *opf:OpenFile, dat : Data, i, p : Int*
>> *read(write(opf, dat, p), len(dat), p).reddata == dat*
>> **converts** *create, open*
>> **exempting**
>>> ∀ *nm : Name, f : File, dat : Data, p: Int*
>>> *write(open(f, READ), dat, p),*
>>> *open(create(nm,READ), WRITE),*
>>> *open(create(nm, READ), READ_WRITE)*

Fig. 14.13   LSL Trait for file

14.3.1
File

The trait in Fig. 14.13 specifies properties common to text files. A text file in disk storage, or in memory can be modeled as a string of bytes. We consider *Byte* as a basic abstraction to model fixed-length sequence of characters. The **includes** clause mentions the trait *String* with two parameters of the sorts *Byte*, and *Data* as a string of bytes to abstract file data. A disk file is described by **tuple** trait *File* with three fields *name: Name, data:Data, mode:Mode*. The trait *Mode* is defined by the **enumeration** of three distinct constants *READ, WRITE, READ_WRITE*. The abstraction of a file in memory is introduced in the trait *Openfile*, as a tuple with four fields: *file* refers to the disk file, *data* refers to the contents of the file, *mode* refers to the mode enumeration, and *fpointer* corresponds to a position in the file. The trait *readeffect* abstracts the effect of reading a file in memory, by resetting the position in the file to the last byte read. The sorts and operations are:

- File on disk corresponds to the sort *File*.
- File in memory corresponds to the sort *Openfile*.
- The data in a file is abstracted as a string of bytes, *Data*.
- When a file is opened, the data in the file in memory is a copy of the data in the corresponding disk file.
- *create*—creates a disk file.
- *open*—opens a disk file in memory with its proper mode set.
- *flush*—updates a disk file with the data from the corresponding memory file.
- *error*—returns true if an I/O error occurred in a memory file.
- *read*—describes the effect of reading a file in memory.
- *write*—describes the effect of writing a file from memory on to disk.

14.3.1.1
Iterator

An iterator is an object associated with a list, a basic container type. By specializing a list and its iterator, one can obtain iterators for hash-dictionaries, bags, and tree-dictionaries. The goal of this example is to construct a theory of iterators. We first extract a simple theory of finite lists from the theory given in Guttag and Horning [6]; we then construct a richer theory of lists; finally, we develop a theory of iterators associated with this list type. The first two steps are motivated by the need for iterator operations in C++ classes in the Rogue Wave library [10].

List Trait Figure 14.14 shows the LSL trait for a finite list. It has operations to construct a list by concatenation, and by adding elements at the front or rear of the list. The element at one end can be extracted and the list following this element can be identified.

Enriching List Trait The trait *ListOp* shown in Fig. 14.15 includes $List(E, C)$ and introduces the following additional operations:

- *isequal*—compares two lists for identical elements occurring in the same order.
- *movepos*—removes a number of elements at one end of the list and returns the rest of the list; this operation is equivalent to a finite number of successive applications of the *tail* operation;
- *occurrencesof*—determines the number of occurrences of an element in a given list;
- *findonlist*—returns *true* if a given element is in the given list, otherwise returns *false*;
- *lastnode*—returns the list containing the last node of a given list;
- *tailrem*—returns the list after removing a given number of elements from its tail;
- *sublist*—extracts a sublist from the given list;

Fig. 14.14 An LSL trait for finite lists

$List\ (E,C)$: **trait**
  includes *Integer*
  introduces
    empty: $\rightarrow C$
    $\_\dashv\_$: $E,\ C \rightarrow C$
    $\_\vdash\_$: $C,\ E \rightarrow C$
    head: $C \rightarrow E$
    tail: $C \rightarrow C$
    len: $C \rightarrow Int$
    $\{\_\}$: $E \rightarrow C$
    $\_\|\_$: $C,\ C \rightarrow C$
  asserts
    C **generated by** *empty*, $\vdash$, $\|$
    C **partitioned by** *len, head, tail*
    $\forall e, e_1, e_2 : E, c, c_1, c_2 : C$
      $e \dashv empty == empty \vdash e$
      $e_1 \dashv (c \vdash e_2) == (e_1 \dashv c) \vdash e_2$
      $head(e \dashv c) == e$
      $tail(e \dashv c) == c$
      $len(empty) == 0$
      $len(e \dashv c) == 1 + len(c)$
      $\{e\} == empty \dashv e$
      $c \| empty == c$
      $(e \dashv c_1) \| c_2 == e \dashv (c_1 \| c_2)$
  implies
    $\forall c: C$
    $c = empty \lor (c = head(c) \dashv tail(c))$
  converts *head, tail, len,* $\|$, $\{\_\}$
    exempting *head(empty), tail(empty)*

Iterator　The iterator is represented as a tuple composed of the fields *Col*, *Head*, where *Col* is a pointer to the collection that is to be iterated, and *Head* points to the current item in the collection. Consequently, the iterator is modeled as a pair of lists. The following operations are provided:

- *create*—returns an iterator to traverse the list in the *Col* field; the *Head* field is undefined.
- *sizecol*—returns the number of items in the collection *Col*.
- *moveiterator*—returns the iterator after moving *Head* by a specified number of positions; when *Head* is undefined or when the number of positions is greater than the number of unvisited elements in the list, the result is undefined.
- *reset*—returns the iterator as it was at its creation time.
- *itemat*—returns the element in the list *Col* at the current position pointed to by *Head*.
- *isfirst*—returns *true* if the current element, as pointed to by *Head*, is the first element of *Col*.
- *islast*—returns *true* if the current element, as pointed to by *Head* is the last element of the list *Col*.
- *first*—returns the iterator with *Head* pointing to the first element of the list *Col*.

ListOp(E, C): **trait**
  includes List(E, C)
  introduces
    isequal: $C, C \rightarrow Bool$
    movepos: $C, Int \rightarrow C$
    occurrencesof: $C, E \rightarrow Int$
    findonlist: $C, E \rightarrow Bool$
    lastnode: $C \rightarrow C$
    sublist: $C, Int, Int \rightarrow C$
    tailrem: $C, Int \rightarrow C$
  asserts
    $\forall c_1, c_2 : C, n, n_1, n_2 : Int, e, e_1, e_2 : E$
      isequal(empty, empty)
      $isequal(e_1 \dashv c_1, e_2 \dashv c_2) == e_1 = e_2 \wedge isequal(c_1, c_2)$
      $movepos(c_1, n) ==$ if $n = 0$ then c_1
          else if $n > 0 \wedge n \leq len(c_1)$ then
               $movepos(tail(c_1), n - 1)$
          else empty
      occurrencesof(empty, e) == 0
      $occurrencesof(e_1 \dashv c, e) ==$ if $e = e_1$ then $1 + occurrencesof(c, e)$
          else occurrencesof(c, e)
      $\neg$ findonlist(empty, e)
      $findonlist(e_1 \dashv c, e) == (e_1 = e) \vee findonlist(c, e)$
      $lastnode(c) == movepos(c, len(c) - 1)$
      tailrem(empty, n) == empty
      tailrem(c, 0) == c
      $tailrem(c \vdash e, n) == tailrem(c, n - 1)$
      $sublist(c, n_1, n_2) ==$ if $(n_1 + n_2) \leq len(c)$ then
          $tailrem(movepos(c, n_1 - 1), n_2)$
          else empty

Fig. 14.15   LSL trait for an enrichment of list trait

- *last*—returns the iterator with *Head* pointing to the last element of the list *Col*.
- *nextitem*—returns the iterator with *Head* pointing to the next item in the list *Col*, equal to a given value.

14.3.2
Date and Zone

Database and network programs use date and zone types. A theory for these data types is described in the traits *Date*, and *Zone*. The trait *Zone* shown in Fig. 14.21 defines the standard and daylight saving zones and their relationship. The trait *Date* shown in Figs. 14.19

Iterator(Iter, C, E): **trait**
    includes *ListOp(E, C)*
    Iter **tuple of** *Col:C, Head:C*
    introduces
        create: C → Iter
        sizecol: Iter → Int
        moveiterator: Iter, Int → Iter
        reset: Iter → Iter
        itemat: Iter → E
        UND: → E
        isfirst: Iter → Bool
        islast: Iter → Bool
        first: Iter → Iter
        last: Iter → Iter
        nextitem: Iter, E → Iter
        remove: Iter → Iter
        removenext: Iter, E → Iter
        insertat: Iter, E → Iter
    asserts
        ∀ *i:Iter, c:C, n:Int, e:E*
          create(c).Head == empty
          create(c).Col == c
          reset(i).Head == empty
          reset(i).Col == i.Col
          moveiterator(i,0) == i
          $n > 0$ ⇒ *(moveiterator(i,n).Head =*
            (if len(i.Head) = 0 ∧ *len(i.Col) > 0*
            then movpos(i.Col, n-1)
            else if len(i.Col) = 0 then empty
              else movepos(i.Head,n))
          $n < 0$ ⇒ *(moveiterator(i,n).Head =*
            (if len(i.Head) = 0 ∧ *len(i.Col) > 0*
            then moveiterator(last(i), n-1).Head
            else if isequal(i.Head, i.Col) ∧ *len(i.Col) = 0 then empty*
            else if len(i.Col) = 0 then empty
            else if ((-n) ≤ *(len(i.Col) - len(i.Head))) then*
              movepos(i.Col, (len(i.Col) - len(i.Head)) + n)
              else empty))

Fig. 14.16 An LSL trait for iterators—Part I

and 14.20 models the dates in a Julian calendar, and operations on the dates. A date is abstracted by a fixed length tuple of *Day, Month, Year* of type *Int*. Constraints on the fields, converting the numeric value of a month to a string to denote its name, and the relationship

$moveiterator(i,n).Col == i.Col$

$itemat(i) == head(i.Head)$

$sizecol(i) == len(i.Col)$

$isfirst(i) == isequal(i.Col, i.Head)$

$islast(i) == isequal(tail(i.Head),empty)$

$first(i).Col == i.Col$

$first(i).Head == i.Col$

$last(i).Col == i.Col$

$last(i).Head == lastnode(i.Col)$

$nextitem(i,e).Head == if\ (itemat(moveiterator(i,1) = e$
$\quad \vee\ itemat(moveiterator(i,1)) = UND)\ then$
$\qquad moveiterator(i,1).Head$
$\quad else\ nextitem(moveiterator(i,1),e).Head$

$nextitem(i,e).Col == i.Col$

$i.Head = empty \Rightarrow itemat(i) = UND$

$remove(i).Col == sublist(i.Col, (len(i.Col) - len(i.Head))) \parallel tail(i.Head)$

$remove(i).Head == movepos(remove(i).Col, (len(i) - len(i.Head) - 1))$

$removenext(i).Head == remove(nextitem(i,e))$

$insertat(i,e).Col == (sublist(i.Col, len(i.Col) - len(i.Head))) \vdash) \parallel i.Head$

$insertat(i,e).Head == movepos(remove(i).Col, (len(i.Col) - len(i.Head)))$

Fig. 14.17 An LSL trait for iterators—Part II

Fig. 14.18 LSL Trait for local format

Locale: **trait**
includes *Integer*
introduces
Localformat: → *Int*

between number of days and month are specified in equations shown in Fig. 14.20. The formatting convention for date is abstracted in the trait *Locale* shown in Fig. 14.18. Date can also be represented as a natural number, the number of days elapsed since *startDay*. The operations in *Date* have the following significance.

- *today*—constructor; creates today's date.
- *date*—constructor; composes a date from the given values.
- *totalDays*—returns the number of days elapsed since *startDay* until the given date.
- *dayConvert*—converts the given number of days into date.
- *isValid*—returns *true* if the given date is valid.
- *week_day*—determines which day of the week the given date is.
- *startDay*—defines which day of the week the starting date.
- *leap*—returns *true* if the given year is a leap year.
- *ConvertY*—determines the number of days elapsed since *startDay*, including the current day.

- *ConvertM*—determines the number of days elapsed in a given year up to the given month, including the given month.
- *ConvertD*—determines which day of the month the given date is.
- *yConvert*—converts a given year into the number of days, that is, 366 for a leap year, and 365 otherwise.
- *mConvert*—determines the number of days in the given month during the given year.
- *dYconvert*—converts the given day in a year into the corresponding date; for example, 32 corresponds to February 1.
- *dtConvert*—converts the given date into the number of days elapsed in the given year.
- *validDay*—returns *true* if the given day is valid.
- *validMonth*—returns *true* if the given month is valid.
- *validYear*—returns *true* if the given year is valid.
- *date_string*—converts the given date into a string.
- *string_date*—converts the given string into a date.
- *name_month*—converts the given name of the month into the corresponding number.
- *month_name*—converts the given number corresponding to a month into its name.
- *name_date*—converts the given name of a day into the corresponding number.
- *day_name*—converts the given number corresponding to a day into its name.
- *toLocale*—transforms the given date into the given locale format.

The trait *Zone* in Fig. 14.21 abstracts the time zones the world as a tuple with four fields. The first two fields assign names to the zone and the Daylight Saving Time (DST) of that zone; the next two fields refer to the standard time offset and the DST offset.

- *standardOffset*—an offset from the Greenwich time with no daylight saving time correction.
- *DSTOffset*—an offset from the Greenwich time with daylight saving time correction.
- *utc*—Greenwich time zone.
- *local*—local time zone with respect to the daylight saving time, if there is any.
- *standard*—local time zone without daylight saving time correction.

14.3.3
Time

Time stamping information is mandatory for legal contracts and communication protocols. The LSL trait *Time* provides necessary abstractions for programming tasks in such applications. Time is abstracted as observed according to daylight saving conventions in the Julian calendar. We have abstracted the notion of time zones and dates in the previous example. These traits are included in the **includes** clause.

The sort *Time* shown in Fig. 14.22, models time as a tuple of *date, hour, minute, second*, and *zone*. The local convention for stating time is abstracted in the trait *Locale*. From the local format, time is converted to an integer, and converted again to the structure imposed by the sort *Time*. In order to do this conversion, we need to know *the origin* of time.

Date : **trait**

    includes *Boolean, Integer, Locale, Zone*

    Weekday **enumeration of** *mon, tue, wed, thu, fri, sat, sun*

    Date **tuple of** *Day, Month, Year* : *Int*

    introduces

        today : $\rightarrow$ *Date*

        date : *Int, Int, Int* $\rightarrow$ *Date*

        totalDays : *Date* $\rightarrow$ *Int*

        dayConvert : *Int* $\rightarrow$ *Date*

        isValid : *Date* $\rightarrow$ *Bool*

        week_day : *Date* $\rightarrow$ *Int*

        startDay : $\rightarrow$ *Int*

        leap : *Int* $\rightarrow$ *Bool*

        ConvertY : *Int* $\rightarrow$ *Int*

        ConvertM : *Int, Int* $\rightarrow$ *Int*

        ConvertD : *Int* $\rightarrow$ *Int*

        yConvert : *Int* $\rightarrow$ *Int*

        mConvert : *Int, Int* $\rightarrow$ *Int*

        dYconvert : *Int, Int* $\rightarrow$ *Date*

        dtConvert : *Date* $\rightarrow$ *Int*

        validDay : *Int* $\rightarrow$ *Bool*

        validMonth : *Int* $\rightarrow$ *Bool*

        validYear : *Int* $\rightarrow$ *Bool*

        date_string : *Date* $\rightarrow$ *Str*

        string_date : *Str* $\rightarrow$ *Date*

        name_month : *Str* $\rightarrow$ *Int*

        month_name : *Int* $\rightarrow$ *Str*

        name_day : *Str* $\rightarrow$ *Int*

        day_name : *Int* $\rightarrow$ *Str*

        toLocale : *Date, Locale* $\rightarrow$ *Date*

        min : *Date, Date* $\rightarrow$ *Date*

        max : *Date, Date* $\rightarrow$ *Date*

Fig. 14.19 LSL trait for date—Part I

This *origin* is fixed at midnight of *startDay*, the abstraction of the first day of the last millennium. The abstraction for Daylight Saving Time depends on the *Zone* and *Date* abstractions. The operations introduced in *Time* are the following:

- *makeStr*—returns a string representation of a given time according to the format specified by the *Locale* parameter.
- *makeTime*—converts a given string to time.
- *toZone*—converts the given time to time in a different zone.
- *observedDST*—returns AHEAD if the clock is changed forward;
- *observedDST*—returns BEHIND if the clock is changed backward.

asserts

Date **generated by** date

$\forall$ d: Int, m:Int, y:Int, dt, dt_1:Date, dn : Int

    ConvertY(dt.Year) == if (dt.Year = 1) then yConvert(dt.Year)

      else yConvert(dt.Year) + ConvertY(dt.Year − 1)

    mConvert(m,y) == if (m = 1 $\vee$ m = 3 $\vee$ m = 5 $\vee$ m = 7 $\vee$

      m = 8 $\vee$ m = 10 $\vee$ m = 12) then 31

      else if (m = 4 $\vee$ m = 6 $\vee$ m = 9 $\vee$ m = 11) then 30

      else if leap(y) then 29 else 28

    yConvert(y) == if leap(y) then 366 else 365

    ConvertM(m, y) == if m = 1 then 31

      else mConvert(m, y) + ConvertM(m − 1, y)

    dtConvert(dt) == ConvertM(dt.Month − 1, dt.Year) + ConvertD(dt.Day)

    validDay(dt.Day) == dt.Day $\leq$ 31 $\wedge$ dt.Day > 0

    validMonth(dt.Month) == dt.Month $\leq$ 12 $\wedge$ dt.Month > 0

    validYear(dt.Year) == dt.Year > 1900

    leap(y) == if (y = 1900) then true

      else if (y > 1903) then leap(y − 4) else false

    week_day(dt) == mod(totalDays(dt)+ startDay, 7)

    totalDays(dt) = ConvertY(dt.Year − 1) +

      ConvertM(dt.Month − 1, dt.Year) + ConvertD(dt.Day)

    isValid(dt) == dt.Month = 1 $\vee$ dt.Month = 3 $\vee$ dt.Month = 5 $\vee$

      dt.Month = 7 $\vee$ dt.Month = 8 $\vee$ dt.Month = 10 $\vee$ dt.Month = 12 $\wedge$

      dt.Day > 0 $\wedge$ dt.Day $\leq$ 31

    isValid(dt) == dt.Month = 4 $\vee$ dt.Month = 6 $\vee$ dt.Month = 9 $\vee$

      dt.Month = 11 $\wedge$ dt.Day > 0 $\wedge$ dt.Day $\leq$ 30

    isValid(dt) == leap(dt.Year) $\wedge$ dt.Day > 0 $\wedge$ dt.Day $\leq$ 29

      $\wedge$ dt.Month = 2

    isValid(dt) == $\neg$ leap(dt.Year) $\wedge$ dt.Day > 0 $\wedge$ dt.Day $\leq$ 28 $\wedge$

      dt.Month = 2

    min(dt, dt_1) == if totalDays(dt) > totalDays(dt_1) then dt_1 else dt

    max(dt, dt_1) == if totalDays(dt) < totalDays(dt_1 then dt_1 else dt

    d < mConvert(1, y) $\Rightarrow$ date(d, 1, y) = dYconvert(d, y)

    d < mConvert(m, y) $\Rightarrow$ date(d − mConvert(m − 1, y), m, y) =

      dYconvert(d, y)

implies

    $\forall$d_1:Date, d, m, y:Int

    validMonth(2) $\Rightarrow$ $\neg$ validDay(30)

Fig. 14.20 LSL trait for date—Part II

- *observedDST*—returns NON if there is no daylight saving clock change in the given zone for a given year.
- *beginDST*—returns the time when clock is changed forward.

Zone : **trait**
>   **includes** *Integer, String*
>   *Zone* **tuple of** *standardName, DSTName : String,*
>   *standardOffset, DSTOffset : Int*
>   **introduces**
>   *utc :* → *Zone*
>   *local :* → *Zone*
>   *standard :* → *Zone*
>   *daylightObserved : Zone* → *Bool*
>   **asserts**
>   *Zone* **partitioned by** *daylightObserved*
>   ∀ *zn : Zone*
>   *utc.DSTOffset == 0*
>   *utc.standardOffset == 0*
>   ¬ *daylightObserved(local)* ⇒ *local.DSTOffset = standard.DSTOffset*
>   *local.standardOffset == standard.standardOffset*
>   ¬ *daylightObserved(zn)* ⇒ *zn.DSTOffset = zn.standardOffset*
>   ¬ *daylightObserved(standard)*

Fig. 14.21   LSL trait for zone

- *endDST*—returns the time when clock is changed backward.
- *convert*—takes a time representation and converts it to number of seconds.
- *reconvert*—takes a number of seconds and converts it to a valid time expression.

Figure 14.22 shows the signature of the trait *Time*, and Fig. 14.23 shows the equations constraining its operations.

14.4
Larch/C++: A Larch Interface Specification Language for C++

An interface is the place where two independent systems meet and communicate with each other. An interface specification defines an interface between program components. Larch/C++ is a formal specification language for specifying C++ program components. A Larch/C++ specification suggests how to use C++ program modules from within C++ programs. The version of Larch/C++ discussed in this chapter is based on the work of Gary Leavens [8].

An interface specification is written from the point of view of clients who will use the module. A C++ class has three interfaces: *public, protected,* and *private*. Figure 14.24 shows the public, protected, and private interfaces for a simple module implementing a data structure for time.

A public interface is used by all clients, including subclasses, member functions of the class, and friends. A public interface of a class *Y* derived from the base class *X* under a

Time : **trait**
  includes *TotalOrder(Time), Date, Integer, Locale, Zone, String(E for E, Str for C)*
  Time **tuple of** *date:Date, hour, minute, second:Int, zone: Zone*
  DSTmethod **enumeration of** *AHEAD, BEHIND, NON*
  introduces
    current_time : → *Time*
    convert : *Time* → *Int*
    reconvert : *Int* → *Time*
    suc : *Time* → *Time*
    pred : *Time* → *Time*
    inc : *Time, Int*→ *Time*
    dec : *Time, Int* → *Time*
    max : *Time, Time* → *ime*
    min : *Time, Time* → *Time*
    ≤ : *Time, Time* → *Bool*
    ≥ : *Time, Time* → *Bool*
    makeStr : *Time, Locale* → *Str*
    makeTime : *Str, Local* → *Time*
    isValid : *Time* →*Bool*
    toZone : *Time, Zone* → *Time*
    observedDST : *Year, Zone* → *DSTmethod*
    beginDST : *Year, Zone* → *Time*
    endDST : *Year, Zone* → *Time*

Fig. 14.22   LSL trait for time—Part I

public subclass relationship includes the public members of X; however, the private and protected members of X maintain their access level in Y. For example, the public members of `display` are also the public members of `time`; however, the private and protected members of `display` maintain their access level in `time`.

If a class Y is derived from the base class X under a protected subclass relationship, then the protected interface of class Y consists of the protected members of class Y and all public and protected members of class X. This interface can be used only by member functions of the class, friends and subclasses of this class. The public and private members of `date` become protected members of time; however, the private members of date retain their access level in `time`.

If a class Y is derived from the base class X under a private subclass relationship, then the private interface of class Y consists of the private members of class Y and all the members of class X. For example, all members of class `zone` become private members of the class `time`. A private interface can be accessed by member functions and friends only.

Documenting the functions in the public interface of a C++ module provides a clean separation between the interface and the implementation of the module. Detailed design decisions can be captured by giving specifications for protected and private interfaces. For example, the specification of the protected interface is useful for programs based on subclasses. However, it is very important to specify public interfaces so that the behavior

asserts

    Time **partitioned by** *convert*

    $\forall$ *t, t_1: Time, d: Date, y: Year, h , m , s: Int, zn,zn_1: Zone*

    i : Int, locale : Locale

        isValid(current_time)

        current_time.zone == local

        isValid(t) == isValid(t.date) $\wedge$ *convert(t) > 0*

        *convert(t) == (3600 * 24 * totalDays (t.date)) + (3600 * t.hour) +*

          *(60 * t.minute) + t.second*

        reconvert(convert(t)) == t

        suc(t) == reconvert((convert(t) + 1))

        pred(t) == reconvert((convert(t) − 1))

        inc(t, i) == reconvert((convert(t) + i))

        dec(t, i) == reconvert(convert(t) − i)

        t $\geq$ *t_1 == convert(t)* $\geq$ *convert(t_1)*

        t $\leq$ *t_1 == convert(t)* $\leq$ *convert(t_1)*

        max(t, t_1) = t == t $\geq$ *t_1*

        min(t ,t_1) = t == t $\leq$ *t_1*

        toZone(t, zn_1).zone == zn_1

        toZone(toZone(t, zn), t.zone) == t

        makeTime(makeStr(t, locale), locale) == t

        (observedDST(y, zn) = AHEAD) $\Rightarrow$

          convert(beginDST(y, zn)) < convert(endDST(y,zn))

        (observedDST(y ,zn) = BEHIND) $\Rightarrow$

          convert(beginDST(y, zn)) > convert(endDST(y, zn))

        (observedDST(y, zn) = NON) $\Rightarrow$

          beginDST(y, zn) = endDST(y,z n)

implies

    $\forall$ *t : Time*

        suc (pred(t)) == t

Fig. 14.23 LSL trait for time—Part II

of public members can be understood independent of the specifications of other interfaces. Henceforth, we focus on the specification of public members.

14.4.1
Relating Larch/C++ to C++

Each Larch/C++ specification is structured similar to a C++ module. It contains the names of imported modules, traits used from the LSL tier, and specifications.

```
class time public display, protected date, private zone {
    public:
        time(int hours, int minutes, int seconds);
        int get_hour();
        int get_min();
        int get_sec();
        void display();
    protected:
        set_hour(int hours);
        set_min(int minutes);
        set_sec(int seconds);
    private:
        int hr,min,sec;
};
```

Fig. 14.24 C++ class for time

14.4.1.1
The Formal Model of Objects, Values and States

A C++ object is a region of storage or a reference to a storage location. Every object has an identifier corresponding to the *address* of the object. Every variable identifier has a type and is associated with a location of that type. *Values* stored in memory locations can be complex or simple, such as the integer 13 or character 'x'. Complex values can be:

- values of data structures constructed; for example, *date(2,10,1995)*.
- values of set expressions, such as *insert(3, insert(2,emptyset))*.
- values of attributes which are themselves objects or references to objects; for example *$*X$, where $*$ indicates that X is a pointer to an object.

Formal parameters passed by value in Larch/C++ are not objects; only formal parameters passed by reference are objects. Pointers passed by value are not objects, but may point to objects. An object in Larch/C++ is either mutable or a constant (immutable). Mutable objects include variables and reference parameters. Objects of sort S are referred to as Obj[S]; that is, Obj[S] is the object of sort S.

A formal model of objects in Larch/C++ has been developed by Leavens [8]. The trait *MutableObj* describes the formal model of mutable objects by adding the mutability to the trait *TypedObj*. The trait *TypedObj* handles the translation between typed objects and values, and untyped objects and values used in the trait *state*. The trait *ConstObj* gives the formal model of constant objects. Constant objects are modeled by sorts with names of the form ConstObj[T], the sort of a constant object containing abstract values of sort T. Traits of interest for Larch/C++ can be built hierarchically by including these library of traits. For example, the trait specifying a dictionary of items, where each item is a tuple of Obj[K] and Obj[V], includes *MutableObj(K)*, *MutableObj(V)*, and *Iterator(Iter[item]* **for** Iter, C, item **for** E).

States are mappings from objects to values. During execution, a program creates objects and binds values to them. A state captures the set of objects that exist at a specific point in time and their bindings. The trait *State* given by Chen [2] gives the formal model of states used in Larch/C++. It defines the sort State as a mapping between untyped objects of sort Obj and abstract values of sort Val.

14.4.1.2
Declarations and Declarators

C++ provides various kinds of declarators for every possible declaration. Larch/C++ has incorporated these declarators both in syntax and semantics. A declaration in Larch/C++ implies that the C++ module that implements the specification must have a matching declaration. There are some minor differences between the syntax of Larch/C++ for declarators and that of C++; these have been deliberately included in Larch/C++ to resolve some ambiguities in the C++ grammar.

In a declaration, a declarator defines a single object, a function or a type, giving it a name. The semantics of each declarator is described by identifying the sort associated with the variables in the declaration. For instance, when declaring a global variable of type integer Larch/C++ implicitly uses the LSL trait *Integer*. A declarator may refine an object's type using the following operators:

pointer	*
pointer to member	:: *
reference	&
array	[ ]
function	()

A variable declared globally, a formal parameter passed to a function, or a quantified variable is of a specific sort. Larch/C++ uses sort generators to automatically introduce certain auxiliary sorts for modeling some features of C++. An example of sort generator is Obj, which can be used to generate the auxiliary sort Obj[int], whose abstract values are of the sort int. Other sort generators in Larch/C++ include Ptr for pointers, Arr for arrays, and ConstObj for constructs and for functions. Tables 14.1 and 14.2 give a summary of the sorts that correspond to global variables, and formal parameters. Larch/C++ describes the semantics of these sorts using LSL traits. In these tables a term x of sort Ptr[Obj[T]] is a pointer that points to an object that contains an abstract value of sort T. To obtain the object pointed to, the operator * must be used. Therefore, *x is of the sort Obj[T]. A term x of sort Arr[Obj[T]] is an array of objects that contain abstract values of sort T. To obtain any of these objects, the operator [] and the integer index of the particular object are used. A *structure* or a *union* declared globally is an object. Since C++ parameters are passed by value (except for reference parameters), a *structure* or a *union* passed as a parameter to a function is not an object but simply a tuple of the respective fields. Thus, in Table 14.1 the sort of the global variable of type IntList is ConstObj[IntList] and in Table 14.2 the sort of the formal parameter of type IntList is Val[IntList].

Table 14.1 Sorts of global variables

Declaration	Sort of x (x is global)
T x	Obj[T]
const T x	ConstObj[T]
T & x	Obj[T]
const T & x	ConstObj[T]
T & const x	Obj[T]
T * x	Obj[Ptr[Obj[T]]]
const T * x	Obj[Ptr[ConstObj[T]]]
T * const x	ConstObj[Ptr[Obj[T]]]
T x[3]	Arr[Obj[T]]
const T x[3]	Arr[ConstObj[T]]
IntList x	ConstObj[IntList]
int x(int i)	ConstObj[cpp_function]

Table 14.2 Sorts of formal parameters

Declaration	Sort of x (x is formal parameter)
T x	T
const T x	T
T & x	Obj[T]
const T & x	ConstObj[T]
T & const x	ConstObj[T]
T * x	Ptr[Obj[T]]
const T * x	Ptr[ConstObj[T]]
T * const x	Ptr[Obj[T]]
T x[]	Ptr[Obj[T]]
const T x[]	Ptr[ConstObj[T]]
IntList x	Val[IntList]

14.4.1.3
State Functions

An object can be in an infinite number of states through its life-time. Some states may not be visible to the client of a class interface; in particular, only a limited number of states are visible. States that are not visible to a client are *internal object states*. States that are of particular interest to the class interface are:

- the *pre-state*, which maps objects to their values just before the function body is run, but after parameter passing,
- the *post-state*, which maps objects to their values at the point of returning from the function call, or signaling an exception, but before the function parameters go out of scope.

A state function must be used to obtain an object's abstract value in a particular state, provided the object is assigned a value in that state. There are four state functions in Larch/C++:

- \pre or ^ : gives the abstract value of an object in the pre-state,
- \post or ' : gives the abstract value of an object in the post-state,
- \any : gives the abstract value of an object without reference to any particular state. This state function is usually used when the object is immutable with the same abstract value in both the pre-state and the post-state.
- \obj : is used to explicitly refer to an object itself, instead of its abstract value. It is only used for emphasis.

State functions can only be applied to terms that denote objects and sorts that are either Obj[T] or ConstObj[T] for some type T. The sort of any object of type T to which has been applied one of the three state functions \pre, \post, \any is the same as the sort of the object but without the leading Obj or ConstObj sort generator. When the \any state function is applied to an object, the sort of the expression is the same as the sort of the object. For example, if the sort of x is Obj[int] then the sort of x' is int and the sort of x\ any is Obj[int].

A type in the interface layer is associated with a sort in the shared layer. The abstract values of a type are the equivalence classes of the sort with which the type is associated. For example, the types int, int[5] are mapped to sorts *Int, Arr[Int]*. However, there may be no type corresponding to a sort. For instance, there is no C++ type corresponding to the sort Obj[int].

14.4.1.4
Larch/C++ Syntax—An Example

Figure 14.25 shows a Larch/C++ interface specification for *IntSet*, a module implementing sets of integers. For each *IntSet* operation, the specification consists of a *header* and a *body*. The header specifies the name of the operation, the names and types of parameters, as well as the return type; it uses the same notation as used in C++. The body of the specification consists of an **ensures** clause as well as optional **requires** and **modifies** clauses. We discuss the body of the specification in the next section.

The link between the *IntSet* interface specification and the LSL tier specification for *SetTrait* is indicated by the clause **uses** *SetTrait (IntSet* **for** *Set, int* **for** *E)*. The trait used in *IntSet* provides the names and meanings of the operators *emptyset, insert, delete, unionn, member*, and *subset* as well as the meaning of the equality symbol, '=', which are referred to in the pre- and post-states of the operations of *IntSet*. The **uses** clause also specifies the *type* to *sort* mapping which indicates which abstract values over which the objects involved in the specification range. For example, the abstract values of *IntSet* objects are represented by terms of the sort *Set*. In summary, the **uses** clause defines the mapping from interface types to LSL sorts; the interface specification is written based on types and values; the used trait gives the names and meanings of the operators referred to in the interface specifications, thus providing meaning to values.

Fig. 14.25 Larch/C++
specification for integer set

```
class IntSet
{
        uses SetTrait(IntSet for S, int for E);
public:
        IntSet( ) {
                modifies self;
                ensures self' = emptyset;
        }
        ~IntSet( ) {
                modifies self;
                ensures trashed(self);
        }
        void add(int i) {
                modifies self;
                ensures self' = insert(i, self^);
        }
        void remove(int i) {
                requires member(i, self^);
                modifies self;
                ensures self' = delete(i, self^);
        }
        IntSet* unionn(IntSet* pS) {
                ensures (*result) = unionn(self^, (*pS)^);
        }
        bool isIn(int x) {
                ensures result = member(x, self^);
        }
};
```

14.4.2
Function Specification

The specification of a function in the interface documents its behavior. This can be under-stood without reference to other functions in the interface. The body of a function consists of a number of clauses. Most function specifications contain **requires, modifies**, and **en-sures** clauses. Other clauses are discussed in the next section.

The **requires** clause defines constraints on the state and parameters at the instance of function invocation. From the point of view of clients, a function must be invoked only when the program state satisfies the predicate in the **requires** clause. Otherwise, the be-havior of the function is unconstrained. The **modifies** and **ensures** clauses state the behav-ior of the function when it is invoked properly. If a function is called when the program state satisfies the predicate in the **requires** clause, the function will terminate in a state that satisfies the predicate in the **ensures** clause. Moreover, the program is allowed to change only those visible objects listed in the **modifies** clause. Thus, the behavior of a function is described relative to two states: the state before the function is entered, called the *pre-state*, and the state after the function returns, called the *post-state*. A **requires** clause refers to variables in the pre-state. An **ensures** clause may refer to variables in both the pre- and the post-state. The **modifies** clause states that no location visible to the user other than those listed in the **modifies** clause may be changed. All these clauses in the function specification are optional. Omitting either the **requires** or the **ensures** clause is equivalent to including the predicate *true* in the corresponding clause. If there is no **modifies** clause, then nothing visible to the client may be changed.

When a client wants to use the program module implementing a function, then it is the responsibility of the client to make the **requires** clause true in its pre-state. Once this is done, the client may assume the behavior as expressed in the **ensures** and **modifies** clauses upon termination of the function. The implementation must ensure that this behavior is achieved.

In Fig. 14.25, the identifier *self* denotes the object which receives the message corresponding to the specified method. The operations *add* and *remove* are allowed to change the state of an *IntSet* object, but the operations *unionn* and *isIn* are not. The predicate in **requires** clause of the *remove* procedure states that the set object from which the integer *i* should be deleted must contain it. The names and meaning of the operators in **requires** and **ensures** clauses come from the LSL trait *SetTrait*.

It is important to note the following points about a Larch/C++ interface specification:

1. The keyword *self* is a shorthand for *(*(this/any))*, which is dereferencing the pointer value of *this* in some visible state. The state function *any* stands for either the *pre* or the *post* state. In C++, *this* represents a pointer to the receiving object, so that

   $$self = ((*this/any))$$

   is a name representing a pointer to the receiving object itself in some visible state. The keyword *self* can be used only in specifications of member functions.
2. A distinction is made between an object and its value. An identifier, such as x denotes an object. A superscripted object identifier such as x' or $x^\wedge$ denotes a value of x: x' denotes the value of x in a post-state, and $x^\wedge$ denotes the value of x in a pre-state. Thus, the assertion $self' = self^\wedge$ says that the value of object self is not changed by the operation.
3. The **modifies** clause specifies which objects are changed. The changes are asserted in the **ensures** clause.
4. Modules defining abstract data type have constructor and destructor functions. For module *IntSet*, these are *IntSet()* and *~IntSet()*, respectively. The constructor function creates an instance of the abstract data type. The destructor function deallocates the storage space associated with the instance of the abstract data type.
5. The keyword *result* denotes the result of a function call. The type of function *unionn* is a pointer to an *IntSet* object. The argument to the function is a pointer *pS* to object *IntSet*. The predicate in the **ensures** clause asserts the union as defined by the LSL trait operator *unionn* to be an object whose pointer is *result*. The keyword *result* cannot be used in functions with return type *void*.

```
typedef int *ratl;
ratl make_ratl(int num, int den)
    requires den ≠ 0;
    ensures assigned(result, post)∧ size(locs(result))= 2 ∧
    (result[0])' = n ∧ (result[1])' = d ∧
    fresh(result[0], result[1]);
```

Fig. 14.26 Use of `fresh` in Larch/C++

14.4.3
Additional Function Specification Features

Keywords recently added to Larch/C++ include `allocated`, `assigned`, and `fresh`. The keyword `allocated` can be used in a predicate for the `requires` and `ensures` clauses, in order to specify that an object is allocated at a certain state. An object can be defined without being allocated. The keyword `assigned` can be used in a predicate for the `requires` and `ensures` clauses, in order to specify that an object has a well-defined value. The keyword `fresh` can only appear within a predicate of an `ensures` clause; it is used to specify that an object was not allocated in the pre-state, and it is allocated in the post-state. The example in Fig. 14.26 illustrates the use of `fresh` in function specifications. Several new clauses have been added lately to Larch/C++. Some of these allow recording implementation design decisions, and some others provide notational convenience.

The **constructs** clause is equivalent of the **modifies** clause. Larch/C++ provides this clause for reading convenience. The clause is used in constructor functions in order to express that an object is not only modified but there is memory allocated for it, and its attributes are initialized.

The **trashes** clause is used for any function that trashes objects. In Larch/C++ the trashing of an object is done whenever the object was assigned in the pre-state and not assigned in the post-state, or when the object was allocated in the pre-state and not allocated in the post-state. The **trashes** clause lists a set of objects that may be trashed from the function.

The **claims** clause contains a predicate which does not affect the meaning of a function specification, but rather describes redundant properties which can be checked by a theorem prover. This is quite similar to the **implies** clause in LSL tier.

The **let** clause can appear in any function specification. It can be used in order to abbreviate expressions that will be used many times in the function specification, in the **requires**, **ensures, example** clauses. The example in Fig. 14.27 illustrates the use of these clauses.

14.5
Proofs in LSL

All assertions stated in the **implies** and **converts** clauses of a trait require proof. When specifications are composed, the resulting specification must be consistent. The various

```
void student_account (& gpa g);
    requires assigned(a, pre) ∧ allocated(g,pre);
    modifies g;
    trashes a;
    ensures
    let new = cumulative(g) in
    if new < 2.5 then trashed(a) else set_gpa(a ^, a^.new);
    claims new > 2.5 ⇒¬ isTrashed(a, pre, post);
```

Fig. 14.27 Use of allocated, assigned, trashed, let and claims in Larch/C++

proof obligations, proof methods, and the features of LP, the Larch Prover are briefly outlined in this section.

14.5.1
Proof Obligations

In general, an LSL specification T consists of a hierarchy of traits. The hierarchy is formed by the **includes** and **assumes** relationships on the traits. These relationships are irreflexive, and transitive. If the **implies** clause of a trait T mentions a trait S, then T implies S, and T cannot transitively include S. Consequently,

- the *assertions* of T consist of the equations in the **asserts** clause of T and those of the traits transitively included in it;
- the *assumptions* of T are those transitively assumed by it;
- the *axioms* of T consist of its assertions and its assumptions;
- the *theory* of T consists of the logical consequence of its axioms.

As mentioned earlier, the **generated by** clause of the **asserts** section adds induction rules, and the **partitioned by** clause of the **asserts** section adds deduction rules. The claims made in the **implies**, and **converts** clauses of an LSL trait require proof obligations. The assertions made in the **implies** clause must follow from the stated axioms. The **converts** clause must follow from its axioms, assertions in its **implies** clause, and the **implies** clauses of the included traits and implied traits.

   The proof techniques for LSL traits include natural deduction method and proof by implication, both discussed in Chap. 10, and proof by structural induction discussed in Chap. 9. The proofs can be developed using LP, the Larch Prover, which has several built-in proof strategies. Below, we demonstrate how to develop a proof for the specifications given in Sect. 14.2.1. The proof steps are not strictly formal.

Example 1 The **implies** clause in the trait *Poset*(T) shown in Fig. 14.4 consists of the two assertions

$x \leq y \wedge y \leq z \Rightarrow x \leq z$
Preorder($\leq$ **for** $\diamond$)

The proof steps for the first claim are:

$$x \leq y == x < y \vee x = y, \qquad\qquad\qquad\qquad \textit{from equation (6)}$$
$$y \leq z == y < z \vee y = z, \qquad\qquad\qquad\qquad \textit{from equation (6)}$$
$$x \leq y \wedge y \leq z \equiv [(x < y \wedge y < z) \vee (x = y \wedge y < z)]$$
$$\vee [(x < y \wedge y = z) \vee (x = y) \wedge y = z)] \quad \textit{distributive law}$$
$$\equiv (x < z \vee x < z) \vee (x < z \vee x = z) \qquad \textit{equation (4)}$$
$$\equiv (x < z \vee x = z) \qquad\qquad\qquad\qquad \textit{idempotent}$$
$$\equiv x \leq z$$

To prove the second claim, we write the axioms after ignoring the operator $<$ from the specification $Poset(T)$:

$$x \leq x$$

$$x \leq y \wedge y \leq x == x = y$$

Substituting $\diamond$ for $\leq$ in the above assertions and in the implication, we get the assertions

$$x \diamond x$$

$$x \diamond y \wedge y \diamond x == x = y$$

$$x \diamond y \wedge y \diamond z \Rightarrow x \diamond z$$

Hence, $Poset(T, \leq) \Rightarrow Preorder(\leq, T)$; that is, if $\leq$ is a partial order on T, then $\leq$ is also a preordering on T. $\Box$

Example 2 The claim that S is **partitioned by** $subset$ is made in the **implies** clause of the trait *SetTrait*. To prove this claim, we must show that two sets S and T are equal if they have the same subsets. Formally stated, it is required to prove the following assertion

$$\forall X \bullet X \subseteq S \wedge X \subseteq T \Rightarrow S = T$$

Let X, S and T denote nonempty sets. Use the fact that *insert* is a generator of *SetTrait* to rewrite the left-hand side of the assertion to obtain

$$subset(insert(e, X'), S) \wedge subset(insert(e, X'), T)$$

Using equation (6) of *SetTrait* we rewrite as

$$member(e, S) \wedge subset(X', S) \wedge member(e, T) \wedge subset(X', T)$$

From this we infer that $member(e, S)$, $member(e, T)$, $subset(X', S)$, and $subset(X', T)$ are true. Continuing with the above two rewriting steps for an element of the set X', and repeating until all the elements of X are accounted, the assertion to be proved can be rewritten as

$$\forall e : X \bullet (member(e, S) == member(e, T)) \Rightarrow S = T$$

This result has already been proved in Sect. 14.2.2. This completes the proof.

Notice that in the first step of the proof it is shown that

$$subset(s, t) \Rightarrow (member(x, s) \Rightarrow member(x, t))$$

which is another claim made in the **implies** clause of *SetTrait*. $\Box$

The **implies** clause of a trait may include a **generated by** clause, in which case a proof is required to show that the set of elements generated by the given operators in the **generated by** clause contains all the elements of the sort. We use induction on the set of generators defined in the **generated by** clause of the trait. For example, we may introduce { } as a unary operator in *SetTrait* with the signature

$$\{\} : E \rightarrow S$$

and an equation

$$\{e\} == insert(e, \{\}).$$

The operator constructs a singleton set for every element from E. The claim

    generated by{ }, *emptyset, unionn*

can be included in the **implies** clause of the trait *SetTrait*. The proof of this claim is left as an exercise.

14.5.2
LP, the Larch Prover

Larch Prover (LP) [6] is a theorem prover for a subset of multi-sorted first-order logic. The basis for proofs in LP is a logical system, consisting of a set of operators, the properties the operators are axiomatized by equations, rewrite rules, operator theories, induction rules, and deduction rules. LP is intended as an interactive proof assistant rather than an automatic theorem prover. LP is designed with the assumption that initial attempts to state a theorem correctly, and to prove it usually fails. As a result, LP provides useful information about the reasons for the failure of a proof. This feature of LP is especially important when used for verification of properties not explicitly stated in the **implies** clause.

14.5.2.1
LP theories

The basis for proofs in LP is a logical system consisting of a set of operators, the properties of which are axiomatized by equations, rewrite rules, operator theories, induction rules, and deduction rules. Each axiom of LP has two semantics, a definitional semantics in first-order logic and an operational semantics that is sound with respect to the definitional semantics but not necessarily complete.

LP sort, operator and variable declarations are semantically the same as those of LSL. LP has built-in sort *Bool*, as well as the operators *true, false, if, not,* =, &*(and)*, |*(or)*, => *(implies)*, and <=> *(if and only if)*. During a proof, LP can generate local variables, constants, and operators.

A term in multi-sorted first-order logic consists of either a variable or an operator with a sequence of terms as arguments. The number of arguments in a term and their sorts agree with the declaration of the operator.

Equations The LP theory consists of equations. An equational theory as defined in Sect. 14.2.1, is a theory axiomatized by a set of equations. The set of terms constructed from a set of variables and operators is called *a free-word algebra* or *term algebra*. A set S of equations defines a congruence relation on a term algebra. This is the smallest relation containing the equations in S and that is closed under reflexivity, symmetry, transitivity, instantiation of free variables, and substitution of terms by their equals. An equation $t_1 == t_2$ is in the equational theory of S , or is an equational consequence of S, if t_1 is congruent to t_2. The notion of congruence is related to reduction to canonical forms and equality of such reduced terms.

Rewrite Rules LP inference mechanisms requires that equations are oriented into rewrite rules. The logical meaning of the rewrite rules is identical to that of equations; however, the operational behavior is different. A rewrite rule is an ordered pair *(u, v)* of terms, usually written as $u \rightarrow v$, such that u is not a variable and that every variable that occurs in v also occurs in u. A *rewriting system* is a set of rewrite rules. LP orients equations into rewrite rules and uses these rules to reduce terms to *normal* forms.

Informally, starting from a rewrite rule $u \rightarrow v$ and a substitution q that matches u to a subterm w of t, we can replace w by $q(v)$ to reduce t to a new term t'. This reduction process, starting with some term t, can continue until no more reduction is possible. A term t is *irreducible* if there is no term t' to which it can be reduced using the rewrite rules; an irreducible term is in normal form.

A term can have many different normal forms; a term with only one normal form, is a *canonical* term. It is usually essential that the rewriting system is terminating. Although in general it is undecidable whether the set of rewrite rules is terminating, LP provides mechanisms that orient sets of the equations into the terminating rewrite system. A terminating rewrite system in which all terms have a canonical form is said to be *convergent*. If a rewrite system is convergent, its rewriting theory, that is, the equations that can be proved by reducing them to identities, is identical to its equational theory. Most rewriting systems are not convergent. In these systems, the rewriting theory is a proper subset of the equational theory.

Operator Theories Some equations cannot be oriented into terminating rewrite rules; these are associativity and commutativity statements. For example, attempting to orient commutativity equation $a + b == b + a$ into rewrite rules will produce non-terminating system:

$$a + b \rightarrow b + a;$$
$$b + a \rightarrow a + b.$$

To avoid this LP uses *equational term-rewriting* to match and unify terms modulo associativity and commutativity. In equational term-rewriting, a substitution q matches $t1$ and $t2$ modulo a set S of equations if $q(t1) = t2$ is in the equational theory of S. For example, if $+$ is associative and commutative, the rewrite rule $a * b \rightarrow c$ will reduce the term $a * c * b$ to $c * c$.

Inductive Rules Inductive rules increase the number of theories that can be axiomatized using a finite set of assertions. Their syntax and semantics are similar to those of the inductive statements in LSL. An example is *Set* **generated by** *emptyset, insert*. The equation

$$delete(insert(s, e), e) == s$$

in *SetTrait* (see Fig. 14.1) produces an infinite number of equations:

$$delete(insert(emptyset, e), e) == new);$$

$$delete(insert(insert(emptyset, b), e), e) == insert(emptyset, b) \dots$$

Thus, **generated by** clause is equivalent to the infinite set of first-order formulas:

$$(E[emptyset] \wedge (\forall s : Set, b : element)(E[s] \Rightarrow E(insert(s, b)))) \Rightarrow$$

$$(\forall s : Set) \bullet E[s],$$

for any well-formed equation E.

Deduction Rules LP uses deduction rules to deduce new equations from existing equations and rewrite rules. LP produces deduction rules from the LSL **partitioned by** clause. For example, LSL statement *Stack* **partitioned by** *isEmpty, top, pop* is reflected in LP theory as

assert when
top(s1) == top(s2),
pop(s1) == pop(s2),
isEmpty(s1) == isEmpty(s2)
yield *s1 == s2*

14.5.2.2
Proof Methods

LP provides mechanisms for proving theorems using both forward and backward inference. Forward inferences produce consequences from a logical system; backward inferences produce a set of subgoals from a goal whose proof will suffice to establish a conjecture.

Normalization Whenever a new rewrite rule is added to its logical system, LP normalizes all equations, rewrite rules, and deduction rules all over again. If an equation or rewrite rule normalizes to an identity, it is discarded. LP uses normalization in forward inference. If a new conjecture is to be proved, LP tries to normalize it to an identity. If successful, the conjecture is proved by normalization; this action is a backward inference applying normalization.

Critical-Pair Equations   A common problem arises when a set of equations is oriented into a rewriting system which is not convergent, and hence, there is more than one way to normalize the logical system. Thus reduction to normal form does not provide a decision procedure for the equational theory. As a consequence, LP can fail, for example, to reduce term v and term u to the same normal form, even if v and u are reducible. The **critical-pair** command provides a method of extending the rewriting theory to approximate its equational theory more closely. Each critical-pair equation captures a way in which a pair of rewrite rules might be used to reduce a single term in two different ways. For example, critical-pair equation between $(x * y) * z \to x * (y * z)$ and $i(w) * w \to e$ produces $e * z == i(y) * (y * z)$, when the substitution $\{i(y)|x, y|w\}$ unifies $i(w) * w$ with subterm of $(x * y) * z$.

Instantiation   Explicit instantiation of variables in equations, rewrite rules, and deduction rules may lead to establishing that the conjecture is an identity. For example, to establish the identity of the theorem $x == x \cup x$ in a logical system that contains the deduction rule

  when $(\forall e)e \in x == e \in y$ **yield** $x == y$

and the rewrite rule

  $e \in (x \cup y) \to e \in x | e \in y,$

we instantiate y by $x \cup x$ in the deduction rule.

Proof by Case   A conjecture can often be simplified by dividing a proof into cases. When a conjecture reduces to an identity in all cases, it is a theorem. For example, the command **prove** $0 < f(c)$ by case $c = 0$, will make LP to consider three cases: $c = 0$, $c < 0$, and $c > 0$. If in all three cases the conjecture is true, then it is a theorem.

Proof by Induction   A proof by induction is based on the induction rules. The command **prove** e **by induction on** x **using** IR directs LP to prove the equation e by induction on variable x using the induction rule IR. LP generates subgoals for the basic and inductive steps in a proof by induction as follows. The basic subgoals involve the equations that result from substituting the basic generators of IR for x in e. Basis generators are those with no variables of the sort of x. Induction subgoals generate one or more hypotheses by substituting one or more new constants for x in e. Each induction subgoal involves proving an equation that results from substituting a non-basic generator of IR for x in e. For example, consider an induction proof over the sort Nat:

  prove $i \le j => i \le (j + k)$ **by induction on** j

  Conjecture $lemma.1$: Subgoals for proof by induction on 'j'
  Basis subgoal:
      $lemma.1.1 : (i < 0) => (i < (0 + k)) == true$
  Induction constant: jc
  Induction hypothesis:
      $lemma.InductHyp.1 : (i < jc) => (i < (jc + k)) == true$
  Induction subgoal:
      $lemma.1.2 : (i < s(jc)) => (i < (s(jc) + k))) == true$

Proof by Implication The command **prove** $t1 \Rightarrow t2$ **by** $\Rightarrow$ directs LP to prove the subgoal t'2 using the hypothesis $t'1 == true$. In general t'1=t1 and t'2 =t2, but in some cases LP has to generate new constants instead of variables in t1 and t2 to form t'1 and t'2 and preserves the soundness of proof. For example: Given the axioms $a \Rightarrow b \rightarrow true$ and $b \Rightarrow c \rightarrow true$, the command **prove** $a \Rightarrow c$ **by** $\Rightarrow$ uses the hypothesis $a \rightarrow true$ to normalize the axiom and to reduce it to identity.

14.6
Case Study—Two Examples from Rogue Wave Library

Rogue Wave Tools.h++ class library [10] is a rich, robust and versatile C++ foundation class library of industrial standard. The library classes are well-structured, well-documented and are usable in isolation.

Tools.h++ consists of a large set of C++ classes that are usable in isolation independent of other classes. The set consists of simple classes, such as date, zone, time, and string, and three families of collection classes, namely collection classes based on templates, collection classes that use preprocessor facilities, and "Smalltalk-like" classes for heterogeneous collections. The library also consists of a set of abstract data types, and corresponding specialized classes that provide a framework for persistence, localization, and other issues. All collection classes have a corresponding iterator.

RWZone is a simple Rogue Wave abstract base class, whose operations are imported into *RWDate* and *RWTime*. We give the interface specifications for the classes *RWFile* and *RWZone* in this section.

14.6.1
RWZone Specification

RWZone is an abstract base class for user-defined zones and accommodates the necessary methods for the derived class when used with *RWTime* and *RWDate* classes. It defines an interface for issues pertaining to various time zones, such as whether or not daylight saving time is in use in a specific zone, the offset from GMT (Greenwich Meridian Time) to the time in a zone, the starting and ending dates for daylight saving time. The Rogue-Wave library provides rules for constructing zone objects for North American (NoAm), and Western Europe (WeEu). This feature is modeled as the values of an enumerated type in the specification. A class such as *RWTime*, which defines operations on time across different time zones in the world, inherits these properties.

The informal descriptions of virtual functions of RWZone abstract class are given in [10]. The basic abstractions for Greenwich time zone, *standard* and *daylight saving time* are defined in the LSL trait *Zone* shown in Fig. 14.21. Interface specification for RWZone is given in Figs. 14.28, 14.29, and 14.30. This specification is consistent with the intended purpose of the virtual functions informally described in [10], and are adequate for specifying the classes *RWTime* and *RWDate*.

14

```
typedef int Zone;
typedef int RWCString;
imports typedefs;
struct RWDaylightRule;
extern Zone local;
extern Zone standard;
enum DstRule {NoDST, NoAm, WeEu};
extern RWDaylightRule *rules[3];
enum StdZone {NewZealand = -12, Japan, Greenwich, Hawai,
        Europe, USEastern } zone;
abstract class RWZone
{
uses Zone, Time(RWBoolean for Bool), string(RWCString for C);
public:
virtual int timeZoneOffset() {
        ensures result = self^.standardOffset;
}
virtual int altZoneOffset() {
        ensures result = self^.DSTOffset;
}
virtual RWBoolean daylightObserved() {
        ensures result = daylightObserved(self^);
}
virtual RWBoolean isDaylight(const struct tm* tspec) {
        requires daylightObserved(self^) ∧ (*tspec)^.tm_wday =
            week_(day(date((*tspec).tm_day, (*tspec)^.tm_month,
                (*tspec)^.tm_year)));
        ensures ∃ t:Time (result = ( t = get((tspec*)^)) ∧
            observedDST(t.year, self^) <> NON ∧
            (observedDST(t.year, self^)= AHEAD ⇒
            (convert(t) ≥ convert(beginDST(t.year, self^)) ∧
            convert(t) ≤ convert(endDST(t.year, self^)))) ∧
            (observedDST(t.year, self^) = BEHIND ⇒
            (convert(t) ≤ convert(beginDST(t.year, self^)) ∧
            convert(t) ≥ convert(endDST(t.year, self^)))));
}
```

Fig. 14.28 Larch/C++ interface specification for RWZone—Part I

14.6.2
RWFile Specification

The class *RWFile* encapsulates binary file operations, using Standard C stream library. Since this class is intended to encapsulate operations on binary files, it is required that

```
virtual void getBeginDaylight(struct tm* tspec) {
        requires validYear((*tspec)^.tm_year);
        modifies (tspec);
        ensures ∃ t:Time((daylightObserved(self ) ⇒
                (t=beginDST((*tspec)^.tm_year, self^) ∧ (*tspec)'=fill(t))) ∧
                (¬ daylightObserved(self^) ⇒ (*tspec)'.all'< 0));
}
virtual void getEndDaylight(struct tm* tspec) {
        requires validYear((*tspec)^.tm_year);
        modifies (tspec);
        ensures ∃ t:Time((daylightObserved(self ) ⇒
                (t=endDST((*tspec)^.tm_year, self^) ∧ (*tspec)'=fill(t))) ∧
                (¬ daylightObserved(self^) ⇒ (*tspec)'.all'< 0));
}
virtual RWCString timeZoneName() {
        ensures result=self^.standardName;
}
virtual RWCString altZoneName() {
        ensures result=self^.DSTName;
}
static const RWZone& local() {
        ensures result=local;
}
static const RWZone& standard() {
        ensures result=standard;
}
static const RWZone& utc() {
        ensures result=utc;
}
static const RWZone& local(const RWZone* zn) {
        modifies local;
        ensures local'=(*zn)^;
}
```

Fig. 14.29 Larch/C++ interface specification for RWZone—Part II

the file be opened in a binary mode. An adequate formal model is to specify a file as a
sequence of bytes. The memory copy of a file is captured by *Open_file*, whereas the disk
copy of the file is considered as a global structure. The specification models the memory
copy to be identical to the disk copy when the file is opened. Proper encapsulation in the
class hides the logic of file creation. Different data structures are used to write and read
a file. Since LSL is strongly typed, explicit type casting from a sequence of bytes to the
target type and vice versa is needed. To improve readability of specification parameterized
function is used. The LSL trait *File* shown in Fig. 14.13 introduces and defines all the

14

$$static\ const\ RWZone\&\ standard(const\ RWZone*\ zn)\ \{$$
$$\quad\quad \textbf{modifies}\ standard;$$
$$\quad\quad \textbf{ensures}\ standard' = (*zn)\,\char94;$$
$$\}$$
$$static\ const\ RWDaylightRule*\ dstRule(DstRule\ x = NoAm)\ \{$$
$$\quad\quad \textbf{ensures}\ result = rules[x];$$
$$\}$$

Fig. 14.30   Larch/C++ interface specification for RWZone—Part III

abstract operators. The interface specification for *RWFile* is shown in Figs. 14.31, 14.32, 14.33, and 14.34.

14.7
Exercises

In the following exercises, use the traits defined in this chapter wherever possible.

1. Give an LSL theory for finite directed line segments. A directed line segment is a *vector*, with a *position* and a *direction*. Include operations so that (i) two vectors can be compared; (ii) the position and orientation of a vector may be obtained; (iii) a vector may be translated to a new position while maintaining its orientation; and (iv) the inner product of two vectors can be calculated. Define simple traits and compose them to construct a trait for directed line segments.
2. Define an LSL theory for triangles; it should include the theory of vectors defined in Question 1. Include an operation for moving a triangle to a new position without changing the orientation of its sides. Derive specialized theories for (i) right-angled triangles; (ii) equilateral triangles; and (iii) isosceles triangles.
3. Give a Larch/C++ specification of the C++ class `Triangle`, which uses the traits developed in Question 2.
4. Enrich the theory of *Rational* given in Sect. 14.2.7 by adding the arithmetic operators $+$, and $*$ for rational numbers. Provide a sufficient number of equations.
5. Prove the claims made in the **implies** clause of the following LSL traits:
   (a) *Rational* shown in Fig. 14.8.
   (b) *NStackTrait* shown in Fig. 14.7.
   (c) *String* shown in Fig. 14.12.
   (d) *File* shown in Fig. 14.13
6. Use the traits discussed in Sect. 14.3 to construct the following Larch traits:
   (a) The trait *DictIterObj* specifies iterators for dictionaries. An item in the dictionary is an ordered pair *Obj[K], Obj[V]*. Include operations for (i) advancing the iterator to the next position where an item whose key matches the given key is found; and (ii) advancing the iterator to the next position where an item equal to the given item is found.

---

typedef unsigned size_t;
typedef char* String;
enum MODE { READ, WRITE, READ_WRITE};
struct Mode {MODE create_mode; MODE open_mode};
typedef int RWBoolean;
class RWFile
{
uses *File(RWFile for OpenFile,String for Name), Types(char for S);*
public:
RWFile(const char* filename, const char* mode = 0) {
        modifies *self;*
        ensures if *mode = 0*
            then ∃ *f: File, of: OpenFile*
                if *f.name=filename* ∧ *of=open(f, READ_WRITE) ∧¬ error(of)*
                then *self' = of*
                else *self' = open(create(filename,*
                    READ_WRITE),READ_WRITE))
            else *self'=open(create(filename, create_mode), open_mode);*
    }
RWFile() {
        modifies *self;*
        ensures *trashed(flush(self^));*
    }
long CurOffset() {
        ensures *result = self^.fpointer;*
    }
RWBoolean Eof() {
        ensures *result = (self^.fpointer = len(self^.date));*
    }
RWBoolean Erase() {
        modifies *self;*
        ensures *self'.data = empty* ∧ *result= ¬ error(self');*
    }
RWBoolean Error() {
        ensures *result = error(self^);*
    }

Fig. 14.31 Larch/C++ interface specification for RWFile—Part I

(b) The trait *crypt* encrypts a string to another string such that no two different strings have the same image.

(c) The trait *filecrypt*, which includes the *file* and *crypt* traits, creates an encrypted copy on disk of a given disk file.

```
RWBoolean Exists() {
        ensures ∃ file:File, name:Name, mode:Mode
            (result = ((self^= open(file, mode)) ∧
                file = create(name, READ_WRITE)));

}
RWBoolean Flush() {
        ensures result = ¬ error(flush(self^));

}
const char* GetName() {
        ensures result' = self^.file.name;

}
RWBoolean ISEmpty() {
        ensures result = (self^.data = empty);

}
RWBoolean isValid() const {
        ensures ∃ f:File, m:Mode (result = (self^= open(f, m)));

}
RWBoolean Read(char& c) {
        requires (len(self^.data) - self^.fpointer ≥ len(toByte(c^)));
        modifies self.fpointer, c;
        ensures result = ¬ error(self') ∧
            (result ⇒ (toByte(c')= read(self^, len(toByte(c^)), self^.fpointer)));

}
RWBoolean Read(char* i, size_t count) {
        requires len(self^.data) - self^.fpointer ≥ count*len(toByte((*i)^))
            ∧ maxIndex(i)+1 ≥ count;
        modifies self.fpointer, *i;
        ensures result = ¬ error(self') ∧∀ ind:Int(¬ error(self')
            ∧ ind ≥ 0 ∧ ind ≤ count ⇒ toByte((*(i+ind))') =
            read(self^, len(toByte((*string)^)), self^.fpointer +
                ind * len(toByte((*i)^)))));

}
```

Fig. 14.32 Larch/C++ interface specification for RWFile—Part II

7. Give a Larch/C++ specification of the C++ class `Intstack`, which uses the *StackTrait* given in Fig. 14.5.

8. Give Larch/C++ specifications for the following C++ classes:
   (a) The class `IntDate` has the following constructors and member functions:
      (i) `IntDate(unsigned day, unsigned year)`—constructs a date with the given day of the year and the given year.
      (ii) `IntDate(unsigned day, char* month, unsigned year, const locale)`—constructs a date with the given day of the month, the given month and the given year. The locale argument is used to convert the month name.

RWBoolean Read(char string) {*
    requires $\exists\, l: int(nullTerminated(substring(self^\wedge, self^\wedge.fpointer, l)))$
        $\wedge\ (maxIndex(string)+1 \geq l*len((*string)^\wedge));$
    modifies *self.fpointer, *string;*
    ensures $result = \neg\ error(self') \wedge$
        $\forall\ ind:Int(ind \geq 0 \wedge ind \leq l \wedge result \Rightarrow$
            $toByte((*(string + ind))')=$
                $read(self^\wedge, len(toByte((*string)^\wedge)),$
                      $self^\wedge.fpointer + ind*len((*string)^\wedge)));$
    }
RWBoolean SeekTo(long offset) {
    modifies *self.fpointer;*
    ensures $result=(self'.fpointer=offset);$
    }
RWBoolean SeekToBegin( ) {
    modifies *self.fpointer;*
    ensures $result=(self'.fpointer = 1);$
    }
RWBoolean SeekToEnd( ) {
    modifies *self.fpointer;*
    ensures $result=(self'.fpointer=len(self^\wedge));$
    }
RWBoolean Write(char i) {
    requires $\exists\, f:File\ (self^\wedge = open(f, WRITE) \vee$
        $self^\wedge = open(f, READ\_WRITE));$
    modifies *self;*
    ensures $result = \neg\ error(self') \wedge (\neg\ error(self') \Rightarrow$
        $self' = write(self^\wedge, toByte(i), self^\wedge.fpointer));$
    }
RWBoolean Write(char i, size_t count) {*
    requires $maxIndex(i)+1 \geq count \wedge$
        $\exists\, f:File\ (self^\wedge = open(f, WRITE) \vee$
        $self^\wedge = open(f, READ\_WRITE));$
    modifies *self;*
    ensures $result = \neg\ error(self') \wedge (result \Rightarrow$
        $\forall\ ind:int((ind \geq 0) \wedge (ind \leq count) \wedge toByte((*(i+ind))^\wedge)=$
            $read(self',len(toByte((*i)^\wedge)),$
                $self^\wedge.fpointer + ind * len(toByte((*i)^\wedge)))));$
    }

Fig. 14.33 Larch/C++ interface specification for RWFile—Part III

(iii) IntDate(const IntTime& t, const IntZone& zone=
LocalZone)—constructs a date from a time and zone in IntTime.

```
RWBoolean Write(const char* string) {
        requires ∃ f:File ( (self^= open (f, WRITE) ∨
              self^= open(f, READ_WRITE)) ∧
              (∃ l: int (nullTerminated(prefix((*string)^, l)))));
        modifies self;
        ensures result= ¬ error(self') wedge
              ∀ ind:Int (ind>=0 ∧ ind≤l ∧
              result ⇒ toByte((*(string + ind))^) =
                    read(self',len(toByte((*string)^)),
                         self^.fpointer + ind*len((*string)^)));
}
RWBoolean Exists(const char* filename) {
        ensures ∃ f:File(result =
              (filename = f.name ∧ file=create(filename, READ_WRITE)));
}
```

Fig. 14.34   Larch/C++ interface specification for RWFile—Part IV

(iv) between(const IntDate& a, const IntDate& b) const—returns true if *this* IntDate is between a and b.

(v) previous(const char* dayName,   const Locale&locale= LocalFormat) const—returns the date of the previous dayName, for example, the date of the previous Saturday. The weekday name is interpreted according to the local conventions in Locale.

(vi) leapyear(unsigned year)—returns true if a given year is a leap year.

(vii) firstdayofmonth(unsigned month)—returns the day of the year corresponding to the first day of the month in this IntDate's year.

(a) The class IntTime has the following constructors and member functions:

(i) IntTime(unsigned long x)—constructs a time with x seconds since *00:00:00 January 1, 1901 UTC.*

(ii) IntTime(unsigned date,   unsigned hour = 0,   unsigned minute = 0,   unsigned second = 0,   const RWZone& local)—constructs the time for the given date, hour, minute, and second, relative to the time zone local, which defaults to local time.

(iii) compare(const IntTime* t)—returns 0 if self ==*t, returns 1 if self > *t, and returns −1 if self < *t.

(iv) isDST(const RWZone& zone=local) const—returns true if self is during Daylight Saving Time in the time zone given by zone, false otherwise.

(v) beginDST(unsigned year,   const RWZone&zone=local)— returns the start of Daylight Savings Time for the given year in the given time zone. Returns a message if DST is not observed in that time zone in that year.

(vi) seconds() const—returns the number of seconds since *00:00:00 January 1, 1901.*

9. The topology of a communication network may be abstracted as a directed graph with a finite number of nodes and links; the network is connected. Typical operations on the network include (i) adding a link between nodes; (ii) adding a node and linking it to some node in the network; (iii) deleting a node in the network; and (iv) deleting a link in the network. Deletions must preserve the connectedness property. Write a Larch/C++ interface specification which provides these functionalities. Define a mathematical model of the network in the LSL layer, and use it in the interface specification. Hint: See Network example in Chap. 16.

14.8
Bibliographic Notes

The Larch family of languages originated from the works of Wing [11, 12], and Guttag and Horning [6]. A specifier can design theories by using and composing the theories in the mathematical toolkit provided by Guttag and Horning [6]. LP, the Larch Prover provides an interactive verification support for checking properties of LSL traits. There are several interface specification languages, each tailored to a specific programming language. Larch/C++ was designed by Gary Leavens [8].

In a Larch/C++ interface specification, implementation design details that are tailored to the C++ programming language can be specified. This feature makes Larch/C++ suitable for industrial applications, where black-box specifications of C++ classes can enhance their effective reuse. Larch/C++ interface specifications for several classes taken from Rogue Wave *tools.h++* [10] can be found in Alagar et al. [1]. The report summarizes the incompleteness of informal class descriptions in Rogue Wave Library, and the experience gained in understanding and writing the interface specifications and the corresponding LSL traits.

A classified Larch bibliography can be found at the Larch home page: http://larch.lcs.mit.edu:8001/larch/index.html

References

1. Alagar VS, Colagrosso P, Loukas A, Narayanan S, Protopsaltou A (1996) Formal specifications for effective black-box reuse. Technical reports (2 volumes), Department of Computer Science, Concordia University, Montreal, Canada, February 1996
2. Chen J (1989) The Larch/Generic interface language. SB thesis, Department of Electrical Engineering and Computer Science, Massachusettes Institute of Technology
3. Cheon Y (1991) Larch/Smalltalk: a specification language for Smalltalk. MSc thesis, Department of Computer Science, Iowa State University
4. Colagrosso P (1993) Formal specification of C++ class interfaces for software reuse. M Comp Sci thesis, Department of Computer Science, Concordia University, Montreal, Canada
5. Guaspari D, Marceau C, Polak W (1990) Formal verification of Ada programs. IEEE Trans Softw Eng 16(9):1058–1075
6. Guttag JV, Horning JJ (1993) Larch: languages and tools for formal specification. Springer, Berlin

7. Jones K (1991) LM3: a Larch interface language for Modula-3: a definition and introduction: version 1.0. Technical report 72, DEC/SRC, Digital Equipment Corporation, MA
8. Leavens GT (1997) Larch/C++ reference manual, draft: revision 5.1, February 1997
9. Leavens GT, Cheon Y (1992) Preliminary design of Larch/C++. In: Martin U, Wing J (eds) Proceedings of the first international workshop on Larch. Workshops in computer science series. Springer, Berlin
10. Rogue Wave (1993) Tools.h++ class library. Version 6.0, Rogue Wave Software
11. Wing J (1983) A two-tiered approach for specifying programs. Technical report TR_299, Massachusetts Institute of Technology, Laboratory for Computer Science
12. Wing J (1987) Writing Larch interface language specifications. ACM Trans Program Lang Syst 9(1):1–24
13. Wing J (1990) A specifier's introduction to formal methods. IEEE Comput 23(9):8–24

Calculus of Communicating Systems   15

In automata theory, a process is modeled as an automaton. In Chaps. 6 and 7, we studied automata models for simple input/output systems with some extensions. In particular we discussed interaction of systems modeled by automata in Chap. 7. We modeled compositions of simple input/output systems as well as composition of reactive systems. In the latter instance, the composition is based on communication between automata, abstracted as "shared transitions". The meaning of composed systems is understood from the behavior that can be observed. It is known to algebraists [8] that "the principle of compositionality of *meaning* requires an algebraic framework." An algebra that allows equational reasoning about automata is the algebra of regular expressions. This is true for extended finite state machine models in which the semantics of concurrency includes all transitions, including synchronous communications whenever they occur.

In Chap. 11, we discussed program graphs and transition systems to model systems with shared variables. They have the Kripke structure as basic formal domain. Since a Kripke structure can be transformed to a Büchi automaton, the algebra here is defined by the language expressions recognized by Büchi automata. Although reasoning was done by model checking which is algorithmic in nature, the underlying principle is the recognition of strings, representing behaviors, by an automata that represents a system. Given that a temporal logic specification can be transformed to a Büchi automaton, we reckon that the interaction models that we have studied so far are based on automata, and they have the basis "algebra on strings". In this chapter, we explore an algebraic specification method, called *Calculus of Communicating Systems* (CCS) for representing and reasoning about concurrent systems. CCS gives a language for introducing processes, and gives rules (axioms) for deriving terms in the language. The derivations of terms are subject to equational laws, similar to but distinct from the equational laws discussed in Chap. 13.

CCS is a *process algebra*, the term first used by Bergstra and Klop [2]. But CCS is not just an algebra, it is also a calculus. The word "process" in "Process algebra" refers to a set of actions that can be performed either sequentially or jointly, and results in a certain *behavior*. The word "algebra" in "Process algebra", denotes that an *algebraic/axiomatic* approach is to be taken. That is, in a process algebraic approach, the behavior of a process will be described algebraically by means of axioms, and a system of equations involving the terms of the algebra. Thus, process algebra is the study of algebraic specification for

V.S. Alagar, K. Periyasamy, *Specification of Software Systems*,
Texts in Computer Science,
DOI 10.1007/978-0-85729-277-3_15, © Springer-Verlag London Limited 2011

concurrent systems. The word "calculus" refers to a method of doing symbolic calculations. The calculations in CCS are purely based on axioms, and done on terms that represent program/system structures. The interpretations of the terms are done over a semantic domain.

In tracing the history of process algebra as an area of research in concurrency theory, Baeten [1] discusses the influence of the following four prominent methods.

- Petri nets [11, 12],
- CSP [6, 7],
- CCS [8, 9], and
- ACP [2].

In net theory, the basic abstraction is the concurrency relation over the *places* (conditions) and *transitions* (events) in a system. If two events are in the relation then they are *causally independent*, and may occur either simultaneously or in some sequential order. That is "simultaneous occurrence" of events is observable in Petri net model. However, in CCS only one event is observable at any moment in time.

CSP is an extension of imperative programming language in which the basic abstraction is direct communication between modules. Another abstraction in CSP is the way the global memory is organized, by forbidding a module from altering the value of a variable mentioned by another module in the system. CCS is not an imperative language, rather it is an algebraic system allowing expressions to be formed from basic terms according to a small set of axioms. CCS and CSP are quite close in handling the communication abstraction and it is expressed in similar notations.

Bergstra and Klop [2] introduced the theory of ACP in which alternative, sequential, and parallel composition of processes are axiomatically defined. ACP is closely related to CCS, but with differences in definitions, expressibility, and methodology. In CCS, axioms are derived after fixing the derivation of the agents in a model. In contrast, ACP is an axiomatic approach, in which axioms are stated and the models satisfying the axioms are studied. The three models CSP, CCS, and ACP have different kinds of communication schemes. The communication scheme in ACP is by means of actions, in CCS, communication is combined with abstraction, and in CSP, communication is combined with restriction. The main motivation to single out CCS from this group of three for its study in this chapter comes from the following characteristics of CCS.

- *Simplicity:* CCS uses a small number of basic concepts. The underlying process algebra is simple to build and easy to comprehend.
- *Expressivity:* CCS offers a richness in expression and also flexibility for manipulation.
- *Generality:* The basic mechanisms in CCS seem sufficient to represent many of the relevant concepts of concurrent computations, and build more complex mechanisms.
- *Reasoning:* The calculus enables the manipulation of terms, yielding equivalent terms. The behavior of a modeled system can be reasoned within CCS, using the notion "equivalence".

15.1
Why a Specific Calculus for Concurrency Is Necessary?

The *intension* of a program or system is in the description of its structure, and program manipulation yields a term with different intension, called its *extension*, but they have identical behaviors. We saw such a transformation in Chap. 11, while introducing modalities in logic. For sequential programs, such transformations are expressed through input/output behavior, which require function computations. In Chap. 5, we have seen that the lambda calculus is *computationally complete*, in the sense that it can express any computable function. It is the fundamental abstraction for sequential systems, in which all computations may be viewed as function computations. The interaction between sequential system objects is deterministic, which can be expressed by function composition. However, the lambda calculus is not sufficient to express concurrent computations, because they involve some aspects that are not expressible as functions. In order to convince ourselves of the need for a new calculus, let us revisit some of the concepts introduced in Chap. 11.

- *Program Interaction:* In Chap. 11, we have seen that program interaction possibilities are much richer for concurrent programs.
- *Nature of nondeterminism:* The notion of nondeterminism for concurrent systems is quite different from the one normally understood for sequential systems. Examples of nondeterministic formalisms for sequential systems include "the nondeterministic Turing machines", and "the semantics of logic languages like Prolog". A nondeterministic finite state automaton can be transformed to a finite state automaton. In algorithm analysis and complexity theory, nondeterminism serves as a tool to simplify the description of algorithms. Nondeterminism can be eliminated in algorithmic explorations by resorting to backtracking or efficient branch and bound techniques. There is no loss of computational power in removing nondeterminism. More significantly, in complexity theory it is sufficient to know the existence of a successful computation, that is, failures do not matter. In concurrent systems, nondeterminism is in the nature of "interesting things happening in the system", and cannot be and should not be avoided. Ignoring even some parts of it would mean a loss of expressive power in the nature of computable results obtained from the interacting objects. However, controlling nondeterminism is essential to ensure safety and liveness properties. By prematurely ignoring parts of nondeterminism, we may be landing in an unsafe situation. Eliminating nondeterminism in sequential systems is possible and its consequence is a loss of efficiency. However, for concurrent systems, eliminating nondeterminism is impossible, because the control is distributed and it may be undesirable because of safety, liveness, and fairness criteria. See Example 5 in Chap. 11.
- *Nature of Communication Abstraction:* In Chap. 11, we have seen different kinds of communications between modules. Depending upon the medium of communication it can be "through channel", or "through shared variable". Each kind of communication can be further specialized as "broadcasting or peer-to-peer", or "bounded/unbounded" or "ordered or unordered". The important aspects of the communication primitives that

we have seen in Chap. 11 are that they are not symmetric and need not be synchronous. In an algebraic setting and a calculus based on it, we would like to have symmetry of communication and time abstraction. Therefore there is a need to choose the right communication abstraction primitives for a calculus of concurrency.

15.2
Informal Introduction to CCS

The two key concepts in CCS are *observations* and *synchrony*. There exists a system and an observer of the system. They are independent. For the observer, the system is a *black box*, and the observer experiences the system by communicating with it. Communication is synchronous, meaning that the system and the observer "shake hands" through a message. That is, communication time is zero. A synchronous composition of the system produces a larger system in which the observer and the system being observed allow each other to be observed.

The expressions in the language of CCS are called *agents*. The agent expression for a process at any instant expresses actions performed by the process until that moment. We assume that a process can perform only a finite set of actions; however, an action can be repeatedly performed. In CCS, there are two kinds of *visible* actions, called *input* actions α, and *output* actions $'\alpha$. The third kind of action is the *internal* action (also called *silent* action) τ. Internal action is not visible.

At any moment in the system's evolution, an agent may either be idle (perform no action) or perform an action specified in it. Agent *Nil* is intended to represent a process which can do nothing. From *Nil* we can construct more interesting agents.

Action Prefix   In a nontrivial behavior expression, there is some action performed by the process. The constructor "·", called *action prefixing*, acts like concatenation operator allowing us to specify action sequencing. The action performed is written to the left of the symbol "·", and agent name that becomes after performing the action is written to the right of the symbol "·". For example, we may describe the behavior of "disposable face mask" by the expression

wear_mask · Nil

The meaning of the above expression is that the process described by it is capable initially of performing the action *wear_mask* and thereafter behaving as the process described by *Nil*. The agent expression for describing the mask that can be worn two times, instead of just once, is

wear_mask · wear_mask · Nil

The agent expression to describe the mask that can be worn k times, where k is arbitrary but finite, becomes a bit tedious to write. To describe the total behavior of a finite process, such as face mask, *Nil* is necessary. The agent expression for the behavior of a process P that can perform an action α infinitely often is

$$\alpha.P$$

Generalizing the above expression for a sequence of actions, we can write the agent expression for the behavior of the traffic light process in Example 6, Chap. 11 as

$$'red \cdot' green \cdot' yellow \cdot P \tag{15.1}$$

An important assumption in writing the above agent expression is "at the moment of starting to observe the traffic light" it is red, then it is green, then it is yellow, and then it continues to repeatedly output the actions $\langle red, green, yellow \rangle$ in the same order forever. If the traffic light was first observed to be yellow, instead of red, then the process behavior expression will be

$$'yellow \cdot' red \cdot' green \cdot P \tag{15.2}$$

The expressions in (15.1) and (15.2) are different. We can expand expressions in (15.1) and (15.2) as infinite sequences, and observe that they are identical but for a prefix of length one. This makes us believe that if we continuously observe the behavior over a long period of time the behaviors of the two agents are indistinguishable. However, the question as to whether these correspond to two *distinct* behaviors or two *similar* behaviors must be formally answered. In CCS, similarity of behavior is formally defined, which we study in Sect. 15.4.

Definition We may introduce agents by means of definitions. We can define an agent *Drop_Catch* as follows:

$$Drop\_Catch \overset{\text{def}}{=} drop\_ball \cdot Nil$$

The intended meaning is that the agent *Drop_Catch* on the left hand side of $\overset{\text{def}}{=}$ is defined to be the agent expression on the right hand side of $\overset{\text{def}}{=}$. A definition may be recursive. For example, the traffic light agent in (15.1) may be defined as in (15.3).

$$TrafficLight \overset{\text{def}}{=} 'red \cdot' green \cdot' yellow \cdot TrafficLight \tag{15.3}$$

So far, we have been looking at processes that "outputs" without receiving any input. Consider a door bell. When it is pressed it responds with a sound. The door bell process receives the input "press" and responds with "buzz" and then stays as a door bell process. The definition of the agent for this process is given in (15.4).

$$Doorbell \overset{\text{def}}{=} press \cdot' buzz \cdot Doorbell \tag{15.4}$$

Parameterizations   The input to a process, or its output, need not be a "constant" as in the preceding examples. By parameterizing process its corresponding agent becomes like a lambda expression. The parameters should be instantiated to invoke the resultant of a specific input. As an example, the expression in (15.5) has one input parameter x and the behavior of the process is to increment the input by 1.

$$Adder \stackrel{\text{def}}{=} x \cdot' (x+1) \cdot Adder \tag{15.5}$$

An advantage of definition notation is that complex agent expressions can be broken down into simpler expressions through the introduction of "placeholder agents". We can rewrite the definition in (15.5) as shown below.

$$Adder \stackrel{\text{def}}{=} x \cdot Temp$$

$$Temp \stackrel{\text{def}}{=} '(x+1) \cdot Temp$$

A process may receive several inputs before giving an output. As an example, the agent expression for a vending machine process which receives 1\$ and a request c for coffee before delivering coffee is given in (15.6).

$$VendingMachine \stackrel{\text{def}}{=} 1\$ \cdot c \cdot' deliverC \cdot VendingMachine \tag{15.6}$$

A currency changing machine, on the other hand, receives one input and returns multiple outputs. The agent expression for a currency changing process that accepts a 50\$ bill and returns two 20\$ bills and one 10\$ bill in that order is given in (15.7).

$$CurrencyChange \stackrel{\text{def}}{=} 50\$ \cdot' 20\$ \cdot' 20\$ \cdot' 10\$ \cdot CurrencyChange \tag{15.7}$$

Sum (Choice)   Suppose a currency changing machine has two input slots. Through one slot it can receive a 50\$ bill, and through the other slot it can receive a 100\$ bill. It gives the change as described above when it receives 50\$. However, when it receives 100\$ bill it returns two 50\$ bills. We can write agent expressions for each behavior separately and "put them together" to describe the full behavior of the currency changer. The constructor $+$ is used, as shown below, to conjoin the capabilities of two currency changing agents.

$$NewCurrencyChange \stackrel{\text{def}}{=} 50\$ \cdot' 20\$ \cdot' 20\$ \cdot' 10\$ \cdot NewCurrencyChange$$

$$+ 100\$ \cdot' 50\$ \cdot' 50\$ \cdot NewCurrencyChange$$

The sum operator $+$ has the same meaning as the choice operator $+$ defined in Chap. 6 for automata. In general, if A_P and A_Q are agents describing, respectively, the observed behaviors of processes P and Q then $A_P + A_Q$ is the agent that describes the capabilities of both agents A_P and A_Q. Equivalently, the meaning of expression $A \stackrel{\text{def}}{=} A_P + A_Q$ is that A starts performing as A_P or as A_Q whichever occurs during the observation.

Many extensions are possible when action prefixing is combined with sum operator. For example, the expression $\alpha \cdot A_P + \beta \cdot A_Q$ represents an agent which describes the behavior of a process performing action α and then behaving as described by the expression A_P or performing action β and then behaving as described by the expression A_Q. Suppose there are two processes with different behaviors but have the common prefix action α, then after performing α they will behave differently. The expression for the conjoined behavior of these two processes is

$$VMD \stackrel{\text{def}}{=} \alpha \cdot (VMD_1 + VMD_2) \tag{15.8}$$

In (15.8) let us replace α by *coin*, and define VMD_1 as the "coffee machine" and VMD_2 as the "tea machine". The resulting agent expression for the vending machine process is

$$VMD_1 \stackrel{\text{def}}{=} {}'coffee \cdot VMD$$

$$VMD_2 \stackrel{\text{def}}{=} {}'tea \cdot VMD \tag{15.9}$$

$$VMD \stackrel{\text{def}}{=} coin \cdot ({}'coffee \cdot VMD +' tea \cdot VMD)$$

After the input action *coin* has occurred in *VMD*, there is a "choice" between coffee and tea. That is, the user gets to exercise this choice. Consequently, the expression for *VMD* in (15.9) describes a deterministic vending machine. However, the behavior of the process as given by the agent expression (15.10), is nondeterministic. The reason is that VMD' can behave either way.

$$VMD' \stackrel{\text{def}}{=} coin \cdot' coffee \cdot VMD' + coin \cdot' tea \cdot VMD' \tag{15.10}$$

Although *VMD* and VMD' have some commonality yet their observed behaviors are distinct. The lesson is that in general

$$\alpha \cdot (\beta \cdot VMD + \gamma \cdot VMD) \neq \alpha \cdot \beta \cdot VMD + \alpha \cdot \gamma \cdot VMD$$

The binary operator $+$ is replaced by the sum operator Σ when an arbitrary number of processes have to be conjoined. That is,

$$\Sigma_{i=1}^{k} A_i = A_1 + A_2 + \cdots + A_k$$

Communication   The concept of *port* is the basis for direct communication between processes. A port is an abstraction of communication point. Ports are to be defined in *complementary* pairs. One port in a complementary pair belongs to the process which receives information (input port) and the other port belongs to the process that sends information (output port). Thus, a pair of complementary ports cannot belong to the same process. In CCS, a *label* is associated with a port and port names are the port labels. Input and output ports are distinguished by complementary labels. The label of an input port is often called the input label, and the label of an output port is called the output label.

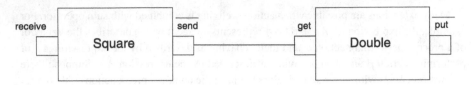

Fig. 15.1 Communicating processes—1

Let us denote the labels for a process P as $\mathcal{L}_P$, input labels of P as $\mathcal{I}_P$, and output labels of P as $\mathcal{O}_P$. The set of all labels through which P actually communicates throughout its lifetime is denoted $sort(P)$, $sort(P) \subset \mathcal{L}_P$. We consider labels restricted with the following properties.

- *Finiteness:* For a process P, $\mathcal{L}_P$ is a finite set.
- *Uniqueness:* Each port must have a unique label. Consequently, $\mathcal{L}_P \cap \mathcal{L}_Q = \emptyset$
- *Complementary completeness for communication:* Let us use the notation X and $\overline{X}$ to denote labels such that for every label in X, its complementary label is in $\overline{X}$. In order for P and Q to communicate in either direction, there must exist nonempty subsets $\mathcal{O}'_P \subset \mathcal{O}_P$ and $\mathcal{I}'_Q \subset \mathcal{I}_Q$ such that $\mathcal{O}'_P$ and $\mathcal{I}'_Q$ are complementary sets of labels. Thus the set $\mathcal{L} = \bigcup_P \mathcal{L}_P$ of labels for all processes in the system is partitioned into $\mathcal{I}$, the set of input labels and $\mathcal{O}$, the set of output labels such that for every communication in the system labels are complementarily complete.

The constructor "$|$" is the *composition* operator for two processes. The expression $P \mid Q$ implies that ports of P and Q with complementary labels are "connected" through "abstract channels" and process P may communicate with process Q through these channels. The two processes in a composition may proceed independently of the other, and in addition there is a possibility of communication between them. The composition operator does not *require* that the processes *must* communicate. It allows the possibility of communication. Without the composition operator, communication is not possible. As a special case of the definition, we have $P \mid Nil = P$. Example 1 illustrates agents for two processes with ports and the expression for the composition of the two processes.

Example 1 Let *receive* and *send* be the input and output port names of process *Square*. The process *Square* receives x and outputs x^2, and is defined by the agent

$$Square \stackrel{def}{=} receive(x) \cdot \overline{send}(x^2) \cdot Square \tag{15.11}$$

Let *get* and *put* be the input and output port names of process *Double*. The process *Double* receives x and outputs $2x$, and is defined by the agent

$$Double \stackrel{def}{=} get(x) \cdot \overline{put}(2x) \cdot Double \tag{15.12}$$

Let $\overline{send}$ and *get* be complementary labels. This allows us to compose process *Square* with process *Double* as in Fig. 15.1. This composed process, denoted *SD*, has the agent expression *Square* | *Double*. Agent *SD* may accept a value v at label *receive* and after

Fig. 15.2 Communicating processes—2

Fig. 15.3 A simple train–controller–gate system

internal communication between the component agents *Square* and *Double* may output the value $2x^2$ at the label $\overline{put}$. If we define *in* and $\overline{put}$ as complementary labels, then it is possible to realize a process as in Fig. 15.2, and its corresponding agent, denoted *DS*, is the composition *Double | Square*. Agent *DS* may accept a value v at label *get* and after internal communication between the component agents *Double* and *Square* may output the value $(2x)^2$ at the label $\overline{send}$.   □

In general, the value of a parameter to a port label may be an event name, or a message, or a numeric constant. If a process P has to communicate with k different processes, we create k different port labels for P and assign the complement of each label to the port label of the process communicating with P. We illustrate this principle in giving a CCS specification for the rail road problem discussed in Chap. 11.

Example 2 Train, *Gate* and *Controller* are the three processes in a railroad model. The *Controller* process needs to communicate with both *Train* and *Gate* processes. Both *Train* and *Gate* need to communicate only with *Controller* process. Figure 15.3 shows the complementary port labels through which the processes may communicate, and the events associated with the port labels.

Train	Gate	Controller
$T : \{'approaching,' exit\}$		$\overline{T} : \{approaching, exit\}$
	$\overline{G} : \{close, raise\}$	$G : \{'close,' raise\}$

In specifying the *Train*, *Gate*, and *Controller* processes, we explicitly shown their *internal* actions, as defined in Chap. 11. However, we can replace all internal action names by the silent action τ. The composition is obtained by first composing *Train* with *Controller* and then composing that process with *Gate*. Agent *TGC* receives messages from *Train*, activate *Controller*, which in turn monitors *Gate*.

$$Train \stackrel{def}{=} T('approaching) \cdot in\_gate \cdot leave\_gate \cdot T('exit) \cdot Train$$

$$Controller \stackrel{\text{def}}{=} \overline{T}(approaching) \cdot wake\_up \cdot G('close) \cdot monitor \cdot G('raise) \cdot Controller$$

$$Gate \stackrel{\text{def}}{=} \overline{G}(close) \cdot down \cdot \overline{G}(raise) \cdot up \cdot Gate$$

$$TGC \stackrel{\text{def}}{=} Train \mid Controller \mid Gate$$

□

Restriction   After a port label of a process P has been used in a communication it becomes unavailable for future use. The constructor \ is used to achieve such a restriction. Given an agent P and a label l then

$$P \backslash l,$$

read as "P restricted on label l ", is an agent whose behavior is that of P except that the capability of agent P for communicating through labels l and $\overline{l}$ have been removed. Note that $P \backslash l$ and $P \backslash \overline{l}$ have the same effect. For any label l, we have $Nil \backslash l = Nil$.

It is possible to restrict an agent on more than one port label. For example, to restrict P on port labels l_1 and l_2 one can write

$$(P \backslash l_1) \backslash l_2$$

In general, the restriction of P on set L of labels is written

$$P \backslash L$$

The agent TGC in Example 2 can be restricted on the set of ports $L = \{T, G\}$. The resulting agent $TGC \backslash L$ cannot communicate with any other agent, and hence represents a closed system in which $Train$, $Controller$, and $Gate$ communicate synchronously.

The restriction constructor may be combined with other constructors. For example, in the expression below

$$(P + Q) \backslash L$$

the conjoined agent's behavior is restricted by the set of ports L. In the expression below

$$P \backslash L + Q \backslash L$$

both processes P and Q are restricted by the set of labels L, and then they are conjoined. Since there is no communication involved between processes and we are dealing only with conjoined processes, it is reasonable to expect the behavior of these two agents to be the same. However, the order in which the compositions and restrictions are performed determines the structure and behavior of the composite system. In general, the agent expressions

$$(P \mid Q) \backslash L$$

$$(P \backslash L) \mid (Q \backslash L)$$

have different effect. Let us illustrate this point with an example.

Example 3 We consider two user programs, denoted U_1 and U_2, which interact with two arbiters, denoted A_1 and A_2. An arbiter receives a request for resource from a user and sends the requested resource. The port labels are defined below.

Process	Port labels
U_1	$\{in_1, recv_1, out_1, \overline{send_1}\}$
U_2	$\{in_1, recv_2, out_2, \overline{send_2}\}$
A_1	$\{send_1, \overline{recv_1}\}$
A_2	$\{send_2, \overline{recv_2}\}$

In the composition $(U_1 \mid A_1)$, the port labels $\{send_1, recv_1\}$ have been used and they are not available for future use. The available port labels for the agent

$$U_1 A_1 \stackrel{\text{def}}{=} (U_1 \mid A_1) \backslash \{send_1, recv_1\}$$

are $\{in_1, out_1\}$. There is no communication possible between the agents in the composition $(U_1 \backslash \{send_1, recv_1\}) \mid A_1$. As such they proceed independently and simultaneously. In the composition $(U_2 \mid A_2)$, the port labels $\{send_2, recv_2\}$ may have been used and they are not available for future use. The available port labels for the agent

$$U_2 A_2 \stackrel{\text{def}}{=} (U_2 \mid A_2) \backslash \{send_2, recv_2\}$$

are $\{\overline{in_1}, out_2\}$. Hence, the agents $U_1 A_1$ and $U_2 A_2$ can communicate through the complementary ports $\{in_1, \overline{in_1}\}$. This composition will give the agent

$$UA_f \stackrel{\text{def}}{=} (U_1 A_1 \mid U_2 A_2) \backslash \{send_1, send_2, recv_1, recv_2\}$$

for which the port labels $\{out_1, out_2\}$ are available. However, the agent

$$UA_c \stackrel{\text{def}}{=} (U_1 A_1 \backslash \{out_1\}) \mid (U_2 A_2 \backslash \{out_2\})$$

has the same effect as UA_f, although it has no available port.   □

From the preceding discussion, the question arises as to the meaning of "equality of effects or equality of behavior". This question will be answered formally in Sect. 15.4.

Conditional Constructor   If P and Q are agents and e is a Boolean expression, then

  if e then P else Q

is an agent which behaves like P when e is true, and behaves like Q when e is false. For example, the agent which squares odd integers and doubles even integers is the expression

  if $(odd(x))$ then $receive(x) \cdot Square$ else $get(x) \cdot Double$

We can combine conditional construct with other constructs. Some instances are listed below.

- *conditional action prefix: a · if e then P else Q*
- *conjoin with one or the other: P + if e then Q else R*
- *conditional selection of a conjoin: if e then P + Q else P + R*
- *composition with one or the other: P | if e then Q else R*
- *conditional selection of a composition: if e then P + Q else P + R*
- *conditional restriction: if e then (P\L) else P*

Relabeling   The relabeling operator is a partial function $f : \mathcal{L} \mapsto \mathcal{L}'$, where $\mathcal{L}$ is the set of labels of agent P and $\mathcal{L}'$ is a set of new labels. The process P in which some ports are relabeled using a function f is written

$P[f]$,

to be read "P relabeled by f". For $l \in \mathcal{L}$, the function f satisfies the property $f(\bar{l}) = \overline{f(l)}$. Process P and $P[f]$ have the same behavior because relabeling does not change the events occurring at the ports. So, relabeling is a tool to construct new identical agents and use them in modeling different systems.

Example 4 We consider the two systems shown in Fig. 15.4(a) and in Fig. 15.4(b). In Fig. 15.4(a), there are two train processes $Train_1$, and $Train_2$, one controller process *Controller*, and one gate process *Gate*. The train processes communicate with the controller process, and the controller process communicates with the gate process, all using the same set of messages as defined in Example 2. The agent expression for this system configuration is

$((Train_1 + Train_2) \mid Controller) \mid Gate$

If the trains have the same behavior, we could relabel the ports of $Train_1$ to get $Train_2$. For a relabeling function f, $f(T_1) = T_2$, we can rewrite the above agent expression as

$((Train_1 + Train_1[f]) \mid Controller) \mid Gate$

In Fig. 15.4(b), the train processes communicate with controller processes on a one-to-one basis, while the controller processes independently communicate with the gate process. The agent expression for this system configuration is

$((Train_1 \mid Controller_1) + (Train_2 \mid Controller_2)) \mid Gate$

If the trains have the same behavior and the controllers have the same behavior then using the relabeling function f, we can rewrite the above agent expression as

$((Train_1 \mid Controller_1) + (Train_1[f] \mid Controller_1[f])) \mid Gate$ □

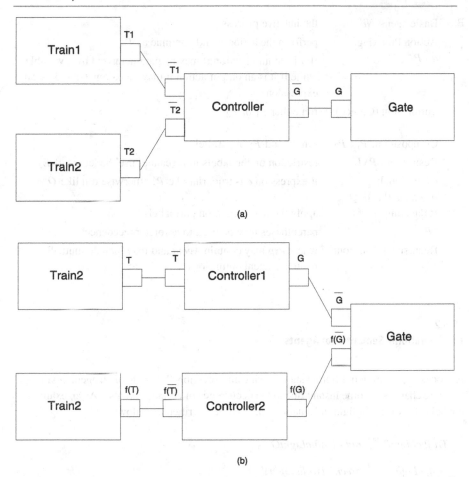

Fig. 15.4 Multiple trains/controllers communicating with one gate

15.3
CCS—Syntax and Semantics

In this section, we present a formal syntax and semantics of CCS. The syntactic definition follows the discussion in Sect. 15.2. The semantics of CCS is based on Labeled Transition Systems (LTS) discussed in Chap. 11.

15.3.1
Syntax

We use uppercase letters to denote processes and lowercase letters to denote actions.

P::   Basic agent: *Nil*   the inactive process

Action Prefixing: perform the action a and continue as P

$a \cdot P$ If a is an input action it may be parameterized by a variable, while if it is an output action it may be parameterized by an expression

Summation (Choice):   run either P_1 or P_2

$P_1 + P_2$

Composition: $P_1 \mid P_2$ run P_1 and P_2 in parallel

Restriction: $P \backslash L$ restriction on the labels in L (cannot use the letters of L)

Conditional: if expression e is true, run like P, otherwise run like Q

if e then P else Q

Relabeling: $P[f]$ apply the mapping f on port labels

(P) parentheses may be used to enforce precedence

Recursive Definition: where *exp* may contain *Agent* and may include mutually

$Agent \stackrel{\text{def}}{=} exp$ recursive agent definitions

15.3.2
The Operational Semantics of Agents

A process goes through different states during an execution. The state of an agent or simply the state changes at some instant due to the occurrence of certain "events". As an example, the behavior of traffic light in Equation 15.3 can be rewritten as follows:

$$TrafficLightR \stackrel{\text{def}}{=} red \cdot TrafficLightG$$

$$TrafficLightG \stackrel{\text{def}}{=} green \cdot TrafficLightY$$

$$TrafficLightY \stackrel{\text{def}}{=} yellow \cdot TrafficLightR$$

We may regard the agents *TrafficLightG* and *TrafficLightR* as representing two states of the traffic light process. In state *TrafficLightG*, it will output *green*, and in state *TrafficLightY*, it will output *yellow*. No input event is required at any of these states. We use the state transition notation discussed in Chap. 11 for LTS.

$$TrafficLightR \stackrel{red}{\longrightarrow} TrafficLightG$$

$$TrafficLightG \stackrel{green}{\longrightarrow} TrafficLightY$$

$$TrafficLightY \stackrel{yellow}{\longrightarrow} TrafficLightR$$

The state transition rules are intended to formalize the explanations for process constructors given in Sect. 15.2. Before describing the rules, we must consider the proper notation for describing the behavior of composite agents. In CCS, the basis of communication in a composition is synchrony: that the two processes "shake hands" on the pair of "complementary actions" involved in the communication. The complementary action of an action a is denoted $\overline{a}$. If a is an input action then $\overline{a}$ is the output action $'a$, and conversely $\overline{'a} = a$. Instead of using a and $'a$ in communication, the notation a and $\overline{a}$ will be used. The principle of "hand-shaking" is that the actions a and $\overline{a}$ involved in the hand-shaking "cancel out", because the internal details of "hand-shaking" are not observable. Consequently, both a and $\overline{a}$ will be replaced by τ in a transition. Let us illustrate this for the vending machine definition in (15.6). We rewrite the definition using transitions.

$$VendingMachine \xrightarrow{1\$} VendingMachine_1$$

$$VendingMachine_1 \xrightarrow{c} VendingMachine_2$$

$$VendingMachine_2 \xrightarrow{deliverC} VendingMachine$$

The agent for a person who interacts with the vending machine can be written as

$$User \stackrel{def}{=} \overline{1\$}\ User_1$$

$$User_1 \stackrel{def}{=} \overline{c}\ User_2$$

$$User_2 \stackrel{def}{=} \overline{deliverC}\ User$$

The definition can be written using transitions as below.

$$User \xrightarrow{\overline{1\$}} User_1$$

$$User_1 \xrightarrow{\overline{c}} User_2$$

$$User \xrightarrow{\overline{deliverC}} User_1$$

When the complementary actions $1\$$ and $\overline{1\$}$ are performed, the agents in the composite agent $VendingMachine \mid User$ shake hands, they undergo state changes simultaneously, which should result in the next state $VendingMachine_1 \mid User_1$. This transition relation is written

$$VendingMachine \mid User \xrightarrow{\tau} VendingMachine_1 \mid User_1$$

Similar reasoning on the next two pairs of complementary actions gives us the transitions

$$VendingMachine_1 \mid User_1 \xrightarrow{\tau} VendingMachine_2 \mid User_2$$

$$VendingMachine_2 \mid User_2 \xrightarrow{\tau} VendingMachine \mid User$$

With this background we are ready to present the transition rules.

Transition rules

But for *Nil* every other construct has at least one transition rule.

- *Nil:* The understanding is that *Nil* represents a process that does not have any action to perform. There is no formal rule for *Nil*.
- *Action prefixing:* If a is an action and P is an agent then $a \cdot P$ is an agent which initially performs the action a, and thereafter behaves like agent P. This is expressed by the rule

$$\mathbf{Act}: \mathit{Infer}\ a \cdot P \xrightarrow{a} P$$

written in sequent calculus notation

$$\mathbf{Act}: \frac{}{a \cdot P \xrightarrow{a} P} \tag{15.13}$$

Input actions may be parameterized by variables and output actions may be parameterized by expressions. For parameterized input actions, values must be bound to variables (as in LST) to enable the correct transition. This is expressed by the rule

$$\mathbf{Act\text{-}inputparameter}: \frac{}{a(x) \cdot P \xrightarrow{a[v/x]} P} \tag{15.14}$$

For an output action parameterized by an expression, the expression must evaluate to a value. This is expressed by the rule

$$\mathbf{Act\text{-}outputparameter}: \frac{}{\overline{a}(e) \cdot P \xrightarrow{\overline{a}[v=e]} P} \tag{15.15}$$

- *Summation:* The agent $P + Q$ has the capabilities of both agents P and Q. This is expressed by rules **Sum1** and **Sum2**. Rule **Sum1** states that if P produces P' under the action a, then $P + Q$ also produces P' under the same action. Rule **Sum2** states likewise for Q.

$$\mathbf{Sum1}: \frac{P \xrightarrow{a} P'}{P + Q \xrightarrow{a} P'} \tag{15.16}$$

$$\mathbf{Sum2}: \frac{Q \xrightarrow{a} Q'}{P + Q \xrightarrow{a} Q'} \tag{15.17}$$

- *Composition:* The agents P and Q in a composition $P \mid Q$ may act independent of the other, while P and Q act synchronously together whenever they are able to perform complementary actions. This behavior is expressed by the rules **Compose1**, **Compose2**, and **Compose3**. Rules **Compose1** and **Compose2** express the concurrent behavior of P and Q. That is, all actions possible for P and Q are admissible for $P \mid Q$. In case P and Q have complementary actions, rule **Compose3** expresses the synchronized action which produces τ action in $P \mid Q$. By introducing τ in the result, the reason for synchronized action is abstracted. Thus rule **Compose3** involves both abstraction and synchrony.

$$\mathbf{Compose1}: \frac{P \xrightarrow{a} P'}{P \mid Q \xrightarrow{a} P' \mid Q} \tag{15.18}$$

$$\text{Compose2} : \frac{Q \xrightarrow{a} Q'}{P \mid Q \xrightarrow{a} P \mid Q'} \tag{15.19}$$

$$\text{Compose3} : \frac{P \xrightarrow{a} P', Q \xrightarrow{\bar{a}} Q'}{P \mid Q \xrightarrow{\tau} P' \mid Q'} \tag{15.20}$$

- *Restriction:* The agent $P \backslash L$ behaves like P except that it may not engage in any action a such that a or $\bar{a}$ is in the set L. The rule is

$$\text{Rest} : \frac{P \xrightarrow{a} P', a, \bar{a} \notin L}{P \backslash L \xrightarrow{a} P' \backslash L} \tag{15.21}$$

Notice that τ cannot be restricted, and P' is restricted on L.

- *Relabeling:* For a relabeling function f, the behavior of agent $P[f]$ is like that of P. The rule is

$$\text{Rel} : \frac{P \xrightarrow{a} P'}{P[f] \xrightarrow{f(a)} P'[f]} \tag{15.22}$$

Notice that τ cannot be relabeled, and P' is relabeled by f.

- *Conditional:* The agent *if e then P else Q* is an agent which behaves like P if e is true, and behaves like Q if e is false. In the rules below we use the definition $R \stackrel{\text{def}}{=} if\ e\ then\ P\ else\ Q$.

$$\text{Cond1} : \frac{P \xrightarrow{a} P', e}{R \xrightarrow{a} P'} \tag{15.23}$$

$$\text{Cond2} : \frac{Q \xrightarrow{a} Q', \neg a}{R \xrightarrow{a} Q'} \tag{15.24}$$

- *Recursive definition:* If $P \stackrel{\text{def}}{=} A$ then the behavior of agent P is that of agent A according the rule below:

$$\text{Rec} : \frac{A \xrightarrow{a} P'}{P \xrightarrow{a} P'} \tag{15.25}$$

- *Reduction for value passing:* The reduction rule combines the action rules (15.14), (15.15), and rule **Compose3** of the composition rule (15.18). The interpretation of the rule is that the value passing is successful only when complementary actions can be performed. Formally, it is expressed as below:
  - The process $a(x) \cdot P$ send a message x along channel a. The process $\bar{b}(y) \cdot Q$ receives the message on channel $\bar{b}$.
  - After sending the message x, the process $a(x) \cdot P$ becomes process P. At the same instant, the process $\bar{b}(y) \cdot Q$ becomes $Q[x/y]$, which is process Q with y substituted by x, the data received on channel $\bar{b}$.

$$\textbf{Red}: \frac{a(x) \cdot P \cdot | \, \overline{b}(y) \cdot Q}{P \, | \, Q[x/y]} \tag{15.26}$$

The set of inference rules given above effectively *partitions* the set of agents into a set of *equivalence* classes. Two expressions in a set are *indistinguishable,* for they have the same effect. This equivalence relation, called *observational equivalence* is discussed Sect. 15.4.

Example 5

- *Action prefixing:* Applying the action-prefix axiom to

$$P \stackrel{\text{def}}{=} a.(b.(c \, | \, (\overline{c} + d)))$$

we may write

$$P \stackrel{a}{\rightarrow} P'$$
$$P' \stackrel{\text{def}}{=} (b.(c \, | \, \overline{c} + d))$$

- *Choice:* Using the action-prefixing axiom on

$$P \stackrel{\text{def}}{=} a \cdot (b \, | \, \overline{b})$$

we infer

$$P \stackrel{a}{\rightarrow} (b \, | \, \overline{b})$$

Thus, we may infer

$$P + Q \stackrel{a}{\rightarrow} (b \, | \, \overline{b})$$

- *Composition:* The process P that does only one action a is $a \cdot Nil$. Using the action-prefixing axiom this is written

$$P \stackrel{a}{\rightarrow} Nil$$

The process Q that does only one action $\overline{a}$ is $\overline{a} \cdot Nil$. Using the action-prefixing axiom this is written

$$Q \stackrel{\overline{a}}{\rightarrow} Nil$$

Applying the composition axiom for P and Q we get

$$P \, | \, Q \stackrel{\tau}{\rightarrow} Nil \, | \, Nil$$
$$P \, | \, Q \stackrel{a}{\rightarrow} Nil \, | \, Q$$
$$P \, | \, Q \stackrel{\overline{a}}{\rightarrow} P \, | \, Nil$$

- *Restriction:* Applying restriction on $\{a\}$ to $P \mid Q$ in the composition above we get

$$(P \mid Q)\backslash\{a\} \xrightarrow{\tau} (Nil \mid Nil)\backslash\{a\} = Nil\backslash\{a\} = Nil$$

- *Reduction:* Let us model a producer (P) and consumer (Q) which communicate through a buffer (B) that can hold only one item. Producer puts items in channel $\overline{in}$ and items are received by buffer in channel in. An item placed in the buffer channel $\overline{out}$ is received in the channel out by the consumer Q. The agent definitions are

$$B \stackrel{\text{def}}{=} in(x) \cdot B'$$

$$B' \stackrel{\text{def}}{=} \overline{out}(x) \cdot B + in(x) \cdot B$$

$$P \stackrel{\text{def}}{=} \overline{in}(y) \cdot P$$

$$Q \stackrel{\text{def}}{=} out(y) \cdot Q$$

$$PC \stackrel{\text{def}}{=} (P \mid B \mid Q)\backslash\{in, out\}$$

- *Conditional:* We give a specification C_e for a container with capacity $M > 0$. Agent C_e, in its initial empty state, receives an item x and becomes agent C_m, a state in which the container has at least one item but is not full. Agent C_m may get an input, in which case either it becomes full or it is less than full. Agent C_f denotes the situation that the container is full. The predicate $Size < M - 1$ is used in defining C_f. Agent C_m may also perform an output action and after performing that action either it becomes empty or it still has at least one item. The predicate $size > 1$ is used to test this situation. Agent C_f can perform only an output action, and after performing it becomes agent C_m. Based on the above behavior the definition of C_e is given below.

$$C_e \stackrel{\text{def}}{=} in(x) \cdot C_m$$

$$C_m \stackrel{\text{def}}{=} if \ (size < m - 1) \ then \ in(x) \cdot C_m \ else \ in(x) \cdot C_f$$

$$+ \ if \ (size > 1) \ then \ \overline{out}(x) \cdot C_m \ else \ \overline{out}(x) \cdot C_e$$

$$c_f \stackrel{\text{def}}{=} \overline{out}(x) \cdot C_m \qquad\qquad \square$$

15.4
Simulation and Equivalence

The transition rules provide an operational semantics for agents of the calculus. Using the rules, the behavior of an agent can be represented by a labeled tree. To construct the tree for an agent P, we start with a node, called root, labeled by P. Then for each agent P_i for which there exists a rule $P \xrightarrow{a_i} P_i$, we create a node labeled P_i, draw an arc from the node labeled P to it, and label that arc a_i. Then we repeat the process for each agent P_j. This process may not terminate if the definition of agent P is recursive. This tree is called the *derivation tree* for agent P. The *sort* of an agent P, denoted $sort(P)$, is the set of labels in $\mathcal{L}$ that label the derivation tree.

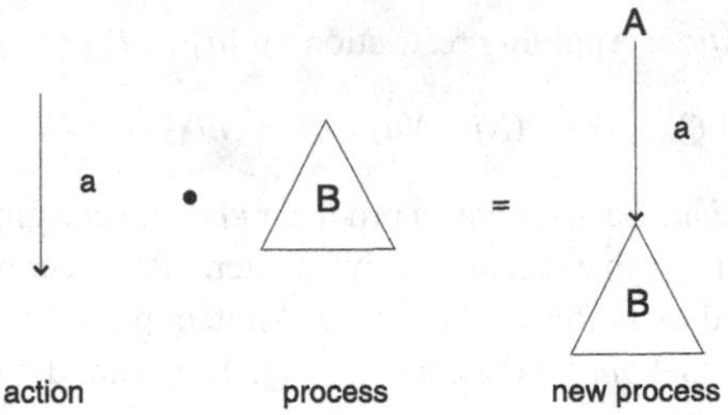

Fig. 15.5 Derivation tree for action-prefixing rule

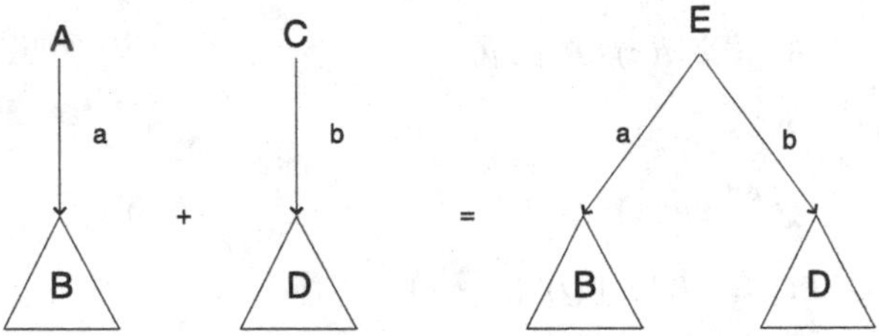

action   process   new process

Fig. 15.6 Derivation tree for summation rule

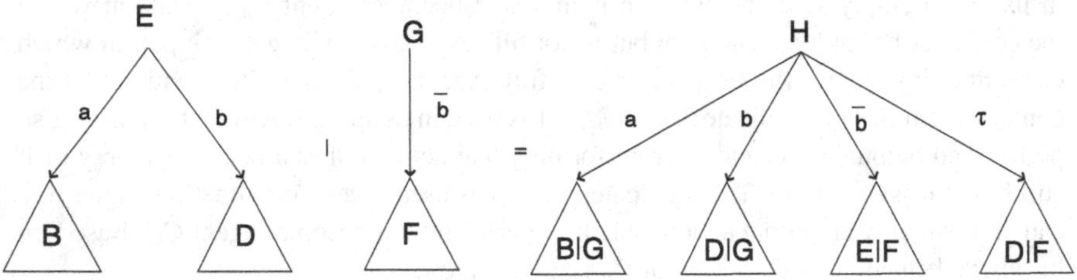

Fig. 15.7 Derivation tree for parallel composition rule

Fig. 15.8 Derivation tree for restriction rule

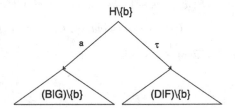

15.4.1
Derivation Trees

Derivation trees corresponding to the transition rules action prefixing, sum, composition, restriction, and relabeling are shown, respectively, in Figs. 15.5, 15.6, 15.7, 15.8, and 15.9. Examples are successively reused in these figures. In all these figures, we use lower case letters for actions, an action labels an arc, and agents are represented by triangles with uppercase labels.

Fig. 15.9 Derivation tree for
relabeling rule

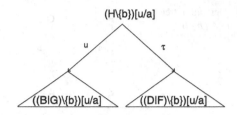

In Fig. 15.5, action a that prefixes agent B gives rise to the derivation tree with root labeled by agent A, a node labeled by agent B, and the arc from A to B with label a. We reuse this tree in Fig. 15.6 to illustrate the construction of the tree for the agent definition $E \stackrel{\text{def}}{=} a \cdot B + b \cdot D$. The trees corresponding to $a \cdot B$ and $b \cdot D$ are combined so that they are the left and right branches of a tree rooted at E. Figure 15.7 illustrates the parallel composition tree corresponding to the expression $H \stackrel{\text{def}}{=} E \mid \overline{b} \cdot F$. The tree for the expression $\overline{b} \cdot F$ and the tree for E are combined using the three parallel composition rules. Applying rule **Compose1**, both a and b actions can be performed independently by E. After a action is performed, B and G should be composed in parallel. This gives the left most branch in the tree rooted at H. Likewise, after b is performed D and G should be composed in parallel. This gives the second branch in the tree rooted at H. Agent G may perform action $\overline{b}$ independent from the actions of E. After $\overline{b}$ is performed E and F must be composed in parallel. This gives the third branch in the tree rooted at H. Finally, the complementary actions may occur synchronously, in which case τ action is produced and following it D and F must be composed in parallel. This gives the right most branch in the tree rooted at H. The tree corresponding to $H \backslash \{b\}$ is shown in Fig. 15.8. The effect of restricting H on $\{b\}$ is to remove the transitions labeled by b and $\overline{b}$ in Fig. 15.7. The effect of relabeling the action a by u is to replace every occurrence of a in the tree for $H \backslash \{b\}$ by the label u. The tree after relabeling is shown in Fig. 15.9.

Example 6 We want to construct the derivation tree for the expression

$$a \cdot A \mid b \cdot B$$

The following steps are to be followed.

- *Step 1:* Let $P \stackrel{\text{def}}{=} a \cdot A$ and $Q \stackrel{\text{def}}{=} b \cdot B$.
- *Step 2:* Construct the trees for P and Q (use Fig. 15.5). The trees are shown in Fig. 15.10(a).
- *Step3:* Construct the parallel composition of the trees, (use Fig. 15.7). The tree is shown in Fig. 15.10(b). The unlabeled branches refer to transitions arising from the actions of agents A and B.   □

Example 7 When an agent expression involves only actions, we can construct the full derivation tree, and understand its total behavior. Consider the expression

$$a \cdot (b \cdot (c \mid \overline{c}) + d)$$

Fig. 15.10 Derivation tree for the agent $a \cdot A \mid b \cdot B$

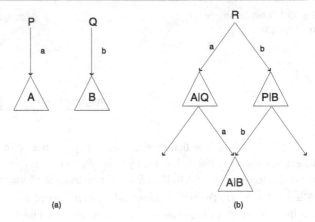

(a)   (b)

Fig. 15.11 Full derivation of the agent in Example 7

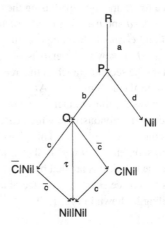

- *Step1:* Let $R \stackrel{\mathrm{def}}{=} a \cdot P$, $P \stackrel{\mathrm{def}}{=} b \cdot Q + d$, and $Q \stackrel{\mathrm{def}}{=} (c \mid \overline{c})$.
- *Step2:* Construct the tree for $R \stackrel{\mathrm{def}}{=} a \cdot P$ using action-prefixing tree construction.
- *Step3:* Construct the two subtrees rooted at P for the expression $b \cdot Q + d$ using sum tree construction. The subtree for the branch labeled d is *Nil*. The left subtree is the action-prefix branch labeled b. The root of the left subtree is Q.
- *Step3:* Expand Q using parallel tree construction. Three possibilities arise: c and $\overline{c}$ may occur independently or they may synchronize. The left branch labeled c has the subtree $Nil \mid c$, the middle branch labeled $\overline{c}$ has the subtree $c \mid Nil$, and the right branch labeled τ has the subtree $Nil \mid Nil$. By performing the $\overline{c}$ action $Nil \mid \overline{c}$ becomes $Nil \mid Nil$. Likewise, $c \mid Nil$ becomes $Nil \mid Nil$ by performing the action a.

The full tree is shown in Fig. 15.11.   □

15.4.2
Milner's Laws

Milner [8, 9] has given a number of laws that can be used as rewrite rules to transform agent expressions to some kind of *normal form*. We can say that two agent expressions are *equal* if they can be reduced to identical normal forms. Equality is hard to achieve, rather "equivalence" is what we should look for. Milner [9] has given several laws of equivalence. Without dwelling into the rigorous reasoning behind these laws, we reproduce below the laws propounded by Milner for *observational congruence*, one of the equivalences for agents that we will study in Sect. 15.4.5. For the present, understand the equality sign "=" to mean "agents on both sides" have the same effect. A strict interpretation is that "=" is the congruence relation as discussed in Sect. 15.4.5.

The laws can be grouped into *Dynamic Laws*, *Static Laws*, *Expansion Laws*, and the *Recursion Laws*. The *Dynamic Laws* express properties of the dynamic constructors, action prefixing and summation. The *Static Laws* describe properties of static constructors, composition, restriction, and relabeling. The *Expansion Principle* relates the static and dynamic constructors. The *Recursion Laws* helps to reason with recursively defined agents. We discuss the *Expansion Laws*, and the *Recursion Laws* in Sect. 15.4.5, and the rest of the laws are given below.

Dynamic Laws

- **Laws of Summation:** These laws express some properties of the summation operator.

The SUM Laws		
1. $P + Q$	$= Q + P$	(commutativity)
2. $P + (Q + R)$	$= (P + Q) + R$	(associativity)
3. $P + Nil$	$= P$	(Nil is unity for +)
4. $P + P$	$= P$	(absorption)

- **Laws of Silent Transition:** These laws enable us to rewrite agents containing τ action.

The TAU Laws	
1. $a \cdot \tau \cdot P$	$= a \cdot P$
2. $P + \tau \cdot P$	$= (\tau \cdot P)$
3. $a \cdot (P + \tau \cdot Q) + a \cdot Q$	$= a \cdot (P + \tau \cdot Q)$
4. $P + \tau \cdot (P + Q)$	$= \tau \cdot (P + Q)$

Notice that $P = \tau \cdot P$ and $a \cdot (P + Q) = a \cdot P + a \cdot Q$ are *not* true in general, and thus are excluded as laws.

Static Laws

- **Laws of Parallel Composition:** Parallel composition is both commutative and associative.

The COMPOSITION Laws

1. $P \mid Q$	$= Q \mid P$	(commutativity)
2. $P \mid (Q \mid R)$	$= (P \mid Q) \mid R$	(associativity)
3. $P \mid Nil$	$= P$	(Nil is unity for $\mid$)

- **Laws of Restriction:** The laws are defined for restricting any set L of labels.

The RESTRICTION Laws

1. $Nil\backslash L$	$= Nil$
2. $(P + Q)\backslash L$	$= P\backslash L + Q\backslash L$
3. $(\alpha \cdot P)\backslash L$	$= Nil, \alpha \in L$
	$= \alpha \cdot (P\backslash L), \alpha \notin L$
4. $P\backslash L$	$= P, sort(P) \cap (L \cap \overline{L}) = \emptyset$
5. $P\backslash L\backslash K$	$= P\backslash (L \cup K)$
6. $(P \mid Q)\backslash L$	$= (P\backslash L \mid Q\backslash L), (L \cup \overline{L}) \cap sort(P) \cap \overline{sort(Q)} = \emptyset$

- **Laws of Relabeling:** Relabeling laws can be specialized. Thus, if a label that is not in $sort(P)$ is used to relabel agent P, it has no effect.

The RELABELLING Laws

1. $Nil[f]$	$= Nil$
2. $(P + Q)[f]$	$= P[f] + Q[f]$
3. $(a \cdot P)[f]$	$= f(a) \cdot P[f]$
4. $P[I]$	$= P, I$ is identity function
5. $P[f]$	$= P[g]$, if $dom(f) = dom(g)$ on $sort(P)$
6. $(P[f])[g]$	$= P[(g \circ f)]$, $\circ$ is function composition
7. $P[f]\backslash L$	$= (P\backslash f^{-1}(L))[f]$
8. $(P \mid Q)[f]$	$= P[f] \mid Q[f]$

An agent expression may be simplified to a normal form (meaning that it cannot be reduced any further) by a careful application of Milner's laws. Some useful tips to a simplification procedure are the following:

1. Using Milner's laws on an agent expression does not change its semantics. Consequently a step of simplification, meaning "rewrite" of the original expression using one of Milner's laws, produces an expression that has the same effect as the original expression.
2. Both $+$ and $\mid$ are commutative and associative. Using this property, a given expression can be "subdivided" and each sub-expression may be simplified.
3. In simplifying expressions involving parallel compositions, such as $P \mid Q \mid R \mid S$, it is better that sub-expressions which have maximum interactions are combined earlier in the reduction process. After applying rule **Compose3** to each interaction, the TAU laws can be applied to reduce an expression.
4. Since the parallel construct $\mid$ "distributes over" the restriction construct $\backslash$ for a label not in the sorts of its arguments, it may be advantageous to restrict first and then compose.

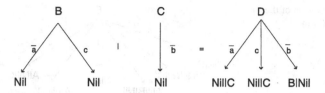

Fig. 15.12 Derivation of the agent $B \mid C$ in Example 8

5. Constructing the derivation tree for an expression and using the reduction laws on the trees, as illustrated in Figs. 15.5, 15.6, 15.7, and 15.8, might be helpful.

We illustrate the usefulness of these tips in Example 8.

Example 8 We want to simplify the expression

$$(A \mid B \mid C)\backslash\{a\},$$

where $A \stackrel{\text{def}}{=} a + b$, $B \stackrel{\text{def}}{=} \overline{a} + c$, and $C \stackrel{\text{def}}{=} \overline{b}$. Expressions A and B have an interaction. Likewise, expressions A and C have an interaction. By distributive law, the given expression can be combined either as in $(A \mid B) \mid C$ or as in $A \mid (B \mid C)$. Since C involves only one action, it is better to evaluate $A \mid (B \mid C)$. We first construct the derivation trees for A, B, and C, next compute $D \stackrel{\text{def}}{=} B \mid C$, and then compute $E \stackrel{\text{def}}{=} A \mid D$. We can use Milner's laws directly to simplify the given expression. However, using the derivation trees we get a better grip in the calculation process.

- *Step1:* Following the construction in Fig. 15.5, the derivation trees for B, and C are constructed. Following the construction in Fig. 15.7 the parallel composition of B and C is constructed. These trees are shown in Fig. 15.12. From the resulting derivation tree the agent expression for D in (15.27) is calculated.

$$D = B \mid C$$
$$= \overline{a} \cdot (Nil \mid C) + c \cdot (Nil \mid C) + \overline{b} \cdot (B \mid Nil)$$
$$= \overline{a} \cdot C + c \cdot C + \overline{b} \cdot B \qquad\qquad (15.27)$$

- *Step2:* Following the construction in Fig. 15.5, the derivation trees for A is constructed. Following the construction in Fig. 15.7 the parallel composition of A and D is constructed. These trees are shown in Fig. 15.13. Notice that each one of the actions a, b, c, $\overline{a}$, and $\overline{b}$ may occur independently. In addition, the action pairs $(a, \overline{a})$, and $(b, \overline{b})$ may occur synchronously. Thus there are seven branches in the tree rooted at E. In this tree, we apply the restriction on label a (and $\overline{a}$), which removes the subtrees under the branches labeled by a and $\overline{a}$. From the remaining tree, shown in Fig. 15.14, the result expression is calculated as the sum of five action prefixes, one corresponding to each subtree. The final expressions are enumerated in the table below.

Fig. 15.13 Derivation of the agent $A \mid (B \mid C)$ in Example 8

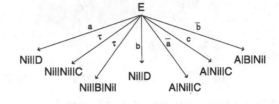

Fig. 15.14 Derivation of the agent $(A \mid (B \mid C))\backslash\{a\}$ in Example 8

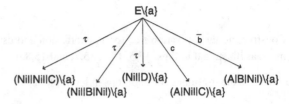

1	$\tau \cdot (Nil \mid Nil \mid C)\backslash\{a\}$	$= \tau \cdot \overline{b}$
2	$\tau \cdot (Nil \mid B \mid Nil)\backslash\{a\}$	$= \tau \cdot c$
3	$b \cdot (Nil \mid D)\backslash\{a\}$	$= b \cdot (c \cdot \overline{b} + \overline{b} \cdot c)$
4	$c \cdot (A \mid Nil \mid C)\backslash\{a\}$	$= c \cdot (b \cdot \overline{b} + \overline{b} \cdot b + \tau)$
5	$\overline{b} \cdot (A \mid B \mid Nil)\backslash\{a\}$	$= \overline{b} \cdot (b \cdot c + c \cdot b + \tau)$

Notice that expressions in column 2 should be reduced, using either Milner's laws or the derivation trees. In (15.28) and (15.29) we, respectively, illustrate the simplification steps for expressions 3 and 4 in the table.

$$b \cdot (Nil \mid D)\backslash\{a\} = (b \cdot D)\backslash\{a\}\,(Composition\ Law\ 3)$$

$$= b \cdot (c \cdot C + \overline{b} \cdot B)\backslash\{a\}\,(Restrction\ Law\ 3\ and$$

$$Substitution\ from\ (15.27))$$

$$= b \cdot ((c \cdot C)\backslash\{a\} + (\overline{b} \cdot B)\backslash\{a\})\,(Restriction\ Law\ 2)$$

$$= b \cdot (c \cdot (C\backslash\{a\}) + \overline{b} \cdot (B\backslash\{a\}))\,(Restriction\ Law\ 3)$$

$$= b \cdot (c \cdot \overline{b} + \overline{b} \cdot c)\,(Definition\ of\ Restriction) \tag{15.28}$$

$$c \cdot (A \mid Nil \mid C)\backslash\{a\} = c \cdot (A \mid C)\backslash\{a\}\,(Composition\ Laws\ 2\ and\ 3)$$

$$= c \cdot (A\backslash\{a\} \mid C\backslash\{a\})\,(Restriction\ Law\ 6)$$

$$= c \cdot (b \mid \overline{b})\,(Definition\ of\ Restriction)$$

$$= c \cdot (b \cdot \overline{b} + \overline{b} \cdot b + \tau)\,(Composition\ Laws) \tag{15.29}$$

$\square$

The derivation tree T_P of an agent P may exhibit a repetitive structure, in which case the tree becomes a graph, called the *transition diagram* of agent P. The transition diagram

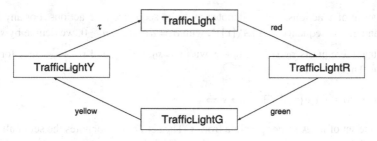

Fig. 15.15 LST for traffic light definition (15.30)

is a labeled transition system (LTS). Thus, corresponding to an agent definition, as defined by its transition rules, we can construct a derivation tree, an LTS if the derivation tree has a repetitive structure. Henceforth we discuss simulation and equivalence of agents in terms of their corresponding LTSs.

As an example, consider definition (15.3) of *TrafficLight* process. We can rewrite it as in (15.30).

$$TrafficLight \stackrel{def}{=} red \cdot TrafficLightR$$

$$TrafficLightR \stackrel{def}{=} green \cdot TrafficLightG$$

$$TrafficLightG \stackrel{def}{=} yellow \cdot TrafficLightY \tag{15.30}$$

$$TrafficLightY \stackrel{def}{=} \tau\, TrafficLight$$

Following the construction process for derivation trees from agents, we get the LTS shown in Fig. 15.15.

15.4.3
Labeled Transition Systems—Some Properties

Recall the formal definition of LTS from Chap. 11. If A is the set of actions associated with an LTS, let $A^\star$ denote the set of all finite sequences of actions in A. An element $\sigma \in A^\star$ is called an *action sequence*. For states s, t in the LTS and action sequence $\sigma = a_1 \ldots a_k, k \geq 0$, if there exists $s_0, s_1, \ldots, s_k \in S$ with $s = s_0, t = s_k$, and $s_i \xrightarrow{a_{i+1}} s_{i+1}$ for all $i, 0 \leq i < k$, then we denote $s \xrightarrow{\sigma} t$. The set

$$Tr(s) = \{\sigma \in A^\star \mid \exists t \in S \bullet s \xrightarrow{\sigma} t\}$$

is called the set of *traces* possible from state s. The set $Tr(s_0)$ is the set of possible traces of the LTS.

We may allow τ actions and consider traces between states on which any number of τ actions occur in between. We introduce a new notation to express transitions that involve any sequence of τ actions. Let τ^* denote any finite sequence of τ actions. For any states s and t and action sequence $\sigma \in \{A\backslash\{\tau\}\}^*$, with $\sigma = a_1 \ldots a_n$, $n \geq 0$, we denote by $s \overset{\underline{a}}{\Rightarrow} t$ the fact that there exists $s_0, s_1, \ldots, s_n \in S$ with $s = s_0$, $t = s_n$, and $s_i \xrightarrow{\tau^* a_{i+1}} s_{i+1}$ for all i, $0 \leq i < n$. The set

$$Tr_w(s) = \{\sigma \in (A \setminus \{\tau\})^* \mid \exists t \in S \bullet s \overset{\underline{a}}{\Rightarrow} t\}$$

is called the set of *weak traces* possible from s. The set $Tr_w(s_0)$ denotes the set of all weak traces possible from the initial state.

In order to complete the definition of LTS of an agent, we let the state in an LTS of an agent P to include the values of all variables that are parameters to the actions in $sort(P)$. That is, with every state of T_P there exists a state vector $(v_1 : D_1, \ldots, v_n : D_n)$ where v_i is a variable name and D_i is the domain for variable v_i. With this background we can address the meaning of "equivalence" and "simulation".

15.4.4
Trace Equivalence

Trace equivalence is very close to language equivalence as studied for deterministic finite state automata in Chap. 6. Informally, two states are trace equivalent if the possible sequences of actions starting from these states are the same. Let T_P and T_Q, respectively, denote the LTS corresponding to agents P and Q. Agents P and Q are *trace equivalent*, written $P \approx_{tr} Q$, if and only if $sort(P) = sort(Q)$, and $Tr(s_0) = Tr(s_0')$. That is, the two agents P and Q perform the same sequence of actions. We may also write $T_P \approx_{tr} T_Q$ instead of $P \approx_{tr} Q$.

An LTS may be *refined* by making explicit in the model some internal actions. A refined LTS is necessary to reason about the functional correctness of the modeled process. Suppose T_Q is a refined LTS of T_P then it is necessary that both T_P and T_Q have the observable behavior and $sort(Q) = sort(P) \cup \{\tau\}$. Thus, we are led to consider the equivalence of traces of T_Q, which involve τ actions and T_P which involve only observable actions. This equivalence, called *weak trace equivalence*, is defined in terms of equality of weak traces. Agents P and Q are *weakly trace equivalent*, written $P \approx_{wtr} Q$ or equivalently as $T_P \approx_{wtr} T_Q$, if and only if $Tr_w(s_0) = Tr_w(s_0')$. It is easy to see that if two LTSs are trace equivalent then they are also weakly trace equivalent.

Consider the two LTS T_P and T_Q shown in Fig. 15.16(a) and Fig. 15.16(b). They represent, respectively, the behavior of two vending machines P and Q. For vending machine P, $Tr(s_0) = \{coin\ coffee, coin\ tea\}$, and for vending machine Q, $Tr(t_o) = \{coin\ coffee, coin\ tea\}$. That is, the two vending machines are trace equivalent. In T_P, starting at s_0 we can perform the action *coin*, and the result is not deterministic, because we will observe the two possible sequences $\{coin\ coffee, coin\ tea\}$. This is exactly the same sequences observed for T_Q, and consequently $T_P \approx_{tr} T_Q$. Yet, there is a difference in their observed behavior. In T_Q, after performing the action *coin* at the state t_0 we have a choice, either the action *coffee* or the action *tea* can be exercised. Thus, a user of these vending

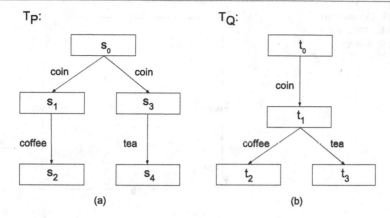

Fig. 15.16 Coffee-tea vending machine LST

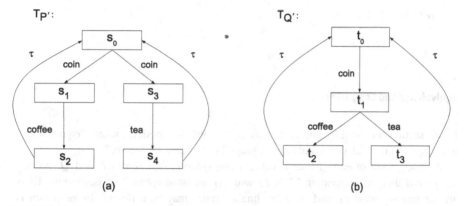

Fig. 15.17 Coffee-tea vending machine LST with τ transitions

machines can observe this difference in the behavior of these machines. Thus, trace equivalence does not reveal the true behavior. We need a different notion of equivalence in order to conclude whether or not two agents have "similar" (identical) behavior.

Consider the two LTS $T_{P'}$ and $T_{Q'}$ shown in Fig. 15.17(a) and Fig. 15.16(b). The LTS $T_{P'}$ is a refinement of the LTS T_P and the LTS $T_{Q'}$ is a refinement of the LTS T_Q. It can be inferred that

$T_P \approx_{tr} T_Q$

$T_{P'} \approx_{tr} T_{Q'}$

$T_P \approx_{wtr} T_{P'}$

$T_Q \approx_{wtr} T_{Q'}$

Fig. 15.18 Commutative
diagram for trace and weak
trace equivalences

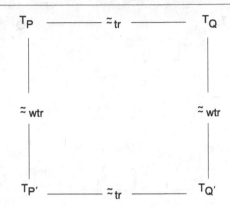

Figure 15.18 illustrates the "commutativity" of the trace equivalence and weak trace equivalence. Following the arrows from T_P in two ways we get the equation

$$\approx_{tr} \circ \approx_{wtr} = \approx_{wtr} \circ \approx_{tr} \tag{15.31}$$

15.4.5
Equivalence and Congruence

In this section, we consider different kinds of "equivalence" notions, where "equivalence" is a property on which two agents can be judged to be "like" or "unlike".

A strong form of equivalence is called *isomorphism*. Two agents P and Q are *isomorphic* if their corresponding LTSs T_P and T_Q are isomorphic. Two isomorphic LTSs are structurally identical and their labeling of states may be different. Isomorphism is the strongest form of equivalence. Formally, two LSTs $T = (S, A, \Sigma, s_0)$, and $T' = (S', A', \Sigma', s_0')$, are isomorphic, if, and only if, $A = A'$ and there exists a bijective function $\phi : S \mapsto S'$ such that

- $\phi : sort(T) \mapsto sort(T')$,
- $\phi(s_0) = s_0'$, and
- for every transition $s \xrightarrow{a} t \in \Sigma$, there exists a unique transition $\phi(s) \xrightarrow{\phi(a)} \phi(t) \in \Sigma'$.

Example 9 Consider processes R and S as defined below.

$$R \stackrel{\text{def}}{=} (P \mid Q) \backslash \{b\}, where$$

$$P \stackrel{\text{def}}{=} a \cdot \overline{b} \cdot P$$

$$Q \stackrel{\text{def}}{=} c \cdot b \cdot Q$$

$$S \stackrel{\text{def}}{=} a \cdot c \cdot \tau \cdot S + c \cdot a \cdot \tau \cdot S$$

It is easy to verify that T_R and T_S are isomorphic graphs. So, R and S are equivalent. □

Let us revisit the producer–consumer reduction in Example 5 and specialize it to a 1-place buffer and a 2-place buffer. The 1-place buffer definition is

$$B \overset{\text{def}}{=} in(x) \cdot B'$$
$$B' \overset{\text{def}}{=} \overline{out}(x) \cdot B \tag{15.32}$$

The 2-place buffer definition is

$$B_2 \overset{\text{def}}{=} in(x) \cdot B_1$$
$$B_1 \overset{\text{def}}{=} in(x) \cdot B_0 + \overline{out}(x) \cdot B_2 \tag{15.33}$$
$$B_0 \overset{\text{def}}{=} \overline{out}(x) \cdot B_1$$

Intuitively, it is suggested that a 2-place buffer can be implemented by using two 1-place buffers, provided we link the $\overline{out}$ channel of the first 1-place buffer to the in channel of the second buffer. This is achieved by relabeling functions f, and g such that $f(in) = newin$ and $g(\overline{out}) = \overline{newin}$, and then composing the two 1-place buffers as

$$TB \overset{\text{def}}{=} B[f] \mid B[g] \tag{15.34}$$

It is necessary to formally prove that TB and B_2 are "equivalent", in some precise sense. Once a proof is given, then we can infer that the systems $P \mid B_2 \mid Q$ and $P \mid (B[f] \mid B[g]) \mid Q$ are also equivalent in the same sense. This precise sense comes out of the relation *weak bisimulation* ($\sim_w$).

Weak bisimulation abstracts τ actions and is a suitable relation for stating the equivalence of processes like those given for producer-consumer systems that communicate through buffers. We extend the notation $P \overset{a}{\Rightarrow} Q$ if P may be transformed to Q by performing the action a preceded and succeeded by a finite number (possibly zero) of τ transitions. That is,

$$P \overset{a}{\Rightarrow} Q$$

stands for

$$P \xrightarrow{(\tau)^m a (\tau)^n} Q$$

For example if $P \overset{\text{def}}{=} \tau \cdot \tau \cdot a \cdot \tau \cdot Nil$ then

$$P \overset{\tau}{\Rightarrow} \tau \cdot a \cdot \tau \cdot Nil$$
$$P \overset{a}{\Rightarrow} a \cdot Nil$$
$$P \overset{a}{\Rightarrow} \tau \cdot Nil$$
$$P \overset{a}{\Rightarrow} Nil$$

We may write $P \stackrel{a}{\Rightarrow} Q$ only if the sequence of actions performed by P has at least one τ. We define the property that takes into account the special status of τ actions described above and would see the agents $a \cdot \tau \cdot Nil$ and $a \cdot Nil$ as "equivalent". This kind of "equivalence" is under the *weak bisimulation* property defined below.

Agents P and Q are *weakly bisimilar* if and only if

- (a) for each action $a \neq \tau$ that P can perform, there exists P' such that $P \stackrel{a}{\rightarrow} P'$, *either*
  (1) there exists Q' such that $Q \stackrel{a}{\Rightarrow} Q'$ and P' and Q' are equivalent, *or* (2) $a = \tau$ and P' is equivalent to Q, **and conversely,**
- (b) for each action $a \neq \tau$ that Q can perform, there exists Q' such that $Q \stackrel{a}{\rightarrow} Q'$, *either*
  (1) there exists P' such that $P \stackrel{a}{\Rightarrow} P'$ and P' and Q' are equivalent, *or* (2) $a = \tau$ and P is equivalent to Q'.

It is possible to prove that the processes TB and B_2 are weakly bisimilar or "equivalent" with respect to the bisimilarity property. Bisimilarity is *not* a relation.

Milner [9] has proved that there exists a relation $\approx$ on the set of agents that satisfy the bisimilarity property, and in fact that relation is the largest among such relations. Milner calls the relation $\approx$ *observational equivalence*, and writes $P \approx Q$ to express that P and Q are "observationally equivalent".

Substitutability and Strong Bisimilarity   In general, observational equivalence does not guarantee "substitutability". That is, if $P \approx Q$ it does *not* follow that $P + Q \approx Q + R$. From our discussion above it follows that $\tau \cdot a \cdot Nil \approx a \cdot Nil$. Let us do a 'sum' of the process $b \cdot Nil$ with the two processes in the above relation. Then we get the processes $P \stackrel{def}{=} \tau \cdot a \cdot Nil + b \cdot Nil$, and $Q \stackrel{def}{=} a \cdot Nil + b \cdot Nil$. The process P can perform a τ action to become $a \cdot Nil$, but the process Q cannot perform any sequence of τ actions with at least one τ in it. As such, $P \approx Q$ is *not* true. This example illustrates the important distinction between "observational equivalence" and the "actual behavior involving internal actions". An occurrence of an internal action, which is not observable in the environment of the system, will drastically affect the behavior of the system. This leads us to look at a much stronger notion of equivalence.

Another kind of bisimilarity is called *strong bisimilarity*, in which τ actions have the same status as visible actions. Agents P and Q are *strongly bisimilar* if and only if the following hold:

- if $P \stackrel{a}{\rightarrow} P'$ there exists a Q' such that $Q \stackrel{a}{\rightarrow} Q'$, and P' and Q' are strongly bisimilar, **and**
- if $Q \stackrel{a}{\rightarrow} Q'$ there exists a P' such that $P \stackrel{a}{\rightarrow} P'$, and P' and Q' are strongly bisimilar.

The processes $a \cdot \tau \cdot b \cdot Nil + c \cdot \tau \cdot b \cdot Nil$ and $c \cdot \tau \cdot b \cdot Nil + a \cdot \tau \cdot b \cdot Nil$ are strongly bisimilar. However, the processes $b \cdot (a \cdot Nil + c \cdot Nil)$ and $b \cdot a \cdot Nil + b \cdot c \cdot Nil)$ are not strongly bisimilar.

Strong bisimilarity allows substitutability. That is if process P is strongly bisimilar to process Q one can replace P with Q within any large system that includes P. Milner [9] showed that there exists a *congruence relation* $(=)$ that satisfies the strong bisimilarity property and it is the largest such relation. The congruence relation for agents is an *equivalence* relation that satisfies the substitution principle. This relation $=$, defined on the set of agents, is called *observational congruence* and is formally expressed below.

- *reflexive:* $P = P$
- *symmetric:* if $P = Q$ then $Q = P$
- *transitive:* if $P = Q$ and $Q = R$ then $P = R$
- *substitutivity:* if $P = Q$ then

$$
\begin{aligned}
a \cdot P &= a \cdot Q \\
P + R &= R + P \\
P \mid R &= R \mid P \\
P \backslash L &= Q \backslash L \\
P[f] &= Q[f] \\
\text{if } e \text{ then } P & \quad \text{if } e \text{ then } Q \\
\text{else } R &= \text{else } R \\
A \stackrel{\text{def}}{=} P & \\
\text{and} & \quad A = B \\
B \stackrel{\text{def}}{=} Q &
\end{aligned}
$$

The "equivalence hierarchy" is

$$
= implies \approx implies \sim_w implies \approx_{tr} implies \approx_{wtr}
$$

Under observational congruence principle we discuss *Expansion* and *Recursion* principles.

Expansion Principle   A system is modeled as a composition of agents. It includes parallel composition, and possibly relabeling, and restriction constructors. The *Expansion Principle* expresses the behavior of such a static agent in terms of the behaviors of its components and dynamic constructors, action prefixing and summation. We state it for the simplest case, a system modeled as a parallel composition of two agents P_1 and P_2. Informally, we need to apply the three compositions laws **Compose1**, **Compose2**, and **Compose3** for all possible combinations of actions (a_1, a_2), $a_1 \in sort(P_1)$, $a_2 \in sort(P_2)$. The result of such an application, written as a set of agents, is

$$
P_1 \mid P_2 = \{ a_1 \cdot (P_1' \mid P_2) + a_2 \cdot (P_1 \mid P_2') \mid P_1 \stackrel{a_1}{\rightarrow} P_1', P_2 \stackrel{a_2}{\rightarrow} P_2' \}
$$

$$
+ \{ \tau \cdot (P_1' \mid P_2') \mid P_1 \stackrel{\bar{1}}{\rightarrow} P_1', P_2 \stackrel{\bar{1}}{\rightarrow} P_2' \}
$$

Generalizing the above for $n > 2$ agents we can write the *Expansion Law* as follows:

$$
P_1 \mid \ldots \mid P_n = \sum_{i=1}^{n} \{ a_i \cdot (P_1 \mid \ldots \mid P_i' \mid \ldots \mid P_n) \mid P_i \stackrel{a_i}{\rightarrow} P_i' \}
$$

$$
= \sum_{1 \leq i < j \leq n} \{ \tau \cdot (P_1 \mid \ldots \mid P_i' \mid \ldots \mid P_j' \ldots \mid P_n) \mid (P_i \stackrel{1}{\rightarrow} P_i'), (P_j \stackrel{\bar{1}}{\rightarrow} P_j') \}
$$

Writing the *Expansion Principle* in the most general case, for an agent involving relabeling and restriction, is more complicated. It is harder to write because we have to avoid relabeled actions in a communication and defer from using restricted events. However, it is rather straightforward to write for specific agents, by just following the transition laws **Rel** and **Rest**.

Recursion Principle   Process definitions are often recursive and involve a finite number of recursive equations, as in

$$C \stackrel{\text{def}}{=} a \cdot C' \tag{15.35}$$

$$C' \stackrel{\text{def}}{=} \overline{b} \cdot C \tag{15.36}$$

The **Recursion Laws** of Milner [9] give the criteria which guarantee unique solutions to recursive equations. The first law ensures that in a recursive definition we obtain an agent congruent to the defining expression.

Law1-Recursion

$$\text{If } A \stackrel{\text{def}}{=} P \text{ then } A = P \tag{15.37}$$

To formulate a law for recursively defined agents, as in (15.35), *agent variables* and *incomplete agents* are defined. Let $\mathcal{V}$ denote a set of agent variables. If $X, Y \in \mathcal{V}$, then $a \cdot X$ and $a \cdot X \mid b \cdot Y$ are examples of incomplete agents. That is, an incomplete agent is an expression involving agent variables and constructors of the calculus. An incomplete agent can be instantiated to an agent by substituting agents for each agent variable. For example, substituting $b \cdot Nil$ for X and $c \cdot Nil + d \cdot Nil$ for Y in the expression $a \cdot X \mid b \cdot Y$, we get the agent $a \cdot b \cdot Nil \mid b \cdot (c \cdot Nil + d \cdot Nil)$. Recursive equations in CCS are of the form $X = E$, where X is an agent variable and E is an expression containing no agent variable other than X. In addition two restrictions are imposed on E.

- *Guardedness:* Every occurrence of X in E must be prefixed by an action. As examples, X is guarded in $a \cdot X + b \cdot Nil$, and in $a \mid b \cdot Nil$, but not in $a \cdot X + X$ or in $X + a \cdot Y$.
- *Sequential:* X should *not* occur in E within static constructors. Thus, X is not sequential in $a \cdot X \mid Y$ or in $a \cdot X + (a \cdot X \mid c \cdot Nil)$, but sequential in $a \cdot X + (b \cdot Nil \mid Y)$. In $X + Y$ the variable X is sequential but is not guarded, and in $a \cdot X \mid Y$ the variable X is guarded but not sequential.

Milner [9] has proved that the conditions of guardedness and sequentiality together are sufficient to guarantee up to $=$ of solutions to recursive equations in a single variable.

Law2-Recursion   Suppose that $X = E$ is an equation in agent variable X, E has no variable other than X, X is guarded in E and is sequential in E. Then any two solutions of the equation are observationally congruent. That is,

$$\text{if } P = E\{P/X\} \text{ and } Q = E\{Q/X\} \text{ then } P = Q \tag{15.38}$$

As an example, let us try to prove $A = B$, where

$$A \stackrel{\text{def}}{=} a \cdot A$$

$$B \stackrel{\mathrm{def}}{=} a \cdot a \cdot B$$

Consider the equation $X = E$, where E is the expression $a \cdot a \cdot X$. The variable X is both guarded and sequential in E. Thus, from **Law2**, if P and Q are both solutions to it then $P = Q$. But from **Law1** we infer that $B = a \cdot a \cdot B$ and hence B is a solution to the equation $X = E$. Likewise, A is a solution to $X = E$. Hence $A = B$.

Example 10 Consider the definitions

$$P \stackrel{\mathrm{def}}{=} a \cdot P + \tau \cdot b \cdot Nil$$

$$Q \stackrel{\mathrm{def}}{=} a \cdot Q + c \cdot Nil$$

$$R \stackrel{\mathrm{def}}{=} \bar{c} \cdot b \cdot Nil$$

$$S \stackrel{\mathrm{def}}{=} (Q \mid R) \backslash c$$

We want to prove $P = S$. It is easy to verify that P satisfies the equation

$$X = a \cdot X + \tau \cdot b \cdot Nil \tag{15.39}$$

and the variable X is guarded and is sequential in the expression $E(X) = a \cdot X + \tau \cdot b \cdot Nil$. In order to prove $P = S$, we must now prove that S satisfies (15.39). The definition of S is not recursive, but involves Q which is recursively defined. We calculate $Q \mid R$ using either expansion laws directly or using derivation tress discussed in Sect. 15.4.1, and then calculate $S = (Q \mid R) \backslash c$ using the restriction laws. We get the following results.

$$Q \mid R = a \cdot (Q \mid R) + c \cdot (Nil \mid R) + \bar{c} \cdot (Q \mid b \cdot Nil) + \tau \cdot (Nil \mid b \cdot Nil)$$

$$S = (Q \mid R) \backslash c$$

$$= a \cdot (Q \mid R) + \tau \cdot (Nil \mid b \cdot Nil)$$

Thus, S satisfies equation (15.39). From **Law2-Recursion** we infer $P = S$. $\qquad\square$

15.5
Exercises

1. Define agents *Sum* and *Difference*, which repeatedly input a number at each of their input ports and then output, respectively, their sum and difference. Using these agents, construct an agent that has the capabilities of both *Sum* and *Difference*.
2. Define an agent *CoinChanger* which has two ports, one for accepting a 1$ coin and the other for delivering 25c and 10c coins. The agents must have the ability to produce any sequence of 25c and 10c coins the sum of whose values is equal to 1$.
3. Define an agent *Divisor* which has two input ports and one output port. At each input port, it can receive an integer value. It behaves conditionally, by outputting the quotient if one of the input number divides the other and outputting the smaller of the two input numbers otherwise.

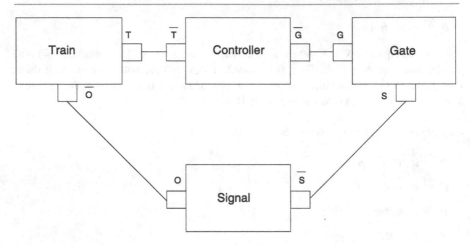

Fig. 15.19 Train-controller-gate-signal System

4. Introduce a new process *Signal* in *TCG* system in order that (1) the *Gate* process communicates with the *Signal* process, and (2) the *Signal* process communicates with the *Train* process. See Fig. 15.19. The new system *TCGS* should have the additional behavior defined as follows:

   - The *Gate* process informs the *Signal* process either to turn *green* or *red*, upon receiving the information *close* from the controller. In case the *Gate* process informs the *Signal* process to turn *red*, it will send the message *not_closing* to the *Controller* process.
   - The *Gate* process triggers the internal action *down* only after it sends the message *green* to the *Signal* process.
   - If the *Controller* process receives the message *not_closing* it sends the message *close* again to the *Gate* process.
   - The *Train* process will *stop* if it receives (sees) *red* signal; otherwise, it will proceed toward the gate.

   Give the port labels for the new set of communication requirements and the full CCS specification of the system *TCGS*.

5. Give an agent definition for the behavior of an elevator that can service two floors. In the ground floor, the elevator can either stay in the first floor or can go up to the second floor. In the second floor, the elevator can either stay in the second floor or go down to the first floor. A user in a floor can get into the elevator only if the elevator is in that floor and then go to the floor as serviced by the elevator.

6. Using the transition rules, find all pairs (a, P') such that $P \xrightarrow{a} P'$ where P is defined by

$$P \stackrel{\text{def}}{=} ((a \cdot P + \overline{b} \cdot \textit{Nil}) \mid (b \cdot P + \overline{a} \cdot \tau \cdot \textit{Nil})) \backslash a$$

7. Draw the derivation trees for the agents

$$a \cdot (b \cdot c \cdot Nil + c \cdot b \cdot Nil)$$

$$a \cdot (b \cdot Nil \mid c \cdot Nil)$$

For the two trees investigate trace equivalence and bisimilarity. Which one holds?

8. Draw the derivation trees for the agents

$$P \stackrel{\text{def}}{=} a \cdot (b \cdot Nil + \tau \cdot P) + a \cdot \tau \cdot P$$

$$Q \stackrel{\text{def}}{=} ((a \cdot \tau \cdot Nil \mid \overline{a} \cdot Nil) + c \cdot Nil) \backslash a) + b \cdot Q$$

$$R \stackrel{\text{def}}{=} (c \cdot P) \mid (a \cdot Q)$$

9. Determine whether or not $R \approx S$ from the following definitions of agents.

$$P \stackrel{\text{def}}{=} get(x) \cdot \overline{hold}(x) \cdot P$$

$$Q \stackrel{\text{def}}{=} hold(x) \cdot \overline{put}(x) \cdot Q$$

$$R \stackrel{\text{def}}{=} (P \mid Q) \backslash \{hold\}$$

$$S \stackrel{\text{def}}{=} get(x) \cdot put(x) \cdot S$$

10. Which of the following expressions satisfy both *guardedness* and *substitutability* properties?
    (a) $a \cdot Nil$
    (b) $\tau \cdot X + X$
    (c) $a \cdot Nil \mid (a \cdot X + \tau \cdot Nil)$
    (d) $a \cdot X + b \cdot Y$
    (e) $a \cdot (X \mid \tau \cdot Y)$

11. For the agent definitions

$$P \stackrel{\text{def}}{=} \overline{a} \cdot c \cdot P$$

$$Q \stackrel{\text{def}}{=} a \cdot Q + \tau \cdot b \cdot Nil$$

calculate $(P \mid Q) \backslash a$ and simplify it to an agent R such that R satisfies an expression $E(X)$ in which X satisfies the guarded and sequential properties.

15.6
Bibliographic Notes

Research in process calculi began in earnest with Robin Milner's seminal work [8, 9] on Calculus of Communicating Systems (CCS) during the period 1973–1980. During the same period, Hoare developed a calculus for Communicating Sequential Processes (CSP) [6, 7]. In 1982, Bergstra and Klopp [2] introduced the basics of Algebra of Communicating Processes (ACP), and in subsequent papers [3, 4], they developed a full version of ACP with synchronization and simulation. The majority of other process calculi work can trace their roots to one of CCS, CSP, and ACP. A comparative study on these three models can be found in [1]. Other models of concurrency include Petri Nets developed by Petri [11] and the Actor Model [5].

An important issue in CCS is the specification of systems composed of agents and verification of certain properties in the modeled systems. We have explained in sufficient detail how systems may be put together. In this endeavor, the notation, sequence of topics, and many examples are either liberally taken or adapted from the lecture notes of Walker [13]. However, verification is not discussed in any detail. It is a subject that requires a study in itself. It requires a much subtler aspects of algebra and logic which is both vast and deep that it cannot be fitted within the scope of this chapter.

Current research on process calculi focuses on developing new process calculi for mobile systems and biological systems. Milner's Pi-calculus [10] is inspiring the work on mobile process calculi. Different kinds of modal logics are studied in order to reason about arbitrary properties of processes, following the basic ideas of Hoare.

References

1. Baeten JCM (2003) Over 30 years of process algebra: past, present, and future. In: Accto L, Ésik Z, Fokkink W, Ingólfsdóttir A (eds) Process algebra: open problems and future directions. BRICS notes series, vol NS-03-3, pp 7–12
2. Bergstra JA, Klop JW (1982) Fixed point semantics in process algebra. Technical report IW 208, Mathematical Center, Amsterdam
3. Bergstra JA, Klop JW (1984) Process algebra for synchronous communication. Inf Control 60(1):109–137
4. Bergstra JA, Klop JW (1985) Algebra of communicating processes with abstraction. Theor Comput Sci 37:77–121
5. Hewitt C, Baker H Jr. (1977) Actors and continuous functionals. MIT/LCS/TR-194
6. Hoare CAR (1978) Communicating sequential processes. Commun ACM 21(8):666–677
7. Hoare CAR (1985) Communicating sequential processes. Prentice-Hall, New York
8. Milner R (1980) A calculus for communicating systems. Lecture notes in computer science, vol 92. Springer, Berlin
9. Milner R (1989) Communication and concurrency. Prentice-Hall, New York
10. Milner R (1999) Communicating and mobile systems, the Pi-Calculus. Springer, Berlin
11. Petri CA (1962) Kommunikation mit automaten. PhD Thesis, Institut fuer Instrumentelle Mathematik, Bonn
12. Petri CA (1980) Introduction to general net theory. In: Brauer W (ed) Proc advanced course on general net theory, processes, systems. Lecture notes in computer science, vol 84. Springer, Berlin, pp 1–20
13. Walker D (1987) Introduction to a Calculus of communicating systems. Technical report ECS-LFCS-87-22, Department of Computer Science, University of Edinburgh, Edinburgh

Part VI
Model-Based Specifications

This part describes the four model-based specification techniques VDM-SL, Z, Object-Z and the B-Method. Each technique is unique in some respect. VDM-SL is based on three-valued logic, while the other methods use classical two-valued logic. There are many similarities between VDM-SL and Z specification languages. The B-Method is based on the notion of abstract machine, and provides syntactic structures and proof obligations for refining an abstract machine into a more concrete representation. Object-Z supports the development of specifications in object-oriented style, and its syntactic structure is closer to many OO programming languages. The learning outcomes from this part are the following:

- VDMl-SL specification language—its syntax and semantics
- specification examples in VDM-SL
- data refinement of VDM-SL specifications
- reasoning about VDM-SL specifications
- Z specification notation—its syntax and semantics
- specification examples in Z
- data refinement of Z specifications
- proving properties using Z specifications
- Object-Z specification language—its syntax and semantics
- OO features in Object-Z-encapsulation, inheritance and polymorphism
- specification examples in Object-Z
- Abstract Mathematical Notation (AMN)
- B-Method and AMN used in the B-Method
- abstract machines in B
- specification examples in B
- refinement of B specifications
- proof obligations in B

Vienna Development Method

16

The *Vienna Development Method* (VDM) is an environment for the modeling and development of sequential software systems. The specification language of VDM has evolved from Meta-IV, the language used at IBM's Vienna development laboratory for specifying the semantics of the PL/I programming language in the early seventies. The current version of the VDM specification language, VDM-SL, has been standardized by the International Standards Organization (ISO). It supports the modeling and analysis of software systems at different levels of abstraction. Using VDM-SL constructs, both data and algorithmic abstractions expressed in one level can be refined to a lower level to derive a concrete model that is closer to the final implementation of the system.

In this chapter, we present a tutorial of VDM-SL, explain refinement techniques, and discuss proof rules. Mathematical proofs are used to demonstrate the consistency of models and also to show that a refined concrete model faithfully conforms to its abstract model. However, we put less emphasis in proof techniques and focus on the use of abstraction to construct precise models. We introduce several examples to illustrate the effective use of VDM-SL features for modeling software systems of reasonable complexity.

16.1
Structure of a VDM Specification

VDM supports two kinds of abstractions—*representational abstraction* and *operational abstraction*. In representational abstraction, the data is abstracted from the representational details of data structures to be used in the final implementation of the system. Operational abstraction describes the abstract algorithmic manipulations of the data introduced in the representational abstraction as first-order predicate logic formulas. These constraints are expressed as functions and operations in the specification.

A VDM specification is structured into various blocks, where each block is identified by a distinct keyword:

V.S. Alagar, K. Periyasamy, *Specification of Software Systems*,
Texts in Computer Science,
DOI 10.1007/978-0-85729-277-3_16, © Springer-Verlag London Limited 2011

types
               \<type definitions>
values
               \<value definitions>
functions
               \<function definitions>
operations
               \<operation definitions>
state \<state name> **of**
               \<state definition>
end

There is no explicit ordering among these blocks. Moreover, not all of them are required to be present in a specification. To illustrate, a portion of the VDM specification for a hotel reservation system is given in Example 1.

Example 1 Specification for a Hotel Reservation System.

types
    RoomNumber = {1, ..., 100};
    RoomStatus = Available | Occupied
state *Reservation* **of**
    rooms: RoomNumber $\xrightarrow{m}$ *RoomStatus*

    init mk-*Reservation (rms)* $\triangleq$
        $\forall$ *rn* $\in$ **dom** *rooms* • *rooms(rn) = Available*
end
operations
    book-room (roomno: RoomNumber)
    ext wr *rooms: RoomNumber* $\xrightarrow{m}$ *RoomStatus*
    pre *roomno* $\in$ **dom** *rooms*
    post
        let *st: RoomStatus = Occupied* **in**
        rooms = $\overleftarrow{rooms}$† {roomno $\mapsto$ st};   □

In Example 1, *RoomNumber* denotes the type of room numbers, numbers ranging from 1 to 100. The status of a room is either available or occupied. The state of the system consists of the rooms and the status of each room in the hotel. The only operation specified in this example is *book-room*. The precondition of the operation checks the validity of the room number. The postcondition ensures that the status of the selected room is occupied.

16.2
Representational Abstraction

Representational abstraction describes the modeling primitives necessary to specify a software. A model of the software is constructed from the data types built into the language and from those data types that can be constructed by composing the already defined types.

Table 16.1 Conventions for identifiers

Convention	Synopsis	Used for
lowercase bold roman	**nil**	keywords
lowercase italics	*student*	variables
lowercase italics with first letter in uppercase italics	*Faculty*	types
uppercase roman	ORANGE	quote type, state variables
lowercase bold	**mk_ ...**	make function
– lowercase roman	– comments	comments

There are five mathematical structures—*set, sequence, map, record* and *tuple*. These structures help us to build composite types.

16.2.1
Identifiers

Identifiers in VDM-SL are formed using alphanumeric characters and Greek letters. The language does not restrict the length of identifiers. Hyphens and primes are permitted within identifiers but they should not appear at the beginning of an identifier. The identifiers in VDM-SL are case sensitive. Thus, the two identifiers *student* and *Student* are different.

Table 16.1 describes conventional font selection followed in this book for various syntactic structures. In addition, we also use subscripts as part of identifiers.

Comments and Separators   Comments in VDM-SL are written with '–' preceding the comment. Any text preceding '–' is part of the specification:

– This is a comment in VDM-SL.
$x \notin S$ – x is not a member of the given set

If comments extend to several lines, it is necessary to start each line of comment with '–'. Each line in VDM-SL corresponds to a line in printed output of the specification.

Within a block of a VDM specification, such as a type definition and an operation definition, individual statements or expressions are separated by semicolons. However, there is no semicolon at the end of the block; instead, the keyword such as **types** and **functions** itself acts as the separator.

16.2.2
Simple Types

Simple types in VDM-SL can be classified into two categories: *primitive types* defined in the language, and *quote types* introduced by the user. These types are called simple because they are treated as basic elements of the current specification. Consequently, these types

Table 16.2 Primitive types in VDM-SL

Symbol	Type
$\mathbb{Z}$	Integer
$\mathbb{N}$	Natural number
$\mathbb{N}_1$	Natural number excluding zero
$\mathbb{R}$	Real number
$\mathbb{Q}$	Rational number
$\mathbb{B}$	Boolean
char	Character
token	Token type

Table 16.3 Arithmetic operators in VDM-SL

Operator	Synopsis	Meaning
↑	a ↑ b	exponentiation
div	a **div** b	integer division
rem	a **rem** b	remainder after integer division
mod	a **mod** b	modulus operator
abs	**abs** a	returns the absolute value
floor	**floor** (a/b)	floor operator

are not further elaborated in the current specification. Representations of these types are left to the implementation level. The operations that can be performed on simple types include testing for equality, inequality and membership.

Primitive Types   The primitive types in VDM-SL are given in Table 16.2. Types other than the **token** type resemble those in a programming language. The **token** type contains a countable collection of distinct values, called *tokens*. There is no internal representation for a token. It is generally used to define a type whose definition is deferred until the later stages of the development process. For example, the type definition

   Person = **token**

introduces the type *Person*, which is left unspecified in the current specification.

Arithmetic and Logic Operators   In addition to the standard set of arithmetic operators such as '+', '−', '∗', '/' and logical operators '<', '>', '≤' and '≥', operators enumerated in Table 16.3 are also available in VDM-SL.

   The sign of 'a **rem** b' is the same as that of 'a'; the sign of 'a **mod** b' is the same as that of 'b'. Other operators in Table 16.3 have their usual meanings.

Quote Types   A quote type, unlike a token, has an internal representation defined by a string of distinguished letters. In this book, we use upper case alphabets in roman fonts to represent quote types. The string representing a quote type denotes both the type and its value. For example, ORANGE is a quote type whose value is ORANGE.

16.2.3
Composite Types

Composite types are constructed from the types already introduced in the specification (simple or composite) using type constructors. In general, a composite type is defined along with its type invariant which constrains the set of elements of the type.

Union Type A *union* type allows us to combine two or more types into one composite type. The syntax is as follows:

$$T = T_1|T_2|\ldots|T_n$$

where T is a union type and $T_1, T_2, \ldots, T_n$ are component types; the symbol '|' is part of the syntax. The semantics of a union type is that an instance of type T can be substituted by an instance of any one of its component types. For example, if the type *User* in a library environment is defined as

$$User = Faculty \mid Student$$

then members of the type *User* are the union of the members of the types *Faculty* and *Student*.

Union and quote types can be composed as in

$$Message = SUCCESS \mid INPUT\text{-}ERROR \mid MISSING\text{-}PARAMETER$$

where *Message* can be used, for example, to denote the return values of a function.

Union type is associative and commutative. The following definitions are equivalent.

$$User = (Faculty \mid Student) \mid Staff$$

$$User = Faculty \mid (Student \mid Staff)$$

$$User = Staff \mid (Faculty \mid Student)$$

VDM-SL uses a special keyword **nil** to denote a null type. As the name implies, **nil** stands for a type having no value. However, **nil** cannot be used by itself. It can only be combined with other types composing a *union* type. For example,

$$B = \textbf{nil}$$

is illegal, and

$$B = \mathbb{N} \mid \textbf{nil}$$

denotes a type B whose instances include natural numbers and null value.

An optional type, represented by $[T]$, consists of the union of some type T and **nil** type; i.e.,

$$[T] \equiv T \mid \textbf{nil}$$

Table 16.4 Set operators

Operator	Synopsis	Meaning
card	**card** S	cardinality of the set S
$\in$	$x \in S$	x is a member of the set S
$\cup$	$S_1 \cup S_2$	set union
$\cap$	$S_1 \cap S_2$	set intersection
$\setminus$	$S_1 \setminus S_2$	set difference
$\subseteq$	$S_1 \subseteq S_2$	subset
$\subset$	$S_1 \subset S_2$	proper subset
$=$	$S_1 = S_2$	set equality
$\neq$	$S_1 \neq S_2$	set inequality
$\bigcup$	$\bigcup SS$	distributed union of the sets SS
$\bigcap$	$\bigcap SS$	distributed intersection of the sets SS
$\{i, \ldots, j\}$	$\{i, \ldots, j\}$	subset of integers from i to j, both inclusive

Set VDM-SL deals with only finite sets [9]. Countable sets, although not finite, are treated as if they are finite. This seems to simplify some proof obligations. VDM-SL uses the notion for set enumeration and set comprehension as discussed in Chap. 12.

The syntax for a declarative definition of a set in VDM-SL is

P–**set**

which denotes the set of elements of type P; the symbol '–' and the keyword **set** are part of the syntax. Some examples for set type definition are given below:

$Digits = \{0, 1, 2, 3, 4, 5, 6, 7, 8, 9\}$
$Even = \{n \in \mathbb{N} \mid n \textbf{ mod } 2 = 0\}$
– no predicate part
$Even = \{n \mid n \in \mathbb{N} \wedge n \textbf{ mod } 2 = 0\}$
– type inferred from declaration; no predicate part
$Even = \{n \mid n \in \mathbb{N} \bullet n \textbf{ mod } 2 = 0\}$
$Person = \textbf{token}$
        $Employee = Person\textbf{-set}$

Empty set is denoted by { }.

Table 16.4 enumerates the VDM-SL operators on sets. The semantics for these operators is derived from set theory.

Notice that there is no symbol in VDM-SL for superset and proper superset; instead, supersets can be specified using the symbols for subset and proper subset.

Sequence A sequence type can be defined using the declarative syntax, as a type or using the constructive style as enumeration and comprehension. The two forms of declarative syntax for sequences are T^* and T^+ in which T denotes the type of elements of the sequence. The declaration T^+ defines a nonempty sequence type, whereas the declaration T^* introduces a general sequence type which includes an empty sequence with no value.

Table 16.5 Sequence operators

Operator	Synopsis	Meaning
len	**len** S	length of the sequence S
$\frown$	$S_1 \frown S_2$	sequence concatenation
conc	**conc** SS	distributed concatenation of the sequence of sequences SS
hd	**hd** S	head of the sequence S
tl	**tl** S	tail of the sequence S
inds	**inds** S	indices of the sequence S; returned as a set of positive integers
elems	**elems** S	set of elements comprising the sequence S
$(i, \ldots, j)$	$S(i, \ldots, j)$	subsequence of S from the ith element to the jth element, both inclusive
$=$	$S_1 = S_2$	sequence equality
$\neq$	$S_1 \neq S_2$	sequence inequality

The syntax for sequence enumeration is similar to that for sets, except the parentheses '{' and '}' in sets are replaced by the square brackets '[' and ']', respectively. For example,

$$Vowels = [\text{'a', 'e', 'i', 'o', 'u'}]$$

introduces the sequence *Vowels* having five members.

Sequence comprehension uses the syntax that is similar to that of set comprehension in which the curly parentheses are replaced by square brackets. Thus,

$$Cubes = [n \uparrow 3 \mid n \in \{1, 2, 3\}]$$

refers to the sequence $[1, 8, 27]$. This sequence can also be written as

$$Cubes = [m \in \mathbb{N} \mid m = n \uparrow 3 \wedge n \in \{1, 2, 3\}]$$

The ordering of the elements in the sequence *Cubes* depends on the natural order of elements in the set $\{1, 2, 3\}$. Thus, the following definitions denote the same sequence.

$$Cubes_1 = [m \in \mathbb{N} \mid m = n \uparrow 3 \wedge n \in \{1, 2, 3\}]$$
$$Cubes_2 = [m \in \mathbb{N} \mid m = n \uparrow 3 \wedge n \in \{1, \ldots, 3\}]$$
$$Cubes_2 = [m \in \mathbb{N} \mid m = n \uparrow 3 \wedge n \in \{3, 2, 1\}]$$

The empty sequence is represented by [ ].

Individual elements of a sequence can be accessed by subscripts as in $d(5)$, $d(i)$ and $d(i + j - k)$. The parentheses are part of the syntax. In the second and third cases, the variable 'i' and the expression 'i + j − k' must be of type $\mathbb{N}_1$. By convention, VDM-SL sequences always start at the index position 1.

Operators on sequences are listed in Table 16.5. The semantics of most of the operators on sequences are given in Chap. 12; this is reinforced in the following example.

Example 2 Operations on a Sequence.
Let $S_1 = [a,b,c,d,e]$, $S_2 = [b,c,d,e,a]$, $S_3 = [f,g,h]$ and $SS = [S_1 \ S_2 \ S_3]$

$S_1 \frown S_2 = [a,b,c,d,e,b,c,d,e,a]$
conc $SS = [a,b,c,d,e,b,c,d,e,a,f,g,h]$
inds $S_1 = \{1,2,3,4,5\}$
inds $S_2 = \{1,2,3,4,5\}$
inds $S_3 = \{1,2,3\}$
elems $S_1 = \{a,b,c,d,e\}$
elems $S_2 = \{a,b,c,d,e\}$
elems $S_3 = \{f,g,h\}$
$S_1 (1, \ldots, 3) = [a,b,c]$
$S_3 (2, \ldots, 2) = [g]$
$S_2 (3, \ldots, 2) = $ **undefined** since j $<$ i   □

Map   A map in VDM-SL is an abstraction of a finite function. As with functions, a map also has a *domain* and a *range*. A map associates each element from the domain to at most one element in the range. It is convenient to think of a map as a finite table of pairs where each domain element appears at most once. A map can be defined declaratively as a type or can be constructively defined by enumeration or comprehension. The VDM-SL syntax for map is

$$D \xrightarrow{m} R$$

where D is the domain of the map and R is its range. The symbol $\xrightarrow{m}$ is part of the syntax. In the following example, M denotes a map type from X to Y:

$X = \{1, 2, 3, 4, 5\}$
$Y = \{1, 8, 27, 64, 125\}$
$M = X \xrightarrow{m} Y$

Individual elements of a map can be enumerated as

$M_1 = \{1 \mapsto 1, 2 \mapsto 8, 3 \mapsto 27, 4 \mapsto 64, 5 \mapsto 125\}$

The symbols '{', '↦' and '}' are part of the syntax. The empty map is represented as $\{\mapsto\}$.

The syntax for map comprehension closely resembles that of set comprehension:

$M_2 = \{n \mapsto m \mid n \in X \wedge m \in Y \bullet m = n \uparrow 3\}$

Notice that maps in VDM-SL are finite. It is possible to define a map type T in which the domain type is infinite (e.g., $\mathbb{N}$). However, when a variable v is declared to be of type T, the domain of v must be constrained to a finite set. This can be achieved by specifying a condition on v. See the following example:

$M_3 = \mathbb{N}_1 \xrightarrow{m} \mathbb{N}_1$
$Cubes : M_3 = \{n \mapsto m \mid n \leq 5 \bullet m = n \uparrow 3\}$

Table 16.6 summarizes map operators in VDM-SL. The semantics for many of these operators have been discussed in Chap. 12. The following example reinforces the semantics:

Table 16.6 Map operators

Operator	Synopsis	Meaning
dom	**dom** M	domain of the map M
rng	**rng** M	range of the map M
M^{-1}	M^{-1}	Inverse of the map M; M should be an injective map; $M^{-1} = \{b \mapsto a \mid a \mapsto b \in M\}$
$\cup$	$M_1 \cup M_2$	map union
$\dagger$	$M_1 \dagger M_2$	map overriding
$\circ$	$M_1 \circ M_2$	map composition
( )	M(a)	map application
$\lhd$	$D \lhd M$	domain restriction
$\lhd\!\!\!-$	$D \lhd\!\!\!- M$	domain subtraction
$\rhd$	$M \rhd R$	range restriction
$-\!\!\!\rhd$	$M -\!\!\!\rhd R$	range subtraction

Example 3 Operations on a map.
Let $M_1 = \{1 \mapsto a, 2 \mapsto b, 3 \mapsto c\}$, $M_2 = \{1 \mapsto a, 3 \mapsto a\}$, $M_3 = \{a \mapsto \theta, b \mapsto \phi, c \mapsto \psi\}$ and $M_4 = \{1 \mapsto a, 4 \mapsto d\}$.

$$M_1^{-1} = \{a \mapsto 1, b \mapsto 2, c \mapsto 3\}$$

Notice that the inverse of a map M need not be a map; however, if M is bijective, the inverse M^{-1} of M is bijective. Note that M_2^{-1} is not a map.

The union of two maps is defined only if they have consistent maplets. $M_1 \cup M_2$ cannot be determined because the maplets $3 \mapsto c$ in M_1 and $3 \mapsto a$ in M_2 are inconsistent. The union of M_1 and M_4 exists and is given by

$$M_1 \cup M_4 = \{1 \mapsto a, 2 \mapsto b, 3 \mapsto c, 4 \mapsto d\}$$

$$M_1 \dagger M_2 = \{1 \mapsto a, 2 \mapsto b, 3 \mapsto a\}$$

Two maps can be composed only if the range of the first map is a subset of the domain of the second map.

$$M_1 \circ M_3 = \{1 \mapsto \theta, 2 \mapsto \phi, 3 \mapsto \psi\}$$

The map composition operator $\circ$ is right associative. The semantics of domain and range restriction operators are carried over from Chap. 12.

$$\{1\} \lhd M_1 = \{1 \mapsto a\}$$

$$\{1\} \lhd\!\!\!- M_1 = \{2 \mapsto b, 3 \mapsto c\}$$

$$M_2 \rhd \{a\} = \{1 \mapsto a, 3 \mapsto a\}$$

$$M_2 -\!\!\!\rhd \{a\} = \{\mapsto\}$$

$$M_1(1) = a, M_2(3) = a, M_4(4) = d \qquad \square$$

Record   While set and sequence types are constructed from the same type of elements, a composite type with different component types can be represented by a *record* type. VDM-SL syntax for a record is

$T :: v_1 : T_1$
$\qquad v_2 : T_2$
$\qquad \dots$
$\qquad v_n : T_n$

where T is a record type and $T_1, T_2, \dots, T_n$ represent the types of components of T. These components, called *fields*, are identified by the variables $v_1, v_2, \dots, v_n$. The symbol '::' is part of the syntax. The record type given below defines a collection of books:

Book :: title : String
*   author : String*
*   year : $\mathbb{N}$*

Individual fields of a composite type can be extracted using the selection operator '.' as in *Book.author* and *Book.year*. An object of the composite type can be constructed using the '**mk-**' (make) function on the values of the individual fields. For example, if *tit, aut* and *y* are the values of the individual fields of a book, the book object can be constructed as

mk-$Book(tit, aut, y)$

The arguments for the **mk-** function can be constants, variables or expressions:

mk-$Book(tit, \text{``John''}, 1984)$

While constructing an object of a record type, the values of the individual fields in the '**mk-**' function should be given to match the order and types of the components in the definition of the record type. For example, the '**mk-**' function

mk-$Book(aut, tit, y)$

is type correct; however, it does not represent the same object as the book

mk-$Book(tit, aut, y)$

Two records r_1 and r_2 of type T are equal if the values of their corresponding fields are equal.

The values of the individual fields of a record can be modified using the μ operator; the syntax for μ operator is

$\mu(< record >, < field_1 > \mapsto < value_1 >, < field_2 > \mapsto < value_2 >, \dots,$
$\quad < field_n > \mapsto < value_n >)$

The expression

$\mu(Book, title \mapsto \text{``Set Theory''}, author \mapsto \text{``Shaw''}, year \mapsto 1945)$

denotes the book "Set Theory" written by "Shaw" with its date of publication "1945".

Cartesian Product A *Cartesian Product* type is an ordered collection of types grouped together by a single name. VDM-SL syntax for Cartesian product type is

$$T = T_1 \times T_2 \times \cdots \times T_n$$

where T is the name of the product type and $T_1, T_2, \ldots, T_n$ are the component types. The symbol '$\times$' is part of the syntax. Cartesian product types are not associative. They can be compared for equality. Two product types T_1 and T_2 are equal if and only if the order and the types of individual components in both product types are the same. For example, if the types *Book*, *Monograph*, *Collection* and *Lecture_notes* are defined as

Book = *String* × *String* × $\mathbb{N}$
Collection = *String* × *String* × $\mathbb{N}$
Monograph = $\mathbb{N}$ × *String* × *String*
Lecture_notes = *String* × (*String* × $\mathbb{N}$)

then

Book = *Collection*
Book ≠ *Monograph*   –ordering different
Book ≠ *Lecture_notes*   –types mismatch

The elements of a Cartesian product type are termed as *tuples*. A tuple belonging to a Cartesian product type can be constructed using '**mk-**' function. As an example, a tuple of type *Book* can be constructed as follows:

mk-(*"Set Theory", "Shaw", 1945*)

Notice that the '**mk-**' function for tuples does not involve any name, which is in contrast to the '**mk-**' function for records. As a result, one cannot infer the product type of a tuple from the '**mk-**' function. For example, the tuple

mk-(*"Set Theory", "Shaw", 1945*)

may belong to either *Book* or *Collection* or both.

Function Types A function type has a domain and a range, and its elements are functions having the same domain and range. Thus, in

$$F = \mathbb{N} \to \mathbb{N}$$

F is a function type which defines the set of all functions from natural numbers to natural numbers. The values of a function type can be given using a lambda expression or using a function definition. The following are some instances of the function type F:

$(\lambda n : \mathbb{N} \bullet n + 2) \in F$
    $- accepts\ n,\ returns\ n + 2$
$(\lambda n : \mathbb{N} \bullet n^2) \in F$
    $- accepts\ n,\ returns\ n^2$
$(\lambda n : \mathbb{N} \bullet n \mathbf{\ mod\ } 2) \in F$
    $- accepts\ n,\ returns\ n\ \mathbf{mod}\ 2$

Flat Types Function types in VDM-SL are treated separately and are called *non-flat types*. Correspondingly, the values of a non-flat type are called *non-flat values*. Non-flat types and non-flat values can be used just like their flat counterparts such as set, sequence, map and Cartesian product, except in the following situations:

1. Non-flat types can neither be passed as parameters to operations nor be returned as results from operations; however, they can be passed as parameters or results of a function.
2. Values of set and map types should not contain non-flat values. For example, in

   $Square = (\lambda n : \mathbb{N} \bullet n^2)$
   $Square\text{-}set = Squares\text{–}\mathbf{set}$

   The type *Square-set* is not valid since elements of this set are non-flat values. Constructors of set and map types cannot be applied to non-flat types.
3. State and local variable declarations should not contain non-flat types.
4. Equality and inequality are not defined for non-flat values.

16.2.4
Patterns, Bindings and Values

A pattern in VDM-SL is a template consisting of a nonempty collection of identifiers, symbols and values. The purpose of a pattern is to match the entities in the template to a set of values of appropriate types. Table 16.7 lists some patterns, the types for the identifiers in the patterns and their matching values. When an identifier in a pattern matches a value, a binding occurs between them. For example, if a pattern (x, y) matches the value (2, 3), then the binding "x to 2 and y to 3" occurs. Pattern matching and binding are tightly coupled in the sense that they always occur together. VDM-SL supports tuple patterns, set patterns, sequence patterns and record patterns. Table 16.7 lists several tuple patterns. While defining a set or a sequence pattern, the set or the sequence cannot be defined using comprehension. Record patterns match with values of records with the same record tag. Record patterns are generally used in defining type invariants, state invariants and initial state conditions. The initial state definition

  init mk-*Reservation(rms)* $\overset{\triangle}{=}$

    $\forall rn \in dom\ rooms \bullet rooms(rn) = Available$

Table 16.7 Simple patterns

Pattern	Type Information	Some Possible Matching Values	Comment
x	$x : \mathbb{Z}$	-15 2478 0 ...	any integer value
(x, y)	$x : \mathbb{N}, y : \mathbb{N}$	(0,0) (1,2) (10,12) ...	pair of natural numbers
(4, n, b)	$n : \mathbb{Z}, b : \mathbb{R}$	(4,0,1.6) (4,-7,-3.68) (4,17,0.0) ...	The first value must be the integer constant '4'
(x, –, y)	$x : \mathbb{Z}, y : \mathbb{Z}$	0, {1,2,3}, 10 15, [3,4,7], 32 1, 2, 3 ...	triple with second element as don't care

in Example 1 involves a record pattern matching the record *Reservation*. Patterns may sometimes include *don't care identifiers* as in (x, -, y). In such a case, the pattern denotes a tuple with three components which matches with any 3-tuple value as long as the types of *x* and that of the first component are the same and the types of *y* and that of the third component are the same. The matching of the second component is ignored. For example, if x and y are both natural numbers, then both tuples (0, {1,2,3}, 10) and (15, [3,4,7], 32) will match the pattern (x, -, y).

Table 16.8 illustrates the values that match some set and sequence patterns:

16.2.5
State Representation

A model of the software system under development can be constructed using the VDM-SL type definitions and structures introduced in the previous sections. A VDM specification for a problem consists of a *state*, which includes data type representations for problem domain objects, and *operations*, which express the changes to the state variables consistent with the requirements of the problem. In other words, the state is a model of the problem and operations on the state bring out the behavior of the model. The following example illustrates the construction of a model from the requirements.

Example 4 Course registration system.

Table 16.8 Set and sequence patterns

Pattern	Type Information	Some Possible Matching Values	Comment
{a,b,c}	a,b,c : $\mathbb{Z}$	{1,2,3} {-100,0,100} …	set of three integers
$s_1 \cup s_2$	s_1, s_2 : $\mathbb{Z}$-**set**	{1,8} $\cup$ {7,8} {} $\cup$ {3,7} …	union of two integer sets
$s_1 \setminus \{5\}$	s_1 : $\mathbb{Z}$-**set**	{} \ {5} {1,5,7} \ {5} …	difference between two integer sets; the second set must be a singleton with its only element as '5'
[a,b,c]	a,b,c : $\mathbb{Z}$-**set**	[{1,2}, {5} , {2, 0, -17}] [{}, {}, {}] …	sequence of three integer sets
$t_1 \frown t_2$	t_1, t_2 : Char*	['a'] $\frown$ ['b'] ['a','b','c'] $\frown$ [ ] …	concatenation of two character sequences

This example constructs a model of a course registration system based on the following set of requirements:

A course registration software system maintains information on the courses offered by a department in one semester. Each course has only one section of offering. Information on the courses completed and the courses currently taken by the students in the department, the times of course offerings, the days on which a course is offered and the faculty members who teach these courses are to be recorded. A course has a unique name and a unique number. A course may have a finite number of prerequisite courses. A teacher teaches a finite number of courses.

The Model:
Every course has a name, a number, a place and time of offering, and has a set of prerequisite courses. So, it can be modeled as a record type consisting of the fields: course-name, course-number, class room, days, start-time, end-time, pre-requisites:

    Course :: course-name : String
             course-number : String
             classroom : Room
             days : WeekDays–**set**
             start-time : Time
             ending-time : Time
             pre-requisites : String–**set**   – course names

The type *String* is assumed to be a basic type for this level of specification and will not be defined further. Therefore it can be defined using the **token** type.

   String = **token**

Every room has a unique room number, possibly prefixed by the building where the room is situated. Based on this domain knowledge, we may define the type *Room* to be a union of subsets of natural numbers where each number uniquely identifies one class room.

   Room = { 100, ..., 120} ∪ {200, ..., 220} ∪ {300, ..., 320}

The type *WeekDays* defines the days in a week and is modeled as a quote type.

   WeekDays = MONDAY | TUESDAY | WEDNESDAY | THURSDAY | FRIDAY

Time can be modeled as an ordered pair of integers, representing hours and minutes. This could be modeled either record type or the Cartesian product type. The latter representation is used here.

   Time = {0, ..., 23} × {0, ..., 59}

The record types *Student* and *Teacher* model students and teachers, respectively. A student has a name and an identification number. Information on courses completed and courses currently taken are modeled as sets of courses. This information is held as part of student record to show the association between a student and courses taken by a student. A teacher has a name and teaches a finite set of courses. From these requirements, the record types for student and teacher entities are constructed.

   Student :: *name* : *String*
               idnumber : *String*
               courses-finished : *Course*–**set**
               courses-taken : *Course*–**set**

   Teacher :: *name* : *String*
               courses-teaching : *Course*–**set**

The state of the course registration system is modeled using the three types *Course*, *Student* and *Teacher*.

   state *Department* **of**
      courses : *Course*–**set**
      students : *Student*–**set**
      teachers : *Teacher*–**set**
   end

The model that we have constructed reflects the requirements and no more. It inherits some domain knowledge, in this case from a University environment, in defining the state to consist of the entities that are relevant to course registration. The three state variables are *courses*, *students* and *teachers*; the identifiers *String*, *Course*, *Room*, *WeekDays*, *Time*, *Student* and *Teacher* are type names. The identifier *Department* is the name of the state. □

16.2.6
Invariants

An invariant of an entity is an assertion constraining the behavior of that entity. The properties implied by the invariant must be preserved before and after every operation performed on that entity in order to ensure the correct behavior of that entity. There are two types of invariants in VDM—*type invariant* and *state invariant*. A type invariant, as the name implies, is associated with a type. A type invariant constrains type construction. All built-in types have well-defined constructors. For each user defined composite type, constraints if any, should be stated as an invariant. Type invariant in VDM is quite similar to integrity constraints in databases. A state invariant, associated with a state space definition, constrains the behavior of the system when it is subject to modifications by the operations specified on the state.

Type Invariant   The invariants for types and the state in the course registration problem are as follows: The type invariant for *Course* can be expressed as a conjunction of two predicates: (i) the starting time of a course should be earlier than its ending time and (ii) the set of prerequisites for a course should not include the course itself:

$$\textbf{inv mk-}Course \ (cn, \ c\#, \ rm, \ d, \ st, \ et, \ pr) \stackrel{\triangle}{=} earlier \ (st, \ et) \wedge cn \notin pr$$

The expression

$$\textbf{mk-}Course \ (cn, \ c\#, \ rm, \ d, \ st, \ et, \ pr)$$

constructs an instance of the type *Course*. The invariant asserts that for every instance, the conjunction

$$earlier \ (st, \ et) \wedge cn \notin pr$$

holds. The boolean function *earlier (st, et)* is not yet defined; its intended meaning is that the function will return the value *true* if *st* precedes *et* in a 24-hour clock time.

A type invariant for *Student* is that a student is not permitted to repeat a completed course. That is, the set of courses completed by a student and the set of courses currently taken by the student should be distinct:

$$\textbf{inv mk-}Student \ (n, \ id, \ cf, \ ct) \stackrel{\triangle}{=} cf \cap ct = \{\}$$

State Invariant   The state invariant for *Department* is a conjunction of the following constraints: (i) All prerequisite courses for a course should be offered by the same department; (ii) The courses completed and the courses currently taken by each student in the department must be offered by the same department; and (iii) The courses taught by every teacher are offered by the same department.

inv mk_Department *(cs, sts, ts)* $\triangleq$
  $\forall c \in cs \bullet c.pre\text{-}requisites \subset cs \wedge$
  $\forall st \in sts \bullet (st.courses\text{-}finished \subseteq cs \wedge st.courses\text{-}taken \subseteq cs) \wedge$
  $\forall t \in ts \bullet t.courses\text{-}teaching \subseteq cs$

A type invariant constrains the values that an object of the type can assume. If the type is composite, it cannot relate a component to another variable or constant outside the definition of a composite type. A state invariant asserts the relationships among the state variables. It can also relate the state variables with other type declarations and global constants. For example, if the type of a state variable is a union type, any assertion involving this state variable will require the definitions of all component types of the union type.

16.3
Operational Abstraction

While representational abstraction describes the objects in the domain of a software system, the observable behavior of the model is captured through operational abstraction. In VDM-SL, operational abstraction is defined by functions and operations. The behavior of the model is defined by describing the effects of functions and operations on the model. The major difference between functions and operations is that functions do not access global variables while operations not only access global variables but may change them.

The syntax for an operation definition in VDM-SL has a separate clause which identifies all global variables accessed in that operation, thereby making the difference between functions and operations explicit. An operation may be defined by either implicitly or explicitly in VDM-SL. In the implicit style, a function or an operation is specified by two sets of assertions, called *precondition* and *postcondition*. Explicit style uses constructive methods for operation definitions.

The precondition of a function is a boolean expression which is true only on those input values to which the function may be applied. The postcondition of a function is another boolean expression which states how the result of the function is related to its input. The precondition of an operation is an assertion on the state of the system which must be true before the operation is invoked in that state. The postcondition of an operation is an assertion which states the relationship among the state variables after a successful termination of the operation. If the function or the operation does not terminate, the postcondition is not valid. If the precondition of a function or an operation fails, the status of the corresponding postcondition is undefined.

16.3.1
Let Expression

When a complex expression is repeatedly used in a specification, it is convenient to assign a name for it and use the name instead of the full expression. This naming convention is only a syntactic sugar which simplifies typing and improves readability of the specification. VDM-SL provides such a syntactic sugar through the **let** expression. A **let** expression has the following syntax:

> **let** *<definition>* **in** *<expression>*

The *<definition>* clause is of the form

> $< variable >$: $< type >=< expression_1 >$ or
>
> $< variable >=< expression_1 >$

The term *<expression>* uses *<definition>* given in the **let** expression and hence defines the scope of the **let** expression. Multiple <expression> definitions can be given, provided they are separated by commas. See the examples below:

> **let** *student : Student* = **mk-***Student ("John Major", "12345", { }, SoftEng)* **in**
>   *validate_student (student)*
>   ...
> **let** *origin* = **mk-***Point (0.0, 0.0)*, *p* = **mk-***Point (x, y)* **in**
>   *distance (p, origin)* = ...
>   ...
> **let** *axis* = **mk-***LineSegment (***mk-***Point (x,y),* **mk-***Point(p,q))* **in**
>   ...

16.3.2
Function Definitions

There are four kinds of function definitions in VDM-SL.

16.3.2.1
Implicit Function

An implicit function in VDM-SL characterizes the result by stating the properties. The syntax is

> *fun* $(p_1 : t_1, p_2 : t_2, \ldots, p_n : t_n) \, p : t$
> **pre** *B*
> **post** *B'*

where *func* is the name of the function, $p_1, p_2, \ldots, p_n$ are input parameters of types t_1, $t_2, \ldots, t_n$, respectively and *p* is the output parameter of type *t*, *B* and *B'* are boolean expressions.

The function *find* given below is an example of an implicit function. If a given element is found in the sequence, the function returns its index. If the element is not a member of the sequence, the function returns zero. The sequence in this example is defined as a nonempty and non-duplicating sequence.

find $(S : X^+, x : X)$ *result* $: \mathbb{N}$
pre card elems $S =$ **len** S – *non-duplicating*
post
     $(\exists\, i \in \{1, \ldots,\, \mathbf{len}\ S\} \bullet S(i) = x) \Rightarrow result = i \wedge$
     $\neg\, (\exists\, i \in \{1, \ldots,\, \mathbf{len}\ S\} \bullet S(i) = x) \Rightarrow result = 0$

Sometimes one may want to introduce only the signature of an implicit function without giving its definition. The signatures of all the functions used in the specification must be stated. Where the definition is not given, the signature of the function is augmented with the phrase **is not yet defined** as in

     fun-one $(p_1 : t_1, p_2 : t_2, \ldots, p_k : t_k)\ p : t$ **is not yet defined**

An implicit function may have an empty set of input parameters in which case the function is treated as a constant. Implicit functions may be recursively defined; however, recursion can occur only in the postcondition.

16.3.2.2
Explicit Function

The explicit style of a function specification has two components—function declaration and function definition. The declaration of a function includes only its signature.

     fun-two $: t_1 \times t_2 \times \cdots \times t_n \rightarrow t$

The syntax for the definition of an explicit function is

     fun-two $(p_1, p_2, \ldots, p_n) \stackrel{\triangle}{=} E$
     pre B

where E denotes an expression of type t and the parameters $p_1, p_2, \ldots, p_n$ are of types t_1, $t_2, \ldots, t_n$, respectively. The precondition is optional.

The function *max* given below is written using the explicit style:

     max $: \mathbb{Z} \times \mathbb{Z} \rightarrow \mathbb{Z}$
     max $(x, y) \stackrel{\triangle}{=}$ **if** $x > y$ **then** x **else** y
     pre $x \neq y$

An explicit function may be recursive and can be defined with or without input parameters. The result of an explicit function can be an undefined value in which case the keyword **undefined** is used to denote the result.

16.3.2.3
Higher Order Function

VDM-SL also permits the definition of higher order functions, known as *curried functions*. A function is a curried function if its output is another function, instead of a value. Curried functions can be defined only explicitly. The exponentiation function for integer arguments can be defined as a curried function:

$$power : \mathbb{N}_1 \rightarrow \mathbb{N} \rightarrow \mathbb{N}_1$$
$$power\ (n)(x) \stackrel{\triangle}{=} n \uparrow x$$

The function takes a positive number n as input and returns a function $f = power(n)$, which can compute $n \uparrow x$ for any argument x.

16.3.2.4
Polymorphic Function

A function is polymorphic or *generic*, if its definition can be given as a template which can be instantiated with appropriate parameters. For example, the function $f[T]$ is a generic function whose definition does not depend on the type of the formal parameter T. Later, when we instantiate f with some element, say a set, the complete definition of f will be available. The built-in function **elems** for sequence types is polymorphic:

$$elems\ [@S] : @S^* \rightarrow @S\text{-set}$$
$$elems\ (s) \stackrel{\triangle}{=} \textbf{if } s = [\ ] \textbf{ then } \{\}$$
$$\textbf{else hd } s \cup \textbf{elems } (\textbf{tl } s)$$

Notice that $@S$ in the above function may be of any type and the definition of **elems** does not depend on the type $@S$. The square bracket surrounding $@S$ is part of VDM-SL syntax for defining generic functions.

The function *subsequence* defined below is also generic which asserts whether or not a given sequence *small* is a subsequence of another sequence *large*:

$$subsequence[@X] : @X^* \times @X^* \rightarrow \mathbb{B}$$
$$subsequence\ (small,\ large) \stackrel{\triangle}{=}$$
$$\exists\ i,j \in \textbf{inds } large \mid j > i \wedge \textbf{len } small = j - i + 1 \bullet$$
$$\exists\ m : (\textbf{inds } small) \xrightarrow{m} i \ldots j \bullet$$
$$\forall\ k \in \textbf{inds } small \bullet small(k) = large(m(k))$$

16.3.3
Operation Definitions

There are two styles of operation definitions in VDM-SL.

16.3.3.1
Implicit Operation

The syntax for implicit operation is given below:

$oper\ (p_1 : t_{11}, p_2 : t_{12}, \ldots, p_n : t_{1n})\ p: t$

ext $<mode>\ g_1 : t_{21}$

$\quad <mode>\ g_2 : t_{22}$

$\quad \ldots$

$\quad <mode>\ g_k : t_{2k}$

pre B

post B'

err $e_1 : B_1 \rightarrow B'_1$

$\quad e_2 : B_2 \rightarrow B'_2$

$\quad \ldots$

$\quad e_m : B_m \rightarrow B'_m$

The syntax of an implicit operation is similar to the syntax of an implicit function; however, it includes the two additional clauses *external clause* **ext** and *error block* **err**. The external clause lists all the global variables that are accessed in this operation. The declaration of each global variable is preceded by <mode> which is either **rd** or **wr** indicating 'read' and 'write' attributes, respectively, of the global variable within the scope of that operation. If the mode is **wr** for a variable, the value of that variable might have been changed when the operation successfully terminates.

The error block contains a list of named error conditions labeled by the identifiers denoted as e_i's. An error condition has its own precondition B_i and a postcondition B'_i. If one or more of the error preconditions hold, then the effect of the operation is the conjunction of the corresponding postconditions.

Let us consider the state space definition of the course registration system. An operation that adds a new student to this system can be written in implicit style as follows:

Message = SUCCESS | ERROR – add these to **types**
add-student (n : String, id : String) report : Message
ext wr *students : Student*–**set**
pre $\forall s \in students \bullet s.idnumber \neq id$
post

$\quad students = \overline{students} \cup \{\mathbf{mk}\text{-}Student\ (n, id, \{\}, \{\})\} \wedge$

$\quad report = SUCCESS$
err *already-exists :*

$\quad (\exists s \in students \bullet s.idnumber = id) \rightarrow report = ERROR$

The hook notation $\overline{students}$ denotes the value of the global variable *students* in the pre-state of the operation. The value of the same variable after the operation is written without the hook. The postcondition asserts the inclusion of a new student record in *students* and reports the success of the operation. The hook notation is applicable only to global variables, thus indicating state changes. Consequently, it should appear only in postconditions.

The definition of an implicit operation can also be left incomplete by adding the phrase **'is not yet defined'**. VDM-SL does not permit recursive operation definitions.

16.3.3.2
Explicit Operation

The signature of an explicit operation in VDM-SL is

$$oper\text{-}two : t_1 \times t_2 \times \cdots \times t_n \xrightarrow{o} t$$

The symbol $\xrightarrow{o}$ makes the syntactic difference between the signature of an explicit function and that of an explicit operation. The definition of an explicit operation is given as follows:

$$oper\text{-}two\,(p_1,\ p_2,\ldots,\ p_n)$$
$$\triangleq\quad St$$
pre B

where $p_1, p_2, \ldots, p_n$ are, respectively, the parameters of type $t_1, t_2, \ldots, t_n$ and St refers to a statement. We discuss statements in detail in the next section. The operation returns a result of type t through a **return** statement.

The following explicit operation adds a new teacher to the course registration system:

$$add\text{-}teacher\colon String \times Course\text{-}\mathbf{set} \xrightarrow{o} Message$$
$$add\text{-}teacher\,(n,\ ct) \triangleq$$
$$\quad teachers := teachers \cup \{\mathbf{mk\text{-}}Teacher\,(n,\ ct)\};$$
$$\quad \mathbf{return}\ SUCCESS$$
$$\quad \mathbf{pre}\ \forall\, t \in teachers \bullet t.name \neq n$$

The definition for *add-teacher* consists of two statements: an assignment statement (indicated by :=) and a return statement. The semi-colon between the two statements indicates sequential composition of statements. Unlike implicit operations, there is no **ext** clause in the definition of an explicit operation. It is assumed that an explicit operation can modify all the variables in the state in which the operation is defined. Thus, the operation *add-teacher* modifies the state variable *teachers*.

16.4
Statements

VDM-SL also supports statements, much similar to those found in programming languages such as Pascal and C. Statements are generally used during refinement of VDM specifications. A specification written in assertional style can be refined into another specification written using statements. The refined specification resembles a program except that execution control is not present. Therefore, it seems easier to map the refined specification into a program in one of the block structured languages. Because of these advantages, VDM is considered as a software development environment or framework rather than a simple specification language.

Table 16.9 gives a partial list of statements supported by VDM-SL; see [19] for a complete list. Below, we discuss some of the distinguishing features of these statements.

Let Statement The semantics of **let** statement is similar to that of the **let** expression in VDM-SL except that the <definition> in **let** statement is applied to a statement, rather than to an expression.

Assignment Statement The <designator> in assignment statement is an identifier whose type is the same as that of <expression> in the assignment statement. This identifier must have been declared before the assignment statement. The semantics of the assignment statement is to overwrite the value previously held by <designator>. Therefore, the assignment statement does not use the hook notation (e.g., $\overline{previous}$) for a variable in <expression>. A major advantage of the assignment statement is that it can be used to modify only a portion of a state variable when the variable is of composite type.

Declare Statement A declare statement is used to introduce local variables to a block of statements. The block of statements are enclosed in parentheses, which also define the scope of variables introduced through the declare statement.

For Statement VDM-SL supports five kinds of **for** statement. The first two of these statements are similar to those found in programming languages. The statement

for all < *pattern* > ∈ < *expression* > **do** < *statement* >

is used to iterate over all elements of a given set. Generally, this kind of **for** statement is used while refining a universally quantified expression. The last two kinds of **for** statements in Table 16.9 are used to iterate over sequences.

Cases Statement The semantics of a **cases** statement is similar to the `case` statement in Pascal or `switch` statement in C. The <expression> is the key or selector which identifies the choice among the several alternatives. For a given <expression>, one of the patterns may match in which case the corresponding statement will be considered. The

Table 16.9 Statements in VDM-SL

Statement	Syntax
let statement	**let** <definition> **in** <statement>
assignment statement	<designator> := <expression>
conditional statement	**if** <expression> **then** <statement> **else** <statement>

case statement	**cases** <expression>:
	     <pattern$_1$ > $\rightarrow$ <statement$_1$ >,
	     <pattern$_2$ > $\rightarrow$ <statement$_2$ >,
	     ...
	     <pattern$_n$ > $\rightarrow$ <statement$_n$ >,
	     others $\rightarrow$ <statement$_k$ >
	 end

declare statement	**dcl** <name> : <type> **dcl** <name> : <type> := <initial value>
block statement	(<statement>; ... ;<statement>)

for statement	**for** <name> = <expression> **to** <expression>
	   do statement
	
	 for <name> = <expression> **by** <expression> **to** <expression>
	   do statement
	
	 for all <pattern> $\in$ <expression>
	   do <statement>
	
	 for <pattern> $\in$ <expression> **in** <expression>
	   do statement
	
	 for <pattern> : <type> **in** <expression>
	   do statement

while statement	**while** <expression> **do** <expression>
return statement	**return** <expression>
exit statement	**exit** <expression>
error statement	**error**

statement corresponding to **others** will be considered when none of the listed patterns matches. The **others** clause is optional; it can be omitted if the listed alternatives cover all possible patterns. The scope of the **cases** statement ends with the **end** keyword.

The following example illustrates the use of some of these statements:

types
    Mark = {*0,...,100*};
    IDNumber = **token**;
    Grade = *A* | *B* | *C* | *D* | *F*
values
    maxtermwork : $\mathbb{N}$:= 5;
state *Grading* **of**
    termwork : *IDNumber* $\xrightarrow{m}$ *Mark*$^+$
    total : *IDNumber* $\xrightarrow{m}$ *Mark*
    grades : *IDNumber* $\xrightarrow{m}$ *Grade*

    inv mk-*Grading (tw, tt, gr)* $\triangleq$
        dom *tw* = **dom** *tt* = **dom** *gr* $\wedge$
        $\forall$ *id* $\in$ **dom** *tw* $\bullet$ **len** *tw(id)* $\leq$ *maxtermwork*

    init mk-*Grading (–, tt, –)* $\triangleq$
        $\forall$ *id* $\in$ **dom** *tt* $\bullet$ *tt(id)* = 0
end
operations
    compute-grade () $\xrightarrow{o}$ *()* $\triangleq$
        for all *id* $\in$ **dom** *termwork* **do**
            (**dcl** *i* : $\mathbb{N}$:= *1*; *sum* : $\mathbb{N}$:= 0;
            while *(i* $\leq$ **len** *termwork(id))* **do**
                (sum := sum + termwork(id)(i);
                i := i + 1;
                );
            if *sum > 100* **then** *total(id) := 100* **else** *total(id) := sum*;
            let *excellent* = {*85,...,100*},
                good = {*70,...,84*},
                fair = {*60,...,69*},
                pass = {*50,...,59*} **in**
            cases *true* :
                total(id) $\in$ *excellent* $\rightarrow$ *grades(id) := A*,
                total(id) $\in$ *good* $\rightarrow$ *grades(id) := B*,
                total(id) $\in$ *fair* $\rightarrow$ *grades(id) := C*,
                total(id) $\in$ *pass* $\rightarrow$ *grades(id) := D*,
                others $\rightarrow$ *grades(id) := F*
            end
        );

The above example specifies the computation of grades for students in a course. The term work for a student is represented by a sequence of marks. The state invariant asserts that the domains of the three maps representing the term work, total and the grades are the same. The operation *compute-grade* is given in explicit style. The **for** statement iterates over all the elements of the three maps. For each entry, the sum of term work is computed using the **while** loop. This while loop uses a local variable i declared using the **dcl** statement. The **if** ... **then** ... **else** statement ensures that the total mark does not exceed 100. The **let** statement introduces four local variables which are used to classify the marks in various grading categories. Finally, the **cases** statement assigns the grade to each student according to the category to which the total mark belongs.

16.5
Specification Examples

VDM-SL specifications consist of type definitions, state space definitions, invariants, functions and operations. Comments are permitted in between the specification text. In this section, we discuss three examples emphasizing the choice of the various structures and type definitions that are appropriate for their modeling. Each example in this section is given in the following format: Problem Description, additional requirements, assumptions, the model, VDM-SL specification and comments on the specification.

Example 5 Employment Exchange.

Problem Description

An employment exchange collects and manages information on two sets of people—*unemployed*, representing the set of people who have registered with the exchange but not yet employed by any employer, and *employed*, representing the set of people who are employed after registering with the exchange. A person cannot be both in *employed* and in *unemployed* at the same time. Operations for registration and changing status of persons must be made available.

Assumptions

1. Personal details of individuals are not stated in the problem description and consequently will not be included in the employment exchange registry.
2. People, once registered, will not be deleted from the exchange.

The Model

Since personal details of individuals are not required to be included in the specification, each person registered with the employment exchange can be modeled as the type *Person*, which is defined to be a **token** type. The state space can be modeled with two collections *employed* and *unemployed*, both of which are of type *Person*-**set**. We choose sets to model the two collections since the problem description does not require an ordering on the registration process.

The state invariant asserts that no person should be in both the sets simultaneously. The initial state of the employment exchange asserts that in the beginning there are no registered members.

The two operations *register* and *change-status* are specified. The operation *register* accepts a person as input, ensures that the person has not been registered with the exchange and modifies the set *unemployed* to include this person. The operation *change-status* changes the status of the given person from *unemployed* to *employed*.

VDM-SL Specification

types
    Person = **token**
state *Emp-Exch* **of**
    employed : *Person*–**set**
    unemployed : *Person*–**set**
    inv mk-*Emp-Exch* (*em, unem*) $\overset{\triangle}{=}$ *em* ∩ *unem* = { }
    init mk-*Emp-Exch* (*em, unem*) $\overset{\triangle}{=}$ *em* = { } ∧ *unem* = { }
end
operations
    register (*p* : *Person*)
    ext
        wr *unemployed* : *Person*–**set**
        rd *employed* : *Person*–**set**
    pre *p* ∉ *unemployed* ∧ *p* ∉ *employed*
    post *unemployed* = $\overleftarrow{unemployed}$ ∪ {*p*};
    change-status (*p* : *Person*)
    ext
        wr *unemployed* : *Person*–**set**
        wr *employed* : *Person*–**set**
    pre *p* ∈ *unemployed*
    post
        unemployed = $\overleftarrow{unemployed}$ \ {*p*}
        employed = $\overleftarrow{employed}$ ∪ {*p*};

Comments
The initialization of the state asserts that none is registered with the exchange initially. Since the operations that modify the state do not have any result parameter, the result of each operation is the truth value of the postcondition of that operation. If the requirements of the employment exchange change, more operations may become necessary. For example, if it is required to re-register a person after the person loses the job, an operation to delete a person from the set of employed persons must be included to the system specification.   □

Example 6 Automated Transaction Machine (ATM).

Problem Description
An automated transaction machine provides fast banking services for depositing and withdrawing cash. Each user of the ATM has a card which is coded with a unique password of

the user. To initiate a transaction, the machine is accessed with a card and password. If the password coded in the card matches the password entered by the user, the user is permitted to execute the transaction; otherwise, the transaction is terminated.

It is assumed that only one account can be accessed with one card. The machine allows only two types of transactions—*withdraw* and *deposit*.

Additional Requirements

1. Each account in the bank is uniquely identified by an account number.
2. A user can have several accounts with the bank; however, the user needs one card for each account.
3. Several users can share an account; however, every user must have a separate card.
4. The machine has a reserve which can hold a fixed amount of cash.
5. If there is a request to withdraw an amount exceeding the balance in that account or in the machine's reserve, the withdrawal request will not be completed. No partial withdrawal is permitted.
6. The machine's reserve can be modified only by an employee of the bank. Each employee of the bank has a distinct card to access a special account. An employee can update the reserve of the machine using the distinct card.
7. Error messages should be given to user stating why a certain operation is not successful.

Assumptions

1. All account holders have equal privileges.
2. Sufficient fund is deposited into the machine's reserve on a regular basis.

The Model

Since no personal details, such as name and address are mandated by the requirements, it is assumed that users themselves need not be modeled. The cards will be the representatives of the users.

Cards and accounts are modeled as record types. A *card* contains a *card number* and a *password*. An *account* contains an *account number, balance* and *holders*, a set of card numbers associated with this account. The cardinality of the set *holders* is the number of cards associated with the account.

Since each card accesses only one account, the relationship between cards and accounts is modeled as a map. ATM's reserve is modeled as a global variable of type $\mathbb{N}$. Since only an employee can update the bank's reserve, the employee has a distinct card which is mapped to a particular account number. The state of ATM system is modeled by the database of card holders (*dbase*), the bank's reserve (*reserve*), and the special account for updating the reserve (*special-Account*).

We provide four operations—*validate-card, withdraw, deposit* and *update-reserve*. The *validate-card* operation is *internal* to the system and is not accessible to any user of ATM. This operation validates the given card before allowing access to an account. The operation *update-reserve* is restricted to a bank employee who is authorized to access it. The other two operations are accessible to all card holders of ATM.

VDM-SL Specification

types

    $Card :: card\text{-}number : \mathbb{N}$

               $code : \mathbb{N};$

    $Account :: account\text{-}number : \mathbb{N}$

                  $balance : \mathbb{N}$

                  $holders : \mathbb{N}\text{-}\textbf{set};$ $-$ *set of card numbers*

    $Message = VALID\text{-}CARD \mid INVALID\text{-}CARD \mid UPDATED \mid$

                    $INSUFFICIENT\text{-}BALANCE \mid NO\text{-}MONEY\text{-}IN\text{-}RESERVE;$

state *ATM* **of**

    $dbase : Card \xrightarrow{m} Account$

    $reserve : \mathbb{N}$

    $special\text{-}account : Account$ $- Account\# for\ employee's\ card.$

    inv mk-$ATM\ (db,-,\ sa) \triangleq$

        $(\forall\ ac_1,\ ac_2 \in \textbf{rng}\ db \bullet ac_1.account\text{-}number = ac_2.account\text{-}number$

        $\Leftrightarrow ac_1 = ac_2)\ \wedge$

        $(\forall\ c \in \textbf{dom}\ db \bullet db(c).holders \neq \{\}\ \wedge$

            $\forall\ h \in db(c).holders \bullet$

                $\exists\ ca \in \textbf{dom}\ db \bullet ca.card\text{-}number = h \wedge db(ca) = db(c))\ \wedge$

        $(\forall\ h \in sa.holders \bullet \exists\ ca \in \textbf{dom}\ db \bullet ca.card\text{-}number = h \wedge db(ca) = sa)\ \wedge$

        $sa.holders \neq \{\}$

      init mk-$ATM\ (-,\ re,\ -) \triangleq re > 0$

end

operations

    $validate\text{-}card : Card \times \mathbb{N} \xrightarrow{o} Message$

    $validate\text{-}card\ (c,\ n) \triangleq$

        if $c.code = n$ **then return** $VALID\text{-}CARD$

               else return $INVALID\text{-}CARD$

        pre $c \in \textbf{dom}\ dbase;$

$update\text{-}reserve : Card \times \mathbb{N} \times \mathbb{N} \xrightarrow{o} Message$

$update\text{-}reserve\ (sc,\ code,\ amount) \triangleq$

$reserve := reserve + amount;$

return $UPDATED$

pre

    $validate\text{-}card\ (sc,\ code) = VALID\text{-}CARD\ \wedge$

    $dbase(sc) = special\text{-}account;$

$withdraw : Card \times \mathbb{N} \times \mathbb{N} \overset{o}{\to} Message$

$withdraw \ (c, \ code, \ amount) \ \overset{\triangle}{=}$
    if $dbase(c).balance \geq amount$ **then**
        if $reserve \geq amount$ **then**
            $(dbase(c).balance := dbase(c).balance - amount;$
             $reserve := reserve - amount;$
              return *UPDATED*)
        else return *NO-MONEY-IN-RESERVE*
    else return *INSUFFICIENT-BALANCE*
pre $validate\text{-}card \ (c, \ code) = VALID\text{-}CARD;$

$deposit : Card \times \mathbb{N} \times \mathbb{N} \overset{o}{\to} Message$

$deposit \ (c, \ code, \ amount) \ \overset{\triangle}{=}$
    $dbase(c).balance := dbase(c).balance + amount;$
    $reserve := reserve + amount;$
    return *UPDATED*
    pre $validate\text{-}card \ (c, \ code) = VALID\text{-}CARD;$

Comments

The state invariant asserts that (i) each account has a unique account number; (ii) each account is accessible by at least one card; (iii) each account that can be accessed by a card should include the corresponding card number in the account; (iv) the number of the card that is used to access the special account must have been recorded in the special account itself. The state invariant in this case is an assertion on the users of the card and not on the reserve of the machine. Consequently, the second parameter to the **mk-** function for the state invariant is not specified. The initial state asserts that there should be some money deposited into the machine's reserve. All operations in this example are given in explicit style. The explicit style enables us to use statements in VDM-SL. In particular, the assignment statement

$$dbase(c).balance := dbase(c).balance - amount;$$

in operation *withdraw* and the assignment statement

$$dbase(c).balance := dbase(c).balance + amount;$$

in operation *deposit* indicate that only part of the record $dbase(c)$ is modified without modifying the rest of the record. This is permissible only in explicit operations. □

Example 7 Home Heating System.

Problem Description

A home heating system controls and maintains temperature in each room of the home according to a predefined pattern corresponding to that room. An entry for a room in the pattern consists of an interval of time in a 24-hour clock and the desired temperature during that interval. The control system maintains the temperature in each room at its stable level as defined in the pattern; however, it can also change the temperature in each room dynamically, depending on the occupancy of the room. Occupancy is true when there is at least one person in the room and is false when there is nobody in the room. A sensor in each room detects the occupancy.

Additional Requirements

1. The home has a finite number of rooms.
2. The three levels of temperature to be maintained in a room are *normal*, *below-normal* and *above-normal*.
3. The system permits the temperature in a room to be maintained at one of the three levels during a certain interval of time. Temperature pattern varies from room to room and can be dynamically changed during system operation.
4. If the occupancy in a room changes from true to false or vice versa and is stable for 5 consecutive minutes, the control system adjusts the room temperature according to the following table:

Current Temp. Level	Occupancy	New Temp. Level
normal	True	normal
normal	False	below normal
below normal	True	normal
below normal	False	below normal
above normal	True	above normal
above normal	False	normal

5. There is a sensor in each room which can read the temperature at any given time.

The home heating system includes the following operations: (i) initialize the pattern; (ii) activate a pattern at a given time; (iii) change the occupancy in a room; and (iv) control temperature in a room based on occupancy change.

Assumptions

1. The smallest time unit is a second.

The Model

We first model the following data types.

Temperature We model the temperature using real numbers. It is difficult to ensure the ordering among the temperature levels if it were to be modeled as an enumerated type. Although temperature varies continuously with time, the temperature can be observed only at discrete time points.

Room-Number A room number is modeled as a natural number not exceeding a maximum value, the number of rooms in the house.

Sensors Both temperature sensors and occupancy sensors are defined using token types because the actual description and operations of these sensors are not relevant for the current specification. However, there are functions to read the values indicated by the sensors at a given time.

Time We model *Time* as a triple representing the hour, minute and second of a clock. The values of these components are constrained by appropriate invariants so that their values lie within the applicable range (for example, minutes must be between 0 and 59). The reason for choosing this representation is that the pattern entries are defined on time intervals based on a 24-hour clock. The clock itself is not represented in the specification; rather, the current time is obtained by invoking the function *current-time( )* which extracts the current value of time from the clock.

Room Information In order to maintain the information on the pattern for each room and the current temperature in that room, we define the data type *Room Information*. For each room, the information includes the current temperature in the room and the last time point at which occupancy change occurred in that room. This information helps to check the stability of the occupancy in the room for 5 consecutive minutes, and to control the temperature against the predefined pattern.

Pattern A pattern is a collection of tuples $\{(t, T)\}$, where T is the temperature to be maintained during the interval t. It is sufficient to represent the starting time of the interval and the temperature in that interval. Therefore, a pattern is modeled as a map from time to temperature.

We define functions for obtaining current time, reading temperature from a temperature sensor and reading the occupancy status returned by an occupancy sensor. Since some operations require a metric notion of time, we define a function called *duration*.

The state of the system includes information on the rooms, the patterns for the rooms, and the temperature and occupancy sensors for the rooms. The state of the system is modeled as a collection of maps from room numbers to each of the data types *Temperature Sensor*, *Occupancy Sensor*, *Room Information* and *Pattern*. The state invariant asserts that the domains of the maps in the state are the same, thereby ensuring consistency among the maps. The state is initialized with an empty pattern for each room.

The following operations are specified for the home heating system.

set-pattern This operation enables the control system to set the pattern for a particular room. The input for this operation consists of the room number and a pattern. The precondition ensures that the room exists in the house and the postcondition asserts that the pattern is replaced.

activate-pattern The room number and the time at which the pattern is to be activated are passed as input to this operation. The precondition ensures that the room exists in the home, the activation time exists in the pattern for that room and the current time matches the activation time of the pattern. The postcondition ensures that the temperature in the room is set to the level defined in the pattern for the given time.

occupied An occupancy change occurs in a room when someone enters into an empty room or when the room becomes empty. The room number is the input to this operation. The postcondition records the change in occupancy and the time at which the occupancy change occurs.

control-temperature This operation changes the temperature in a room depending upon the occupancy change in the room. The precondition ensures that the occupancy change is stable for 5 consecutive minutes. The postcondition asserts that the change in temperature level happens according to the requirements.

VDM-SL Specification

types
>   *Temperature* = $\mathbb{R}$;
>   *Room-Number* = $\mathbb{N}$
>   **inv** *rm* $\overset{\triangle}{=}$ *rm* $\leq$ *maxrooms*;
>   *Temperature-Sensor* = **token**;
>   *Occupancy-Sensor* = **token**;
>   *Time* :: *hour* : $\mathbb{Z}$
>   *minute* : $\mathbb{Z}$
>   *second* : $\mathbb{Z}$
>   **inv mk-***Time* $\overset{\triangle}{=}$
> $(0 \leq h \wedge h \leq 23) \wedge$
> $(0 \leq m \wedge m \leq 59) \wedge$
> $(0 \leq m \wedge m \leq 59)$;
>   *Room-Information* :: *set-temperature* : *Temperature*
>   *last-occupancy-change* : *Time*;
>   *Pattern* = *Time* $\overset{m}{\longrightarrow}$ *Temperature*
>   **inv** *pat* $\overset{\triangle}{=}$
>   *pat(t)* = *normal* $\vee$ *pat(t)* = *below-normal* $\vee$ *pat(t)* = *above-normal*;

values
>   *maxrooms* : $\mathbb{N}_1$:= *10*;
>   *stable-occupancy* : *Time* := **mk-***Time* (0,5,0);
>   *normal* : *Temperature* := *28.0*;
>   *below-normal* : *Temperature* := *25.0*;
>   *above-normal* : *Temperature* := *31.0*;

functions
>   *current-time* : () $\rightarrow$ *Time*;
>   *read-temperature* : *Temperature-Sensor* $\times$ *Time* $\rightarrow$ *Temperature*;
>   *check-occupancy* : *Occupancy-Sensor* $\times$ *Time* $\rightarrow$ $\mathbb{B}$;
>   *normalize-time* : $\mathbb{Z} \times \mathbb{Z} \times \mathbb{Z} \rightarrow$ *Time*
>   *normalize-time* (h, m, s) $\overset{\triangle}{=}$
>   **if** *s* < *0* **then** *normalize-time* (h, m−1, s+60)
>   **else if** *m* < *0* **then** *normalize-time* (h−1, m+60, s)
>   **else if** *h* < *0* **then** **mk-***Time* (h+24, m, s)
>   **else mk-***Time* (h, m, s)
>   **pre**
> $h \geq 0 \Rightarrow 0 \leq h \leq 23 \wedge$
> $m \geq 0 \Rightarrow 0 \leq m \leq 59 \wedge$
> $s \geq 0 \Rightarrow 0 \leq s \leq 59$;
>   *duration* : *Time* $\times$ *Time* $\rightarrow$ *Time*
>   *duration* (t₁, t₂) $\overset{\triangle}{=}$
>   *normalize-time* (t_1.hour − t_2.hour, t_1.minute − t_2.minute,
> t_1.second − t_2.second);

state *Heating-System* **of**
  temp-sensors : Room-Number $\xrightarrow{m}$ *Temperature-Sensor*
  occ-sensors : Room-Number $\xrightarrow{m}$ *Occupancy-Sensor*
  rooms : Room-Number $\xrightarrow{m}$ *Room-Information*
  patterns : Room-Number $\xrightarrow{m}$ *Pattern*
  inv mk-*Heating-System (ts, is, rms, pts)* $\overset{\triangle}{=}$
    dom *ts* = **dom** *is* = **dom** *rms* = **dom** *pts*
  init mk-*Heating-System (-, -, rms, pts)* $\overset{\triangle}{=}$
    ($\forall$ *rm* $\in$ **dom** *pts* •
       pts(rm) = {$\mapsto$} $\wedge$
       rms(rm).last-occupancy-change = **mk-***Time (0, 0, 0))*
end

operations
  set-pattern (rm : Room-Number, pat : Pattern)
  ext wr *patterns : Room-Number* $\xrightarrow{m}$ *Pattern*
  pre *rm* $\in$ **dom** *patterns*
  post *patterns* = $\overleftarrow{patterns}$ † {*rm* $\mapsto$ *pat*};

activate-pattern (rm : Room-Number, at : Time)
ext
  wr *rooms : Room-Number* $\xrightarrow{m}$ *Room-Information*
  rd *patterns : Room-Number* $\xrightarrow{m}$ *Pattern*
pre
  rm $\in$ **dom** *rooms* $\wedge$
  at $\in$ **dom** *(patterns(rm))* $\wedge$
  current-time( ) = *at*
post *rooms* = $\overleftarrow{rooms}$ † {*rm* $\mapsto$
    mk-*Room-Information (($\overleftarrow{patterns}(rm))(at)$,
       ($\overleftarrow{rooms}(rm)).last-occupancy-change$)};

occupied (rm : Room-Number)
ext
  wr *rooms : Room-Number* $\xrightarrow{m}$ *Room-Information*
  rd *occ-sensors : Room-Number* $\xrightarrow{m}$ *Occupancy-Sensor*
pre
  rm $\in$ **dom** *rooms* $\wedge$
  check-occupancy (occ-sensors(rm), current-time( )) =
    $\neg$ *check-occupancy (occ-sensor(rm),*
       duration (current-time( ), **mk-***Time (0,0,1)))*
post *rooms* = $\overleftarrow{rooms}$ † {*rm* $\mapsto$
    mk-*Room-Information (rooms(rm).set-temperature, current-time( ))*};

control-temperature (rm : Room-Number)
ext
    rd *temp-sensors : Room-Number* $\xrightarrow{m}$ *Temperature-Sensor*
    wr *rooms : Room-Number* $\xrightarrow{m}$ *Room-Information*
    rd *occ-sensors : Room-Number* $\xrightarrow{m}$ *Occupancy-Sensor*
pre
    rm ∈ **dom** *rooms* ∧
    duration (current-time( ), rooms(rm).last-occupancy-change)
        = *stable-occupancy*
post
    let *previous = $\overleftarrow{rooms}$(rm).last-occupancy-change,*
        occupancy = check-occupancy ($\overleftarrow{occ-sensors}$(rm), current-time( )) **in**
    cases *read-temperature (temp-sensors(rm), previous) :*
        normal →
            cases *occupancy :*
                true → *rooms = $\overleftarrow{rooms}$,*
                false → *rooms = $\overleftarrow{rooms}$* † *{rm* ↦
                    mk-*Room-Information (below-normal,*
                      rooms(rm).last-occupancy-change)},
                others → *rooms = $\overleftarrow{rooms}$*
            end,
        below-normal →
            cases *occupancy :*
                true → *rooms = $\overleftarrow{rooms}$* † *{rm* ↦
                    mk-*Room-Information (normal, rooms(rm).last-occupancy-*
                    change)},
                false → *rooms = $\overleftarrow{rooms}$,*
                others → *rooms = $\overleftarrow{rooms}$*
            end,
        above-normal →
            cases *occupancy :*
                true → *rooms = $\overleftarrow{rooms}$,*
                false → *rooms =$\overleftarrow{rooms}$* † *{rm* ↦
                    mk-*Room-Information(normal, rooms(rm).last-occupancy-*
                    change)},
                others → *rooms = $\overleftarrow{rooms}$*
            end,
        others → *rooms = $\overleftarrow{rooms}$*
    end*;*

Comments

The function *normalize-time* converts a given triple of integers into a value of type *Time*. If the parameters represent positive integers which are within the limits of the three components for *Time*, the function constructs and returns a valid time value. If one of the parameters is negative, the function modifies the three parameters until the invariant for *Time* is satisfied. For example, if "seconds" is negative, it is made positive by adding 60; at the same time, "minutes" is reduced by one. Notice that after this change, "minutes" may become negative. So, the function is recursively applied until all the three parameters are in proper range. The function *duration* subtracts the second parameter from the first and returns the normalized time.

Every operation modifies some state variable, which is of map type. The postcondition ensures the modification by using the overwrite operation on map type objects. The operation *occupied* can be invoked when either an occupied room becomes empty or an empty room becomes occupied. The precondition ensures that the status of the room at the current time and that at one second preceding the current time are different. There is no mechanism in VDM to specify that this operation is periodically performed, say regularly at 1-minute intervals.   □

16.6
Case Study—Computer Network

A computer network consists of a set of nodes and a set of links connecting the nodes. Every link connects exactly two distinct nodes. A node may be active or inactive. A link is up if both the nodes connected by the link are active; otherwise, the link is down. Messages can be transmitted from an active node to any other active node in the network through a sequence of links that are up. All message transmissions are handled by a network manager. When a node wants to send a message to another node, it submits the message and the address of the recipient to the network manager. It is the responsibility of the network manager to choose a path between the sender and receiver nodes and route the message in the path. Each node maintains a buffer to hold messages deposited by the network manager. An active node periodically reads the messages in its buffer, and (i) deletes a message if it is addressed to the current node, or (ii) forwards the message to the next node in the path.

Additional Requirements

1. Each node has a unique address.
2. Every node on a path chosen by the network manager for message transmission remains active until it forwards it to the next node on the path.
3. No message is lost; every message dispatched by the network manager will eventually be received.
4. The network remains connected at all times.
5. The network manager queues all requests for sending messages based on the order in which these messages are received.

Assumptions

1. No message is corrupted.

The Model
We first consider modeling the data types in the network.

Node A node has an address, a status indicating whether it is active or inactive, and a buffer to hold the messages. Putting these requirements together, we can model a node by a record type with three fields: one for the address, another for the status and the third one for the buffer which is a queue of messages.

Link Since a link is uniquely identified by the two nodes connected by the link, both the nodes are included in its model In addition, a link also includes a status variable. Therefore, a record type is chosen to model a link. The invariant for the link asserts that the two nodes are distinct and the status of the link depends on the status of the two nodes connected by the link.

Path A path is modeled as a sequence of links. Every link, except for the first and last in the sequence, is connected to the link on either side in the path. In addition, no link appears more than once in the path. These constraints are expressed as a type invariant for the path.

Message A message is modeled as a record consisting of the message body and the path through which the message is routed.

Request This data type denotes records which a node uses when it submits a message to the network manager. It consists of the message body, and the sender and receiver information.

The state of the network includes a set of nodes and a set of links and a queue of messages. The state invariant is a conjunction of the following constraints: (i) node identifiers are unique; (ii) each link is uniquely identified by the two nodes it connects; (iii) the network is connected; and (iv) for each request submitted to the network manager, the sender and receiver nodes must be in the network.

We specify the following operations in the network:

addnode This operation adds a new node to the network. Since the network must remain connected at all times, the new node must be connected to at least one other node in the network. The new node must have a unique identifier which must be different from the identifiers of all other nodes in the network. As a result of adding this new node, the set of nodes and links in the network are modified.

addlink The purpose of this operation is to establish a link between two existing nodes in the network. The precondition ensures that the two nodes are present and there is no link between them. The postcondition asserts that a new link is established between the two nodes.

read-message Every node checks its buffer periodically to read the message at the front of its buffer which must be addressed to the current node. This can be ensured by checking that the path encoded in the message is empty. The postcondition asserts that the buffer retains only those messages that are to be forwarded.

forward-message When a node checks the message at the front of its buffer and the path associated with the message is not empty, then the current node is not the receiver of the message. Consequently, the current node is expected to forward the message to the next node in the path and to delete its name from the path.

post-message When a node wants to send a message to another node, it encodes the message text along with the sender and receiver information and submits a request to the network manager by invoking this operation. The precondition ensures that both nodes are present in the network. The postcondition ensures that the message is added to the queue of the network manager.

dispatch-message This operation selects a path for each message submitted to the network manager, encodes the path in the message and puts it into successor of the first node in the path. At the time of selection, the status of all links on the path is UP. It is assumed that this status is valid for every subpath during message transmission.

delete-node The delete operation accepts the node to be deleted. This node must be present in the network. The precondition also ensures that there are at least three nodes in the network. The postcondition asserts that the node as well as all the links associated with the node are deleted from the network. It is assumed that a node is deleted only when all the messages in the buffer of the node have been deleted.

VDM-SL Specification

types
$\qquad$ *Node :: nodeID : NodeAddress*
$\qquad\qquad$ *status : NodeStatus*
$\qquad\qquad$ *messages : Message*;*
$\qquad$ *NodeAddress =* **token***;*

$\qquad$ *NodeStatus = ACTIVE | INACTIVE;*

$\qquad$ *Link :: node1 : Node*
$\qquad\qquad$ *node2 : Node*
$\qquad\qquad$ *status : LinkStatus*

$\qquad$ **inv mk-***Link (n1,n2,st)* $\overset{\Delta}{=}$ *n1.nodeID* $\neq$ *n2.nodeID* $\wedge$
$\qquad\qquad$ *(n1.status = INACTIVE* $\vee$ *n2.status = INACTIVE)* $\Rightarrow$ *st = DOWN* $\wedge$
$\qquad\qquad$ *(n1.status = ACTIVE* $\wedge$ *n2.status = ACTIVE)* $\Rightarrow$ *st = UP;*

$\qquad$ *LinkStatus = UP | DOWN;*

$\qquad$ *Path = Link**
$\qquad$ **inv** *lns* $\overset{\Delta}{=}$ *injective (lns)* $\wedge$
$\qquad\qquad$ $\forall i \in$ **inds** *lns* $\bullet$ $i \geq 2 \Rightarrow lns(i).node1 = lns(i-1).node2;$

$\qquad$ *MessageBody = Char$^+$;*

Message :: *text* : *MessageBody*
             path : *Path*;
Request :: *sender* : *Node*
             receiver : *Node*
             text : *MessageBody*;
Report = *SUCCESS* | *CONNECTING-NON-EXISTING-NODE* |
     NODE-ALREADY-EXISTS | *LINK-ALREADY-EXISTS* |
     NO-MESSAGE-TO-DISPATCH | *NODE-DOES-NOT-EXIST* |
     NO-MESSAGE | *MESSAGE-IN-TRANSIT* |
     MESSAGE-AT-DESTINATION | *NODE-HAS-MESSAGES*;

state *Network* **of**
     nodes : *Node*-**set**
     links : *Link*-**set**
     requests : *Request**

 inv mk-*Network (nodes, links, requests)* $\triangleq$
  (∀ n1, n2 ∈ nodes • n1.nodeID ≠ n2.nodeID ⇒
   connected (n1, n2, links)) ∧
  (∀ ln ∈ links • ln.node1 ∈ nodes ∧ ln.node2 ∈ nodes) ∧
  (∀ rq ∈ requests • rq.sender ∈ nodes ∧ rq.receiver ∈ nodes) ∧
  (∀ ln1, ln2 ∈ links • ln1 = ln2 ⇔
   ln1.node1 = ln2.node1 ∧ ln1.node2 = ln2.node2) ∧
  (∀ n1, n2 ∈ nodes • n1 = n2 ⇔ n1.nodeID = n2.nodeID)

 init mk-*Network (nodes, links, requests)* $\triangleq$
  nodes = {**mk-***Node(***mk-***token(1), ACTIVE, [ ])*,
   mk-*Node(***mk-***token(2), ACTIVE, [ ])}* ∧
  links = {**mk-***Link(***mk-***Node(***mk-***token(1), ACTIVE, [ ])*,
   mk-*Node(***mk-***token(2), ACTIVE, [ ]), UP)}* ∧
  requests = [ ]
end

functions
 injective : *Link** → $\mathbb{B}$
 injective (lns) $\triangleq$ **len** *lns* = **card elems** *lns*;

 connected : *Node* × *Node* × *Link*-**set** → $\mathbb{B}$
 connected (n1, n2, lns) $\triangleq$
  *∃ p ∈{path | path : Path • **elems** path ⊆ lns ∧ **len** p > 0} •*
   *p(1).node1 = n1 ∧ p(**len** p).node2 = n2;*

 links-incident-at : *Node* × *Link*-**set** → *Link*-**set**
 links-incident-at (n, lns) $\triangleq$
  {ln | ln : Link • ln ∈ lns ∧ (ln.node1 = n ∨ ln.node2 = n)};

16

operations

   addnode (new : Node, old : Node) rep : Report

  ext

     wr *nodes : Node*-**set**

     wr *links : Link*-**set**

  pre

     old ∈ nodes ∧

     ∀ n ∈ nodes • n.nodeID ≠ new.nodeID

  post

     nodes = $\overleftarrow{nodes}$ ∪ {$\mathbf{mk\text{-}Node}$ (new.nodeID, new.status, [ ])} ∧

     let *up : LinkStatus := UP, down : LinkStatus := DOWN* **in**

        (new.status = ACTIVE ∧ old.status = ACTIVE) ⇒

           links = $\overleftarrow{links}$ ∪ {$\mathbf{mk\text{-}Link}$ (old, new, up)} ∧

        (new.status = INACTIVE ∨ old.status = INACTIVE) ⇒

           links = $\overleftarrow{links}$ ∪ {$\mathbf{mk\text{-}Link}$ (old, new, down)} ∧

     rep = SUCCESS

  errs

     DOES-NOT-EXIST : old ∉ nodes →

        nodes = $\overleftarrow{nodes}$ ∧

        links = $\overleftarrow{links}$ ∧

        rep = CONNECTING-NON-EXISTING-NODE

     EXISTS : ∃ n ∈ nodes • n.nodeID = new.nodeID →   *'*

        nodes = $\overleftarrow{nodes}$ ∧

        links = $\overleftarrow{links}$ ∧

        rep = NODE-ALREADY-EXISTS;

  addlink (from : Node, to: Node) rep : Report

  ext

     rd *nodes : Node*-**set**

     wr *links : Link*-**set**

  pre

     from ∈ nodes ∧ to ∈ nodes ∧

     ∀ ln ∈ links • ¬ (ln.node1 = from ∧ ln.node2 = to)

  post

     let *up : LinkStatus := UP, down : LinkStatus := DOWN* **in**

        (from.status = ACTIVE ∧ to.status = ACTIVE) ⇒

           links = $\overleftarrow{links}$ ∪ {$\mathbf{mk\text{-}Link}$ (from, to, up)} ∧

        (from.status = INACTIVE ∨ to.status = INACTIVE) ⇒

           links = $\overleftarrow{links}$ ∪ {$\mathbf{mk\text{-}Link}$ (from, to, down)} ∧

     rep = SUCCESS

errs

    DOES-NOT-EXIST : from $\notin$ nodes $\lor$ to $\notin$ nodes $\rightarrow$

        links = $\overleftarrow{links}$ $\land$

        rep = CONNECTING-NON-EXISTING-NODE

    EXISTS : $\exists$ ln $\in$ links $\bullet$ (ln.node1 = from $\land$ ln.node2 = to) $\rightarrow$

        links = $\overleftarrow{links}$ $\land$

        rep = LINK-ALREADY-EXISTS;

post-message (from : Node, to : Node, msg : MessageBody) rep : Report
ext

    rd *nodes : Node-**set***

    wr *requests : Request**

pre *from $\in$ nodes $\land$ to $\in$ nodes*

post *requests = $\overleftarrow{requests}$ $\curvearrowright$ [**mk-**Request (from, to, msg)] $\land$*

    rep = SUCCESS

errs

    DOES-NOT-EXIST : from $\notin$ nodes $\lor$ to $\notin$ nodes $\rightarrow$

        requests = $\overleftarrow{requests}$ $\land$

        rep = NODE-DOES-NOT-EXIST;

dispatch-message () rep : Report
ext

    wr *nodes : Node-**set***

    rd *links : Link-**set***

    wr *requests : Request**

pre len *requests > 0*

post

    *requests = **tl** $\overleftarrow{requests}$ $\land$*

    *$\exists$ path $\in$ {p | p : Path $\bullet$ **len** p > 0 $\land$ **elems** p $\subseteq$ links $\land$*

        *p(1).node1 = (**hd** $\overleftarrow{requests}$).sender $\land$*

        *p(**len** p).node2 = (**hd** $\overleftarrow{requests}$).receiver} $\land$*

        *($\forall$ ln $\in$ **elems** p $\bullet$ ln.status = UP) $\bullet$*

    nodes = $\overleftarrow{nodes}$ \ {path(1).node2} $\cup$

        *{**mk-**Node (path(1).node2.nodeID, path(1).node2.status,*

        path(1).node2.messages $\curvearrowright$

            *[**mk-**Message ((**hd** $\overleftarrow{requests}$).text, **tl** path)]} $\land$*

    rep = SUCCESS

errs

    *NOTHING : **len** requests = 0 $\rightarrow$*

        nodes = $\overleftarrow{nodes}$`$\land$

        requests = $\overleftarrow{requests}$

        rep = NO-MESSAGE-TO-DISPATCH;

read-message (current : Node) rep : Report
ext wr *nodes : Node-***set**
pre
 current $\in$ *nodes* $\wedge$ **len** *(current.messages)* > 0 $\wedge$
 *(***hd** *(current.messages)).path* = [ ]
post
 nodes = $\overleftarrow{nodes}$ \ {*current*} $\cup$
  {**mk-***Node (current.nodeID, current.status,* **tl** *current.messages)*} $\wedge$
 rep = *SUCCESS*
errs
 DOES-NOT-EXIST : current $\notin$ *nodes* $\rightarrow$
  nodes = $\overleftarrow{nodes}$ $\wedge$
  rep = *NODE-DOES-NOT-EXIST*
 NOTHING : **len** *current.messages* = 0 $\rightarrow$
  nodes = $\overleftarrow{nodes}$ $\wedge$
  rep = *NO-MESSAGE*
 *TRANSIT : (***hd** *(current.messages)).path* $\neq$ [ ] $\rightarrow$
  nodes = $\overleftarrow{nodes}$
  rep = *MESSAGE-IN-TRANSIT;*

forward-message (current : Node) rep : Report
ext wr *nodes : Node-***set**
pre
 current $\in$ *nodes* $\wedge$ **len** *(current.messages)* > 0 $\wedge$
 hd *(current.messages).path* $\neq$ [ ]
post
 let *next* = *(***hd** *(current.messages)).path(1).node2* **in**
  nodes = $\overleftarrow{nodes}$ \ {*current, next*} $\cup$
   {**mk-***Node (current.nodeID, current.status,* **tl** *current.messages),*
   mk-*Node (next.nodeID, next.status, next.messages)* $\curvearrowright$
    [**mk-***Message ((***hd** *(current.messages)).text,*
     tl*((***hd** *(current.messages)).path))])*} $\wedge$
 rep = *SUCCESS*
errs
 DOES-NOT-EXIST : current $\notin$ *nodes* $\rightarrow$
  nodes = $\overleftarrow{nodes}$ $\wedge$
  rep = *NODE-DOES-NOT-EXIST*
 NOTHING : **len** *current.messages* = 0 $\rightarrow$
  nodes = $\overleftarrow{nodes}$ $\wedge$
  rep = *NO-MESSAGE*
 DESTINATION : **hd** *(current.messages).path* = [ ] $\rightarrow$
  nodes = $\overleftarrow{nodes}$
  rep = *MESSAGE-AT-DESTINATION;*

delete-node (n : Node) rep : Report

ext

    wr *nodes : Node*-**set**

    wr *links : Link*-**set**

    wr *requests : Request*[*]

pre

    #nodes $\geq$ 3 $\wedge$ n $\in$ nodes $\wedge$ n.messages = [ ]

post

    n $\notin$ nodes $\wedge$

    links = $\overleftarrow{links}$ \ links-incident-at (n, $\overleftarrow{links}$) $\wedge$

    *requests = [$\overleftarrow{requests}$(i) | i $\in$ **inds** $\overleftarrow{requests}$ •*

        ($\overleftarrow{requests}$(i).sender $\neq$ n $\vee$ $\overleftarrow{requests}$(i).receiver $\neq$ n)] $\wedge$

    rep = SUCCESS

errs

    DOES-NOT-EXIST : n $\notin$ nodes $\rightarrow$

        nodes = $\overleftarrow{nodes}$ $\wedge$

        links = $\overleftarrow{links}$ $\wedge$

        requests = $\overleftarrow{requests}$ $\wedge$

        rep = NODE-DOES-NOT-EXIST

    MESSAGE-EXISTS : n.messages $\neq$ [ ] $\rightarrow$

        nodes = $\overleftarrow{nodes}$ $\wedge$

        links = $\overleftarrow{links}$ $\wedge$

        requests = $\overleftarrow{requests}$ $\wedge$

        rep = NODE-HAS-MESSAGES;

<u>Comments</u>

The function *injective* asserts that no link appears more than once in the sequence of links. The function *connected* specifies that two nodes are connected by a given set of links if there exists a path between them. The links comprising the path should be among those links passed as input to the function. Given a node and a set of links, the function *links-incident-at* returns the set of links incident at the node.   □

16.7
Rigorous Reasoning

In this section, we give a rigorous proof for the security property:

> Every message dispatched by the network manager is read only by the node to which the message is addressed.

Let a node X send a message m to a node Y; assume both X and Y exist in the network. The node X constructs a request and submits it to the network manager. When the network manager finds the record $r = (X, Y, m)$ in front of its buffer, the precondition for the operation *dispatch-message* is satisfied for the record r. The postcondition of *dispatch-message* asserts the following:

1. A path from sender to receiver exists, and the status of all links on this path is UP.
2. The first node of the first link on the path is the sender, and the second node of the last link on the path is the receiver.
3. The message, and the path excluding the first link are placed in the buffer of the second node of the first link on the path.

Accordingly, the network manager chooses a path p, where

$$p(1).node1 = X, \text{ and } p(k).node2 = Y, k = \textbf{len } p, k \geq 1$$

It is also true that the status of all links in p are UP. If $p(1).node2 = Z$, the tuple $(m, \textbf{tl } p)$ is appended to the buffer of Z. For the rest of the proof, we need to assume that operations *read-message*, and *forward-message* will be eventually invoked by every node whose buffer is not empty. Note that the preconditions for the operations *read-message* and *forward-message* are independent. In particular, a node can invoke *read-message* operation only when the tuple to be processed in its buffer is of the form (m, q), where q = [ ]. However, for the same node to invoke the *forward-message* operation, the second component q must be nonempty. There are two cases to consider.

Case 1 $k = 1$
Infer from the postcondition of *dispatch-message* that the message structure $(m, [\ ])$ is inserted in the buffer of $Z = p(1).node2 = p(k).node2 = Y$. When this message is at the front of $Z's$ buffer, the precondition for the operation *read-message* becomes true. The postcondition for *read-message* ensures that this tuple is deleted; that is, node Z has received the message sent from X, and no node along the path has read the message.

Case 2 $k > 1$
Infer from the postcondition of *dispatch-message* that the message structure (m, p'), where $p' = \textbf{tl } p$, is inserted in the buffer of node Z. Since $Z = p(1).node2 \neq p(k).node2 = Y$, and $p' \neq [\ ]$, when the tuple (m, p') is at the front of $Z's$ buffer, only the precondition of *forward-message* can become true. The postcondition of the operation *forward-message* ensures that the message m is encoded in the structure $(m, \textbf{tl } p')$, and placed in the buffer of node W, where $p'(1).node1 = Z, p'(1).node2 = W$. Notice that $\textbf{len } p' = k' = k - 1$, and the encoded message is deleted from the buffer of node Z; that is, the message is not read by node Z. If k' = 0, then case 1 applies to node W at some future time; otherwise, case 2 applies.

Since the length of the path encoded in the message is decremented every time the message is forwarded by a node, eventually the length of the encoded path becomes zero. We observe from case 2 that when the path length is greater than zero, the message is not read. From case 1 it follows that the message is read when the path length is zero by the node to which the message is addressed. This proves that no node other than the receiver can read the message.

16.8
Refinement and Proof Obligations

In addition to providing a formalism for specification, VDM also provides the techniques for stepwise refinement of specifications. Such a systematic development approach of VDM makes it suitable for the development of large complex software systems for which the set of initial requirements continuously evolve over a period of time. VDM specifications in this case are given as a layer of models, each model being a refined version of the previous model. A lower-level model adds design and implementation details. Thus the last level of refinement will be closer to the implementation from which a program could be obtained by directly mapping the specification constructs onto those of the underlying programming language. There are two ways by which a specification in VDM can be refined—*data refinement* and *operation decomposition*. In the former approach, abstract data types are mapped into concrete data types. A proof obligation for the refinement establishes that for every abstract data type there exists at least one concrete type which implements it. In addition, it must be proved that every operation performed on concrete data types satisfies the constraints imposed on the abstract data types. In an operation refinement, operations in one level are refined to one or more operations in which computational details are explicit. The effect of performing the low level operations must be proved to be consistent with the abstract operation. The following sections explain the refinement techniques in detail. For a rigorous treatment on refinement, refer to [22, 23].

16.8.1
Data Refinement

In data refinement, an abstract data type is refined into one or more concrete data types. One familiar example is refining a set into a sequence with a proof that the refined data type sequence does not contain duplicate elements. A refinement should neither add more data nor lose any existing data. This requires a proof to establish that every element in the set occurs somewhere in the sequence. With these two proofs, it would be established that the sequence contains all the elements of the set, each element once, and nothing more. Hence, the length of the sequence in the refinement is equal to the size of the set. Next, it is also to be shown that for every operation performed on the set, there exists a unique operation performed on the sequence so that the constraints imposed for the set operation are still satisfied in the sequence.

In general, proof obligation for a data refinement requires (1) showing that no data is lost and no new data is introduced; and (2) for every operation that modify data in the abstract level, the data in the refined data type is modified to yield the same effect. In the proof obligations for data refinement,we use the following notations:

$$pre\text{-}Op\ (x,\ \overline{state})$$

$$post\text{-}Op\ (x,\ \overline{state},\ state)$$

where $\overline{state}$ refers to the state of the system before the operation is invoked, and $state$ denotes the state of the system after the operation terminates and x refers to the set of parameters of the operation Op. Since functions do not affect state spaces, the precondition and postcondition of a function are denoted as

$$pre\text{-}f\,(x)$$

$$post\text{-}f\,(x)$$

16.8.1.1
Proof Obligations

It is necessary to define a *retrieve function* which maps a concrete state space into its abstract state space. There are five components in a proof obligation [23].

Signature Verification First, one must show that the retrieve function is of correct type; that is, if the abstract state is denoted as Abs and the concrete state is denoted as Con, then

$$\boxed{Signature}\ \vdash retrf : Con \rightarrow Abs$$

Adequacy Obligation For every abstract state Abs, we show that there exists at least one concrete state Con which implements the abstract state using the retrieve function. Formally,

$$\boxed{Adequacy}\ \frac{Abs}{\exists Con \bullet retrf(Con) = Abs}$$

Initial State Validation The retrieve function should match the initial concrete state $init\_C$ to the initial abstract state $init\_A$ as defined by the initialization functions in both state spaces. Formally,

$$\boxed{Init}\ \frac{init\_C}{init\_A}$$

Domain Obligation For every concrete operation Op_C, the precondition of the corresponding abstract operation Op_A in conjunction with the retrieve function ensures the precondition of Op_C; i.e.,

$$\boxed{Domain\ Rule}\ \frac{Abs, Con, Abs = retrf(Con), pre\text{-}Op_A(x, Abs)}{pre\text{-}Op_C(x, Con)}$$

Informally, domain obligation ensures that the precondition of the concrete operation is weaker than that of its corresponding abstract operation.

Result Obligation For every abstract operation Op_A, the postcondition of its corresponding concrete operation Op_C, in conjunction with the retrieve function, ensures the postcondition of Op_A. That is, we show that the postcondition of the concrete operation is stronger than that of the corresponding abstract operation. Formally, if $\overleftarrow{Con}$ represents the concrete state before the operation Op_C and Con refers to the concrete state after Op_C successfully terminates, then

$$\text{Result Rule} \quad \frac{\overleftarrow{Con}, Con, \overleftarrow{Abs} = retrf(\overleftarrow{Con}), Abs = retrf(Con),}{pre\text{-}Op_A(x, oldAbs, post\text{-}Op_C(\overleftarrow{Con}, Con)}{post\text{-}Op_A(\overleftarrow{Abs}, Abs)}$$

16.8.2
Example for Data Refinement

In this section, we discuss the data refinement for the employment exchange specification given in the previous section is refined. The state variables *employed* and *unemployed* are refined into sequences. The refined specification is given below:

state *Emp-Exch₁* **of**
    *employed₁ : Person**
    *unemployed₁ : Person**
    inv mk_*Emp-Exch₁ (em, unem)* $\triangleq$
        elems *em* $\cap$ **elems** *unem* = { } $\wedge$
        no-duplicates (em) $\wedge$ *no-duplicates (unem)*
    init mk_*Emp-Exch₁ (em, unem)* $\triangleq$ *em* = [ ] $\wedge$ *unem* = [ ]
end
functions
    *no-duplicates : Person** $\rightarrow \mathbb{B}$
    no-duplicates (plist) $\triangleq$ $\forall i,j \in$ **inds** *plist* $\bullet$ $i \neq j \Rightarrow plist(i) \neq plist(j)$

operations
    register₁ (p : Person)
    ext
        wr *unemployed₁ : Person**
        rd *employed₁ : Person**
    pre
        $(\forall i \in$ **inds** *employed₁* $\bullet$ *employed₁(i)* $\neq p) \wedge$
        $(\forall j \in$ **inds** *unemployed₁* $\bullet$ *unemployed₁(j)* $\neq p)$
    post *unemployed₁* = $\overleftarrow{unemployed_1} \frown [p];$

change-status$_1$ (p : Person)
ext
    wr *unemployed$_1$: Person***
    wr *employed$_1$: Person***
pre $\exists\, i \in$ **inds** *unemployed$_1$* $\bullet$ *unemployed$_1$(i) = p*
post

$\quad$ *($\exists\, i \in$ **inds** $\overleftarrow{unemployed_1}$ $\bullet$ $\overleftarrow{unemployed_1}(i) = p \wedge$*

$\qquad$ *($\forall j \in \{1,\ldots,(i-1)\}$ $\bullet$ unemployed$_1$(j) = $\overleftarrow{unemployed_1}(j)$) $\wedge$*

$\qquad$ *($\forall k \in \{(i+1),\ldots,$**len** $\overleftarrow{unemployed_1}$ $\}$ $\bullet$ unemployed$_1$(k$-$1) =*

$\qquad$ *$\overleftarrow{unemployed_1}(k)$)) $\wedge$*

$\quad$ *employed$_1$ = $\overleftarrow{employed}_1$ $\curvearrowright$ [p];*

Signature Verification   The retrieve function for this refinement is defined as follows:

retrf : Emp-Exch$_1$ $\twoheadrightarrow$ Emp-exch
retrf (mk_Emp-Exch$_1$ (em$_1$, unem$_1$)) $\overset{\triangle}{=}$
$\quad$ *mk_Emp-Exch (**elems** em$_1$, **elems** unem$_1$)*

Adequacy Proof   It is shown in [23, page 40] that

$$\forall s \in S\text{–}\mathbf{set} \bullet \exists \ell \in X^* \bullet s = \mathbf{elems}\, \ell$$

This is the adequacy proof for the current example. From this proof, it can be safely concluded that

retrf (Emp-Exch$_1$) = Emp-Exch
$\overleftarrow{retrf (Emp\text{-}Exch_1)}$ = $\overleftarrow{Emp\text{-}Exch}$

The invariant of *Emp_Exch$_1$* ensures that *em$_1$* and *unem$_1$* do not contain any duplicates.

Initial State Validation   The proof is given below:

from **init** *mk_Emp-Exch$_1$ (em$_1$, unem$_1$); retrf*
1 $\quad$ *em$_1$ = [ ]; unem$_1$ = [ ]* $\qquad\qquad\qquad$ **init** *mk_Emp-Exch$_1$*
2 $\quad$ *em = **elems** [ ]; unem = **elems** [ ]* $\qquad\qquad$ *retrf*
3 $\quad$ *em = { }; unem = { }* $\qquad\qquad\qquad\qquad$ *sequence*
infer **init** *mk_Emp-Exch (em, unem)* $\qquad$ **init** *mk_Emp-Exch*

Domain Obligation   For simplicity, the proof for only one operation, say, *register* is given below; proof for the other operation is left as an exercise. For domain obligation, we have to show that

$\quad$ *$\forall p \in Person$ $\bullet$ (pre-register (p, $\overleftarrow{Emp\text{-}Exch}$) $\wedge$ retrf ($\overleftarrow{Emp\text{-}Exch_1}$)*

$\qquad$ *$\Rightarrow$ pre-register$_1$ (p, $\overleftarrow{Emp\text{-}Exch_1}$)*

from *pre-register (p, $\overline{\textit{Emp-Exch}}$); retrf ($\overline{\textit{Emp-Exch}_1}$)*

1	$p \notin \textit{unemployed} \land p \notin \textit{employed}$	*pre-register*
2	$p \notin \textbf{elems } \textit{unemployed}_1 \land p \notin \textbf{elems } \textit{employed}_1$	*retrf*
3	$(\forall i \in \textbf{inds } \textit{unemployed}_1 \bullet \textit{unemployed}_1(i) \neq p) \land$	
	$(\forall i \in \textbf{inds } \textit{employed}_1 \bullet \textit{employed}_1(i) \neq p)$	*sequence*

infer *pre-register₁ (p, $\overline{\textit{Emp-Exch}_1}$)*   *3*

Result Obligation   We give the proof only for the *register* operation. It is required to prove that

$$\forall p \in \textit{Person} \bullet \textit{pre-register} (p, \overline{\textit{Emp-Exch}}) \land \textit{retrf} (\overline{\textit{Emp-Exch}_1}) \land$$
$$\textit{post-register}_1 (p, \overline{\textit{Emp-Exch}_1}, \textit{Emp-Exch}_1) \land \overline{\textit{Emp-Exch}_1} \land \textit{Emp-Exch}_1$$
$$\Rightarrow \textit{post-register} (p, \overline{\textit{Emp-Exch}}, \textit{Emp-Exch})$$

from *hypotheses*

1	$\textit{unemployed} = \textbf{elems } \textit{unemployed}_1$	*retrf, Emp-Exch₁*
2	$\textit{unemployed} = \textbf{elems } (\overline{\textit{unemployed}_1} \frown [p])$	*post-register₁*
3	$\cdot\textit{unemployed} = \textbf{elems } \overline{\textit{unemployed}_1} \cup \textbf{elems } [p]$	*sequence*
4	$\textit{unemployed} = \textbf{elems } \overline{\textit{unemployed}_1} \cup \{p\}$	*sequence*
5	$\textit{unemployed} = \overline{\textit{unemployed}} \cup \{p\}$	*retrf*

infer *post-register(p, $\overline{\textit{Emp-Exch}}$, Emp-Exch)*   *5, hypotheses*

Since a map is a finite set of maplets, the proof obligation for the refinement of a map type to sequence type is quite similar to that from set type to sequence type. That is, a map can be refined into two sequences of same size, one representing the domain elements and another representing the range elements.

16.8.3
Operation Decomposition

The purpose of an *operation decomposition* process is to refine an abstract operation into a concrete operation with computational details. In order to achieve this goal, the operations in the concrete specification are chosen to reflect those operations supported by programming languages. These include *sequential composition of operations*, *control structures* (**if-then-else** and **case**) and *iterative structures* (**while**, **repeat** and **for**). The operation decomposition process requires a proof; i.e., the combined effect of all operations in the concrete specification should be proved to satisfy the behavior of the abstract operation. Therefore, proof rules are introduced in the operation decomposition process to support formal verification.

We discuss operation decomposition technique for the *delete-node* operation of the network example given in the case study and informally justify the refinement. See [22, 24] for proof rules for operation decomposition.

16.8.4
Example for Operation Decomposition

We assume that the state variables *nodes* and *links* in the network example are refined as follows:

nodes : Node*
links : Links*

We omit the proof obligations for this data refinement. We refine the functions *connected* and *links-incident-at* for the refined data types.

connected : Node × Node × Link* → $\mathbb{B}$
connected (n1, n2, lns) $\triangleq$
    ∃ *p* ∈ {*path | path : Path • **elems** path ⊆ **elems** lns*} •
        (*p(1).node1 = n1* ∨ *p(**len** p).node2 = n2*)
pre len *lns > 0;*

links-incident-at : Node × Link* → Link*
links-incident-at (n, lns) $\triangleq$
    [*ln | ln : Link • ln* ∈ **elems** *lns* ∧ (*ln.node1 = n* ∨ *ln.node2 = n*)];

We now define the refinement of the operation *delete-node*.

delete-node (n : Node) $\triangleq$
    (**dcl** *nds : Node* := [];*
    dcl *lns : Link* := [];*
    dcl *reqs : Request* := [];*

    (**let** *lnks = links-incident-at (n, links)* **in**
        for *ln* **in** *links* **do**
            if *ln* ∉ *lnks* **then**
                lns := lns ⌢ [ln];
        links = lns);
    (**for** *nd* **in** *nodes* **do**
        if *nd* ≠ *n* **then**
            nds := nds ⌢ [nd];
      nodes := nds);
    (**let** *upstat : LinkStatus := UP,*
           downstat : LinkStatus := DOWN **in**
      for *nd1* **in** *nodes* **do**
        for *nd2* **in** *nodes* **do**
            if *nd1* ≠ *nd2* ∧ ¬ *connected (nd1, nd2, links)* **then**
                if (*nd1.status = ACTIVE* ∧ *nd2.status = ACTIVE*) **then**
                    links := links ⌢ **mk-Link** *(nd1, nd2, upstat)*
                else *links := links ⌢* **mk-Link** *(nd1, nd2, downstat)*
            else);
    (**for** *req* **in** *requests* **do**
        if *req.sender* ≠ *n* ∧ *req.receiver* ≠ *n* **then**
            reqs := reqs ⌢ [req]);
)
    pre *n* ∈ **elems** *nodes*

In the refined version, the links incident at the given node are deleted first; this is specified by the first **for** loop. Next, the given node under consideration is deleted from the set of nodes. By deleting the node and the links associated with the node, the network may be left with several unconnected branches. Since the network must be connected at all times as stated in the requirements, we establish links between the unconnected branches and make the network connected.

The refined operation contains a block of statements which is a sequential composition of four statements. The first statement is the **for** statement which collects the sequence of links not associated with the node n. The precondition for this statement is that the node n must be present in the sequence of nodes. If n is not present in the sequence of nodes in the network, the operation fails. Since in VDM-SL an explicit operation does not specify exception, we have ignored the error conditions stated in the abstract operation *delete-node*. The postcondition of the first statement asserts that only links not associated with n remain in the network. The precondition for the second statement is the same as that of the first statement. The postcondition of the second statement asserts that the network no longer contains the node n. There is no precondition for the third statement. The postcondition asserts that new links and their respective status are created, and added to the network. The fourth statement does not depend on the sequential composition of the other three statements. It specifies that the messages submitted by the node n and the messages sent to the node n are removed from the network buffer. This is done by scanning each request in the network buffer and deleting the ones addressed by and addressed to the node n.

16.9
Exercises

1. In the specification for employment exchange given in Example 5, one of the assumptions states that registered people will not be deleted from the exchange. Remove this assumption and specify two operations: *delete-unemployed (p : Person)* and *delete-employed (p : Person)*, which will remove persons from the *unemployed* and *employed* sets, respectively.
2. The specification for course registration system given in Example 4 has an assumption that the course offerings are considered for only one semester. Remove this restriction and modify the specification so that the database maintains information on course offerings for more than one semester. Include constraints such as "pre-requisites for a course should not be held concurrently in the same semester".
3. The specification for automated transaction machine in Example 6 assumes that each user has a distinct card even if the user accesses a shared account. Change this restriction and include personal details for users. Introduce mappings between personal details and card numbers so that the bank knows the users of an account. Modify the specification incorporating these changes. Add new operations if necessary. Notice that a user may have more than one account.

   Specify the following new operations for the ATM example: (i) Issue a new card to a user; include more assumptions, if necessary. (ii) Check the balance in an account.

(iii) Modify the type *Account* so that for a given time interval, the number of deposits and withdrawals can be printed when required.

4. The specification for a computer network in the case study ensures that no link appears more than once in a path. However, it does permit that a path may include a simple loop; i.e., a node can appear twice in a path, still obeying the previous invariant. Impose a restriction that a path should be linear so that no node can appear more than once in a path. Modify the specification to incorporate this change.

   Set a limit to the number of messages that can be stored in the buffer of a node. Modify the specification so that if the buffer in a particular node is full, no message can be forwarded to this node, until the node reads or forwards at least one message from its buffer.

   Set a limit to the number of requests that can be stored in the buffer in the state space. Modify the specification so that, if this buffer is full, no more requests will be accepted by the network manager until the network manager dispatches at least one message from this buffer.

5. Discuss data refinement and proof obligations for data abstractions in the network example.

6. Give a data refinement for the specification of ATM given Example 6 along with proofs.

7. Specify a data type called "Line Segment" with appropriate invariant. You may need to specify "Point" first. Define the following operations on line segments: (i) Determine whether or not two line segments are parallel to each other; (ii) Determine whether or not two line segments are perpendicular to each other; (iii) Determine whether or not two line segments intersect at a common point; (iv) Determine whether or not two line segments share at least one common point; and (v) Determine the length of a line segment.

8. Specify a "Circle" and a "Line Segment" (you may use the specification in the previous question) and define the following operations: Determine whether (i) the circle encloses the line segment; (ii) the line segment touches the circle; and (iii) the line segment intersects the circle.

9. Define the *bag* data type described in Chap. 12 in VDM-SL. Specify operations to count and re-shelve books in a simple library check-out system using *bag*.

10. A simple cryptographic system uses its own code for each printable character. When a message (consisting of a sequence of printable and non-printable characters) is sent, it is encoded by the corresponding codes for each character in the message. The receiver, knowing the code dictionary, can decode the message at the other end. Notice that each station has its own coding dictionary and so the receiver must identify the sender first and then chooses the appropriate dictionary. Moreover, each station must store the dictionaries of all the other stations in the system. Any change in the dictionary in any of the stations must be broadcast to all other stations.

    Write a VDM-SL specification to specify this simple cryptographic system. Include appropriate operations and error messages.

11. Figure 16.1 represents homothetic polygons P_1 and P_2 in which the sides of P_1 are parallel to the sides of P_2, and the distance between every pair of parallel sides is the same. Specify a data type called "Polygon", and define a function to determine whether or not two polygons are homothetic.

Fig. 16.1 Homethetic polygons

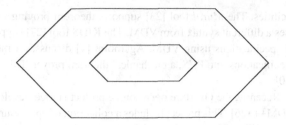

16.10 Bibliographic Notes

Peter Lucas [28] gives a historical overview of VDM, particularly describing its evolution during the last decade. The report describes the evolution of Meta-IV, the specification language associated with VDM until 1987. The standardization process then replaced Meta-IV by VDM-SL. A precise description of VDM-SL is given by [31]; its full description appears in [20].

Since the language for VDM was evolving continuously over the last decade, only a few books on VDM were published during that period. Cohen, Harwood and Jackson describe the Meta-IV language [8, 18] with some simple examples. Hekmatpour and Ince used the same language to describe how VDM can be used for software prototyping. Dawes describes the initial concrete syntax of VDM-SL [9]. The current standard version is slightly different from the version of VDM-SL appeared in [9]. Andrew and Ince [2] also used the same version as in [9]; their book contains several examples and techniques for proving properties using VDM specifications.

In spite of the changes to the VDM specification language, VDM-SL and its predecessor Meta-IV have been used to specify a number of applications. These include a document on Message Authentication Algorithm developed by Parkin and Neil [30] and the Modula-2 programming language by Pronk and Schonhacker [32]. The edited monograph by Jones and Shaw [24] contains several specification case studies using VDM.

VDM originated as a software development framework and is still considered as a vehicle for software synthesis. Consequently, refinement theory has become an integral part of VDM. A number of publications have been reported in the literature on refinement of VDM specifications. Jones's work [21, 22] on refinements is a primary and relevant source of refinement theory. Others in this category include Clement's work on data refinement [6, 7] and Goldsack and Lano's work on data decomposition [16].

The only object-oriented extension reported in the literature is the VDM++ specification language. A detailed description of VDM++ can be found in [11]. Object refinement, similar to data refinement, using VDM++ has been described in [15]. In addition, VDM++ has been used for developing specifications of real-time and concurrent systems as reported in [12, 14, 29]. The application of VDM++ to the development of firmware has been reported in [25].

Several tools are available for developing specifications, refinement and proofs using VDM. The IFAD Toolbox [19] enables one to develop a VDM-SL specification, check its syntax and type correctness, generate proof obligations and prove some properties using its static and dynamic semantic checker. The tool box also includes code generation facilities. The *Mural* tool [23] supports theorem proving using VDM specifications, but uses a different syntax from VDM. The KIDS tool [27] supports proof-based development of specifications using VDM. Agerholm [1] discusses a methodology to translate VDM specifications into PVS, a mechanical theorem prover. This was later extended by Droschl [10].

Recently, the Overture open source project started developing tools for both VDM and VDM++ [26]. This project includes a collection of open source VDM tools. More information on this tool set can be found at https://sourceforge.net/projects/overture. Another tool set called **VDMTools** is available from CSK Systems. This tool set supports both VDM and VDM++, and includes features such as syntax and type checking, interpreter and debugger, test coverage analysis and linking with OO languages such as C++ and Java. VDMTools is an upgraded version of the IFAD Toolbox. This can be obtained from CSK Systems at www.csk.com.

References

1. Agerholm S (1996) Translating specifications in VDM-SL to PVS. In: v. Wright J, Grundy J, Harrison J (eds) Proceedings of the international conference on theorem proving in higher order logics (TPHOL'96). Springer, Berlin
2. Andrews A, Ince D (1991) Practical formal methods using VDM. McGraw Hill, New York
3. Bicarregui JC et al (1994) Proof in VDM: a practitioner's guide. Springer, Berlin
4. Bicarregui J, Ritchie B (1991) Reasoning about VDM developments using the VDM tool support in *mural*. In: Prehn S, Toetenel WJ (eds) VDM'91: formal software development methods. Lecture notes in computer science, vol 552. Springer, Berlin, pp 371–388
5. Bicarregui J, Matthews B (1995) Formal methods in practice: a comparison of two support systems for proof. In: Bartosek A et al (eds) SOFSEM'95: theory and practice of informatics. Lecture notes in computer science, vol 1012. Springer, Berlin
6. Clement T (1994) Comparing approaches to data reification. In: Naftalin M, Denvir T, Bertran M (eds) FME'94: industrial benefits of formal methods. Lecture notes in computer science, vol 893. Springer, Berlin, pp 118–133
7. Clement T (1996) Data reification without explicit abstraction functions. In: Gaudel MC, Woodcock JCP (eds) FME'96: industrial benefits and advances in formal methods. Lecture notes in computer science, vol 1051. Springer, Berlin, pp 195–213
8. Cohen B, Harwood WT, Jackson MI (1986) The specification of complex systems. Addison-Wesley, Reading
9. Dawes J (1991) The VDM-SL reference guide. Pitman, London
10. Droschl G (1999) On the integration of formal methods: events and scenarios in PVS and VDM. In: Third Irish workshop on formal methods, Galway, Eire, July 1999
11. Durr EH, Plat N (eds) (1995) VDM++: language reference manual, Afrodite (ESPRIT-III, project number 6500) document, Cap Volmac, Aug 1995
12. Durr EH, Goldsack S (1996) Formal methods and object technology. In: Concurrency and real-time in VDM++. Springer, Berlin, pp 86–112
13. Elvang-Goransson M (1991) Reasoning about VDM specifications. In: Prehn S, Toetenel WJ (eds) VDM'91: formal software development methods. Lecture notes in computer science, vol 552. Springer, Berlin, pp 343–355
14. Fitzgerald JS et al (2007) Validation support for real-time embedded systems in VDM++. In: Proceedings of the 10th IEEE high assurance systems engineering symposium (HAS 2007), Nov 2007, pp 331–340

15. Goldsack SJ, Durr EH, Plat N (1995) Object reification in VDM++. In: Wirsing M (ed) ICSE-17: workshop on formal methods application in software engineering practice, April 1995, pp 194–201
16. Goldsack S, Lano K (1996) Annealing and data decomposition in VDM. ACM SIGPLAN Not 31(4):32–38
17. Harry A (1996) Formal methods fact file: VDM and Z. Wiley, New York
18. Hekmatpour S, Ince D (1988) Software prototyping, formal methods and VDM. Addison-Wesley, Reading
19. The VDM-SL Tool Group (1995) User manual for the IFAD VDM-SL toolbox, IFAD, The Institute of Applied Computer Science, Forskerparken 10, DK-5230 Odense M, Denmark, June 1995
20. Larsen PG et al. (1996) Information technology—programming languages, their environments and system software interfaces—Vienna development method—Specification language—Part 1: Base language. ISO document, December 1996
21. Jones CB (1986) The systematic software development using VDM. Series in Computer Science. Prentice Hall International, Englewood Cliffs
22. Jones CB (1990) The systematic software development using VDM, 2nd edn. Series in computer science. Prentice Hall International, Englewood Cliffs
23. Jones CB, Jones KD, Lindsay PA, Moore R (1991) Mural: a formal development support system. Springer, Berlin
24. Jones CB, Shaw RC (1990) Case Studies in systematic software development. Series in computer science. Prentice Hall International, Englewood Cliffs
25. Kurita T, Nakatsugawa Y (2009) The application of VDM++ to the development of firmware for a smart card IC chip. Int J Softw Informatics 3(2–3)
26. Larsen PG et al. (2010) The overture initiative—integrating tools for VDM. ACM Softw Eng Notes 35(1)
27. Ledru Y (1996) Using KIDS as a tool support for VDM. In: Proceedings of the 18th international conference on software engineering, March 1996, pp 236–245
28. Lucas P (1987) VDM: origins, hopes and achievements. In: Bjorner D et al (eds) VDM'87: VDM—a formal method at work. Lecture notes in computer science, vol 252. Springer, Berlin, pp 1–8
29. Mukherjee P et al (2000) Exploring timing properties using VDM++ on an industrial application. In: Proceedings of the second VDM workshop, Sep 2000
30. Parkin GI, O'Neil G (1991) Specification of the MAA standard in VDM. In: VDM'91: formal software development methods. Lecture notes in computer science, vol 552. Springer, Berlin, pp 526–544
31. Parkin GI (1994) Vienna development method specification language (VDM-SL). Comput Stand Interfaces 16:527–530
32. Pronk C, Schonhacker M (1996) ISO/IEC 10514-1, the standard for Modula-2: process aspects. ACM SIGPLAN Not 31(8):74–83

The Z Notation

17

The Z notation (pronounced as *zed*, named after the German mathematician *Ernst Zermelo*) originated at the Oxford University Computing Laboratory, UK and has evolved over the last decade into a conceptually clear and mathematically well-defined specification language. The mathematical bases for Z notation are ZF set theory and the classical two-valued predicate logic. An interesting feature of the Z specification language is the schema notation. Using schemas, one can develop modular specifications in Z and compose them using schema calculus.

This chapter presents a tutorial of the Z notation, brings out the differences between the Z notation and other model-based specification languages such as VDM-SL through informal discussions and motivates the reader to understand the principles of modular specification supported by the Z notation. As was done in previous chapters, a number of examples are given to make the reader become familiar with basics of the Z notation and acquire skills in writing Z specifications. All the examples in this chapter have been type-checked by the *fuzz* type checker [11].

17.1
Abstractions in Z

Like VDM, the Z notation supports two types of abstractions—*representational abstraction* and *operational abstraction*. Representational abstraction is described by type definitions, global constants and state space declarations. Operational abstraction is captured by operation definitions and function definitions. Sections 10.2 and 10.3 describe these two abstractions in detail.

17.2
Representational Abstraction

The syntactic structures in Z that form the basis of representational abstraction can be broadly classified into two categories: *mathematical preliminaries* and *schemas*. The mathematical preliminaries include sets, functions, relations and sequences which are already discussed in Chap. 12. Subsequent sections in this chapter focuses only on notational differences for these structures within the Z specification language.

The distinguishing feature of Z is the *schema* notation. A schema has a unique name, a structure described by a set of declarations, and a property described by a set of predicates; these predicates express the invariant relationships among the structural components. The schema notation enables a specification to be split into small manageable pieces, allowing the development of modular specifications. Schemas can be composed using schema calculus. Thus, larger specifications are obtained from smaller specification pieces. Later subsections in this section describe in detail the syntax for schema notation and that for composing schemas.

17.2.1
Types

Types are interpreted as sets in Z. The set of values associated with a type is called the *carrier set* of that type. This set describes the collection of values that an object of the concerned type can assume. Thus, an object of a type in Z is actually a member of the carrier set of that type.

The Z notation is strongly typed. That is, every variable, constant and expression in a Z specification must be associated with a type. Such a strict type system brings out two major advantages [10]: (i) it is easier to spot errors in a specification, and (ii) the type system enforces a discipline in writing good specifications. Moreover, the notion of strong typing enables type checking of a Z specification to be automated.

Types in Z fall into two categories: *simple types* and *composite types*. Composite types are derived from simple types using type constructors. The type of a composite structure such as a schema or that of a compound expression is generally derived from the types of its constituents.

17.2.1.1
Simple Types

There are two kinds of simple types in Z—*primitive types* (already defined in Z) and *basic types* (user defined). Integers ($\mathbb{Z}$) is the only primitive type defined in Z. Basic types are assumed to be defined for the current specification (the specification in which they are declared) and are not further elaborated. The assumption is that these basic types will be defined later. As an example, the users of an automated teller machine in a banking system can be modeled as a basic type. The syntax for this basic type is

[USERS]

The square parentheses are part of the syntax. Several basic types may be introduced in one line as in

[USERS, STAFF, CLIENTS]

Several basic type definitions may be introduced in a specification.

Since types are treated as sets in Z, equality $(=)$ and membership $(\in)$ operators are defined for all types. Hence, objects of basic types can be compared for equality and membership:

[*USERS*]

$\forall u_1, u_2 : USERS \bullet u_1 \neq u_2 \Rightarrow \ldots$

$\ldots$

$u \in USERS \Rightarrow \ldots$

The arithmetic operators $+$, $-$, $*$, div and mod, and the relational operators $<$, $>$, $\leq$ and $\geq$ are defined for integers.

17.2.1.2
Composite Types

There are three composite types in Z: *power set types, Cartesian product types* and *schema types*. Other composite types can be built from them and from simple types.

Sets and Power Set Types In Z, a set can be declared in three ways: set as a type, set by enumeration and set by comprehension. These notations have been introduced in Chap. 12. Set operators built into Z are given in Table 17.1. The symbol $\mathbb{F}$ is used to denote finite subsets of a set, while the symbol $\mathbb{P}$ is used to define the set of all subsets of a set. Mathematically speaking, a finite set is the one whose members can be put into one-to-one correspondence with the elements of the set $\{1, \ldots, n\}$ for some natural number n. Whether to use $\mathbb{F}$ or $\mathbb{P}$ in a specification depends on the application. As an example, to denote a subset of natural numbers without any indication as how it is to be used, one would choose $\mathbb{P}\mathbb{N}$, whereas if it is used to denote a finite subset such as a set of room numbers in a building, the declaration $\mathbb{F}\mathbb{N}$ must be used.

Tuples and Cartesian Product Types The notation for Cartesian product type, as defined in Chap. 12, is used in Z. In the declaration,

$book : Title \times Author \times CallNumber \times Year$

the variable *book* is a quadruple (t, a, c, y) indicating, respectively, the title, author, call number and year of publication of a book. Thus, if t_1, a_1, c_1 and y_1 are variables of type *Title, Author, CallNumber* and *Year*, respectively, then the following equality holds:

$book = (t_1, a_1, c_1, y_1)$

Table 17.1 Set operators in Z

Operator	Synopsis	Meaning
$\in$	$x \in S$	set membership
$\cup$	$S_1 \cup S_2$	set union
$\cap$	$S_1 \cap S_2$	set intersection
$\setminus$	$S_1 \setminus S_2$	set difference
#	#S	cardinality of a set
$\subseteq$	$S_1 \subseteq S_2$	subset
$\subset$	$S_1 \subset S_2$	proper subset
=	$S_1 = S_2$	set equality
$\bigcup$	$\bigcup SS$	generalized union of sets SS
$\bigcap$	$\bigcap SS$	generalized intersection of sets SS
$\mathbb{P}$	$\mathbb{P}\, S$	power set of the set S
$\mathbb{F}$	$\mathbb{F}\, S$	finite subsets of the set S

17.2.2
Abbreviation

Often, it is convenient to introduce a new name for a complex expression so that the new name can be used in place of the complex expression. For example, a type such as

$Title \times Author \times CallNumber \times Year$

can be renamed as *Book* which is easier to use. This is achieved in Z by the following syntax:

$Book == Title \times Author \times CallNumber \times Year$

The notation $==$ is called *abbreviation*, meaning that the expression to the right side of $==$ is abbreviated to the name on the left side. The semantics of the abbreviation

$X == Y$

is that X is of type $\mathbb{P}Y$. Generally, abbreviation definition is used for defining a type as in

$RoomNumber == \mathbb{N}_1$

Here, *RoomNumber* defines a new type which is represented by a subset of $\mathbb{N}_1$. This new type can further be constrained to assume only a finite subset of values using global constraints as in the following:

$\forall r : RoomNumber \bullet 100 \leq r \leq 199$

Table 17.2 Notations for functions

Symbol	Meaning
→	Total function
⇸	Partial function
↣	Total injective function
⤔	Partial injective function
↠	Total surjective function
⤀	Partial surjective function
⤗	Partial bijective function
⤖	Total bijective function
⇻	Finite partial function
⤕	Finite partial injective function

17.2.3
Relations and Functions

Relations and functions are composite mathematical objects, described using sets and Cartesian products. The formal definitions of relations and functions introduced in Chap. 12 are the basis for Z specifications. The kinds of functions supported in Z and their corresponding notations are listed in Table 17.2. The operators on functions and relations and their corresponding notations in Z are given in Table 17.3. The meanings of these operators are the same as discussed in Chap. 12. Mathematical functions in Z are different from computable functions in programming languages, even though during refinement, the mathematical functions are generally implemented using computable functions. Since a function is synonymous to a relation and has a type $\mathbb{P}(X \times Y)$, one can think of a function as a precomputed set of ordered pairs. Consequently, the values of the function are assumed to be known. In fact, both constant definitions and functions use the same syntax in Z as shown below:

$$maximum : \mathbb{N}$$
$$\overline{}$$
$$maximum = 1000$$

$$half : \mathbb{N} \to \mathbb{N}$$
$$\overline{}$$
$$half = \{n : \mathbb{N} \bullet n \mapsto n \operatorname{div} 2\}$$

Function types such as

$$password : UserId \nrightarrow Password$$

may be used in declarations.

Table 17.3 Operators on relations and functions in Z

Operator	Synopsis	Meaning
$\leftrightarrow$	$X \leftrightarrow Y$	declaration of a binary relation between X and Y
$\mapsto$	$x \mapsto y$	maplet
dom	dom R	domain of the relation R
ran	ran R	range of the relation R
id	id X	identity relation
$\overset{\circ}{\underset{9}{}}$	$R_1 \overset{\circ}{\underset{9}{}} R_2$	relational composition
$\circ$	$R_1 \circ R_2$	backward relational composition
$\lhd$	$S \lhd R$	domain restriction
$\rhd$	$R \rhd S$	range restriction
$\lhd\!\!\!-$	$S \lhd\!\!\!- R$	domain subtraction (domain anti-restriction)
$-\!\!\!\rhd$	$R -\!\!\!\rhd S$	range subtraction (range anti-restriction)
$\sim$	$R^{\sim}$	relational inverse
$\_(\!\|\_\|\!)$	$R (\!\| S \|\!)$	relational image
$\oplus$	$R_1 \oplus R_2$	relational overriding
	R^k	relational iteration
	$R+$	transitive closure of the relation R
	R^*	reflexive transitive closure of the relation R

17.2.4
Sequences

The mathematical basis for sequences has been discussed in Chap. 12. Below, we mention their syntax and specific built-in operations defined in Z. In Z, a sequence is treated as a function from $\mathbb{N}_1$ (representing the indexes of the sequence) to the type of objects in the sequence. Hence, the operators defined for functions (in fact, those defined for relations) can be equally applied to sequences.

Sequences can be specified in two ways. A sequence, empty or nonempty, can be declared using the keyword *seq* (e.g., seq$\mathbb{N}$). Nonempty sequences can be explicitly declared using the keyword *seq*$_1$ (e.g., seq$_1$ *Char*). Sequences with no duplicate elements (also called *injective sequences*) are declared using a special keyword *iseq* (e.g., iseq *Person*). A sequence can also be enumerated by explicitly introducing the objects and their relative positions within the sequence.

The notation $S(i)$ denotes the ith element of the sequence S. An empty sequence is represented by $\langle \rangle$. Table 17.4 lists the notations and the meanings of operators on sequences. The following example illustrates the application of some of these operators.

Example 1 Operators on Sequences.

Let $\quad S_1 = \langle a, b, c, d \rangle, \quad S_2 = \langle a, b \rangle, \quad S_3 = \langle f, g, h \rangle,$
$\qquad S_4 = \langle b, c \rangle, \quad S_5 = \langle c, d \rangle, \quad SS = \langle S_1, S_2, S_3 \rangle.$

Table 17.4 Operators on sequences in Z

Operator	Synopsis	Meaning
#	# S	length of the sequence S
⁀	$S_1 ⁀ S_2$	concatenation of sequence S_1 with S_2
rev	*rev* S	reverse of the sequence S
head	*head* S	first element of the sequence S
last	*last* S	last element of the sequence S
tail	*tail* S	sequence S with its first element removed
front	*front* S	sequence S with its last element removed
⁀/	⁀/ SS	distributed concatenation of the sequence of sequences SS
⊆	S ⊆ T	S is a sequence forming the prefix of the sequence T
suffix	S suffix T	S is a sequence forming the suffix of the sequence T
in	S in T	S is a segment inside the sequence T
↿	U ↿ S	extract the elements from the sequence S corresponding to the index set U; the result is also a sequence, maintaining the same order as in S
↾	S ↾ V	extract the elements of the set V from the sequence S; the result is also a sequence, maintaining the same order as in S
disjoint	disjoint SeqSet	SeqSet is an indexed family of mutually distinct sets
partitions	SeqSet partitions T	the indexed family of mutually disjoint sets whose distributed union is T

$S_1 ⁀ S_2 = \langle a,b,c,d,a,b \rangle$
$rev\ S_1 = \langle d,c,b,a \rangle$
$⁀/ SS = \langle a,b,c,d,a,b,f,g,h \rangle$
$S_2 \subseteq S_1$ is true
S_4 suffix S_1 is false
S_5 in S_1 is true
$\{2,3\} ↿ S_1 = \langle b,c \rangle$
$S_1 ↾ \{b,d,f,g\} = \langle b,d \rangle$
disjoint $\langle \{a,b\}, \{c,d\}, \{f,g\} \rangle$ is true
disjoint $\langle \{a,b\}, \{c,d\}, \{f,g,a\} \rangle$ is false
$\langle \{a,b,c\}, \{d\}, \{f,g,h\} \rangle$ partitions $\{a,b,c,d,f,g,h\}$

□

17.2.5
Bags

Like the *schema notation* (to be discussed shortly), *bag* is another distinguishing feature of the Z notation, which is not included in many model-based specification languages including VDM-SL. However, it can be easily modeled using functions or maps. The introduction of *bag* and the set of operators on bags simply provides additional modeling facility.

A bag is a set of elements which also encodes the number of occurrences of each element in the bag. Formally, a bag is defined as a partial function from the type of elements to the number of occurrences of the elements.

$$\text{bag } X == X \nrightarrow \mathbb{N}_1$$

Notice that the range of a bag is denoted by positive numbers ($\mathbb{N}_1$). This is to indicate that a bag does not maintain the information about those elements that are not in the bag.

As an example, consider a bag of coins with varying denominations: 2 pennies, 7 nickels and 12 quarters. Let the type *coins* be defined as

$$coins == \{penny, nickel, dime, quarter\}$$

The coin bag under consideration is then denoted as

$$coinbag = \{penny \mapsto 2, nickel \mapsto 7, quarter \mapsto 12\}$$

17.2.5.1
Operators on Bags

The following operators on bags are available in Z.

<u>count</u> The operator *count* is actually a higher order function which accepts a bag as input and returns a total function from the type of elements in the bag to their corresponding number of occurrences. Typically, *count* elaborates the partial function in the formal definition of the bag into a total function by explicitly checking each element in the domain and associating a zero as the number of occurrences to those elements which are not present in the domain.

The application of the *count* operator is illustrated below:

$$count\ coinbag\ quarter = 12$$
$$count\ coinbag\ dime = 0$$

The infix notation $\sharp$ for *count* may also be used in Z. Using $\sharp$, we can rewrite the example as

$$coinbag \sharp quarter = 12$$
$$coinbag \sharp dime = 0$$

<u>Membership</u> The presence of an element in a bag is checked by the bag membership operator $\sqsubseteq$ whose semantics is similar to the set membership operator. The following example illustrates the application of the bag membership operator:

$$nickel \sqsubseteq coinbag$$
$$dime \not\sqsubseteq coinbag$$

Union, Difference and Sub-bag Operators Similar to sets, there are three operators to compose bags: bag union operator ($\uplus$), bag difference operator ($\uplus$) and sub-bag operator ($\sqsubseteq$). These three operators are binary infix operators and require that both operands be of the same type of bag.

When two bags are joined under the bag union operator, the domain of the new bag includes all the elements in both bags. The number of occurrences of common elements in both bags are summed up in the new bag. Non-common elements in both bags are retained as such in the new bag.

For the difference operator, the domain of the new bag is a subset of the domain of the bag on the left side of the operator. The number of occurrences of elements in the new bag is decreased from that in the left operand according to the count in the right operand. It becomes zero if the result of subtraction is negative. As a result, those elements whose counts become zero due to the difference operation will be eliminated from the bag since the bag does not retain count for elements that are not present.

The sub-bag operator returns true if the domain of the left operand is a subset of the domain of the right operand and the number of occurrences of each element in the left operand is the same or less than that of the same element in the right operand.

The example below illustrates the application of these operators:

Let two new bags be defined as

$$newbag_1 = \{dime \mapsto 3, penny \mapsto 1\}$$
$$newbag_2 = \{nickel \mapsto 2, quarter \mapsto 2\}$$

Some bag expressions are

$$coinbag \uplus newbag_1 = \{penny \mapsto 3, nickel \mapsto 7, dime \mapsto 3, quarter \mapsto 12\}$$
$$coinbag \uplus newbag_2 = \{penny \mapsto 2, nickel \mapsto 5, quarter \mapsto 10\}$$
$$newbag_2 \sqsubseteq coinbag$$

Bag from a Sequence A sequence represents an ordered collection of elements emphasizing the position of each element in the sequence. Given a sequence, therefore, it is possible to count the number of occurrences of each distinct element in the sequence, thus obtain a bag. The prefix operator $items$ performs this operation. Thus, if $coinseq$ is a sequence defined as

$$coinseq = \langle nickel, nickel, penny, nickel, dime, quarter, quarter, dime, penny \rangle$$

then

$$items\ coinseq = \{penny \mapsto 2, nickel \mapsto 3, dime \mapsto 2, quarter \mapsto 2\}$$

17.2.6
Free Types

The primary purpose of a free type definition is to introduce enumerated constants and recursive type definitions. Like type abbreviation, every free type definition introduces a new type name into the current specification.

The syntax of a free type definition is

$$FreeType ::= constant_1 \mid \ldots \mid constant_n \mid$$
$$constructor_1 \langle\!\langle source_1 \rangle\!\rangle \mid \ldots \mid constructor_m \langle\!\langle source_m \rangle\!\rangle$$

The symbols ':$:=$', '$\mid$', '$\langle\!\langle$' and '$\rangle\!\rangle$' are part of the full syntax. The terms $constant_1, \ldots,$ $constant_n$ refer to distinct constants which belong to the carrier set of the free type. The symbols for these constants, as given in the free type definition, stand for their values and they are similar to enumerated type definition in programming languages such as Pascal. The term $constructor_i \langle\!\langle source_i \rangle\!\rangle$ refers to an injective function which accepts an object of type $source_i$ as input and returns an object of type $FreeType$. The definition for $FreeType$ is said to be closed in the sense that

$$\langle \{constant_1\}, \ldots, \{constant_n\}, \operatorname{ran} constructor_1, \ldots, \operatorname{ran} constructor_m \rangle$$
$$\text{partitions } FreeType$$

That is, the sets $\{constant_1\}, \ldots, \{constant_n\}, \operatorname{ran} constructor_1, \ldots, \operatorname{ran} constructor_m$ are pairwise disjoint and their union make up the entire set $FreeType$. Thus a free type definition explicitly defines all the members of its carrier set.

The following examples illustrate the application of free type definitions in several contexts:

Example 2 The different types of coins in a currency system can be defined as an enumerated type.

$$Coins ::= Penny \mid Nickel \mid Dime \mid Quarter \qquad \square$$

Example 3 The users of an automated banking system are drawn from three categories of people:

$$Users ::= cust\langle\!\langle Customer \rangle\!\rangle \mid stf\langle\!\langle Staff \rangle\!\rangle \mid mgr\langle\!\langle Manager \rangle\!\rangle$$

Notice that the above definition is similar to the union type definition in VDM-SL, except for the notation for constructor functions. $\qquad \square$

Example 4 The abstract data type 'List' can be defined using the syntax for free type definition. Following is the recursive definition for a list of natural numbers.

$$List ::= nil \mid cons\langle\!\langle \mathbb{N} \times List \rangle\!\rangle$$

In the definition *List*, the symbol *nil* stands for a unique value of *List* (similar to *quote* types in VDM-SL); *cons* is a constructor function which adds an element to a list. Notice that the definition *List* does not indicate whether *cons* adds the element to the front or to the back of the list. Such constraints must be specified separately outside the free type definition, possibly as global constraints. □

17.2.7
Schemas

A *schema* is a formal mathematical text describing some aspect of the software system being developed. A schema has a *unique name*, a *declaration part* and a *predicate part*. The name of a schema can be used anywhere in the document after its declaration to refer to the text. This name can also serve as a type name (to be discussed in detail shortly). The declaration part introduces some variables along with their types which are local to the schema. The predicate part describes some invariant relationships between the local variables themselves and/or some relationships between the local variables, and global constants and global variables that are declared before the schema.

As an example, a user of a computer system can be specified by the schema:

$[Char]$

```
┌─ User_1 ────────────────────────────────────
│  name : seq Char
│  password : seq Char
│  storage_limit : ℕ
│
└──────────────────────────────────────────────
```

Generally, schemas are defined using the box notation as shown above. The name of the box (in this case *User_*1) is the name of the schema. A schema of this style without any additional constraints is a simple schema. If there are constraints imposed on components of the schema then these constraints are listed below the declaration part, separated by a horizontal line.

```
┌─ User_2 ────────────────────────────────────
│  name : seq Char
│  password : seq Char
│  storage_limit : ℕ
├──────────────────────────────────────────────
│  name ≠ password
└──────────────────────────────────────────────
```

The constraints are generally expressed as well-formed formulas in predicate logic. Alternatively, several well-formed formulas, one on each separate line in the predicate part of the schema, can be given. In this case, an implicit conjunction is assumed between the predicates. For example, the predicate in the schema

$$\begin{array}{|l}
\hline
\_User\_3 \underline{\hspace{8cm}} \\
\quad name : \text{seq } Char \\
\quad password : \text{seq } Char \\
\quad storage\_limit : \mathbb{N} \\
\hline
\quad name \neq password \\
\quad \#password < 8 \\
\hline
\end{array}$$

is equivalent to

$$name \neq password \land \#password < 8$$

A schema can be also be specified in a horizontal style as

$$User\_4 == [name : \text{seq } Char;\ password : \text{seq } Char;\ storage\_limit : \mathbb{N}\ |$$
$$name \neq password \land \#password < 8]$$

The variables in the declaration part of a horizontal schema must be separated by semi-colons, and all constraints in one schema should be stated by one well-formed formula. The square brackets on the right side of $==$ are part of the syntax.

17.2.7.1
Signature and Properties

A *signature* is a collection of variables, each variable being associated with a type. For example,

$$name : \text{seq } char;\ \ age : \mathbb{N}_1$$

is a signature with two variables *name* and *age*; the type of *name* is a sequence of characters and the type of *age* is $\mathbb{N}_1$.

The *property* of a schema is a predicate that is obtained from the predicate part of the schema and the predicate implicit in the declaration part. Thus, the property of the schema *User_3* is the following predicate:

$$name \in \text{seq } char \land password \in \text{seq } char \land storage\_limit \in \mathbb{N} \land$$
$$name \neq password \land \#password < 8$$

17.2.7.2
Schema Types and Bindings

The definition of schema *User_3* introduces the name *User_3* as a type. A *schema type* is an association or a *binding* between names (derived from the schema name and the names of the local variables) and types of the local variables. The type of a schema is completely determined by the names and types in the declaration part. The predicate part is irrelevant in establishing the type of the schema. Two schema types are regarded as identical if they differ only in the order of presentation of their signatures. Thus, the schemas $User\_1$ and $User\_2$ define the same type, even though their predicate parts are different. The schema $User\_3$ defines a type different from $User\_1$ (and $User\_2$), since the signatures are different. An object u with the schema type $User\_3$ has components $u.name$, $u.password$ and $u.storage\_limit$. If N, P and S are objects of types seq $char$, seq $char$ and $\mathbb{N}$, respectively, we can establish a binding between the component names of the schema $User\_3$ and the objects N, P and S as

$$\theta\ User\_3 \equiv (name \Rightarrow N, password \Rightarrow P, storage\_limit \Rightarrow S)$$

which assigns the objects N, P and S to the schema components $u.name$, $u.password$ and $u.storage\_limit$, respectively. The symbol $\Rightarrow$ is used to describe bindings in Z, but is not part of the Z notation. The expression $\theta\ S$ where S is a schema, has a binding as its value. That is, $\theta\ S$ is an instance of S with its components as declared in S. The set comprehension expression $\{User\_3\}$ is interpreted to mean $\{User\_3 \bullet \theta\ User\_3\}$, which denotes a set of users and its type is $\mathbb{P}\ User\_3$.

17.2.7.3
Type Compatibility of Signatures

Two signatures are said to be *type compatible* if and only if every variable common to both signatures has the same type. Thus the signature

> $name$: seq $Char$
> $password$: seq $Char$

is type compatible with the signature

> $name$: seq $Char$
> $social\_insurance\_number$: $\mathbb{N}_1$

since the only common variable $name$ has the same type in both signatures. As another example, the two signatures

> x, y : $\mathbb{N}$ and
> x, t : $\mathbb{Z}$

are also type compatible. Here, the type of the common variable x in both signatures is $\mathbb{Z}$. The term $\mathbb{N}$ denotes a set of non-negative integers with a constraint that

> $\forall n : \mathbb{N} \bullet n \geq 0$

The type of $\mathbb{N}$ is $\mathbb{Z}$, the maximal set.

17.2.7.4
Schema Inclusion

Schema inclusion is a mechanism by which a previously defined schema definition can be reused in the definition of another schema. This could be done in two ways: (i) a schema S_1 can be included in the declaration part of another schema S_2; (ii) S_1 can be included in the predicate part of S_2.

When a schema S_1 is included in the declaration part of another schema S_2, the signature of S_2 includes that of S_1 and the newly declared <variable, type> pairs introduced in the declaration part of S_2. The signature of S_1 must be type compatible with that of S_2. The predicate part of S_1 is conjoined with the newly declared predicates of S_2. As an example, consider the definition of a schema *Student* which includes the schema *User_3*.

$$
\begin{array}{|l}
\_Student_____ \\
User\_3 \\
idnumber : \mathbb{N}_1 \\
\hline
storage\_limit \leq 1000 \\
\end{array}
$$

This is equivalent to the schema

$$
\begin{array}{|l}
\_Student_____ \\
name : \text{seq } Char \\
password : \text{seq } Char \\
storage\_limit : \mathbb{N} \\
idnumber : \mathbb{N}_1 \\
\hline
name \neq password \\
\#password < 8 \\
storage\_limit \leq 1000 \\
\end{array}
$$

A schema S_1 can be included in the predicate part of another schema S_2 in two ways: (i) the name S_1 can be placed on a separate line in the predicate part of S_2; (ii) S_1 can be included using a quantified expression. In both cases, the signature of S_1 must be type compatible with that of S_2. See the two examples below, which illustrate these concepts.

The schema

$$
\begin{array}{|l}
\_Student\_0_____ \\
name : \text{seq } Char \\
password : \text{seq } Char \\
storage\_limit : \mathbb{N} \\
idnumber : \mathbb{N}_1 \\
\hline
User\_3 \\
storage\_limit \leq 1000 \\
\end{array}
$$

is equivalent to the schema

$\begin{array}{|l|}\hline \text{\textit{Student\_0}} \\ \hline \textit{name} : \text{seq } \textit{Char} \\ \textit{password} : \text{seq } \textit{Char} \\ \textit{storage\_limit} : \mathbb{N} \\ \textit{idnumber} : \mathbb{N}_1 \\ \hline \textit{name} \neq \textit{password} \\ \#\textit{password} < 8 \\ \textit{storage\_limit} \leq 1000 \\ \hline \end{array}$

The schema

$\begin{array}{|l|}\hline \text{\textit{Student\_1}} \\ \hline \textit{idnumber} : \mathbb{N}_1 \\ \hline \exists \, \textit{User\_3} \bullet \textit{storage\_limit} \leq 1000 \\ \hline \end{array}$

is equivalent to the schema

$\begin{array}{|l|}\hline \text{\textit{Student\_1}} \\ \hline \textit{idnumber} : \mathbb{N}_1 \\ \hline \exists \, \textit{name} : \text{seq } \textit{Char}; \ \textit{password} : \text{seq } \textit{Char}; \ \textit{storage\_limt} : \mathbb{N} \bullet \\ \quad \textit{name} \neq \textit{password} \wedge \#\textit{password} < 8 \wedge \textit{storage\_limit} \leq 1000 \\ \hline \end{array}$

Remarks   Notice that the constraints defined in the three schemas *Student*, *Student_0* and *Student_1* are the same as seen from their expanded definitions. However, the three schemas are not identical. The subtle differences are:

- The types of the schemas *Student* and *Student_0* are the same, namely the bindings defined by

  $\langle\!\langle \textit{name} : \text{seq } \textit{Char}; \ \textit{password} : \text{seq } \textit{Char}; \ \textit{idnumber} : \mathbb{N}_1;$
  $\quad \textit{storage\_limit} : \mathbb{N}\rangle\!\rangle$

- The type of the schema *Student_1* is $\langle\!\langle \textit{idnumber} : \mathbb{N}\rangle\!\rangle$, which is different from the types of *Student* and *Student_0*.
- The declaration and predicate parts of *User_3* are automatically brought into the respective declaration and predicate parts of *Student*, whereas to create *Student_0* we have to retype the declarations of *User_3* in *Student_0* in order to bring the variables in scope; only the predicate part of *User_3* is automatically conjoined with the newly declared predicate of *Student_0*.

17.2.7.5
Schema as a Type

As stated earlier, a schema can be used as a type name after it has been introduced. The carrier set of this type is the set of all instances of the schema satisfying the binding of the schema. To illustrate, consider the schema *Users* defined below:

$$
\begin{array}{l}
\underline{\quad Users \underline{\hspace{6cm}}} \\
all : \mathbb{P}\,User\_3 \\
\hline
\forall u_1, u_2 : User\_3 \mid u_1 \neq u_2 \wedge u_1 \in all \wedge u_2 \in all \bullet \\
\quad u_1.name \neq u_2.name \\
\end{array}
$$

The predicate part of *Users* asserts that the names of users of type *User_3* must all be unique. A variable u of type *Users* is an instance of *Users* schema. To refer to a particular component of a schema, the $\_\,.\,\_$ operator is used; thus, the name $u.all$ refers to the instance in u of the variable *all* in *Users*.

17.2.7.6
Generic Schema

The generic constructs in Z allow a family of concepts to be captured in a single definition. For example, a table can be defined as a generic schema:

$$
\begin{array}{l}
\underline{\quad Table \underline{\hspace{6cm}} T,X} \\
first\_column : \text{seq}\,T \\
second\_column : \text{seq}\,X \\
\end{array}
$$

The schema *Table* defines a two-column table pattern with entries of type T in the first column and entries of type X in the second column. The structure of a specific table can be described as an instance of this generic pattern. For example,

$$[Person, PhoneNumber]$$
$$PhoneBook == Table[Person, PhoneNumber]$$

defines a table with objects of type *Person* in the first column and objects of type *PhoneNumber* in the second column. The instantiation of the generic parameters T and X by the actual parameters *Person* and *PhoneNumber*, respectively, provides a strict binding defined as

$$\langle\!\langle first\_column : \text{seq}\,Person; \; second\_column : \text{seq}\,PhoneNumber \rangle\!\rangle$$

Notice that the two columns in $Table[T, X]$ need not be of same length. If there is such a restriction, it will be stated in the predicate part of $Table[T, X]$ such as

$\#first\_column = \#second\_column$

This restriction will be carried over when $Table[T, X]$ is instantiated with actual parameters. Thus, *PhoneBook* has the same restriction as that of $Table[T, X]$. One may further constrain the instantiation. For example, if the phone book is required to be sorted on alphabetical ordering of *Person*, then a global constraint such as

$\forall phb : PhoneBook\bullet$
  $\forall i, j : 1..\#(phb.first\_column)\bullet$
    $i \leq j \Rightarrow (phb.first\_column)(i) \leq_p (phb.first\_column)(j)$

provided that the operator $\leq_p$ is defined for objects of type *Person*.

17.2.7.7
Schema Expressions

Type compatible schemas can be composed using the logical operators $\neg$, $\vee$, $\wedge$, $\Rightarrow$ and $\Leftrightarrow$. When the unary operator $\neg$ is applied to a schema S, the result is a schema denoted by $\neg S$ whose signature is the same as that of S and whose predicate part is obtained by negating the property of S. As an example, consider the schema S defined as

```
_ S _____
  x, y : ℕ
_____
  x > y
_____
```

Before considering $\neg S$, we should rewrite S so that the implicit predicates of S are visible. Thus, S can be rewritten as

```
_ S _____
  x, y : ℤ
_____
  x ≥ 0
  y ≥ 0
  x > y
_____
```

Now, $\neg S$ can be defined as

```
_ ¬ S _____
  x, y : ℤ
_____
  ¬ (x ≥ 0 ∧ y ≥ 0 ∧ x > y)
_____
```

As another example, consider the schema S_1 defined as

```
┌─ S_1 ────────────────────────────────
│ x : 1..10
│ y : ℕ₁
├──────────────────────────────────────
│ y > x * x
└──────────────────────────────────────
```

S_1 has an implicit predicate in its declaration part. To obtain its negation, S_1 is first rewritten as

```
┌─ S_1 ────────────────────────────────
│ x, y : ℤ
├──────────────────────────────────────
│ 1 ≤ x ≤ 10
│ y > 0
│ y > x * x
└──────────────────────────────────────
```

and then $\neg S_1$ is obtained:

```
┌─ ¬ S_1 ──────────────────────────────
│ x, y : ℤ
├──────────────────────────────────────
│ ¬ (1 ≤ x ≤ 10) ∨
│ ¬ (y > 0) ∨
│ ¬ (y > x * x)
└──────────────────────────────────────
```

The signature of the schema $S \wedge T$ is the union of the signatures of S and T. The predicate part of $S \wedge T$ is the conjunction of the predicate parts of S and T. Similar definitions are given for $S \vee T$, $S \Rightarrow T$, and $S \Leftrightarrow T$. In all the four cases, the signatures of S and T must be type compatible. The following example illustrates schema composition operations:

Example 5 Logical operators applied to schemas.

Let $S == [x, y : \mathbb{N} \mid x > y]$ and $T == [x : \mathbb{Z} \mid x > 100]$

$$S \vee T == [x : \mathbb{Z}; \ y : \mathbb{N} \mid x > y \vee x > 100]$$
$$S \wedge T == [x : \mathbb{Z}; \ y : \mathbb{N} \mid x > y \wedge x > 100]$$
$$S \Rightarrow T == [x : \mathbb{Z}; \ y : \mathbb{N} \mid x > y \Rightarrow x > 100]$$
$$S \Leftrightarrow T == [x : \mathbb{Z}; \ y : \mathbb{N} \mid x > y \Leftrightarrow x > 100]$$
□

Schemas can appear in quantified expressions. Given two schemas S and T, each one of the expressions $\exists T \bullet S$, $\exists_1 T \bullet S$, and $\forall T \bullet S$ results in a new schema. In all these cases, the signatures of S and T must be type compatible. The resulting schema in each case has its signature as the signature of S with components of T removed from S. The property of the new schema is true under all the bindings for which the property of S is true constrained by the property of T. This requires that the components of T which are not present in the signature of the resulting schema be brought back into the predicate part of the result through the same quantifier. The example below illustrates this concept:

Example 6 Schemas in quantified expressions.

Let $S == [x, y : \mathbb{N} \mid x > y]$, $T == [x : \mathbb{Z} \mid x > 100]$ and $U == [x, w : \mathbb{Z} \mid x > w]$

$$\exists T \bullet S == [y : \mathbb{N} \mid \exists x : \mathbb{Z} \mid x > 100 \bullet x > y]$$
$$\exists_1 T \bullet S == [y : \mathbb{N} \mid \exists_1 x : \mathbb{Z} \mid x > y \bullet x > 100]$$
$$\exists_1 U \bullet S == [y : \mathbb{N} \mid \exists_1 x : \mathbb{Z}; w : \mathbb{Z} \mid x > w \bullet x > y]$$
$$\forall T \bullet S == [y : \mathbb{N} \mid \forall x : \mathbb{Z} \mid x > 100 \bullet x > y] \qquad \square$$

We next define a schema expression. A schema expression SE is a member of the smallest set generated by the following rules:

1. A schema S is an SE.
2. If SE_1 and SE_2 are schema expressions, then their compositions through the logical operators $\neg$, $\vee$, $\wedge$, $\Rightarrow$ and $\Leftrightarrow$ are also schema expressions; i.c., $\neg SE_1$, $SE_1 \vee SE_2$, $SE_1 \wedge SE_2$, $SE_1 \Rightarrow SE_2$, $SE_1 \Leftrightarrow SE_2$ are all schema expressions.
3. If SE is a schema expression and T is a schema, then the quantified expressions $\exists T \bullet SE$, $\exists_1 T \bullet SE$, $\forall T \bullet SE$ are schema expressions.

17.2.7.8
Schema Renaming

The variables $x_1, \ldots, x_n$ of a schema S can be renamed using the notation $S[y_1/x_1, \ldots, y_n/x_n]$ where $y_1, \ldots, y_n$ are new identifiers replacing the existing identifiers $x_1, \ldots, x_n$. The new identifiers y_i need not be distinct from one another and may even be the same identifiers already present in S. The following conditions must be true for the validity of schema renaming:

- The signature of S and that of $S[y_1/x_1, \ldots, y_n/x_n]$ must be type compatible.
- For every binding under which the property of S is true, the property of $S[y_1/x_1, \ldots, y_n/x_n]$ must also be true after renaming. Thus, if S is defined as

$$S == [x, y : \mathbb{N} \mid x > y]$$

then the renaming $S[p/x, q/y]$ results in a valid schema

$$S[p/x, q/y] == [p, q : \mathbb{N} \mid p > q]$$

whereas the renaming $S[y/x]$ results in an invalid schema

$$S[y/x] == [y : \mathbb{N} \mid y > y]$$

because the property $y > y$ is false under all bindings.[1]

- Schema renaming is merely a process of changing identifiers; hence, substitution of expressions to replace components of a schema using schema renaming is invalid.

17.2.7.9
Schema Hiding and Projection

The purpose of schema hiding is to hide some components of a schema from its declaration part. However, these components will be reintroduced in the predicate part of the schema through existential quantifier. The reason is to bring these components in scope so that the property of the new schema will be true under all bindings for which the property of the original schema is true. Since these components are removed from the declaration part, the type of the resulting schema will be different from the original schema.

The notation $S\backslash(x_1, \ldots, x_n)$ is used to hide the components $x_1, \ldots, x_n$ from the schema S. As an example, $User\_3\backslash(name)$ is the schema

```
┌─ User_3 \ (name) ──────────────────────────────────────────
│  password : seq Char
│  storage_limit : ℕ
│ ─────────────────────────────────────────────────────────
│  ∃ name : seq Char | name ≠ password • #password < 8
└───────────────────────────────────────────────────────────
```

For schema hiding such as $S\backslash(x_1, x_2, \ldots, x_n)$ to be valid, the variables $x_1, x_2, \ldots, x_n$ must be present in the declaration part of S.

A schema S can be projected into another schema T using the schema projection operator. The result is a schema, written as $S \upharpoonright T$ whose signature is the same as that of T. The property of $S \upharpoonright T$ is satisfied by exactly those bindings under which the property of $S \wedge T$ is true, but are restricted by the components $x_1, \ldots, x_n$ such that $x_1, \ldots, x_n$ are in S but not in T. Typically,

$$S \upharpoonright T \equiv (S \wedge T)\backslash(x_1, \ldots, x_n)$$

For the schema projection to be valid, the signatures of S and T must be type compatible; see the following example:

---

[1] Strictly speaking, this condition is not mandatory. Thus, the schema $S[y/x]$ is a valid Z specification for which there is no model. However, we impose this restriction for the usefulness of schema renaming.

Example 7 Type Compatibility.

Let $S == [x, y : \mathbb{N} \mid x > y \wedge x > 100]$ and $T == [y, z : \mathbb{Z} \mid y > z]$

$$S \upharpoonright T == [y, z : \mathbb{Z} \mid y > z \wedge y \geq 0 \wedge (\exists x : \mathbb{N} \bullet x > y \wedge x > 100)]$$

Notice that the variable y in T is an integer whereas y in $S \upharpoonright T$ is a natural number, because y is declared as a natural number in S. In order to maintain type compatibility, the constraint $y \geq 0$ is introduced in $S \upharpoonright T$. $\square$

17.2.8
State Representation

A schema can be used to describe the abstract state of a software system in Z. The declaration part of the schema contains the state space variables and the predicate part describes the state invariant. Unlike VDM, substates can be independently specified and combined using schema calculus operators. Modularity, achieved in this fashion, promotes comprehension, analysis, and reuse of schemas.

The instances or snap shots of a state representation in Z correspond to the bindings of the state components to various objects, which satisfy the state invariant. For illustration, consider the state space schema

---

ComputerSystem

$valid, active, inactive : \mathbb{P}\, UserId$
$password : UserId \nrightarrow Password$

$active = \mathrm{dom}\, password$
$active \cap inactive = \emptyset$
$valid = active \cup inactive$

The state *ComputerSystem* describes three types of users. The variable *valid* denotes the set of users who have registered with the system. This set is partitioned into two groups, *active* who are currently using the system and *inactive* whose accounts are frozen and therefore are not used. The state variable *password* in *ComputerSystem* stands for a file which maintains the names and respective passwords of the users. The state invariant of *ComputerSystem* asserts the following: (i) The variable *password* maintains the passwords of active users only; notice that it is defined as a partial function. (ii) A user's account will not be active and inactive at the same time. Stated otherwise, the set of active users and the set of inactive users are mutually exclusive. (iii) The valid users of the system include the sets of active and inactive users.

Table 17.5 shows some snap shots of the state specified by *ComputerSystem* (in this table, John, Mary and Tom refer to distinct objects of type *UserId*; animal, clown and crazy refer to distinct objects of type *Password*).

Table 17.5 Some bindings of the state represented by *ComputerSystem*

valid	active	inactive	password
∅	∅	∅	∅
{John, Mary}	{John}	{Mary}	{John ↦ animal}
{John, Mary, Tom}	{Mary, Tom}	{John}	{Mary ↦ clown, Tom ↦ crazy}

17.3
Operational Abstraction

The operational abstraction formalizes operations and functions on an abstract state. The major difference between operations and functions is, as in VDM-SL, that operations access state space variables while functions do not.

17.3.1
Operations

An operation, defined over an abstract state space, may or may not change the state space and unlike functions, does not return any value explicitly. The schema notation is used to define operations. The declaration part of an operation schema includes the names of the state variables before and after the operation, and input and output parameters for the operation. The predicate part describes how the values of variables in the declaration part are constrained.

Let us consider how to specify the state and operations for a simplified model of a store which issues credit cards to its customers. For each customer, the store maintains the information such as the name of the customer, the card number issued to the customer and the current balance in the customer's account. The schema *Customer* defined below specifies the type of customers for this store.

[*STRING*]

```
┌─ Customer ─────────────────────────────────────
  name : STRING
  cardnumber : N
  balance : N
└─────────────────────────────────────────────────
```

The state space of the system consists of the set of all customers of the store. The schema *Company* describes this state space. It has only one state variable: *customers* which is defined as a set of *Customer*. The state invariant asserts that card numbers issued to customers are unique.

```
  Company
  customers : PCustomer

  ∀ c₁, c₂ : Customer | c₁ ∈ customers ∧ c₂ ∈ customers •
    c₁ = c₂ ⇔ c₁.cardnumber = c₂.cardnumber
```

To enroll a new customer, we need an operation *AddCustomer*, which ensures that the card number for the new customer is different from any other card that has already been issued. This is the precondition for the operation. The postcondition asserts that the database of customers has been modified to include the new customer's information.

```
  AddCustomer
  customers, customers' : PCustomer
  new_customer? : Customer

  (∀ cust : Customer | cust ∈ customers •
    cust.cardnumber ≠ new_customer?.cardnumber)
  customers' = customers ∪ {new_customer?}
```

The declaration part of *AddCustomer* consists of three components: *customers* represents the set of customers before the operation, *customers'* represents the customers after the operation successfully terminates and *new_customer?* is the input parameter to the operation. Unprimed names like *customers* are used to denote the values of the components of the state before the operation, the pre-state. Names with primes like *customers'* are used to denote the values of the same components of the state after the operation, the post-state. Names like *new_customer?* denote input parameters to the operation. Names like *result!* with a ! at the end are used to denote output parameters from the operation. These decorations are conventionally used for these intended purposes, although the Z notation does not prevent a specifier from using the decorations for other purposes. For example, if the state space schema *Company* contains a variable *customer?*, it is still valid. However, experienced Z users may find such declarations unconventional.

The predicate part of *AddCustomer* consists of two predicates: the first one is the precondition for the operation which, asserts that the card number of the new customer must not be the same as the card number of any other customer in the system. The second predicate is the postcondition which ensures that the new customer is added to the database of the system.

Recall that the specification of an operation in VDM-SL may include an **error** clause; the error clause asserts the conditions that must be satisfied when the precondition fails. In Z, such error conditions may be specified as separate schemas and then they may be combined with the operation schema using schema composition. In the store example discussed above, we may wish to include messages indicating a successful or an unsuccessful addition of a new customer to the store. So, we first define a message type:

Message ::= *CUSTOMER_ADDED* | *CARD_NUMBER_EXISTS*

$$\boxed{\begin{array}{l}
\_AddCustomer\_0 _____ \\
customers, customers' : \mathbb{P}Customer \\
new\_customer? : Customer \\
message! : Message \\
\hline
(\forall\, cust : Customer \mid cust \in customers \bullet \\
\quad cust.cardnumber \neq new\_customer?.cardnumber) \\
customers' = customers \cup \{new\_customer?\} \\
message! = CUSTOMER\_ADDED
\end{array}}$$

The operation *AddCustomer_0* is enriched with a message in *AddCustomer*.

$$\boxed{\begin{array}{l}
\_Customer\_Exists _____ \\
customers : \mathbb{P}Customer \\
new\_customer? : Customer \\
message! : Message \\
\hline
(\exists\, cust : Customer \mid cust \in customers \bullet \\
\quad cust.cardnumber = new\_customer?.cardnumber) \\
message! = CARD\_NUMBER\_EXISTS
\end{array}}$$

The operation *Customer_Exists* affirms the presence of a customer in the database whose card number matches the card number of the new customer.

$$AddCustomer\_new == AddCustomer\_0 \vee Customer\_Exists$$

The operation *AddCustomer_new* composes *AddCustomer_0* and *Customer_Exists* to incorporate both messages into one single operation.

Remarks   It should be noted that both *AddCustomer* and *AddCustomer_new* assert only the conditions that must be true of the state variables before and after the operation. However, they do not guarantee the validity of the state invariant after the termination of the operation. It requires a proof obligation; see Sect. 10.4.

17.3.2
Schema Decorators and Conventions

The conventions for schema decorations allow specifications to be written with clarity and reused in other schemas. Among the three decorators (prime, question mark and exclamation mark) discussed earlier for variable names, the use of prime deserves further elaboration. When an operation schema includes the variables of a state, it should include all the variables in that state plus their primed counterparts. This is in contrast to the specification of an operation in VDM-SL where only those state variables which are modified by the operation are specified through the **ext** clause. An important consequence of including all the state variables and their primed counterparts in a schema is that the specifier must explicitly show what state variables are changed by the operation (by specifying how they are modified) and must also report that all other state variables remain unchanged. In order to simplify the writing of all the state variables and their primed counterparts in an operation schema, Z has two conventions: the Δ and the Ξ notations.

The Δ notation: The Δ notation is used as an abbreviation to include schemas S and S' into a single schema ΔS. Note that Δ is part of a schema name, and not an operator.

$$\begin{array}{|l}\hline\ S \\ \hline x:X \\ y:Y \\ \hline P(x,y) \\ \hline\end{array}$$

$$\begin{array}{|l}\hline\ S' \\ \hline x':X \\ y':Y \\ \hline P[x'/x,y'/y] \\ \hline\end{array}$$

$$\begin{array}{|l}\hline\ \Delta S \\ \hline S \\ S' \\ \hline\end{array}$$

Having defined ΔS, we can include it in an operation schema to introduce all state variables of S before and after the operation. We illustrate below the Δ convention by rewriting *AddCustomer* operation defined previously:

$$\begin{array}{|l}\hline\ AddCustomer\_1 \\ \hline \Delta Company \\ new\_customer?:Customer \\ \hline (\forall\,cust:Customer\mid cust\in customers \\ \quad cust.cardnumber\neq new\_customer?.cardnumber) \\ customers'=customers\cup\{new\_customer?\} \\ \hline\end{array}$$

The above operation definition is equivalent to

```
┌─ AddCustomer_1 ─────────────────────────────────────────────
│ customers : ℙCustomer
│ customers' : ℙCustomer
│ new_customer? : Customer
├─────────────────────────────────────────────────────────────
│ (∀ c₁, c₂ : Customer | c₁ ∈ customers ∧ c₂ ∈ customers •
│    c₁ = c₂ ⇔ c₁.cardnumber = c₂.cardnumber)
│ (∀ c₁, c₂ : Customer | c₁ ∈ customers' ∧ c₂ ∈ customers' •
│    c₁ = c₂ ⇔ c₁.cardnumber = c₂.cardnumber)
│ (∀ cust : Customer | cust ∈ customers •
│    cust.cardnumber ≠ new_customer?.cardnumber)
│ customers' = customers ∪ {new_customer?}
└─────────────────────────────────────────────────────────────
```

Notice that the operation *AddCustomer_1* includes the state invariant before and after the operation as part of its meaning. This ensures the validity of state invariant before and after the operation.

The Ξ notation: When the Δ notation is used in an operation schema, the intention is that the operation changes the values of some of the state variables. This is synonymous to read/write operation in programming languages. If the operation is an inquiry operation such as to find or read the value of a state variable, then the Ξ notation is used. The formal definition of ΞS is given below:

```
┌─ ΞS ─────────────────────────────────────────────────────────
│ ΔS
├─────────────────────────────────────────────────────────────
│ S = S'
└─────────────────────────────────────────────────────────────
```

The following is a revised specification of the operation *Customer_Exists*:

```
┌─ Customer_Exists ───────────────────────────────────────────
│ ΞCompany
│ new_customer? : Customer
│ message! : Message
├─────────────────────────────────────────────────────────────
│ (∃ cust : Customer | cust ∈ customers •
│    cust.cardnumber = new_customer?.cardnumber)
│ message! = CARD_NUMBER_EXISTS
└─────────────────────────────────────────────────────────────
```

Unlike VDM-SL, an operation in Z can act on several state spaces at the same time. These state spaces will be included in the definition of the operation schema using the Δ or Ξ notations. The semantics for schema inclusion will be applied to merge common declarations in these state spaces. The invariants of the state spaces are conjoined with the predicate part of the operation schema.

17.3.3
Sequential Composition

Schema calculus uses logical connectives on predefined schemas to create new schemas. In addition, there is a *sequential composition operator* denoted by $\frac{9}{9}$ which is primarily used to compose operation schemas.

The sequential composition of operations describes the combined effect of the operations, applied in the specified sequence, on the state of the system. The sequential composition $S == S_1 \frac{9}{9} S_2$ defines S as an operation for which the input is the input of S_1 and the result is that from S_2 when the result of S_1 is fed as input to S_2. That is to say that the postcondition of S_1 implies the precondition of S_2. For sequential composition to remain meaningful, the signatures of the two schemas S_1 and S_2 must be type compatible and both S_1 and S_2 should address the same abstract state. If this abstract state is represented as T, then S_1 will describe the states T and T'. Since T' is fed as input to S_2, S_2 describes the states T' and T''; all the Ts are of same type. S will contain T and T'' as its initial and final states. The signature of S consists of the unprimed components of S_1, the primed components of S_2, and the input and output parameters of both S_1 and S_2.

Sequential composition operator can be used to specify the changes in profile of a customer in the database of a credit card company, an example discussed earlier. The following operation deletes a customer record:

$$
\begin{array}{|l}
\hline
\underline{\quad DeleteCustomer\qquad\qquad\qquad\qquad\qquad\qquad\qquad\qquad}\\
\Delta Company \\
old\_customer? : Customer \\
\hline
(\exists\, cust : Customer \mid cust \in customers \bullet \\
\quad cust.cardnumber = old\_customer?.cardnumber) \\
customers' = customers \setminus \{old\_customer?\} \\
\hline
\end{array}
$$

Assuming that the operation *AddCustomer* is the same as defined earlier, we can now define *ChangeCustomer* operation as a sequential composition of *DeleteCustomer* and *AddCustomer*:

$ChangeCustomer\_0 == DeleteCustomer \frac{9}{9} AddCustomer$

$ChangeCustomer == [ChangeCustomer\_0 \mid$

$\quad old\_customer?.cardnumber = new\_customer?.cardnumber]$

The syntax of Z does not allow constrained sequential composition. So, we first introduce the operation *ChangeCustomer_0* and then introduce the additional constraint that the card numbers of *old_customer?* and *new_customer?* are the same.

The fully expanded version of the operation *ChangeCustomer_0* is given below:

$\boxed{\begin{array}{l} \_\mathit{ChangeCustomer\_0}_____ \\ customers, customers' : \mathbb{P}Customer \\ old\_customer? : Customer \\ customers', customers'' : \mathbb{P}Customer \\ new\_customer? : Customer \\ \hline (\forall c_1, c_2 : Customer \mid c_1 \in customers \wedge c_2 \in customers \bullet \\ \quad c_1 = c_2 \Leftrightarrow c_1.cardnumber = c_2.cardnumber) \\ (\forall c_1, c_2 : Customer \mid c_1 \in customers' \wedge c_2 \in customers' \bullet \\ \quad c_1 = c_2 \Leftrightarrow c_1.cardnumber = c_2.cardnumber) \\ (\exists cust : Customer \mid cust \in customers \bullet \\ \quad cust.cardnumber = old\_customer?.cardnumber) \\ customers' = customers \setminus \{old\_customer?\} \\ (\forall c_1, c_2 : Customer \mid c_1 \in customers' \wedge c_2 \in customers \bullet \\ \quad c_1 = c_2 \Leftrightarrow c_1.cardnumber = c_2.cardnumber) \\ (\forall c_1, c_2 : Customer \mid c_1 \in customers'' \wedge c_2 \in customers' \bullet \\ \quad c_1 = c_2 \Leftrightarrow c_1.cardnumber = c_2.cardnumber) \\ (\forall cust : Customer \mid cust \in customers' \bullet \\ \quad cust.cardnumber \neq new\_customer?.cardnumber) \\ customers'' = customers' \cup \{new\_customer?\} \end{array}}$

Next, we simplify the schema: the state implied by single primed variables are first merged; to maintain consistency with the Δ notation, the single primed variables are removed and the double primed variables are changed into single primed variables. Thus, the simplified definition of *ChangeCustomer_0* is

$\boxed{\begin{array}{l} \_\mathit{ChangeCustomer\_0}_____ \\ \Delta Company \\ old\_customer? : Customer \\ new\_customer? : Customer \\ \hline (\exists cust : Customer \mid cust \in customers \bullet \\ \quad cust.cardnumber = old\_customer?.cardnumber) \\ (\forall cust : Customer \mid cust \in customers \bullet \\ \quad cust.cardnumber \neq new\_customer?.cardnumber) \\ customers' = customers \setminus \{old\_customer?\} \cup \{new\_customer?\} \end{array}}$

17.3.4
Functions

The specification of a function has two parts—signature and definition. The signature consists of names and types of input and output parameters. Like VDM-SL, one can define a function in two ways in Z: using *explicit style* or using *implicit style*. The definition of an explicit function is constructive in the sense that the function definition explicitly shows how the output parameter is obtained. For example, the function *Sqr* which squares its input parameter can be explicitly stated as follows:

$$
\begin{array}{|l}
Sqr : \mathbb{N} \to \mathbb{N} \\
\hline
\forall n : \mathbb{N} \bullet Sqr(n) = n * n
\end{array}
$$

An implicit function states the relationships between the input parameters and the result of the function as shown in the example below:

$$
\begin{array}{|l}
max : \mathbb{F}_1 \mathbb{N} \to \mathbb{N} \\
\hline
\forall nset : \mathbb{F}_1 \mathbb{N};\ n : \mathbb{N} \bullet max(nset) = n \Leftrightarrow \\
\quad n \in nset \wedge (\forall i : \mathbb{N} \bullet i \in nset \Rightarrow i \le n)
\end{array}
$$

A function definition can also be recursive. For example, the function *sum_list* defined below sums up all integers in an integer list and returns the sum. It uses the free type definition *List* defined as

$$List ::= nil \mid cons\langle\!\langle \mathbb{Z} \times List \rangle\!\rangle$$

$$
\begin{array}{|l}
sum\_list : List \to \mathbb{Z} \\
\hline
\forall n : \mathbb{Z};\ l : List \bullet \\
\quad sum\_list(nil) = 0 \wedge \\
\quad sum\_list(cons(n, l)) = n + sum\_list(l)
\end{array}
$$

The definition of *sum_list* asserts that the sum of integers of an empty integer list is zero. If the list is nonempty, then the list has been constructed by adding an integer n to a sublist l. In this case, the resulting sum is the sum of integers in l and the integer n.

17.3.5
Generic Functions

Generic functions are those that produce results for arguments of arbitrary types. We have seen examples of generic functions in Chap. 12. The syntax for defining a generic function in Z is a box with a double line at the top containing the name of the generic parameters. The generic function *length* defined below recursively determines the length of a sequence (of elements of some type).

$$
\begin{array}{|l}
\hline
[T] \\
\hline
length : \text{seq}\, T \rightarrow \mathbb{N} \\
\hline
\forall\, inseq : \text{seq}\, T \bullet \\
\quad inseq = \langle\rangle \Rightarrow length(inseq) = 0\ \land \\
\quad inseq \neq \langle\rangle \Rightarrow length(inseq) = 1 + length(tail\ inseq) \\
\hline
\end{array}
$$

17.4
Specification Examples

A Z specification consists of a series of paragraphs, where each paragraph can be a type definition, global constant, global constraint, state space declaration or an operation. Z follows the principle of "define before use"; accordingly, every entity (type declaration, operation, function) must be defined before being used. The scope of an entity starts from the point at which it is declared and extends to the end of the current specification (except for the structural components of a schema, whose scope ends at the end of the schema definition itself). A specifier can introduce any Z paragraph as and when it is needed. In addition, each paragraph can be augmented with informal descriptions. This helps the specifier to explain the purpose of a piece of specification immediately after it is introduced. The reader should note how this feature differs from VDM-SL syntax, where an entire specification must be written in one piece, under one state space.

In this section, three Z specification examples are given to illustrate the syntactic structures discussed so far. In all examples, the specifications are accompanied by informal descriptions.

Example 8 Login Subsystem Management.

Problem Statement
A login subsystem maintains a set of accounts, one for each user of the system. Each account consists of a user name and a password. It is required that the names of users must be unique in the system. A user can have multiple accounts in the system with different user names. It should be possible to (i) add a new account to the system ,(ii) delete an existing account, and (iii) change the password of an account.

Additional Requirement

1. Suitable error messages must be given.

The Model
User names and passwords are modeled as basic types. The rationale for this decision is that user attributes are neither stated in the problem, nor are they required to specify the operations. An account is a composite entity which consists of a user name and a password. This can be modeled either as a Cartesian product or a schema. We have chosen the schema notation to model an account. The state space is represented by a schema which consists

of only one component: *the set of accounts*. Since no ordering is implied by the problem statement the state variable can be modeled as a set. The state invariant ensures that no two accounts have the same user name. Three operations, add an account, delete an account and change the password of an account, are given.

Z Specification
An account in the login subsystem consists of a user name and a password.

[*Username*, *Password*]

Account
---
name : *Username*
password : *Password*

The state space is described by the schema *LoginSubsystem*.

LoginSubsystem
---
users : $\mathbb{P}\,Account$

$\forall u_1, u_2 : Account \mid u_1 \in users \land u_2 \in users \bullet$
    $u_1.name = u_2.name \Leftrightarrow u_1 = u_2$

The state invariant in the above schema asserts that if two accounts have the same name, then the two accounts are identical. That is, no two users in the system have the same name.

It is possible to rewrite the state invariant as

$$\forall u_1, u_2 : users \bullet u_1.name = u_2.name \Leftrightarrow u_1 = u_2$$

We follow the former style in this book so that the types of variables are explicit from their declarations.

The operation *AddAccount* accepts a new account as input. It modifies the state space to include the new account, if the precondition is satisfied.

AddAccount

$\Delta LoginSubsystem$
a? : *Account*

$(\forall a : Account \mid a \in users \bullet a.name \neq a?.name)$
$users' = users \cup \{a?\}$

The precondition ensures that there is no user in the system having the same name as that of the user name in the new account. The postcondition asserts that the state space is modified to include the new account.

To delete an existing account, it is sufficient to present the user name of that account since user names are unique in the system.

```
┌─ DeleteAccount ──────────────────────────────────────────────
│ ΔLoginSubsystem
│ uname? : Username
├──────────────────────────────────────────────────────────────
│ users' = users \ {a : Account | a ∈ users ∧ a.name = uname? • a}
└──────────────────────────────────────────────────────────────
```

The predicate in *DeleteAccount* asserts that the user's account whose name matches with the input parameter is deleted from the database.

In order to change the password of an existing account, the user name of the account to be modified and the new password must be presented.

```
┌─ ChangePassword ─────────────────────────────────────────────
│ ΔLoginSubsystem
│ uname? : Username
│ pnew? : Password
├──────────────────────────────────────────────────────────────
│ ∃ a : Account | a ∈ users ∧ a.name = uname? ∧ a.password ≠ pnew? •
│     users' = users \ {a} ∪
│         {(μ acc : Account | acc.name = uname? ∧ acc.password = pnew?)}
└──────────────────────────────────────────────────────────────
```

The operation *ChangePassword* first checks whether the new password is different from the old password. If this condition is satisfied, the account corresponding to the old password is deleted from the database and a new account having the same user name and the new password is created.

The operation *ChangePassword* uses a μ expression which has the following syntax in Z:

$$(\mu < \text{declaration} > | < \text{predicate} > • < \text{expression} >)$$

The parentheses at both ends of the μ expression are part of the syntax. The semantics of a μ expression is the same as that of set comprehension except that a μ expression returns only one value. This value is determined by the expression after • symbol in the μ expression. If the expression after • is omitted, then the result of the μ expression is the same as that of the declaration constrained by the predicate after the | symbol.

The types of error messages for the chosen problem are

Message ::= *Success* | *UsernameAlreadyExists* | *UsernameUnknown* |
             SamePassword

The success of an operation will be prompted by the message *Success*; this is given by the schema *Successful*.

```
┌─ Successful ─────────────────────────────────────────────────
│ message! : Message
├──────────────────────────────────────────────────────────────
│ message! = Success
└──────────────────────────────────────────────────────────────
```

The operation *AlreadyExists* returns the message *UsernameAlreadyExists* when a match for the input name is found in the database. The operation *Unknown* returns the message *UsernameUnknown* if no match for the given input name is found. Finally, the operation *Repeated* returns the message *SamePassword* when a user invoked *ChangePassword* but does not give a new password; it inputs the same password.

AlreadyExists
$\Xi LoginSubsystem$
uname? : *Username*
message! : *Message*

$(\exists a : Account \mid a \in users \bullet a.name = uname?)$
$message! = UsernameAlreadyExists$

Unknown
$\Xi LoginSubsystem$
uname? : *Username*
message! : *Message*

$\neg\ (\exists a : Account \mid a \in users \bullet a.name = uname?)$
$message! = UsernameUnknown$

Repeated
$\Xi LoginSubsystem$
uname? : *Username*
pnew? : *Password*
message! : *Message*

$\exists a : Account \mid a \in users \wedge a.name = uname? \wedge a.password = pnew?$
$message = SamePassword$

The seven operations described so far can be combined to produce three new operations corresponding to the required functionalities of the problem statement.

$CAddAccount == (AddAccount \wedge Successful) \vee AlreadyExists$

$CDeleteAccount == (DeleteAccount \wedge Successful) \vee Unknown$

$CChangePassword == (ChangePassword \wedge Successful) \vee Unknown \vee Repeated$

The meaning of each one of these operations will be best understood if we expand them using the semantics for schema composition. For example, the operation *CAddAccount* can be viewed as

___ *CAddAccount* _____
$\Delta LoginSubsystem$
$a? : Account$
$message! : Message$

$(\neg(\exists\, a : Account \mid a \in users \bullet a.name = a?.name) \land$
$\quad users' = users \cup \{a?\} \land$
$\quad message! = Success)$
$\lor (\exists\, a : Account \mid a \in users \bullet a.name = a?.name) \land$
$\quad message! = UsernameAlreadyExists)$
_____

□

Example 9 University Accounts Office.

Problem Statement

An accounts office in a university is required to maintain a database of information on courses in which students are registered and enrolled. A student pays a fee for each course taken during a semester. In addition, each student also pays a fixed fee for administration and student activity. Graduate students are required to pay additional fees toward thesis registration and graduation. Only after full payment of fees, students will be registered in courses. The accounts office expects to perform three operations: (i) enroll a student, (ii) register a student in a course, and (iii) collect fees.

Additional Requirement

1. A student cannot register for the same course more than once.

The Model

A student's record can be modeled as a schema consisting of *identification number, status* (undergraduate or graduate) and *the courses registered*. The courses registered by a student is modeled as a set of course numbers. The details of a course such as course name, instructor and time at which the course is offered are irrelevant for the current problem. Therefore, courses can be uniquely represented by course numbers.

The state space is represented by a schema which consists of two state variables, one representing the collection of students who have already paid their fees, and the other representing the collection who have not yet paid the fees. These collections can be modeled either as sets or sequences. We choose sequences to model them. This choice enables us to modify the specification, if necessary, later; for example, the students records can be sorted based on their identification numbers. The state invariant ensures that no student is included in both collections at the same time.

Z Specification

The course numbers are derived from the basic type *COURSENO*.

$[COURSENO]$

We declare *IDNUMBER* as a finite nonempty subset of natural numbers.

$IDNUMBER : \mathbb{F}_1 \mathbb{N}$

Notice that *COURSENO* is defined as a basic type while *IDNUMBER* is declared as a global variable. In particular, *IDNUMBER* has been declared as of type $\mathbb{Z}$. The reason for this choice is that identification numbers must be compared when ordering the students records. However, no such comparison is necessary for course numbers.

The free type *Status* declares the two student categories managed by the system.

$Status ::= Ugrad \mid Grad$

A student's record is modeled by the schema *Student*.

```
Student
  id : IDNUMBER
  status : Status
  courses : ℙCOURSENO
```

The following is a global constraint which asserts that no two students have the same identification number.

$\forall s_1, s_2 : Student \bullet s_1.id = s_2.id \Leftrightarrow s_1 = s_2$

The state space is represented by the schema *Accounts*.

```
Accounts
  paid, unpaid : iseq Student

  ran paid ∩ ran unpaid = ∅
  (∀ i, j : 1..#paid • i ≤ j ⇒ (paid i).id ≤ (paid j).id)
  (∀ k, l : 1..#unpaid • k ≤ l ⇒ (unpaid k).id ≤ (unpaid l).id)
```

The sequence *paid* is the collection of enrolled students who have paid the fee. The sequence *unpaid* is the collection of enrolled students who have not registered in any course. Since these are injective sequences, no student is included more than once in a sequence. The state invariant asserts that (i) the two collections are mutually exclusive; and (ii) each sequence is ordered on the identification numbers of the students. The term *paid i* uses a functional notation and is equivalent to *paid(i)*.

The operation *Enrol* accepts a student, who has not been previously enrolled, and puts the student in the *unpaid* list of students so that the ordering in the sequence is maintained.

To simplify the writing of *Enrol* operation, the function *insert* has been introduced; this function places a student's record at the appropriate location in an injective sequence of student records maintaining the ordering on identification numbers. The operation *Enrol* will use this function in the postcondition.

$$insert : \text{iseq } Student \times Student \nrightarrow \text{iseq } Student$$

$\forall \, inseq, outseq : \text{iseq } Student; \; s : Student \bullet outseq = insert(inseq, s) \Leftrightarrow$
$\quad (\exists \, prior, after : \text{iseq } Student \mid$
$\quad\quad prior \subseteq inseq \wedge$
$\quad\quad after \textbf{ suffix } inseq \wedge$
$\quad\quad inseq = prior \frown after \bullet$
$\quad\quad (last \, prior).id < s.id \wedge$
$\quad\quad s.id < (head \, after).id \wedge$
$\quad\quad outseq = prior \frown \langle s \rangle \frown after)$

The function *insert* splits the input sequence *inseq* into two subsequences *prior* and *after* such that *s* is greater than the last element in *prior* and *s* is smaller than the first element in *after*. It constructs a new sequence by concatenating *prior*, *s* and *after*. The function assumes that *inseq* is a non-decreasing sequence and does not check whether or not *s* occurs in *inseq*. If these assumptions change, the function *insert* must be rewritten. The operation *Enrol* and the nature of sequencing are separated in this design.

The definition for *Enrol* is

Enrol

$\Delta Accounts$
$new? : Student$

$\neg \, (\exists \, s : Student \mid s \in (\text{ran } paid \cup \text{ran } unpaid) \bullet s.id = new?.id)$
$unpaid' = insert(unpaid, new?)$
$paid' = paid$

An enrolled student may register for one or more courses. A student cannot register for a course after fees for one set of registered courses have been paid. So, at the time of registration the student record must belong to *unpaid* sequence. The operation *Register* modifies the sequence *unpaid* reflecting course registration. This operation uses the function *update*, which modifies the set of courses in one student record.

$$update : \text{iseq } Student \times Student \nrightarrow \text{iseq } Student$$

$\forall \, inseq, outseq : \text{iseq } Student; \; snew : Student \bullet$
$\quad outseq = update(inseq, snew) \Rightarrow$
$\quad\quad (\exists \, prior, after : \text{iseq } Student; \; sold : Student \mid sold.id = snew.id \bullet$
$\quad\quad\quad inseq = prior \frown \langle sold \rangle \frown after \wedge$
$\quad\quad\quad outseq = prior \frown \langle snew \rangle \frown after)$

The schema for *Register* follows:

Register
ΔAccounts
s? : *Student*
c? : *COURSENO*

$s? \in \text{ran } unpaid$
$unpaid' = update(unpaid, (\mu s : Student \mid s.id = s?.id \wedge$
    $s.status = s?.status \wedge s.courses = s?.courses \cup \{c?\}))$
$paid' = paid$

The operation *PayFees* calculates the fee to be paid by a student, deletes the student record
from *unpaid* and inserts it in *paid*. The fee calculation is based on the student's status and
the number of courses registered. The tuition fee for each course, administration fee and
thesis fee are defined as global constants:

$course\_fee, admin\_fee, thesis\_fee : \mathbb{N}_1$

The *delete* function removes a student record from a sequence.

$delete$: iseq *Student* $\times$ *Student* $\nrightarrow$ iseq *Student*

$\forall inseq, outseq : \text{iseq } Student; \; s : Student \bullet outseq = delete(inseq, s) \Leftrightarrow$
    $(\exists prior, after : \text{iseq } Student \mid prior \frown \langle s \rangle \frown after = inseq \bullet$
    $outseq = prior \frown after)$

Notice that *delete* operation does not depend on the sequence type. It depends only on the
ordering of elements in the sequence. Therefore, it can be defined as a generic function as
shown below:

$=[X]=$
$delete\_from\_sequence$: iseq $X \times X \nrightarrow$ iseq X

$\forall inseq, outseq : \text{iseq } X; \; x : X \bullet$
    $outseq = delete\_from\_sequence(inseq, x) \Leftrightarrow$
        $(\exists prior, after : \text{iseq } X \mid prior \frown \langle x \rangle \frown after = inseq \bullet$
        $outseq = prior \frown after)$

---PayFees_____
$\Delta Accounts$
$paid\_by? : Student$
$total! : \mathbb{N}$
_____

$paid\_by? \in \operatorname{ran} unpaid \wedge paid\_by?.courses \neq \emptyset$
$(paid\_by?.status = Ugrad \Rightarrow$
$\quad total! = \#(paid\_by?.courses) * course\_fee + admin\_fee)$
$(paid\_by?.status = Grad \Rightarrow$
$\quad total! = \#(paid\_by?.courses) * course\_fee + admin\_fee + thesis\_fee)$
$paid' = insert(paid, paid\_by?)$
$unpaid' = delete(unpaid, paid\_by?)$

The precondition for *PayFees* ensures that the student *paid_by?* has already registered for some courses. The postcondition asserts that (i) the fee is calculated; and (ii) the student's record is moved from *unpaid* to *paid*. □

Example 10 Resource Allocation in a Computer System.

Problem Statement
Every computer system manages the allocation and deallocation of resources to processes. A process, when created, is assumed to indicate the resource types and the number of resources for each type that it will require in fulfilling its task. Process creation fails if (1) resource types unknown to the system are requested by a process; (2) the number of resources of any one type exceeds the number of resources of that type available in the system. The resource allocator maintains information on the resources allocated to processes, and resources requested by processes. Based on the availability of resources, either resources are allocated to the process and the process is executed, or the request is queued. Upon release of resources, queued requests are serviced on first-in-first-out basis.

Additional Requirements
There are two additional requirements: (i) Process and resource instances have unique identifications. (ii) When a process is destroyed, all resources that were held by the process must be returned to the system.

Assumptions
The following assumptions are made: (i) The types of resources and the number of instances of each type are fixed. (ii) Processes are created and destroyed dynamically during the operation of the system. (iii) All processes have equal privileges in acquiring the resources.

The Model
There are two basic types, one for process identifiers and another for resource identifiers. A free type, called *ResourceType*, enumerates the resource types. A resource has a unique type, a unique identifier, and a status (free or in use). Since a process requests a resource by type, we model *resources* as a function from *ResourceType* to the power set of

ResourceInstance, where *ResourceInstance* is a schema containing the *id* and *status* of the resource modeled by it. In this model, resource instances of a given type can be looked up efficiently.

All requests that have not been met are queued. Since different resource types may have been requested by a process, an appropriate model would be a total function *waiting_queues* from *ResourceType* to iseq *PROCESS_ID*. The injective sequence will ensure that no process is added more than once to any queue.

A process has a unique identifier, status (running or waiting), and information on resources needed to complete its task. The structure of a process is modeled by a schema *ProcessStructure* with two components: *status*, and *resources_needed*. The variable *resources_needed* is a partial function from *ResourceType* to $\mathbb{N}$ giving the number of resources of each type required by the process. Since process identifiers are unique, the set of all processes in the system is a partial function *processes* from *PROCESS_ID* to *ProcessStructure*.

A resource instance can be allocated to at most one process. So, all resource allocations can be modeled by a partial injective function *allocated* from *RESOURCE_ID* to *PROCESS_ID*. Being injective, it asserts that no resource instance will be allocated to more than one process.

The state of the computer system includes the declarations of *resources*, *processes*, *waiting_queues*, and *allocated*.

Z Specification

[*PROCESS_ID*, *RESOURCE_ID*]

We define three distinct types of resources:

ResourceType ::= *Terminal* | *Printer* | *Disk*
ProcessStatus ::= *Running* | *Waiting*
ResourceStatus ::= *Free* | *In_Use*

```
__ ResourceInstance _____
  id : RESOURCE_ID
  status : ResourceStatus
```

Every resource instance is unique, irrespective of its type; this condition is ensured by the following global constraint:

$$\forall rins_1, rins_2 : ResourceInstance \bullet rins_1.id = rins_2.id \Leftrightarrow rins_1 = rins_2$$

A process structure is a schema containing the status and resource requirements of a process.

```
__ ProcessStructure _____
  status : ProcessStatus
  resources_needed : ResourceType \nrightarrow \mathbb{N}
```

Notice that a process identification is not part of the process structure since a process is a dynamic entity. It is assigned a unique identification as and when it is created. The schema *ComputerSystem* given below describes the state space of the computer system.

```
┌─ ComputerSystem ──────────────────────────────────────────────
│  resources : ResourceType ↣ ℙResourceInstance
│  waiting_queues : ResourceType → iseq PROCESS_ID
│  processes : PROCESS_ID ↦ ProcessStructure
│  allocated : RESOURCE_ID ↦ PROCESS_ID
│ ──────────────────────────────────────────────────────────────
│  (∀ r₁, r₂ : ResourceType | r₁ ∈ dom resources ∧ r₂ ∈ dom resources •
│      resources r₁ ∩ resources r2 = ∅)
│  (∀ r : ResourceType | r ∈ dom waiting_queues •
│      ran(waiting_queues r) ⊆ dom processes)
│  ran allocated ⊆ dom processes
│  (∀ rid : RESOURCE_ID | rid ∈ dom allocated •
│      (∃ rinset : ℙResourceInstance | rinset ∈ ran resources •
│          rid ∈ {rins : ResourceInstance | rins ∈ rinset ∧
│              rins.status = In_Use • rins.id}))
│  (∀ pid : PROCESS_ID | pid ∈ dom processes •
│      (processes pid).status = Running ⇒
│          ¬ (∃ r : ResourceType | r ∈ dom waiting_queues •
│              pid ∈ ran(waiting_queues r)))
└──────────────────────────────────────────────────────────────
```

The state invariant asserts the following:

- Each resource instance belongs to a unique type. Stated otherwise, the sets of resource instances in the range of *resources* are pairwise disjoint.
- The set of processes waiting for a resource type r must be a subset of the processes that already exist in the system.
- The set of processes currently holding some resources must be a subset of the processes already existing in the system.
- The status of every resource instance that is allocated to some process is *In_Use*.
- If the status of a process is *Running*, then the process should not be waiting for any resource. Stated otherwise, the process's identifier should not appear in the range of the waiting queues.

Initialization

The initialization of a software system is specified by a separate state schema which has the same components as that of the state space of the system. The initial state schema, named as *InitComputerSystem*, is defined below:

```
┌─ InitComputerSystem ─────────────────────────────────────────────────────┐
│ ComputerSystem'                                                           │
├──────────────────────────────────────────────────────────────────────────┤
│ ∀r : ResourceType | r ∈ dom resources' • #(resources' r) > 0             │
│ ∀r : ResourceType | r ∈ dom waiting_queues' • waiting_queues' r = ⟨⟩      │
│ dom processes' = ∅                                                        │
│ dom allocated' = ∅                                                        │
└──────────────────────────────────────────────────────────────────────────┘
```

The predicate part of *InitComputerSystem* asserts the following conditions: (i) Every resource type must have at least one instance. (ii) The waiting queues of all resource types are initially empty. (iii) Initially, there is no process in the system. (iv) All resources are initially free.

The schema *CreateProcess* given below describes the creation of a process:

```
┌─ CreateProcess ──────────────────────────────────────────────────────────┐
│ ΔComputerSystem                                                          │
│ pstruct? : ProcessStructure                                              │
├──────────────────────────────────────────────────────────────────────────┤
│ dom(pstruct?.resources_needed) ⊆ dom resources                           │
│ (∀r : ResourceType | r ∈ dom(pstruct?.resources_needed) •                │
│   (pstruct?.resources_needed) r ≤ #(resources r))                        │
│ (∃pid : PROCESS_ID | pid ∉ dom processes •                               │
│   processes' = processes ∪ {pid ↦ (μps : ProcessStructure |              │
│     ps.status = Running ∧                                                 │
│     ps.resources_needed = pstruct?.resources_needed)})                   │
│ resources' = resources                                                   │
│ waiting_queues' = waiting_queues                                         │
│ allocated' = allocated                                                   │
└──────────────────────────────────────────────────────────────────────────┘
```

The *CreateProcess* operation accepts a process structure (denoted by *pstruct?*) as input. The processor identifier is internally generated (not specified) within this operation. The precondition for *CreateProcess* ensures that the types of resources and the number of instances of each type required by the new process are available in the system. The postcondition for the operation asserts that the new process is added to the set of processes after a new identifier was assigned to it and its status is set to *Running*. Other state variables are not modified by *CreateProcess*.

When a process is destroyed, all the resources held by the process are returned to the system. The process identifier of the deleted process will be removed from the waiting queues, in which the process has registered. The entire process description is also removed from the set of processes in the system. To simplify the writing of this operation and several others to follow, three functions are introduced.

Given a set of resource instances, the function *set_status* sets the status of one particular instance to *In_Use*; others in the set are not modified.

$set\_status : \mathbb{P}ResourceInstance \times RESOURCE\_ID \nrightarrow \mathbb{P}ResourceInstance$

$\forall\, rinset : \mathbb{P}ResourceInstance;\ rid : RESOURCE\_ID \bullet$
$\quad set\_status(rinset, rid) = rinset \backslash$
$\qquad \{rins : ResourceInstance \mid rins \in rinset \land rins.id = rid\} \cup$
$\qquad \{rnew : ResourceInstance \mid rnew.id = rid \land rnew.status = In\_Use\}$

Unlike *set_status*, the function *reset_status* resets a subset of resource instances among a given set of resource instances to *Free*. The reason for this subtle change is that the computer system might set the status of only one resource instance at a time. However, when a process is deleted, all resource instances held by the process need to be reset. Therefore, it would be appropriate to define *reset_status* in such way to reset a set of resource instances. Even when a particular resource instance is required to be reset individually (for example, when a resource instance is released by a process), *reset_status* can still be used with a singleton set as the parameter.

$reset\_status : \mathbb{P}ResourceInstance \times \mathbb{P}RESOURCE\_ID \nrightarrow \mathbb{P}ResourceInstance$

$\forall\, rinset : \mathbb{P}ResourceInstance;\ rids : \mathbb{P}RESOURCE\_ID \bullet$
$\quad reset\_status(rinset, rids) = rinset \backslash$
$\qquad \{rins : ResourceInstance \mid rins \in rinset \land rins.id \in rids\} \cup$
$\qquad \{rnew : ResourceInstance \mid rnew.id \in rids \land rnew.status = Free\}$

The third function, *delete_process*, is defined to remove a process identification from an injective sequence of process identifiers. Typically, this function will be used to delete a process from a waiting queue.

$delete\_process : \text{iseq}\, PROCESS\_ID \times PROCESS\_ID \rightarrow \text{iseq}\, PROCESS\_ID$

$\forall\, \_procids : \text{iseq}\, PROCESS\_ID;\ pid : PROCESS\_ID \bullet$
$\quad (\_procids = \langle\rangle \Rightarrow delete\_process(\_procids, pid) = \langle\rangle) \land$
$\quad (\_procids \neq \langle\rangle \Rightarrow$
$\qquad (pid = head\ \_procids \Rightarrow delete\_process(\_procids, pid) = tail\ \_procids \land$
$\qquad pid \neq head\ \_procids \Rightarrow delete\_process(\_procids, pid) =$
$\qquad\quad \langle pid \rangle \frown delete\_process(tail\ \_procids, pid)))$

The operation *DestroyProcess* uses both *reset_status* and *delete_process*.

```
┌─ DestroyProcess ──────────────────────────────────────────────
│ ΔComputerSystem
│ pid? : PROCESS_ID
├───────────────────────────────────────────────────────────────
│ pid? ∈ dom processes
│ processes′ = {pid?} ⊲ processes
│ allocated′ = allocated ⊳ {pid?}
│ (let rids == {rid : RESOURCE_ID | allocated(rid) = pid?} •
│    resources′ = resources ⊕ {r : ResourceType | r ∈ dom resources •
│       r ↦ reset_status(resources r, rids)})
│ waiting_queues′ = waiting_queues ⊕
│    {r : ResourceType; ps : iseq PROCESS_ID | (r ↦ ps) ∈ waiting_queues •
│       (r ↦ delete_process(ps, pid?))}
└───────────────────────────────────────────────────────────────
```

The schema *DestroyProcess* uses the **let** clause which needs further explanation. The **let** clause is used in Z to dynamically introduce local variables whose scope ends with the current paragraph (a paragraph may contain a schema, an axiomatic definition, a generic definition or a global constraint). The general form of a **let** clause is

let *variable* == *expression* • . . .

In this case, *expression* is abbreviated to *variable* and thereafter *variable* is used in the paragraph. In essence, *variable* stands for a textual substitution of *expression* wherever *variable* is used in the rest of the paragraph. The type of *variable* is power set of the type of the expression, following the semantics of type abbreviation. In the schema *DestroyProcess*, the variable *rids* stands for a set of resource identifiers that are allocated to the process *pid?* (indicated by the constraint *allocated(rid) = pid?*).

When a process P requests a resource, it specifies the type *rtype* of the resource. If at least one instance *rins* of *rtype* is free, then *rins* is allocated to P. If no such instance can be found, P is placed at the end of the waiting queue for *rtype*. The allocation is defined by the schema *Allocate*.

```
┌─ Allocate ────────────────────────────────────────────────────
│ ΔComputerSystem
│ pid? : PROCESS_ID
│ rtype? : ResourceType
├───────────────────────────────────────────────────────────────
│ pid? ∈ dom processes
│ rtype? ∈ dom resources
│ (∃ rins : ResourceInstance |
│    rins ∈ resources rtype? ∧ rins.status = Free •
│    allocated′ = allocated ∪ {rins.id ↦ pid?} ∧
│    (resources′ = resources ⊕ {r : ResourceType | r ∈ dom resources •
│       if r = rtype? then r ↦ set_status(resources r, rins.id)
```

else $r \mapsto resources\ r\}) \wedge$
$waiting\_queues' = waiting\_queues \wedge$
$processes' = processes)$
$\neg\ (\exists\ rins : ResourceInstance \bullet$
$rins \in resources\ rtype? \wedge rins.status = Free) \Rightarrow$
$resources' = resources \wedge$
$allocated' = allocated \wedge$
$(waiting\_queues' = waiting\_queues \oplus$
$\{rtype? \mapsto (waiting\_queues\ rtype?) \frown \langle pid? \rangle\}) \wedge$
$(processes' = processes \oplus$
$\{pid? \mapsto (\mu\,ps : ProcessStructure \mid$
$ps.status = Waiting \wedge$
$ps.resources\_needed = (processes\ pid?).resources\_needed)\})$

The operation *Allocate* has two preconditions: the process requesting a resource must exist in the system and the resource type which the process requests must be known to the system. The first part of the postcondition of *Allocate* is for the case when a free instance is found. The state variables *allocated* and *resources* are modified to indicate that the resource instance has been allocated to the requesting process and the status of the allocated resource is set to *In_Use*. The other two variables, *waiting_queues* and *processes*, are not modified.

The second part of the postcondition for *Allocate* is for the condition that no instance of the resource type can be found. The state components *waiting_queues* and *processes* are modified to indicate that the requesting process must be placed in the waiting queue of the resource type and that the status of the requesting process is set to *Waiting*. The other two state variables are not modified.

Note the following facts regarding the specification of *Allocate*: When a resource instance *rins* is allocated to a process, the status of *rins* is updated. This modification does not affect the status of any other resource instance in the system. Such a modification on a portion of a state variable (in this case *resources*) cannot be specified in isolation because the primed variables in an operation schema correspond to only state variables. Therefore, it becomes necessary to specify the effect of the change in one resource instance on the whole set of resource instances which are collectively referred to by *resources'*.
The expression

$(resources' = resources \oplus \{r : ResourceType \mid r \in \text{dom}\ resources \bullet$
$\quad$ **if** $r = rtype?$ **then** $r \mapsto set\_status(resources\ r, rins.id)$
$\quad$ **else** $r \mapsto resources\ r)$

in the postcondition asserts that the function *resources* is overwritten (indicated by $\oplus$) by the changes in the resource instances of one particular resource type (indicated by $r = rtype?$); instances of other resource types are not modified (indicated by $r \mapsto resources\ r$).

Finally, the *DeAllocate* operation is specified. When a resource instance is released by a process, it is returned to the pool of resources in the system.

```
┌─ DeAllocate ──────────────────────────────────────────────────
│  ΔComputerSystem
│  rid? : RESOURCE_ID
├───────────────────────────────────────────────────────────────
│  rid? ∈ dom allocated
│  allocated' = {rid?} ◁ allocated
│  processes' = processes
│  waiting_queues' = waiting_queues
│  (∃ rtype : ResourceType; rins : ResourceInstance |
│     rtype ∈ dom resources ∧
│     rins ∈ resources rtype ∧
│     rins.id = rid? •
│        resources' = resources ⊕
│           {rtype ↦ reset_status(resources rtype, {rid?})})
└───────────────────────────────────────────────────────────────
```

It would be appropriate to allocate a deallocated resource *rins* belonging to a resource type *rtype* to the process in the front of the waiting queue for *rtype*. This can be specified by the sequential composition of three operations

$$DeAllocate \; _9^° \; SelectProcess \; _9^° \; Allocate$$

where the operation *SelectProcess* retrieves the first process in the waiting queue of *rtype* whose instance is deallocated in *DeAllocate*. Specification of *SelectProcess* is left as an exercise for the reader.   □

17.5
Proving Properties from Z Specifications

A specification must be inspected by the specifiers and developers to ensure that it captures all the requirements of the software system being specified. The inspection process, also called *consistency checking*, includes the following steps: (i) Check the syntactic and type correctness of the specification. Ensure that all operations strictly use the state model. (ii) Ensure that the specification captures the required functionalities and properties. (iii) Analyze the formal text to bring out inconsistent and missing information in the documented requirements.

In this section, we illustrate how we could ensure consistency of Z specifications and how some properties can be derived by formal analysis. The consistency of a Z specification is established (i) by showing that there exists a valid initial state for the state space of the system, and (ii) by showing that every operation respects the state invariant (that is, if the state invariant is true before the operation, then it must be true after the operation as well).

17.5.1
Initial State Validation

The validity of an initial state is established by the *initialization theorem* which asserts that

$$\exists\, S' \bullet Init\ S$$

where S refers to the state space schema and *Init S* is the initial state schema. Informally, the initialization theorem asserts that it is possible to find a state S' with the initialization asserted by *Init S*. The proof obligation in this case is to show that the initialization is type correct and it indeed satisfies the state invariant. We illustrate the initialization theorem for the two examples: the login subsystem and resource allocation system. Generally, the proof for the initialization theorem uses a technique called the *one-point-rule* in order to eliminate the quantifier in the initialization theorem.

17.5.1.1
One-Point-Rule

The one-point-rule eliminates the existential quantifier from a quantified statement if the bound variables in the existentially quantified statement can be substituted by other terms in the same statement, and the types of the substituting terms are compatible with those of the bound variables. Formally, one-point-rule may be stated as

$$\exists\, x : X \bullet P \wedge (x = y)\ \ \equiv\ \ y \in X \wedge P[y/x]$$

The right side of the equivalence asserts that y can be substituted for x provided that (i) y is of the same type as that of x, and (ii) the property P inside the quantified expression must still be satisfied even after substituting y for x. An important constraint for the application of one-point-rule is that x should not be a free variable in the expression y.

Example 11 Login Subsystem—revisited.

One of the possible initial states for the login subsystem (not given earlier) is

```
┌─ InitLoginSubsystem ─────────────────────────────
│  LoginSubsystem'
│ ─────────────────────────────────────────────────
│  users' = ∅
└──────────────────────────────────────────────────
```

The corresponding initialization theorem would be

$$\exists\, LoginSubsystem' \bullet InitLoginSubsystem$$

By expanding *LoginSubsystem'*, we get

$\vdash \exists\, users' : \mathbb{P}Account \mid (\forall\, u_1, u_2 : Account \mid u_1 \in users' \wedge u_2 \in users' \bullet$
$u_1.name = u_2.name \Leftrightarrow u_1 = u_2) \bullet$
$users' = \emptyset$

The symbol $\vdash$ denotes syntactic derivation as explained in Chap. 9. Using *one-point-rule*, the above statement is simplified to

$\emptyset \in \mathbb{P}Account \wedge$
$\forall\, u_1, u_2 : Account \mid u_1 \in \emptyset \wedge u_2 \in \emptyset \bullet$
$u_1.name = u_2..name \Leftrightarrow u_1 = u_2$

The first conjunct is true because the formal definition of $\emptyset$ in the mathematical toolkit for Z [12] is defined as

$\emptyset[X] == \{x : X \mid false\}$

The above definition asserts that $\emptyset$ is defined as a generic type which can be instantiated for any type X. Accordingly,

$\emptyset[Account] \in \mathbb{P}Account$

The second conjunct in the proof is vacuously true because the predicate $u_1 \in \emptyset \wedge u_2 \in \emptyset$ is false and hence the quantified statement as a whole is true.

Therefore, the initial state *InitLoginSubsystem* is valid.   □

Example 12   Resource Allocation in a Computer System—revisited.

For convenience, the initial state of the computer system given earlier is repeated here:

```
┌─ InitComputerSystem ──────────────────────────────────────
│  ComputerSystem'
│  ─────────────────────────────────────────────────────────
│  ∀ r : ResourceType | r ∈ dom resources' • #(resources' r) > 0
│  ∀ r : ResourceType | r ∈ dom waiting_queues' • waiting_queues' r = ⟨⟩
│  dom processes' = ∅
│  dom allocated' = ∅
└────────────────────────────────────────────────────────────
```

The initialization theorem for this example would be

$\exists\, ComputerSystem' \bullet InitComputerSystem$

which when expanded gives rise to the following derivation:

$\vdash \exists\, resources' : ResourceType \rightarrowtail \mathbb{P}ResourceInstance;$

$waiting\_queues' : ResourceType \rightarrow iseq\,PROCESS\_ID;$
$processes' : PROCESS\_ID \nrightarrow ProcessStructure;$
$allocated' : RESOURCE\_ID \nrightarrow PROCESS\_ID\ |$
$\quad (\forall r : ResourceType \mid r \in dom\,waiting\_queues' \bullet$
$\quad\quad ran(waiting\_queues'\,r) \subseteq dom\,processes') \wedge$
$\quad ran\,allocated' \subseteq dom\,processes' \wedge$
$\quad (\forall rid : RESOURCE\_ID \mid rid \in dom\,allocated' \bullet$
$\quad\quad (\exists rinset : \mathbb{P}ResourceInstance \mid rinset \in ran\,resources' \bullet$
$\quad\quad\quad rid \in \{rins : ResourceInstance \mid rins \in rinset \wedge$
$\quad\quad\quad\quad rins.status = In\_Use \bullet rins.id\})) \wedge$
$\quad (\forall pid : PROCESS\_ID \mid pid \in dom\,processes' \bullet$
$\quad\quad (processes'\,pid).status = Running \Rightarrow$
$\quad\quad\quad \neg\,(\exists r : ResourceType \mid r \in dom\,waiting\_queues' \bullet$
$\quad\quad\quad\quad pid \in ran(waiting\_queues'\,r))) \bullet$
$\quad (\forall r : ResourceType \mid r \in dom\,resources' \bullet \#(resources'\,r) > 0) \wedge$
$\quad (\forall r : ResourceType \mid r \in dom\,waiting\_queues' \bullet$
$\quad\quad waiting\_queues'\,r = \langle\rangle) \wedge$
$\quad dom\,processes' = \emptyset \wedge dom\,allocated' = \emptyset$

With regard to type correctness, it must be shown that

$\langle\rangle \in iseq\,PROCESS\_ID \wedge \emptyset \in \mathbb{P}PROCESS\_ID \wedge \emptyset \in \mathbb{P}RESOURCE\_ID$

From the definition of $\emptyset$, the last two conjuncts are trivial. The formal definitions of '$\langle\rangle$', 'seq', and 'iseq' are

$seq\,X == \{f : \mathbb{N} \nrightarrow X \mid dom\,f = 1..\#f\}$
$\langle\rangle\,X == \{f : \mathbb{N} \nrightarrow X \mid dom\,f = \emptyset\}$
$iseq\ X == seq\,X \cap (\mathbb{N} \rightarrowtail X)$

From these formal definitions, one can infer that the type of $\langle\rangle$ is the same as that of seq X and so is the type of iseq X. Therefore, the first conjunct in the derivation, namely

$\langle\rangle \in iseq\,PROCESS\_ID$

is type correct. Next, it must be shown that the initializations satisfy the state invariant. The state invariant is defined by four conjuncts. Using the initializations, the state invariant can be rewritten as

$(\forall r : ResourceType \mid r \in dom\,waiting\_queues \bullet ran\,\emptyset \subseteq \emptyset) \wedge$
$\emptyset \subseteq \emptyset \wedge$
$(\forall rid : RESOURCE\_ID \mid rid \in \emptyset \bullet$
$\quad (\exists rinset : \mathbb{P}ResourceInstance \mid rinset \in ran\,resources \bullet$

$$rid \in \{rins : ResourceInstance \mid rins \in rinset \land$$
$$rins.status = In\_Use \bullet rins.id\})) \land$$
$$(\forall pid : PROCESS\_ID \mid pid \in \emptyset \bullet$$
$$(processes\ pid).status = Running \Rightarrow$$
$$\neg\ (\exists r : ResourceType \mid r \in \mathrm{dom}\ waiting\_queues \bullet$$
$$pid \in \mathrm{ran}(waiting\_queues\ r)))$$

The four conjuncts are vacuously true for the same reason explained in proving the initialization theorem for the login subsystem example.

Therefore, the initial state for the computer system is valid. $\quad\Box$

17.5.2
Consistency of Operations

The specification for an operation is ensured to be consistent if it can be shown that the pre- and postconditions of the operation respect the state invariant. That is, the property 'if the state invariant is true before the operation is invoked, the invariant remains true after the operation terminates' should be proved for every operation. Formally, for every operation Op, if S and S' refer to the states before and after the operation, respectively, $inv\ (S)$, and $inv\ (S')$ refer to the invariant evaluated at S and S', respectively, the consistency of Op is established by proving

$$pred\ (Op) \land inv\ (S) \Rightarrow inv\ (S')$$

where $pred\ (Op)$ denotes the predicate part of the operation schema Op.

We prove the consistency of $AddAccount$ operation given in the $LoginSubsystem$ example. In this case, it must be shown that

$$(\forall u_1, u_2 : Account \mid u_1 \in users \land u_2 \in users \bullet$$
$$u_1.name = u_2.name \Leftrightarrow u_1 = u_2) \land$$
$$\neg\ (\exists a : Account \mid a \in users \bullet a.name = a?.name) \land$$
$$users' = users \cup \{a?\}$$
$$\Rightarrow$$
$$(\forall u_1, u_2 : Account \mid u_1 \in users' \land u_2 \in users' \bullet$$
$$u_1.name = u_2.name \Leftrightarrow u_1 = u_2)$$

Replacing $users'$ in the right side of the implication by $users \cup \{a?\}$, the right side is rewritten as

$$(\forall u_1, u_2 : Account \mid u_1 \in users \cup \{a?\} \land u_2 \in users \cup \{a?\} \bullet$$
$$u_1.name = u_2.name \Leftrightarrow u_1 = u_2)$$

There are three possibilities that must be considered: (i) both u_1 and u_2 are identical and refer to $a?$; (ii) one of them refers to $a?$ and the other is different from $a?$; and (iii) both of them are different from $a?$.

<u>Case 1</u> $u_1 = a? \wedge u_2 = a?$ Hypothesis

In this case, both u_1 and u_2 have been selected to denote the same account, namely the input parameter. The formal proof below shows that the invariant is true after the operation.

1.1 **from** $u_1 = a?$
          $u_1.name = a?.name \wedge$ schema equality
          $u_1.password = a?.password$
        infer $u_1.name = a?.name$ $\wedge$-elimination
1.2 **from** $u_2 = a?$
          $u_2.name = a?.name \wedge$ schema equality
          $u_2.password = a?.password$
        infer $u_2.name = a?.name$ $\wedge$-elimination
1.3 **from** 1.1, 1.2
        infer $u_1.name = u_2.name$ equality
1.4 **from** $u_1 = a?$
          $u_1.name = a?.name \wedge$ schema equality
          $u_1.password = a?.password$
        infer $u_1.password = a?.password$ $\wedge$-elimination
1.5 **from** $u_2 = a?$
          $u_2.name = a?.name \wedge$ schema equality
          $u_2.password = a?.password$
        infer $u_2.password = a?.password$ $\wedge$-elimination
1.6 **from** 1.1, 1.2
        infer $u_1.password = u_2.password$ equality
1.7 **from** 1.3, 1.6
        infer $u_1.name = u_2.name \wedge$ $\wedge$-introduction
          $u_1.password = u_2.password$
1.8 **from** 1.7
        infer $u_1 = u_2$ schema equality
1.9 **from** 1.3, 1.7
        infer $u_1.name = u_2.name \Rightarrow u_1 = u_2$ $\Rightarrow$-introduction
1.10 **from** 1.8
        infer $u_1.name = u_2.name$ schema equality
1.11 **from** 1.8, 1.10
        infer $u_1 = u_2 \Rightarrow u_1.name = u_2.name$ $\Rightarrow$-introduction
1.12 **from** 1.9, 1.11
        infer $u_1.name = u_2.name \Leftrightarrow u_1 = u_2$ $\Leftrightarrow$-introduction

<u>Case 2</u> $u_1 = a? \wedge u_2 \neq a?$ Hypothesis

The variable u_1 denotes the input parameter and u_2 denotes some other account already existing in the system. One expects u_1 and u_2 to be different because the system does not maintain duplicate accounts. The formal proof below not only ensures this fact but also shows that accounts are compared based on user names.

2.1 **from** $u_1 = a?$

       $u_1.name = u_2.name \land$ schema equality

        $u_1.password = a?.password$

    infer $u_1.name = a?.name$ $\land$-elimination

2.2 **from** $u_1 = a?$

       $u_1.name = u_2.name \land$ schema equality

        $u_1.password = a?.password$

    infer $u_1.password = a?.password$ $\land$-elimination

2.3 **from** $u_2 \in users \cup \{a?\}$ and $u_2 \neq a?$

       $u_2 \in users$ set union

    infer $u_2.name \neq a?.name$ precondition of *AddAccount*

2.4 **from** $u_2 \neq a?$

       $\neg \, (u_2.name = a?.name \land$ schema inequality

         $u_2.password = a?.password)$

       $u_2.name \neq a?.name \lor$ DeMorgan's law

       $u_2.password \neq a?.password$

    infer $u_2.name \neq a?.name$ 2.3

2.5 **from** 2.1, 2.4

    infer $u_1.name \neq u_2.name$ inequality

2.6 **from** 2.5

    infer $u_1 \neq u_2$ schema inequality

2.7 **from** 2.5, 2.6

    infer $u_1.name \neq u_2.name \Rightarrow u_1 \neq u_2$ $\Rightarrow$-introduction

2.8 **from** Hypothesis

    infer $u_1 \neq u_2$ inequality

2.9 **from** 2.8

       $u_1.name \neq u_2.name \lor$ schema inequality

       $u_1.password \neq u_2.password$

    infer $u_1.name \neq u_2.name$ 2.5

2.10 **from** 2.8, 2.9

    infer $u_1 \neq u_2 \Rightarrow u_1.name \neq u_2.name$ $\Rightarrow$-introduction

2.11 **from** 2.7, 2.10

    infer $u_1.name \neq u_2.name \Leftrightarrow u_1 \neq u_2$ $\Leftrightarrow$-introduction

A similar proof applies for the case $u_1 \neq a? \land u_2 = a$.

<u>Case 3</u> $u_1 \neq a? \land u_2 \neq a?$ Hypothesis

Since both u_1 and u_2 are different from the input parameter $a?$, they denote two accounts that already exist in the system. Since the invariant is true before the operation, it is trivial to prove that u_1 and u_2 are equal if and only if the user names in these two accounts are the same.

3.1 **from** $u_1 \in users \cup \{a?\}$ and $u_1 \neq a?$

    infer $u_1 \in users$ set union

3.2 **from** $u_2 \in users \cup \{a?\}$ and $u_2 \neq a?$

    infer $u_2 \in users$ set union

3.3 **from** 3.1, 3.2

  infer $u_1.name = u_2.name \Leftrightarrow u_1 = u_2$ invariant before

Formal proofs, as seen from the above example, requires a number of proof steps where in each step an inference rule is used to derive a new fact. For most non-trivial applications formal proofs are very hard to produce. Even with the help of a proof assistant, deriving a formal proof can be a tedious and difficult process. The major difficulty lies in managing the large number of proof steps and in the generation of intermediate inference rules.

  To alleviate the problems in deriving formal proofs, but still support reasoning based on formal specifications, software developers use a *rigorous approach*. A rigorous proof is not formal, but it is not informal either. A rigorous proof resembles a mathematical proof.

  In this approach, proofs include rigorous arguments and informal descriptions. The rigorous arguments are justified by quoting the formal specification components. The inference rules are ignored and fundamental properties of basic types are assumed. Below, we rigorously prove that the operation *ChangePassword* in the *LoginSubsystem* example is consistent.

Example 13 Login Subsystem—Revisited.

The operation *ChangePassword* in the *LoginSubsystem* example should not modify any account other than the account selected for modification. Formally stated:

$$ChangePassword \vdash (\forall u : Account \mid u \in users' \bullet$$
$$u.name \neq uname? \Rightarrow (\exists v : Account \mid v \in users \bullet v = u)$$

In the expression above, u denotes any account in the state after the operation terminates (indicated by $u \in users'$). There are two cases to be considered for the proof:

Case 1: $u \in users' \wedge u.name = uname?$

The variable u refers to the account being modified. Since $u \in users'$ and $u.name = uname?$ is the negation of the constraint given in the quantified expression

$$\forall u : Account \mid u \in users' \bullet u.name \neq uname? \Rightarrow \dots$$

the implication is vacuously true. This means that the stated property is derivable from *ChangePassword*. Notice that the variables and their types in the hypothesis are derived from the declaration of the schema *ChangePassword* as indicated by the semantics of the notation $\vdash$.

Case 2: $u \in users' \wedge u.name \neq uname?$

The predicate part in *ChangePassword* has been reproduced below for the sake of understanding:

```
┌─ ChangePassword ─────────────────────────────────────
│ ΔLoginSubsystem
│ uname? : Username
│ pnew? : Password
├──────────────────────────────────────────────────────
│ ∃ a : Account | a ∈ users ∧ a.name = uname? ∧ a.password ≠ pnew? •
│    users' = users \ {a}∪
│       {(μ acc : Account | acc.name = uname? ∧ acc.password = pnew?)}
└──────────────────────────────────────────────────────
```

ChangePassword describes the construction of *users'*: i.e., *a* is removed from *users* and *acc* is inserted in *users*. From

$u.name \neq uname?$ (hypothesis)

$a.name = uname?$ (precondition),

we conclude

$u.name \neq a.name$

From the state invariant

$\forall u_1, u_2 : Account \mid u_1 \in users \land u_2 \in users \bullet$

$u_1.name = u_2.name \Leftrightarrow u_1 = u_2$

one can derive

$u \neq a$

Therefore, u is not the account which is being deleted by *ChangePassword*. Since u exists in the state after the operation terminates (indicated by $u \in users'$), either it exists in the state before the operation or it is the newly created account(i.e., $u = acc$). In the predicate part of the specification, notice that

$u.name \neq uname?$ and

$acc.name = uname?$

The state invariant asserts that

$u \neq acc$

Therefore, u is not changed by the operation *ChangePassword*. □

17.6
Case Study: An Automated Billing System

In this section, we describe the specification of an automated billing system for work schedule in a software firm. Most of the Z notation discussed so far are used in this specification.

Problem Statement

Software consulting firms generally deal with several clients where each client contracts out a project to the firm and receives a set of services related to the project. An employee in the firm may work on multiple projects at any one time, with interleaved work schedule. A customer is billed at an hourly rate and an employee is paid at another hourly rate. The focus of the problem is to develop an automated billing system which can be used both for billing the customers for their projects and for calculating the salaries of employees.

Additional Requirements

1. A project employs one or more employees.
2. The hourly rate charged for projects is the same for all the projects and is assigned at the initiation of the project.
3. The hourly salary is the same for all employees in the firm. The salary is independent of the project(s) assigned to the employee.
4. The estimated number of hours for completing a project is fixed for billing purposes, whether or not the project is completed by the deadline. If a project is not completed within its estimated time, the customer who initiated this project will not be billed for the extra hours required by the firm to complete the project. However, employees who work on this project during the extra hours will be paid according to their salary rate.
5. Depending on the rate of progress and the nature of a project, employees may be assigned to a project or be removed from a project.
6. A project, once initiated, will not be terminated until it is completed.
7. It must be possible to perform the following operations: (i) add a new employee to the firm, (ii) add a new customer, (iii) initiate a project (by a known customer), (iv) assign an employee to a project, (v) release an employee from a project, (vi) report the work done by an employee, (vii) calculate the salary of an employee for a given month and year, and (viii) bill a customer for a given month and year.

The Model

The requirements reveal that *Employee*, *Customer* and *Project* are three composite data types to be modeled with a number of static and dynamic relationships among them. For example, "a project is initiated by a customer" is a static relationship between *Project* and *Customer*, while "an employee is assigned to a particular project" defines a dynamic relationship between *Employee* and *Project*. These relationships must be captured succinctly in their models.

Schema type or Cartesian product type may be used to construct the data model for *Employee*, *Project* and *Customer*. However, that may lead to a clumsy specification. For example, a schema for *Employee* would have to include project information as well. This necessitates using expressions of the form *e.project* in operation specifications. If the Cartesian product type were to be used as in

$$Customer == CUSTOMER\_ID \times \mathbb{P}(PROJECT\_ID \times DATE \times HOURS)$$

two projection operations are required to select the number of hours spent on a project initiated by a customer. So we avoid these two modeling approaches and instead use a modular approach to building data types required for the problem. First, primitive types

and operations on them are defined. Next, composite types are constructed and curried
functions (higher order functions) are defined to capture the relationships among the composite types. Finally, these are used to form aggregates modeling the three types *Employee*,
Customer and *Project*.

Z Specification

We first define several basic types and auxiliary functions that are necessary in the system
specification.

Basic Types

The identifiers for employees, customers and projects are represented by three distinct
basic types.

$$[EMPLOYEE\_ID, CUSTOMER\_ID, PROJECT\_ID]$$

Date

The requirements state that salaries of employees and customer invoices are based on the
number of hours devoted to the projects on a daily basis. So, we need to model *Date*. *Date*
is a triple $(day, month, year)$ and so Cartesian product is an appropriate model for it.

$Day == 1..31$

$Month ::= January \mid February \mid March \mid April \mid May \mid June \mid July \mid$
$\qquad\qquad August \mid September \mid October \mid November \mid December$

$Year == 1991..2999$

$Date == Day \times Month \times Year$

The enumerated values for *Year* are chosen arbitrarily. We next specify three projection
functions *day*, *month* and *year* to select the fields of a date.

> $day : Date \rightarrow Day$
> $month : Date \rightarrow Month$
> $year : Date \rightarrow Year$
> _____
> $\forall dt : Date \bullet$
> $\quad \exists d : Day; \ m : Month; \ y : Year \mid (d, m, y) = dt \bullet$
> $\qquad day(dt) = d \wedge month(dt) = m \wedge year(dt) = y$

The following global constraint asserts the validity of instances of type *Date*.

> $\forall dt : Date \bullet$
> $\quad month(dt) \in \{April, June, September, November\} \Rightarrow day(dt) \leq 30 \wedge$
> $\quad (month(dt) = February \Rightarrow$
> $\qquad ((year(dt) \bmod 4 = 0 \wedge year(dt) \bmod 100 \neq 0) \Rightarrow day(dt) \leq 29) \wedge$
> $\qquad ((year(dt) \bmod 4 \neq 0 \vee year(dt) \bmod 100 = 0) \Rightarrow day(dt) \leq 28))$

Work hours

An employee may work for a maximum of 24 hours during a 24-hour day. We therefore define *Hours* as an enumerated set of values 0..24.

$$Hours == 0..24$$

Timesheet

Combining *Date* and *Hours*, we define the data type *TimeSheet* which shows the dates and the number of hours worked by an employee during each day on a particular project. A time sheet cannot show two different work hours for a given date, since a *TimeSheet* is a function from *Date* to *Hours*.

$$TimeSheet == Date \nrightarrow Hours$$

A *TimeSheet* may also be used as part of a customer's record to enter the work hours completed on a particular project.

Two time sheets may be combined into one. The resulting time sheet will show the number of hours worked by an employee on two different projects on a given day.

$update\_timesheet : TimeSheet \times TimeSheet \nrightarrow TimeSheet$

$\forall tsh_1, tsh_2, tsh : TimeSheet \bullet update\_timesheet(tsh_1, tsh_2) = tsh \Rightarrow$
$\quad \text{dom}\, tsh = \text{dom}\, tsh_1 \cup \text{dom}\, tsh_2 \wedge$
$\quad (\forall dt : Date \mid dt \in \text{dom}\, tsh \bullet$
$\quad\quad (dt \in \text{dom}\, tsh_1 \wedge dt \in \text{dom}\, tsh_2 \Rightarrow$
$\quad\quad\quad tsh\, dt = tsh_1\, dt + tsh_2\, dt) \wedge$
$\quad\quad (dt \in \text{dom}\, tsh_1 \Rightarrow tsh\, dt = tsh_1\, dt) \wedge$
$\quad\quad (dt \in \text{dom}\, tsh_2 \Rightarrow tsh\, dt = tsh_2\, dt))$

Given a time sheet, we can sum up all the entries in the second column, which is the number of hours worked by an employee on different dates. This sum can be used to calculate the salary of an employee (or to prepare a bill for the customer). The function *sum_timesheet* computes this sum for a given time sheet.

$sum\_timesheet : TimeSheet \rightarrow \mathbb{N}$

$\forall tsh : TimeSheet \bullet$
$\quad tsh = \emptyset \Rightarrow sum\_timesheet(tsh) = 0 \wedge$
$\quad tsh \neq \emptyset \Rightarrow (\exists dt : Date \mid dt \in \text{dom}\, tsh \bullet$
$\quad\quad sum\_timesheet(tsh) = (tsh\, dt) + sum\_timesheet(\{dt\} \lhd tsh))$

Notice that the expression

$$sum\_timesheet(\{dt\} \lhd tsh)$$

recursively defines the sum on the time sheet entries after deleting the entry corresponding to *dt* from the domain of *tsh*. Since there can be only finitely many entries in a time sheet, the terminating condition stated in the postcondition is satisfied.

Worksheet

There is at most one (logical) time sheet for a project. A worksheet records for each project
the time sheet associated with that project.

$$WorkSheet == PROJECT\_ID \nrightarrow TimeSheet$$

The number of work hours completed for a project can be calculated from a work sheet
by projecting the project identifier and the work hours in the work sheet. The function
project_hours discards the date component in *TimeSheet* of a work sheet and returns the
project identification with the number of hours completed for that project.

$project\_hours : WorkSheet \nrightarrow (PROJECT\_ID \nrightarrow \mathbb{N})$

$\forall work : WorkSheet \bullet project\_hours(work) =$
$\quad \{pid : PROJECT\_ID;\ hrs : Hours\ |$
$\quad\quad pid \in \operatorname{dom} work \land hrs = sum\_timesheet(work\ pid) \bullet$
$\quad\quad\quad (pid \mapsto hrs)\}$

The function *sum_workhours* accepts a work sheet as input and returns the total number
of hours in all the time sheets contained in the work sheet. This function is necessary to
calculate the salary of an employee as well as the amount to be billed to a customer.

$sum\_workhours : WorkSheet \nrightarrow \mathbb{N}$

$\forall work : WorkSheet \bullet$
$\quad work = \emptyset \Rightarrow sum\_workhours(work) = 0 \land$
$\quad work \neq \emptyset \Rightarrow (\exists pid : PROJECT\_ID \mid pid \in \operatorname{dom} work \bullet$
$\quad\quad sum\_workhours(work) = sum\_timesheet(work\ pid) +$
$\quad\quad\quad sum\_workhours(\{pid\} \ntriangleleft work))$

In order to know the monthly salary of an employee or cost on a project to a customer, we
need to select the time sheets corresponding to the particular month under consideration
from the set of time sheets given in a work sheet.

$select\_timesheets : WorkSheet \times Month \times Year \nrightarrow WorkSheet$

$\forall work : WorkSheet;\ m : Month;\ y : Year \bullet$
$\quad select\_timesheets(work, m, y) = \{pid : PROJECT\_ID;\ tsh : TimeSheet \mid$
$\quad\quad pid \mapsto tsh \in work \land$
$\quad\quad (\forall dt : Date \mid dt \in \operatorname{dom} tsh \bullet month(dt) = m \land year(dt) = y) \bullet$
$\quad\quad\quad (pid \mapsto tsh)\}$

Like the function *update_timesheet*, we also define another function *update_worksheet* to
update a worksheet.

$update\_worksheet : WorkSheet \times WorkSheet \nrightarrow WorkSheet$

$\forall\, work_1, work_2, work : WorkSheet \bullet update\_worksheet(work_1, work_2) = work \Rightarrow$
  $\mathrm{dom}\, work = \mathrm{dom}\, work_1 \cup \mathrm{dom}\, work_2 \wedge$
  $(\forall pid : PROJECT\_ID \mid pid \in \mathrm{dom}\, work \bullet$
    $(pid \in \mathrm{dom}\, work_1 \wedge dt \in \mathrm{dom}\, work_2 \Rightarrow$
      $work\, pid = update\_timesheet(work_1\, pid, work_2\, pid) \wedge$
    $(pid \in \mathrm{dom}\, work_1 \Rightarrow work\, dt = work_1\, dt) \wedge$
    $(pid \in \mathrm{dom}\, work_2 \Rightarrow work\, dt = work_2\, dt))$

State of the system

There are three constants in the state model: *project_rate* denoting the hourly rate used to charge a customer; *employee_rate* denoting the hourly rate for calculating the salaries of employees; and *bill_charge* indicating the fixed monthly charge to be added to the bill for each customer.

$project\_rate : \mathbb{N}_1$
$employee\_rate : \mathbb{N}_1$
$bill\_charge : \mathbb{N}_1$

  Organization
$employees : EMPLOYEE\_ID \nrightarrow WorkSheet$
$customers : CUSTOMER\_ID \nrightarrow WorkSheet$
$projects : PROJECT\_ID \nrightarrow (\mathbb{N}_1 \times \mathbb{N})$

$(\forall eid : EMPLOYEE\_ID \mid eid \in \mathrm{dom}\, employees \bullet$
  $\mathrm{dom}(employees\, eid) \subseteq \mathrm{dom}\, projects \wedge$
  $(\forall pid : PROJECT\_ID \mid pid \in \mathrm{dom}(employees\, eid) \bullet$
    $second(projects\, pid) \geq sum\_timesheet((employees\, eid)\, pid))) \wedge$
$(\forall cid : CUSTOMER\_ID \mid cid \in \mathrm{dom}\, customers \bullet$
  $\mathrm{dom}(customers\, cid) \subseteq \mathrm{dom}\, projects \wedge$
  $(\forall pid : PROJECT\_ID \mid pid \in \mathrm{dom}(customers\, cid) \bullet$
    $second(projects\, pid) = sum\_timesheet((customers\, cid)\, pid))) \wedge$
$(\forall pid : PROJECT\_ID \mid pid \in \mathrm{dom}\, projects \bullet$
  $second(projects\, pid) \leq first(projects\, pid))$

The state space schema *Organization* defines three entities: *employees*, a function from employee identifiers to worksheet; *customers*, a function from customer identifiers to worksheet; and *projects*, a function from project identifiers to a pair of integers, where the first integer denotes the estimated time for the completion of a project, and the second denotes the actual number of hours put in.

The state invariant is a conjunction of the following constraints:

- Every project assigned to an employee is a project contracted out to the firm:

  $\mathrm{dom}(employees\, eid) \subseteq \mathrm{dom}\, projects$

- The number of work hours reported by an employee on a project cannot exceed the total number of hours completed on that project:

$$second(projects\ pid) \geq sum\_timesheet((employees\ eid)\ pid)))$$

- The number of hours completed on a project must agree with the number of hours reported to the customer of that project:

$$second(projects\ pid) = sum\_timesheet((customers\ cid)\ pid)))$$

- For every project, the number of work hours completed must be less than or equal to the number of work hours estimated for the project:

$$second(projects\ pid) \leq first(projects\ pid)$$

Initialization

The initial state for the organization is one in which there is no employee, customer or project.

$$
\begin{array}{|l}
\hline
\_InitOrganization \underline{\hspace{8cm}} \\
Organization' \\
\hline
employees' = \emptyset \\
customers' = \emptyset \\
projects' = \emptyset \\
\hline
\end{array}
$$

Operations

The operation *AddEmployee* adds a new employee to the organization, who is not yet assigned to any project.

$$
\begin{array}{|l}
\hline
\_AddEmployee \underline{\hspace{8cm}} \\
\Delta Organization \\
\hline
(\exists eid : EMPLOYEE\_ID \mid eid \notin \mathrm{dom}\ employees \bullet \\
\quad employees' = employees \oplus \{eid \mapsto \emptyset\}) \\
customers' = customers \\
projects' = projects \\
\hline
\end{array}
$$

The identifier for the new employee is generated by *AddEmployee* operation and ensures that the identifier is unique.

The operations *InitiateProject* and *AddCustomer* are similar; however, there are some minor differences between them. Only a customer of the organization can initiate projects. That is, a project initiation by a customer happens only after the customer has been included in the database of customers in the organization. When a customer is added to the database, the customer is assigned a unique identification number and no project has been initiated at that instant. Below, the *InitiateProject* operation is shown; *AddCustomer* is left as an exercise.

InitiateProject
$\Delta Organization$
$cid? : CUSTOMER\_ID$
$estimate? : \mathbb{N}_1$

$cid? \in \text{dom } customers$
$(\exists pid : PROJECT\_ID \mid pid \notin \text{dom } projects \bullet$
$\quad customers' = customers \oplus \{cid? \mapsto$
$\qquad (customers\, cid?) \oplus \{pid \mapsto \emptyset\}\} \wedge$
$\quad projects' = projects \oplus \{pid \mapsto (estimate?, 0)\})$
$employees' = employees$

AssignEmployee
$\Delta Organization$
$eid? : EMPLOYEE\_ID$
$pid? : PROJECT\_ID$

$eid? \in \text{dom } employees$
$pid? \in \text{dom } projects$
$\neg\, (pid? \in \text{dom}(employees\, eid?))$
$employees' = employees \oplus \{eid? \mapsto (employees\, eid?) \oplus \{pid? \mapsto \emptyset\}\}$
$customers' = customers$
$projects' = projects$

The operation *AssignEmployee* assigns an employee to a project (or a project to an employee). The employee identifier *eid* and the project identifier *pid* are input parameters. The precondition checks the validity of these identifiers. In addition, the precondition ensures that the project *pid?* has not been assigned previously to the employee *eid?*. The postcondition asserts that the employee has been assigned the project.

The operation *ReleaseEmployee*, a complement of the operation *AssignEmployee*, is left for the exercises.

ReportWork
$\Delta Organization$
$eid? : EMPLOYEE\_ID$
$work? : WorkSheet$

$eid? \in \text{dom } employees$
$\text{dom } work? \subseteq \text{dom}(employees\, eid?)$
$employees' = employees \oplus \{eid? \mapsto$

$$update\_worksheet(employees\ eid?, work?)\}$$
$$customers' = customers \oplus \{cid : CUSTOMER\_ID \mid cid \in \text{dom}\ customers \bullet$$
$$cid \mapsto update\_worksheet(customers\ cid, work?)\}$$
$$(\textbf{let}\ updates == project\_hours(work?) \bullet$$
$$projects' = projects \oplus \{pid : PROJECT\_ID \mid pid \in \text{dom}\ updates \bullet$$
$$pid \mapsto (first(projects\ pid), second(projects\ pid) + (updates\ pid))\})$$

Since the date/time at which the employee reports the completion of work has not been modeled, the operation *ReportWork* only specifies the functionality of updating the work sheet for a particular employee without regard to the date and time of update. The precondition checks for the validity of the employee identification and the legitimacy of the work reported. The postcondition uses the two functions *update_worksheet* and *project_hours* to modify the state variables.

CalculateSalary
Ξ*Organization*
eid? : *EMPLOYEE_ID*
month? : *Month*
year? : *Year*
salary! : $\mathbb{N}$

---
eid? $\in$ dom *employees*
(**let** *worksheet* == *select_timesheets*((*employees eid?*), *month?*, *year?*) $\bullet$
salary! = *sum_workhours*(*worksheet*) $*$ *employee_rate*)

The salary for an employee is calculated for a given month and so the operation *CalculateSalary* receives three input parameters: the employee identifier *eid* whose salary is to be calculated, the month and year for which the salary is to be calculated. The **let** clause in the predicate part of *CalculateSalary* projects only those time sheets that correspond to the selected month from the employee's record. Since *CalculateSalary* does not modify the state (indicated by Ξ), it is not necessary to include those constraints which assert that the state variables are not changed by this operation.

The operation *BillCustomer* is similar to the operation *CalculateSalary* and is left to the Exercises.

17.7
Additional Features in Z

In this section, we discuss *precondition calculation* and *promotion*, two additional features in Z. The predicate part of a schema consists of several predicates, some denoting preconditions and some denoting postconditions for the specified operation. However, the Z

17

notation does not explicitly separate the precondition from the postcondition. Therefore, a procedure to calculate the precondition is introduced. Promotion effectively describes the influence of an operation defined for a local state space on a global state space; the local state space must be part of the global state space.

17.7.1
Precondition Calculation

The precondition of an operation describes the set of possible assignments of values to the state variables and input variables such that the operation terminates in a consistent state and generates an expected output. If the precondition of an operation fails, the consequences of invoking that operation are unpredictable or are unacceptable. Unlike in VDM-SL, there is no explicit notation to denote the precondition of an operation in Z. Instead, one has to calculate the precondition from the definition of the operation. *pre op* will be used to denote the schema derived by the precondition calculation on the schema *op*.

The main question to be answered in a precondition calculation is "for what combinations of inputs and starting states one can find the ending states and outputs that satisfy the predicates?". Informally, the answer to the above question is to assert the existence of outputs and ending states such that the predicate part of the *op* schema is satisfied for the unprimed variables. So, the precondition calculation is done as follows: from the given schema remove the outputs and ending states (primed variables) from the declaration part, and bind them in the predicate part with an existential quantifier.

As an example, in the specification *LoginSubsystem* consider the operation *AddAccount*. For convenience, we reproduce the specification of *AddAccount* here with its declaration and predicate parts expanded.

$$
\begin{array}{l}
\rule{0.5pt}{40pt}\!\!\underline{\;AddAccount\;}\underline{} \\[4pt]
\quad users, users' : \mathbb{P}\,Account \\[2pt]
\quad a? : Account \\[6pt]
\rule{0pt}{2pt}\\
\quad (\forall\, u_1, u_2 : Account \mid u_1 \in users \wedge u_2 \in users \bullet \\[2pt]
\qquad u_1.name = u_2.name \Leftrightarrow u_1 = u_2) \\[2pt]
\quad (\forall\, u_1, u_2 : Account \mid u_1 \in users' \wedge u_2 \in users' \bullet \\[2pt]
\qquad u_1.name = u_2.name \Leftrightarrow u_1 = u_2) \\[2pt]
\quad \neg\,(\exists\, a : Account \mid a \in users \bullet a.name = a?.name) \\[2pt]
\quad users' = users \cup \{a?\}
\end{array}
$$

No implicit predicate arises from the declaration. We need to remove the outputs and ending states from the declaration and bind them with existential quantifier in the predicate part. The expression *pre AddAccount* results in the following unnamed schema:

$$
\begin{array}{l}
users : \mathbb{P}Account \\
a? : Account \\
\hline
\exists\, users' : \mathbb{P}Account \bullet \\
\quad (\forall u_1, u_2 : Account \mid u_1 \in users \wedge u_2 \in users \bullet \\
\qquad u_1.name = u_2.name \Leftrightarrow u_1 = u_2) \wedge \\
\quad (\forall u_1, u_2 : Account \mid u_1 \in users' \wedge u_2 \in users' \bullet \\
\qquad u_1.name = u_2.name \Leftrightarrow u_1 = u_2) \wedge \\
\quad (\neg\, (\exists\, a : Account \mid a \in users \bullet a.name = a?.name)) \wedge \\
\quad (users' = users \cup \{a?\})
\end{array}
$$

The application of *pre* always results in an unnamed schema, because the result is neither a state space schema nor an operation schema. It is generally used in proofs or part of another schema expression. The predicate part of the precondition schema can be further simplified by applying predefined inference rules [16] and techniques such as the *one-point-rule*.

17.7.1.1
Precondition Simplification

Using the one-point-rule, *pre AddAccount* can be further simplified. The term $users'$ will be substituted by $users \cup \{a?\}$ and the existential quantifier in $\exists\, users' : \mathbb{P}Account \ldots$ will be removed. The constraint $users \cup \{a?\} \in \mathbb{P}Account$ will be conjoined with the predicate part. The modified schema is shown below:

$$
\begin{array}{l}
users : \mathbb{P}Account \\
a? : Account \\
\hline
(\forall u_1, u_2 : Account \mid u_1 \in users \wedge u_2 \in users \bullet \\
\quad u_1.name = u_2.name \Leftrightarrow u_1 = u_2) \\
(\forall u_1, u_2 : Account \mid u_1 \in users \cup \{a?\} \wedge u_2 \in users \cup \{a?\} \bullet \\
\quad u_1.name = u_2.name \Leftrightarrow u_1 = u_2) \\
\neg\, (\exists\, a : Account \mid a \in users \bullet a.name = a?.name) \\
users \cup \{a?\} \in \mathbb{P}Account
\end{array}
$$

The predicate

$$users \cup \{a?\} \in \mathbb{P}\,Account$$

can be removed because it is easily provable from the declarations of $users$ and $a?$ and from set union. The constraint

$$
\forall u_1, u_2 : Account \mid u_1 \in users \wedge u_2 \in users \bullet \\
\quad u_1.name = u_2.name \Leftrightarrow u_1 = u_2
$$

can be removed because it is subsumed by the other two constraints. Therefore, *pre AddAccount* will effectively reduce to

---

$users : \mathbb{P}Account$
$a? : Account$

$(\forall u_1, u_2 : Account \mid u_1 \in users \cup \{a?\} \land u_2 \in users \cup \{a?\} \bullet$
$\quad u_1.name = u_2.name \Leftrightarrow u_1 = u_2)$
$\neg\, (\exists a : Account \mid a \in users \bullet a.name = a?.name)$

Since the universally quantified statement in *pre AddAccount* is the state invariant which is inherent in every operation schema, we specify only the other constraint as precondition when we write the specification for *AddAccount*.

17.7.2
Promotion

Promotion is a technique by which an operation on a component (referred to as local state space) of a large system (referred to as global state space) is promoted or upgraded to the large system. The major advantage of promotion is the reuse of smaller notations in more elaborate situations.

Consider the following schema definitions:

__User_____
$name : STRING$
$id : \mathbb{N}_1$

__AllUsers_____
$all : \mathbb{P}User$

$\forall u_1, u_2 : User \mid u_1 \neq u_2 \land u_1 \in all \land u_2 \in all \bullet$
$\quad u_1.name \neq u_2.name$

In this case, the local state space is defined by the schema *User*. An operation such as *ChangeName* can be defined to change the name of a user. The schema *AllUsers* defines the global state space in which *User* is a component. In order to change the name of one user within the set of users defined by *AllUsers*, one can make use of the operation *ChangeName* and promote it to the global state *AllUsers*.

In general, if *Local* denotes a local state space, *Global* denotes a global state space which contains *Local*, *Local$_{op}$* denotes an operation on *Local* and *Global$_{op}$* denotes an operation on *Global* which has the same effect as that of *Local_op* (modifying only *Local* in *Global* and the rest of *Global* being unaffected), then we can define an operation called *Promote* such that

$$Global_{op} \equiv \exists \, \Delta Local \bullet Local_{op} \land Promote$$

For promotion to be valid, the global state must be an aggregate of the local state space; that is, there must exist a component of *Global* whose type is *Local*. The following example illustrates the concept of promotion.

Consider the operation *Register* in the accounts system example, which is reproduced below:

Register
$\Delta Accounts$
$s? : Student$
$c? : COURSENO$

$s? \in \text{ran } unpaid$
$unpaid' = update(unpaid, (\mu \, s : Student \mid s.id = s?.id \land$
$\quad s.status = s?.status \land s.courses = s?.courses \cup \{c?\}))$
$paid' = paid$

Register is a global operation which operates on the global state *Accounts*. The local state in this case is *Student*. We now introduce the operation *Register_Local* which operates on *Student* and updates the set of courses included in *Student*. Finally, we define the promotion operation called *Promote*.

Register_Local
$\Delta Student$
$c? : COURSENO$

$id' = id$
$status' = status$
$courses' = courses \cup \{c?\}$

Promote
$\Delta Accounts$
$\Delta Student$
$s? : Student$

$\exists \, s : Student \mid s \in \text{ran } unpaid \land s.id = s?.id \bullet \theta Student = s$
$unpaid' = update(unpaid, \theta Student')$
$paid' = paid$

In principle, the operation *Promote* establishes a binding between the global state *Accounts* and local state *Student*. The expression

$$\exists\, s : Student \mid s \in \mathrm{ran}\, unpaid \wedge s.id = s?.id \bullet \theta Student = s$$

asserts that the local state before the operation corresponds to a copy of a student record already existing in the system. The expression

$$unpaid' = update(unpaid, \theta Student')$$

indicates that the global state variable *unpaid'* is updated using the modified local state $\theta Student'$. The change in local state is established by the operation *Register_Local*. Therefore, the equation

$$Register \equiv \exists\, \Delta Student \bullet Register\_Local \wedge Promote$$

confirms that the operation *Register_Local* is promoted to the global state.

The use of θ operator in *Promote* has a significance. The term $\theta Student$ refer to any instance of the schema *Student* which in this case is bound to the input student record. That is, the connection between the local state and the global state is established through the input variable *s?*. The term $\theta Student'$ refers to the same instance of *Student* after being updated by an operation on a local state which in this case is bound to *Register_Local* through the equation for promotion. By the use of θ operator, *Promote* asserts that whenever the local state is updated, the global state is also modified. But *Promote* does not specify which local operation causes this change. Therefore, the same *Promote* operation can be conjoined with another local operation to promote it to the global state. For example, if there is an operation *Withdraw_Local* on *Student*, which is defined as

$$
\begin{array}{l}
\underline{\quad Withdraw\_Local\ } \\
\Delta Student \\
c? : COURSENO \\
\hline
id' = id \\
status' = status \\
courses' = courses \setminus \{c?\}
\end{array}
$$

then it can be promoted to *Accounts* in the same way as *Register_Local*. Thus,

$$Withdraw \equiv \exists\, \Delta Student \bullet Withdraw\_Local \wedge Promote$$

17.8
Refinement and Proof Obligations

The goal of a refinement process is to develop a detailed design and/or an implementation from formal specification of requirements. A refinement process requires a proof obligation to ensure that successive designs are consistent. We use the term 'abstract specification' to denote the specification that is the source of refinement (the one that is supposed to be refined) and the term 'concrete specification' for the specification obtained after refinement.

Morgan and Vickers discuss refinement calculus for model-based specification techniques with sufficient rigor [9]. In this section, we describe refinement of Z specifications as described by Spivey in [12].

The two possible refinements of a Z specification are *data refinement* and *operation refinement*. In data refinement, a data type in an abstract state space is refined into another data type in the concrete state space. The data type in the concrete state space is selected in such a way that it is more easily implementable. One of the obligations for data refinement is that every operation that uses the abstract data type must be proved to be correct if it also uses the concrete data type. Operation refinement, on the other hand, focuses on mapping an operation in the abstract state space to one or more operations in the concrete state space. In particular, operation refinement describes algorithmic details of concrete operations thereby justifying that the specification is implementable. Unlike VDM-SL, the Z notation does not directly support programming language-like constructs. Hence, there is a semantic gap between Z and a programming language implementing specifications in Z. For this reason, we do not consider operation refinement in this book.

17.8.1
Data Refinement

In data refinement, there exist three possible mappings between abstract and concrete state spaces:

- There exists exactly one concrete state space for every abstract state space.
  This is the ideal situation. Proof obligations in this case are easy and straightforward.
- For every abstract state space, there exist possibly many concrete state spaces.
  This is the most general case. The proof obligations for this case are very similar to those of the ideal case.
- One concrete state space serves as the refinement of several abstract state spaces.
  Such a situation occurs only when some aspects of each one of the abstract state spaces are not implementable. The concrete state space implements those features which are common to all the abstract state spaces. Naturally, any feature of an abstract state space that is not implementable is not interesting and hence is not worthy of refinement.

We now consider proof obligations for the first two cases. A data refinement process requires an abstraction schema which maps concrete state spaces to abstract state spaces. For the rest of the discussion in this chapter, we use the following terminology:

AbsState An abstract state space.

ConState The concrete state space mapped to AbsState.

AbsOp   An operation on the abstract state space AbsState.

ConOp   The operation on the concrete state space ConState which implements AbsOp.

Refine   The abstraction schema which maps ConState to AbsState.

AbsInit   An initial state for the abstract specification.

ConInit   An initial state for the concrete specification which implements AbsInit.

A data refinement process must satisfy the following three conditions.

- Every initial state for the concrete state space corresponds to a valid initial state for the abstract state space. Formally, for the ideal case

$$\forall AbsState;\ ConState \bullet ConInit \wedge Refine \Rightarrow AbsInit$$

and for the general case

$$\forall ConState;\ ConInit \Rightarrow (\exists AbsState \bullet Refine \wedge AbsInit)$$

- A concrete operation terminates whenever the corresponding abstract operation is guaranteed to terminate. That is to say that the precondition of the concrete operation must be weaker than that of the abstract operation. This can be formally stated for the ideal case as follows:

$$\forall AbsState;\ ConState;\ x? : X \bullet pre\ AbsOp \wedge Refine \Rightarrow pre\ ConOp$$

The term $x? : X$ denotes the set of input parameters to the operation. The formal expression for the general case is the same as that of the ideal case.

- Every state in which a concrete operation terminates corresponds to a member of those abstract states in which the corresponding abstract operation could terminate. This condition indirectly asserts that the postcondition of the concrete operation is stronger than that of the abstract operation. The formal expression describing this condition for the ideal case is

$$\forall AbsState;\ AbsState';\ ConState;\ ConState';\ x? : X;\ y! : Y \bullet$$
$$pre\ AbsOp \wedge Refine \wedge ConOp \wedge Refine' \Rightarrow AbsOp$$

and the formal expression for the general case is

$$\forall AbsState;\ ConState;\ ConState';\ x? : X;\ y! : Y \bullet$$
$$pre\ AbsOp \wedge Refine \wedge ConOp \Rightarrow$$
$$(\exists AbsState' \bullet Refine' \wedge AbsOp)$$

Notice that both these formal expressions contain the subexpression

$$pre\ AbsOp \wedge Refine$$

which denotes that *pre ConOp* is satisfied according to the second condition. Therefore, the left side of the implication asserts that *ConOp* is invoked in *ConState* resulting in *ConState'*. The refinement schema *Refine'* when conjoined with *ConState'* results in *AbsState'* which is one of the terminating states obtained from *AbsState*. The existence of *AbsState* and *AbsState'* thereby indicates the presence and validity of *AbsOp*.

It is interesting to notice that the three conditions for data refinement in Z correspond to *initial state validation, domain obligation* and *result obligation* for data refinement in VDM. The only difference is that the mapping of concrete state spaces to abstract state spaces is defined as a function (*retrieve function*) in VDM, whereas it is defined by a schema in Z. By including the abstract and concrete states in the declaration part of the refinement schema, the latter satisfies the *signature* and *adequacy* obligations warranted by data refinement. Thus, the refinement theory for VDM and Z specifications are one and the same, except for notational differences.

Example 14 Personal Phone Book.

A simple model of a personal phone book contains pairs of names and phone numbers. It is assumed that every name is associated with only one phone number. Two names, however, may be associated with the same phone number.   □

17.8.1.1
Abstract Specification

For simplicity, *Name* and *Phone* are assumed to be basic types in this specification.

$$[Name, Phone]$$

The state of the phone book contains only one variable, *entries*, which denotes the mapping between names and phone numbers.

```
__PhoneBook_____
  entries : Name ↦ Phone

```

There is no state invariant for this abstract state. A possible initial state is given below.

```
__InitPhoneBook_____
  PhoneBook
  _____
  entries = ∅

```

We illustrate data refinement on only one operation *AddPhone*. This operation adds a new pair of name and phone number to the book. The precondition for this operation ensures that the new name does not already exist in the book.

```
__AddPhone_____
  ΔPhoneBook
  n? : Name
  ph? : Phone
_____
  n? ∉ dom entries
  entries' = entries ∪ {n? ↦ ph?}
```

The postcondition asserts that the new pair is added to the book.

17.8.1.2
Concrete Specification

In the refined specification, each entry is modeled as a record. This record is described by the schema *Entry* as shown below:

```
__Entry_____
  name : Name
  phone : Phone
```

Since the names are assumed to be unique in the phone book, we introduce a global constraint on entries asserting that two entries are equal if and only if their names are equal.

$$\forall e_1, e_2 : Entry \bullet e_1.name = e_2.name \Leftrightarrow e_1 = e_2$$

In the refined version of the phone book, the entries are arranged in a sequence. The ordering of entries depends on the order in which they are entered in the phone book. It is therefore clear that a new entry will be placed at the end of the sequence.

```
__PhoneBook_1_____
  entries_1 : iseq Entry
```

Like the abstract state, there is no state invariant for the concrete state. The declaration 'iseq' in the concrete state *PhoneBook_1* denotes an injective sequence and hence there are no duplicate entries in the concrete state. This declaration, in conjunction with the global constraint defined earlier, asserts that the names in the concrete state are unique.
In the schema *InitPhoneBook_1* a possible initial state for the concrete specification is shown.

```
__InitPhoneBook_1_____
  PhoneBook_1
_____
  entries_1 = ⟨⟩
```

We now specify the concrete operation *AddPhone_1*.

```
__AddPhone_1_____
ΔPhoneBook_1
n? : Name
ph? : Phone
_____
¬ (∃e : Entry | e ∈ ran entries_1 • e.name = n?)
entries_1' = entries_1 ⌢ ⟨(μe : Entry | e.name = n? ∧ e.phone = ph?)⟩
```

The precondition for *AddPhone_1* ensures that the new name does not exist in the book before the operation is invoked. The postcondition ensures that a new record is constructed with the input parameters and is concatenated to the sequence of entries in the book.

17.8.1.3
Refinement Schema

The refinement schema for the above example is given below:

```
__Refine_____
PhoneBook
PhoneBook_1
_____
dom entries = {e : Entry | e ∈ ran entries_1 • e.name}
∀i : 1..#entries_1 •
    (entries_1 i).phone = entries((entries_1 i).name)
```

The schema *Refine* maps the concrete space *PhoneBook_1* to the abstract space *PhoneBook*. The first predicate in *Refine* asserts that both *PhoneBook* and *PhoneBook_1* contain the same set of names. The second predicate ensures that the phone number associated with each name in *PhoneBook* and that associated with the same name in *PhoneBook_1* are identical.

17.8.2
Proof Obligations

We give a rigorous proof that *PhoneBook_1* implements *PhoneBook*. The proof shows that the refinement described by *Refine* satisfies all the three conditions for data refinement.

Initial State Validation
For the initial state validation, it must be proved that

∀ *PhoneBook*; *PhoneBook_1* •
    InitPhoneBook_1 ∧ *Refine* ⇒ *InitPhoneBook*

Since there is no state invariant both in *PhoneBook* and in *PhoneBook_1*, we need to consider only the predicate parts of *InitPhoneBook_1*, *Refine* and *InitPhoneBook*. Expanding the predicate parts of all the three schemas, the left side of the implication becomes

$entries\_1 = \langle \rangle \wedge$
$\operatorname{dom} entries = \{e : Entry \mid e \in \operatorname{ran} entries\_1 \bullet e.name\} \wedge$
$(\forall i : 1..\#entries\_1 \bullet$
$\quad (entries\_1\ i).phone = entries((entries\_1\ i).name)$

Since $entries\_1 = \langle \rangle$, there is no entry in $entries\_1$. Hence,

$\{e : Entry \mid e \in \operatorname{ran} entries\_1 \bullet e.name\} = \emptyset$

From the second predicate, we can therefore infer that

$\operatorname{dom} entries = \emptyset$

which is the same as

$entries = \emptyset$

This is the predicate part of *InitPhoneBook* which is the right side of the implication. Therefore, every initial state of *PhoneBook_1* also serves as an initial state for *PhoneBook*.

Domain Obligation
For the second condition, we have to prove that the precondition of *PhoneBook* in conjunction with *Refine* implies the precondition of *PhoneBook_1*. That is,

$\forall PhoneBook;\ PhoneBook\_1;\ n? : Name;\ ph? : Phone \bullet$
$\quad pre\ AddPhone \wedge Refine \Rightarrow pre\ AddPhone\_1$

Since the specifications are simple, we do not show the precondition evaluation of *AddPhone* and that of *AddPhone_1*. Instead, we directly use the results. Thus, we need to prove

$n \notin \operatorname{dom} entries \wedge$
$\operatorname{dom} entries = \{e : Entry \mid e \in \operatorname{ran} entries\_1 \bullet e.name\} \wedge$
$(\forall i : 1..\#entries\_1 \bullet$
$\quad (entries\_1\ i).phone = entries((entries\_1\ i).name) \Rightarrow$
$\quad\quad \neg\,(\exists e : Entry \mid e\operatorname{ran} entries\_1 \bullet e.name = n?)$

From

$n \notin \operatorname{dom} entries \wedge$
$\operatorname{dom} entries = \{e : Entry \mid e \in \operatorname{ran} entries\_1 \bullet e.name\}$

we can infer that

$$n? \notin \{e : Entry \mid e \in \text{ran } entries\_1 \bullet e.name\}$$

Using the semantics of set membership, we can rewrite this expression as

$$\forall e : Entry \mid e \in \text{ran } entries\_1 \bullet e.name \neq n?$$

which is the same as

$$\neg (\exists e : Entry \mid e \text{ ran } entries\_1 \bullet e.name = n?)$$

Result Obligation

Finally, we have to prove that the postcondition of *AddPhone_1* is stronger than that of *AddPhone*. Formally,

$$\forall PhoneBook; PhoneBook'; PhoneBook\_1; PhoneBook\_1';$$
$$n? : Name; ph? : Phone \bullet$$
$$\text{pre } AddPhone \wedge Refine \wedge AddPhone\_1 \wedge Refine' \Rightarrow AddPhone$$

By expanding the predicate parts of the respective schemas, we obtain

$$n? \notin \text{dom } entries \wedge$$
$$\text{dom } entries = \{e : Entry \mid e \in \text{ran } entries\_1 \bullet e.name\} \wedge$$
$$(\forall i : 1..\#entries\_1 \bullet$$
$$\quad (entries\_1\ i).phone = entries((entries\_1\ i).name) \wedge$$
$$\neg (\exists e : Entry \mid e \in \text{ran } entries\_1 \bullet e.name = n?) \wedge$$
$$entries\_1' = entries\_1 \frown \langle (\mu e : Entry \mid e.name = n? \wedge e.phone = ph?) \rangle \wedge$$
$$\text{dom } entries' = \{e : Entry \mid e \in \text{ran } entries\_1' \bullet e.name\} \wedge$$
$$(\forall i : 1..\#entries\_1' \bullet$$
$$\quad (entries\_1'\ i).phone = entries'((entries\_1'\ i).name) \Rightarrow$$
$$n? \notin \text{dom } entries \wedge$$
$$entries' = entries \cup \{n? \mapsto ph?\}$$

The right side of the implication contains two conjuncts of which the first one occurs as one of the conjuncts on the left side of the implication. Hence, it is sufficient to derive only the second conjunct from the left side of the implication. This conjunct asserts that the new name and phone number are added to the entries of the phone book in the abstract state. We prove this conjunct in two parts: (i) $n?$ is in the domain of *entries'* and (ii) the phone number corresponding to $n?$ in *entries'* is $ph?$.

Part 1 To prove that $n? \in \text{dom } entries'$

In the predicate

$$\text{dom } entries' = \{e : Entry \mid e \in \text{ran } entries\_1' \bullet e.name\}$$

substitute for *entries_1'*. For ease of understanding, we rename the bound variables in the expression.

$$\text{dom } entries' = \{e : Entry \mid e \in \text{ran}(entries\_1 \frown \langle(\mu\, e_1 : Entry \mid e_1.name =$$
$$n? \land e_1.phone = ph?)\rangle) \bullet e.name\}$$

Using the semantics of sequence concatenation, we infer that the right side of the equality contains an entry corresponding to $n?$ and so does the left side. Therefore, we can conclude that $n? \in \text{dom } entries'$.

Part 2 To prove that $entries'(n?) = ph?$

From Part 1 and from the predicate

$$(\forall i : 1..\#entries\_1' \bullet$$
$$(entries\_1' \, i).phone = entries'((entries\_1' \, i).name))$$

we can infer that

$$entries'(n?) = \{i : 1..\#entries\_1' \mid (entries\_1' \, i).name = n? \bullet$$
$$(entries\_1' \, i).phone\} \tag{17.1}$$

From the predicate

$$entries\_1' = entries\_1 \frown \langle(\mu\, e : Entry \mid e.name = n? \land e.phone = ph?)\rangle$$

we can conclude using the one-point-rule that

$$\exists i : 1..\#entries\_1' \bullet e.name = n? \land e.phone = ph? \tag{17.2}$$

From equations (17.1) and (17.2), we assert that the phone number corresponding to $n?$ in *entries'* is $ph?$.

17.9
Exercises

1. Given two sequences s_1 and s_2, prove
   (a) $items\,(s_1 \frown s_2) = items\, s_1 \uplus items\, s_2$
   (b) if s_2 in s_2, then $items\, s_2 \sqsubseteq items\, s_1$
   (c) if $s_2 = I \upharpoonright s_1$ for some $I \subseteq 1..\#s_1$, then $items\, s_2 \sqsubseteq items\, s_1$
2. Modify the specification for the login subsystem given in Example 8 as stated below:
   (a) Instead of the schema definition *Account*, use the function definition *Username* $\nrightarrow$ *Password* in the *LoginSubsystem* schema.
   (b) The specification in the text considers only one class of users. Introduce at least two different categories of users: *normal* and *system* users. With this change, modify the specification for the login subsystem example to satisfy the following requirements:

(i) A user belongs to only one category.

(ii) Adding and deleting accounts can be performed only by a system user.

(iii) The password of an account can be changed either by the owner of that account or by a system user. A normal user who is not the owner of a particular account cannot access that account.

3. In the specification for an university accounts office in Example 9, introduce a schema called *Course* which contains course number, prerequisites for a course and the maximum number of seats available in that course. Modify the specification to reflect these changes. It should accommodate the following condition: *a student registering for a course must have completed all the prerequisites for that course.*

   Modify the specification such that the information for more than one semester can also be maintained by the registration system.

4. The operation *SelectProcess* in the specification for resource allocation in a computer system (Example 10) is not given in the text. Complete the specification by introducing an operation schema *SelectProcess*.

   If it is assumed that there is only one instance for each resource type, what changes are required in the specification?

5. Give the specification for an initial state for the university accounts office example, and prove its validation.

6. Prove the consistency of operations *Enrol*, *Register* and *PayFees* given in the specification for the university accounts office.

7. One of the requirements for the accounts office example is that a student cannot register for the same course more than once. Prove that the operation *Register* satisfies this requirement.

8. Do the following for the specification discussed in the case study:

   (a) Give the specification for the following additional operations:

   - *ListProject* which will list all the projects initiated by a particular customer.
   - *DeleteProject* which will delete a particular project.
   - *ListEmployees* which determines all the employees working in projects initiated by a particular customer.

   (b) Consider the following new set of requirements for the billing system:

   (i) There are three categories of employees: *programmer, supervisor* and *manager*. Employees in each category have the same hourly rate, but the hourly rate will be different for the three categories.

   (ii) There are three categories of customers: *individual, corporation* and *government*.

   (iii) There are three categories of projects: *small, medium* and *large*.

   (iv) A project is charged differently depending on the category of the project and the category of the customer who initiates that project. *

   Discuss necessary changes in the data types, state space and operations in the specification of the billing system given in the text, and rewrite the specification to capture the requirements mentioned above in addition to the original requirements.

9. Calculate the preconditions for the following operations:

   (a) *PayFees* in the specification for university accounts office (Example 9).

(b) *DeAllocate* in the specification for resource allocation (Example 10).

(c) *ReportWork* in the specification for the automated billing system (case study).

10. In the specification for the login subsystem, define a local operation called *ChangePassword_Local* which operates on *Account* and changes the password for that account. Promote this operation to the global state *LoginSubsystem*.

11. Model *TimeSheet* and *WorkSheet* as schemas in the specification for the automated billing discussed in the case study. Define all functions on time sheets and worksheets as local operations to the respective state spaces defined by *TimeSheet* and *WorkSheet*. Promote these operations to the global state *Organization*. Notice that you may want to promote operations defined on *TimeSheet* to the state space defined by *WorkSheet* and then promote them again to *Organization*.

12. The specification for login subsystem models accounts as sets. Refine the data type *users* using sequences and modify the specification accordingly. Prove the correctness of this refinement.

13. The *waiting_queues* in the specification of resource allocation system is modeled using a partial function. Refine this model using sequences, modify the specification accordingly and prove the correctness of the refinement.

14. (Project) A post office handles three types of mails: *Regular mails*, *Express mails*, *Fast or Courier mails* and so on. Mails may arrive from different locations at different times, including the mails handed over in person at the post office itself. Mails are sorted by three different processes: the first process sorts mails based on the zone to which the mails are to be delivered (may be identified by the first three letters of the postal code), the second process sorts mails based on the location within that zone (may be identified by the last three letters of the postal code) and the third process sorts them based on the street number. After the third sorting process, mails are classified based on the type of mail. At the end of this classification, the mails are sent out from the post office for delivery.

Model the mail handling subsystem in the post office. You may introduce additional requirements and assumptions, if necessary.

17.10
Bibliographic Notes

Much of the earlier work on Z can be found in [6]. The syntax of the Z notation evolved continuously over several years; a somewhat more stable version has been described by Spivey which can be found in [10, 12]. Currently, the Z notation is being standardized by International Standards Organization (ISO). The most recent version of the Z notation described in [16] is slightly different from the earlier version described in [10, 12]. We have used the earlier version [12] in this book.

Spivey's version includes the notion of piping which is discarded in the Standard version. We have not discussed piping in this chapter.

Woodcock and Davies [14] discuss refinement theory for Z specifications which is not dealt with in such great detail in this book. A somewhat simple refinement method for both data refinement and operation refinement can be found in [15]. The readers can also find a detailed and formal treatment of the precondition calculation in [14].

Among all the books for Z, Spivey's book [12] seems to be the only one which describes formal definitions of symbols in Z; these are collectively described as the *mathematical toolkit*. The ISO Standards draft [16] also includes formal definitions of the symbols in the mathematical toolkit, but with minor modifications.

Several object-oriented extensions to the Z notation have been reported in the literature. These include the languages MooZ [8], Object-Z [5] and Z++. All these extensions are based on Spivey's version. A comprehensive overview of these can be found in [13]. As a result of the standardization process, these object-oriented languages are also evolving.

Coombes and McDermid [4], and Baumann and Lermer [2] discussed real-time specifications using Z, without extending the syntax of Z. Hayes and Mahony [7] have described extensions to the Z notation to specify real-time systems. Carrido [3], and Alagar and Periyasamy [1] have extended Object-Z toward real-time specifications; in both these cases, the semantics of the extensions have been developed as extensions of the semantics for the Z language.

The Computing Laboratory at Oxford University in the UK maintains a web site for the Z notation: http://www.comlab.ac.uk/zforum. This web site contains a current Z bibliography, information on tool support for Z notation and pointers to work achieved by the standardization process. A separate moderated newsgroup called comp.specification.z is also maintained by the Oxford Computing Laboratory, which is a useful source for beginners to find out more about the Z notation. In addition, proceedings of the annual conference, called *The Z Users Meeting*, are also an invaluable source for up-to-date developments in Z.

References

1. Alagar VS, Periyasamy K (1996) Real-time object-Z: a language for the specification and design of real-time reactive systems. Technical report, Department of Computer Science, Concordia University, Montreal, Quebec, Canada, June 1996
2. Baumann P, Lermer K (1995) A framework for the specification of reactive and concurrent systems in Z. In: Proceedings of the fifteenth conference on foundations of software technology and theoretical computer science. Lecture notes in computer science, vol 1026. Springer, Berlin, pp 62–79
3. Carrido JM (1995) Specification of real-time systems with extensions to object-Z. In: Proceedings of technology of object-oriented languages and systems (TOOLS), Santa Barbara, CA, pp 167–179
4. Coombes AC, McDermid JA (1992) Specifying temporal requirements for distributed real-time systems in Z. Technical report YCS176, Computer Science Department, University of York, Heslington, York, UK
5. Duke R, Rose G, Smith G (1995) Object-Z: a specification language for the description of standards. Comput Stand Interfaces 17:511–533
6. Hayes IJ (ed) (1987) Specification case studies. Series in computer science. Prentice Hall International, Englewood Cliffs
7. Mahony BP, Hayes IJ (1992) A case-study in timed refinement: a mine pump. IEEE Trans Softw Eng 18(9):817–826

8. Meira SL, Cavalcanti ALC (1992) The *MooZ* specification language. Technical report, Departamento de Informática, Universidade Federal de Pernambuco, Recife—PE, Brasil

9. Morgan C, Vickers T (eds) (1994) On the refinement calculus. Springer, Berlin

10. Potter B, Sinclair J, Till D (1991) An introduction to formal specification and Z. Series in computer science. Prentice Hall International, Englewood Cliffs

11. Spivey JM (1992) The fuzz reference manual. JM Spivey Computing Science Consultancy, Oxford OX44 9AN, UK

12. Spivey JM (1992) The Z notation—a reference manual, 2nd edn. Series in computer science. Prentice Hall International, Englewood Cliffs

13. Stepney S, Barden R, Cooper D (eds) (1992) Object-orientation in Z. Workshops in Computing Series. Springer, Berlin

14. Woodcock JCP, Davies J (1996) Using Z: specification, refinement and proof. Series in computer science. Prentice Hall International, Englewood Cliffs

15. Wordsworth JB (1992) Software development with Z. Addison-Wesley, Reading

16. The Z Notation, ISO/IEC JTC 1/SC22 CD 13568, September 1995

The Object-Z Specification Language   18

The Z notation is more popular and is easy to use, but it is procedural in nature. A Z specification starts with a global state definition. Operations are then specified to manipulate the state variables. The procedural nature of Z specification makes the specifiers to think in terms of one global state space, and operations and functions to act on that global state. Practitioners of the object-oriented approach attempted to use the Z notation in an object-oriented style [46]. They tried to model each object as a separate Z specification and thereby made each object as an independent and reusable entity. Composition of objects and interactions among objects were specified using schema calculus. However, this effort was not fruitful because the intrinsic properties of object-orientation such as encapsulation, inheritance and polymorphism were not captured by the Z specification written in object-oriented style. In order to utilize the full expressive power of the object-oriented approach, several object-oriented extensions of the Z notations were developed. MooZ [4, 5], ZEST [46], Z++ [46] and Object-Z [10, 38] are some of them. Among these extensions, Object-Z became more popular because of its literature support and tool support.

The Object-Z notation is a conservative extension of the Z notation. Most of the syntactic structures of Z such as primitive types, schema notation, set, sequence, function and relation are retained in Object-Z with their respective semantics. Additionally, Object-Z introduces the class notation and some unique features of object-orientation such as visibility (to declare the public interface of a class), inheritance, polymorphism and composition operators (to define message passing between objects).

18.1
Basic Structure of an Object-Z Specification

Before looking at the structure of an Object-Z specification, it is important to revise the syntax of the Z language because a major portion of an Object-Z specification uses the

V.S. Alagar, K. Periyasamy, *Specification of Software Systems*,
Texts in Computer Science,
DOI 10.1007/978-0-85729-277-3_18, © Springer-Verlag London Limited 2011

same syntax and semantics of the Z language. The readers are therefore advised to revise Sect. 17.2 in Chap. 17.

An Object-Z specification consists of several class definitions preceded by global definitions. Generally, global definitions are given as Z paragraphs the beginning of an Object-Z specification. The global definitions include types, constants and functions that are shared by all classes.

A template of an Object-Z specification is given below.

```
__ Classname _____
< visibility list >
< inherited class names >
< local definitions >
< state definition >
< initial state definition >
< operation definitions >
```

The class name of a class serves as the unique identifier of the class.

The visibility list includes the names of the features (state variables and operation names) that will be exported (made public) from this class. If no such list is specified, then all features of the class are exported. The visibility list will not be inherited by any subclass. Hence, a subclass can export a private feature of a superclass or can hide a public feature of a superclass. The terms 'subclass' and 'superclass' are used with the same meaning as in Object-Oriented programming. The list of superclasses is listed next to the visibility list. Local definitions within a class definition may include types, constants, and functions they are local to the class.

The state definition is represented by an unnamed schema. This includes the state variables which are the attributes of the class. The predicate of the state schema represents the class invariant. The initial state definition is a schema with the keyword 'INIT' and includes the conditions corresponding to the initial state of an object instantiated from this class definition. While it is the specifier's responsibility to include the state name in the initial state definition in a Z specification, the initial state definition inside a class does not have any state name. This is because it is associated with only the state of the class in which it is declared. An operation definition in a class is very similar to that of an operation definition in a Z specification, except for the semantics of Δ. The Δ symbol in Object-Z is associated with a list of state variables that are modified by the operation.

Object-Z also enforces that the various components of a class must be listed in the same order as shown above. Among these components, the state definition is mandatory; others are optional.

Example 1 Employees in a small company.

A small software development company has a set of employees. The following specification models the employees and their salaries.

[*EMPLOYEE*]

┌─ *EmployeeSalaries* ──
│ ⇃ (*AddEmployee*, *ModifySalary*, *DeleteEmployee*)
│ ┌──
│ │ *employeeSalary* : *EMPLOYEE* $\rightarrowtail \mathbb{R}$
│ ├──
│ │ $\forall d : \mathrm{dom}\, employeeSalary \bullet employeeSalary(d) > 0.0$
│ └──
│
│ ┌─ *INIT* ──────────────────────────────────────
│ │ *employeeSalary* $= \emptyset$
│ └──
│
│ ┌─ *AddEmployee* ───────────────────────────────
│ │ $\Delta(employeeSalary)$
│ │ *newEmployee?* : *EMPLOYEE*
│ │ *salary?* : $\mathbb{R}$
│ ├──
│ │ *salary?* > 0.0
│ │ *newEmployee?* $\notin \mathrm{dom}\, employeeSalary$
│ │ *employeeSalary'* $= employeeSalary \cup \{newEmployee? \mapsto salary?\}$
│ └──
│
│ ┌─ *ModifySalary* ──────────────────────────────
│ │ $\Delta(employeeSalary)$
│ │ *employee?* : *EMPLOYEE*
│ │ *newSalary?* : $\mathbb{R}$
│ ├──
│ │ *newSalary?* > 0.0
│ │ *employee?* $\in \mathrm{dom}\, employeeSalary$
│ │ *employeeSalary'* $= employeeSalary \oplus \{employee? \mapsto newSalary?\}$
│ └──
│
│ ┌─ *DeleteEmployee* ────────────────────────────
│ │ $\Delta(employeeSalary)$
│ │ *who?* : *EMPLOYEE*
│ ├──
│ │ *who?* $\in \mathrm{dom}\, employeeSalary$
│ │ *employeeSalary'* $= \{who?\} \mathbin{⩤} employeeSalary$
│ └──
└──

The class *EmployeeSalaries* uses the basic type *EMPLOYEE* which is declared outside of the class as a global type definition. The visibility list indicates that this class exports the three operations *AddEmployee*, *ModifySalary* and *DeleteEmployee*. The state of the class consists of a mapping from employees to their salaries; the salaries are modeled as real numbers. The state invariant asserts that the salaries must be positive real numbers. The state uses a partial function to model the mapping and hence each employee has only one salary recorded in the system. The state schema in a class is unnamed.

Initially, the system has no records, as indicated by the *INIT* state. The keyword *INIT* is used to denote the initial state of the objects instantiated from a class. Thus, every class has its own *INIT* state.

Operations in a class are defined in the same way as operations in a Z specification, except for the difference in Δ list as described below. The semantics of Δ list in Object-Z is different from that in the Z specification language. While in Z, the Δ list indicates the names of the state space schemas, in Object-Z, they indicate the state variables of the class in which the operation is located. Further, the Δ list in Object-Z only includes those state variables that are modified by the operation. Other state variables may be used by the operation but not included in the Δ list.

The operation *AddEmployee* will be invoked to add a new employee to the system. This operation will modify the state variable *employeeSalary* as indicated by the Δ list. The operation accepts the new employee and his/her salary as inputs. The precondition for this operation ensures that the salary must be a positive number and the employee must not be in system before. The postcondition asserts that the employee record is added to the system.

The *ModifySalary* operation describes how the salary of an employee can be modified. The employee identification and the new salary are passed as inputs. The salary must be a positive number and the employee must be in the system before. The postcondition in this case asserts that the salary for this employee is overwritten by the new salary, as indicated by the relational override operator.

The last operation in the *EmployeeSalaries* class is used to delete an employee from the system. The only input parameter is the employee identification. The precondition ensures that the employee is found in the system records. The postcondition asserts that the employee record is removed from the system. The operation uses the domain subtraction operator for this purpose.

Object-Z syntax also includes operations specified in horizontal style, just like horizontal schemas in the Z notation. For example, the operation *DeleteEmployee* can be specified in the horizontal style as follows:

$$DeleteEmployee \,\widehat{=}\, \left[who? : EMPLOYEE \mid who? \in \mathrm{dom}\, employeeSalary \wedge \right.$$
$$\left. employeeSalary' = \{who?\} \vartriangleleft employeeSalary \right]$$

The Δ list is not specified in the horizontal style. This style is used in composition of operations, to be discussed later in this chapter. $\qquad\qquad\Box$

18.1.1
Parameterized Class

A class can have parameters but they are optional. If present, they must be included in the name of the class as shown below:

$$\_\,ClassName[<Parameters>]\,_____$$
$$\qquad \ldots$$

The specification of a parameterized class can make use of the parameters in the same way as basic types and cannot anticipate any other property of the parameters. Consequently, any variable of the parameter types can only be compared for equality and inequality just like variables of basic types. The parameters of a class can be instantiated only by set values, and not by any scalar value. The concept of parameterized class is similar to that of parameterized schema in Z. Example 2 illustrates how a parameterized class can be defined and used.

Example 2 Generic Queue.

$$
\begin{array}{|l|}
\hline
\textit{Queue}[T] \\
\hline
\upharpoonright (\textit{Join}, \textit{Remove}) \\
\hline
\textit{elements} : \text{seq}\, T \\
\hline
\begin{array}{|l|}
\hline
\textit{INIT} \\
\hline
\textit{elements} = \langle\,\rangle \\
\hline
\end{array} \\
\begin{array}{|l|}
\hline
\textit{Join} \\
\hline
\Delta(\textit{elements}) \\
t? : T \\
\hline
\textit{elements}' = \textit{elements} \frown \langle t? \rangle \\
\hline
\end{array} \\
\begin{array}{|l|}
\hline
\textit{Remove} \\
\hline
\Delta(\textit{elements}) \\
t! : T \\
\hline
\#\textit{elements} > 0 \\
\textit{elements}' = \textit{tail}\,\textit{elements} \\
t! = \textit{head}\,\textit{elements} \\
\hline
\end{array} \\
\hline
\end{array}
$$

The class *Buffer* uses the generic queue and instantiates it with integers.

$$
\begin{array}{|l|}
\hline
\textit{Buffer} \\
\hline
\textit{items} : \textit{Queue}[\mathbb{Z}] \\
\hline
\textit{AddItems} \mathrel{\widehat{=}} \textit{items}.\textit{Join} \\
\textit{DeleteItems} \mathrel{\widehat{=}} \textit{items}.\textit{Remove} \\
\hline
\end{array}
$$

Just like in Z, an operation schema can be specified in box notation as well as in horizontal style as shown in the *Buffer* class. The operations of a class can be invoked using the dot notation, commonly used in object-oriented design and programming. The class *Buffer* thus uses this dot notation to invoke the *Join* and *Remove* operations from the class *Queue*[$\mathbb{Z}$].   □

18.2
Distinguished Features of Object-Orientation

Among the many differences between procedural and object-oriented paradigms, three features are dominant. These are *encapsulation*, *inheritance* and *polymorphism*.

18.2.1
Encapsulation

Encapsulation is a property by which the internal features of a class are separated from external (public) features. In short, *encapsulation* enforces access restrictions on the features of a class. In Object-Z, *encapsulation* is implemented by the *visibility list* operator in a class definition. For example, in the *EmployeeSalaries* class described in Example 1, the line

$\quad$ ↾ *(AddEmployee, ModifySalary, DeleteEmployee)*

indicates the public features that are exported from the class. All other features that are not exported will be considered as private.

In many object-oriented programming languages, three levels of restrictions are used to enforce encapsulation. These are called *public, private* and *protected*. In Object-Z, only the first two levels are used. The items listed in the visibility list of a class are public in the sense that they can be accessed by another class. Any feature that is not included in the visibility list is deemed private. The private features can thus be used only within the scope of the class definition in which they are defined.

18.2.2
Inheritance

The discussion on inheritance requires the notion of *subclass* and *superclass* made clear. Even though these two terms can be found in every reference on object-orientation, a brief description here will help the readers understand their roles in Object-Z specifications.

A class X is said to be a *subclass* of another class Y if X is a specialization of Y. That is, X acquires some features of Y but may add its own features and/or modify some of the features acquired from Y. The class Y is called the *superclass* in this case. Specialization denotes the concept of acquiring the features in this way, and inheritance is the mechanism that implements the specialization concept. The inheritance mechanism may specifically state the features from the superclass that are acquired and the actions that a subclass is allowed to do.

In Object-Z, a subclass X can inherit from a superclass Y by including the name of the superclass (i.e. Y in this case) after the visibility list in X. If there is no such visibility list in X, then the superclass name will be the first one listed inside the class definition. The inheritance mechanism in Object-Z allows the subclass to inherit every feature that is defined in the superclass ignoring the visibility list. That is, the visibility list of the superclass is not inherited. However, the subclass can make any of the inherited features to become public even if these features are private in the superclass. At the same time, the subclass can also make some of the inherited features to be private by not listing them in its visibility list even though these features may be listed as public in the visibility list of the superclass. The consequences of inheritance are summarized below:

- All local type definitions and constant definitions of the superclass are included in the subclass. Notice that the subclass should not have another definition for the same type or constant; otherwise, it will lead to a nondeterministic choice.
- The state variables of the superclass are merged with those of the subclass. If the subclass redefines the type of a superclass state variable, then two types must be compatible (e.g., $\mathbb{N}$ and $\mathbb{Z}$). This occurs when there is a state variable in the subclass with the same name as that of a state variable in the superclass but with a different type. In this case, a subclass may expand or restrict the horizon of a superclass state variable. As an example, the type $\mathbb{N}$ of a variable x in the superclass may be expanded to the type $\mathbb{Z}$ of the same variable in the subclass. Likewise, the type $\mathbb{Z}$ of a superclass variable may be restricted to the type $\mathbb{N}$ of the same variable in the subclass.
- The state invariant of the superclass is conjoined with that of the subclass. Care must be taken to ensure that there is no contradiction after conjoining.
- The initial state of the superclass is conjoined with that of the subclass.
- If an operation Op is redefined in the subclass, the declaration of Op in the superclass is merged with that of the same operation in the subclass. If any input or output parameter has the same name both in the superclass and in the subclass, then their types must be compatible. The predicate part of Op in the superclass is conjoined with that of the same operation in the subclass. Once again, it is the specifier's responsibility to ensure that there is no contradiction after conjoining.

Object-Z supports multiple inheritance and hence a subclass can inherit more than one superclass at the same time.

To illustrate the inheritance mechanism in Object-Z, consider the class *Account* in a bank:

```
┌─Account ─────────────────────────────────────────────────
│ ↾ (accountNumber, Deposit, Withdraw)
│ ┌─────────────────────────────────────────────────────
│ │ accountNumber : None
│ │ ownerID : None
│ │ balance : ℝ
│ │
│ └─────────────────────────────────────────────────────
```

$$\begin{array}{|l}
\_Deposit_____ \\
\Delta(balance) \\
amount? : \mathbb{R} \\
\hline
amount? > 0.0 \\
balance' = balance + amount?
\end{array}$$

$$\begin{array}{|l}
\_Withdraw_____ \\
\Delta(balance) \\
amount? : \mathbb{R} \\
\hline
amount? \geq 0.0 \\
balance' = balance - amount?
\end{array}$$

The *Withdraw* operation includes an unconditional withdrawal of *amount?* from the balance. This may lead to a negative balance in the account if there is not sufficient balance in the account. The subclasses derived from *Account* may enforce restrictions on withdrawals to keep the balance zero or positive. One such account is *SavingsAccount*, which is specified below.

$$\begin{array}{|l}
\_SavingsAccount_____ \\
\upharpoonright (accountNumber, balance, Deposit, Withdraw) \\
Account \\
\hline
minimumBalance : \mathbb{R} \\
\hline
minimumBalance = 1000 \\
\hline
balance \geq minimumBalance \\
\hline
\_Withdraw_____ \\
balance - amount? \geq minimumBalance
\end{array}$$

The class *SavingsAccount* inherits *Account* and then exports the state variable *balance* along with the three features already exported by *Account*. A minimum balance of 1000 is expected to be maintained at all times by the savings account. This constant is introduced inside the class *SavingsAccount* and the constraint on minimum balance is included as a state invariant. Since the class *Account* does not have any state invariant, no conflicts will arise in *SavingsAccount*. The operation *Withdraw* has a precondition to ensure that the balance in the account is sufficiently high to allow the withdrawal and at the same time to maintain the minimum balance. This precondition will be conjoined with the predicate

$$amount? \geq 0$$
$$balance' = balance - amount?$$

already stated in *Withdraw* in the class *Account*.

18.2.3
Polymorphism

Object-Z supports *universal polymorphism* in which a subclass object can be *substituted* for a superclass object. In order to do this, the superclass object must be declared polymorphic in the first place. For example, consider the classes *Account* and its subclass *SavingsAccount* for the bank example described in the previous section. The declaration

$$account : \downarrow Account$$

means that the variable *account* belongs to the superclass *Account* but any object of the class *Account* or its descendant *SavingsAccount* can be assigned to *account*. Using this syntax, a bank class can be given as below:

__Bank_____

$accounts : \mathbb{P} \downarrow Account$

$\forall a_1, a_2 : accounts \bullet a_1.accountNumber = a_2.accountNumber \Leftrightarrow a_1 = a_2$

__INIT_____
$accounts = \emptyset$

__AddAccount_____
$\Delta(accounts)$
$sac? : SavingsAccount$

$sac?.accountNumber \notin \{a : Account \mid a \in accounts \bullet a.accountNumber\}$
$accounts' = accounts \cup \{sac?\}$

The class *Bank* includes a set of accounts. The declaration

$$accounts : \mathbb{P} \downarrow Account$$

indicates that *accounts* is a set of elements of the polymorphic type *Account*. Therefore, this set can contain elements from *Account* as well as elements from its subclasses.

The state invariant asserts that an account is uniquely identified by its account number.

The operation *AddAccount* receives an object of *SavingsAccount* as a parameter. The precondition of this operation ensures that the savings account number is not already included in any of the accounts in the bank. The postcondition asserts that the savings account is added to the set of accounts. The predicate

$$accounts' = accounts \cup \{sac\}$$

illustrates the polymorphic substitution because *sac* is an object of type *SavingsAccount*, while *accounts* is declared to be a set of *Account*.

18.3
Composition of Operations

In object-oriented approach, a class is expected to be highly cohesive and fairly independent. This means that the state of an object instantiated from a class must be changed only by the operations defined within the class. In order to execute a common task that involves several operations possibly from different classes, a mechanism for method communication is used. Object-Z supports specification of the method communication mechanism through *Composition of Operations*. There are five composition operators defined in Object-Z; these are *sequential composition operator* ($\S$), *concurrency operator* ($\wedge$), *parallel composition operator* ($\|$), *nondeterministic choice operator* ($\|$), and *environment enrichment operator* ($\bullet$). All the five of them are binary infix operators. The semantics of each of these operators is explained in detail in subsequent sections.

It is important to notice that the composition operators can only be used in the horizontal schema style. This is because, they define composition of operations while the box notation for schema is meant for including declarations and predicates. Thus, the box notation should be used only for single standalone operation.

18.3.1
Sequential Composition Operator

The sequential composition operator is used when a specifier wants to realize the effect of two operations performed in a sequence. It is similar to sequential composition of operation schemas in Z.

<u>Syntax</u>

$$Op \mathrel{\widehat{=}} Op_1 \mathbin{\S} Op_2$$

<u>Semantics</u>
The signature of Op is the union of the signatures of Op_1 and Op_2 and the predicate part of Op is the conjunction of the predicate part of Op_1 and that of Op_2.

The operation Op_2 starts in the state where Op_1 finishes, thus they are in a sequence. The communication between the two operations occurs through input and output variables. Accordingly, the input variables of Op_2 are equated to the output variables of Op_1. In order for this to happen, the communicating variables in both operations must have the same base name. These communicating variables are hidden in Op and so is the intermediate state between Op_1 and Op_2.

To illustrate how the sequential composition operator can be used, consider a crafts store that sells several items. A customer can buy an item and ask the store to paint it. However, the customer must pay for the item first before asking the store to paint. These two tasks can be specified as below:

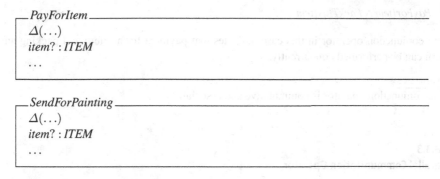

$\_$ PayForItem $_____$
$\Delta(\ldots)$
$item? : ITEM$
$\ldots$

$\_$ SendForPainting $_____$
$\Delta(\ldots)$
$item? : ITEM$
$\ldots$

$PayForItem \; \overset{\circ}{,} \; SendForPainting$

Since both operations use *item?* as input, the composition operation merges the two declarations which indicate that the same item is purchased and sent for painting. Alternatively, the operation *PayForItem* can output *item!* which can be absorbed into *SendForPainting* through sequential composition.

Properties
The sequential composition operator is neither commutative nor associative.

18.3.2
Concurrency Operator

This operator is used to specify the situation when two operations are invoked at the same time. It is similar to the schema conjunction operator in Z.

Syntax

$$Op \stackrel{\frown}{=} Op_1 \wedge Op_2$$

Semantics
Like in sequential composition, the signature of Op is the union of the signatures of Op_1 and Op_2, and the predicate part of Op is the conjunction of the predicates of the two constituent operations.

The operations Op_1 and Op_2 are started at the same time, even if they terminate at different times. There is no direct communication involved between Op_1 and Op_2. It is important to notice that the individual behavior of the constituent operations is hard to observe within the composition, especially when both Op_1 and Op_2 access or modify the same state variable. An example of a concurrency operator is given below using the crafts store example discussed in the previous section:

$\_$ PackThisItem $_____$
$\Delta(\ldots)$
$item? : ITEM$
$\ldots$

PayForItem ∧ *PackThisItem*

The conjunction operator in this case indicates that payment for an item and packing an item can be performed concurrently.

Properties
The conjunction operator is commutative and associative.

18.3.3
Parallel Communication Operator

This operator is also called *handshaking communication operator* because the constituent operations involved in the communication exchange information with each other.

Syntax

$$Op \mathbin{\widehat{=}} Op_1 \parallel Op_2$$

Semantics
The signature and predicates of *Op* are derived from the constituent operations in the same way as in sequential communication.

In this handshaking communication mode, Op_1 and Op_2 exchange information with each other through input and output variables. Accordingly, if Op_1 has an output variable and Op_2 has an input variable of the same base name, then the output of Op_1 is absorbed as input by Op_2. Similarly, if Op_2 has an output variable and Op_1 has an input variable of the same base name, then the output of Op_2 is absorbed as input by Op_1. While the information exchange is strictly one way in sequential communication, it occurs in both directions in parallel communication. As before, the communicating variables are hidden in *Op*. The following example illustrates the parallel communication using the crafts store example.

DeliverPaintedItem
$\Delta(\dots)$
item! : *ITEM* ...

PayForItem ⨾ *SendForPainting* ⨾ (*PackThisItem* ∥ *DeliverPaintedItem*)

The parallel composition in this case indicates that the item is delivered by the paint shop and is given for packaging.

Properties
The parallel communication operator is commutative but not associative. An associative version of the parallel operator denoted by $\parallel_!$ is also available. Apart from the associativity, another difference between the two parallel operators is that the output variables are not hidden when the associative parallel operator is used, and hence these variables may be equated with other input variables in subsequent parallel operations [38].

18.3.4
Nondeterministic Choice Operator

This binary operator exclusively selects one of the two constituent operations.

Syntax

$$Op \mathrel{\widehat{=}} Op_1 [\![Op_2$$

Semantics

The signature of Op is the union of the signatures of both Op_1 and Op_2. The predicate of Op is formed by the disjunction of the predicates of the two constituent operations.

If Op_1 is enabled, i.e., when its precondition is true, Op_1 will be executed when Op is called. Similarly, if Op_2 is enabled, then Op_2 will be executed when Op is called. However, if both of them are enabled, then one of them is selected to occur. The choice is determined at design or implementation time and hence this operator is called *nondeterministic*. One of the restrictions of the choice operator is that Op_1 and Op_2 must have the same set of auxiliary variables. Auxiliary variables are the variables declared in the operation excluding those listed in the Δ-list of the operation.

As an example for the choice operator, consider the situation of an overbooked flight. Assume that the economy seats are full but the flight has few more seats in the business class. The airlines generally chooses someone who has paid regular price for the economy ticket or someone who has an Elite membership. If the airlines can find people from both the categories, then it chooses one arbitrarily. This can be shown using the choice operator as follows:

$$PomoteSeating \mathrel{\widehat{=}} PaidRegularPrice \; [\![\; HasEliteMembership$$

Properties

The choice operator is commutative and associative.

18.3.5
Environment Enrichment Operator

The environment enrichment operator is somewhat similar to the sequential composition operator. It is denoted by the symbol •. If two operations Op_1 and Op_2 are composed as $Op_1 \bullet Op_2$, then Op_2 starts in the state where Op_1 ends. In this aspect, • behaves like $\mathrel{{}_9^\circ}$. The difference between the two operators is that the environment enrichment operator extends the full signature of Op_1 to Op_2. In other words, this operator enriches the environment of Op_2 by allowing it to access the variables declared in the signature of Op_1.

Syntax

$$Op \mathrel{\widehat{=}} Op_1 \bullet Op_2$$

Semantics

The signature of Op is the union of the signature of Op_1 and Op_2 and its predicate part is the conjunction of the predicate parts of the two constituent operations.

In this composition, Op_2 can access any variable declared in the signature of Op_1. For illustration, consider the flight overbooking example given in the previous section. Assume that the two operations *PaidRegularPrice* and *HasEliteMembership* both have an input parameter of type *EconomySeatPassenger* but have different names. In this case, an unnamed operation can be introduced for passing the input parameter and its signature can be extended to the two operations using the environment enrichment operator.

$$PromoteSeating \,\widehat{=}\, \left[\, x? : EconomySeatPassenger \,\right] \bullet$$
$$(PaidRegularPrice[x?/passenger?] \| HasEliteMembership[x?/member?]$$

The syntax *PaidRegularPrice*[$x?/passenger?$] indicates that the parameter *passenger*? is renamed by $x?$. This renaming of components in a schema is described in Chap. 17.

Properties

The environment enrichment operator is neither commutative nor associative.

The case study given in Sect. 18.5 illustrates the use of all the five composition operators.

18.4
Specification Examples

Example 3 The *Transcript* class.

This example is on modeling a student's transcript. In addition to demonstrating how to model a simple data-oriented application using Object-Z, this example also shows how to use the axiomatic definitions within a class.

Problem Description

A student's transcript includes the student's name, the courses taken by the student and the mark for each course. Mark is a number between 0 and 100. The specification must support operations (i) to add a course to the student's transcript, (ii) to remove a course from the transcript, (iii) to change the mark for a course already entered in the transcript, and (iv) to find the average of marks in all the courses taken by the student. No course can exist in the transcript without a mark. Stated otherwise, whenever a course is added to the transcript, the mark in that course must also be added at the same time.

Assumptions

1. There is only one mark for each course in the transcript. If the student takes the course again, the new mark for the course will override the previous mark entered for that course.

The Model

The application is modeled as one class called *Transcript* with some global types that can be used inside the class.

Mark is a number ranging from 1 to 100, both inclusive, and hence it is appropriate to model it as an enumerated type. The course and mark are tightly related and hence can be modeled as a relation. Since there is only one mark for a course, the relation between course and mark should be modeled as a function. The state of the system will include a variable that corresponds to the mapping between courses and the marks in these courses. The student's name is included as another state variable, even though this variable does not contribute to any operations in the class.

It is required to compute the average of the marks for a student. This means that the marks in all the courses must be summed up to find the average. Consequently, the sum function must be defined using an axiomatic definition.

Since the course to mark relationship is modeled as a function data type in the state space, we can include another function to extract the mark in each course. Because two courses may have the same mark, the output of the extraction function will be modeled as a sequence. This output will be fed as an input to the sum function. Although the average can be computed within an operation, the specification includes a third function to compute the average. This function can be used to compute the average of a sequence of numbers and hence can be used in other context as well.

Initially, the mapping from courses to marks will be empty. The operations of the *Transcript* class follow:

AddRecord This operation describes how to add a new course record to the transcript. The precondition must ensure that the course name must not exist in the transcript before.

RemoveRecord In order to remove a record from the transcript, the course name corresponding to the record must exist already in the transcript. This should be stated as a precondition. Since *courses* is a function, it guarantees that there is only one record for each course in the transcript.

ReportAverage The purpose of this operation is to find the average of marks for all the courses reported in the transcript. This operation will make use of the function *findAverage* which, in turn, calls the function *findSum*. The sequence of marks from the transcript are extracted using the function *extractMarks*.

The Object-Z Specification

$[COURSE, STRING]$

$Mark == 0..100$

$\qquad$ *Transcript* $\underline{\qquad\qquad\qquad\qquad\qquad\qquad\qquad\qquad\qquad\qquad\qquad\qquad}$
$\upharpoonright (name, courses, AddRecord, RemoveRecord, ReportAverage)$

$\quad extractMarks : (COURSE \nrightarrow Mark) \nrightarrow \text{seq} \, Mark$

$\rule{3cm}{0.4pt}$

$\quad \forall \, cours : (COURSE \nrightarrow Mark) \bullet$
$\qquad (cours = \emptyset \Rightarrow extractMarks(cours) = \langle \rangle) \land$
$\qquad (cours \neq \emptyset \Rightarrow$
$\qquad\quad (\exists \, c : COURSE \mid c \in \text{dom} \, cours \bullet$
$\qquad\qquad extractMarks(cours) = \langle cours(c) \rangle \frown extractMarks(\{c\} \lhd cours)))$

$$findSum : \text{seq } Mark \nrightarrow \mathbb{N}$$

$$\forall s : \text{seq } Mark \bullet$$
$$(s = \langle \rangle \Rightarrow findSum(s) = 0) \wedge$$
$$(s \neq \langle \rangle \Rightarrow findSum(s) = head\ s + findSum(tail\ s))$$

$$findAverage : \text{seq } Mark \nrightarrow \mathbb{N}$$

$$\forall s : \text{seq } Mark \mid s \neq \langle \rangle \bullet findAverage(s) = findSum(s)\ \text{div}\ (\#s)$$

$name : STRING$
$courses : COURSE \nrightarrow Mark$

___ INIT _____

$courses = \emptyset$

___ AddRecord _____
$\Delta(courses)$
$newCourse? : COURSE$
$mark? : Mark$

$newCourse? \notin \text{dom}\ courses$
$courses' = courses \cup \{newCourse? \mapsto mark?\}$

___ RemoveRecord _____
$\Delta(courses)$
$courseToRemove? : COURSE$

$courseToRemove? \in \text{dom}\ courses$
$courses' = \{courseToRemove?\} \ntriangleleft courses$

___ ReportAverage _____
$average! : \mathbb{R}$

$average! = findAverage(extractMarks(courses))$

□

Example 4 Access Rights to Computers.

Problem Description

This example is about the specification of authorized access to a set of computers in a
department. The department has a set of computers and a set of student users. Each user

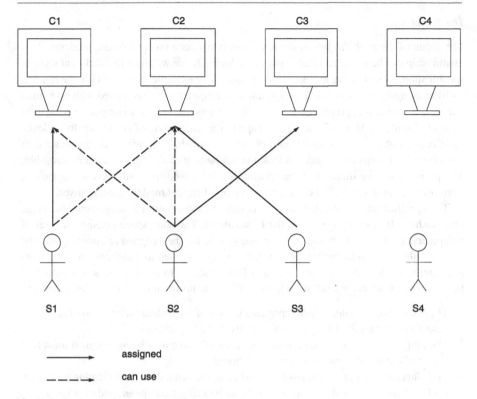

Fig. 18.1 A scenario in the Access Rights example

is assigned at most one computer for his/her use. The user U assigned to a computer C is responsible for maintaining C. Each computer can be assigned to at most one student. In addition to using the computer assigned to him/her, a student is also allowed to use a subset of computers that are already assigned to other users. This authorization must be given by the department. Notice that no one can use a computer that is not assigned to anyone because no one can maintain (is responsible for) that computer. Also, a student who has not been assigned to any computer cannot use any other computer.

To better understand the problem, consider the scenario as shown in Fig. 18.1: There are four students and four computers in this scenario. Student S1 is assigned the computer C1 but can also use C2. Student S2 is assigned C3 but can also use C1 and C2. Student S3 is assigned C2. The computer C4 is not assigned to anyone and student S4 is not assigned to any computer.

The department must be able (i) to add a new student, (ii) to add a new computer, (iii) to assign a computer to a student, (iv) to de-assign a computer that was assigned to a student, (v) to give authorization for a student to use a computer other than the one assigned to him/her, and (vi) to remove authorization for a student from using a computer.

Assumptions

1. The set of computers that a student can use includes the computer he/she is assigned to.

The Model

The focus of the problem lies in the relationship between computers and students. This relationship can be modeled in different ways. Each choice will lead to a different style of specification, some leaning to easier to understand. For example, one could use the relation $\leftrightarrow$ from computers to students. This will allow a computer to be associated with more than one student which is appropriate for the usage relationship. That is, a computer can be used by several students. However, in order to capture the assignment of computers to students, additional constraints must be imposed on this relationship, because each computer is at most assigned to only one student. A function is a natural choice for the latter relationship. The problem will be different if the relationship is viewed from students to computers. Thus, this example serves as a candidate to explore different modeling alternatives.

The specification given below uses functions to model both the assignment and usage relationships. It has only one class, the *Department*. The state space consists of a set of computers, a set of students and two mappings—one for the assigned relationship and the other for the usage relationship. Both mappings are modeled as functions from students to computers. Thus, *assigned* is a function from students to computers, and *canUse* is a function from students to a set of computers. The state invariant must assert the following:

1. The domain of *assigned* which represents the set of all students who are assigned computers must be a subset of the set of students in the department.
2. The range of *assigned* which denotes the set of all computers being assigned must be a subset of the set of computers in the department.
3. Both functions *assigned* and *canUse* must have the same domain indicating that every student who is assigned a computer must also be using a computer, and vice versa.
4. The set of all computers that are assigned must also be used, and vice versa.
5. The constraint that each user can be assigned at most one computer is taken care of by the function data type. However, an additional constraint is needed to assert that each computer is assigned to at most one student. Stated otherwise, no two students must have been assigned the same computer.
6. Every student who is assigned a computer can use that computer.

The operations *AddStudent* and *AddComputer* are straightforward. The operation *Assign* should check whether the student is not assigned any computer, and the computer is not assigned to any student. If these two conditions are true, both the functions *assigned* and *canUse* should be updated to include a new entry for the given student and the given computer.

The operation *Authorize* allows a student to use a computer. It must check whether the computer is already assigned to a student, because only those computers that are assigned can be authorized to use. Similarly, the operation must also check whether the student has been assigned a computer. If these two conditions are met, the set of computers used by this student should be updated to include the computer given as the parameter.

The purpose of the *DeAssign* operation is to remove the assignment of a computer from a student. Since this will remove the person who is in charge of the computer, all usage relationships to this computer must also be removed. Further, the student who was assigned to this computer must also be removed from all usage relationships because a student cannot use any computer if he/she does not have any computer assigned to him/her. The operation *DeAssign* accepts two input parameters—*student?* and *computer?*. The precondition must ensure that *computer?* is assigned to *student?* before this operation. The postcondition must (i) remove the entry corresponding to *student?* $\mapsto$ *computer?* from the function *assigned*; (ii) remove all entries corresponding to the use of this computer in *canUse*; and (iii) remove all entries corresponding to *student?* from *canUse*.

The operation *RemoveAuthorization* will be invoked to remove authorization of a student from using a computer. It accepts *student?* and *computer?* as inputs. The student must be using this computer before and hence there must be an entry *student?* $\mapsto$ *computer?* in *canUse*. It is also important to check that *computer?* is not assigned to *student?*. Otherwise, there will be no one to administer *computer?*. Further, de-assigning a computer will be taken care of by the *DeAssign* operation, and not by *RemoveAuthorization*. The postcondition for the *RemoveAuthorization* must assert that *computer?* is removed from the set of computers used by *student?*.

Object-Z specification

[*USERNAME, COMPUTER*]

The state of the class *Department* includes two relations, called *assigned* and *canUse* which, respectively, define the relationships from students to assigned computers and from students to the set of computers that they can use. For the above example, these two relations will be

$$assigned = \{(S1, C1), (S2, C3), (S3, C2)\}$$
$$canUse = \{(S1, \{C2, C1\}), (S2, \{C3, C1, C2\}), (S3, \{C2\})\}$$

Notice that $S4$ is not included in the relation *canUse*, because $S4$ cannot use any computer. It is possible to include the ordered pair (S4, { }) in the relation *canUse* but it will be a slightly different model.

Department

$students : \mathbb{P}USERNAME$
$computers : \mathbb{P}COMPUTER$
$assigned : USERNAME \nrightarrow COMPUTER$
$canUse : USERNAME \nrightarrow \mathbb{P}COMPUTER$

$\operatorname{dom} assigned \subseteq students$
$\operatorname{ran} assigned \subseteq computers$
$\operatorname{dom} canUse = \operatorname{dom} assigned$
$\bigcup(\operatorname{ran} canUse) = \operatorname{ran} assigned$
$\forall u_1, u_2 : \operatorname{dom} assigned \bullet u_1 \neq u_2 \Rightarrow assigned(u_1) \neq assigned(u_2)$
$\forall u : \operatorname{dom} assigned \bullet assigned(u) \in canUse(u)$

INIT
$students = \emptyset$
$computers = \emptyset$
$assigned = \emptyset$
$canUse = \emptyset$

AddStudent
$\Delta(students)$
$newStudent? : USERNAME$

$newStudent? \notin students$
$students' = students \cup \{newStudent?\}$

AddComputer
$\Delta(students)$
$newComputer? : COMPUTER$

$newComputer? \notin computers$
$computers' = computers \cup \{newComputer?\}$

Assign
$\Delta(assigned, canUse)$
$student? : USERNAME$
$computer? : COMPUTER$

$student? \in students$
$computer? \in computers$
$student? \notin \mathrm{dom}\, assigned$
$computer? \notin \mathrm{ran}\, assigned$
$assigned' = assigned \cup \{student? \mapsto computer?\}$
$canUse' = canUse \cup \{student? \mapsto \{computer?\}\}$

DeAssign
$\Delta(assigned, canUse)$
$student? : USERNAME$
$computer? : COMPUTER$

$(student? \mapsto computer?) \in assigned$
$assigned' = \{student?\} \mathbin{\lhd\mkern-9mu-} assigned$
$\forall s : \mathrm{dom}\, canUse \mid computer? \in canUse(s) \bullet$
$\quad canUse' = (canUse \oplus \{s \mapsto canUse(s) \setminus \{computer?\}\})$
$\quad\quad \cup (\{student?\} \mathbin{\lhd\mkern-9mu-} canUse)$

Authorize
$\Delta(canUse)$
$student? : USERNAME$
$computer? : COMPUTER$

$student? \in \text{dom}\,assigned$
$computer? \in \text{ran}\,assigned$
$computer? \notin canUse(student?)$
$canUse' = canUse \oplus \{student? \mapsto canUse(student?) \cup \{computer?\}\}$

RemoveAuthorization
$\Delta(canUse)$
$student? : USERNAME$
$computer? : COMPUTER$

$student? \in \text{dom}\,canUse$
$computer? \in canUse(student?)$
$student? \mapsto computer? \notin assigned$
$canUse' = canUse \oplus \{student? \mapsto canUse(student?) \setminus \{computer?\}\}$

□

Example 5 University Sports Management.

Problem Description

A computerized system maintains information about players and teams in several universities and games played between the universities. Each university has a set of players, considered to be the sportsmen of the university. The players for a team are selected from the set of players of the university. A university may have more than one team whose players are selected from the same pool, and so a player from a university may play for more than one team. The following rules must be obeyed by the universities and their teams:

- Each team is associated with exactly one university.
- Each player is associated with exactly one university.
- A university may have more than one team.
- The players for a team are chosen from the players of the same university.
- A player from a university may play for more than one team of the same university.
- No two teams from the same university play against each other.

The system must include operations (i) to add a new player to a team, (ii) to add a new player to the university, (iii) to add a new team to a university, (iv) to delete a player from a team, (v) to delete a player from the university, (vi) to delete a team from a university, (vii) to replace a player in a team, (viii) to add a game between two universities and (ix) to delete a game between two universities.

Assumptions

1. Since the problem is concerned with the relationships between teams, players and games, no personal information about players will be included.
2. A team will have a team name and a set of players. No additional information such as captain or team logo will be included in the specification.
3. Team names are assumed to be unique throughout the system.
4. University names are assumed to be unique.
5. For a game, only the two team names playing in the game will be maintained in the system. No additional information such as game timings or location will be included.

The Model

Based on the assumptions, it is appropriate to model the player, team name and university name as basic types. Like the computer access rights problem given in Example 4, this problem can be modeled in several ways. For example, the relationship between team and player can be modeled as a relation or as a function, and the relationship between team and university can be modeled in the same way. The specification below uses functions to model the relationships between the entities.

There will be two classes, *University* and *SportsManagementSystem*. Further, one could model a team as a separate class and then include it in the *University* class. However, the only information needed for a team is its name and the set of players in the team. This could be modeled as a relation within the *University* class, thus eliminating the need forone more class. If the problem is expanded to include additional information, such as the caption of the team, then it is appropriate to consider team as a separate class.

For the *University* class, the state space will include the name of the university, the set of players of the university, and the set of teams along with their players. As stated earlier, teams and their players can be modeled as a function from team names to a set of players. The state invariant must assert the players of all teams within the university must be coming from the pool of players belonging to the university. Initially, there is no player and no team in the university. The operations will be modeled next.

The operations *AddPlayerToUniversity*, *AddTeam*, *AddPlayerToTeam*, *DeletePlayer-FromTeam* and *DeleteTeam* in the *University* class are straightforward. The readers are urged to think of the specifications for these operations by themselves and then compare their solutions with the ones given in the specification below.

The operation *DeletePlayerFromUniversity* needs special attention because a player when deleted from a university must also be deleted from all the teams in which he/she participates.

The operation *ReplacePlayerFromTeam* can be defined as a composition of deleting a player from the team and adding a new player.

The class *SportsManagementSystem* maintains the information about games between the teams. Since teams are associated with the universities, the state space for this class consists of a set of universities and games. A game is modeled as a relation between two teams. Since team names are unique, and the information about a game only requires the team names, it is appropriate to model this relation between two team names. This also justifies why it is not necessary to model the team as a class. The state invariant for this class must assert the following:

1. The names of all universities are unique.
2. No player is associated with more than one university. Stated otherwise, the set of players of two different universities are mutually exclusive.
3. The team names are all unique. That is, no two teams, whether belonging to the same university or different universities, will have the same name.
4. For every game, the two teams playing the game must come from two different universities. This asserts the fact that two teams of the same university cannot play against each other.

There are only two operations in the *SportsManagementSystem* class—*AddGame* and *DeleteGame*. Deleting a game from the system is straightforward; it simply removes the entry from the relation *games*. To add a game, the precondition must ensure that the two teams must belong to two different universities.

Object-Z specification

$[PLAYER, TEAM\_NAME, UNIVERSITY\_NAME]$

University

$name : UNIVERSITY\_NAME$
$players : \mathbb{P}\,PLAYER$
$teams : TEAM\_NAME \nrightarrow \mathbb{P}\,PLAYER$

$\bigcup(\operatorname{ran} teams) \subseteq players$

INIT
$players = \emptyset$
$teams = \emptyset$

AddPlayerToUniversity
$\Delta(players)$
$newPlayer? : PLAYER$

$newPlayer? \notin players$
$players' = players \cup \{newPlayer?\}$

AddTeam
$\Delta(teams)$
$newTeamName : TEAM\_NAME$
$newTeamPlayers : \mathbb{P}\,PLAYER$

$newTeamName \notin \operatorname{dom} teams$
$newTeamPlayers \subseteq players$
$teams' = teams \cup \{newTeamName \mapsto newTeamPlayers\}$

┌─ *AddPlayerToTeam* ──────────────────────────────────────
│ $\Delta(teams)$
│ $newPlayer? : PLAYER$
│ $teamName? : TEAM\_NAME$
├──────────────────────
│ $teamName? \in \operatorname{dom} teams$
│ $newPlayer? \in players$
│ $newPlayer? \notin teams(teamName?)$
│ $teams' = teams \oplus \{teamName? \mapsto (teams(teamName?) \cup \{newPlayer?\})\}$
└──

┌─ *DeletePlayerFromTeam* ─────────────────────────────────
│ $\Delta(teams)$
│ $player? : PLAYER$
│ $teamName? : TEAM\_NAME$
├──────────────────────
│ $teamName? \in \operatorname{dom} teams$
│ $player? \in teams(teamName?)$
│ $teams' = teams \oplus \{teamName? \mapsto (teams(teamName?) \setminus \{player?\})\}$
└──

┌─ *DeletePlayerFromUniversity* ───────────────────────────
│ $\Delta(players, teams)$
│ $player? : PLAYER$
├──────────────────────
│ $player? \in players$
│ $players' = players \setminus \{player?\}$
│ $\forall teamName : TEAM\_NAME \mid$
│ $\quad teamName \in \operatorname{dom} teams \land player? \in teams(teamName) \bullet$
│ $\quad\quad teams' = teams \oplus \{teamName \mapsto$
│ $\quad\quad\quad (teams(teamName) \setminus \{player?\})\}$
└──

┌─ *DeleteTeam* ───
│ $\Delta(teams)$
│ $teamName? : TEAM\_NAME$
├──────────────────────
│ $teams' = \{teamName?\} \ntriangleleft teams$
└──

$ReplacePlayerFromTeam \mathrel{\widehat{=}} DeletePlayerFromTeam \mathbin{\overset{\circ}{\scriptscriptstyle 9}} AddPlayerToTeam$

```
┌─ SportsManagementSystem ─────────────────────────────────────────
│ ┌───────────────────────────────────────────────────────────────
│ │ universities : ℙUniversity
│ │ games : TEAM_NAME ↔ TEAM_NAME
│ ├───────────────────────────────────────────────────────────────
│ │ ∀ univ1, univ2 : universities •
│ │   (univ1.name = univ2.name ⇔ univ1 = univ2) ∧
│ │   (univ1 ≠ univ2 ⇒
│ │   (univ1.players ∩ univ2.players − ∅) ∧
│ │   ({tn : TEAM_NAME | tn ∈ dom univ1.teams} ∩
│ │   {tn : TEAM_NAME | tn ∈ dom univ2.teams} = ∅))
│ │ ∀ team1, team2 : TEAM_NAME | (team1, team2) ∈ games •
│ │   team1 ≠ team2 ∧
│ │   (∃ univ1, univ2 : University | univ1 ∈ universities ∧
│ │     univ2 ∈ universities ∧ univ1.name ≠ univ2.name •
│ │       team1 ∈ dom univ1.teams ∧ team2 ∈ dom univ2.teams)
│ └───────────────────────────────────────────────────────────────
```

```
┌─ INIT ────────────────────────────────────────────────────────────
│ universities ≠ ∅
│ games = ∅
└───────────────────────────────────────────────────────────────────
```

```
┌─ AddGame ─────────────────────────────────────────────────────────
│ Δ(games)
│ team1?, team2? : TEAM_NAME
├───────────────────────────────────────────────────────────────────
│ (∃ univ1, univ2 : University | univ1 ∈ universities ∧
│   univ2 ∈ universities ∧ univ1.name ≠ univ2.name •
│     team1? ∈ dom univ1.teams ∧ team2? ∈ dom univ2.teams)
│ games' = games ∪ {team1? ↦ team2?}
└───────────────────────────────────────────────────────────────────
```

```
┌─ DeleteGame ──────────────────────────────────────────────────────
│ Δ(games)
│ team1?, team2? : TEAM_NAME
├───────────────────────────────────────────────────────────────────
│ (team1?, team2?) ∈ games
│ games' = games \ {(team1?, team2?)}
└───────────────────────────────────────────────────────────────────
```

Comments

Replacing a player in a team is the same as deleting the player from the team and adding a new player. So, a sequential composition is used for this operation. Notice that there is no communication between *DeletePlayerFromTeam* and *AddPlayerToTeam*, but the sequence of executions is still defined by this operation. □

18.5
Case Study

In Chap. 16, the case study is given on a computer network. The focus of that problem is to model the nodes, the paths and network protocol. The case study in this chapter is on modeling an electronic mail system which focuses on client side mail operations such as sending, receiving, reading and forwarding mails, as well as network manager operations in distributing the mails. These two case studies are derived from the same application domain but each has a different focus and hence the modeling are different. Further, the specification for the case study in this chapter utilizes the composition operators in Object-Z.

Problem Description

An electronic mail system supports transactions of mails across a set of nodes. It is assumed that a network manager handles communication of mails between nodes. A node wishing to send a mail (hereafter referred to as *sender*) must compose the mail first and submit it to the network manager. The sender will get an acknowledgment from the network manager whether or not the mail has been accepted by the network manager, depending on the availability of space in the network manager's buffer to hold the mail. The network manager maintains two queues for holding mails—*regular queue*, which is used to hold the incoming mails, and *retry queue*, which is used to hold the mails that are not dispatched in the first attempt. The network manager concurrently dispatches mails from both the queues.

Receiving a mail at a node is different from reading the mail. While receiving a mail, the network manager attempts to put the mail in the incoming tray of the receiver. If the tray is not full, the receive operation will be successful; if the tray is full, then the network manager will place the mail in its *retry_queue* and attempt to dispatch the mail again at a later time. The network manager attempts at most two times to deliver a mail. In case the mail could not delivered within two attempts, the network manager sends a message to the sender and discards the mail.

When a node reads a mail, it moves the mail from its incoming tray to an internal mailbox. The mails in the internal mailbox are grouped based on sender identifications.

Assumptions

1. If a sender receives a notification from the network manager that a mail sent by the sender is not accepted, the sender can decide to send the mail again or to ignore the mail.
2. Each mail is addressed to only one recipient. Therefore, if a sender wants to send a mail to more than one recipient, the sender must send a separate mail to each recipient.
3. A node can send a new mail, reply to a mail or can forward a mail.
4. When a mail is forwarded by a node, it does not change the contents of the mail. Only the *to* address of the mail is changed.

5. When a node replies back to a mail, the contents of the mail must be changed. The *from* and *to* addresses of the incoming mail are switched in the outgoing mail.

The Model

This problem is quite complex in terms of the number of entities involved and the communication between them. For example, from the problem description, one could identify the entities *Mail*, *Node*, *Queue*, *Buffer* and *Network Manager*. Each of these entities has its own private data and operations to manipulate the data, thus qualifying for a class definition. This type of analysis is done in object-oriented design to identify the set of classes from the problem description.

The Object-Z Specification

The following basic types are introduced in the specification.

[*NODEID*, *CHAR*]

The following global types are used in the specification.

MailContent == seq *CHAR*
Acknowledgement ::= *Accepted* | *NotAccepted*
DeliveryMessage ::= *Delivered* | *TimeOut*
SpaceAvailability ::= *Full* | *NotFull*

The type *MailContent* is used to describe the contents of a mail as one string. Other global entities are enumerated types.

The class *Mail* contains three state variables. The variable *from* identifies the sender node, *to* identifies the receiver and *body* describes the contents of the mail. The two edit operations given in the class allow one to edit the *to* address of a mail and the *body* of the mail, respectively.

┌─ *Mail* ───
│ ┌───
│ │ *from* : *NODEID*
│ │ *to* : *NODEID*
│ │ *body* : *MailContent*
│ ├───
│ │ *body* ≠ ⟨ ⟩
│ └───
│ ┌─ *EditTo* ────────────────────────────────────
│ │ Δ(*to*)
│ ├───
│ │ *to'* ≠ *to*
│ └───
└──

$$\begin{array}{|l}
\underline{\quad EditBody} \underline{} \\
\Delta(body) \\
\hline
body' \neq body \\
\end{array}$$

The class *MailQueue* describes a queue of mails. From the problem description, there are at least three places where mails are queued in this example: the *intray* of a node, which holds the incoming mails, the *regular queue* in the network manager, which holds the mails submitted by nodes, and the *retry queue* in the network manager, which holds the mails that are not delivered in the first attempt. Each mail queue has its constant called *buffer_capacity*, which denotes the maximum size of the queue. There are three operations included in the *MailQueue* class:

AddMail This operation is to add a mail to the queue. It must ensure that there is enough space in the buffer of the queue.

ExtractMail This operation will be invoked to remove the first element in the queue and output the same.

IsFull This is a boolean operation that asserts whether or not the queue is full.

$$\begin{array}{|l}
\underline{\quad MailQueue} \underline{} \\
\quad buffer\_capacity : \mathbb{N}_1 \\
\hline
buffer : \text{iseq } Mail \\
\hline
\#buffer \leq buffer\_capacity \\
\hline
\underline{\quad INIT} \underline{} \\
buffer = \langle \, \rangle \\
\hline
\underline{\quad AddMail} \underline{} \\
\Delta(buffer) \\
new? : Mail \\
\hline
\#buffer < buffer\_capacity \\
buffer' = buffer ^\frown \langle new? \rangle \\
\hline
\underline{\quad ExtractMail} \underline{} \\
\Delta(buffer) \\
out! : Mail \\
\hline
\#buffer > 0 \\
buffer' = tail \; buffer \\
out! = head \; buffer \\
\end{array}$$

$\underline{\quad IsFull\quad}$
$result!$: $SpaceAvailability$

$\#buffer = buffer\_capacity \Rightarrow result! = Full$
$\#buffer \neq buffer\_capacity \Rightarrow result! = NotFull$

A node contains a unique identifier for the node, a mail queue called *intray* to store the incoming mails and an internal mailbox indicated as *mbox* in the class *Node*. The internal mailbox is defined as a function from sender identifiers to a set of mails. Each entry in this function shows the mails received from a particular sender. The state invariant of the class *Node* asserts the following:

- Every mail in *intray* of the current node has its *to* address corresponding to the node id of this node. In other words, every node n has only those mails addressed to n in its *intray*.
- If there is an entry for a node n in *mbox*, then there must be at least one mail received from n. In other words, no entry in *mbox* will have an empty set mapped to a node.
- Every mail in *mbox* has its *from* address corresponding to the entry in *mbox* and *to* address corresponding to the id of the current node.
- When a mail is read, it is moved from *intray* to *mbox*. Therefore, there is no duplicate copy of any mail held in *intray*. Consequently, the set of mails in *intray* and the set of mails in *mbox* are mutually exclusive.

Initially, both *intray* and *mbox* must be empty. The operations in the class *Node* are summarized below:

Send This operation is used when a node wants to send a mail. Typically, this operation lets the user compose a mail. The *from* address of the new mail must be the sender's id.

ReceiveACK This operation will be invoked when the node wants to receive acknowledgment from the network manager after sending a mail. Currently, this operation is specified with no predicates because the primary purpose of this operation is to receive the acknowledgment only.

ReceiveDeliveryMessage Similar to *ReceiveACK*, this operation will be invoked when a network manager sends a delivery message for a mail submitted by this node.

SendAndWait This is a composite operation defined as a sequential composition of *Send* and *ReceiveACK*.

Receive This operation will be invoked by the network manager to put the incoming mails into the *intray*. It is defined as a composite operation using environment enrichment operator. The unnamed operation on the left side of the • operator is used to declare the input variable *new*? which will be used by the *intray.AddMail* operation.

UpdateMailbox The *UpdateMailbox* operation is used to add a mail to *mbox*. It checks whether there is a mail already from the same sender in *mbox*. If so, it adds the new mail to the set of mails already received from this sender. Otherwise, a new entry will be created for this sender and the new mail is added to this entry.

Read The process of reading a mail is defined as moving a mail from *intray* to *mbox*.

Forward The *Forward* operation is supposed to be defined as a sequential composition of *Read*, followed by *EditTo* in the incoming mail which is then followed by *SendAndWait*. Conceptually, a forwarding operation reads the mail, enters the new destination in *to* field and then sends it to the new destination.

Reply When a node replies back to a message, the sender and receiver addresses are switched as indicated by the unnamed operation in the definition of *Reply*. The *Reply* operation itself is defined as a sequential composition of *Read*, followed by *EditBody* of the incoming mail and then followed by *SendAndWait*.

__*Node*_____

$nid : NODEID$
$intray : MailQueue$
$mbox : NODEID \nrightarrow \mathbb{P}\,Mail$

$\forall m : Mail \mid \langle m \rangle \text{ in } intray.buffer \bullet m.to = nid$
$\forall id : NODEID \mid id \in \text{dom}\,mbox \bullet$
   $(mbox(id) \neq \emptyset) \wedge$
   $(\forall m : Mail \mid m \in mbox(id) \bullet m.from = id \wedge nid = m.to) \wedge$
   $(mbox(id) \cap \text{ran}(intray.buffer) = \emptyset)$

___*INIT*_____
$intray.buffer = \emptyset$
$mbox = \emptyset$

___*Send*_____
$to? : NODEID$
$body? : MailContent$
$m! : Mail$

$m!.from = nid$
$m!.to = to?$
$m!.body = body?$

___*ReceiveACK*_____
$ack? : Acknowledgement$

___*ReceiveDeliveryMessage*_____
$message? : DeliveryMessage$

$SendAndWait \mathrel{\widehat{=}} Send \mathbin{\circ}^{\circ} ReceiveACK$
$Receive \mathrel{\widehat{=}} \left[\, new? : Mail \mid nid = new?.to \,\right] \bullet intray.AddMail$

```
┌─ UpdateMailbox ─────────────────────────────────────────
│ Δ(mbox)
│ m? : Mail
├─────────────────────────────────────────────────────────
│ (m?.from ∈ dom mbox ⇒
│    mbox' = mbox ⊕ {m?.from ↦ mbox(m?.from) ∪ {m?}})
│ (m?.from ∉ dom mbox ⇒
│    mbox' = mbox ⊕ {m?.from ↦ {m?}})
├─────────────────────────────────────────────────────────
│ Read ≙ intray.ExtractMail • UpdateMailbox[out!/m?]
│ Forward ≙ [m?, m! : Mail | m!.from = nid] •
│   (Read ⨾ m?.EditTo ⨾ SendAndWait)
│ Reply ≙ [m?, m! : Mail | m!.from = nid ∧ m!.to = m?.from] •
│   (Read ⨾ m?.EditBody ⨾ SendAndWait)
└─────────────────────────────────────────────────────────
```

Comments on the class Node

The operation *Read* is defined as sequential composition of the two operations *intray.ExtractMail* and it UpdateMailbox. Notice that the output variable *out!* of *intray.ExtractMail* is substituted for the input variable *m?* of *UpdateMailbox*.

The unnamed operation in *Forward* before the sequential composition declares the input and output variables and ensures that the sender of the new mail is the current node.

The *NetworkManager* class is given next. It consists of a set of nodes and two mail queues—the *regular_queue* that holds all mails submitted by other nodes, and the *retry_queue* that holds the mails that were not delivered in the first attempt. The state invariant of this class asserts that no mail is duplicated between the two queues, and every mail stored in the two queues is sent by a node known to the network manager and is also addressed to one of the nodes known to the manager. Initially, the two queues in the network manager are empty. All the operations of the network manager are defined as composite operations.

```
┌─ NetworkManager ────────────────────────────────────────
│
│  nodes : ℙNODEID
│  regular_queue : MailQueue
│  retry_queue : MailQueue
│ ────────────────────────────────────────────────────────
│  ran(regular_queue.buffer) ∩ ran(retry_queue.buffer) = ∅
│  ∀ m : Mail | m ∈ ran(regular_queue.buffer) ∪ ran(retry_queue.buffer) •
│    m.from ∈ nodes ∧ m.to ∈ nodes
│
└─────────────────────────────────────────────────────────
```

$\boxed{\begin{array}{l} \_INIT _____ \\ \quad regular\_queue.INIT \\ \quad retry\_queue.INIT \end{array}}$

$AcceptMail \,\widehat{=}$
  $[\,ack! : Acknowledgement;\; result! : SpaceAvailability;\; m! : Mail;$
    $sender : Node \mid sender.nid \in nodes\,]\;\bullet$
  $(\,(sender.SendAndWait \parallel$
    $(regular\_queue.IsFull \bullet [\,result! = NotFull \land ack! = Accepted\,])$
  $)\,\raisebox{0.2ex}{\scriptsize$\,\substack{\circ \\ \circ}$}$
  $regular\_queue.AddMail[m!/new?]$
  $)$

$RefuseMail \,\widehat{=}$
  $[\,ack! : Acknowledgement;\; result! : SpaceAvailability;\; m! : Mail;$
    $sender : Node \mid sender.nid \in nodes\,]\;\bullet$
  $(sender.SendAndWait \parallel$
    $(regular\_queue.IsFull \bullet [\,result! = Full \land ack! = NotAccepted\,])$
  $)$

$Receive \,\widehat{=}\, AcceptMail \parallel RefuseMail$

$Regular\_dispatch\_successful \,\widehat{=}$
  $[\,receiver : Node;\; out! : Mail;\; result! : SpaceAvailability;$
    $delivery! : DeliveryMessage;\; tray : MailQueue;\; sender : Node\mid$
    $receiver.nid \in nodes \land out!.to = receiver.nid \,\land$
    $tray = receiver.intray \land out!.from = sender.nid\,]\;\bullet$
  $(\,((regular\_queue.ExtractMail \land tray.IsFull) \bullet [\,result! = NotFull\,]$
  $)\,\raisebox{0.2ex}{\scriptsize$\,\substack{\circ \\ \circ}$}$
  $((receiver.Receive[out!/new?] \land [\,delivery! = Delivered\,])$
  $\raisebox{0.2ex}{\scriptsize$\,\substack{\circ \\ \circ}$}\; sender.ReceiveDeliveryMessage$
  $)$
  $)$

$Retry\_dispatch\_successful \,\widehat{=}$
  $[\,receiver : Node;\; out! : Mail;\; result! : SpaceAvailability;$
    $delivery! : DeliveryMessage;\; tray : MailQueue;\; sender : Node\mid$
    $receiver.nid \in nodes \land out!.to = receiver.nid \,\land$
    $tray = receiver.intray \land out!.from = sender.nid\,]\;\bullet$
  $(\,((retry\_queue.ExtractMail \land tray.IsFull) \bullet [\,result! = NotFull\,]$
  $)\,\raisebox{0.2ex}{\scriptsize$\,\substack{\circ \\ \circ}$}$
  $((receiver.Receive[out!/new?] \land [\,delivery! = Delivered\,])$
  $\raisebox{0.2ex}{\scriptsize$\,\substack{\circ \\ \circ}$}\; sender.ReceiveDeliveryMessage$
  $)$
  $)$

$Regular\_dispatch\_fail \,\widehat{=}$
$[\,receiver : Node;\; out! : Mail;\; result! : SpaceAvailability;\; tray : MailQueue\,|$
  $receiver.nid \in nodes \wedge out!.to = receiver.nid \wedge tray = receiver.intray\,] \; \bullet$
  $(\,(\,(regular\_queue.ExtractMail \wedge tray.IsFull) \bullet [\,result! = Full\,]$
  $)\, _9^o$
  $retry\_queue.AddMail[out!/new?]$
  $)$

$Retry\_dispatch\_fail \,\widehat{=}$
$[\,receiver : Node;\; out! : Mail;\; result! : SpaceAvailability;$
  $delivery! : DeliveryMessage;\; tray : MailQueue;\; sender : Node\,|$
  $receiver.nid \in nodes \wedge out!.to = receiver.nid \wedge$
  $tray = receiver.intray \wedge out!.from = sender.nid\,] \; \bullet$
  $(\,(\,(retry\_queue.ExtractMail \wedge tray.IsFull) \bullet [\,result! = Full \wedge delivery! =$
  $TimeOut\,]$
  $)\, _9^o$
  $sender.ReceiveDeliveryMessage$
  $)$

The explanation for one of the composite operations is given below:

AcceptMail The *AcceptMail* operation defines the constraints that must be true when a submitted mail is accepted by the network manager. For the purpose of explanation, the *AcceptMail* operation can be viewed as

$$AcceptMail \,\widehat{=} Op_1 \bullet ((Op_2 \parallel (Op_3 \bullet Op_4))\, _9^o\, Op_5)$$

Op_1 is an unnamed operation that introduces the input and output parameters, and other variables that are used by the other components. These variables are accessed by the other component operations through the environment enrichment operator. Op_2 refers the sender's action of submitting the mail to the network manager. Op_3 corresponds to checking whether the regular queue in the network manager is full. Since *AcceptMail* describes only the success scenario, Op_3 is expected to return the value asserting that the regular queue is not full. This is indicated by the unnamed operation Op_4, which also indicates that the acknowledgment to be sent to the sender must say "Accepted". Following the checking, the submitted mail is added to the regular queue of the network manager which is described by Op_5.

Other operations in the class *NetworkManager* can be interpreted in a similar way.

18.6
Exercises

1. In Example 1, all employees are modeled into one set. Modify this example so that the state space now contains two divisions of employees—Managers and Developers. The

salary for each manager must be greater than the salary of every developer. No employee will be in both divisions; i.e., the set of developers and the set of managers are mutually exclusive. Modify the operations with these changes in the state space. Include one more operation by which an employee is promoted to a manager and his/her salary is increased.

2. The Example 4 uses functions from students to computers to model the relationships.

   (a) Model the relationships using functions from computers to students.

   (b) Model the relationships using relations from computers to students.

   (c) Model the relationships using relations from students to computers.

   In all the three cases, you may need to rewrite the whole specification.

3. Modify the class *Transcript* given in Example 3 to add an operation that overwrites a mark for a given course already entered in the transcript.

4. Modify the class *Transcript* given in Example 3 to add an operation which allows more than one mark for a course to be entered. This situation corresponds to taking the course more than once in order to get a better mark. However, when the average is calculated, it should take only the highest mark for any course.

5. Modify the university sports management system example to include the following:

   • Every team has a captain who is one of the players of the team. A captain cannot play for more than one team. This is because a captain has more responsibilities and cannot afford for spending time for more than one team.

   • The university maintains a list of players who qualify to serve as captains. Therefore, the captain of a team must be selected only from this list.

6. Model a double-sided generic queue. It should be possible to add items into this queue and delete items from the queue on both sides. Show how to use this queue for modeling a queue in a bank. The regular customers will join the queue at the back while privileged customers join the queue at the front. When the queue is served, it always removes the customer from the front of the queue. However, if the last person in the queue leaves, it should be possible to remove the person from the tail end of the queue.

7. This problem is an expanded version of the crafts store example already used in this chapter. A crafts store sells several items. Some of these items can be painted or re-painted at the store for an extra cost. Customers who want an item to be painted must first pay for the item. An item requested for painting will be sent to the paint shop. After painting, it is delivered back to the store. It is then packed and the customer will pick it up from the store. If a customer buys an item without painting, the item is packed after payment and given to the customer. Model the crafts store mentioned above. Use as many composition operators as possible. You may also consider the paint shop as a separate entity rather than part of the store. This will change the model considerably.

8. A car dealer sells several types of vehicles. Each vehicle has a Vehicle Identification Number (VIN), 'make' (Toyota, Honda, Ford etc.), 'model' under each 'make' (Carolla and Camery under Toyota, Civic and Pilot under Honda and so on), price and a set of features of the vehicle. Write Object-Z specification for this car dealer shop using inheritance. You can use the 'models' as subclasses under the superclass corresponding to the 'make'. For example, there is a superclass for Toyota vehicle and every 'model'

of Toyota can be defined as a subclass. Include operations to add new vehicles, to sell vehicles, to change features and report sales for a given 'make' or 'model'.

9. (project) An electronic repair shop accepts electronic items for repair. Each item may require some repair work to be done and/or some parts to be replaced. If parts need to be replaced, the shop takes the parts from its storage. Obviously, the store needs to maintain a parts storage. If the parts are not available in the storage, the shop orders them from a warehouse. Assume that the warehouse has sufficient parts for all electronic items. Model this electronic repair shop. You may want to consider each entity such as the shop, storage, warehouse, and electronic item as a separate class. Include relevant operations for each entity.

18.7
Bibliographic Notes

Object-Z was developed by Graeme Smith [34] at the Software Verification Research Center (SVRC) associated with the University of Queensland, Australia. A detailed description of the language can be found in [10, 38]. Smith described the formal semantics of the language in [35] which was later extended by Griffiths [13]. Griffiths worked further on the semantics of recursive operation definitions [14], which was later refined by Smith [39].

Since its inception, Object-Z has been extensively used for many applications. Most of them were research projects supported by SVRC. Interested readers can find a good collection of technical reports and publications at SVRC as well as from Smith's web site http://www.itee.uq.edu.au/~smith/publications.html. Some of these applications include multi-agent systems [16], mobile systems [41, 49], user interface design [17, 18], specification of concurrent systems [44], and specification-based testing [3, 30].

Recently, Object-Z has been combined with CSP for developing the specification of concurrent systems [8, 43]. Taguchi and others [50] have reported the close relationships between Pi-Calculus and Object-Z, though there was no integration between the two methods. Some researchers have used UML with Object-Z [2]. Notable among these is using the use case diagrams as the front end for Object-Z [27]. Kim and Carrington explained the mapping between UML models and Object-Z [21]. Roe and others have extended this approach to include OCL [33].

There are quite a few type checkers available for Object-Z. Wendy Johnson developed the *Wizard* tool at SVRC. It is a LaTeX-based tool and is freely available. *Wizard* is available at http://www.itee.uq.edu.au/~smith/tools.html and its associated documentation can be found in [19]. *ZML* is another type checker for Object-Z that is freely available. This tool is XML-based and was developed at National University of Singapore. In fact, *ZML* handles three specification languages, Z, Object-Z and TCOZ, a temporal extension of Object-Z. This tool and its associated documentation can also be found at http://www.itee.uq.edu.au/~smith/tools.html. A GUI-based editor and type checker for Object-Z called *TOZE* was developed by Tim Parker at the University of Wisconsin-La Crosse [29]. This tool was developed in Java and is easily portable to any platform. Moreover, this tool is also freely available. The CSP-Object-Z formal specifications can be type checked by *FDR* tool developed at Oxford University, London. In addition to type check-ers, there are some animation tools also available for Object-Z. These include the XML-based tool by Sun and others [9, 47] and *CZT* [24]. *CZT* is a collection of Z-based tools that include type checking and animation tools.

Refinement of Object-Z specifications mostly follow the same approach as that of Z specifications, despite the semantic differences between the two languages. Derrick and Boiten discussed this common approach these two languages in [7]. Smith discussed rea-soning about Object-Z specifications and formal verification using Object-Z specifications in [36, 37]. More recently, the refinement of the combined specifications and their usage in modeling of concurrent systems have been described in [8, 42].

Though there are specific languages for the specification of temporal and real-time sys-tems, the real-time extension of Object-Z seems to be appealing. This is because Object-Z can be used to develop the static model of the application and then temporal constraints can be embedded onto the model. An overview of real-time extensions of Object-Z is given in [45]. *Timed Communication in Object-Z (TCOZ)* is a temporal extension of Object-Z re-ported in [23, 32]. The *Real-Time Object-Z (RTOZ)* is a real-time extension of Object-Z reported in [1, 31]. *RTOZ* uses a layered approach in which the static model lies at the bottom and the real-time model is placed over the static model. Both models use the same class structure.

References

1. Alagar VS, Periyasamy K (1996) Real-time Object-Z: a language for the specification and design of real-time reactive system. Technical report, Department of Computer Science, Con-cordia University
2. Amálio N, Polack F (2003) Comparison of formalisation approaches of UML class constructs in Z and Object-Z. In: International conference of Z and B users (ZB 2003). Lecture notes in computer science, vol 2561. Springer, Berlin
3. Carrington D, MacColl I, McDonald J, Murray L, Strooper P (2000) From Object-Z specifi-cations to ClassBench test suites. Softw Test Verif Reliab 10(2):111–137
4. Cornelio M, Borba P (2000) Structuring mechanisms for an object-oriented formal specifica-tion language. In: Software reuse: advances in software reusability. Lecture notes in computer science series, vol 1844. Springer, Berlin, pp 47–102
5. Cordeiro VAO, Sampaio A, Meira SL (1994) From MooZ to Eiffel—a rigorous approach to system development. In: FME'94: industrial benefits of formal methods. Lecture notes in computer science, vol 873, pp 306–325
6. Derrick J (2003) Timed CSP and Object-Z. In: International conference of Z and B users (ZB 2003). Lecture notes in computer science, vol 2561. Springer, Berlin
7. Derrick J, Boiten E (2001) Refinement in Z and Object-Z, foundations and advanced applica-tions. Springer, Berlin
8. Derrick J, Smith G (2003) Structural refinement of systems specified in Object-Z and CSP. Formal Aspects Comput 15(1):1–27
9. Dong JS, Li YF, Sun J, Sun J, Wong H (2002) XML-based static type checking and dynamic visualisation for TCOZ. In: International conference on formal engineering methods (ICFEM 2002). Lecture notes in computer science, vol 2495. Springer, Berlin
10. Duke R, Rose G (2000) Formal object-oriented specification using Object-Z. MacMillan, New York

11. Fukagawa M, Hikita T, Yamazaki H (1994) A mapping system from Object-Z to C++. In: 1st Asia-Pacific software engineering conference (APSEC94). IEEE Computer Society, Los Alamitos
12. Griffiths A (1995) From Object-Z to Eiffel: a rigorous development method. In: Technology of object-oriented languages and systems: TOOLS 18. Prentice Hall, New York
13. Griffiths A (1996) An extended semantic foundation for Object-Z. In: Asia-Pacific software engineering conference (APSEC'96). IEEE Computer Society, Los Alamitos
14. Griffiths A (1997) A semantics for recursive operations in Object-Z. In: Formal methods Pacific (FMP'97). Springer, Berlin
15. Gruer P, Hilaire V, Koukam A (2004) Heterogeneous formal specification based on Object-Z and state charts: semantics and verification. J Syst Softw 70(1–2):95–105
16. Hilaire V, Simonin O, Koukam A, Ferber J (2004) A formal approach to design and reuse agent and multiagent models. In: Agent oriented software engineering (AOSE 04). Lecture notes in computer science
17. Hussey A (1999) Formal object-oriented user-interface design. Technical report 99-09, Software Verification Research Center, University of Queensland, Australia
18. Hussey A, Carrington D (1998) An empirical study of formal user-interface design. HCI Lett 1(1):19–24
19. Johnston W (1996) A type checker for Object-Z. SVRC technical report No 96–24
20. Kassel G, Smith G (2001) Model checking Object-Z classes: some experiments with FDR. In: Asia-Pacific software engineering conference (APSEC). IEEE Press, New York
21. Kim S-K, Carrington D (2002) A formal metamodeling approach to transformation between the UML state machine and Object-Z. In: International conference on formal engineering methods (ICFEM 2002). Lecture notes in computer science, vol 2495. Springer, Berlin
22. Lano K, Haughton H (eds) (1994) Object oriented specification case studies. Prentice Hall, New York
23. Mahony B, Dong JS (2000) Timed communicating Object Z. IEEE Trans Softw Eng 26(2):150–177
24. Malik P, Utting M (2005) CZT: a framework for Z tools. In: Lecture notes in computer science, vol 3455, pp 65–84
25. McComb T, Smith G (2003) Animation of Object-Z specifications using a Z animator. In: International conference on software engineering and formal methods (SEFM). IEEE Computer Society, Los Alamitos
26. Miao H, Lui L, Li L (2002) Formalizing UML models with Object-Z. In: International conference on formal engineering methods (ICFEM 2002). Lecture notes in computer science, vol 2495. Springer, Berlin
27. Moreira A, Arau'jo J (2000) Generating Object Z specifications from use cases. In: Filipe J (ed) Enterprise information systems. Kluwer Academic, Norwell, pp 43–51. ISBN 0-7923-6239-X
28. Moller M, Olderog E-R, Rasch H, Wehrheim H (2004) Linking CSP-OZ with UML and Java: a case study. In: International conference on integrated formal methods (IFM 2004). Lecture notes in computer science, vol 2999. Springer, Berlin
29. Parker T (2008) TOZE: a graphical editor and type checker for Object-Z. Masters thesis, Department of Computer Science, University of Wisconsin-La Crosse
30. Periyasamy K, Alagar VS, Subramanian S (1998) Deriving test cases from Object-Z specifications. In: TOOLS USA'98 (technology of object-oriented languages and systems). IEEE Computer Society, Los Alamitos
31. Periyasamy K, Alagar VS (1998) Extending Obejct-Z for specifying real-time systems. In: TOOLS USA'97: technology of object-oriented languages and systems. IEEE Computer Society, Los Alamitos
32. Qin SC, Dong JS, Chin WN (2003) A semantic foundation of TCOZ in unifying theory of programming. In: International FME symposium (FM'03). Lecture notes in computer science. Springer, Berlin

33. Roe D, Broda K, Russo A (2003) Mapping UML models incorporating OCL constraints into Object-Z. Technical report 2003/9, Imperial College, London
34. Smith G (1992) An object-oriented approach to formal specification. PhD thesis, University of Queensland
35. Smith G (1995) A fully abstract semantics of classes for Object-Z. Formal Aspects Comput 7(3):289–313
36. Smith G (1995) Reasoning about Object-Z specifications. In: Asia-Pacific software engineering conference (APSEC '95). IEEE Computer Society, Los Alamitos
37. Smith G (1995) Formal verification of Object-Z specifications. SVRC Technical report 95-55
38. Smith G (2000) The Object-Z specification language. Kluwer Academic, Norwell
39. Smith G (2000) Recursive schema definitions in Object-Z. In: ZB2000: international conference of B and Z users. Lecture notes in computer science, vol 1878. Springer, Berlin
40. Smith G (2002) An integration of real-time Object-Z and CSP for specifying concurrent real-time systems. In: International conference on integrated formal methods (IFM 2002). Lecture notes in computer science, vol 2335. Springer, Berlin
41. Smith G (2004) A formal framework for modelling and analysing mobile systems. In: Australasian computer science conference (ACSC). Australian Computer Society, Sydney
42. Smith G, Derrick J (2001) Specification, refinement and verification of concurrent systems—an integration of Object-Z and CSP. Form Methods Syst Des 18(3):249–284
43. Smith G, Derrick J (2002) Abstract specification in Object-Z and CSP. In: International conference on formal engineering methods (ICFEM 2002). Lecture notes in computer science, vol 2495. Springer, Berlin
44. Smith G, Duke R (1992) Specifying concurrent systems using Object-Z. In: 15th Australian computer science conference (ACSC-15)
45. Smith G, Hayes I (2002) An introduction to real-time Object-Z. Form Aspects Comput 13(2):128–141
46. Stepney S, Barden R, Cooper D (eds) (1992) In: Object orientation in Z. Springer, Berlin
47. Sun J, Dong JS, Liu J, Wang H (2001) An XML/XSL approach to visualize and animate TCOZ. In: 8th Asia-Pacific software engineering conference (APSEC'01). IEEE Press, New York
48. Taylor C, Derrick J, Boiten E (2000) A case study in partial specification: consistency and refinement for Object-Z. In: International conference on formal engineering methods (ICFEM). IEEE Computer Society, Los Alamitos
49. Taguchi K, Dong JS (2002) An overview of mobile Object-Z. In: International conference on formal engineering methods (ICFEM 2002). Lecture notes in computer science, vol 2495. Springer, Berlin
50. Taguchi K, Dong JS, Ciobanu G (2004) Relating Pi-calculus to Object-Z. In: IEEE international conference on engineering complex computer systems (ICECCS'04). IEEE Press, New York

The B-Method

19

Formal software development requires specifications that are both abstract and concrete, and in addition a mechanism to refine abstract specifications to concrete specifications. The B-Method is purposively designed to accomplish the goal of specification and refinement together along with proof obligations. Introduced by Jean-Raymond Abrial in the early 1990s, the B-Method includes the B language, refinement methods and proof methods to verify the satisfaction of refinements. This chapter provides a sound tutorial of the B-Method and includes several examples at varying levels of complexity. The specifications given in this chapter have been type checked using the **Atelier-B**-tool. As a result of using this tool, some of the symbols that were quite frequently used in previous chapters may look different in this chapter. For example, in this chapter, $\mathcal{P}$ denotes the power set, $\mathcal{N}$ denotes the natural numbers, $\mathcal{N}_1$ denotes the positive numbers, and $\mathcal{Z}$ denotes the integers.

19.1
Abstract Machine Notation (AMN)

The B-Method uses Abstract Machine Notation (AMN), which is a wide-spectrum language that supports both abstract specification and its refinement. This makes it easier for a specifier to start with an abstract specification, refine it toward an implementation and generate code from a fairly detailed level of specification. The proof obligations discharged at each level guarantees the correctness of the refinement at that level and hence the final implementation [1, 20]. The specification is given as a collection of abstract machines. Each machine includes encapsulated data and operations, and invariants. Like other model-based specification languages such as VDM and Z, the B-Method is also based on set theory and first-order predicate logic.

V.S. Alagar, K. Periyasamy, *Specification of Software Systems,*
Texts in Computer Science,
DOI 10.1007/978-0-85729-277-3_19, © Springer-Verlag London Limited 2011

19.1.1
Structure of a B Specification

A template of a B specification is given below.

> **MACHINE** *MName(p)*
> **CONSTRAINTS** *C*
> **SETS** *S*
> **CONSTANTS** *K*
> **PROPERTIES** *B*
> **DEFINITIONS** *M*
> **VARIABLES** *V*
> **INVARIANT** *I*
> **INITIALIZATION** *T*
> **OPERATIONS**
> $\quad$ *y* ← *operation(x)* =
> $\qquad$ **PRE** *pre*
> $\qquad$ **THEN** *stat*
> $\qquad$ **END**;
> $\quad$ . . .
> **END**

The clauses in uppercase bold letters such as **MACHINE** and **CONSTRAINTS** are keywords in the notation. Most of these keywords are self-explanatory in terms of the purposes they serve.

MACHINE and **CONSTRAINTS** clauses

Each abstract machine comes with a unique name (in the above template, *MName*). A machine may be parametrized; in this case, the parameters of the machine are supplied with the machine name. The machine name *MName* has a parameter *p*. A machine may have any number of parameters but their relative ordering is not important. There are two types of parameters—scalar valued parameters and set valued parameters. A scalar valued parameter must be instantiated with a scalar value during implementation of the machine. A set valued parameter must be instantiated with a nonempty set. The parameters of a machine may be subject to some constraints which are provided in the **CONSTRAINTS** clause after the machine name.

SETS, **CONSTANTS** and **PROPERTIES** clauses

Every specification starts at an abstract level. Some types are assumed to be defined at that level. Z and Object-Z languages call these *Basic Types*. The equivalent of basic types in B is the **SETS** clause. Being sets, this also confirms that types and sets are treated equally within the B-Method. Constants used within the machine are defined in the **CONSTANTS** clause. Any constraints and relationships between the sets, constants and machine parameters are introduced in the **PROPERTIES** clause.

DEFINITIONS clause

Sometimes it will be useful to rename some of the complex structures into a simple name. The **DEFINITIONS** clause will be used in this case. All definitions given in this clause will be textually expanded just like macro substitutions.

VARIABLES, INVARIANT and **INITIALIZATION** clauses

The **VARIABLES** clause introduces the state variables of the machine. The invariant of the machine is specified under the heading **INVARIANT** which also establishes the relationships between state variables, constants, sets and parameters. Generally, the invariant of the machine describes the static properties of the machine that should be preserved at any time and is expressed using the state variables in relation with the constants, sets and parameters. The **INVARIANTS** clause must include the type for each state variable.

An initial state of the machine is described by assigning an initial value for each variable based on its type. These initial assignments are given in the **INITIALIZATION** clause.

OPERATIONS clause

The dynamic behavior of the machine is described by a set of operations, each of which is given under the heading **OPERATIONS**. The signature of each operation is given in functional style with its output parameter name, followed by the left arrow, and the name of the operation together with the names of the input parameters. The set of input parameters and the output parameter are both optional, but the name of the operation is mandatory.

Each operation consists of a precondition given under the heading **PRE**, and a body stated after the **THEN** clause. Precondition of an operation includes the types for the parameters. The body of an operation is described by a set of statements (also called *generalized substitutions*) that either set values to output variables or change some state variables or both. The set of statements include assignment statements, conditional statements using **IF ... THEN ... ELSE** clauses, and **CASE** selections. The syntax for these statements is similar to that found in many imperative programming languages.

Assignment statements in the body of an operation are sometimes referred to as *substitutions*. Since, in a formal specification, sequencing of actions will not be specified, the statements of an operation are always specified as parallel statements. An example for parallel statements is given below:

$$x := x + 1 \quad \| \quad z := result$$

The B-Method provides a facility by which multiple assignments can be specified in a single statement, such as

$$a, b := x, y$$

The number of variables on the left side of the assignment must be equal to the number of expressions on the right side. Hence, the ordering of variables and their corresponding expressions is implicit. The variables on the left side must be all distinct.

The end of an operation is signified by the keyword **END**. Operation definitions are separated by semicolons. The entire specification ends with another keyword **END**.

Table 19.1 Visibility Rules within an Abstract Machine. ©Abrial, 1996

	CONSTRAINTS	PROPERTIES	INVARIANT	OPERATIONS
Machine parameters	√		√	√
SETS		√	√	√
CONSTANTS		√	√	√
VARIABLES			√	√

Visibility Rules

Table 19.1 shows the visibility rules for various entities within an abstract machine. The symbol √ in the ith row and jth column of the table indicates that the object in row i is accessible to the object in column j.

Notice that the visibility rules given in Table 19.1 excludes the **DEFINITIONS** clause because the definitions are textually substituted in the rest of the specification before the specification is type checked. The definitions, therefore, do not have any impact on the rest of the specification by themselves.

The B-Method includes some additional clauses such as **INCLUDES**, **SEES** and **USES** which will be discussed later in this chapter.

Though each clause is written on a separate line, formatting of the specification is completely left with the specifier and tool support. In this chapter, the specifications are written in the same style as in [20].

To understand the AMN structure of a B specification, consider Example 1, which describes a student council. It consists of a set of students, one of whom is elected as the president of the council. It includes three operations—to add a new student to the council, to delete an existing student from the council and to change the president of the council.

Example 1 The *StudentCouncil* machine.

> **MACHINE**
>   *StudentCouncil (limit)*
> **CONSTRAINTS**
>   *limit* $\in \mathcal{N}_1$
> **SETS**
>   *STUDENT*
> **VARIABLES**
>   *council, president*
> **INVARIANT**
>   *council* $\in \mathcal{P}$ *(STUDENT)* $\wedge$ **card**(*council*) $\leq$ *limit* $\wedge$
>   *president* $\in$ *STUDENT* $\wedge$
>   (*council* $\neq \emptyset \Rightarrow$ *president* $\in$ *council*)
> **INITIALIZATION**
>   *council* $:= \emptyset \parallel$
>   *president* $:\in$ *STUDENT*
> **OPERATIONS**

AddStudent(*nn*) =
  PRE
    nn ∈ *STUDENT* ∧ *nn* ∉ *council* ∧ **card**(*council*) < *limit*
  THEN
    IF *council* = ∅ **THEN**
      president := *nn*
    END ‖
    council := *council* ∪ {*nn*}
  END;

DeleteStudent(*nn*) =
  PRE
    nn ∈ *STUDENT* ∧ *nn* ∈ *council* ∧ *nn* ≠ *president*
  THEN
    council := *council* - {*nn*}
  END;

ChangePresident(*nn*) =
  PRE
    nn ∈ *STUDENT* ∧ *nn* ∈ *council*
  THEN
    president := *nn*
  END
END

The *StudentCounil* machine is declared with a parameter *limit* which is a positive number (see the **CONSTRAINTS** clause). The parameter *limit* in this case indicates the maximum size of the student council. The type *STUDENT* denotes the set of all students used in this specification. There are two state variables for this specification, namely *council* and *president*, which are listed under **VARIABLES**. The **INVARIANT** clause starts with the type declarations of the state variables; the variable *council* is declared as a set of *STUDENT* while the variable *president* is declared of type *STUDENT*. In addition to these two type declarations, the state invariant also asserts that (i) the number of students in the council must be less than or equal to *limit*, and (ii) the president must be a member of the council whenever the council is nonempty. The **INITIALIZATION** clause indicates that the council is initially empty. It also shows that the value for *president* is set to some value of type *STUDENT*. The operator :∈ denotes a nondeterministic choice from the set *STUDENT*. Nondeterministic operators will be discussed in detail in a later section.

The specification includes three operations. The **AddStudent** operation accepts a student as a parameter. The precondition of this operation ensures that the student is not in the council already (otherwise, there is no need to add the student again). If the precondition is satisfied, the council is updated to include the student. If the council is empty before this operation, then this student will be the only member of the council and hence will automatically become the president of the council. The **DeleteStudent** operation removes a student from the council if the student is already a member of the council. The

Table 19.2   Arithmetic and Set Notations in B-Method

Arithmetic notations		Set notations	
Symbol	Meaning	Symbol	Meaning
$\mathcal{N}$	Natural numbers	$S \cup T$	Set union
$\mathcal{N}_1$	Positive numbers	$S \cap T$	Set intersection
$m..n$	Range of numbers from m to $n, m \leq n$	$S - T$	Set difference
max(S)	Maximum of a set of numbers	$e \in S$	Set membership
min(S)	Minimum of a set of numbers	$S \subseteq T$	Subset
m div n	Integer division	$S \subset T$	Proper subset
m mod n	m modulo n	$\mathcal{P} S$	Power set of S
$\sum x . (P \mid E)$	Summation of all E(x) for which P(x) holds	$\{ \}, \emptyset$	Empty set
		$\bigcup X$	Generalized union of the set of sets X
$\Pi x . (P \mid E)$	Product of all E(x) for which P(x) holds	$\bigcap X$	Generalized intersection of the set of sets X
		card(S)	Cardinality of the set S

operation **ChangePresident** changes the president of the council to a person input to the operation. The precondition here ensures that the new president is a student and is a member of the council. If the precondition is satisfied, the state variable *president* is set to this new student.   □

19.2
Notations

Being a model-based specification method, the B-Method shares a majority of symbols with other model-based specification languages such as VDM-SL and Z. Tables 19.2 and 19.3 display the symbols and their meanings used by the B-Method.

The summation and product notations are new in the B-Method. These two notations are used in assignment statements in operations.

The notation perm(S) denotes a bijective sequence of type S and is also called the set of permutations of S.

19.2.1
Arrays

Arrays are formally modeled through functions and sequences in many specification languages. The B-Method provides additional syntax for arrays. In B, functions and sequences

Table 19.3 Sequence and Relation Notations in B-Method

Sequence notations		Relation notations	
Symbol	Meaning	Symbol	Meaning
[ ]	Empty sequence	$x \mapsto y$	x maps to y
seq(S)	Sequence of type S	dom(R)	Domain of relation R
seq_1(S)	Nonempty sequence of type S	ran(R)	Range of relation R
iseq(S)	Injective sequence of type S	$U \lhd R$	Domain restriction
perm(S)	Bijective sequence of type S	$U \ntriangleleft R$	Domain subtraction
$s_1 \frown s_2$	Sequence concatenation	$R \rhd U$	Range restriction
size(s)	Cardinality of the sequence s	$R \ntriangleright U$	Range subtraction
rev(s)	Reverse of the sequence s	$S \times T$	Cartesian product
first(s)	First element of sequence s	R[U]	Relational image of the set U
last(s)	Last element of sequence s	R^{-1}	Relational inverse
tail(s)	Sequence s with first element removed	$R0 \mathbin{;} R1$	Relational composition
front(s)	Sequence s with last element removed	$R0 \ntriangleleft R1$	Relational override
$e \rightarrow s$	Prefix sequence s with sequence e	id(S)	Identity relation on S
$s \leftarrow e$	Append sequence e to sequence s	R^n	nth iteration of relation R
$s \uparrow n$	Truncate sequence s after n elements	R^*	Transitive closure of relation R
$s \downarrow n$	Remove first n elements of sequence s		

Table 19.4 Syntax for Arrays in B-Method

Symbol	Meaning
arr $\in$ 1..N $\nrightarrow$ T	Array declaration
arr := Exp	Substitution of an entire array; 'Exp' must be of the same type as 'arr'
arr(i) := Exp	assigning the result of expression 'Exp' to the ith element of the array 'arr'

are generally used in assertions such as in **CONSTRAINTS** and **PROPERTIES**. Arrays, on the other hand, are used in substitutions inside operations. Since the abstraction of an array is a function, arrays in B use the same syntax as a function application. Table 19.4 shows the syntax for arrays.

Since arrays are formally modeled as functions, the following equivalence holds:

$$arr(i) := Exp \equiv arr := arr \ntriangleleft \{i \mapsto Exp\}$$

In a multiple assignment statement, the variables on the left hand side must all be distinct. Hence, the statement

$$arr(i), arr(j) := Exp_1, Exp_2$$

which involves the same array variable *arr* on the left hand side is not permitted. However, the statement

$$arr(i), brr(j) := Exp_1, Exp_2$$

is correct.

19.3
Nondeterministic Statements

The B-Method allows nondeterminism and provides several constructs to specify it. Informally, when a set of nondeterministic statements are included, the refinement steps and hence the desired implementation can exercise a choice in selecting only those statements that satisfy the additional constraints imposed by the refinement steps.

19.3.1
ANY Statement

The purpose of the **ANY** statement is to execute a particular statement based on any of the permissible values of a control variable. The syntax of the **ANY** statement is given below:

ANY a **WHERE** C **THEN** S **END**

In this structure, the control variable a may have several permissible values, and C is a condition on a. The condition C can be any logical expression but it must provide the type of the control variable a. If a satisfies the condition C, then the statement S is executed. It is possible that more than one value of a may satisfy the condition C and hence S is nondeterministically executed when any one of the values of a satisfies the condition C. The control variable a must be local to the **ANY** statement, and therefore, should not be part of the state space (state variables, input and output variables) of the operation in which the **ANY** statement is executed. As an example, consider the following **ANY** statement:

ANY n **WHERE** $n \in \mathcal{N}_1$ **THEN** $n := n + 1$ **END**

In this case, any positive value of n will cause the statement $n := n + 1$ to be executed. An extension of the **ANY** statement includes multiple control variables and their associated conditions as in

ANY $a_1, a_2, \ldots, a_m$ **WHERE** $C_1 \wedge C_2 \wedge \cdots \wedge C_n$ **THEN** S **END**

It is important to notice that there should be at least one condition associated with each control variable. In addition, the type of each control variable must also be provided by the predicate $C_1 \wedge C_2 \wedge \cdots \wedge C_n$.

19.3.1.1
LET Statement

The **LET** statement is a special form of **ANY** statement in which there is only one value for the control variable. Its syntax is as follows:

LET a **BE** $a = Exp$ **IN** S **END**

The value of a in the above **LET** statement is constrained to the value evaluated by the expression Exp. The **LET** statement given above can be equivalently expressed using the **ANY** statement as follows:

ANY a **WHERE** $a = Exp$ **THEN** S **END**

The type of the control variable a is derived from the type of the expression Exp.

19.3.2
CHOICE Statement

Instead of executing a statement based on an arbitrary value of a control variable, sometimes it may be useful to specify an arbitrary choice of statements without constraints. This is achieved using the **CHOICE** statement. Its purpose is to arbitrarily choose a statement for execution giving full freedom to the implementer. The syntax of the **CHOICE** statement is

CHOICE S_1 **OR** S_2 **OR** ... **OR** S_n **END**

where each S_i is a statement. If the above **CHOICE** statement is executed, it results in one of the statements S_i being executed nondeterministically. To illustrate, consider the following example:

CHOICE courseResult := Pass

OR courseResult := Fail

OR courseResult := Undecided || action := RepeatCourse

The above example shows the result of a course which describes one of the three possible outcomes—Pass, Fail or Repeat the course. The **CHOICE** statement indicates that one of these will be chosen for execution, but does not indicate how the choice is made. Perhaps it can be chosen from the user interface.

19.3.3
SELECT Statement

The **SELECT** statement can be considered as an extension of the **CHOICE** statement in which the selection is included in the specification. The syntax for the **SELECT** statement is given below:

> **SELECT** C_1 **THEN** S_1
> **WHEN** C_2 **THEN** S_2
> ...
> **WHEN** C_n **THEN** S_n
> **ELSE** $S_{default}$
> **END**

The semantics of the **SELECT** statement is as follows: When any of the conditions C_i is satisfied exclusively and all other conditions fail, its associated statement S_i is executed. However, if more than one condition is satisfied, then a nondeterministic choice is made to execute one of the corresponding statements. The order in which the conditions C_i are checked is immaterial, because the selection of the executable statement is nondeterministic.

If none of the conditions from C_1 to C_n is satisfied, then the statement $S_{default}$ associated with the **ELSE** clause is executed. The **ELSE** clause is optional in which case, one of the conditions must be satisfied when the **SELECT** statement is executed. It is the specifier's responsibility to ensure that one of the conditions becomes true if there is no **ELSE** clause. The following is an example for the **SELECT** statement.

> **SELECT** marks $\geq$ 60 **THEN** courseResult := Pass
> **WHEN** marks $\geq$ 50 $\wedge$ marks $<$ 60 **THEN** courseResult := Undecided $\parallel$
>   action := RepeatCourse
> **WHEN** marks $\geq$ 0 $\wedge$ marks $<$ 50 **THEN** courseResult := Fail
> **ELSE** action := ReportErrorInMarks
> **END**

The **ELSE** clause in the **SELECT** statement insists that *marks* must be zero or above; otherwise, there is an error in the marks.

19.3.4
PRE Statement

The **PRE** statement includes a precondition for a statement to be executed. It has the following syntax:

> **PRE** C **THEN** S **END**

The statement S will be executed only if the precondition C is true. This is used in most of the operations. The readers are urged to refer to the *StudentCouncil* machine in Example 1 for illustration of the **PRE** statement.

19.4
Structured Specifications

This section discusses the constructs for structuring B specifications. In particular, these constructs enable a disciplined development of incremental specifications.

19.4.1
The INCLUDES Clause

The inclusion mechanism in the B-Method is similar to the aggregation relationship used in object-orientation. It allows one machine M_1 to be completely embodied into another machine M_2. Such an inclusion makes M_1 an inherent part of M_2. This is achieved by using the **INCLUDES** clause as follows:

MACHINE M_2
   $\boxed{\textbf{INCLUDES } M_1}$
SETS ...
END

The consequences of the **INCLUDES** clause are summarized below:

General Conditions

The sets, constants and variables of M_1, the included machine, must be distinct from those of M_2, the including machine. In fact, if M_2 includes several machines, the sets, constants and variables of every machine including M_2 must all be distinct. The reason for this condition is explained below under the heading *invariant inclusion*.

Parameter Instantiation

If M_1 is parameterized, the parameters of M_1 must be instantiated while including M_1 in M_2. Therefore, the inclusion mechanism expects a particular instance of a parameterized machine, and not a template.

Access to Sets and Constants

The sets and constants of M_1 are accessible in M_2. So, M_2 is free to use any set or constant declared in M_1, along with those additionally declared in M_2.

Invariant Inclusion

The state of M_1 becomes a part of the state of M_2. This indicates that the invariant of M_2 includes the invariant of M_1. Thus, every operation invoked from M_2 must satisfy both the invariant of M_2 as well as the invariant of M_1. However, the state of M_1 included within M_2 can only be updated by invoking the operations in M_1. Stated otherwise, the operations of M_2 can invoke the operations of M_1 but they cannot directly access or modify the state variables of M_1. Since the invariant may use the sets, constants and variables of the corresponding machine, it is necessary that the sets, constants and invariants of the two machines are distinct; otherwise, there will be a conflict.

Exclusivity of Included Machine

Because the state space of M_1 is included in the state space of M_2, M_1 cannot be included in any other machine. The reason is that the invariant of M_2 depends on the invariant of M_1. If M_1 is allowed to be included in another machine, the other machine may change the state of M_1 by invoking one of the operations on M_1 while M_2 is not aware of such invocation.

Order of Invocation

The initialization of M_2 will invoke the initialization of M_1.

Promotion of Operations

By default, operations of M_1 are accessible only within M_1 and M_2 and are not accessible from outside of M_2. However, M_2 can make an operation Op of M_1 to be available for its clients through its interface. This requires the **PROMOTES** clause; its syntax is shown below:

> **MACHINE** M_2
>   &boxed;**INCLUDES** M_1&boxed;
>   &boxed;**PROMOTES** Op&boxed;
> **SETS** ...
> **END**

In effect, M_2 promotes the operation Op to an outer level. The **PROMOTES** clause must occur in conjunction with the **INCLUDES** clause.

Exporting All Operations

It would be cumbersome to use the **PROMOTES** clause if M_2 wants to promote every operation from M_1, especially when M_1 has many operations. In this case, M_2 can use the **EXTENDS** clause in place of the **INCLUDES** clause. Thus,

> **MACHINE** M_2
>   &boxed;**EXTENDS** M_1&boxed;
> **SETS** ...
> **END**

is equivalent to

> **MACHINE** M_2
>   &boxed;**INCLUDES** M_1&boxed;
>   &boxed;**PROMOTES** $Op_1, Op_2, \ldots, Op_n$&boxed;
> **SETS** ...
> **END**

Table 19.5 Visibility rules for the **INCLUDES** clause

	PROPERTIES of including machine	**INVARIANT** of including machine	**OPERATIONS** of including machine
Parameters of included machine			
SETS of included machine	✓	✓	✓
CONSTANTS of included machine	✓	✓	✓
VARIABLES of included machine		✓	read-only
OPERATIONS of included machine			✓

where $Op_1, Op_2, \ldots, Op_n$ are all the operations in M_1.

Invocation of Included Operations

Though M_2 can invoke any operation of M_1, it can invoke only one operation of M_1 at any one time. This is because it would not be possible to guarantee the invariant satisfaction if more than one operation is invoked. Remember that invocation of any operation of M_1 or M_2 requires to satisfy the invariants of both the machines.

If M_2 includes several machines, the operations of different machines can be executed in parallel, still maintaining the constraint that only one operation from each machine is invoked at a time.

Visibility Rules

For ease of quick references, Table 19.5 describes the visibility of different elements of M_1 in M_2 under the inclusion relationship, taken from [1].

Transitivity

The inclusion mechanism is transitive. Thus, if a machine M_3 includes M_2, and M_2, in turn, includes the machine M_1, then M_3 includes M_1 as well. There is one exception to the transitivity: M_3 cannot invoke any operation of M_1 directly but can invoke the operations of M_1 through M_2. Even if M_2 promotes any operation Op from M_1, op is considered to be a part of M_2 as far as M_3 is concerned.

To illustrate the **INCLUDES** clause, consider the relationship between a car and its engine. The car naturally includes the engine. Example 2 describes an engine in a car.

Example 2 The *Engine* machine and *Car* machine.

    MACHINE *Engine*
    SETS *STATUS* $=$ {*Running, Stopped*}
    VARIABLES *status*
    INVARIANT *status* $\in$ *STATUS*
    INITIALIZATION *status* $:=$ *Stopped*
    OPERATIONS
        run $=$

      PRE *status* = *Stopped*
      THEN *status* := *Running*
      END;
   stop =
      PRE *status* = *Running*
      THEN *status* := *Stopped*
      END
END

MACHINE *Car*
   INCLUDES *Engine*
SETS *CARSTATUS* = {*On*, *Off*}
VARIABLES *carStatus*, *engineStatus*
INVARIANT
   carStatus ∈ *CARSTATUS* ∧ *engineStatus* ∈ *STATUS* ∧
   (*engineStatus* = *Running* ⇒ *carStatus* = *On*)
INITIALIZATION
   carStatus, *engineStatus* := *Off*, *Stopped*
OPERATIONS
   start =
      PRE *carStatus* = *Off*
      THEN run ‖ *carStatus* := *On*
      END;
   turnOff =
      PRE *carStatus* = *On*
      THEN stop ‖ *carStatus* := *Off*
      END;
   turnOn = *carStatus* := *On*
END

The car machine has two state variables—the variable *carStatus* is of type *CARSTATUS* which is declared as a set inside the car machine. The other variable *engineStatus* is declared as of type *STATUS* which is a set defined in the engine machine. This is accessible because car includes engine. Even though the variable *engineStatus* is not used anywhere else in the *Car* machine, it is introduced in this example mainly to show that the sets and constants of the included machine are accessible by the including machine.

There are three scenarios described by the operations of the car machine. Initially, the engine is stopped and the car ignition switch is turned off. In the first scenario, the car is started by turning it on and the engine is running. This is illustrated by the operation *start*() in the car machine. Notice that this operation invokes the *run*() operation inside the engine machine. In the second scenario, the car is stopped by invoking the *turnOff*() operation, which in turn invokes the *stop*() operation in the engine machine. The third scenario describes the possibility of turning on the car without starting the engine, as illustrated by the *turnOn*() operation.

The *Car* machine does not promote any operation from the *Engine* machine and hence none of the operations of *Engine* is accessible from outside of the *Car* machine.   □

19.4.2
The USES Clause

The inclusion mechanism incorporates one machine M_1 into another machine M_2. Machine M_2, in this case, has complete control over M_1. The fact that M_1 cannot be included in or accessed by any other machine shows a strict aggregation relationship between M_1 and M_2. However, there are some other situations where a machine is required to be shared by several other machines but in read-only format. This is achieved by the **USES** clause. Thus, when a machine M_2 uses a machine M_1, M_2 can only make use of the static environment of M_1, described the **SETS**, and **CONSTANTS** clauses of M_1. In addition, M_2 can also make use of the variables of M_1 in the invariant of M_2, thus establishing a strong binding between the invariant of M_2 and M_1. In other words, the invariant of M_2 depends on the state of M_1. However, M_2 cannot change the state of M_1 because it does not have access to the operations of M_1. This shows the read-only access of M_1 from M_2.

The dependency relationship of the invariant of M_2 on the state of M_1 raises an important issue. How would M_2 ensure the satisfaction of its own invariant when it does not have control over the state of M_1? In fact, M_2 would not be able to guarantee that its own invariant is satisfied at all times. This must be done by a machine that includes both M_1 and M_2. Therefore, the **USES** clause is used only in a situation where M_1 and M_2 are both part of another machine M, but M_2 uses M_1 for some of its definitions. More details on the *USES* relationship can be found in [1].

The *INCLUDES* and *USES* mechanisms in the B-Method are similar to the concepts of *composite aggregation* and *shared aggregation*, respectively, in the Unified Modeling Language (UML) [9], a design notation commonly used for object-oriented software development.

The following is the syntax of the **USES** clause:

MACHINE M_2
> **USES** M_1

SETS ...
END

The semantics of the **USES** clause is described below. The description refers to the situation where machine M_2 uses machine M_1.

Parameter Instantiation

Unlike in the **INCLUDES** clause, the parameters of M_1 are not instantiated in M_2. This is mainly because M_1 can be shared by any other machine. However, M_2 can make use of the parameters of M_1 in its invariant and operations because the state (and hence the invariant) of M_2 depends on the state of M_1.

Table 19.6 Visibility Rules of the **USES** clause

	PROPERTIES of using machine	INVARIANT of using machine	OPERATIONS of using machine
Parameters of used machine		√	√
SETS of used machine	√	√	√
CONSTANTS of used machine	√	√	√
VARIABLES of used machine		√	read-only
OPERATIONS of used machine			

Access to Sets and Constants

The sets and constants of M_1 are available within M_2 which can be used anywhere in M_2.

Inclusion of Invariant

The variables of M_1 are visible to M_2. So the **INVARIANT** and **INITIALIZATION** clauses of M_2 can use the variables of M_1.

Inclusion of Query Operations

According to Schneider [20], the machine M_2 can use only the query operations of M_1 since these operations do not change the state of M_1. Because the query operations can reveal the state of M_1, it can be stated that M_2 can visualize the state of M_1 indirectly, but not directly through the state variables of M_1. However, Abrial indicated in his B-Book that none of the operations of M_1 are accessible in M_2 [1].

Visibility Rules

The visibility rules concerning the various elements of M_1 with respect to M_2 are given in Table 19.6 under the uses relationship, taken from [1].

Transitivity

When the machine M_1 includes another machine M_3, machine M_2 can also use the machine M_3. However, when M_1 uses another machine M_4, M_2 cannot use M_4. This means that the relationship given by the **USES** clause is not transitive.

As an example for the **USAGE** class, consider a water meter that reads water level in a boiler. The water meter can read values between -1000 and 1000 units. It simply reads and stores the value internally. The water meter is used in conjunction with a water controller. This controller takes some actions depending on the water level recorded. For example, when the water level goes below 10 units, the controller opens a pump. When the water level exceeds 100 units, the controller closes the pumps. The descriptions of these two machines are given in Example 3.

Example 3 The *WaterMeter* machine.

> **MACHINE** *WaterMeter*
> **CONSTANTS** *MIN_W, MAX_W*
> **PROPERTIES** $MIN\_W = -1000 \land MAX\_W = 1000$
> **VARIABLES** *currentLevel*
> **INVARIANT**
> > $currentLevel \in \mathbb{Z} \land$
> > $MIN\_W \le currentLevel \land$
> > $currentLevel \le MAX\_W$
>
> **INITIALIZATION** $currentLevel := 0$
> **OPERATIONS**
> > **changeWaterLevel**(*nn*) =
> > > **PRE** $nn \in \mathbb{Z} \land nn \ge MIN\_W \land nn \le MAX\_W$
> > > **THEN** $currentLevel := nn$
> > > **END**;
> >
> > /* ... */
>
> **END**

> **MACHINE** *WaterController*
> **USES** *WaterMeter*
> **CONSTANTS** *MIN_ALLOWED, MAX_ALLOWED*
> **PROPERTIES** $MIN\_ALLOWED = 10 \land MAX\_ALLOWED = 100$
> ...
> **OPERATIONS**
> > **OpenPump** =
> > > **PRE** $currentLevel < MIN\_ALLOWED$
> > > **THEN**
> > > > ...
> > > **END**;
> >
> > **ClosePump** =
> > > **PRE** $currentLevel > MAX\_ALLOWED$
> > > **THEN**
> > > > ...
> > > **END**;
> >
> > ...
>
> **END**

Clearly, the machine *WaterController* uses the state of the *WaterMeter* machine by using its state variable inside the operations **OpenPump** and **ClosePump**. □

19.4.3
The SEES Clause

The B-Method has another clause, called the **SEES** clause, which has several characteristics similar to those of the **USES** clauses. But it was introduced mainly to share machines at the refinement and implementation levels. In other words, the **USES** clause is used at the specification level, while the **SEES** clause can be used at the specification, refinement and implementation levels. This will be clear when looking at the visibility rules, given later in this section.

When a machine M_2 sees a machine M_1, the invariant of M_2 is no longer dependent on the state of M_1. This is the major difference between the **USES** and **SEES** clauses.

The syntax of the **SEES** clause is as follows:

MACHINE M_2
    SEES M_1
SETS ...
END

When a machine M_2 sees a machine M_1, M_2 has read-only access to M_1. Only the sets, constants and query operations of M_1 are visible to and are accessible from M_2. The semantics of the **SEES** clause is given next; the description assumes that machine M_2 sees machine M_1.

Parameters

The **SEES** clause does not include the parameters of M_1. Therefore, the parameters of M_1 are not visible to M_2. The **SEES** mechanism is expected to be used at the implementation level and hence if a machine M_2 sees a machine M_1, then the implementation of M_2 must import the implementation of M_1. Since at the specification level there is no information available corresponding to implementation details, M_2 does not know how to instantiate M_1 and therefore, the parameters of M_1 are not visible to M_2.

Access to Sets and Constants

The sets and constants of M_1 are available for M_2 and they can be used anywhere in M_2.

Exclusion of Invariant

The variables of M_1 are not visible to M_2. Otherwise, M_2 may be able to change the state of M_1. Consequently, M_2 cannot use the invariant or the initialization of M_1.

Inclusion of Query Operations

According to Schneider [20], the machine M_2 can use only the query operations of M_1 since these operations do not change the state of M_1. The machine M_2 can thus observe the state of M_1. However, Abrial indicated that none of the operations of M_1 are accessible in M_2 [1].

Table 19.7 Visibility Rules of the **SEES** clause

	PROPERTIES of seeing machine	**INVARIANT** of seeing machine	**OPERATIONS** of seeing machine
Parameters of seen machine			
SETS of seen machine	✓	✓	✓
CONSTANTS of seen machine	✓	✓	✓
VARIABLES of seen machine		✓	read-only
OPERATIONS of seen machine			

Visibility Rules

The visibility rules concerning the various elements of M_1 with respect to M_2 are given in Table 19.7 under the SEES relationship, taken from [1].

Transitivity

When the machine M_1 includes another machine M_3, machine M_2 can also see the machine M_3. However, when M_1 sees another machine M_4, M_2 cannot see M_4. This means that the relationship given by the **SEES** clause is not transitive.

Example 4 illustrates how a **SEES** clause can be used. Consider a clock that outputs the time in hours and minutes in 24-hour format.

Example 4 The *Clock* machine.

MACHINE *Clock*
CONSTANTS *HOUR, MINUTE, TIME, Hour, Minute*
PROPERTIES
    $HOUR = 0 .. 23 \wedge$
    $MINUTE = 0 .. 59 \wedge$
    $TIME = HOUR \times MINUTE \wedge$
    $Hour \in TIME \rightarrow HOUR \wedge$
    $Minute \in TIME \rightarrow MINUTE \wedge$
    $\forall (hh, mm).((hh, mm) \in TIME \Rightarrow$
        $Hour(hh, mm) = hh \wedge Minute(hh, mm) = mm)$
VARIABLES *time*
INVARIANT $time \in TIME$
INITIALIZATION $time := 0 \mapsto 0$ /* equivalent to (0, 0) */
OPERATIONS
    tick $=$
        IF $Minute(time) = 59$
        THEN $time := ((Hour(time) + 1) \textbf{ mod } 24) \mapsto 0$
        ELSE $time := Hour(time) \mapsto (Minute(time) + 1)$
        END;

$hh \leftarrow$ **hours** $= hh := Hour(time);$

$mm \leftarrow$ **minutes** $= mm := Minute\ (time)$
END

An office machine that sees this clock is described next.

The *Office* machine.

MACHINE
  Office
  SEES *Clock*
OPERATIONS
  $hh, mm \leftarrow currentTime =$
  BEGIN $hh \leftarrow$ **hours** $\|$ $mm \leftarrow$ **minutes END**
END

The office machine is able to get the current time from the clock machine by calling the *hours* and *minutes* functions. However, it cannot access the *tick* function which actually changes the time. Notice that the office machine access the two operations of the clock machine at the same time. This is allowed because they are both query operations and they do not affect the invariant of either machine.   □

19.5
Refinement

The B-Method, Like VDM-SL, includes several AMN notations which look like programming language notations that support refinement of abstract specifications. For example, the B-Method supports assignment statements, conditional statements, iterative statements and notations for sequential and parallel composition of statements. It also includes notations to declare local variables within an operation just like in programming languages. Using the same AMN structure, a specifier can therefore develop a design specification by refining an abstract specification. This section describes the AMN structure for refinement with the additional syntax.

19.5.1
Sequential Composition of Statements

The statements in the body of an operation can be composed using a sequential composition operator; the syntax is

  S ; T

The semantics of this operator is that the statement T is executed in a state in which S terminates. If, however, S does not terminate, then the sequential composition fails. The same is true when T does not terminate. So, the sequential composition will be valid only if both S and T terminate and T starts in the state in which S terminates. Several statements can be sequentially composed as in

S ; T ; Q ; R

19.5.2
Local Variables

An operation can declare a local variable using the syntax

VAR x **IN** S **END**

The variable x is local only to the statement S and hence will not be accessible outside of S. Because x is local to S, it must be assigned some value within S before it is being used. Otherwise, the value of x becomes undefined. The syntax of local variables declaration can be extended to include multiple variables within the same declaration as in

VAR $x_1, x_2, \ldots, x_n$ **IN** S **END**

As before, every one of x_i must be assigned a value within S before it is used.

19.5.3
Refinement Machine

Refinement is supported through refinement machines which use the same interface as the abstract machine they refine. The data types inside the refinement machine will be different and hence the refinement process in the B-Method is considered to be data refinement. A refinement machine R will have the same set of operations, input and output parameters of the abstract machine M it refines. This set of operations include the operations of any machine that is included or extended by M. There are two clauses required of a refinement machine as indicated below:

REFINEMENT R
REFINES M
. . .

The **REFINEMENT** clause introduces the name of the refinement machine and the **REFINES** clause introduces the name of the abstract machine that is refined. The rest of the structure for the refinement machine is similar to that of an abstract machine. Thus, the refinement machine uses the same AMN structure which is easier for a specifier.

One of the obligations of a refinement machine is that it must provide some relationship between its own state space and the state space of the abstract machine that it refines. For example, if the state space of the refinement machine includes a variable called *refinedVariable* which is of type $N \rightarrowtail NAME$, and the state space of the abstract machine includes a variable called *absVariable* whose type is $\mathcal{P}NAME$, then a relationship between these two variables could be that ran *refinedVariable* = *absVariable*. That is, the set of names addressed by *refinedVariable* is the same set as described by *absVariable*. However, *refinedVariable* includes an ordering of these names through the injective function. This relationship between the two state spaces is called a *linking invariant*. It is required that the linking invariant must include some relationship for every state variable of the abstract machine and thus ensuring data refinement.

The **REFINES** clause is somewhat similar to that of the **INCLUDES** clause but not exactly the same. The reason for this assumption is that the state variables of the abstract machine are accessible directly in the linking invariant in order to establish the relationship between the two state spaces. The refinement machine does not need to redeclare these variables. In addition, the refinement machine preserves the signature of all the operations declared in the abstract machine.

Suppose $y \leftarrow Op(x)$ is an operation introduced in the abstract machine, the refinement machine will automatically have this operation with the same signature. Moreover, the type of the input variables (in this case, the variable x) and the precondition on these input variables, namely the **PRE** clause in operation Op are inherited into the operation in the refinement machine. Therefore, the refinement machine does not need to repeat the precondition. The assumption is that the refinement works if and only if it satisfies the conditions in the abstract machine and hence the precondition of the operation must be true before the refined operation is invoked.

While the refinement machine uses the same AMN structure as the abstract machine, there are a few restrictions.

- A refinement machine can only include abstract machines through the **INCLUDES** clause. This is because refinement machines includes specifications and not implementations.
- A refinement machine can have **INCLUDES**, **EXTENDS**, **PROMOTES** and **SEES** clauses but cannot have **USES** clause. The **USES** clause is a specification construct that establishes a relationship between the state variables of the two machines. Since the refinement machine explicitly does this through the linked invariant, it is not appropriate to have a **USES** clause.

As an example for refinement, consider an abstract machine *Collection* that describes a collection of books maintained, say, in a personal library. It includes two operations: *add* that adds a new book to the collection and *search* that confirms whether or a not a given book is in the collection. The collection machine is shown in Example 5.

Example 5 The *Collection* machine.

    MACHINE *Collection*
      SETS *BOOK*; *ANSWER* = {*yes*, *no*}

```
    VARIABLES books
    INVARIANT books ∈ 𝒫 (BOOK)
    INITIALIZATION books := ∅
    OPERATIONS
        add(bb) =
            PRE bb ∈ BOOK ∧ bb ∉ books
            THEN books := books ∪ {bb}
            END;

        cc ← search(bb) =
            PRE bb ∈ BOOK
            THEN
                IF bb ∈ books
                THEN cc := yes
                ELSE cc := no
                END
            END
    END
```

□

A refinement machine called *Shelf* puts the collection of books in order so that each book has an index. The index starts at 1. Every time a new book is added, it is always placed at the end of the collection. It is assumed that no book is deleted from this collection and therefore the index of a book in the collection never changes. The refinement machine *Shelf* is given in Example 6.

Example 6 The *Shelf* machine.

```
    REFINEMENT Shelf
        REFINES Collection
        VARIABLES sBooks, count
        INVARIANT
            sBooks ∈ 𝒩₁ ⤖ BOOK ∧
            count ∈ 𝒩 ∧
            ran(sBooks) = books
        INITIALIZATION sBooks, count := ∅ , 0
        OPERATIONS
            add(bb) =
                BEGIN
                    count := count + 1; sBooks(count) := bb
                END;

            cc ← search(bb) =
                IF bb ∈ sBooks[1 .. count]
                THEN cc := yes
```

           ELSE $cc := no$
           END
    END

The machine *Shelf* uses an additional variable called *count* to maintain the number of books in the collection. The syntax *sBooks*[1..*count*] in the operation *search* indicates the set of all books held in the shelf indexed from 1 to *count*. This could have been alternatively specified as

    IF $(\exists i.(i \in 1..count \wedge sBooks(i) = bb))$

The machine *Shelf* thus refines the machine *Collection*. $\square$

19.6
Specification Examples

This section includes several examples with varying complexity. They together illustrate the expressive power of the B-Method.

Example 7 Synonyms and Antonyms.

Problem Description

A personal dictionary includes a set of words. Each word also comes with a set of synonyms and antonyms, though a given word may neither have a synonym nor have an antonym. The synonyms and antonyms are themselves words in the same dictionary. It is required to develop an on-line version of the personal dictionary that includes the operations (i) to add a new word into the dictionary, (ii) to add a synonym to a word in the dictionary, (iii) to add an antonym to a word in the dictionary, (iv) to query the number of words that have the given word as a synonym, and (v) to query the number of words that have the given word as an antonym.

Assumptions

1. If a word w has another word w_1 as a synonym, then w_1 need not have w as the synonym. The same is true for antonyms.

The Model

The personal dictionary will be modeled as an abstract machine. The state of the machine will consist of a set of words in the dictionary, and two mappings—one for maintaining the synonyms and the other for antonyms. Since one word may have several synonyms (and several antonyms), the mappings are designed as functions from words to a set of words. The following invariants must be specified:

- Synonyms and antonyms can only be found for those words in the dictionary.
- Synonyms and antonyms themselves are words in the same dictionary.

- The synonyms and antonyms of a particular word are mutually exclusive; i.e., no word can be the synonym and antonym of the same word.

The machine will include five operations as requested in the problem description:

AddWord This operation will add a new word into the dictionary. It should ensure that the word is not in the dictionary before. No synonyms or antonyms will be added at this time; these will be taken care of by the next two operations.

AddSynonym In order to add a word *ss* as a synonym to a word *ww*, both words must exist in the dictionary. One of the preconditions is to ensure that the word *ss* must neither be in the synonyms of *ww* nor in its antonyms. Care must also be taken to ensure that *ss* is not the same as *ww* because a word cannot be its own synonym.

AddAntonym This operation is very similar to *AddSynonym* but for antonyms.

QueryNumberOfWordsWithSameSynonym This is a read-only operation which returns the number of words that have the same word *ss* in their list of synonyms. A precondition for this operation must ensure that the word *ss* is in the dictionary.

QueryNumberOfWordsWithSameAntonym This operation is similar to **QueryNumberOfWordsWithSameSynonym** but it returns the number of words that contain the same word *aa* as antonym.

The *PersonalDictionary* machine is given below.

> **MACHINE** *PersonalDictionary*
> **SETS** *WORD*
> **VARIABLES** *words, synonyms, antonyms*
> **INVARIANT**
>> *words* $\in \mathcal{P}$ (*WORD*) $\wedge$
>> *synonyms* $\in$ *WORD* $\nrightarrow \mathcal{P}$ (*WORD*) $\wedge$
>> *antonyms* $\in$ *WORD* $\nrightarrow \mathcal{P}$ (*WORD*) $\wedge$
>> **dom**(*synonyms*) $\cup$ **dom**(*antonyms*) $\subseteq$ *words* $\wedge$
>> **union**(**ran**(*synonyms*) $\cup$ **ran**(*antonyms*)) $\subseteq$ *words* $\wedge$
>> $\forall$ (*ww*).(*ww* $\in$ **dom**(*synonyms*) $\cap$ **dom**(*antonyms*) $\Rightarrow$
>>> *synonyms*(*ww*) $\cap$ *antonyms*(*ww*) = $\emptyset$)
>
> **INITIALIZATION**
>> *words, synonyms, antonyms* := $\emptyset$, $\emptyset$, $\emptyset$
>
> **OPERATIONS**
>> **AddWord**(*ww*) =
>>> **PRE**
>>>> *ww* $\in$ *WORD* $\wedge$ *ww* $\notin$ *words*
>>> **THEN**
>>>> *words* := *words* $\cup$ {*ww*}
>>> **END**;
>>
>> **AddSynonym**(*ww, ss*) =
>>> **PRE**

$ww \in WORD \land ss \in WORD \land$

$ww \neq ss \land \{ww, ss\} \subseteq words \land$

$(ww \in \mathbf{dom}(synonyms) \Rightarrow ss \notin synonyms(ww)) \land$

$(ww \in \mathbf{dom}(antonyms) \Rightarrow ss \notin antonyms(ww))$

THEN

    IF $ww \in \mathbf{dom}(synonyms)$ **THEN**

        $synonyms(ww) := synonyms(ww) \cup \{ss\}$

    ELSE

        $synonyms(ww) := \{ss\}$

    END

  END;

AddAntonym(ww, aa) =

PRE

    $ww \in WORD \land aa \in WORD \land$

    $ww \neq aa \land \{ww, aa\} \subseteq words \land$

    $(ww \in \mathbf{dom}(antonyms) \Rightarrow aa \notin antonyms(ww)) \land$

    $(ww \in \mathbf{dom}(synonyms) \Rightarrow aa \notin synonyms(ww))$

THEN

    IF $ww \in \mathbf{dom}(antonyms)$ **THEN**

        $antonyms(ww) := antonyms(ww) \cup \{aa\}$

    ELSE

        $antonyms(ww) := \{aa\}$

    END

END;

$count \leftarrow$ **QueryNumberOfWordsWithSameSynonym**(ss) =

PRE

    $ss \in WORD \land ss \in words$

THEN

    $count := \mathbf{card}(\{ww \mid ww \in \mathbf{dom}(synonyms) \land ss \in synonyms(ww)\})$

END;

$count \leftarrow$ **QueryNumberOfWordsWithSameAntonym**(aa) =

PRE

    $aa \in WORD \land aa \in words$

THEN

    $count := \mathbf{card}(\{ww \mid ww \in \mathbf{dom}(antonyms) \land aa \in antonyms(ww)\})$

END

END

Comments

The state of the personal dictionary is defined by three variables, namely *words*, *synonyms* and *antonyms*. The variable *words* is of type of set of *WORD*, and *synonyms* and *antonyms* are both functions from *WORD* to a set of *WORD*. Typically, for a given word w, *synonyms* will return a set of words which are recorded as the synonyms of w. Similarly, *antonyms* will return a set of antonyms for a given word. In addition to defining the types of the state variables, the invariant of the machine asserts the following:

1. If a word ww has its synonym recorded in the system (indicated by dom(*synonym*)), then ww must be a word in the dictionary; the same is true for antonyms.
2. The collection of words recorded as synonyms and antonyms (indicated by $\bigcup(\mathrm{ran}(synonym) \cup \mathrm{ran}(antonym)))$ must be words in the dictionary.
3. For every word ww for which synonyms and antonyms are both recorded, the synonyms and antonyms must be mutually exclusive.

Initially, all the three state variables are set to empty.
The operations of the machine are self-explanatory. □

Example 8 File Access Control.

Problem Description

A computer system has a set of files and a set of users. Each user is given read/write access to the files according to the following criteria:

- If a user has write access to a file f, then the user must have read access to f as well. However, a user may have read-only access to a file.
- Every file must have at least one user who has read access to it.
- A user may not have any access to a given file.

Assumptions

1. If a user u is deleted from the system and a file f has u as the only user who has read or write access to it, then f must also be deleted from the system. Thus, the system does not maintain any file which is not accessible by any user.
2. File ownership will not be included in this level of specification. Only low level operations such as adding users and files, deleting users and files and changing access rights for a user to a given file will be included.

The computer system must include operations (i) to add a new user to the system, (ii) to add a new file to the system, (iii) to delete a user from the system, (iv) to delete a file from the system, and (v) to change the access rights of a user to a given file.

The Model

The file access control system must maintain three entities: a set of users, a set of files and the access rights of users for each file. The access rights can be modeled in two ways: (i) For each file f, the set of users who have access rights to f can be maintained as a list. (ii) For each user u, the set of files to which u has access rights can be maintained as a list. In both approaches, the read and write accesses must be separately maintained. The specification in this example uses the first approach, namely from files to the set of users.

19

The access control subsystem for the computer system will be modeled as an abstract machine. The state of the machine will contain a set of files, a set of users, and two mappings, one for read access and the other for write access. The access criteria as mentioned in the problem description above must be specified as state invariant. The machine will include the following operations:

AddNewUser   The precondition for this operation must ensure that the user is not already present in the computer system.

AddNewFile   When a new file is added to the system, there must be at least one user in the system who has read access to the file. Otherwise, no one will be able to use the file. So, the operation should accept three parameters, the file ff to be added, the user uu who is given access right to this file, and the access right rr itself. It is possible that uu is given write access to ff which, in turn, requires read access to be included. The precondition for the operation must ensure that the file ff is not already present in the system, but the user uu is. In addition, it should also ensure that the access right parameter rr must indicate read or write access to the file.

DeleteFile   Deleting an existing file will remove all entries for this file from the two mappings—read access and write access. Also, the file itself must be removed from the state of the system.

DeleteUser   When an existing user uu is deleted from the system, not only that uu is removed from the state of the system, but the access rights given to the user must also be removed. This requires that the two mappings must be updated to remove all entries corresponding to the user uu. In addition, if there is any file ff in the system which has uu as the only person who has access rights, then ff also must be removed from the state of the system.

ChangeAccessRight   This operation takes three parameters—the file ff whose mapping is to be changed, the user uu who is given new access rights, and the access right rr. The intention is to give the access right rr for the user uu to the file ff. The operation does not check what access rights uu has on file ff before the operation. It only ensures that both ff and uu exist in the state of the system. Care must be taken to ensure that if the access right rr indicates 'NONE', then there must be at least one user other than uu who has read access to ff. Otherwise, the file may become an orphan after changing the access rights.

The *FileAccessControl* machine is given below.

> **MACHINE** *FileAccessControl*
> **SETS** *FILE*; *USER*; *RIGHT* = {*RD, WR, NONE*}
> **VARIABLES**
>   *files, users, readAccess, writeAccess*
>
> **INVARIANT**
>   *files* $\in \mathcal{P}$ (*FILE*) $\wedge$ *users* $\in \mathcal{P}$ (*USER*) $\wedge$
>   *readAccess* $\in$ *FILE* $\leftrightarrow$ *USER* $\wedge$ *writeAccess* $\in$ *FILE* $\leftrightarrow$ *USER* $\wedge$
> $\forall$ *ff*.(*ff* $\in$ **dom**(*writeAccess*) $\Rightarrow$ *writeAccess*[{*ff*}] $\subseteq$ *readAccess*[{*ff*}]) $\wedge$
>   **dom**(*readAccess*) = *files* $\wedge$
>   **dom**(*writeAccess*) $\subseteq$ *files* $\wedge$

$\mathbf{ran}(readAccess) \cup \mathbf{ran}(writeAccess) \subseteq users$

INITIALIZATION

    $files, users, readAccess, writeAccess := \emptyset , \emptyset , \emptyset , \emptyset$

OPERATIONS

    AddNewUser(*newUser*) =

        PRE

            $newUser \in USER \wedge newUser \notin users$

        THEN

            $users := users \cup \{newUser\}$

        END;

    AddNewFile(*newFile, initUser, initRight*) =

        PRE

            $newFile \in FILE \wedge newFile \notin files \wedge$

            $initUser \in USER \wedge initUser \in users \wedge$

            $initRight \in RIGHT \wedge initRight \neq NONE$

        THEN

            $files := files \cup \{newFile\} \parallel$

            $readAccess := readAccess \cup \{newFile \mapsto initUser\} \parallel$

            IF $initRight = WR$ **THEN**

                $writeAccess := writeAccess \cup \{newFile \mapsto initUser\}$

            END

        END;

    DeleteFile(*ff*) =

        PRE

            $ff \in FILE \wedge ff \in files$

        THEN

            $writeAccess := \{ff\} \lhd writeAccess \parallel$

            $readAccess := \{ff\} \lhd readAccess \parallel$

            $files := files - \{ff\}$

        END;

    DeleteUser(*uu*) =

        PRE

            $uu \in USER \wedge uu \in users$

        THEN

            $writeAccess := writeAccess \rhd \{uu\} \parallel$

            $readAccess := readAccess \rhd \{uu\} \parallel$

            /* Delete orphan files */

            $files := files - \{ff \mid ff \in files \wedge uu \in readAccess[\{ff\}] \wedge$

                                   $\mathbf{card}(readAccess[\{ff\}]) = 1\} \parallel$

$$users := users - \{uu\}$$
END;

ChangeAccessRight(ff, uu, rr) =
  PRE
    $ff \in FILE \land ff \in files \land$
    $uu \in USER \land uu \in users \land$
    $rr \in RIGHT \land$
    $(rr = NONE \land uu \in readAccess[\{ff\}] \Rightarrow$
               $\mathbf{card}(readAccess[\{ff\}\,]) > 1)$
  THEN
    IF $rr = WR$ **THEN**
      $readAccess := readAccess \cup \{ff \mapsto uu\} \,\|$
      $writeAccess := writeAccess \cup \{ff \mapsto uu\}$
    ELSIF $rr = RD$ **THEN**
      $readAccess := readAccess \cup \{ff \mapsto uu\} \,\|$
      $writeAccess := writeAccess - \{ff \mapsto uu\}$
    ELSE
      $readAccess := readAccess - \{ff \mapsto uu\} \,\|$
      $writeAccess := writeAccess - \{ff \mapsto uu\}$
    END
  END
END

Comments

The invariant, in addition to describing the types of these four variables, asserts the following conditions.

- The set of users who has write access to a given file ff also has read access to the same file.
- Every file in the system must be readable. That is, there is at least one user for every file who has read access to it. Otherwise, the file becomes an orphan which cannot be used.
- Some files may not have write access; i.e., these files have read-only access. So, the set of files that do have write access is actually a subset of the entire file system.
- Some users in the system may not have read or write access to any file. Stated otherwise, the union of the set of users who have read access to at least one file and the set of users who have write access to at least one file is a subset of the users of the system.

Initially all the four state variables are assigned empty sets. It is not possible to add a new file until a user is added because the operation **AddNewFile** requires an existing user as one of the inputs.

In the **DeletUser** operation, the statement

$$files := files - \{ff \mid ff \in files \land uu \in readAccess[\{ff\}] \land$$
$$\mathbf{card}(readAccess[\{ff\}]) = 1$$

collects all the files that the user has read access to it and also ensures that *uu* is the only user who has read access to it. These files will eventually be deleted from the system as well because they become orphans as a result of deleting the user *uu*. Notice that the files for which the user has write access are not checked because the user will have read access to every file for which he/she has write access.

There are three choices to be considered in **ChangeAccessRight** operation:

1. If the access right *rr* is 'WR', then the user is given both read and write access to the files. Consequently, the two maps *readAccess* and *writeAccess* will both be updated to include an entry for this user.

2. If the access right *rr* is 'RD', then the user is given read-only access. This is achieved by adding an entry for this user in the map *readAccess* and removing the entry of this user from *writeAccess*. If the user already has write access to the file, this operation will remove such access. If the user does not have write access to the file, then the second action will not have any effect. So, at the end, the user will have read-only access to the file.

3. In the third case, the user is revoked both read access and write access for this file. Hence, the user entry from *readAccess* and *writeAccess* is removed, no matter whether or not this user had read access or write access to the file before.   □

Example 9 Seating arrangement in a Theater.

Problem Description

This problem is concerned with ticketing and seating arrangements in a theater. The theater sells tickets for various events. There are three types of tickets: REGULAR, FRONT_ROW and BALCONY. Each ticket type has a different price. Tickets can be bought individually or as a group. A sample seating arrangement for the three types of tickets is shown in Fig. 19.1. As seen in Fig. 19.1, the seats that correspond to one type of ticket must all be consecutive. The number of tickets in each ticket type may be different.

The following minimal set of operations must be specified: (1) Buy an individual ticket. (2) Buy a group ticket. (3) Report the revenue collected through ticket sales at any time. (4) Cancel a ticket.

Additional Requirements

1. While purchasing a group ticket, all tickets in the group must be of same type and the seat numbers for the tickets must be consecutive. For example, if someone buys a group ticket for seven people in FRONT_ROW, there must be seven consecutive seats available in FONT_ROW ticket type. Otherwise, the group ticket for this party will not be sold.

Assumptions

1. The total number of seats is fixed.
2. The number of tickets in each ticket type is fixed.

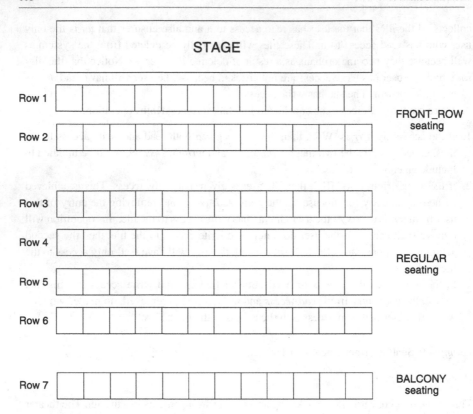

Fig. 19.1 Seating arrangement for the three types of tickets

The Model

The focus of this problem is on the seating arrangement. It is decided to use a two-dimensional array for modeling the seating arrangement. The maximum number of rows and columns must be specified as constants and hence they will not change. There is more than one option to model the seating for each type of ticket. One of the options would be to fix some specific rows of seats for each type of ticket. Figure 19.1 shows such an arrangement. Another option would be to give the choice for the implementer to decide which rows belong to a given ticket type. The specification in this example uses the second option. In this case, each seat is defined to belong to a particular type of ticket and hence the seat number must be checked for the ticket type before the seat is sold. The implementer of this specification has the freedom to change the number of rows for each ticket type. However, once implemented, there is no operation to change the number of rows dynamically during the operation of the system. Thus, the system still maintains the second condition stated in the assumptions.

The ticketing system will be modeled as an abstract machine named *TheaterTicketingSystem*. The machine must include appropriate types—one to define the status of a seat to indicate whether or not it is occupied/sold, and another to define the type of ticket. Both are modeled as sets in the machine. The total number of seats, described by the multiplication of number of rows and number of columns, should be defined as a constant since it is fixed. It is assumed that each row has the same number of seats as shown in Fig. 19.1. Instead of modeling one single number to indicate the total number of seats, the specification models two constants *max_row* and *max_column* that define the maximum number of rows and columns, respectively. The prices for each type of ticket must also be included as constants because they do not change.

Since the seating arrangement is modeled as a two-dimensional array, it is appropriate to define projection functions on this array to identify the row number and column number of a particular seat. Apart from these two projection functions, additional functions are needed to assert the positional relationships between two seats. For example, we would like to know whether one seat is before the next seat. This is defined by the function *precedes* in the specification. We also want to know whether a given seat is in between two seats. This would be useful to find out whether a ticket in a group is inside a range of consecutive seat numbers. The specification includes a function called *inRange* which asserts whether or not a given seat number is inside a range of seat numbers.

The state of the system includes two variables—*seat* and *type*, both are modeled as functions. The mapping *seat* is defined from seat numbers to the status of a seat; the mapping *type* denotes the ticket type of a given seat number. Initially, all the seats must have the status as unoccupied or empty.

The operations of the *TheaterTicketingSystem* machine are described in detail below:

- The operation **SellIndividualTicket** allows a user to buy an individual ticket. It should take the seat number, its type the amount paid as parameters. The operation should return the change if the amount is more than the ticket price. The precondition must ensure that the seat is empty, the type requested by the user matches with the type of the seat in the seating, and the amount is greater than or equal to the amount of the ticket. If all constraints in the precondition are satisfied, then the seat should be declared to be *occupied* and the change should be calculated.

- The operation **SellGroupTickets** will be invoked when a user wants to buy a group of tickets. There are two ways to model this operation: The user can input the number of tickets needed and the type of tickets, and the system can find a set of consecutive seats for the tickets. There could be more than one possible set of seats available for this purchase. The other option would be to ask the user to select the particular seat numbers they want, of course, all belonging to the same ticket type. This second approach is used in this specification. Accordingly, when a user buys a group of tickets, the user must provide the starting seat number *fr_seat*, the ending seat number *to_seat*, the ticket type *seatType* and the amount *paidAmount* as parameters to the operation. The precondition must ensure that the seat number *fr_seat* must precede *to_seat*. Further, every seat in this range must be empty and must have the same type. Remember that a group ticket can be bought only if the tickets are all of same type and consecutive seats are available for these tickets. The precondition must also ensure that the amount paid is greater than or equal to the total amount for all the tickets in the range specified. If the precondition is true, the operation will set all the seats in the given range to be *occupied* and also will calculate the change for this purchase.

- An individual ticket can be canceled by invoking the **CancelTicket** operation. It accepts the seat number of the ticket to be canceled and returns the refund amount. The precondition for this operation must ensure that the seat is indeed occupied meaning that the ticket is purchased. If the precondition is true, the operation should set the seat to be empty and calculate the refund. There is no separate operation provided for canceling a group of tickets. It is assumed that the **CancelTicket** operation can be invoked individually for every ticket in a group ticket in order to cancel a group of tickets.
- The operation **RevenueQuery** returns the revenue collected so far. It comes from all the tickets sold. However, the specification does not keep track of ticket counts or ticket numbers but this information is gathered from seat numbers that are occupied. So, the revenue is calculated by checking every seat whether or not it is occupied, and then summing up its price value.

The *TheaterTicketingSystem* machine is given next.

MACHINE *TheaterTicketingSystem*
SETS
 $SEATSTATUS = \{empty, occupied\}$;
 $SEATTYPE = \{regular, front\_row, balcony\}$

CONSTANTS
 max_row, max_column,
 $reg\_price, front\_price, balcony\_price$,
 $row, column, price$ /* functions */

PROPERTIES
 $max\_row \in \mathcal{N}_1 \wedge max\_column \in \mathcal{N}_1 \wedge$
 $reg\_price \in \mathcal{N}_1 \wedge front\_price \in \mathcal{N}_1 \wedge balcony\_price \in \mathcal{N}_1 \wedge$
 $row \in \mathcal{N}_1 \times \mathcal{N}_1 \rightarrow \mathcal{N}_1 \wedge$
 $column \in \mathcal{N}_1 \times \mathcal{N}_1 \rightarrow \mathcal{N}_1 \wedge$
 $\forall (rr, cc).((rr, cc) \in \mathcal{N}_1 \times \mathcal{N}_1 \Rightarrow$
   $row(rr, cc) = rr \wedge column(rr, cc) = cc) \wedge$
 $price \in SEATTYPE \rightarrow \mathcal{N}_1 \wedge$
 $price = \{regular \mapsto reg\_price,$
    $front\_row \mapsto front\_price,$
    $balcony \mapsto balcony\_price\}$

DEFINITIONS
 $SEATNO == (1 .. max\_row) \times (1 .. max\_column)$;

 /* s1 precedes s2 */
 $precedes(s1, s2) ==$ $($
  $row(s1) < row(s2) \vee$
  $row(s1) = row(s2) \wedge column(s1) < column(s2)$
 $)$;

/* ss inRange [s1, s2] */
$inRange(ss, s1, s2) == ($
   $ss = s1 \lor ss = s2 \lor (precedes(s1, ss) \land precedes(ss, s2))$
$)$

VARIABLES

seat, type

INVARIANT

$seat \in SEATNO \rightarrow SEATSTATUS \land$
$type \in SEATNO \rightarrow SEATTYPE$

INITIALIZATION

$seat := \lambda sn.(sn \in SEATNO \mid empty) \parallel$
/* Another way to init. seat()
seat := SEATNO $\times$ {empty}
*/
$type :\in SEATNO \rightarrow SEATTYPE$

OPERATIONS

$change \leftarrow$ **SellIndividualTicket**(*seatNumber, seatType, paidAmount*) =
  PRE
    $seatNumber \in SEATNO \land seat(seatNumber) = empty \land$
    $seatType \in SEATTYPE \land type(seatNumber) = seatType \land$
    $paidAmount \in \mathcal{N}_1 \land paidAmount \geq (type\ ;\ price)(seatNumber)$
  THEN
    seat(*seatNumber*) := *occupied* $\parallel$
    $change := paidAmount - (type\ ;\ price)(seatNumber)$
  END;

$change \leftarrow$ **SellGroupTickets**(*fr_seat, to_seat, seatType, paidAmount*) =
  PRE
    $fr\_seat \in SEATNO \land to\_seat \in SEATNO \land$
    $precedes(fr\_seat, to\_seat) \land$
    $seatType \in SEATTYPE \land$
    $\forall ss.(ss \in SEATNO \land inRange(ss, fr\_seat, to\_seat)$
                $\Rightarrow seat(ss) = empty \land type(ss) = seatType) \land$
    $paidAmount \in \mathcal{N}_1 \land$
    $paidAmount \geq price(seatType) \times$
                card($\{ss\cdot \mid ss \in SEATNO \land inRange(ss, fr\_seat, to\_seat)\}$)
  THEN
    LET *sellingSeats* **BE**
      $sellingSeats = \{ss \mid ss \in SEATNO \land$
                       $inRange(ss, fr\_seat, to\_seat)\}$
    IN

$$seat := seat \triangleleft sellingSeats \times \{occupied\} \parallel$$
$$change := paidAmount - price(seatType) \times \textbf{card}(sellingSeats)$$
        END
    END;

$refund \leftarrow$ **CancelTicket**$(seatNumber) =$
    PRE
        $seatNumber \in SEATNO \wedge seat(seatNumber) = occupied$
    THEN
        seat$(seatNumber) := empty \parallel$
        $refund := (type \; ; \; price)(seatNumber)$
    END;

$revenue \leftarrow$ **RevenueQuery** $=$
    $revenue := \sum (ss).($
            $ss \in SEATNO \wedge$
            $seat(ss) = occupied \mid (type \; ; \; price)(ss))$
END

Comments

This specification includes three definitions: *SEATNO* is used as an abbreviation for a two-dimensional array. Each element of this array uniquely identifies a seat. The other two definitions are boolean functions. The function *precedes* takes two seats as parameters and returns true if the first seat precedes the second seat in the seating. The function *inRange* accepts three parameters. It asserts whether or not the seat passed as the first argument lies in between the two seats that are passed as the second and third parameters. It is interesting to notice that the types of parameters for the two functions are not given in these definitions but are inferred from the definitions themselves.

The **INITIALIZATION** clause shows that the variable *type* is assigned some arbitrary value from the type $SEATNO \rightarrow SEATTYPE$. This is indicated by the nondeterministic operator $:\in$.

The expression $(type \; ; \; price)$ in the operation **SellIndividualTicket** shows functional composition which results in a function that takes a seat number as a parameter and returns its price. The same compositional function is used in two other operations—**CancelTicket** and **RevenueQuery**.

The operation **SellGroupsTickets** uses the **LET** clause that introduces a local variable *sellingSeats* that is used in the statements corresponding to changing the seat status as well as calculating the change.   □

19.7
Case Study—A Ticketing System in a Parking Lot

In this section, we present a case study for the specification of an automated ticketing system in a parking lot. The case study uses several syntactic structures discussed in this chapter.

Problem Description

A parking lot generally has several parking spaces; some might have been reserved for specific purposes such as handicapped parking. Vehicles enter the parking lot through one or more entry points. While entering into the parking lot, every vehicle must take a ticket issued by the automated ticketing system. The system records the date and time of entry on the ticket but does not note anything specific to the vehicle such as license plate number. It is also important to note that the driver and the vehicle are together treated as one entity. So, the actions of a driver implies that of the vehicle and vice versa. Vehicles leave the parking lot through one or more exit points. While leaving, the driver must first insert the ticket into the ticketing system. The system, in turn, calculates and displays the amount to be paid. The driver then inserts money (cash or credit card) into the appropriate slots in the machine. It is expected that the driver pays in full. If paid in cash, and if the driver pays in excess, then a change will be returned.

Modeling a problem with such a general description may become too complex. For example, when there is more than one entry point, it would be hard for the system to find out how many vehicles enter into the lot at any one time. If there is only one space available and two vehicles enter the lot, it may be difficult for the system to allocate the one available space to one of the two vehicles. In order to develop such automated ticketing system, it is therefore necessary to consider some assumptions that provide the boundary within which the ticketing system operates. In this case study, the following assumptions are made in order to simplify the development of the automated ticketing system.

Assumptions

1. All spaces in the parking lot are identical. Consequently, no space is reserved for any particular vehicle type.
2. There is only one entry point and one exit point for vehicles.
3. Vehicles and drivers are treated as one entity. Vehicles are uniquely identified by the ticket numbers they take while entering the parking lot. Since no additional information about a vehicle is required other than its unique identification, vehicles will not be modeled separately.
4. Vehicles are charged from 6:00 A.M. to 9:00 P.M. only. No vehicle is allowed to park in the lot between 9:00 P.M. and 6:00 A.M. The specification will not include any penalty or overnight charges. It is assumed that the parking lot management somehow forces the vehicles to clear the lot after 9:00 P.M.
5. All vehicles are charged at a flat rate of $15 per hour. Parking hours are rounded to the nearest hour. This means that even if a vehicle is parked for one minute, it will be charged for one hour.

6. Only cash payments are accepted. It is further assumed that the ticketing machine has sufficient money at all times to render correct change.
7. Every vehicle/driver pays in full when leaving the parking lot.

The specification will include operations to (i) issue a ticket to a vehicle when it enters, (ii) pay for a ticket when the vehicle holding the ticket leaves the parking lot, (iii) report the number of tickets sold for a given period of time (a day, a week or a month), and (iv) report the revenue generated for a given period of time (a day, a week or a month).

The Model

Since the specification of the ticketing system requires date and time to be used in tickets and in calculations, the specification of date and time is given as a separate machine and is used by the parking lot. This machine is called *DateTime* and its model is discussed first.

The *DateTime* machine

The main purpose of the *DateTime* machine is to validate a given date or time, and to provide some services to compare dates and times. Hence, it is appropriate to design the *DateTime* machine as a stateless machine, meaning without a state space. Accordingly, the machine includes several services which are modeled as constants. These are described below:

DATE This is a triple consisting of three other constants, *DAY*, *MONTH* and *YEAR*. Validation of a date is given as a property of this constant that checks whether a given date is correct with respect to the number of days in a given month and the number of days for the month of February in a leap year.

TIME This is a tuple comprising two other constants, *HOUR* and *MINUTE*. As in the case of *DATE*, the validation of a given time is stated as a property in the specification.

Day, *Month*, *Year* These are projection functions which return the day, month and year components of a given date.

Hour, *Minute* These are projection functions which return the hour and minute of components of a given time.

In addition to the constants mentioned above, the machine needs to provide comparative functions for dates and times. These functions are also modeled as constants and their definitions are given as properties. The following functions are defined:

DateCmp This function compares two dates and returns an indicator showing whether the first argument is earlier, later or on the same date as the second argument. The three types of indicators themselves are defined as constants in the specification.

DateDiffInDays This function returns the number of days elapsed between two given dates.

TimeCmp This function is similar to *DateCmp* but compares two times, instead of dates.

TimeDiffInHours This function returns the number of hours elapsed between two given times.

TimeDiffInMinutes This is similar to the function *TimeDiffInHours* but returns the number of minutes elapsed.

The *DateTime* machine.

MACHINE *DateTime*
CONSTANTS
    DAY, MONTH, YEAR, DATE,
    HOUR, MINUTE, TIME,

    /* Constants used in comparison */
    EARLIER, SAME, LATER,

    /* Projection functions */
    Day, Month, Year, Hour, Minute,

    /* DATE comparison functions */
    DateCmp, DateDiffInDays,
    ComputeDayOffset,   /*   Aux function */

    /* TIME comparison functions */
    TimeCmp, TimeDiffInHoursSameDay, TimeDiffInMinutesSameDay

PROPERTIES
    /* DATE/TIME defs */
    $DAY = 1 .. 31 \land MONTH = 1 .. 12 \land YEAR = 1900 .. 3000 \land$
    $HOUR = 0 .. 23 \land MINUTE = 0 .. 59 \land$
    $DATE = DAY \times MONTH \times YEAR \land$
    $TIME = HOUR \times MINUTE \land$

    /* DATE validation */
    $\forall (dd, mm, yy).((dd, mm, yy) \in DATE \Rightarrow ($
        $(mm \in \{1, 3, 5, 7, 8, 10, 12\} \Rightarrow dd \in 1 .. 31) \land$
        $(mm \in \{4, 6, 9, 11\} \Rightarrow dd \in 1 .. 30) \land$
        $(mm = 2 \land ($
            $yy \bmod 400 = 0 \lor$
            $(yy \bmod 4 = 0 \land yy \bmod 100 \neq 0)$
        $) \Rightarrow dd \in 1 .. 29) \land$
        $(mm = 2 \land \neg ($
            $yy \bmod 400 = 0 \lor$
            $(yy \bmod 4 = 0 \land yy \bmod 100 \neq 0)$
        $) \Rightarrow dd \in 1 .. 28)$
    $)) \land$

    /* Constants used in comparison */
    $EARLIER = -1 \land SAME = 0 \land LATER = 1 \land$

    /* Projection functions */

$Day \in DATE \rightarrow DAY \wedge$
$Month \in DATE \rightarrow MONTH \wedge$
$Year \in DATE \rightarrow YEAR \wedge$
$Hour \in TIME \rightarrow HOUR \wedge$
$Minute \in TIME \rightarrow MINUTE \wedge$

/* Defs. of Day(), Month(), Year(), Hour(), Minute() */
$\forall (dd, mm, yy).((dd, mm, yy) \in DATE \Rightarrow$
$\quad Day(dd, mm, yy) = dd \wedge$
$\quad Month(dd, mm, yy) = mm \wedge$
$\quad Year(dd, mm, yy) = yy$
$) \wedge$
$\forall (hh, mm).((hh, mm) \in TIME \Rightarrow$
$\quad Hour(hh, mm) = hh \wedge$
$\quad Minute(hh, mm) = mm$
$) \wedge$

*/ DATE comparison functions */
$DateCmp \in DATE \times DATE \rightarrow \mathbb{Z} \wedge$
$DateDiffInDays \in DATE \times DATE \rightarrow \mathcal{N} \wedge$
$ComputeDayOffset \in DATE \rightarrow \mathcal{N} \wedge$

/**
* Defs of DATE comparison functions
*/
/* Def. DateCmp() */
$\forall (d1, d2).(d1 \in DATE \wedge d2 \in DATE \Rightarrow$
$\quad (DateCmp(d1, d2) = LATER \Leftrightarrow ($
$\quad\quad Year(d1) > Year(d2) \vee$
$\quad\quad Year(d1) = Year(d2) \wedge Month(d1) > Month(d2) \vee$
$\quad\quad Year(d1) = Year(d2) \wedge$
$\quad\quad\quad Month(d1) = Month(d2) \wedge Day(d1) > Day(d2)$
$\quad)) \wedge$
$\quad (DateCmp(d1, d2) = EARLIER \Leftrightarrow ($
$\quad\quad Year(d1) < Year(d2) \vee$
$\quad\quad Year(d1) = Year(d2) \wedge Month(d1) < Month(d2) \vee$
$\quad\quad Year(d1) = Year(d2) \wedge$
$\quad\quad\quad Month(d1) = Month(d2) \wedge Day(d1) < Day(d2)$
$\quad)) \wedge$
$\quad (DateCmp(d1, d2) = SAME \Leftrightarrow (d1 = d2))$
$) \wedge$

/* Def. ComputeDayOffset */
$\forall (yy, mm, dd, tm, ty).$
$\quad ((yy, mm, dd) \in DATE \wedge$

$tm \in \mathcal{N} \wedge ty \in \mathcal{N} \wedge$
$tm = (mm + 9) \bmod 12 \wedge$
$ty = yy - tm \operatorname{div} 10 \Rightarrow$
   $ComputeDayOffset(yy, mm, dd) =$
       $365 \times ty + ty \operatorname{div} 4 - ty \operatorname{div} 100 + ty \operatorname{div} 400 +$
       $(306 \times tm + 5) \operatorname{div} 10 +$
       $(dd - 1)$
) $\wedge$

/* Def. DateDiffInDays */
$\forall (d1, d2).(d1 \in DATE \wedge d2 \in DATE \Rightarrow$
   $(DateCmp(d1, d2) \in \{EARLIER, SAME\} \Rightarrow$
       $DateDiffInDays(d1, d2) =$
           $ComputeDayOffset(d2) - ComputeDayOffset(d1)$
) $\wedge$
   $(DateCmp(d1, d2) - LATER \Rightarrow$
       $DateDiffInDays(d1, d2) = DateDiffInDays(d2, d1)$
)
) $\wedge$

/**
 * TIME comparison functions
 */
$TimeCmp \in TIME \times TIME \rightarrow \mathcal{Z} \wedge$
$TimeDiffInHoursSameDay \in TIME \times TIME \rightarrow \mathcal{Z} \wedge$
$TimeDiffInMinutesSameDay \in TIME \times TIME \rightarrow \mathcal{N} \wedge$

/**
 * Defs. of TIME comparison functions
 */
/* Def. TimeCmp() */
$\forall (t1, t2).(t1 \in TIME \wedge t2 \in TIME \Rightarrow$
   $(TimeCmp(t1, t2) = LATER \Leftrightarrow ($
       $Hour(t1) > Hour(t2) \vee$
       $Hour(t1) = Hour(t2) \wedge Minute(t1) > Minute(t2)$
   )) $\wedge$
   $(TimeCmp(t1, t2) = EARLIER \Leftrightarrow ($
       $Hour(t1) < Hour(t2) \vee$
       $Hour(t1) = Hour(t2) \wedge Minute(t1) < Minute(t2)$
   )) $\wedge$
   $(TimeCmp(t1, t2) = SAME \Leftrightarrow (t1 = t2))$
) $\wedge$

/* Def. TimeDiffInHoursSameDay */
$\forall (t1, t2).(t1 \in TIME \wedge t2 \in TIME \Rightarrow$

$(TimeCmp(t1, t2) \in \{EARLIER, SAME\} \Rightarrow$
$\quad (Minute(t1) \geq Minute(t2) \Leftrightarrow$
$\quad\quad (TimeDiffInHoursSameDay(t1, t2) =$
$\quad\quad\quad Hour(t2) - Hour(t1))) \wedge$
$\quad (Minute(t1) < Minute(t2) \Leftrightarrow$ /* One-hour rounding */
$\quad\quad (TimeDiffInHoursSameDay(t1, t2) =$
$\quad\quad\quad Hour(t2) - Hour(t1) + 1))$
$) \wedge$
$(TimeCmp(t1, t2) = LATER \Rightarrow$
$\quad TimeDiffInHoursSameDay(t1, t2) =$
$\quad\quad TimeDiffInHoursSameDay(t2, t1))$
$) \wedge$

/* Def. TimeDiffInMinutesSameDay */
$\forall (t1, t2).(t1 \in TIME \wedge t2 \in TIME \Rightarrow$
$\quad (TimeCmp(t1, t2) \in \{EARLIER, SAME\} \Rightarrow$
$\quad\quad (TimeDiffInMinutesSameDay(t1, t2) =$
$\quad\quad\quad (Hour(t2) - Hour(t1)) \times 60 + Minute(t2) - Minute(t1))$
$\quad) \wedge$
$\quad (TimeCmp(t1, t2) = LATER \Rightarrow$
$\quad\quad (TimeDiffInMinutesSameDay(t1, t2) =$
$\quad\quad\quad TimeDiffInMinutesSameDay(t2, t1))$
$\quad)$
$)$

END

Comments

The function *ComputeDayOffset* is an auxiliary function used in the calculation of the number of days elapsed between two given dates. Consequently, this function is used by *DateDiffInDays* function. The algorithm implemented in this function is given in http://alcor.concordia.ca/~gpkatch/gdate-method.html.

Though it would be appropriate to use the **DEFINITIONS** clause for some of the constants such as *DAY, MONTH, YEAR, DATE, HOUR, MINUTE* and *TIME*, it was decided to define them in the **CONSTANTS** clause instead because these definitions will not be visible to other machines when the *DateTime* machine is used through the **SEES** clause or **USES** clause of another machine.

The AutomatedTicketingSystem machine

We now discuss the details of the automated ticketing machine that makes use of the *DateTime* machine. Among the three relationships discussed in the previous sections in this chapter, the inclusion relationship is not appropriate because it exclusively includes the component inside an aggregate machine. Since *DateTime* machine can be shared by many other machines, either the *DateTime* machine can be seen by the ticketing machine or used by it. As stated in Sect. 19.4.2, if the ticketing machine uses the *DateTime* machine, the invariant of the ticketing machine is not guaranteed when the state of the *DateTime* machine changes. Since, the *DateTime* machine does not have a state, it is possible for the ticketing machine to use the *DateTime* machine. However, the SEES relationship seems to be quite appropriate in this case because the invariant of the ticketing machine does not depend on the invariant of the *DateTime* machine. Therefore, the SEES relationship has been used in the specification.

The parking lot has a fixed capacity; that is, the number of available spaces is fixed. In order to demonstrate that this specification can be used for different parking lots of varying sizes, it is decided to use a machine parameter to denote the capacity.

The machine must include a function to compute the charges based on the time a vehicle is parked. This is defined as *Computer_Charge* in the **CONSTANTS** clause. Three other constants are required for computing the charge—*RATE* which defines the rate per hour for parking, *START_CHARGE_TIME* and *END_CHARGE_TIME* which, respectively, denote the opening and closing time of the parking lot.

The state space must maintain information about the tickets that are issued and the tickets that are paid. Every ticket must have a date stamp on it. This is used to ensure that the ticket is paid on the same day and hence the vehicle leaves the parking lot on the same day. The state of the machine must also include the status of each ticket. Finally, the state space should include a count on the number of spaces available at any time. This count will be used to check whether there is a free space when a vehicle enters the parking lot.

The state invariant must assert the following constraints:

- The set of vehicles that are checked out must be a subset of the vehicles that were checked in.
- There should be a date stamp on the ticket and a status for every vehicles that is checked in.
- A vehicle that is not checked out must have its status *Unpaid*. In contrast, if the status of a vehicle is *Paid*, then it must have checked out.
- The check out time stamp must be later than the check in time stamp.
- Both check in and check out time stamps must be within the allowable parking times (*START_CHARGE_TIME* and *END_CHARGE_TIME*).

The initialization of the machine should set the number of available spaces to the capacity of the parking lot and set all ticket entries to null.

The operations on the ticketing machine are explained below.

The **IssueTicket** operation will be invoked when a vehicle checks in. This operation should accept three parameters: the ticket, check in date and check in time. The precondition must ensure that the ticket is not used by another vehicle before. That is, a ticket uniquely identifies a vehicle. If one vehicle comes back to the parking lot after check out, it is considered to be a different vehicle because it is issued a different ticket number. The precondition also must ensure that there is at least one space available for the vehicle that is checking in. If the precondition is satisfied, then the check in time of the vehicle must be updated and its status must be set to *Unpaid*.

When a vehicle leaves the parking lot, two things should be taken care of. (i) The charges must be computed for this vehicle when the driver inserts the ticket into the machine. Only after computing and displaying the charges, the driver will know how much to pay. (ii) The driver must pay in full for this vehicle. The status of the vehicle should be updated. These two tasks are described separately by the operations **Checkout** and **PayTicket**, respectively.

The **Checkout** operation should accept the ticket and check out time as input parameters. The precondition must ensure that the vehicle is checked in but not checked out, and the check in time (entered in the ticket) is earlier than check out time. If the precondition is true, the check out time should be recorded, the number of available spaces should be increased by one, and the charge should be computed based on the check in and check out times.

The **PayTicket** operation should take a ticket and amount paid by the driver as input parameters. The precondition for this operation must ensure that the vehicle is checked out but not paid. This indirectly enforces the sequencing of tasks by **Checkout** and **PayTicket**. The precondition must also ensure that the amount is greater than or equal to the charges computed. If the precondition is true, the operation must update the status of the ticket to *Paid* and should return the change after payment.

Two query operations are to be included in the specification. The first one is **QueryNumberOfTicketsSold** which is invoked to query the number of tickets sold in a given period of time. It takes two dates *fromDt* and *toDt* as input parameters which define the period in which the calculation is to be performed. Obviously, the precondition must ensure that *fromDt* is earlier than *toDt* or the same. The operation should count the number of tickets whose status is *Paid* and the date stamp in the ticket is in the range *fromDt .. toDt*.

The second query operation **QueryRevenue** is very similar to that of **QueryNumberOfTicketsSold**, but in addition to counting the tickets, it should also compute the charge for each ticket based on the check in and check out times entered on the ticket.

The *AutomatedTicketingSystem* machine is given below.

> **MACHINE** *AutomatedTicketingSystem* (*Capacity*)
> **CONSTRAINTS** *Capacity* $\in \mathcal{N}_1$
> **SEES** *DateTime*
> **SETS**
> > *TICKETNO*;
> > *TICKETSTAT* = {*Paid, Unpaid*}
>
> **CONSTANTS**
> > *RATE, START_CHARGE_TIME, END_CHARGE_TIME,*
> > *Compute_Charge*   /* functions */
>
> **PROPERTIES**
> > *RATE* = 15 $\wedge$
> > *START_CHARGE_TIME* = (6, 0) $\wedge$
> > *END_CHARGE_TIME* = (21, 0) $\wedge$
> > *Compute_Charge* $\in$ *TIME* $\times$ *TIME* $\rightarrow$ $\mathcal{N}$ $\wedge$
> > $\forall$ (*t1, t2*).(
> > > *t1* $\in$ *TIME* $\wedge$ *t2* $\in$ *TIME* $\wedge$

$$TimeCmp(t1, t2) \in \{EARLIER, SAME\} \Rightarrow$$
$$Compute\_Charge(t1, t2) =$$
$$RATE \times TimeDiffInHoursSameDay(t1, t2)$$
)

VARIABLES

checkin, checkout, date, status,   /* functions */
availableSpace

INVARIANT

checkin $\in$ *TICKETNO* $\rightarrowtail$ *TIME* $\wedge$
checkout $\in$ *TICKETNO* $\rightarrowtail$ *TIME* $\wedge$
date $\in$ *TICKETNO* $\rightarrowtail$ *DATE* $\wedge$
status $\in$ *TICKETNO* $\rightarrowtail$ *TICKETSTAT* $\wedge$
availableSpace $\in \mathcal{N}$ $\wedge$

/* relationship */
dom(*checkout*) $\subseteq$ **dom**(*checkin*) $\wedge$
dom(*date*) = **dom**(*checkin*) $\wedge$
dom(*status*) = **dom**(*checkin*) $\wedge$
$\forall$ (*tk*).(
    tk $\in$ **dom**(*checkin*) $\wedge$ *tk* $\notin$ **dom**(*checkout*) $\Rightarrow$ *status*(*tk*) = *Unpaid*
) $\wedge$
$\forall$ (*tk*).(
    tk $\in$ **dom**(*checkin*) $\Rightarrow$
        TimeCmp(*checkin*(*tk*), *START_ CHARGE_TIME*) $\in$ \{*SAME, LATER*\} $\wedge$
        TimeCmp(*checkin*(*tk*), *END_ CHARGE_TIME*) = *EARLIER*
) $\wedge$
$\forall$ (*tk*).(
    tk $\in$ **dom**(*checkout*) $\Rightarrow$
        TimeCmp(*checkin*(*tk*), *checkout*(*tk*)) = *EARLIER* $\wedge$
        TimeCmp(*checkout*(*tk*), *START_ CHARGE_TIME*) = *LATER* $\wedge$
        TimeCmp(*checkout*(*tk*), *END_ CHARGE_TIME*) $\in$ \{*EARLIER, SAME*\}
) $\wedge$
$\forall$ (*tk*).(*tk* $\in$ **dom**(*status*) $\wedge$ *status*(*tk*) = *Paid* $\Rightarrow$ *tk* $\in$ **dom**(*checkout*))

INITIALIZATION

availableSpace := *Capacity* $\parallel$
checkin, checkout, date, status := $\emptyset$, $\emptyset$, $\emptyset$, $\emptyset$

OPERATIONS

IssueTicket(*tk*, *checkinDate*, *checkinTime*) =
    PRE
        tk $\in$ *TICKETNO* $\wedge$ *tk* $\notin$ **dom**(*checkin*) $\wedge$
        checkinDate $\in$ *DATE* $\wedge$ *checkinTime* $\in$ *TIME* $\wedge$

$TimeCmp(checkinTime, START\_CHARGE\_TIME) \in \{SAME, LATER\} \land$
$TimeCmp(checkinTime, END\_CHARGE\_TIME) = EARLIER \land$
$availableSpace > 0$

THEN

$availableSpace := availableSpace - 1 \parallel$
checkin$(tk) := checkinTime \parallel$
date$(tk) := checkinDate \parallel$
status$(tk) := Unpaid$

END;

$charge \leftarrow$ **Checkout**$(tk, checkoutTime) =$
    PRE
        $tk \in TICKETNO \land checkoutTime \in TIME \land$
        $tk \in \mathbf{dom}(checkin) - \mathbf{dom}(checkout) \land$
        $TimeCmp(checkoutTime, checkin(tk)) = LATER \land$
        $TimeCmp(checkoutTime, END\_CHARGE\_TIME) \in \{EARLIER, SAME\}$
    THEN
        checkout$(tk) := checkoutTime \parallel$
        $availableSpace := availableSpace + 1 \parallel$
        $charge := Compute\_Charge(checkin(tk), checkoutTime)$
    END;

$change \leftarrow$ **PayTicket**$(tk, amount) =$
    PRE
        $tk \in TICKETNO \land tk \in \mathbf{dom}(checkout) \land status(tk) = Unpaid \land$
        $amount \in \mathcal{N} \land$
        $amount \geq Compute\_Charge(checkin(tk), checkout(tk))$
    THEN
        status$(tk) := Paid \parallel$
        $change := amount - Compute\_Charge(checkin(tk), checkout(tk))$
    END;

$count \leftarrow$ **QueryNumberOfTicketsSold**$(fromDt, toDt) =$
    PRE
        $fromDt \in DATE \land toDt \in DATE \land$
        $DateCmp(fromDt, toDt) \in \{EARLIER, SAME\}$
    THEN
        $count := \mathbf{card}(\{tk \mid tk \in \mathbf{dom}(status) \land status(tk) = Paid \land$
                $DateCmp(fromDt, date(tk)) \in \{EARLIER, SAME\} \land$
                $DateCmp(date(tk), toDt) \in \{EARLIER, SAME\}\})$
    END;

$revenue \leftarrow$ **QueryRevenue**$(fromDt, toDt) =$
    PRE
        $fromDt \in DATE \land toDt \in DATE \land$

$$DateCmp(fromDt, toDt) \in \{EARLIER, SAME\}$$

THEN

$$revenue := \sum (tk).($$

$$tk \in \mathbf{dom}(status) \wedge status(tk) = Paid \wedge$$
$$DateCmp(fromDt, date(tk)) \in \{EARLIER, SAME\} \wedge$$
$$DateCmp(date(tk), toDt) \in \{EARLIER, SAME\} \mid$$
$$Compute\_Charge(checkin(tk), checkout(tk)))$$

END;

$$count \leftarrow \mathbf{QueryAvailableSpaces} = count := availableSpace$$

END

19.8
Proof Obligations

An abstract machine must be proved to be well-founded by showing that it is internally consistent. A general abstract machine is described by the following AMN structure:

MACHINE *MName(p)*
CONSTRAINTS *C*
SETS *S*
CONSTANTS *K*
PROPERTIES *B*
VARIABLES *V*
INVARIANT *I*
INITIALIZATION *T*
OPERATIONS
  $y \leftarrow operation(x) =$
  PRE *pre*
  THEN *stat*
  END;
  ...
END

The above structure does not include the **DEFINITIONS** clause because they are macro substitutions and hence must be textually expanded before showing internal consistency of the machine. Given this structure, there are five proof obligations that must be discharged to ensure internal consistency of the machine.

Parameter Existence

If a machine has parameters, then for every parameter, it is required to show that there exists at least one instantiation that can be used to instantiate the machine. Otherwise, the machine becomes useless. The parameters must satisfy the conditions given in the **CONSTRAINTS** clause. This proof obligation is stated as

$$\exists p . C$$

If there is no parameter for the machine, there will be no constraints to satisfy and so there is no proof obligation with respect to the parameters.

Existence of Sets and Constants

If a machine has the **SETS** and/or **CONSTANTS** clauses, then, as in the case of parameters, showing the existence of such sets and constants becomes a proof obligation. Formally, it is stated as

$$C \Rightarrow \exists S, K . B$$

The formal statement asserts that, given that the parameters of the machine have been shown to exist, there must exist some sets and constants as described in the machine that satisfy the properties stated in the machine. Since the **PROPERTIES** clause may use the parameters, it is important to assert the existence of parameters first.

Invariant Satisfaction

Generally, every machine will have at least one variable to define the state space of the machine. A necessary condition is that the existence of state variable must satisfy the invariant.

$$C \wedge B \Rightarrow \exists v . I$$

If a machine does not have a state variable, there will be no invariant. See the *DateTime* machine given in the case study for an example of a machine without state variables. Such stateless machines will be useful for providing some services.

Initialization and Invariant

The initialization conditions must satisfy the invariant. This is formally stated as

$$C \wedge B \Rightarrow [T]I$$

The notation $[T]I$ denotes that I must be satisfied after executing T. In other words, I is the postcondition of executing T.

Maintaining the Invariant

Every operation of the machine must satisfy the invariant. The proof obligation for operation definition follows:

$$C \wedge B \wedge I \wedge pre \Rightarrow [stat]I$$

Informally, for every operation, if the constraints, properties and invariant of the machine are true along with the precondition of the operation, then the execution of the substitutions must satisfy the invariant. The parameters of the operation need not be explicitly addressed in the proof obligation since they will be covered under *pre* and *stat*.

To illustrate the process of checking internal consistency, consider the Student Council example given in Example 1.

Parameter Existence   The *StudentCouncil* machine has one parameter of type positive numbers. Any positive number such as 30 that represents a reasonable size of the student council will enable us to discharge this proof obligation.

Existence of Sets and Constants   There is only one set *STUDENT* included in this machine. Since there is no property stated in the specification, the proof obligation can be discharged easily.

Invariant Satisfaction   If the machine is instantiated with a positive number *limit* and given the set *STUDENT*, we need to show that there exist two variables *council* and *president* such that

$$council \in \mathcal{P}(STUDENT) \wedge \mathbf{card}(council) \leq limit \wedge$$

$$president \in STUDENT \wedge council \neq \emptyset \Rightarrow president \in council$$

This requires that we need to find values for *council* and *president* that satisfy the two conditions

$$\mathbf{card}(council) \leq limit \wedge council \neq \emptyset \Rightarrow president \in council$$

If *limit* is 30 and there is only one student in the council, these constraints will be satisfied.

Initialization and Invariant   The substitution *council* := 0 in the **INITIALIZATION** clause shows that $\mathbf{card}(council) \leq limit$ since *limit* is a positive number. Further, since council is empty, the other part of the state invariant is automatically true. Thus, the initial state satisfies the state invariant.

Maintaining the State Invariant   Consider the **AddStudent** operation. The precondition of this operation ensures that the parameter is of type *STUDENT* and is not a member of the council. Further, there is a space for at least one more member in the council. Given that the parameter is instantiated, the set *STUDENT* exists, the invariant of the machine is true, and the precondition is true, the proof obligation requires that the substitution for this operation satisfies the state invariant. That is, the substitution

$$council = \emptyset \Rightarrow president := nn \quad \| \quad council := council \cup \{nn\}$$

must imply the invariant

$$\mathbf{card}(council) \leq limit \wedge (council \neq \emptyset \Rightarrow president \in council)$$

There are two cases to consider here.

<u>Case 1</u> Council was empty before this operation.

In this case, the substitution results in a one-member council after the operation and the only member will be the president. This satisfies both the constraints in the invariant. The fact that **card**(*council*) < *limit* before the operation ensures that the new addition will not exceed the limit.

<u>Case 2</u> Council was not empty before this operation.

In this case, the cardinality constraint, as stated in Case 1, ensures that the size of the council will not exceed the limit. The president of the council is not changed by the operation in this case, and hence the second constraint *president* $\in$ *council* is satisfied because it is supposed to be true before the operation.

Thus, the **AddStudent** operation maintains the state invariant. The proof for other two operations are left as exercise.

19.8.1
Proof Obligations for INCLUDES Clause

When a machine M_2 includes a machine M_1, additional proof obligations need to be discharged in addition to those that are required for ensuring internal consistency. This section gives the complete proof obligations for the machine M_2 when it includes machine M_1. The following discussion uses subscripts to distinguish various components of the two machines. For example, p_1 refers to the parameters of the machine M_1.

Parameter Existence

If M_2 has parameters, the proof obligation requires the existence of some values for its parameters. This is formally stated as

$$\exists p_2 . C_2$$

Existence of Sets and Constants

The machine M_1 is an inherent part of M_2. This shows that sets and constants of M_1 are also part of those in M_2. Hence, the existence of sets and constants in M_2 warrants the existence of sets and constants in M_1 as well. Formally,

$$C_1 \wedge C_2 \Rightarrow \exists S_1, K_1, S_2, K_2 . B_1 \wedge B_2$$

The sets and constants of both machines together must satisfy the properties of both the machines.

Invariant Satisfaction

If parameter existence and sets and constants existence are satisfied for both machines, then the existence of variables on both machines must satisfy the invariants of both machines. A formal statement follows:

$$C_1 \wedge C_2 \wedge B_1 \wedge B_2 \Rightarrow \exists V_1, V_2 . I_1 \wedge I_2$$

Initialization and Invariant

The initialization process of M_2 uses the initialization of M_1 first. The entire initialization process must satisfy the invariant of M_2.

$$C_1 \wedge C_2 \wedge B_1 \wedge B_2 \Rightarrow [T_1 \, {}^\circ_9 \, T_2] I_2$$

The expression $T_1 \, {}^\circ_9 \, T_2$ denotes sequential composition of the initializations of the two machines. Notice that the initialization of M_1 must satisfy the invariant of M_1 as a standalone machine and hence it is not brought into the above statement.

Maintaining the Invariant

Every operation in M_2 must satisfy the invariant of M_2. Since, during inclusion, M_2 may invoke some operations of M_1, it is required that the invariant of M_2 is also satisfied by every operation of M_1. The proof obligation for this step uses the same structure for individual machine.

$$C_1 \wedge C_2 \wedge B_1 \wedge B_2 \wedge I_1 \wedge I_2 \wedge pre \Rightarrow [stat] I_2$$

The satisfaction of I_1 will be taken care of inside M_1.

19.8.2
Proof Obligations for USES Clause

Consider a machine M_2 that uses a machine M_1. Since M_2 does not alter the state space of M_1, the proof obligations mostly concern with the invariant of M_2.

Parameter Existence

This is the same for an individual machine; i.e.,

$$\exists p_2 . C_2$$

Existence of Sets and Constants

The sets and constants of M_1 must exist already for M_2 to use it. The proof obligation for M_2 in this case becomes

$$C_1 \wedge C_2 \wedge B_1 \Rightarrow \exists S_2, K_2 . B_2$$

Invariant Satisfaction

The invariant of M_2 may use the invariant of M_1 and hence the variables of both the machines must exist and they must satisfy the invariants of both machines. Formally,

$$C_1 \wedge C_2 \wedge B_1 \wedge B_2 \Rightarrow \exists V_1, V_2 . I_1 \wedge I_2$$

Initialization and Invariant

As in the case of inclusion, the initialization of M_1 must be done prior to the initialization of M_2. The latter must satisfy the state invariant of M_2.

$$C_1 \wedge C_2 \wedge B_1 \wedge B_2 \Rightarrow [T_1 \, \mathbin{\substack{\circ \\ \circ}} \, T_2]I_2$$

Since M_1 must exist already, initialization of M_1 must satisfy its invariant.

Maintaining the invariant

This is the same as the corresponding rule for the *INCLUDES* clause. That is,

$$C_1 \wedge C_2 \wedge B_1 \wedge B_2 \wedge I_1 \wedge I_2 \wedge pre \Rightarrow [stat]I_2$$

19.8.3
Proof Obligations for SEES Clause

The only difference between the **USES** clause and the **SEES** clause is that in the case of the latter, the machine M_2 cannot use the invariant of M_1. Therefore, the proof obligation for invariant satisfaction of M_2 does not include I_1. Formally, this is stated as

$$C_1 \wedge C_2 \wedge B_1 \wedge B_2 \Rightarrow \exists V_2 . I_2$$

Other proof rules are the same for both the clauses.

19.8.4
Proof Obligations for Refinement

As discussed in the Sect. 19.5, the refinement machine refers to several entities in the abstract machine including the preconditions of operations. It has a linking invariant which relates the state of the abstract machine and that of the refinement machine. The refinement machine must have the same signature for operations as that of the abstract machine. These unique characteristics of the refinement process make the proof obligations for refinement different from those for establishing internal consistency. Consider the structure for the abstract machine as given at the beginning of this section, and consider the structure of a refinement machine given below:

> **REFINEMENT** *RName*
> **REFINES** *MName*
> **SETS** *S*
> **CONSTANTS** *K*
> **PROPERTIES** *B*
> **VARIABLES** *V*

INVARIANT I
INITIALIZATION T
OPERATIONS
   $y \leftarrow operation(x) =$
    PRE pre
    THEN $stat$
    END;

  ...

END

Notice that the refinement machine cannot have parameters and hence there is no proof obligation concerning parameters. The rest of the proof obligations are given next.

Existence of Sets and Constants

Since the abstract machine may have parameters, the proof obligation for this step requires the existence of values for those parameters. If there exist parameters for the abstract machine that satisfy the constraints of the abstract machine, then the sets and constants of both the abstract and refined machines must exist that together satisfy the properties of both the machines. This is stated formally as

$$C_a \Rightarrow \exists S_a, S_r, K_a, K_r \,.\, B_a \wedge B_r$$

The above statement uses the subscript 'a' for components of the abstract machine and 'r' for those of the refined machine.

Initialization and Invariant

Any transition by the initial state of the refinement machine must reach a state in which some transition of the abstract state can establish the linking invariant, which is the invariant of the refinement machine. In other words, every valid initial state T_r of the refinement machine must correspond to some initial state T_a of the abstract machine for which the linking invariant I_r is true. This is expressed as

$$\neg\,[T_a]\neg\,I_r$$

which states that not every transition of T_a guarantees that I_r is false. In other words, some transition of T_a guarantees that I_r is true. For T_r to be a refinement of T_a, it is required that $\neg\,[T_a]\neg\,I_r$ must be true for any state that T_r can reach. That is, T_r must guarantee to reach a state in which $\neg\,[T_a]\neg\,I_r$ is true. This is expressed as

$$[T_r](\neg\,[T_a]\neg\,I_r)$$

Formally, the proof obligation is

$$C_a \wedge B_a \wedge B_r \Rightarrow [T_r](\neg\,[T_a]\neg\,I_r)$$

Operations Without Output

For operations without output, the proof obligation is reduced to satisfying the precondition of the refined operation.

$$C_a \wedge B_a \wedge B_r \wedge I_a \wedge I_r \wedge pre_a \Rightarrow pre_r$$

Since the refined machine does not include a separate precondition, the above proof rules thus reduces to the satisfaction of the precondition in the abstract operation.

For operations with output y, the proof obligation becomes

$$C_a \wedge B_a \wedge B_r \wedge I_a \wedge I_r \wedge pre_a \Rightarrow [stat_r[y'/y]](\neg [stat_a] \neg (i_r \wedge y' = y))$$

Since the refinement operation has exactly the same signature as that of the abstract operation, the renaming of the output variable y into y' is necessary in this proof obligation.

19.9
Exercises

1. Rewrite the *StudentCouncil* machine given in Example 1 using arrays to model the council.
2. In Sect. 19.3.3, it is mentioned that the **SELECT** statement is an extension of the **CHOICE** statement. Prove that is true.
   Hint: Write a **SELECT** statement that is equivalent to a **CHOICE** statement.
3. The *DateTime* machine given in the case study includes two functions *TimeDiffInHoursSameDay* and *TimeDiffInMinutesSameDay*. These functions return the elapsed time between two times passed as input in hours and minutes, respectively. However, they assume that the times occur on the same day. Include two other functions in this machine named *TimeDiffInHours* and *TimeDiffInMinutes* which relax the assumption. In other words, these new functions must return the elapsed time between any two given times. Choose the input parameters for these functions appropriately.
4. Modify the *PersonalDictionary* machine given in Example 7 to include the additional constraint: "For every word w in the dictionary, if w_1 is a synonym of w, then w must be included in the synonym of w_1 as well. A similar constraint must be included for antonyms as well".
5. Modify the *FileAccessControl* machine given in Example 8 to include file ownership. Include the following additional constraints: (i) The owner of a file will automatically get read and write access to the file. It is possible that the owner can modify the access rights later. (ii) Only the owner of the file can change the access rights of a file. Consequently, in order for a user to get access to a file that he/she does not own, the user must request the owner to grant access rights.
6. Write the specification for a simple TV remote control that supports three functionalities for channel selection: (1) A user must be able to select any specific channel by giving the channel number. (2) If the user does not select any channel, the remote

control should arbitrarily select a channel for display. (3) The user may specify a criteria such as SPORTS and PAY PER VIEW and the remote control selects one of the channels from this group arbitrarily.

Hint: Use nondeterministic statements in the operations.

7. A simple library collection management system includes only books. Model this system and include the following functionalities: (i) add a new book to the collection; (ii) borrow a book from the library; (iii) return a book to the library; and (iv) reserve a book that is borrowed by another user. You may make use of the *DateTime* machine given in the case study.

8. Show that the *PersonalDictionary* machine given in Example 7 is internally consistent.

9. Give the proof obligations for the refinement of the *Collection* machine and its refinement shown in Examples 5 and 6, respectively.

10. (Project) The case study on automated ticketing machine for a parking lot includes the assumption that no vehicle is allowed to park between 9:00 P.M. and 6:00 A.M. Relax this assumption and rewrite the specification. This will involve changing the model and computing charges.

11. (Research) Critically compare the refinement techniques supported by specification languages VDM-SL and Z, and the one supported by the B-Method.

19.10
Bibliographic Notes

The B-Method was invented by Jean-Raymond Abrial. A detailed discussion of the first version of the B-Method is given in his B-Book [1]. The inclusion of a specification language, refinements and proof all under one umbrella attracted many researchers to use the B-Method for various applications. These applications include smart card application [10], component-based software development [12], model-based testing [19, 24], validation of strategies in space applications [22], reliability assessment [23], and verification of work flow applications [27]. This list shows the diversity of applications in which the B-Method is used and hence its expressive power for specification and verification of systems. A major industrial application of the B-Method has been reported in [17, 18] in which the B-Method was applied to the specification and development of a control system for Paris Metro Rail System. In particular, the safety properties in the control system have been proved using the B-Method. Several other case studies using the B-Method have been reported in [8, 21].

Several researchers have combined the B-Method with other modeling notations, specifically for proving the correctness of models specified in other notations. Thus, the power of the B-Method lies in its influence in proving the correctness of the system being specified. Notable modeling notations that have been used in this approach include Model Checking using SPIN [3], Timed Automata [4], and Personal Software Process (PSP) [6]. In some cases, informal or semi-formal requirements engineering methods have been combined with the B-Method in order to provide a rigorous requirements analysis [5, 7].

19

Abrial also developed an extension of the B-Method which includes specification of events. This method is called Event-B [2] and has become more popular than B because of its ability to specify and prove interactive systems such as web-based systems. Both B and Event-B use the AMN syntactic structure to describe the dynamics of systems (called machines). However, Event-B is more flexible in terms of adding newer syntax and in combining with other notations [14, 27]. More information about current work on Event-B can be found at www.event-b.org.

There are two tools for the B-Method that are quite popular. The B-Core company in UK provides the *B-Tool* which is widely used. This can be obtained from the B-core web site at www.b-core.com/btool.html. Recently, ClearSy System Engineering has provided another tool called *Atelier-B*, named after the founder of the company. This tool is free for academic purposes and can be obtained from www.atelierb.eu/index-en.php.

References

1. Abrial J-R (1996) The B-book: assigning programs to meanings. Cambridge University Press, Cambridge
2. Abrial J-R (2009) Modeling in event-B: system and software design. Cambridge University Press, Cambridge
3. Attiogbe JC (2004) A mechanically proved development combining B abstract systems with spin. In: International conference on quality software (QSIC 2004), pp 42–49
4. Ayoub A, Wahba A, Sheirah M (2008) Mapping timed automata to B. In: Third international design and test workshop (IDT 2008), Monstir, pp 255–259
5. Ayed LJB, Younes AB (2006) From graphical design in STATEMATE to formal specification in event B. In: International conference on information and communication technologies (ICITA'06), Damascus, pp 2837–2842
6. Babar A, Potter J (2005) Adapting the personal software process (PSP) to formal methods. In: Proceedings of the Australian software engineering conference, pp 192–201
7. Babar A, Tosic V, Potter J (2007) Aligning the map requirements modeling with the B-method for formal software development. In: Asia Pacific software engineering conference (APSEC 2007), Aichi, pp 17–24
8. Bicarregui JC et al (1997) Formal methods into practice: case studies in the application of the B method. IEE Proc Softw Eng 144(2):119–133
9. Eirksson H-E et al (2004) UML 2 toolkit. Wiley, Indianapolis
10. Gomes B, Deharbe D, Moreira A, Moraes K (2010) Applying the B method for the rigorous development of smart card applications. In: Abstract state machines, alloy, B and Z (ABZ 2010). LNCS, vol 5977, pp 203–216
11. Habrias H, Griech B (1997) Formal specification of dynamic constraints with the B-method. In: International conference on formal engineering methods (ICFEM 1997), Hiroshima, Japan, pp 304–314
12. Hatebur D, Heisel M, Souquieres J (2006) A method for component-based software and system development. In: EUROMICRO conference on software engineering and advanced applications (SEAA'06), Cavtat, Dubrovnik, pp 72–80
13. Hoang TS, Furst A, Abrial J-R (2009) Event-B patterns and their tool support. In: IEEE international conference on software engineering and formal methods (SEFM'09), Hanoi, pp 210–219
14. Iliasov A et al (2010) Supporting reuse in event B development: modularisation approach. In: Abstract state machines, alloy, B and Z (ABZ 2010). LNCS, vol 5977, pp 174–188

15. Lano K (1996) The B language and method: a guide to practical formal development. Springer, London
16. Lano K, Haughton H (1996) Specification in B: an introduction using the B-toolkit. Imperial College Press, London
17. Lecomte T (2008) Safe and reliable metro platform screen doors control/command systems. In: International symposium on formal methods (FM 2008), Turku, Finland, pp 430–434
18. Lecomte T, Servat T, Pouzancre G (2007) Formal methods in safety-critical railway systems. In: SBMF Conference, Brazil
19. Malik QA, Truscan D, Lilius J (2010) Using UML models and formal verification in model-based testing. In: IEEE international conference and workshops on engineering of computer-based systems. Oxford, England, pp 50–56
20. Schneider S (2001) The B-method: an introduction. Palgrave Macmillan, Basingstoke
21. Sekerinski E, Sere K (1999) Program development and refinement: case studies using the B method, FACIT. Springer, London
22. Sabatier D, Dellandrea B, Chemouil D (2008) FDIR Strategy validation with the B method. DASIA
23. Tarasyuk A, Troubitsyna E, Laibinis L (2010) From formal specification in event-B to probabilistic reliability assessment. In: Third international conference on dependability, Venice, Italy, pp 24–31
24. Utting M, Legeard B (2007) Practical model-based testing: a tools approach. Morgan Kaufmann, San Mateo
25. Waeselynck H, Behnia S (1998) B model animation for external verification. In: International conference on formal engineering methods (ICFEM 1998), Brisbane, Australia, pp 36–45
26. Wang S, Li Y, Huang G (2007) PostB: the postcondition extension onto the B-method. In: ACIS international conference on software engineering research, management & applications (SERA 2007), Busan, pp 195–202
27. Younes AB, Ayed LJB (2008) From UML activity diagrams to event B for the specification and the verification of workflow applications. In: IEEE international conference on computer software and applications (COMPSAC'08), Turku, pp 643–648

Index

V.S. Alagar, K. Periyasamy, *Specification of Software Systems*,
Texts in Computer Science,
DOI 10.1007/978-0-85729-277-3, © Springer-Verlag London Limited 2011

Printed in the United States
by Baker & Taylor Publisher Services